1787

The Imaginary Institution of Society

The Imaginary Institution of Society

CORNELIUS CASTORIADIS

Translated by Kathleen Blamey

The MIT Press
Cambridge, Massachusetts

First MIT Press edition, 1987

This translation © 1987 by Polity Press. This work originally appeared in French under the title *L'institution imaginaire de la société*, © 1975 by Éditions du Seuil, Paris, France.

Library of Congress Cataloging-in-Publication Data

Castoriadis, Cornelius
  The imaginary institution of society.

  Translation of: L'institution imaginaire de la société,
  Includes index.
  1. Revolutions. 2. Communism. 3. History—Philosophy.
4. Social institutions. I. Title.
JC491.C28913 1987   321.09   87–3393
ISBN 0–262–03134–5

Printed and bound in Great Britain.

Contents

Preface

This book may appear heterogeneous. In a sense, it is, and some explanation regarding the circumstances of its composition might be useful to the reader.

The first part is formed by the text 'Marxism and Revolutionary Theory' published in *Socialisme ou Barbarie* from April 1964 to June 1965.[1] This text was itself the never-ending development of a 'Note on the Marxist philosophy and theory of history', which accompanied 'The revolutionary movement under modern capitalism' and was circulated along with it among the group *Socialisme ou Barbarie* (Spring 1959). When the publication of *Socialisme ou Barbarie* was suspended, the remaining part of 'Marxism and Revolutionary Theory' yet unpublished, although for the most part already drafted, was left among my papers.

Written under the pressure of deadlines imposed by the publication of the journal, this part is itself not a completed work but a work in the making. Contrary to all the rules of composition, the walls of the building are displayed one after the other as they are erected, surrounded by the remains of scaffolding, piles of sand and rocks, odds and ends of wooden supports and dirty trowels. Without making this into a thesis, I am assuming this presentation as my own, dictated at first by 'external' factors. It should be merely a commonplace, recognized by everyone, that in the case of a work of reflection, removing the scaffolding and cleaning up the area around the building not only is of no benefit to the reader, but deprives him of something essential. Unlike the work of art, there is no finished edifice here, nor an edifice to be finished; just as much as, and even more than the results, what is important is the work of reflection and it is perhaps mostly this that an author can make us see, if he can make us see anything at all. Presenting the result as a systematic and polished totality, which in truth it never is; or even presenting the construction process – as is often the case, pedagogically but erroneously, in so many philosophical works – in the form of a well-ordered and wholly mastered logical process, can only serve to reinforce in the reader the disastrous illusion towards which he, like all of us, is already naturally inclined, that the edifice was constructed for him and that he has only, if he so desires, to move in and live there. Thinking is not building cathedrals or composing symphonies. If the symphony exists, it is the reader who must create it in his own ears.

When the possibility of publishing the whole of the work presented itself, it became clearly evident to me that the unpublished follow up of 'Marxism and Revolutionary Theory' had to be taken up again and reworked. The ideas which had already been brought out and formulated in the part of 'Marxism and Revolutionary Theory' published in 1964–5 – those of history as creation *ex nihilo*, of instituting society and instituted society, of the social imaginary, of the institution of society as its own work, of the social–historical as a mode of being unrecognized by inherited thought – had in the meantime been transformed for me from arrival points to starting points, thereby demanding that everything be rethought on this new basis. A reconsideration of psychoanalytic theory (to which I devoted the better part of the years 1965–8), a reflection on language (from 1968–71), a new study, over the past few years, of traditional philosophy, reinforced me in this conviction while at the same time they showed me that, in inherited thought, everything held up, held together and went along with the world which produced it and which this thought had, in its turn, helped to shape. And the hold exerted on our minds by the patterns of this thought, produced by an effort of over three thousand years on the part of so many incomparable geniuses, but also – and this is one of the central ideas of this book – in and through which is expressed, refined and elaborated everything that humanity has thought for hundreds of thousands of years and which, in a sense, reflects the very tendencies of the institution of society, could be shaken, if indeed it can be, only by a precise and detailed demonstration, case by case, of the limits of this thought and of the internal necessities, corresponding to its mode of being, which brought it to conceal what to me appears essential. This cannot be accomplished in one book or even in many books. It was therefore necessary to eliminate, or only to hint at questions which, in my eyes, are just as important as those discussed in the second part of this book: in particular, those of the institution and the functioning of instituted society, the division of society, the universality and the unity of history, the very possibility of an elucidation of the social–historical as the one attempted here, and the political relevance and implications of this work. Likewise, the properly philosophical aspect of the question of the imaginary and of the imagination has been reserved for another work, *l'Élément imaginaire*, which will be published soon. In this sense, the second part of the book is not a completed edifice either.

It would be ridiculous to attempt to replace the discussion of these questions by a few sentences or paragraphs here. I should only like to draw the attention of the reader to a single point in an effort to avoid any misunderstanding. That which, since 1964, I have termed the social imaginary – a term which has since been used and misused in a number of different ways – and, more generally, that which I call the imaginary has nothing to do with the representations currently circulating under this heading. In particular, it has nothing to do with that which is presented as 'imaginary' by certain currents in psychoanalysis: namely, the 'specular' which is obviously only an image *of* and a reflected image, in other words a *reflection*, and in yet other words a byproduct of Platonic ontology (*eidolon*) even if those who speak of it are unaware of its origin. The imaginary does not come from the image in the mirror or from the gaze of the other. Instead, the 'mirror' itself and its possibility, and the other as mirror, are the works of the imaginary, which is creation *ex nihilo*. Those who speak of 'imaginary', understanding by this the 'specular', the reflection of the 'fictive', do no more than repeat, usually without realizing it, the affirmation which has for all time chained them to the underground of the famous cave: it is necessary that this world be an image *of* something. The imaginary of which I am speaking is not an image *of*. It is the unceasing and essentially *undetermined* (social–historical and psychical) creation of figures/forms/images, on the basis of which alone there can ever be a question *of* 'something'. What we call 'reality' and 'rationality' are its works.

This same idea, that of the image *of* something, is what has always promoted theory as a Gaze inspecting what is. What I am attempting here is not a theory of society and of history, in the inherited sense of the term 'theory'. It is instead an elucidation, and this elucidation, even if it inevitably takes an abstract turn, is inseparable from a political aim and a political project. More than in any other area, here the idea of pure theory is an incoherent fiction. There exists no place, no point of view outside of history and society, or 'logically prior' to them, where one could be placed in order to construct the theory of them – a place from which to inspect them, contemplate them, affirm the determined necessity of their being-thus, 'constitute' them, reflect upon them or reflect them in their totality. Every thought of society and of history itself belongs to society and to history. Every thought, whatever it may be and whatever may be its 'object', is but a mode and a form of social–historical *doing*. It may be unaware of itself as such – and this is most often the case, by a necessity which is, so to speak, internal to it. And the fact that it knows itself as such does not take it out of its mode of being as a dimension of social–historical doing. But this can enable it to be lucid about itself. What I term elucidation is the labour by means of which individuals attempt to think about what they do and to know what they think. This, too, is a social–historical creation. The Aristotelian division into *theoria*, *praxis* and *poiesis* is derivative and secondary. History is essentially *poiesis*, not imitative poetry, but creation and ontological genesis in and through individuals'

doing and representing/saying. This doing and this representing/saying
are also instituted historically, at a given moment, as thoughtful doing
or as thought in the making.

This thoughtful doing is pre-eminently such when it is a matter of
political thinking and of the elucidation of the social–historical which
it implies. The illusion of *theoria* has, for a long time, concealed this
fact. An additional parricide is once more unavoidable here. The evil
commences when Heraclitus dared to state: Listening not to me but to
the *logos*, it is wise to agree that .... To be sure, one must struggle
against personal authority as well as against mere opinion, incoherent
arbitrariness, the refusal to give others an account of an explanation
for what one says – *logon didonai*. But do not listen to Heraclitus. His
humility is but the height of arrogance. It is never the *logos* that you
are listening to but always *someone*, such as he is, speaking from the
place where he is at his own risk, but at yours too. And that which in
the 'pure theorist' can be posited as a necessary postulate of responsibility and of the control over his words has become, necessarily, in
political thinkers the philosophical cover behind which they speak –
they speak. They speak in the name of being and of the *eidos* of man
and of the city – like Plato. They speak in the name of the laws of
history or of the proletariat – like Marx. They want to shield what they
have to say – which may be, and certainly has been, of immense
importance – behind being, nature, reason, history, or the interests of
a class 'in the name of which' they are expressing themselves. But no
one ever speaks in the name of someone else – unless he has been
explicitly delegated to do so. At most, others may recognize themselves
in what is said – and even this 'proves' nothing, for what is said may
and sometimes does induce a 'recognition' which nothing permits us to
assert that it would have existed without this discourse, or that it
validates it. Millions of Germans 'recognized themselves' in Hitler's
discourse, millions of 'communists' in that of Stalin.

The political individual and the political thinker offer a discourse under
their own responsibility. This does not mean that their discourse is
unverifiable – it demands to be tested by all; nor does this mean that
it is merely 'arbitrary' – if it is, no one will listen to it. The political
individual, however, cannot propose, prefer or project anything by
calling upon an allegedly 'rigorous' theory – any more than by presenting himself as the spokesman for a determined category. As for a
rigorously rigorous theory, there is none in mathematics; how could
there be one in politics? And no one is ever, except as a result of
circumstances, the true spokesman for a determined category – and, if
he were, he would still have to demonstrate that the point of view of
this category holds for everyone, and this brings us back to the preceding problem. You must not listen to a political speaker who speaks *in
the name of* ...; as soon as he has uttered these words, he is fooling us

or himself, little matter. More than anyone else the political figure and the political thinker speak in their own name and assume what they say as their own responsibility. This is, to be sure, the ultimate modesty.

The discourse of a political individual and the project he proposes are publicly verifiable in many different aspects. It is easy to imagine and even to display historical examples of incoherent pseudo-projects. But such a project is not so incoherent in its central core, if this core has any value – any more than is the movement of individuals with which it must link up or run the risk of disappearing altogether. For the former and the latter and their junction posit, create and institute not only new forms of intelligibility but new forms of social–historical doing, representing and value – forms which cannot simply be discussed and gauged on the basis of prior criteria belonging to instituted reason. The first, the second and their junction are but as moments and forms of instituting doing, of the self-creation of society.

December 1974

I
Marxism and Revolutionary Theory

1

Marxism: A Provisional Assessment

i THE HISTORICAL SITUATION OF MARXISM AND THE NOTION OF ORTHODOXY

For anyone who is preoccupied with the question of society, the encounter with Marxism is immediate and inevitable. Even to speak of an encounter in this case is inappropriate, inasmuch as this word denotes a contingent and external event. Ceasing to be a particular theory or a political programme professed by a few, Marxism has so impregnated language, ideas, and reality that it has become part of the atmosphere we breathe when we come into the social world, part of the historical landscape that frames our comings and goings.

For this very reason, however, to speak of Marxism has become one of the most difficult tasks imaginable. To begin with, we ourselves are implicated in a thousand different ways in this matter. And Marxism, in 'realizing' itself, has become ungraspable. Of which Marxism, in fact, should we be speaking? That of Khrushchev, of Mao Tse-tung, of Togliatti or Thorez? Or that of Castro, of the Yugoslavs, of the Polish revisionists? Or rather of the Trotskyites (and here again, this depends on geography: French and English Trotskyites, those from the United States and those from Latin America fight among themselves and denounce one another), Bordiguists, or any given far-left group that accuses all the others of betraying the spirit of 'true' Marxism, which it alone would possess? There is not simply the gulf that separates official Marxisms and opposition Marxisms. There is an enormous range of variants, each presenting itself as excluding all the others.

No simple criterion allows us to reduce this complexity all at once. There is obviously no factual test that speaks for itself, since both the public official and the political prisoner find themselves in particular social situations, which, as such, confer no privilege on their views and, on the contrary, render indispensable a double interpretation of what they say. The consecration of power must not carry greater weight for us than the halo of irreducible opposition, and it is Marxism itself that forbids us to forget the suspicion that is cast on established power as well as on the oppositions that remain indefinitely in the margins of historical reality.

Nor could the solution be 'a return to Marx', pure and simple whereby the historical evolution of ideas and practices over the past 80 years[1] would be considered no more than a layer of impurities concealing the resplendent body of a doctrine intact. Not only is the doctrine of Marx itself, as is well known and as I shall attempt once more to show, far from possessing the systematic simplicity and the consistency that some would like to attribute to it. Nor is it that such a 'return' necessarily involves an academic character – since, at the best, it could do no more than to restore the correct theoretical content belonging to a past doctrine, as could be done for Descartes or Thomas Aquinas, while at the same time leaving entirely in the shadows the problem that counts above all the others, namely the importance and the meaning of Marxism for us and for contemporary history. The return to Marx is impossible because, under the pretext of being faithful to Marx and in order to realize this fidelity, it begins by violating some essential principles posited by Marx himself.

Marx was, in fact, the first to show that the meaning of a theory cannot be understood in isolation from the historical and social practice to which it corresponds, which is an extension of it or which it serves to cover. Who today would dare to claim that the one and only sense of Christianity is that which restores a purified reading of the Evangelists, and that the social reality and the historical practice of the Churches and of Christianity over two millenia has nothing essential to teach us on this account? The 'faithfulness to Marx' that brackets the historical fate of Marxism is no less laughable. It is even more so, because for a Christian the revelation of Scripture has a transcendent ground and a timeless truth that no theory could possess in the eyes of a Marxist. To want to find the sense of Marxism exclusively in what Marx wrote, ignoring what this doctrine has become in history, is to claim, in direct contradiction to the central ideas of this doctrine, that real history does not count, that the truth of a theory is always and exclusively 'beyond', and, finally, it is to replace revolution by revelation and the reflection on facts by the exegesis of texts.

This in itself would be serious enough. But there is more to it, for the necessity of confrontation with historical reality[2] is explicitly inscribed in Marx's work and bound up with its most profound meaning. The Marxism of Marx did not aspire to be, and could not have been, a theory like another, paying no attention to its rootedness and its historical resonance. The point was no longer 'to interpret but to change the world',[3] and the full sense of the theory *is*, according to the theory itself, that which appears in the practice that it inspires. Those who say, believing they thus 'exonerate' Marxist theory: none of the historical practices that claim to belong to Marxism are 'truly' inspired by it, these very people, in saying this, 'condemn' Marxism as a 'mere theory' and level an irrevocable judgement on it. This could even be called, quite literally, a Last Judgement, for Marx assumed entirely as his own Hegel's great idea: *Weltgeschichte ist Weltgericht.*[4]

In fact, if the practice inspired by Marxism actually was revolutionary during certain phases of modern history, it was also the opposite during other periods. And if these two phenomena require interpretation (I shall return to this), it is nevertheless the case that they indicate beyond any doubt the essential ambiguity of Marxism. It is also the case, and this is even more important, that in history and in politics, the present carries infinitely greater weight than the past. Now, this 'present' is the fact that for over 40 years Marxism has become an *ideology* in the very sense that Marx gave to this term: a set of ideas that relate to a reality not in order to shed light on it and to change it, but in order to veil it and to justify it in the imaginary, which permits people to say one thing and do another, to appear as other than they are.

Marxism first became an ideology as the official dogma of the established powers in countries described ironically as 'socialist'. Invoked by governments that visibly do not embody the power of the proletariat and are no more 'controlled' by the latter than any bourgeois government; represented by brilliant leaders treated by their equally brilliant successors as no more than criminal madmen, without further ado; serving as a foundation for the policies of Tito as well as those of the Albanians, the policies of Khrushchev as well as those of Mao, Marxism has become the 'solemn complement of justification' discussed by Marx, which allows one to teach students the mandatory work, *The State and the Revolution*, and at the same time to maintain the most oppressive and most rigid state apparatus ever known,[5] thereby helping the bureaucracy to conceal itself behind the 'collective ownership' of the means of production.

Marxism has also become an ideology as the doctrine of the multitude of sects that proliferated as a result of the degeneration of the official Marxist movement. The word 'sect' is not used here simply as an epithet, it has a precise sociological and historical sense. A group with few members is not necessarily a sect; Marx and Engels did not form a sect even at the times they were most isolated. A sect is a group that sets up as an absolute a single side, aspect, or phase of the movement it stems from, making this aspect the truth of the doctrine and *the* truth as such, subordinating everything else to it and, in order to maintain its 'faithfulness' to this aspect, severs itself radically from the world, living henceforth in 'its' own world. The appeal to Marxism by these sects allows them to think of themselves and to present themselves as something other than what they really are, that is as the future revolutionary party of the proletariat, in which they are unable to take root.

Finally, Marxism has become an ideology in an entirely different sense as well: for the past several decades, it is no longer, even as a simple theory, a living theory, and it is useless to search in the literature of the last 40 years for any fecund applications of the theory, and even less for any attempts to extend it or deepen it.

It may be that what we are saying will be received as a scandal by those who, making it their profession to 'defend Marx', bury his remains every day a little deeper under the thick layers of their lies or their stupidity. I could not care less about this. It is clear that by analysing the historical destiny of Marxism, I am not, in any ethical sense, 'imputing' the responsibility to Marx. It is Marxism itself in what is best in its spirit, in its merciless denunciation of empty phrases and of ideologies, in its continual demand for self-criticism, that forces us to concern ourselves with its real fate.

Moreover, the question goes far beyond Marxism. For, just as the degeneration of the Russian revolution poses the problem: is it the fate of *every* socialist revolution that is indicated by this degeneration? So, too, we must ask: is it the lot of *every* revolutionary theory that is indicated by the fate of Marxism? This is the question that I shall deal with at length at the end of this text.[6]

It is therefore not possible to maintain or to rediscover any sort of 'orthodoxy' – whether in the laughable and comically complementary form given to it at once by the Stalinist pontiffs and the sectarian hermits, that of a doctrine alleged to be intact and 'amended', 'improved' or 'brought up to date' by one or the other at their convenience on a particular point; or in the dramatic and ultimatum-like form given to it by Trotsky in 1940,[7] stating more or less as follows: we know that Marxism is an imperfect theory, bound to a given historical epoch, and that its theoretical development must continue, but, since revolution is the order of the day, this task can and must wait. Acceptable on the very day of armed insurrection, when it is anyhow useless, this argument, after a quarter of a century, serves only to conceal the inertia and sterility that have indeed characterized the Trotskyite movement since the death of its founder.

Nor is it possible to attempt to maintain an orthodoxy as Lukács did in 1919 by limiting it to Marxist *method*, which is held to be separate from its content and, so to speak, indifferent to it.[8] Although it marks an advance with respect to the diverse varieties of 'orthodox' cretinism, this position is untenable for a reason that Lukács, who was nonetheless steeped in dialectic, overlooked: unless we are to take the term in its most superficial sense, method cannot be separated from content in this way, especially not when it is a question of historical and social theory. Method, in the philosophical sense, is simply the operating set of categories. A rigid distinction between method and content belongs only to the most naive forms of transcendental idealism or criticism, which, in its initial steps, separates and opposes a finite or indefinite matter or content and the categories that the eternal flow of the material cannot affect, categories that are the form without which this matter could not be grasped. But this rigid distinction is already superseded in the more advanced, more dialectical phases of critical thinking. For the problem immediately appears: how are we to know which category corresponds to which material? If the material bears in itself the 'distinctive sign' allowing it to be subsumed under a given category, it is therefore not merely shapeless matter; and if it is truly without form, then the application of this or that category becomes indifferent, and the distinction between true and false collapses. It is precisely this antinomy that has led, upon a number of occasions in the history of philosophy, from critical thinking to thinking of a dialectical type.[9]

Such is the way the question is posed on the level of logic. And, on the historical–genetic level, that is to say, when the process of the development of knowledge is considered from the point of view of its unfolding as *history*, it is most often the 'unfolding of the material' that leads to the revision or the shattering of the categories. The properly philosophical revolution produced in modern physics as a result of relativity and quantum theory is only one striking example among others.[10]

However, the impossibility of establishing a rigid distinction between method and content, between category and material, appears even more clearly when we consider not knowledge of nature, but knowledge of history. For in this case there is not simply the fact that the further exploration of the material already given or the appearance of new material can lead to a modification of the categories, that is of method. There is especially, and more profoundly, another fact, one brought to light, precisely, by Marx and by Lukács himself:[11] the categories that we use to think of history are, for an essential part, the real products of historical development. These categories can clearly and effectively become forms of *knowledge* of history only when they are embodied or realized in forms of *actual social life*.

To cite the simplest example: if in antiquity, the dominant categories under which social and historical relations are grasped are essentially *political* categories (power in the city-state, relations between city-states, the relation between force and right, etc.), and if the economic receives only marginal attention, this is neither because understanding or reflection was less 'advanced', nor because the economic material was absent or neglected. The reason is that, in the reality of the ancient world, the economy was not yet constituted as a separate, 'autonomous' moment (as Marx would say), 'for itself', of human activity. A genuine analysis of the economy itself and of its importance for society could occur only after the seventeenth, and in particular, after the eighteenth century, that is with the birth of capitalism, which in fact set up the economy as the dominant moment of social life. And the central importance accorded by Marx and the Marxists to the economic likewise translates this historical reality.

It is therefore clear that there can be no 'method' in history which would remain unaffected by real historical development. And this for reasons more profound than the notions of the 'progress of knowledge', 'new discoveries', and so on, reasons that concern directly the very *structure* of historical knowledge, and first and foremost the structure of its object, that is the mode of being proper to history. Since the object of historical knowledge is itself a meaningful object, or an object constituted by significations, the development of the historical world is *ipso facto* the unfolding of a world of significations. There can thus be no break between matter and category, between fact and sense. And since this world of significations is that in which the 'subject' of historical knowledge lives, it is also that through which this subject necessarily grasps, to begin with, the whole of the historical material.

Of course, these observations, too, are to be relativized. They cannot imply that at every instant every category and every method are put into question, superseded, or destroyed by the evolution of real history at the very moment we think it. In other words, it is in every instance a concrete question whether historical change has reached the point where the old categories and the old method are to be reconsidered. But it then becomes apparent that this cannot be done independently of a discussion on content which, if necessary, by using the old method to begin with shows the need to go beyond it when it is placed in contact with the material.

To say that being Marxist is being faithful to the method of Marx which continues to be true, is to say that nothing in the content of the history of the past 100 years either authorizes us or compels us to put Marx's categories into question, that everything can be understood by means of his method. This is, therefore, to take a position with reference to content, to have a definite theory about it, and yet to refuse to state it.

In fact, it is precisely the elaboration of the content that forces us to reconsider the method and hence the Marxist system. If we have been led to pose, at first gradually and in the end bluntly, the question of Marxism, it is because we have been forced to recognize, not only and not so much that this or that particular theory of Marx, this or that precise idea of traditional Marxism were 'false', but that the history we are living can no longer be grasped with the help of Marxist categories as they stand, not even when they are 'amended', 'extended', etc. It appeared to us that this history can be neither understood nor changed with this method. The re-examination of Marxism that we have undertaken does not occur in a void, nor are we speaking by placing ourselves anywhere at all or nowhere at all. Starting from revolutionary Marxism, we have arrived at the point where we have to choose between remaining Marxist and remaining revolutionaries, between faithfulness to a doctrine that, for a long time now, has ceased to fuel either reflection or action, and faithfulness to the project of a radical change of society, which demands that we first understand what we want to change and that we identify what in society truly challenges this society and is struggling against its present form. Method cannot be separated from content, and their unity, that is to say, theory, cannot in its turn be separated from the requirements of a revolutionary action which, as the example of both great parties and sects has shown, can no longer be clarified and guided by traditional schemata.

ii MARXIST THEORY OF HISTORY

We therefore can, indeed we must, begin our study by considering what has become of the most concrete content of Marxist theory, namely the economic analysis of capitalism. Far from representing a contingent and accidental empirical application to a particular historical phenomenon, this analysis forms the honed point where the entire substance of the theory is to be concentrated, where the theory at last shows that it is capable, not only of producing a few general ideas, but of making its own dialectic coincide with the dialectic of historical reality, and finally, of extracting out of this movement of reality itself both the basic principles of revolutionary action and its orientation. It is not insignificant that Marx devoted the greater part of his life to this analysis (nor that the Marxist movement after him always granted a capital importance to the economy). Today's sophisticated Marxists who only want to hear about Marx's early manuscripts prove themselves to be both superficial and extremely arrrogant, for their attitude amounts to saying that after the age of 30 Marx no longer knew what he was doing.

We know that for Marx the capitalist economy is subject to insurmountable contradictions which are manifested by periodic crises of overproduction as well as by long-term tendencies, which act to shake the system with an increasing intensity: the increase in the rate of exploitation (hence, greater poverty, whether absolute or relative, of the proletariat); the rise in the organic composition of capital (hence the growth of the industrial reserve army, in other words, continuing unemployment); the fall in the rate of profit (hence the slow-down of the accumulation and expansion of production). What is expressed by this, in the final analysis, is *the* contradiction of capitalism as Marx saw it: the incompatibility between the development of the productive forces and the 'relations of production' or the capitalist 'forms of ownership'.[12]

Now, the experience of the past 20 years leads us to think that the periodic crises of overproduction are by no means inevitable in modern capitalism (except in the extremely attenuated form of minor and transitory 'recessions'). And the experience of the past 100 years has shown, in the developed capitalist countries, neither the (absolute or relative) pauperization of the proletariat, nor the secular increase of unemployment, nor any fall in the rate of profit, much less a slow-down in the development of the productive forces, which has instead accelerated in proportions that were unimaginable in an earlier time.

Of course, this experience 'demonstrates' nothing by itself. But it forces us to reconsider Marx's economic theory in order to see whether the contradiction between theory and facts is simply apparent or transitory, whether a suitable modification of the theory would not enable us to account for the facts without giving up anything essential, or whether, finally, it is the very substance of the theory that is in question.

Once we make this return, we are led to conclude that Marx's economic theory is tenable neither in its premises, nor in its method, nor in its structure.[13] Briefly, the theory as such 'ignores' the action of social classes. It 'ignores' the effect of class struggles on the redistribution of the social product and through this, necessarily, on all aspects of the economy, in particular on the constant expansion of the market for consumer goods. It 'ignores' the effect of the progressive organization of the capitalist class, aimed precisely at dominating the 'spontaneous' tendencies of the economy. This derives from its basic premise: in the capitalist economy, individuals, whether proletarians or capitalists, are actually and wholly transformed into things, i.e. reified; they are submitted to the action of economic laws that differ in no way from natural laws,[14] except that they use the 'conscious' actions of individuals as the *unconscious* instrument of their realization.

This premise is an abstraction that corresponds, so to speak, with only half of reality, and as such it is ultimately false. Reification, the essential tendency of capitalism, can never be wholly realized. If it were, if the system were actually able to change individuals into things moved only by economic 'forces', it would collapse not in the long run, but immediately. The struggle of people against reification is, just as much as the tendency towards reification, the condition for the functioning of capitalism. A factory in which the workers were really and totally mere cogs in the machine, blindly executing the orders of management, would come to a stop in a quarter of an hour. Capitalism can function only by continually drawing upon the genuinely *human* activity of those subject to it, while at the same time trying to level and dehumanize them as much as possible. It can continue to function only to the extent that its profound tendency, which actually is reification, is not realized, to the extent that its norms are continually countered in their application. Analysis shows that the final contradiction of capitalism resides here,[15] and not in the so to speak mechanical incompatibilities presented by the economic gravitation of human molecules in the system. These incompatibilities are ultimately illusory, even though they go beyond particular and localized phenomena.

From this reconsideration, there follows a whole series of conclusions. We shall discuss only the most important ones.

First of all, we can no longer maintain the central importance that Marx (and the entire Marxist movement) ascribes to the *economy* as such. The term 'economy' is taken here in the relatively precise sense conferred upon it by the very contents of *Capital*: the system of abstract and quantifiable relations which, starting from a certain type of appropriation of the productive resources (whether this appropriation possesses the legal guarantee of ownership or simply translates a *de facto* power of control) determines the formation, exchange and distribution of values. These relations, whose functioning is held to be governed by specific laws, independently of other social relations, cannot be set up as an autonomous system. This cannot be done in the case of capitalism, and since, precisely, it is under capitalism that the economy has shown the greatest tendency to 'become autonomous' as a sphere of social activity, we can only suspect that such systematization would be even more difficult in the case of previous societies. Even under capitalism, the economy remains an abstraction. Society is not transformed into economic society to the extent that all other social relations can be considered as secondary.

Next, if the category of reification is to be re-examined, this signifies that the entire philosophy of history underlying the analysis in *Capital* must also be re-examined. We shall consider this question later.

Finally, it becomes clear that the conception Marx had of the most general historical and social dynamics is put into question in the very area where it had been most concretely worked out. If *Capital* takes on such great importance in the work of Marx and in the ideology of Marxists, this is because it was to show scientifically in the precise case which is of the highest interest (that of capitalist society) the theoretical and practical truth of a general conception of the dynamics of history, namely that 'at a certain stage of development, the material productive forces of society come into conflict with the existing relations of production or – this merely expresses the same thing in juridical terms – with the property relations within the framework of which they have operated hitherto'.[16]

In fact, *Capital* is permeated from beginning to end by this essential intuition: that nothing can henceforth stop the development of technology and, along with it, that of the concomitant productivity of labour. What *Capital* thus attempts to show is that the capitalist relations of production, which in the beginning were the most adequate expression and the most effective instrument of the development of the productive forces, become 'at a certain stage' a brake on this development and so must *for this very reason* break apart.

As much as the hymns of praise addressed to the bourgeoisie in its progressive phase glorify the development of the productive forces, of which it is the historical instrument,[17] so the condemnation of the bourgeoisie, by Marx as well as by later Marxists, is based on the idea that this development is henceforth blocked by the capitalist mode of production. 'The great forces of production – that shock factor in historical development – were choked in those obsolete institutions of the superstructure (private property and the national state) in which they found themselves locked by all preceding development. Engendered by capitalism, the forces of production were knocking at all the walls of the bourgeois national state, demanding their emancipation by means of the socialist organisation of economic life on a world scale,' Trotsky wrote in 1919,[18] and in 1936 he based his *Transitional Programme* on the observation that 'the productive forces of humanity had ceased to develop ...', because in the interim the capitalist relations, from a relative brake, had become a provisionally absolute brake on their development.

Today we know that such is not the case and that, for the past 25 years, the productive forces have known a development that far surpasses anything that could have been imagined in the past. This development was, of course, influenced by modifications in the organization of capitalism, and it in turn has led to a number of others, but it has not put into question the substance of the capitalist relations of production. What appeared to Marx and to the Marxists as a 'contradiction' that was to destroy the system, has instead been 'resolved' within the system.

This is, first of all, because there never was a *contradiction*. To speak of a 'contradiction' between the productive forces and the relations of production is worse than an abuse of language; it is a phraseology that lends a dialectical appearance to what is simply a model of mechanistic thinking. When a gas is heated inside a container, and it exerts on the walls an increasing pressure that can finally make them burst, there is no sense in saying that there is a 'contradiction' between the gas pressure and the rigidity of the walls – any more than there is a 'contradiction' between two forces applied to the same point and acting in opposite directions. In the same way, in the case of society one can, at the very most, speak of a tension, of an opposition or a conflict between the productive forces (whether actual production or the productive capacity of society), which, for their development, require at each stage a certain type of organization of social relations, and those types of organization that, sooner or later, 'lag behind' the productive forces and cease to be adequate to them. When the tension becomes too great, the conflict too sharp, a revolution sweeps away the old social organization and opens the way for a new stage in the development of the productive forces.

This mechanical schema, however, is not tenable even at the simplest empirical level. It represents an improper extrapolation to history as a whole of a process that has been realized during just one phase of this history, the phase of bourgeois revolution. It more or less faithfully describes what took place at the time of the transition from feudal society: from the hybrid societies of western Europe from 1650 to 1850 (where a well-developed and economically dominant bourgeoisie ran up against absolute monarchy *and* the remains of feudalism in agrarian property and in legal and political structures) to capitalist society. But it corresponds neither to the breakdown of ancient society and the subsequent appearance of the feudal world, nor to the birth of the bourgeoisie, which emerged precisely outside of and on the fringes of feudal relations. It corresponds neither to the constitution of the bureaucracy as the dominant order today in countries that are in the process of industrialization, nor finally to the historical evolution of non-European peoples. In none of these cases can we speak of a development of the productive forces embodied in the emergence of a social class within the given social system, a development which 'at a certain stage' would have become incompatible with the maintenance of the system and would therefore lead to a revolution giving the power to the 'rising' class.

Here again, beyond the 'confirmation' or 'refutation' of the theory by the facts, we must reflect on the *meaning* of the theory, on its deepest content, on its categories, and the type of relation it attempts to establish with reality.

It is one thing to recognize the fundamental importance of Marx's teaching concerning the profound relation that links production to the rest of social life. No one after Marx can continue to think of history while 'forgetting' that every society has to assure the production of the material conditions of its existence and that all aspects of social life are deeply bound up with labour, with the mode of organization of this production, and with the social divisions that correspond to it.

It is something else again to reduce production, human activity mediated by instruments and objects, labour, to 'productive forces', that is to say, ultimately, to technique[19] and to ascribe to the latter a development which 'in the final analysis' is deemed autonomous. For this is to construct a mechanical system of social relations based on an eternal, and eternally identical, opposition between a technique (or productive forces) that would have its own specific activity and everything else in social relations and in human existence (the 'superstructure') that would be endowed, just as arbitrarily, with passivity and essential inertia.

In fact, there is neither any autonomy of technique nor any immanent tendency of technique towards autonomous development. During 99.5 per cent of its span – that is to say, for all but the last five centuries – the known or presumed history of humanity has unfolded on the basis of what today appears to us as stagnation and which was lived by people at the time as a self-evident stability of technique. Civilizations and empires rose and fell, over thousands of years, against the backdrop of the same technical 'infrastructures'.

In Greek antiquity, the fact that the techniques applied to production remained certainly far behind the possibilities offered by the scientific development already attained cannot be separated from the social and cultural conditions of the Greek world, nor, most likely, from the attitude of the Greeks towards nature, labour and knowledge. In the same way, the vast technical development of modern times cannot be separated from the radical change in these attitudes – even if this came about gradually. The idea that nature is *only* there to be exploited by human beings, for example, is anything but self-evident from the point of view of all of humanity up to now, and even today would be questioned in non-industrial societies. To make *scientific* knowledge essentially a means of industrial development, to give it a predominantly instrumental character, also corresponds to a new attitude. The appearance of these attitudes is inseparable from the birth of the bourgeoisie, which initially takes place on the basis of old techniques. It is only with the flowering of the bourgeoisie that, in appearance, one can observe a sort of autonomous dynamics of technological evolution. But in appearance only. For, not only is this evolution dependent on the philosophical and scientific development set in motion (or accelerated) by the Renaissance, which has incontestable ties to the whole of bourgeois culture and society, but it is increasingly influenced by the development of the proletariat and the class struggle within capitalism, leading to a *selection* of the techniques applied in production from among all possible techniques.[20] Finally, in the present phase of capitalism technological research is planned, controlled and directed explicitly towards objectives that are set by the dominant levels of society. What is the sense of speaking of the autonomous evolution of technology, when the United States government spends a billion dollars on research for missile fuels and one million dollars on research into the causes of cancer?

With respect to earlier phases of history, where an invention or a method was, so to speak, hit upon by chance and where the basis of production (just as in war or other social activities) was a sort of technological scarcity, the idea of a relative autonomy of technique can retain some meaning – even though it is false to say that this technique was a 'determinant' in any exclusive sense for the structure and evolution of society, as is proved by the great variety of cultures, both archaic *and* historical (Asiatic cultures, for example) built on 'the same technical bases'. Even for these phases, the problem of the relation between the type of technique and the type of culture and of society remains whole and entire. In contemporary societies, however, the constantly increasing range of technical possibilities and the continuous action of society on methods of labour, of communication, of war and so on definitively refutes the idea of the autonomy of the technical factor and makes absolutely explicit the reciprocal relation, the uninterrupted circular feed-back between the methods of production, social organization and the total content of culture.[21]

What we have just said shows that there is not, nor has there ever been, an inertia of the rest of social life, nor a privileged passivity of the 'superstructures'. These superstructures are no more than a fabric of social relations, neither more nor less 'real', neither more nor less 'inert' than the others, and just as 'conditioned' by the infrastructures as the infrastructures are by them, if the word 'conditioned' can be used to designate the mode of coexistence of the various moments or aspects of social activities.

The famous phrase about consciousness 'lagging behind reality' is only a phrase. It represents an empirical observation valid for the right half of any phenomenon and false for the left half. In the speech and in the unconscious of Marxists it has become a theological phrase, and as such it has no meaning. Without consciousness, there is neither life nor social reality, and to say that consciousness lags behind reality is tantamount to saying that the head of a man who is walking constantly lags behind the man himself. Even if we take 'consciousness' in a narrow sense (that of explicit consciousness, of 'thinking of', of the theoretical elaboration of data) the phrase still remains false as often as true, for just as consciousness can 'lag behind' reality, so too can reality 'lag behind' consciousness. In other words, there is a correspondence as well as a difference between what people do or experience and what they think. And what they think is not only the arduous elaboration of what is already there, following breathless in its tracks. It is also the *relativization* of what is given, its setting at a distance, a projection. History is just as much a conscious creation as it is an unconscious repetition. What Marx called the superstructure was itself no more a passive and belated reflection of a social 'materialness' (moreover, undefinable) than human perception and knowledge are imprecise and cloudy 'reflections' of an external world, which would be perfectly formed, coloured and scented in itself.

To be sure, human consciousness – considered as a transforming and creative agent in history – is essentially a *practical* consciousness, an operative, active reason rather than a theoretical reason to which practice would be appended like the corollary to the theorem, merely serving to materialize the consequences. This practice, however, is not simply a modification of the material world; it is just as much and even more so the modification of human behaviour and relations. The *Sermon on the Mount* and the *Communist Manifesto* belong to historical practice just as much as a technical invention and, with regard to their real effects on history, carry infinitely greater weight.

The present ideological confusion and the neglect of elementary truths are such that what we are saying here will doubtless appear to many 'Marxists' as idealism. But idealism, indeed the crudest and most naive form of it, is actually to be found in this attempt to reduce the whole of historical reality to the effects of the action of a single factor, which is necessarily *abstracted* from the rest and thus *abstract* purely and simply; and which is, moreover, something on the order of an *idea*. Ideas are, in fact, what make history progress in the conception called 'historical materialism', except that instead of being philosophical, political, religious ideas, these are technological ideas. It is true that, to become operative, these ideas must be 'embodied' in the instruments and methods of labour. This embodiment, however, is determined by the ideas themselves. A new instrument is new inasmuch as it realizes a new manner of conceiving of the relations between the productive activity, its means and its object. Technical ideas thus remain a kind of prime mover. These, then, are the alternatives: either one stops here, and this 'scientific' conception appears to base all of history on a mystery, the mystery of the autonomous and unexplainable evolution of a particular category of ideas. Or else one plunges technique back into the whole social reality, and then it can no longer be accorded a privilege, whether *a priori* or even *a posteriori*. Engels' attempt to get out of this dilemma by explaining that although the superstructures do act on the infrastructures, the latter continue to be determinant 'in the final analysis', has scarcely any meaning.[22] In a causal explanation there is no final analysis, each link refers ineluctably to another. Either Engels' concession remains merely verbal and we are left with a factor that determines history without being determined by it, or else it is real, and it defeats the claim of having localized the ultimate explanation of historical phenomena in a specific factor.

The genuinely idealistic character of the conception appears even more clearly when we consider another aspect of the categories of infrastructure and superstructure as these were used by Marx. It is not simply that the infrastructure has a determining weight, in fact it *alone* carries weight, because it produces the movement of history. It is also that the infrastructure possesses a *truth* which the rest does not have. Consciousness can be, and in fact most of the time is, 'false consciousness'; it is mystified, its content is 'ideological'. The superstructures are always ambiguous: they express the 'real situation' and to the same extent they mask it. Their function is essentially double. The constitution of the bourgeois republic, for example, or civil law have an explicit or apparent sense – the one presented in their text. They also have a latent sense, a real sense – the one unveiled by Marxist analysis, showing behind the equality of citizens the division of society into classes, behind the 'people's sovereignty' the *de facto* power of the bourgeoisie. Anyone who wanted to understand current law by confining himself to its explicit, manifest meaning would be guilty of legal cretinism. Law, like politics, religion, etc., can acquire its full and true sense only when it is bound up with a reference to all the other social phenomena of an epoch. But this ambiguity, this truncated character belonging to any particular signification in the historical world is held to come to an end once we enter the 'infrastructure'. Here, things can be understood in themselves, a technical fact is held to have an immediate and full significance, there is no ambiguity; it is what it 'says' and it says what it is. It even says all the rest: the handmill says feudal society, and the steam mill says capitalist society. We therefore have things that *are* meanings complete in themselves, and which at the same time are meanings fully and immediately[23] understandable by us. Technical facts are not only '*backward*' ideas (meaning that they have been embodied), they are also '*forward*' ideas (they *signify* actively all that 'results' from them, conferring a determined sense on all that surrounds them).

That history is the domain in which meanings are 'embodied' and in which things become meaningful is certain beyond the shadow of a doubt. However, none of these meanings is ever complete and closed in on itself; each always refers to something else, and no thing, no particular historical fact can deliver a meaning that in and of itself would be inscribed on it. No technical fact has an assignable meaning if it is isolated from the society in which it is produced and none imposes a univocal and ineluctable sense to the human activities that it underlies, even these. At a distance of only a few kilometres, in the same jungle, with the same weapons and instruments, two primitive tribes develop social structures and cultures as dissimilar as possible. Is it God who wanted it thus, is it the singular 'soul' of the tribe that is behind this? Not at all. A study of the *total history* of each one, of its relations with the others, etc. would permit an understanding of how the various evolutions took place (although it would not enable us to understand 'everything', and even less to isolate a 'cause' of this evolution). The English automobile industry works on the same 'technical base' as the French automobile industry, with the same types of machines and the same methods to produce the same objects. The 'relations of production' are the same in both cases: capitalist firms producing for the market hire workers. But the situation in the factories is completely different: in England, wildcat strikes are common, there is continuous guerrilla warfare between workers and management, and they have established a form of worker representation, the shop stewards, as democratic, as effective, as combative as possible under capitalist conditions. In France, the apathy and subservience of the workers is the rule and worker 'delegates' are entirely transformed into buffers between workers and management. And the *real* 'relations of production', that is to say, precisely, the degree of actual control that the 'purchase of the labour power' confers to management differs considerably as a result of this. Only an analysis of the whole of each of the societies considered, of their previous history, and so on, can permit us to understand, up to a certain point, how situations so different from one another could have come about.

Up to now we have situated ourselves, for the most part, on the level of the *content* of the 'materialist conception of history', attempting to see to what extent the precise propositions following from this conception can be held to be true, or even whether they are meaningful. Our conclusion is, obviously, that this content is not tenable, that the Marxist conception of history does not offer the explanation of it that it claims to provide.

The problem, however, does not end with these considerations. If the Marxist conception does not offer the explanation of history that it seeks, there is perhaps some other conception that might offer it, and would not the construction of a new and 'better' conception be the most urgent task?

This question is of much greater importance than the first one, for, after all, the fact that a scientific theory proves to be insufficient or erroneous is the very law governing the progress of knowledge. The condition for this progress is, nevertheless, that we understand why a theory has proved to be inadequate or false.

The preceding considerations have already allowed us to see that what is at cause in the failure of the materialist conception of history is, much more than the relevance of any particular idea belonging to the content of the theory, the very *type* of theory and what it is aiming at. Behind the attempt to set up the productive forces as an autonomous and determinant factor of historical evolution, there lies the idea of condensing into one simple schema the 'forces' which have dominated this evolution. And the simplicity of the schema results from the belief that the same forces, acting on the same objects, will produce the same series of effects.

But to what extent can we categorize history in this way? To what extent does the historical material lend itself to this treatment?

The idea, for example, that in all societies the development of the productive forces has 'determined' the relations of production and, as a result, legal, political, religious, etc. relations, presupposes that in all societies the same articulation of human activities exists, that technology, the economy, law, politics and religion are always and necessarily separated or separable, for otherwise this assertion is meaningless. But this is to extrapolate to the whole of history the articulations and the structuration characteristic of *our* society, which do not necessarily have a meaning outside of it. Now this articulation, this structuration are, precisely, *products* of historical development. Marx already pointed out that 'the individual is a social product', meaning by this not that the existence of the individual presupposes that of society, or that society determines what the individual will be, but that the *category* of individual as a person freely detachable from the family, the tribe, or the city is itself nothing natural and appears only at a certain stage of history. In the same way, the various aspects or sectors of social activity become 'autonomous', as Marx also said, only in a certain type of society and in relation to a certain degree of historical development.[24] However, if this is the case, it is impossible to give, once and for all, a model of relations or 'determinations' valid for every society. These relations are not fixed to any set points; the movement of history reconstitutes and redeploys social structures in a totally different way each time (and not necessarily in the sense of an ever increasing differentiation: in this respect at least, the feudal domain represents an *involution*, a recondensation of moments that were clearly separated in the Greco-Roman world). In short, there are not in history, even less than there are in nature or in life, separate and fixed *substances* that act on one another from outside. One cannot say that in general 'the economy determines ideology', nor that 'ideology determines the economy', nor, finally, that 'the economy and ideology mutually determine one another,' for the simple reason that economy and ideology, taken as separate spheres that may or may not act on one another, are themselves the products of a given stage (in fact, a very recent one) of historical development.[25]

In the same way, the Marxist theory of history, and every general and simple theory of the same type, is necessarily led to postulate that the basic motivations of individuals are, and have always been, the same in all societies. Productive or other kinds of 'forces' can act in history only through the actions of individuals and to say that the same forces play the same determining role everywhere signifies that they correspond to motives that are constant and that are found everywhere. Thus the theory that makes the 'development of the productive forces' the motor of history implicitly presupposes an invariable type of basic motivation for all individuals, broadly speaking, an economic motivation: from all time, human societies are held to have aimed (whether consciously or unconsciously, little matter) first and foremost to increase their production and their consumption. But this idea is not simply false in a material sense; it overlooks the fact that the types of motivation (and the corresponding values that polarize and direct human lives) are social creations, that each culture establishes its own values and rears individuals in relation to these. This training is practically all-powerful[26] for there is no 'human nature' that could offer resistance to it; in other words, man is not born with the sense of his life already laid out. The maximum amount of consumption, or saintliness, or power are not innate objectives in children; it is the culture in which they live that teaches them that they 'need' one or the other. And it is inadmissible to mix with the examination of history[27] *biological* 'need' or the 'instinct' of self-preservation. Biological 'need' or the 'instinct' of self-preservation is the abstract and universal presupposition of *every* human society and of every living species in general, and it can tell us nothing about any one of them in particular. It is absurd to want to base history, which by definition is always different, on the permanence of the 'instinct' of self-preservation, which by definition is always the same, just as it would be absurd to want to explain by the *constancy* of the libido the infinite variety of types of family organization, of neuroses or sexual perversions that are encountered in human societies. So once a theory postulates that the development of the productive forces has been a determining factor everywhere, it does not mean that men have always had to feed themselves (for in this case they would have remained monkeys). On the contrary, it means that men have always gone *beyond* biological 'needs', that they have formed needs of another sort – and in this, it is actually a theory that speaks of the history of *men*. At the same time, however, it says that these other 'needs' have been always and everywhere and predominantly, economic needs. And in this the theory no longer speaks of history in general, it speaks only of the history of capitalism. To say, in fact, that men have always sought the greatest possible development of the productive

forces, and that the only obstacle they have encountered in this endeavour was the state of technique – or to claim that societies have always
been 'objectively' dominated by this tendency, and organized on this
basis – is to extrapolate unwarrantedly to the whole of history the
motivations, the values, the movement and organization of present
society – more precisely, the capitalist half of present society. The idea
that the meaning of life consists in the accumulation and conservation
of wealth would be madness for the Kwakiutl Indians, who amass
wealth *in order* to destroy it. The idea of seeking power and the
authority to command would be sheer madness for the Zuni Indians,
for whom making someone the leader of the tribe means beating him
until he accepts.[28] Myopic Marxists laugh when one cites these
examples, which they consider to be ethnological curiosities. But the
real ethnological curiosities are precisely these 'revolutionaries', who
have set up the capitalist mentality as the eternal content of human
nature considered everywhere the same, and who, while gabbing on
interminably about colonialism and underdeveloped countries, overlook in their reasoning two-thirds of the population of the globe. For
one of the major obstacles that the penetration of capitalism has met,
and that it will always meet, is the absence of economic motivations and
of the capitalistic type of mentality in people of 'backward' countries. A
classic and still current case is that of the Africans who, after working
for awhile, quit their jobs as soon as they have amassed the amount
decided upon and return to their village to take up again what, in their
eyes, is the only normal existence. Whenever it succeeded in constituting among these peoples a class of wage earners, capitalism has
not only, as Marx has already shown, had to reduce them to poverty
by systematically destroying the material bases of their independent
existence. It has simultaneously had to destroy pitilessly the values and
the significations of their culture and their life – that is to say, actually
to turn them into that combination of an empty stomach and of muscle
ready to perform meaningless labour, which is the capitalist image of
humanity.[29]

It is false to claim that the technical–economic categories have always
been determinant ones, since they were not present either as categories
realized in the life of society, or as poles and values. And it is false to
claim that they always were present, but hidden under mystifying
appearances – whether political, religious, or other – and that capitalism, by demystifying or disenchanting the world, allowed us to see the
'true' meanings of human acts which escaped their authors. Of course,
the technical or the economic 'have always been present' in a certain
manner, since every society must produce its life and socially organize
this production. But it is this 'in a certain manner' that makes all the
difference. For how can we claim that the mode of integrating the
economic into other social relations (relations of authority and
allegiance, for example, in feudal society) does not affect, first of all,
the nature of the economic relations in the society considered and, at

the same time, the manner in which these relations act upon one another? It is certain that once capitalism has been constituted, the redistribution of productive resources among the various social levels and among the capitalists themselves is essentially the result of the play of the economy and is continually modified by the latter. But an analogous assertion would be senseless in the case of a feudal (or 'Asiatic') economy.[30] Let us also admit that in a *laissez-faire* capitalist society, the State (and political relations) can be treated as a 'super-structure', with a one-way dependence on the economy. But what is the sense of this idea when the State is the owner and possessor of the means of production, and when it is peopled by a hierarchy of bureau-crats whose relation with production and exploitation is *necessarily* mediated by their relation to the State and subordinated to this relation? This was the case for the ethnological curiosities represented for thou-sands of years by Asiatic monarchies, as it is the case today for such sociological curiosities as the USSR, China, and the other 'socialist' countries. What is the sense of saying today that in the USSR the 'true' bureaucracy is that of the factory directors and that the bureaucracy of the Party, the Army, the State, and so on, is secondary?

How, too, is it possible to claim that the manner, which differs so widely from one society to another and from one epoch to another, of living these relations is of no importance? How is it possible to claim that the meanings, motivations and values created by each culture have no function, perform no action other than to veil an economic psychology that is held always to have been there? This is not just the paradoxical postulate of an inalterable human nature. It is the no less paradoxical attempt to treat human lives, as they are actually lived (consciously as well as unconsciously) as a mere illusion with respect to the 'real' (economic) forces that govern it. It is the invention of another unconscious beneath the unconscious, the unconscious of the unconscious, which would be at once 'objective' (because totally inde-pendent of the history of subjects and of their action) and 'rational' (because constantly directed towards a definable and even measurable end, the economic end). But if we do not want to believe in magic, the action of individuals, consciously or unconsciously motivated, is obviously an indispensable relay for any action of 'forces' or of 'laws' in history. It would therefore be necessary to construct an 'economic psychoanalysis' which would reveal as the cause of human actions, their 'true' (economic) latent sense, and in which 'economic impulse' would take the place of the libido.

To be sure, a latent economic sense can often be discovered in acts that appear not to possess it. But this does not mean either that it is the only one or that it is the primary one. It certainly does not mean that its content is always and in every instance the maximalization of 'economic satisfaction' in the sense of western capitalism. The fact that the 'economic impulse' – the 'pleasure principle', if you like, turned towards consumption or appropriation – takes this or that direction, fixes itself on a particular objective, and is orchestrated in a given mode of conduct, this depends on all of the factors in play. This depends, in particular, on its relation to the sexual drive (the way in which this drive becomes 'specified' in the society considered) and to the world of meanings and values created by the culture in which the individual lives.[31] It would finally be less false to say that *homo economicus* is a product of capitalist culture than to say that capitalist culture is a product of *homo economicus*. But we should say neither one nor the other. In each case there is a deep homology and correspondence between the structure of the personality and the content of the culture, and there is no sense in predetermining one by the other.

Thus when, as in the cultivation of maize by certain Indian tribes in Mexico, or in the cultivation of rice in Indonesian villages, agricultural labour is lived not only as a means of providing food but at the same time as the cult of a god, as a festival, and as a dance, and when a theoretician appears on the scene and interprets all in those gestures that is not specifically productive as no more than mystification, illusion and cunning of reason, it must be forcefully asserted that this theoretician is a much more complete incarnation of capitalism than any boss. For not only does he remain a lamentable prisoner of the categories specific to capitalism, but he wants to submit all the rest of the history of humanity to them, claiming broadly that all that people have done or sought to do for thousands of years is but an imperfect sketch of the *factory system*.[32] Nothing allows us to assert that the framework of gestures comprising productive labour in the narrow sense is 'truer' or more 'real' than the ensemble of meanings in which these gestures have been interwoven by those who perform them. Nothing, if not the postulate that the true nature of man is to be a productive–economic animal, a totally arbitrary postulate and one which implies, if it were true, that socialism is forever impossible.

If, in order to have a theory of history, it were necessary to exclude from history almost everything, except what has occurred over a few centuries on a narrow strip of land bordering the North Atlantic, the price to pay is really too high. It would be better to keep history and reject theory. But we are not reduced to this dilemma. As revolutionaries, we do not have to reduce the previous history of humanity to simple schemata. We first have to understand and interpret our own society. And we can do this only by *relativizing* it, by showing that none of the present forms of social alienation is inevitable for humanity, since they have not always been there, and not by transforming our society into an absolute and unconsciously projecting onto the past schemata and categories that express, precisely, the deepest aspects of the capitalist reality against which we are struggling.

We have therefore seen why what we call the materialist conception of history seems to us untenable today. Briefly, because this conception:

- makes the development of technology the motor of history 'in the final analysis', and attributes to it an autonomous evolution and a closed and definite meaning.
- attempts to submit all of history to categories that have a sense only for capitalist society in developed countries, whilst the application of these categories to previous forms of social life poses more problems than it solves.
- is based on the hidden postulate of a human nature considered essentially unalterable, whose predominant motivation would be an economic motivation.

These considerations concern the content of the materialist conception of history, which is an *economic* determinism (a denomination often used, moreover, by those who advocate this conception). But the theory is just as unacceptable in that it is pure and simple *determinism*, that is to say inasmuch as it claims that one can reduce history to the effects of a system of forces themselves subjected to laws that can be grasped and defined once and for all, on the basis of which these effects can be integrally and exhaustively produced (and hence *deduced* as well). Since behind this conception, there is inevitably a thesis concerning *what history is*, hence a philosophical thesis, we shall return to this in the third part of this chapter.

Economic Determinism and Class Struggle

To economic determinism seems to be opposed another aspect of Marxism: 'the history of humanity is the history of the class struggle'. But this only *seems* to be the case. For, to the extent to which the essential assertions of the materialist conception of history are upheld, class struggle is not, in reality, a separate factor.[33] It is only a link in the causal connections established unambiguously at any given moment by the state of the technical–economic infrastructure. What the classes do, what they have to do, is necessarily spelled out in each case by their situation in the relations of production, which they can do nothing about, for this situation precedes them causally as well as logically. In fact, the classes are simply the instrument in which the action of the productive forces is embodied. If they are actors, they are so in exactly the same sense as actors in the theatre who recite a text given to them in advance and who make predetermined gestures, and whether they play well or poorly, they cannot prevent the tragedy from moving on to its inexorable conclusion. One class is required to make a socio-economic system function in accordance with its laws, and one is required to overthrow the system – when it becomes 'incompatible with the development of the productive forces' and when its interests lead it just as ineluctably to establish a new system, whose functioning it will have to ensure in its turn. The classes are the agents of the historical process, but its unconscious agents (the expression recurs again and again in Marx's and Engels' writings); they are acted upon rather than acting themselves, says Lukács. Or rather, they act in terms of their class-consciousness, and we know that 'it is not men's consciousness that determines their being, but their social being which determines their consciousness.' It is not simply that the class in power is conservative and the rising class revolutionary. This conservatism, this revolutionary spirit are held to be predetermined in their content, in all their 'important' details[34] by the situation of each class in the productive process.

It is not by accident that the idea of more or less 'intelligent' capitalist policy always appears, to a Marxist, as a stupidity that conceals a mystification. If one is even to agree to speak of a policy being intelligent or not, one must admit that this intelligence or its absence can *make a difference* as to the real evolution. But how can they, since this evolution is determined by factors of another order – 'objective' factors? One shall not even argue that this policy does not fall from heaven, that it acts in a given situation and cannot go beyond certain limits sketched out by the historical context, can find no echo in reality unless other conditions are present – all obvious things. The Marxist will talk as if this intelligence could change nothing (except for the style of discourse, grandiose in Mirabeau, lamentable in Laniel)[35] and, at the very most, will strive to show that Napoleon's 'genius', just as Kerensky's 'stupidity' were necessarily 'called for' and generated by the historical situation.

Nor is it by accident that stringent resistance is opposed to the idea that modern capitalism has attempted to adapt itself to historical evolution and to social struggle, and has been modified as a consequence. This would be to admit that the history of the last century has not been determined exclusively by economic laws, and that the actions of groups and social classes have been able to modify the conditions under which these laws act and, thereby, their very functioning.

This example, moreover, most clearly shows that economic determinism, on the one hand, and the class struggle, on the other, propose two modes of explanation which are irreducible one to the other. It shows us that in Marxism there is not a genuine 'synthesis', but a triumph of determinism over class struggle. Is the essential factor in the evolution of capitalism the technological revolution and the effects of the economic laws that govern the system? Or is it the struggle of classes and social groups? In reading *Capital* we see that the first response is correct. Once its sociological conditions are established, once what can be called the 'axioms of the system' are posited in historical reality (that is, the degree and specific type of technical development, the existence of accumulated capital, and of a sufficient number of proletarians, etc.) and under the continuous impetus of an autonomous technical progress, capitalism evolves solely in terms of the effects of the economic laws it contains, and which Marx has formulated. Class struggle nowhere comes into it.[36] If a more nuanced and more subtle Marxism, based if need be on other texts of Marx, refuses this unilateral view and affirms that class struggle plays an important role in the history of the system, that it can alter the functioning of the economy but that simply one must not forget that this struggle is situated in every instance within a given framework which marks out its limits and defines its meaning – these concessions are useless, the lion and the lamb are not reconciled for all that. For these economic 'laws' formulated by Marx are, properly speaking, *meaningless* outside of class struggle; they have no precise content. When the 'law of value' must be applied to the basic commodity, labour power, it becomes meaningless: it is an empty formula which can be provided with a content only by the struggle between workers and employers, a struggle which is the main determinant of the absolute level of wages and their evolution in time. And since all the other 'laws' presuppose a *given* distribution of the social product, the system as a whole remains suspended in mid-air, completely undetermined.[37] And this is not simply a theoretical 'lacuna', but a 'lacuna' so critical that the theory is immediately destroyed. There is also a world of difference in practice. Between the capitalism of *Capital*, in which the 'economic laws' lead to a stagnation of workers' wages, to growing unemployment, to more and more violent crises, and finally to the quasi-impossibility of the system's functioning, and real capitalism, in which wages increase in the long run along with production and in which the expansion of the system continues without encountering any insurmountable *economic* antinomy, there is not simply the gap that separates the mythical from the real. These are two different universes each of which contains its own fate, its own philosophy, its own politics, its own conception of revolution.

Finally, the idea that the autonomous action of the masses can constitute the central element of the socialist revolution, whether admitted or not, will always remain of secondary importance to a coherent Marxist, for it is without any genuine interest and even without any theoretical or philosophical status. The Marxist knows where history *must* go. If the autonomous action of the masses does go in this direction, it teaches the Marxist nothing; if it goes somewhere else, it is a bad autonomy, or rather it is not an autonomy at all, since if the masses are not directed towards the correct aims, this is because they still remain under the influence of capitalism. When the truth is given, all the rest is error, but error means nothing in a determinist universe: error is only the product or enemy class action and of the system of exploitation.

However, the action of *one* particular class and this class's awareness of its interests and of its situation, appears to have a separate status in Marxism: the action and self-awareness of the proletariat. But this is true only in a special and limited sense. This is not true with respect to what the proletariat is to do:[38] it is to make the socialist revolution, and we know what the socialist revolution is to do (briefly speaking, to develop the productive forces until abundance makes possible communist society and a free humanity). This is only true with respect to knowing whether it will do so or not. For, along with the idea that socialism is inevitable, there also exists in Marx and in the great Marxists (Lenin or Trotsky, for instance) the idea of society's possible incapacity to surmount its crisis, the idea of a 'mutual destruction of both of the classes in conflict', in short the historical alternative of socialism *or* barbarism. This idea, however, represents the system's limit and in a certain manner the limit of any coherent reflection. It is never absolutely excluded that history may 'fail', and so reveal itself to be absurd, but in this case not only this theory, but every theory collapses. Consequently, the fact that the proletariat will or will not carry out the revolution, even if it is uncertain, conditions everything else, and any discussion is possible only given the hypothesis that it will do so. Once this hypothesis is admitted, the sense in which it will do so is determined. The liberty granted the proletariat in this way is no different from the freedom to be mad which we can accord ourselves: a freedom which has value, which exists only on the condition that we do not make use of it, for its exercise would abolish it along with all coherence in the world.[39]

However, if we eliminate the idea that the classes and their action serve merely as relays, if we admit that 'self-awareness' and the activity of classes and of social groups (like that of individuals) give rise to new, unpredetermined, and unpredeterminable elements (which does not, of course, mean that any of these activities is independent of the situations in which it occurs), then we are forced to move outside the classical Marxist schema and to conceive of history in an essentially different way. We shall return to this later in the text.

The conclusion to be drawn here is not that the materialist conception of history is 'false' as to its content. It is that the type of theory at which this conception is aimed has no meaning, that this sort of theory is impossible to establish, and that, moreover, we have no need of it. To say that we possess at last the secret of past and present history (and even up to a certain point, of history yet to come) is no less absurd than to say that we possess at last the secret of nature. It is even more so, precisely because of what makes history a history and of historical knowledge an historical knowledge.

Subject and Object of Historical Knowledge

When we speak of history, *who* is speaking? It is someone of a given period, class and society – in short, someone who is himself an historical being. And this very fact, which founds the possibility of an historical knowledge (for only an historical being can have an experience of history and can talk about it) prevents this knowledge from ever acquiring the status of complete and transparent knowledge – since it is itself, in its essence, an historical phenomenon which demands to be apprehended and interpreted as such. The discourse on history is included within history.

This idea must not be confused with assertions of scepticism or naive relativism, e.g. that what each person says is never more than an opinion, in speaking one betrays oneself more than one conveys anything of reality. There is indeed something more than mere opinion (otherwise discourse, action, and society would not be possible); we can control or get rid of prejudices, preferences, hates, and apply the rules of 'scientific objectivity'. We are not simply left with opinions, one as good as another; Marx, for example, is a great economist even when he is wrong, while François Perroux is only a windbag,[40] even when he is not mistaken. But after making all the purges, applying all the rules, and respecting all the facts, it remains that the person who speaks is not a 'transcendental consciousness', but an historical being, and this is not an unfortunate accident, it is a logical condition (a 'transcendental condition') for historical knowledge. Just as only natural beings – natural *too* – can raise the problem of a science of nature, for only flesh and blood beings can have an experience of nature,[41] only historical beings can raise the problem of knowledge of history, for only they can have history as an object of experience. And, just as experiencing nature is not to go outside the universe and contemplate it, in the same way, having an experience of history is not to consider it from the outside as a finished object placed in front of us – for this sort of history has never existed and will never be given to anyone as an object of inquiry.

To have an experience of history as an historical being is to be *in* and *of* history, as it is also to be *in* and *of* society. And, leaving aside other aspects of this implication, this means:

- thinking of history necessarily in terms of the categories of one's own epoch and one's own society – categories which are themselves the product of historical evolution;
- thinking of history in terms of a practical intention or a project – a project which is itself a part of history.

Not only was Marx aware of this, he was the first to say it clearly. When he scoffed at those who believed they 'could jump beyond their epoch', he was denouncing the idea that there could ever be a pure theoretical subject producing a pure knowledge of history, the idea that one could ever deduce a priori *the* categories valid for all historical material (other than as flat and empty abstractions).[42] When at the same time he denounced the bourgeois thinkers of his period, who were at once naively applying to previous periods categories that have a meaning only in relation to capitalism and refusing to relativize these categories historically ('for them, there has been history, but there is no longer', Marx said in a sentence one would believe coined with contemporary 'Marxists' in mind) and affirmed that his own theory corresponded to the point of view of one class, the revolutionary proletariat, he posited for the first time the problem which has since received the name of socio-centrism (the fact that every society considers itself as the centre of the world and regards all others from its own point of view), and attempted to respond to it.

We tried to show above that Marx finally did not overcome this socio-centrism and that, we find in him the paradox of a thinker who is fully conscious of the historical relativity of capitalist categories and who at the same time projects them (or retro-jects them) onto the whole of human history. It should be well understood that this is not a criticism of Marx but a criticism of historical knowledge in general. *The paradox in question is constitutive of any effort to think history.*[43] It is necessary, it is inevitable that, from our vantage point of one century later, we can relativize certain categories more thoroughly, and can more clearly isolate those elements of a grand theory that tie it solidly to its particular epoch and root it there. But it is *because* it is rooted in its epoch that the theory is grand. To become aware of the problem of socio-centrism, to try to eliminate all the socio-centric elements that can be apprehended is the inevitable first step of all serious thought. To believe that this rootedness is *only* negative and that one should and actually could get rid of it through some infinite purification of reason, is the illusion of a naive rationalism. It is not simply that this rootedness is the condition for our knowledge, that we are able to reflect upon history only because, as historical beings, we are caught up in a society in motion, and have an experience of structuration and of social struggle. It is also a *positive* condition, for it is our own particularity which allows us access to the universal. It is because we are attached to a given view, categorial structure, and project that we are able to say something meaningful about the past. It is only when the present is intensely present that it makes us see in the past something different and something more than the past saw in itself. In a certain way, it is because Marx projected something onto the past that he discovered something in it. It is one thing to criticize these projections, as we have done, when they are presented as truths that are whole, exhaustive and systematic. It is something else again to forget that, however 'arbitrary' it might be, the effort to comprehend preceding societies under capitalist categories proved, in Marx, to be immensely fecund – even if it violated the 'truth specific to' each of these societies. For ultimately there is no such 'specific truth' – not that resulting from historical materialism, of course, but also not that revealed by the quite utopian, and in the end utterly socio-centric, effort to 'think each society for itself and from its own point of view'. What can be termed the truth of each society is its truth in history, for itself but also for all the others, for the paradox of history consists in the fact that every civilization and every epoch, because it is particular and dominated by its own obsessions, manages to evoke and to unveil new meanings in the societies that preceded or surround it. But they can never exhaust or permanently fix their object, even if only because they themselves sooner or later become the object of interpretation (today we attempt to understand how and why the Renaissance, the seventeenth and eighteenth centuries viewed classical antiquity in such different ways). Neither can they ever be reduced to the obsessions of the epoch that apprehended them, for then history would be simply the juxtaposition of ravings and we could not even read a book of the past.

Marxism, as we know, tries to supersede this paradox which is constitutive of any historical thinking.

This supersession results from a twofold movement. On the one hand, there is a dialectic of history, which means that the successive points of view of various epochs, classes and societies have a definite relation to one another, albeit a very complex one. They conform to a certain order; together they form a system which unfolds in time, in such a way that what comes after supersedes (suppresses while preserving) what came before. The present is seen to encompass the past (as a 'superseded' moment and for this reason the present can better understand what the past did not understand in itself. This dialectic is, in essence, the Hegelian dialectic. The fact that what in Hegel was the movement of *logos* becomes in Marx the development of the productive forces and the succession of social classes which marks out the various steps in this development is, in this regard, of no importance. For both of them, Kant 'supersedes' Plato and bourgeois society is 'superior' to ancient society. But this takes on importance in another regard – and this is the second term of the movement. Precisely because this dialectic is the dialectic of the successive appearances of the various *classes* in history, it is no longer necessarily infinite *de jure*.[44] Historical analysis shows that the succession can and must end with the appearance of the 'last class', the proletariat. Marxism is therefore a privileged theory because it represents 'the point of view of the proletariat' and because the proletariat is the last class – not simply the last to date, for then we would always be bound, within the historical dialectic, to a particular point of view destined to be relativized at some later point. It is last absolutely, to the extent that it must realize the suppression of classes and the passage to the 'true history of humanity'. The proletariat is the universal class; it is because the proletariat has no particular interests to defend that it can realize the classless society as well as command a 'true' point of view on past history.[45]

Today, we can no longer maintain this way of seeing things for a number of reasons. We cannot supply ourselves in advance with a dialectic of history that is complete or on the verge of being completed, even if this is termed a dialectic of 'pre-history'. We cannot give ourselves the solution before the problem. We cannot give ourselves as a starting point a dialectic of any kind, for a dialectic postulates the rationality of the world and of history, and this rationality is a problem, both a theoretical and a practical problem. We cannot conceive of history as a unity, thereby hiding from ourselves the enormous problems that this expression poses as soon as it is given a meaning other than a purely formal one. Nor can we conceive of history as a progressive dialectical unification, for Plato cannot be absorbed into Kant, nor the gothic into the rococo, and to say that the superiority of the Spanish culture over the Aztec was demonstrated by the extermination of the latter satisfies neither the surviving Aztec nor ourselves, for we do not understand how and why pre-Columbian America was preparing its dialectical negation through its encounter with cavalrymen bearing firearms. We cannot base the final reply to the ultimate problems of thought and practice on the exactitude of Marx's analysis of the dynamic of capitalism, now that we know that this exactitude is an illusion, but even if we were unaware of this. We cannot directly present a theory, even our own, as 'representing the point of view of the proletariat', for the history of the past century has shown that, far from offering the solution to all the problems, the point of view of the proletariat is itself a problem, for which only the proletariat (let us say, to avoid quibbling, labouring humanity) will be able to invent, or will fail to invent, a solution. At any rate, we cannot present Marxism as representing this point of view for it contains, deeply engrained in its very substance, capitalist elements and because, not unrelated to the former, it is today the ideology-in-act of the bureaucracy everywhere and that of the proletariat nowhere. We cannot believe that, even if the proletariat were the last class and Marxism its authentic representative, its vision of history is *the* vision that will definitively bring an end to all discussion. The relativity of historical knowledge is not only related to its production by a class, it is also related to its production in a culture, at a given epoch, and the latter cannot simply be reduced to the former. The disappearance of classes in future society will not automatically eliminate all differences concerning views of the past which may exist, will not give them an immediate coincidence with their object, and will not shield them from an historical evolution. Lukács, in 1919, as minister of Culture in the Hungarian Revolutionary Government, stated in an official speech, as an aside: 'Now that the proletariat is in power, we need no longer maintain a unilateral view of the past.'[45] In 1964, when the proletariat is nowhere in power, we are even less in a position to do so.

In short, we can no longer maintain the Marxist philosophy of history.

Additional Remarks on the Marxist Theory of History [47]

Concerning the technological evolution and its rhythm
When the question of technological 'stagnation' is discussed, whether during the feudal period or in general, two elements must be clearly distinguished.

In the first place, we must enquire into the technological evolution in Western Europe from the collapse of the Roman Empire (or even before this, from the beginning of the fourth century of our era) up to the eleventh or twelfth century. There are six or seven centuries of human history contained within this extraordinarily important, para-digmatic, and Hegelian–Marxist segment of history which comprises 'European' history (or 'Graeco-Western' history as it is called by phil-osophers). This segment can be termed paradigmatic and Hegelian–Marxist, for it in fact represents the only case where a quasi-'dialectical' development can be constructed (at the cost of innumerable violations of historical facts, but that is another question) both in the socio-economic sphere and in the philosophical, 'spiritual' (Hegelian), sphere. This construction, however, can be made only on the condition of covering over the six or seven centuries which, taken together and compared to the Graeco-Roman world, represent a period of considerable *regression*. Marxists never talk about these lost centuries. When they mention the 'technical progress during the Middle Ages', they in fact mean the twelfth, thirteenth or fourteenth centuries. Ter-minological disputes are not of much interest – except that, here too, as is usually the case terminological imprecision serves to conceal confused thought or sophistic methods. What is important is that we observe in this instance not an 'accident' or a 'seasonal variation' but an extremely long historical period during which, if we consider the social edifice as a whole – even though there were gradual changes in some specific points (for example, replacing the light plow with the heavy plow) – most of the achievements of the previous period were lost. This shows that technology does not necessarily progress in an uninterrupted fashion and that its evolution is in no sense 'autonomous', not even in the loosest sense of the term.

In the second place, there is the question of technological change and of its rhythm throughout history in general. What we observe is that *most* societies have traversed *the greater part* of their history on the basis of stable technical conditions. Conditions so stable that they appear to Western man of the past few centuries as being equivalent to a pure and simple technological *stagnation* within the societies and the periods considered. This is the case, broadly speaking, of long periods of Chinese history, of the history of India since the fourth century BC up to the Islamic invasions, and then from that time until the English conquest, not to speak of 'archaic' societies. There is all the difference in the world between living in a society in which an important new invention is born daily, or even every ten years (as in the West in the past three centuries), and living in a society in which significant inventions appear only every three centuries. Human history has unfolded primarily in the latter context, not in the former.

Concerning 'progress', Marx and the Greeks
Of course, Marx never explicitly asserted the 'superiority' of bourgeois society and culture over Greek society and culture. But this is the

inevitable logical implication of the 'dialectic' applied to history *and* the alleged dependence of the 'superstructure' in relation to the 'infrastructure'. Precisely because he was not a philistine, no more than he was the absolute Spirit made man, Marx 'contradicts' himself on this point – which is all to his honour.

In the unfinished manuscript of 1857,[48] Marx attempts to illustrate the dependence of art on real life and in particular on the technology of the period considered in a manner that is open to criticism, mixing together necessary and sufficient conditions, or rather trivial, negative conditions and genuine, sufficient reasons. He asks whether

> the idea of nature and of the social relations that nourish the Greek imagination and hence Greek mythology [is] compatible with automatic spinning machines, locomotives, and the electric telegraph? What is Vulcan alongside Roberts and Co., Jupiter alongside the lightening rod, and Hermes alongside securities? ... What becomes of *Fama* with regard to the Printing-house Square? ... Is Achilles still possible in the age of powder and lead? Or the *Iliad*, in general, with printing and the printing-press? Songs, legends, Muses, do they not all disappear necessarily before the printer's bar? And have not the conditions necessary for epic poetry vanished?

He then observes that 'the difficulty is not understanding that Greek art and epic are tied to certain forms of social development' (a trivial assertion if it signifies that Achilles could not have worn bluejeans or played with a gun, empty otherwise since we cannot *explain* the correspondence, otherwise self-evident, between the epic and antiquity or the novel and the modern period, and in particular since these same 'forms of social development' *have not* produced analogous works elsewhere) but instead understanding why 'they still offer us artistic enjoyment and, in certain respects, they serve as norms, being for us an inaccessible model.' Let us note that if history has ever produced an inaccessible (or even simply an unsurpassable) model, any discussion in terms of 'progress' becomes sheer nonsense. The solution that Marx proposes for this difficulty consists in attributing 'the charm that we find in works of art' produced by the Greeks to the fact that they were 'normal children'. It is supposed to be 'the historical childhood of humanity, in full blossom' which 'exerted the eternal attraction of the moment that will not come again'. A 'solution' in which the great thinker, for once, proves to be childish himself. One can only laugh at the supposition that *Oedipus Rex* charms us by its 'naivety' and its 'sincerity'. And what can we say about philosophy? Do we find ourselves still reading Plato and Aristotle, heaping up interpretation upon interpretation, because we are under the charm of their infantile normality? The text breaks off abruptly at this point, and we have no reason to dwell upon the formulations of a manuscript left unpublished by its author – unless it is to observe that the problem remains, whole, and wholly inconceivable within the Marxist system of reference. How, indeed, is it possible that reading Kant and Hegel does not dispense

us from the necessity of reading Plato and Aristotle (whereas reading
a good treatise on physics does dispense us from having to read Newton,
except if we are *historians* of science)? How does it happen that a few
sentences by these authors provide us with more food for thought than
99 per cent of the sentences contained in the volumes published today
by the millions? If Plato belonged to a happy childhood of humanity,
then Kant would be less charming perhaps, but certainly more intelligent than Plato. He should be. But he is not. If humanity passes
through a 'childhood' and then arrives at 'adulthood' (granting all that
is to be granted in the use of metaphors), then Spinoza should of
necessity be more 'mature' than Aristotle. But he is not. These statements are meaningless. Kant is not superior to Plato – nor inferior to
him (although we would do well to recall that a 'scientific' and not a
'literary' philosopher, A. N. Whitehead, has written that the best way
to understand the whole of Western philosophy is to consider it as a
series of marginal annotations to Plato's texts).

Nevertheless, contemporary technology *as* technology *is* infinitely
'superior' to Greek technology. What do Marx and Marxists (the vulgar
or the refined) have to say about this divorce? Nothing. At best they
can juggle with words, saying, for example, that bourgeois society is
more 'progressive' than ancient society, but not 'superior' to it.
However, these apparently innocent distinctions destroy completely
and irreversibly the entire Marxist conception of history. If 'pro-
gressiveness' and 'inferiority' can go hand in hand, or, conversely, if
one society can be 'materially' more 'backward' than another but
'culturally' superior to it, what remains of the materialist conception
of history, of its 'dialectical development'?

Concerning the 'unity of history', socio-centrism and relativism
English comrades have objected to what is said above concerning the
antinomy constitutive of historical knowledge, holding that one thereby
denies the unity of history and that one is led towards historical eclec-
ticism.

But what is the 'unity' of history, outside of purely descriptive
definitions, as for example the totality of the acts of speaking bipeds?
The 'dialectical unity' of history is a myth. The only clear starting point
for reflecting on the problem is that every society posits a 'view of
itself' which is at the same time a 'view of the world' (including the
other societies it may know) and that this 'view' is part of its 'truth' or
its 'reflected reality', to speak with Hegel, without being reducible to
it.

We know nothing of Greece, if we do not know what the Greeks
knew, thought and felt with respect to themselves. But obviously, there
were things just as important concerning Greece that the Greeks did
not know and could not have known. We can see these things, but
from our place and through our present perspective. And seeing is just
that. I shall never see anything from all possible places at once; each

time I see from a determined place, I see an 'aspect', and I see through a 'perspective'. And *I* see signifies that I see *because* I am myself, and I do not see only with my eyes. When I see something my whole life is there, incarnate in this vision, in this act of seeing. All this is not some 'fault' in our vision, it *is* vision. The rest is the eternal phantasy of theology and of philosophy.

Now this phantasy re-emerges in the claim to establish a total view of history. A total view which Marxists believe they already possess, or instead postulate for the future, implying, for example, that socio-centrism will be eliminated in a socialist society. This amounts to the absurd assertion that in a socialist society one will be able to see from 'nowhere' (seeing from somewhere is seeing from a given perspective) and to see everything, absolutely everything, including the future. For if one does not see the future, how can one speak of a total view of history? How can a meaning be ascribed to the 'past' if one does not know what comes after? Was the meaning of the Russian Revolution 'the same' in 1918, in 1925, in 1936 and today? Or does there exist in some supra-celestial place an idea, a 'meaning-in-itself', of the Russian Revolution, including, as would be necessary, all the consequences of this event up to the end of time which would be accessible to Marxists? How come, then, for the past 50 years they have not understood a thing about what has been going on?

To recognize these facts as self-evident by no means leads to a simple scepticism or relativism. The fact that we can never explore more than the successive 'aspects' of a given object does not abolish the distinction between a blind man and man who sees, between someone who is colour-blind and someone who is normal, between someone who is subject to hallucinations and someone who is not. It does not abolish the distinction between someone who does not know that the bent stick in the water is an optical illusion and someone who knows it, and who, as a result, *sees* at the same time a straight stick. Aiming at truth, whether in respect of history or anything else is nothing other than this project to clarify other aspects of the object and of ourselves, to situate the illusions and the reasons why they appear, and to connect all this up together in a manner we call – another mysterious expression – coherent. This is, of course, an infinite project. And contrary to what the Marxists (and at times even Marx himself) thought, the 'possession of truth' taken in an 'absolute', hence mythical, sense is not the premise of the revolution and of a radical reconstruction of society. The idea of this sort of 'possession' is not only intrinsically absurd (implying the completion of this infinite project), it is profoundly reactionary, for the belief in a truth that is complete and acquired once and for all (and so able to be possessed by somebody or some bodies) is one of the bases for adhering to fascism or Stalinism.

iii MARXIST PHILOSOPHY OF HISTORY

The Marxist theory of history presents itself in the first place as a scientific theory, and so as a generalization that can be demonstrated or challenged on the level of empirical investigation. This it is indisputably. And, as such, it was unavoidable that it should suffer the fate of every important scientific theory. After having produced an immense and irreversible impact on our way of seeing the historical world, it has been superseded by the enquiries that it has itself provoked. It must, therefore, take its place in the history of theories, without, for all that, erasing the knowledge we have inherited from it. Today, we can say, with Che Guevara, that there is no longer any need to say that we are Marxists, any more than to call ourselves Pasteurians or Newtonians – on the condition that we truly understand what is meant by this statement: everyone is 'Newtonian' in the sense that there is no question of returning to pre-Newtonian categories or ways of posing problems. Yet no one is really 'Newtonian' any more, for no one can continue to be the proponent of a theory that is purely and simply *false*.[49]

At the base of this theory of history there is a philosophy of history, bound up with it deeply yet in a contradictory way and, as we shall see, itself contradictory. It is neither an ornament nor is it complementary; it is necessarily a foundation. It is the foundation of the theory of past history, as well as that of the political conception, the perspective and the programme of revolution. What is essential is that it is a rationalist philosophy and, like all rationalist philosophies, it provides itself beforehand with the solution to all the problems it poses.

Objectivist Rationalism

Marxist philosophy of history is first and foremost an objectivist rationalism. This can already be seen in the Marxist theory of history applied to past history. The object of the theory of history is a natural object, and the model which is applied to it is analogous to that of the natural sciences. Forces acting on precise points of application produce predetermined results in accordance with a grand causal schema which is held to explain both the statics and the dynamics of history, the constitution and functioning of each society as well as the imbalance and the upheaval that are to carry it into a new form. Past history, therefore, is rational in the sense that everything occurred there in accordance with causes that were perfectly adequate and transparent to *our* reason in the state it was in in 1859. The real can be explained perfectly; in principle, it has been explained now and forever (monographs can be written on the economic causes of the birth of Islam in the seventh century, they will verify the materialist theory of history and will teach us nothing new about the latter). Humanity's past concords with reason in the sense that to each thing a reason can be ascribed and that these reasons together form a consistent and exhaustive system.

But also, history to come is just as rational for it will make reason concrete, and this time in a second sense: not simply the sense of making it a fact, but in the sense of value. History to come will be what it ought to be, it will see the birth of a rational society that will embody the aspirations of humanity, where man will finally be human (which means that his existence will coincide with his essence and his actual being will realize his concept).

Finally, history is rational in a third sense: that of the connection between the past and the future, that of facts which will necessarily become values, that of an ensemble of blind quasi-natural laws which blindly work towards the production of the state the least blind of all, that of free humanity. There is thus a reason to be found immanent in things and it will give rise to a society conforming miraculously to our reason.

Hegelianism, as we see, is not actually superseded. All that is and all that will be real is and will be rational. The fact that Hegel arrests this reality and this rationality at the moment his own philosophy appears, whereas Marx prolongs them indefinitely, up to and including communist humanity, does not disprove what we were saying but instead reinforces it. The empire of reason which, in the first case, embraced (by a necessary, speculative postulate) what was already given, is extended now to include all that will ever be given in history. What one can now *say* about what will be becomes increasingly vague as one moves further away from the present; this has to do with contingent limitations on our knowledge and especially with the fact that we have to do what there is to do today and not 'provide recipes for the socialist kitchens of the future'. This future, however, is from now on determined in its principle: it will be freedom, just as the past and the present were and are necessity.

There is thus a 'cunning of reason', as old Hegel used to say; there is a reason at work in history, guaranteeing that past history is comprehensible, that history to come is desirable and that the apparently blind necessity of the facts is secretly arranged to give birth to the Good.

Merely stating this idea is enough to make apparent the extraordinary number of problems that it masks. We can only take up, briefly, a few of these.

Determinism

To say that past history is comprehensible, in the sense of the Marxist conception of history, means that there exists a causal determinism without any 'important' gaps[50] and that this determinism is, to the second degree, so to speak, the bearer of meanings that are linked together in totalities which themselves are meaningful. Yet neither of these ideas can be accepted as it stands.

To be sure, we cannot conceive of history without employing the category of causality and it is even true that, contrary to what idealist philosophers have asserted, history is the domain *par excellence* where causality has a meaning for us, since it takes to begin with the form of motivation and thus enables us to understand a 'causal' chain, something we can never do in the case of natural phenomena. The fact that the movement of electrical current makes the bulb incandescent, or that due to the law of gravity the Moon is at a particular place in the sky at a particular moment, these are and will always remain necessary connections to us, but external ones, predictable but incomprehensible. But when A steps on B's feet, B insults A, and A replies with a slap in the face, we *understand* the necessity of the chain of events, even when we may consider it to be contingent (reproaching the participants for having allowed themselves to get 'carried away' when they 'could have' restrained themselves – all the while knowing from our own experience that at certain moments one cannot help but get carried away). More generally, whether it is in the form of motivation, in that of an indispensable technical means, whether it involves a result that occurs because the conditions were intentionally posited or is the inevitable effect of an involuntary act, we think and we constantly make our own life, and the lives of others, in the mode of causality.

There is a causal element in social and historical life because there is a 'subjective rational element': the deployment of the Carthaginian troops at Cannae (and their victory) results from a rational plan conceived by Hannibal. There is a causal element also because there is an 'objective rational element', because natural causal relations and purely logical necessities are constantly present in historical relations: under certain technical and economic conditions the production of steel and the extraction of coal are bound together in a constant and quantifiable relation (more generally, a functional relation). There is also a 'raw causal element' which we observe without being able to reduce it to subjective or objective causal relations, there are established correlations whose basis is unknown, regularities of behaviour, whether individual or social, which remain pure facts.

The existence of these causal relations of various sorts allows us, beyond the simple comprehension of individual behaviour or its regularity, to place this behaviour under 'laws' and to give to these laws abstract expressions from which the 'real' content of the lived behaviour of individuals has been eliminated. These laws can provide the basis for satisfactory predictions (which are verified with a given degree of probability). There is in this way, for example, in the economic functioning of capitalism an extraordinary wealth of observable and measurable regularities, which can be termed, as an initial approximation, 'laws' and which make many aspects of this functioning appear both explainable and comprehensible and, up to a certain point, in fact predictable. Even beyond the economy, we find a series of partial 'objective dynamics'. However, we are not able to integrate these partial dynamics into a total determinism of the system, and this is so in an entirely different sense than that conveyed by the crisis of determinism in modern physics. This is not due to the fact that the determinism collapses or becomes problematic at the limits of the system or that cracks appear within it. The opposite is rather the case: it is as if only a few aspects, a few cross-sections of social life were subject to determinism, themselves being caught up in networks of no deterministic relations.

We must well understand the source of this impossibility. The partial dynamics that we estabish are, of course, incomplete; they continually refer to one another, and any modification of one modifies all the others. But if this creates immense difficulties in practice, it creates none in principle. In the physical universe as well a relation holds only with the proviso 'all other things being equal'.

The impossibility in question is not due to the complexity of the social material, it belongs to the very nature of this material. It is due to the fact that the social (or the historical) contains the non-causal as one of its essential moments.

This non-causal element appears on two levels. The first, which is of less importance to us, is that of the deviations presented by the real behaviour of individuals in relation to 'typical' behaviour. This introduces an element of unpredictability, but one which cannot as such prevent a deterministic treatment at least on the global level. If these deviations are systematic, they can be submitted to a causal investigation; if they are random, they are amenable to a statistical analysis. The unpredictability of the movement of individual molecules has not prevented the kinetic theory of gases from being one of the more rigorous branches of physics; unpredictability on the individual level is even what founds the extraordinary power of the theory.

The non-causal, however, appears at another level and this is what is important. It appears as behaviour that is not merely 'unpredictable' but *creative* (on the level of individuals, groups, classes or entire societies). It appears not as a simple deviation in relation to an existing type but as the *positing* of a new type of behaviour, as the *institution* of a new social rule, as the *invention* of a new object or a new form – in short, as an emergence or a production which cannot be deduced on the basis of a previous situation, as a conclusion that goes beyond the premises or as the positing of new premises. It has already been observed that the living being goes beyond a simple mechanism because it can provide new responses to new situations. But the historical being goes beyond the simply living being because it can provide new responses to the '*same*' situations or create new situations.

History cannot be thought in accordance with the determinist schema (nor, moreover, in accordance with a simple 'dialectical' schema) because it is the domain of *creation*. We shall return to this point later in our text.

The Concatenation of Significations and the 'Cunning of Reason'

Beyond the problem of determinism in history, there is a problem of 'historical' significations. To begin with, history appears as the place of the conscious actions of conscious beings. This self-evidence, however, is swept away as soon as we take a closer look at it. We then observe, with Engels, that 'history is the domain of unconscious intentions and unintended ends'. The *real* results of men's historical action are, as it were, never those the authors had wanted. This is perhaps not so hard to understand. But what poses a major problem is that these results, which no one intended as such, are presented as being 'coherent' in a certain way, possess a 'meaning' and seem to obey a logic which is neither a 'subjective' logic (carried by a consciousness, posited by someone) nor an 'objective' logic like that we think we see in nature – and which we can term an historical logic.

Hundreds of bourgeois, whether moved or not by the spirit of Calvin and the idea of worldly asceticism, set themselves to accumulating riches. Thousands of ruined craftsmen and starving farmers are available to enter the factories. Someone invents a steam-engine, someone else a new loom. Philosophers and physicists attempt to conceive of the universe as a great machine and to discover its laws. Kings continue to emasculate the nobility and to subject it to their own power and create national institutions. Each of the individuals and each of the groups in question pursues its own particular ends, no one aims at the social totality as such. And yet the result is of an entirely different order; it is capitalism. It is absolutely indifferent, in this context, that the result may be perfectly well determined by the ensemble of causes and conditions. Let us admit that for all these facts, up to and including the colour of Colbert's breeches, one can show all the multidimensional, causal connections that tie them to one another and all together to the 'initial conditions of the system'. What is important here is that this result possesses a coherence which nobody and nothing intended or guaranteed at the start or even later on, and that it possesses a signification (or rather, appears to incarnate a virtually inexhaustible system of significations), making that there indeed is a sort of historical entity which is *capitalism* as such.

This signification appears in a number of different ways. Throughout all the causal connections and beyond them, it is what confers a kind of unity on all the manifestations of capitalist society and makes us immediately recognize a given phenomenon as a phenomenon of this culture, makes us immediately classify in this period objects, books, instruments, sentences of which we otherwise know nothing and at the same time makes us immediately exclude an infinite number of others.

This signification appears as the simultaneous existence of an infinite set of possibilities and of an infinite set of impossibilities, given, as it were, immediately. It also appears in the fact that everything that occurs within the system is produced not only in conformity to something like 'the spirit of the system' but contributes to its solidity (even when it is opposed to it and ultimately tends to upset it as a real order).

Everything occurs as if this global signification belonging to the system were given as it were beforehand, as if it 'predetermined' and overdetermined the causal chains, as if it subjugated them and made them produce results conforming to an 'intention', which, of course, is only a metaphorical expression, since it is no one's intention. Marx says somewhere, 'if there were no chance, then history would be sorcery' – a phrase that is deeply true. But what is surprising is that chance in history itself most often takes on the form of meaningful chance, of 'objective' chance, of '*as if* by chance', as popular irony says so well. What can give to the incalculable number of gestures, acts, thoughts, individual and collective behaviour that make up a society this unity of a *world*, in which a certain order (an order of sense and not necessarily of causes and effects) can always be found woven into the chaos? What is it that gives to great historical events this appearance, which is more than an appearance, of a tragedy that is admirably worked out and staged, in which at times the obvious mistakes of the actors are absolutely unable to prevent the result from occurring, in which the 'internal logic' of the process proves to be capable of inventing and of producing at the right moment the pushes and checks, the compensations and the trickery necessary for the process to reach its end – and in which at other times the actor, infallible up to then, makes the *only* mistake of his life, which in turn was indispensable for producing the 'intended' result?

This signification, which is already different from the signification actually experienced with respect to the determined acts of specific individuals, poses in itself an interminable problem. For signification is irreducible to causation, since significations construct an order of interconnections other than, and yet inextricably linked up with, that of causal connections.

Consider, for example, the question of the *coherence* of a given society – an archaic society or a capitalist society. What makes this society 'hold together'; what makes the rules (legal or moral) that govern the behaviour of adults coherent with their motivations; what makes them not only compatible but deeply and mysteriously akin to the mode of labour and production; what makes all this in its turn correspond to the family structure, the mode of nursing, weaning, the education of children; what produces a well-defined structure of the human personality in this culture; what makes this culture susceptible to certain neuroses and not to others; and what makes all of this connect up with a view of the world, a religion, and a particular way of eating and dancing? In studying an archaic society[51] at times one has the staggering sensation that a team of psychoanalysts, economists, sociologists, etc. possessing superhuman capacities and knowledge, has already worked on the problem of its coherence and has dictated a series of rules to ensure this coherence. Even if our ethnologists, in analysing the workings of these societies and in expounding on them, introduce more coherence than there is in fact, this impression is not and cannot be entirely illusory: after all, these societies are functional, they are stable, they are even 'self-stabilising' and capable of absorbing massive shocks (except, of course, the shock of contact with 'civilization').

Certainly, an important causal reduction can be made in the mystery of this coherence – and this is what constitutes the 'exact' study of a society. If adults behave in a certain manner, it is because they were brought up in a certain way. If the religion of the people has a particular content, this corresponds to the 'basic personality' of this culture. If the relations of power are organised in a given way, this is conditioned by the economic factors or conversely, and so on. However, this causal reduction does not exhaust the problem; it simply makes its skeleton apparent in the end. The connections that it discerns are, for example, the connections of individual acts which are situated within an already given framework, including both a social life which itself is already coherent at every moment as a concrete totality[52] (without which there could be no individual behaviour) and a set of explicit, and also implicit, rules, an organization, a structure, which is at once an aspect of this totality and something different from it. These rules are themselves the product, in a certain way, of this social life and in a large number of cases (almost never in the case of archaic societies, quite often in the case of historical societies) their production can be inserted into social causation (for example, the abolition of serfdom or the market competition introduced by the bourgeoisie serve its ends and are explicitly intended for this reason). But even when one manages to 'produce' them in this way, it remains that their authors were not and could not have been conscious of the totality of their effects and of their implications – and that, nevertheless, these effects and these implications 'concord' inexplicably with what already existed or with what others were producing at the same time in other sectors of social activity.[53] And it remains that, in the majority of cases, conscious 'authors' simply did not exist (basically, the evolution of the forms of family life, fundamental for the understanding of all cultures, does not depend on explicit legislative acts, and even less have such acts resulted from an awareness of the obscure psychoanalytic mechanisms at work in the family). There also remains the fact that these rules are posited at the start of every society,[54] and that they are coherent with one another regardless of the distance separating the domains concerned.

(When we speak of coherence in this context, we are taking the word in its broadest possible sense: for a given society, even its tensions and its crises can, in a certain way, convey its coherence, for they take their place within its functioning, and they never lead to its utter collapse and atomization for these are its 'crises' and 'its' incoherence. The great depression of 1929, just as the two world wars, are indeed 'coherent' manifestations of capitalism, not simply because they fit within its causal connections, but because they take this functioning further as the functioning of capitalism. In what in a thousand different ways seems to be their non-sense, one can still make out in a thousand different ways the sense of capitalism.)

There is a second reduction we can make: if all the societies that we observe, in the present or the past, are coherent, there is no reason for surprise since, by definition, only coherent societies are observable. Incoherent societies would have collapsed immediately and we would have nothing to say about them. This idea, however important it may be, does not put an end to the discussion. It can make us 'understand' the coherence of the societies observed only by referring back to a process of 'trial and error' through which, by a kind of natural selection, only 'viable' societies would have continued to exist. However, already in biology, where evolution takes millions of years and involves a process of infinitely rich random variations, natural selection through trial and error does not appear to be enough to reply to the problem of the genesis of the species. It indeed appears that 'viable' forms are produced in a proportion far greater than the statistical probability of their appearance. In history the reference to random variation and to a selection process seems gratuitous and, moreover, the problem is posed at a prior level (in biology as well!): while the disappearance of peoples and nations described by Herodotus may well be the result of the encounter with other peoples who crushed them or absorbed them, this does not preclude the fact that the former already had an organized and coherent life, which, if it were not for this encounter, would have continued. Moreover, we have seen, either with our own eyes or metaphorically, the birth of societies, and we know that things do not happen this way. What we see in twelfth- to nineteenth-century Europe is not a great number of different types of society appearing, and then all dying a way except for one because they are incapable of surviving. We see one phenomenon, the birth (accidental in relation to the system that preceded it) of the bourgeoisie, which, through its thousands of ramifications and its most contradictory manifestations, from the Lombardian bankers to Calvin, and from Giordano Bruno to the use of the compass, makes apparent from the start a coherent sense which will continue to assert itself and to develop.

These considerations allow us to grasp a second aspect of the problem. It is not only on the level of one society that the superposition of a system of meanings and a network of causes is manifested; this is also the case in the *succession* of historical societies, or simply in every historical process. Consider for example the process of the appearance of the bourgeoisie, which we mentioned above, or better yet that, which we think we know so well, leading first to the Russian Revolution of 1917 and then to the power of the bureaucracy.

It is not possible here – and anyway hardly seems necessary – to recall the deep causes at work in Russian society, directing it towards a second violent social crisis following that of 1905 and establishing the principal actors in the drama in the person of the basic classes of society. We do not find it hard to understand that Russian society was pregnant with revolution, nor that, in this revolution, the proletariat was to play a determining role – in any case, we shall not insist on this. This comprehensible necessity, however, remains 'sociological' and abstract; it has to be mediated in specific processes, it has to be embodied in acts (or omissions) and signed by definite persons and groups and moving in the direction intended. It must also find at the start a number of preconditions, whose presence cannot always be guaranteed by the very factors that created the 'general necessity' of the revolution. One aspect of the question – a minor one, granted, but one that allows us to see easily and clearly what is meant here – is the role of individuals. Trotsky, in his *History of the Russian Revolution*, by no means neglects this aspect. He is at time struck – and able to share this with the reader – by the perfect adequation of personal characters to the 'historical roles' they are called to play. He is also struck by the fact that when the situation 'requires' a specific type of character, this person steps forth (we recall the parallels he establishes between Nicolas II and Louis XVI, between the Tzarina and Marie-Antoinette). What, then, is the key to this mystery? The reply given by Trotsky still seems to be sociological in nature. Everything in the life and the historical existence of a privileged class in decay leads it to produce individuals lacking ideas or character, and if, as an exception to the rule, a different type of individual were to appear, he would be able to do nothing with these materials, and nothing against 'historical necessity'; and everything in the life and existence of the revolutionary class tends to produce individuals of sturdy character and strong views. The reply doubtless contains a good amount of truth, yet it is not sufficient, or rather, it says both too much and not enough. It says too much because it should hold in every case, yet it holds only in the cases, precisely, where the revolution has triumphed. Why did the Hungarian proletariat produce as its hardened leader Bela Kun, whom Trotsky assails with his most scornful irony? Why was the German proletariat unable to recognize or to replace Rosa Luxemburg and Karl Liebknecht? Where was the French Lenin in 1936? To say that in these cases the situation was not ripe enough for the appropriate leaders to emerge is precisely to leave behind the sociological interpretation that can legitimately claim a certain intelligibility and to return to the mystery of a singular situation which requires this or forbids that. Moreover, the situation that is supposed to forbid a certain occurrence does not always do so: for the past half-century the dominant classes have been able to provide themselves with leaders who, regardless of their role in history, have been neither Prince Lvovs nor Kerenskys. But neither does the explanation say enough, for it cannot show why chance is excluded from the processes where it seems to be at work in the most obvious way, why it always acts 'in the right direction', and why the infinite range of chance that would work in the opposite direction does not appear. For the Revolution to attain its goal, are required the inertia of the Tzar and the character of the Tzarina, Rasputin and the absurdities of the court, Kerensky and Kornilov; it is also required that Lenin and Trotsky return to Petrograd, and this in turn requires an error on the part of the German High Command and another on that of the British government – not to mention the diphtherias and pneumonias which conscientiously avoided these two persons from the time of their birth. Trotsky bluntly raises the question: without Lenin could the revolution have carried through to its end? And after discussing it, he replies in the negative. We are inclined to think that he is right and that, moreover, the same thing could be said about him.[55] But in what sense can we say that the internal necessity of the revolution guaranteed the appearance of individuals like Lenin and Trotsky, their survival until 1917, and their presence – itself more than improbable – in Petrograd at the right moment? We are forced to see that the meaning of the revolution is asserted and carried to its conclusion through an interconnection of causes which are unrelated to it, yet which are inextricably bound up with it.

The birth of the bureaucracy in Russia after the revolution allows us to see the problem again at another level. In this case, too, the analysis brings to light profound and comprehensible factors which are at work, but which we are unable to go over again here.[56] The birth of the bureaucracy in Russia is not pure hazard, certainly, and the proof is that bureaucratization has since emerged as the dominant tendency of the modern world. However, in order to understand the bureaucratization of capitalist countries, we appeal to tendencies immanent in the organization of production, of the economy and of the capitalist State. In order to understand the bureaucratization of Russia at the beginning, we appeal to totally different processes, like the relation between the revolutionary class and its party, the 'maturity' of the former and the ideology of the latter. Now, from a sociological point of view, there is no doubt that the canonical form of bureaucracy is that which emerges at an advanced stage of capitalism. And yet the bureaucracy which is first historically is the one that appears in Russia following the revolution, established on the social and material ruins of capitalism. And it is this bureaucracy which, by a thousand direct and indirect influences, has done much to induce and accelerate the movement towards bureaucratization in capitalism. Everything happened as if the modern world contained bureaucracy within itself, and that in order to produce it, it was able to put everything to this use, even what seemed least suitable for its purposes, that is to say Marxism, the workers' movement and the proletarian revolution.

Just as in the problem of the coherence of society, here too there is a causal reduction that one can and must make – and this is the basis for any exact and rational study of history. This causal reduction, however, as we have seen, does not abolish the problem. There is, also, an illusion which must be dissipated: the illusion of retrospective rationalization. This historical material, in which we cannot help but see meaningful relations, well-defined entities, possessing as it were a personal figure – the Peloponnesian War, the revolt of Spartacus, the Reformation, the French Revolution – is itself what has forged our idea about what historical meaning and figures themselves are. These events have themselves taught us what an event is, and the rationality we then find in them after the fact surprises us only because we have forgotten that we first extracted it from these events. When Hegel says more or less that Alexander necessarily had to die at 33 years of age because dying young is part of the essence of a hero and because we cannot imagine Alexander in old age, and when he thus transforms an accidental fever into a manifestation of the hidden Reason in history, we can observe that, as a matter of fact, our image of what a hero is was forged on the basis of the actual case of Alexander and other analogous cases, and that, therefore, there is nothing surprising in the fact that we discover in events a form which has been constituted for us on the basis of the events themselves. A similar demystification has to be made in a great number of cases. This does not, however, exhaust the problem. First of all, because we encounter here something analogous to what occurs in the knowledge of nature:[57] when one has performed the reduction of everything that can appear as rational in the physical world and ascribed it to the rationalizing activity of the knowing subject, there still remains the fact that this arational world must itself be such that this activity can grasp it, which excludes its being chaotic. Next, because historical meaning (that is, a meaning which goes beyond that actually experienced and borne by individuals) does indeed seem to be preconstituted in the material offered to us by history. To return to the example cited above, the myth of Achilles, who also dies young (and of numerous other heroes who suffered the same fate), was not forged on the basis of Alexander's example (the opposite would rather be the case).[58] The meaning articulated 'Heroes always die young' seems to have fascinated humanity since the beginning, despite – or because of – the absurdity it implies, and reality appears to have provided enough support for it to have become 'obvious'. Likewise, the myth of the birth of the hero, which presents analogous features across the most diverse cultures and epochs (at once deforming and reproducing actual facts), and finally all myths attest to the fact that events and meanings are mixed together in historical reality long before the historian's or the philosopher's rationalizing consciousness intervenes. Finally, because history constantly appears to be dominated by *tendencies*, because we find in it something like an 'internal logic' of the processes which confers a central position to a meaning or a complex of meanings (we referred above to the birth and the development of the bourgeoisie and of bureaucracy) and ties together causal series which have no internal connection and supplies itself with all the necessary 'accidental' conditions. The first astonishment one experiences in looking at history is that, if indeed Cleopatra's nose had been shorter, the face of the earth would have been changed. The second astonishment, even stronger than the first, comes when we notice that most of the time these noses were just the right size.

We thus face a basic problem: there are meanings that go beyond immediate and actually experienced meanings and these are carried by causation processes which, in themselves, have no meaning – or not *that* meaning. Sensed by humanity since the beginning of time, explicitly, although metaphorically, posited in myth and in tragedy (in which necessity takes on the figure of an accident), this problem was clearly faced by Hegel. The reply that he gives, however, the 'cunning of reason' which manages to make apparently meaningless events serve the ends of its own realization in history, is obviously no more than a phrase which solves nothing and ultimately participates in the old obscurity of the ways of Providence.

  The problem becomes even sharper in Marxism. For Marxism at one and the same time maintains the idea that meanings can be ascribed to events and to historical phases, affirms the force of the internal logic of historical processes more than any other conception, totalizes these meanings into one meaning, already given for history as a whole (the production of communism) – and claims to be able to reduce the level of meaning in its entirety to the level of causation. The two terms of the antinomy are thus pushed to their greatest degree of intensity, but their synthesis remains purely verbal. When Lukács says, in order to show that Marx has, in this regard as well, resolved the problem that Hegel was able only to raise: 'The "cunning of reason" can be no more than a mythology unless real reason is discovered and shown in a genuinely concrete manner. Then it is a brilliant explanation for the stages of history that are not yet conscious,'[59] he in fact says nothing at all. It is not simply that this 'real reason ... shown in a genuinely concrete manner' is reduced, in fact, by Marx to technical–economic factors and that these are insufficient even on the level of causation itself in order to 'explain' fully the production of results. The question is: how can technical–economic factors have a rationality that far surpasses them, how can their functioning throughout history embody a unity of meaning which itself carries another unity of meaning on a different level? To transform technical–economic evolution into a 'dialectic of the productive forces' is already a feat in itself; to superimpose on this dialectic another one which produces freedom out of necessity is a second feat; and to claim that the latter can be wholly reduced to the former is a third feat. Even if communism could be reduced simply to a question of sufficient development of the productive forces, and even if this development resulted inexorably from the functioning of objective laws established with utter certainty, the mystery would remain whole and entire: how can the functioning of blind laws produce a result which has both a meaning and a positive value for humanity?

In an even more precise and more striking manner, we discover this mystery again in the Marxist idea of an objective dynamics of the contradictions of capitalism. This is more precise because the idea is upheld by a specific analysis of the capitalist economy. And more striking, because here a series of negative meanings is totalized. The mystery seems to be resolved in appearance because the attempt is made to show, in the functioning of the economic system, the series of causes and effects which lead to the crisis of this system and prepare the way for another social order. Actually, the mystery remains untouched. By accepting the Marxist analysis of the capitalist economy, we find ourselves faced with a dynamics of contradictions that is unique, coherent and directed, with this chimaera which is supposed to be the beautiful rationality of the irrational, this philosophical enigma of a world of nonsense producing meaning on all levels and, finally, realizing our desire. In fact, the analysis is false and the projection contained in its conclusion is obvious. Little matter; the enigma does exist and Marxism does not solve it, quite the opposite. By asserting that everything must be grasped in terms of causation and at the same time that everything must be thought in terms of meaning, that there is but one immense causal chain which is simultaneously one immense chain of meaning, it exacerbates the two poles of the enigma to the point of making it impossible to think rationally about it.

Marxism, therefore, does not go beyond the philosophy of history; it is simply another philosophy of history. The rationality it seems to elicit from the facts, it imposes on them. The 'historical necessity' it speaks of (in the sense this expression has commonly had, precisely that of a series of events that leads history towards progress) differs in no way, philosophically speaking, from Hegelian Reason. In both cases, it is a question of an alienation of man which is properly theological. A communist Providence which is held to have set out history with a view to producing our freedom is no less a Providence. In both cases, the central problem of all reflection, that is the rationality of the natural or historical world, is eliminated by providing oneself from the start with a rational world by construction. Obviously, nothing is solved in this way, for a completely rational world would, for this very reason, be infinitely more mysterious than the world in which we are struggling. A history that would be rational through and through would be much more incomprehensible on the whole than the history we know. Its complete rationality would be based on a complete irrationality, for it would be of the nature of a pure fact, a fact so brutal, solid and encompassing that it would stifle us. Finally, under these conditions the primary problem of practice disappears: the fact that men have to give their individual and collective life a signification that is not pre-assigned, a signification that they have to make while they are at grips with real conditions, which neither exclude nor guarantee the accomplishment of their projects.

Dialectic and 'Materialism'

When Marx's rationalism takes on an explicit philosophical expression, it presents itself as a dialectic. And not as a dialectic in general, but as the Hegelian dialectic, from which 'the mystified idealist form' has been removed.

Thus have generations of Marxists mechanically repeated Marx's phrase: 'in Hegel the dialectic was on its head; I have put it back on its feet', without asking themselves whether such an operation was actually possible and especially whether it was capable of transforming the nature of its object. Is it enough to turn something over to modify its substance? Was the 'content' of Hegelianism so loosely tied to its dialectical 'method' that one could substitute another, radically opposed, content? And all the while keeping in mind that this is said of a philosophy which claimed that its content was 'produced' by its method, or rather that method and content were but two moments of the production of the system.

This obviously cannot be so, and if Marx preserved the Hegelian dialectic, he also preserved its true philosophical content – rationalism. What he modified in it is simply its costume, which, 'spiritualist' in Hegel, is 'materialist' in Marx. Used in this way, however, these are only words.

A *closed* dialectic, like the Hegelian dialectic, is necessarily rationalist. It at once presupposes and 'demonstrates' that the whole of experience is exhaustively reducible to rational determinations. (The fact that, in addition, these determinations are found in every instance to coincide miraculously with the 'reason' of a given thinker or a given society, that there is thus at the core of all rationalism an anthropomorphism or socio-centrism, that, in other words, all rationalism sets up as Reason a particular reason, this is clearly evident and would already suffice to put an end to the discussion). This dialectic is the necessary conclusion to any speculative and systematic philosophy which wants to reply to the problem: how can we have true knowledge? and which presents the truth as a complete system of relations, without ambiguity and without residues. Little matter in this respect if its rationalism takes on an 'objectivist' tinge (as in Marx and Engels), the world *being* rational in itself, a system of laws governing without limit an absolutely neutral substratum, and our penetration of these laws following from the character (incomprehensible, it must be admitted) of our knowledge as a *reflection*.[60] If it should take a 'subjectivist' turn (as in the philosophies of German idealism, including finally that of Hegel) the world concerned (in actual fact, the universe of discourse) then becomes the product of the subject's activity, which thereby guarantees its rationality.[61]

Reciprocally, every rationalist dialectic is necessarily a closed dialectic. Without this closed character, the whole system would continue to be suspended in mid-air. The 'truth' of each determination is nothing but its referral to the totality of determinations, for otherwise each of the moments of the system would remain at once arbitrary and indefinite. One thus has to give onself the totality without any remainder; nothing must be left outside of it, or else the system is not merely incomplete, it is nothing at all. Every systematic dialectic must lead to an 'end to history', whether in the form of Hegel's absolute knowledge or of Marx's 'total man'.

The essence of the Hegelian dialectic is not found in the assertion that the *logos* 'precedes' nature, and even less in the vocabulary that forms its 'theological vestment'. It lies in the method itself, in the fundamental postulate according to which 'all that is real is rational', in the inevitable claim to be able to produce the totality of the possible determinations of its object. This essence cannot be destroyed by setting the dialectic 'on its feet', since evidently this will leave the animal unchanged. A revolutionary surpassing of the Hegelian dialectic demands not that it be set on its feet but that, to begin with, its head be cut off.

The nature and the sense of the Hegelian dialectic cannot, in fact, change just because one would henceforth call 'matter' what one formerly called *logos* or 'spirit' – at least if by 'spirit' one does not mean a gentleman with a white beard dwelling in the heavens and if one knows that 'material' nature is not a mass of coloured and solid objects. It is completely indifferent in this respect to say that nature is a moment of *logos*, or that the *logos* springs forth at a given stage in the evolution of matter, since in both cases the two entitites are posited straightaway as possessing the same essence, namely a rational essence. Moreover, neither of the two assertions has any meaning, since no one can say what spirit or matter is outside of purely empty in so far as these are purely nominal definitions: matter (or spirit) is all that is, and so forth. Matter and spirit in these philosophies are finally nothing but pure Being, that is, as Hegel precisely said, pure Nothingness. Calling oneself 'materialist' in no way differs from calling oneself 'spiritualist', if by matter is meant an entity otherwise undefinable, yet entirely subject to laws that are themselves consubstantial and co-extensive with our reason, and hence capable already now of being penetrated by us in principle (and even in actual fact, since the 'laws of these laws', the 'supreme principles of nature and knowledge' are henceforth known to us: these are the 'principles' or the 'laws of the dialectic' discovered 50 years ago and now even numbered thanks to comrade Mao Tse-tung). When a spiritualist astronomer like Sir James Jeans says that God is a mathematician, and when dialectical materialists fiercely assert that matter, life and history are wholly subject to a determinism whose mathematical expression will one day be found, it is sad to think that under certain historical conditions the partisans of each of these schools could have (and actually did) execute those of the other. For they all say exactly the same thing, just giving a different name to it.

A 'non-spiritualist' dialectic must also be a 'non-materialist' dialectic, in the sense that it refuses to posit an absolute Being, whether as spirit, as matter or as the totality, already given in principle, of all possible determinations. It must eliminate closure and completion, pushing aside the completed system of the world. It must set aside the rationalist illusion, seriously accept the idea that there is both the infinite and the indefinite, and admit, without for all that giving up its labour, that all rational determination leaves outside of it an undetermined and non-rational remainder, that the remainder is just as essential as what has been analysed, that necessity and contingency are constantly bound up with one another, that 'nature' outside of us and within us is always something other and something more than what consciousness constructs, and that all of this is valid not only for the 'object' but also for the subject, and not only for the 'empirical' subject but also for the 'transcendental' subject since all transcendental legislation of consciousness presupposes the brute fact that a consciousness exists in a world (order and disorder, apprehendable and inexhaustible), and this is a fact which consciousness cannot produce itself, either really or symbolically. It is only on this condition that a dialectic can truly come to grips with living history, which the rationalist dialectic is obliged to kill in order to stretch it out on the pallets of its laboratories.

But such a transformation of the dialectic is possible, in its turn, only if the traditional and secular idea of theory as a closed system and as contemplation is superseded. And this was indeed one of the essential intuitions of the young Marx.

iv   THE TWO ELEMENTS OF MARXISM AND THEIR HISTORICAL FATE

There are in Marxism two elements whose meaning and historical fate have been radically opposed.

The revolutionary element burst forth in the youthful works of Marx; it continues to appear from time to time in the works of maturity. It reappears at times in the works of the greatest Marxists – Rosa Luxemburg, Lenin, Trotsky – and springs out for a last time in G. Lukács. Its appearance represents an essential twist in the history of humanity. It is this element that wants to unseat speculative philosophy by proclaiming that it is no longer a question of interpreting the world but of changing it, and that philosophy must be surpassed by being realized. It is this element that refuses to grant itself in advance the solution to the problem of history and a completed dialectic and asserts that communism is not an ideal state towards which society is progressing, but the real movement that suppresses the existing state of things. It stresses the fact that men make their own history under concrete conditions and declares that the emancipation of the workers will be the work of the workers themselves. It is this element that will be capable of recognizing in the Paris Commune or in the Russian Soviets not only insurrectional events but the creation by the masses-in-action of new forms of social life. Little matter for the moment if this recognition has remained partial and theoretical, if the ideas mentioned above are only starting points, raising new problems or sidestepping others. One would have to be blind not to see here the announcement of a new world, the project of a radical transformation of society, the search for its conditions in actual history and for its sense in the situation and activity of the men who could bring it about. We are not in the world to look at it or to submit to it; our fate is not servitude; there is a type of action that can be based on what is in order to bring into existence what we want to be. To understand that we are sorcerers' apprentices is already a step outside the condition of the sorcerer's apprentice, and to understand why we are is a second step. Beyond an activity unconscious of its true ends and its real results, beyond a technique which modifies an object in accordance with precise calculations without anything new resulting from this, there can and there must be an historical praxis which transforms the world by transforming itself, which allows itself to be instructed by instructing, and which prepares the new by refusing to predetermine it, for it knows that men make their own history.

These intuitions, however, were to remain intuitions, they were never really to be developed.[62] The announcement of the new world was quickly to be stifled by the expansion of a second element which was to be developed in the form of a system. This second element rapidly predominates; it relegates the first to oblivion or uses it – infrequently – only as an ideological and philosophical alibi. The second element reaffirms and extends capitalist culture and society in its deepest tendencies, even if it does so through the negation of a series of apparently (and genuinely) important aspects of capitalism; it weaves together the social logic of capitalism and the positivism of nineteenth-century science. It is this element that makes Marx compare social evolution to a natural process,[63] that stresses economic determinism, hailing in Darwin's theory a discovery which parallels Marx's.[64] As always, this scientific positivism immediately turns into rationalism and idealism as soon as it poses ultimate questions and replies to them. History is a rational system ruled by given laws, whose principles can be defined already now. Knowledge forms a system, one we already possess in its principle. Of course, there is 'asymptotic' progress.[65] but this is but the verification and the refinement of a solid core of acquired truths, the 'laws of the dialectic'. Correlatively, the theory keeps its eminent place, its primacy, regardless of invocations to 'the green tree of life', references to practice as the ultimate verification.[66]

Everything in this conception fits together: the analysis of capitalism, general philosophy, the theory of history, the status of the proletariat, the political programme. And the most extreme consequences follow from it – in good logic and in good history, as experience has proved in the past half-century. The development of the productive forces commands the rest in social life. Hence, even if it is not an ultimate end in itself, it is an ultimate end in practice since all the rest is determined by it and results from it 'as an addition', since 'the realm of freedom can be constructed only on the realm of necessity',[67] for it presupposes abundance and the reduction of the workday, and these in turn presuppose a given degree of development of the productive forces. This development is progress. Of course, the vulgar ideology of progress is denounced and derided, and capitalist progress is shown to be based on the misery of the masses. This misery itself, however, is part of an ascending process. The exploitation of the proletariat is justified 'historically' as long as the bourgeoisie uses its fruits to accumulate and thus continues its economic expansion. The bourgeoisie, the exploiting class from the start, is a progressive class as long as it develops the productive forces.[68] In the grand realist tradition of Hegel, not just this exploitation but all the crimes of the bourgeoisie, described and denounced at a certain level, are recovered by the rationality of history at another level and finally, because there is no other criterion, justified. 'Universal history is not the place of felicity', Hegel said.

It has often been asked how Marxists could have been Stalinists. But if the bosses are progressive, on the condition that they build factories, how could the commissars who build just as many and even more of them not be so as well?[69] As for the development of the productive forces, it is univocal and univocally determined by the state of technique. There is only one technique at any given stage, and there is also only a single rational ensemble of means of production. There is no question of trying to develop a society by other paths than that of 'industrialization', nor would there be any sense in doing so, the term 'industrialization' being apparently neutral, but finally giving birth to its full capitalist content. The rationalization of production is the rationalization already created by capitalism, the sovereignty of the 'economic' in all the senses of the term; it is quantification, the plan that treats men and their activites as measurable variables. Reactionary under capitalism once it no longer develops the productive forces and uses them only for an increasingly 'parasitic' exploitation, all this becomes progressive under the 'dictatorship of the proletariat'. This 'dialectical' transformation of the sense of Taylorism, for example, will be clarified by Trotsky as early as 1919.[70] It is of no matter that this situation leaves a number of philosophical problems unanswered, since it is not apparent how, under these conditions, identical 'infrastructures' can support opposing social edifices; of no matter that it also leaves unanswered a number of real problems, inasmuch as insufficiently mature workers do not understand the difference between the Taylorism of the bosses and that of the socialist State. The first will be skipped over with the help of the 'dialectic', the second will be silenced by gunshots. Universal history is not the place for subtlety.

Finally, if there is a true theory of history, if there is a rationality at work in things, it is clear that the direction this development takes should be left to the specialists of this theory, to the technicians of this rationality. The Party's absolute power – and within the Party, the 'coryphaei of Marxist–Leninist science', in the remarkable expression coined by Stalin for his own use – has a philosophical status. It is based in actual fact more genuinely on the 'materialist conception of history' than on Kautsky's ideas, taken up again by Lenin, concerning 'the introduction of socialist consciousness in the proletariat by middle-class intellectuals'. If this conception is true, this power *must* be absolute; democracy is then only a concession to the human fallibility of the leaders or a pedagogical method of which they alone can administer the correct dosage. The choice indeed is absolute. Either this conception is true, hence defines what is to be done, and what the workers do is valid only inasmuch as they conform to it. The theory itself cannot be confirmed or infirmed by their action, for the criterion lies within it and it is the workers who show whether or not they have been lifted to 'the consciousness of their historical interests' by acting in accordance with the watchwords which concretize the theory in given circumstances.[71] Or the activity of the masses is an autonomous and creative historical factor, in which case any theoretical conception can be no more than a link in the long process of realizing the revolutionary project. It can, and it even must be overturned by this process. The theory, then, no longer takes for itself history as given in advance and no longer posits itself as the standard of reality but accepts entering truly into history and being jostled and judged by it.[72] All historical privilege, all 'primogeniture' is then denied to the organization based on the theory.

The overvalued status of the Party, unavoidable consequence of the classical conception, finds its counterpart in what is, despite appearances, the undervalued status of the proletariat. If the latter has a privileged historical role, this is because, as the exploited class, it can in the end do no more than struggle against capitalism in a sense predetermined by the theory. This is also because, placed at the heart of capitalist production, it forms the greatest force within society and 'trained, educated, and disciplined' by this production, it is, *par excellence*, the bearer of this rational discipline. It counts, not as the creator of new historical forms, but as the human materialization of capitalist positivity, rid of its negative element: it is the epitome of the 'productive force', possessing nothing within it that might hinder the development of the productive forces.

Thus history was found, once again, to have produced something quite different than what it seemed to be preparing: under the cover of revolutionary theory, the ideology of a force and a social form that was yet to be born – the ideology of bureaucracy – was constituted and began to develop.

It is not possible for us to attempt here to give an explanation for the birth and the victory of this second element in Marxism: this would require an examination of the history of the workers' movement and of capitalist society over the last century. We can only sum up briefly what seems to us to be the decisive factors. The development of Marxism as a theory took place within the intellectual and philosophical environment of the second half of the nineteenth century. This period was dominated, as no other in history, by 'scientism' and positivism, triumphantly borne by the accumulation of scientific discoveries, their experimental verification, and especially, for the first time on this scale, 'the rational application of science to industry'. The apparent all-powerfulness of technique was 'demonstrated' daily, the face of entire countries transforming rapidly by the extension of the industrial revolution. What appears to us today in technical progress not only as ambiguous, but even as undetermined with respect to its social significance, had not yet emerged. The economy presented itself as the essence of social relations and the economic problem as *the* central problem of society. The milieu offered both the materials and the form for a 'scientific' theory of society and of history; it even made this a requirement, by predetermining to a large extent the dominant categories. However, the reader who has understood what we have been trying to say in the preceding pages, will also understand that we do not think that these factors provide 'the *explanation*' of the fate of Marxism. The fate of the revolutionary element in Marxism simply expresses, on the level of ideology, the fate of the revolutionary movement in capitalist society up to now. To say that Marxism has, over the past century, gradually been transformed into an ideology which has its place in existing society is simply to say that capitalism has been able to maintain and even to strengthen itself as a social system, that we cannot conceive of a society in which, in the long run, the power of the dominant classes is affirmed and in which, simultaneously, a revolutionary theory lives and develops. The evolution of Marxism is indissociable from the evolution of the society in which it has existed.

This development is irreversible, and there can be no 'restoration' of Marxism in its original purity, nor a return to its 'better half'. One still runs into subtle and tender 'Marxists' (who, as a general rule, have never concerned themselves with politics) for whom, surprisingly enough, all subsequent history is to be understood on the basis of Marx's early writings – instead of understanding these writings on the basis of subsequent history. In this way they try to support the claim that Marxism has 'superseded' philosophy, by uniting it to both the concrete (economic) analysis of society and to practice, and that it,

nevertheless, is no longer and never could have been a type of specu-
lation or a theoretical system. These claims (which are based on a
particular reading of a few passages of Marx and on the omission of
an infinitely greater number of texts) are not 'false'; in these ideas lie
certain seeds which, as we stated above, are essential. But what we
must see is not simply that these seeds were buried under a 100-year
frost. Rather, once we go beyond the stage of inspirations, intuitions
and intentions of a programmatic nature, once these ideas have to be
embodied, once they become the flesh of a thought that attempts to
embrace the real world and to inspire action, this fine unity is dissolved.
It is dissolved because what was supposed to be a philosophical description of the reality of capitalism, the integration of philosophy and
economics, is decomposed into two phases: the absorption of philosophy into an economics which is no more than economics, and the
illegitimate reappearance of philosophy at the end of the economic
analysis. It is dissolved because what was to be the union of theory
and practice is separated in real history into a rigidified doctrine left
in the state in which it was found at the death of its inventor and a
practice for which this doctrine, at best, serves as an ideological cover.
It is dissolved because, outside of a few rare moments (like 1917),
which moreover have yet to be interpreted – for this is not an easy
matter – *praxis* remains a mere word, and because the problem of the
relation between an activity that claims to be conscious and actual
history, as the relation between the revolutionaries and the masses,
remains whole and entire.

If there can be a philosophy which is something other than and
something more than philosophy, this remains to be proved. If there
can be a politics that is something other and something more than
politics, this also remains to be seen. If there can be a union of
reflection and action, and if this reflection and this action, instead of
separating those who practise it from all the others, carries them
towards a new society, this union remains to be accomplished. The
intention of this union was present at the origin of Marxism. It has
remained a mere intention – but, in a new context, it continues, a
century later, to define our task.

Since the beginning of the recorded history of human thought, innumerable philosophical doctrines have succeeded one another. For as long
as we can trace the evolution of societies, political ideas and movements
have been present. And all historical societies can be said to have been
dominated by the open or latent conflict between social strata or
groups, by class struggle. However, in each case, the world-view, the
ideas on the organization of society and of power and the actual
antagonisms between the classes have been tied together only in an
underground, implicit and unconscious manner. And in each case a
new philosophy has appeared, one that was going to reply to the
problems that the preceding ones had left unresolved, a new political

movement established its claims, in a society torn by a new social conflict – and yet always the same one.

In its beginnings, Marxism presented an entirely new demand. The union of philosophy, politics and the real movement of the exploited class in society was not going to be a mere addition but a genuine synthesis, a superior union in which each of the elements would be transformed. Philosophy could be something different and something more than philosophy, more than a refuge from impotence and a solution to human problems in the realm of ideas,[73] to the extent that it would translate its demands into a new politics. Politics could be something other and more than politics, technique, manipulation, the use of power for particular ends, to the extent that it would become the conscious expression of the aspirations and interests of the great majority of people. The struggle of the exploited class could be something other than a defence of particular interests, to the extent that this class would aim at the suppression of all exploitation through the suppression of its own exploitation, at the liberation of all through its own liberation and the establishment of a human community – the highest of abstract ideas to which traditional philosophy had been capable of aspiring.

In this way, Marxism posed the project of a union of reflection and action, of the highest sort of reflection and the most everyday action. It set out the project of uniting those who practice this reflection and this action and the others, eliminating the separation between an elite or an avant-garde and the mass of society. In the divided and contradictory world of the present it wanted to see something other than a new version of the eternal incoherence of human societies; it especially wanted *to make something* else of it. It asked that, in the challenges put to society by the people who live in it, we see more than a raw fact or the workings of fate, the first babblings of the language of a society to come. It aimed at the conscious transformation of society by the autonomous activity of men, whose real situation leads them to struggle against it. And it saw this transformation neither as a blind explosion, nor as an empirical practice, but as a revolutionary praxis, as a conscious activity that remains lucid about itself and is not alienated from itself in a new 'ideology'.

This new requirement is the most profound and most durable contribution made by Marxism. This is what has effectively made Marxism something more than another philosophical school or another political party. This is what, on the level of ideas, justifies the fact that we continue to speak of Marxism today, and even forces us to do so. The mere fact that this requirement appeared at a particular stage of history is in itself of immense significance. For, if it is not true that 'humanity only raises the problems it can solve', nevertheless, the fact that a new problem comes to be posed does convey important changes in the depths of human existence. It is also of immense significance that Marxism was able to realize its intention in a certain way and for a certain time, not by remaining a mere theory, but by uniting with the workers' movement struggling against capitalism, to the point of becoming almost indiscernible from it for a long time and in a number of different countries.

However, for us living now, the dawn of promises has given way to full light of problems. The organized workers' movement is, everywhere and without exception, thoroughly bureaucratized, and its 'objectives', when these exist, have no relation to the creation of a new society. The bureaucracy that dominates the workers' organizations, and in any case the bureaucracy that reigns supreme in countries said to be, by antiphrasis, 'worker' and 'socialist' States, claims to be Marxist and makes Marxism the official ideology of regimes in which exploitation, oppression and alienation continue. This Marxism, whether the official ideology of States or the credo of sects, has ceased to exist as a living theory. Whatever their definition, their affiliation, or their specific colour, 'Marxists', for decades, have produced no more than compilations and glosses, the laughingstock of theory. Marxism is dead as theory, and when one looks at it closely one sees that it died for good reasons. An historical cycle thus seems to have come to completion.

The problems posed at the outset are not, however, resolved; they have instead been greatly enriched and made more complicated. The conflicts that divide society have not been overcome, far from it. Although the challenge put to society by those who live in it may, for a certain period of time and in certain countries, take on more embryonic and fragmentary forms, this does not change the fact that the problem of the organization of society is posed in actual situations and by each society itself. Today, just as 100 years ago, and in contrast to 1,000 years ago, those who raise social questions are not reformers who want to impose their obsessions on a humanity which has not asked for their advice. Instead, they are simply part of a continuous debate; they extend and clarify the preoccupations of entire sectors of the population, discussing a problem that is kept open by the perpetual reformism of the dominant classes themselves. If this is indeed the case, it is not only because exploitation, alienation and oppression continue. It is because they continue to be accepted by no one and, in particular, because, for the first time in history, they are no longer openly defended by anyone. However, to this universally recognized problem, no one any longer claims to have an answer. Politics has not ceased to be a manipulation that denounces itself, since it remains the pursuit by particular groups of their particular ends under the mask of the general interest and by means of a universal instrument, the State. The universe of theory is more than ever in a problematic and fragmentary state, and philosophy, if it is not simply dead, can no longer maintain its claims of yesteryear, without, for all that, being in a position to define a new role for itself, to say what it is and what it is aiming at.

The conditions which gave rise to Marxism's new requirement not only have not disappeared, they have been exacerbated and this requirement presents itself to us in much sharper terms than it did a century ago. But now we also have the experience of a century which appears, finally, to have held it in check. How is this to be interpreted? How are we to understand this double conclusion, the fact that this requirement seems constantly to re-emerge out of reality and that experience shows that it has not been able to be maintained? What is signified by the downfall of Marxism, the deterioration of the worker movement? What are they the result of and what do they convey? Do they indicate the fatal destiny of all theory, of any revolutionary movement? Just as it is impossible to make of it a mere accident, and to want to start again on the same bases promising to do better this time, so too it is impossible to see, in a theory and in a movement that claimed radically to change the course of history, merely a passing aberration, a state of collective inebriation, unexplainable but transitory, after which we shall find ourselves happily and sadly sober again.

Of course, these questions can be examined as they deserve to be only on the plane of real history: how and why did the workers' movement lead to the point where it now finds itself, and what are the current perspectives for a revolutionary movement? This angle, undoubtedly the most important, cannot be ours here.[74] We must instead confine ourselves to concluding our analysis of Marxist theory by looking at equivalent questions on the plane of ideas: what were the properly theoretical factors which led to the petrification and the downfall of Marxism as an ideology? Under what conditions can we satisfy today the requirement that we defined above, embody it in a conception that does not contain from the start the seeds of its own corruption, as this determined the fate of Marxism?

This terrain – the terrain of theory – is, of course, limited. And in accordance with the very content of what we are saying, it is not a matter of establishing once and for all a new theory – yet one more! – but of formulating a conception that can inspire an indefinite *development* and, in particular, give rise to and clarify an effective activity – which, in the long run, will be the test of this conception. But the importance of this should not be underestimated. If theoretical experience, from a certain point of view, forms only one part of historical experience, it is, from another point of view, an almost unabridged translation of it into another language. And this is even more true of a theory like Marxism which has shaped real history and has allowed itself to be shaped by it in so many ways. And in speaking of the scoresheet of Marxism and of the possibility of a new conception, we are still speaking, in this transposition, of a century of actual experience and of the perspectives of the present. We know perfectly well that the problems that concern us cannot be resolved by theoretical means, but we also know that they will not find a solution without an elucidation of ideas. Socialist revolution as we see it is impossible without lucidity, which does not exclude but, on the contrary, requires

that lucidity be lucid on its own account, that is to say, the acknowl-
edgement by lucidity of its own limits.

The original inspiration of Marxism was aimed at overcoming the
alienation of man in relation to the products of his theoretical activity,
what was later to be termed 'the regression from act to thought'.[75] The
point was to reintegrate the theoretical into historical practice, to which
it, in truth, had never ceased to belong, but most often in a mystified
form, that of a 'shifting of questions' of a fictive solution to real
problems. The dialectic was no longer to be the self-production of the
Absolute; henceforth it was to incorporate the relation between the
thinker and the object, to become the concrete search for the mysterious tie between the singular and the universal in history, to relate
the implicit and the explicit sense of human actions, to unveil the
contradictions at work in reality, perpetually to go beyond what is
already given, and to refuse to set itself up as a final system without
for all that dissolving itself into the indeterminate.[76] Its task was not
to establish eternal truths, but to think the real. This real, the real *par
excellence* – history – was thinkable to the extent that it was, not
rational in itself or by divine construction, but the product of our own
activity, this activity itself in the infinite variety of its forms. However,
to say that history can be thought, that we are not caught in an obscure
trap (whether maleficent or beneficial, little matter) did not mean that
everything had already been thought out. 'As soon as we have once
realized ... that the task of philosophy thus stated means nothing but
the task that a single philosopher should accomplish that which can
only be accomplished by the entire human race in its progressive
development – as soon as we realize that, there is an end[77] of all
philosophy in the hitherto accepted sense of the word.'
   This original inspiration corresponded to essential realities in modern
history. It came as the ineluctable conclusion to the completion of
classical philosophy, the only means of getting out of the impasse in
which the most elaborate, the most finished form of classical philosophy
– Hegelianism – had ended. As soon as it was formulated, it merged
with the needs and the deepest significance of the nascent workers'
movement. It anticipated – if these are correctly understood – the sense
of the discoveries and the upheavals that have marked the present
century: contemporary physics as well as the modern crisis of the
personality, the bureaucratization of society as well as psychoanalysis.
   These, however, were only germs; they never bore fruit. Mixed from
the start with elements of an opposing inspiration,[78] with mythical or
fantastic conceptions (the communist man as the 'total man', once again
Hegel's Absolute-Subject stepping down from his pedestal and walking
on the earth), they either remained vague about essential problems or
covered them over. In particular, the central question for *this sort* of
conception, that of the relation between the theoretical and the practical, remained totally obscure. 'The point is no longer to interpret the
world, but to change it,' the blinding light of this statement does not

clarify the relation between interpretation and change. In fact, most of the time it was intimated that theory was *only* ideology, sublimation, compensation (which later had to be heavily counterweighted, when theory was made the supreme court and the ultimate guarantor). And, symmetrically, praxis remained a word whose meaning was in no way determined or clarified.

The development of Marxism in a systematic form took the opposite direction, so that finally the Marxism set up as a theory (and by this we do not mean the popular versions, which of course also had a great historical importance, but precisely the major works of Marx and Engels, in their maturity), the Marxism which indeed claims to provide responses to the problems that we have just mentioned, is situated at the furthest remove from this original inspiration. In its essence, this Marxism is no more than a pseudo-scientific objectivism to which a rationalist philosophy is appended. We have attempted to show this in previous sections of our text. Here, we simply want to recall a few essential points.

In the completed Marxist theory, what was at the start to be the critical description of the capitalist economy, rapidly becomes an attempt to explain this economy in terms of the operation of laws independent of the action of men, groups or classes. A 'materialist conception of history' is established, one that claims to explain the structure and the functioning of every society on the basis of the state of technique, and the transition from one society to another by means of the evolution of this technique. In this way, a complete knowledge is postulated in principle (one that has already been acquired in its essential features) of all of past history, which is held everywhere to reveal, 'in the last analysis', the action of these same objective laws. Thus men no more make their own history than the planets 'make' their revolutions; they themselves are 'made' by it, or rather both are made by something else – a Dialectic of history which produces the forms of society and their necessary supersession, assures the progressive, ascending movement and the final passage, after a long alienation, of humanity into communism. This communism is no longer 'the real movement that suppresses the existing state of things', it is split into the idea of a future society that will follow the present one and a real movement which is a mere means or instrument, which has no more internal affinity, either in its structure or in its actual life, to what it serves to realize than the hammer and the anvil have to the products they help to produce. It is no longer a matter of transforming the world instead of interpreting it. It is a matter of thrusting to the fore the one and only true interpretation of the world, which assures that it must and will be transformed in the sense deduced by the theory. It is no longer a question of praxis but actually of practice in the ordinary sense of the term, the industrial or the vulgar political sense. The idea of verification by 'experimentation or industrial practice' takes the place of what the idea of praxis presupposes, namely that historical reality as the reality of human actions is the only place in which ideas and projects can acquire their true meaning. The old bugbear of a rationalist–materialist philosophy reappears and imposes itself, proclaiming that all that is, is 'matter' and that this matter is 'rational' through and through, for it is governed by the 'laws of the dialectic', which, moreover, we already possess.

It is hardly necessary to remark that this conception could not help but pave the way for the utter petrification of theory. Within the framework of a system that is closed in on itself in this way – and that makes this closure both the proof and the consequence of the necessity to pass to another historical phase – how could there be anything more than efforts of application, more or less correct, and additions, more or less brilliant? We must also remember that it unfailingly leads to a 'rationalist' politics – a bureaucratic politics. Briefly, if an Absolute knowledge concerning history exists, then the autonomous action of individuals has no sense (at the most it will be one of the disguises of the cunning of reason). Those who are imbued with this knowledge have, therefore, to decide on the most effective and the most rapid means of reaching the goal. Political action becomes a *technical* action, the differences that separate it from the other techniques are not differences of principle but of degree (knowledge gaps, imprecision of information, etc.). Conversely, the practice and the dominance of the bureaucratic layers claiming their Marxist faith, have found in it the best 'solemn complement for their justification', the best ideological cover. Getting rid of the everyday and the concrete by invoking tomorrow as it is assured by the direction of history, the adoration of capitalist 'effectiveness' and 'rationalization', the overwhelming emphasis placed on the development of the productive forces, which is held to rule the rest – all these aspects, of bureaucratic ideology and thousands of others, derive directly from Marxist objectivism and progressivism.[79]

By making Marxism the effective ideology of bureaucracy, historical evolution has stripped of all meaning the question of whether, in order to restore to Marxism its initial character and to make it once again a revolutionary theory, one should attempt to correct it, reform it, revise it or straighten it out. For history makes us see in the facts what theoretical analysis, on its side, shows in ideas: the Marxist system participates in capitalist culture, in the most general sense of the term, and it is therefore absurd to want to make it the instrument of revolution. This is absolutely the case for Marxism taken as a system, as a whole. It is true that the system is not completely consistent, and that in the mature Marx or in his heirs, one can often find ideas and formulations that continue the truly revolutionary and innovative inspiration of the beginning. But, either these ideas are taken seriously and the system breaks apart, or the system is maintained, and then these beautiful formulas become ornaments, which have no use except to justify the indignation of unofficial Marxism's delicate souls in the face of 'vulgar' or Stalinist Marxism. What one must by no means do is to play both sides at the same time: to claim that Marx was not a philosopher like the others, by invoking *Capital* as the depository of rigorous science and the workers' movement as the verification of its conception; to cover over the genuine sense of the degeneration of the workers' movement by appealing to the economic mechanisms that would lead to the overcoming of alienation; and to defend against the accusation of mechanism by referring to a hidden meaning of the economy and to a philosophy of man, neither of which is defined anywhere.

The Philosophical Foundation of the Decay

We have already indicated a number of times that the factors that conditioned what appears to us as the decay of Marxism, the abandonment of its original inspiration, are to be sought in real history, that they are of the same nature as those that have led to the bureaucratic decline of the workers' movement, and that, in a certain way, they convey the almost insurmountable obstacles that prevent the development of a revolutionary movement, the survival and the rebirth of capitalism in the very thing that combats it with the greatest vigour. This is to say that, for us, it is not a matter of seeking the origin of this decay in a theoretical error made by Marx, of detecting the false idea that would only have to be replaced by the true idea to ensure the rectification.

However, precisely because the social world is unitary even in its conflicts, there are equivalences, real attitudes have theoretical counterparts. What on the theoretical level corresponds to bureaucratization must be on the level of the real separated out, discussed as such, and, if not 'refuted'; at least clarified in its profound relation to the world which one is combatting on other fronts. If the socialist revolution is a conscious enterprise, this is a necessary if not a sufficient condition of any new start.

The theoretical origin of the decay of Marxism, the ideological equivalent of the bureaucratic degeneration of the workers' movement, is to be sought in the rapid transformation of the new conception into a theoretical system which is complete and whole in its intention, in the return to the contemplative and the speculative as the dominant mode for solving the problems posed to humanity.

The transformation of theoretical *activity* into a theoretical *system* which considers itself to be closed is the return to the most profound sense of the dominant culture.[80] It is the alienation to what is already there, already created; it is the negation of the most profound content of the revolutionary project, the elimination of the real activity of human beings as the final source of all meaning, the forgetting of revolution as a radical upheaval and of autonomy as the supreme principle. It is the theoretician's claim to take on his own shoulders the weight of solving the problems of humanity. A completed theory claims to provide replies to what cannot be resolved except, if this be possible, by historical praxis. Thus it can close its system only by making people comply in advance to its schemata, by submitting them to its categories, by leaving aside historical creation, all the while glorifying it in words. It can accept what happens in history only if it appears as a confirmation of theory, otherwise it combats it – which is the clearest way of expressing its intention to bring history to a halt.[81]

A closed theoretical system must of necessity posit people as *passive* objects of its theoretical truth, for it must submit them to this *past* to which it is itself subjugated. This is due to the fact that, on the one hand, it remains almost unavoidably the development and the condensation of experience already acquired,[82] and that, even if it foresees something 'new', this is always in every respect the *repetition* on some other level, the 'linear transformation' of what has already occurred. The main reason, however, why a completed theory is compatible only with an essentially static world lies on a deeper level, that of the categorial structure or of the logical essence of a closed system. How can a theory be defined as a complete theory if it does not posit fixed and stable relations embracing the totality of the real, without gaps and without remainder? We have already tried to show that a theory of history like the one Marxism aims at, a general explanatory scheme which draws out the laws of the evolution of societies, can be defined only by postulating constant relations between entities which themselves are constant. Of course, the historical material it is dealing with, and which it has to 'explain', is highly variable and changeable, and at the start it recognizes this and is the first to proclaim it. However, the very aim of the theory conceived of in this way is to reduce this variability, this change, to eliminate them logically, to take them back to the functioning of the *same* laws. The multicolour phenomenal cloak must be torn off, if we are finally to perceive the essence of reality, which is identity – but, obviously, *ideal* identity, the naked identity of laws. This remains true even when the variability of laws at a certain level is acknowledged. Marx rightly says that there are no demographic laws in general, that each type of society entails its own demography. The same thing holds, both in its conception and in its reality, for the 'economic laws' of each type of society. However, the appearance of a given sub-system of demographic or economic laws corresponding to the society considered is itself governed once and for all by the more general system of laws that determine the evolution of history. In this respect, little matter if the theory draws these laws, consciously or unconsciously, from the past, from the present, or even from a future that it constructs or 'projects'. What it is aiming at is in any event something *intemporal*, possessing an *ideal* substance. Time is no longer for it, what we are taught both by our most direct experience and by our furthest-reaching reflection: the perpetual seeping of the new into the porousness of being, which alters what is identical even when leaving it intact; it is the neutral medium of what unfolds, the abstract condition for successive coexistence, the means of ordering a past and a future which have always ideally pre-existed to themselves. The necessary twofold illusion of theory closed in on itself is that the world has been always already made and that it can be possessed by thought. But the central idea of revolution is that humanity has a genuine future before it, and that this future is not simply to be thought but to be *made*.

This transformation of Marxism into a finished theory[83] contained within it the death of its initial revolutionary inspiration. It signified a new alienation with respect to the speculative, for it transformed living theoretical activity into the contemplation of a system of relations given once and for all. It contained the seed of the transformation of politics into technique and bureaucratic manipulation, since politics was now able to be the application of acquired knowledge to a well-defined domain and to precise ends. This alienation did not consist, of course, in theorizing as such, but in the transformation of this theorizing into an absolute, into the allegedly full knowledge of the historical being, as a given being and as a meaning (as an empirical reality and as an essence). This allegedly full knowledge can only be based on a complete misunderstanding of things historical; we have seen this and we shall see it again. But it is also based on a thorough misunderstanding of what true theory is, for, by an obvious dialectic which has been repeated a hundred times in history, this transformation of theory into an absolute is just what can do it the most harm, crushing it under claims it can never make good. Only by returning theory to its rightful place can its true function and dignity be restored. But returning theory to its place is inseparable from returning practice to its rightful place; only when they are in proper relation to one another can they both become true.

2

Theory and Revolutionary Project

---

i PRAXIS AND PROJECT

Knowing and Doing

If what we say is true, if not only the specific content of Marxism as a theory is unacceptable, but the very idea of a complete and definitive theory is a pipe dream and a mystification, can we then still speak of a socialist revolution and maintain the project of a radical transformation of society? Is not a revolution, like the one aimed at by Marxism and like the one we continue to aim at, a conscious enterprise? Does it not presuppose both a rational knowledge of present society and the possibility of rationally anticipating future society? To say that a socialist transformation is possible and desirable, is this not to say that our actual knowledge of present society ensures this possibility, that our expected knowledge of future society justifies this choice? In both cases, do we not raise the claim that our thought possesses present and future social organization as totalities in act and that it provides at the same time a criterion permitting us to judge them? On what can we base all this, if there is not and cannot be a theory, or even, behind it, a philosophy of history and of society?

These questions, these objections can be – and indeed are – formulated from two diametrically opposed points of view, which, nevertheless, ultimately share the same premises.

For the first, the critique of the alleged absolute certainties of Marxism is interesting, perhaps even true – yet unacceptable because it would destroy the revolutionary movement. Since this movement must be supported, the theory must be preserved whatever the cost, even if this means cutting back on claims and requirements, or, if need be, shutting our eyes.

For the second group, since a total theory cannot exist, we are forced to give up the revolutionary project, unless it is posited, in utter contradiction with its content, as the blind will to transform at any price something one does not know into something one knows even less.

In both instances the implicit postulate is the same: without a total theory there can be no conscious action. In both cases, the phantasy of absolute knowledge remains sovereign. And in both cases the same ironic reversal of values occurs. The person who considers himself a man of action grants, instead, the primacy of theory; he sets up as the supreme criterion the possibility of safeguarding revolutionary activity, while making this possibility dependent on maintaining, in appearance anyway, a definitive theory. The philosopher who wants to be radical remains a prisoner of what has been criticized. A conscious revolution, it is said, would presuppose absolute knowledge. Eternally absent, this knowledge nevertheless remains the measure of our acts and of our life.

This postulate, however, is worthless. We already have an inkling that by forcing us to choose between geometry and chaos, between absolute Knowledge and blind reflex, between God and beast, these objections move within a world of fiction and allow to slip through unnoticed a trifle: all that is and ever will be given to us, human reality. Nothing we do, nothing we have ever to do with affords complete transparence, any more than it displays utter molecular disorder. The historical and human world (that is to say, with the exception of an infinitely distant point, as mathematicians say, the world as such) is of a different order. It cannot even be called 'the mingling' for it is not made of a mixture. Total order and total disorder are not the components of the real, but limiting concepts which we abstract from it, pure constructions which, taken in absolute terms, become illegitimate and incoherent. They belong to the mythical extension of the world created by philosophy over the past 25 centuries, and this is something we must rid ourselves of, if we want to stop including our own phantasies in what is to be thought.

The historical world is the world of human *doing*. This doing is always related to knowledge, but the relation itself has to be clarified. For this clarification, we shall look to two examples, two extremes – the limiting cases of 'reflex action' and 'technique'.

Consider a 'purely reflexive' human activity, one that is absolutely unconscious. By definition, this sort of activity would have no relation to any type of knowledge. But it is also clear that it would not belong to the domain of history.[1]

Consider, at the other extreme, a 'purely rational' activity. This would be based on an exhaustive, or practically exhaustive, knowledge of its domain. By practically exhaustive, we mean that any question relevant for practice and arising out of this domain would be decidable.[2] In terms of this knowledge and in conclusion to the reasoning that it permits, action would be confined to positing in reality the means to reach the ends it aims at, and establishing the causes that would lead to the intended results. An activity of this sort is realised approximately in history; it is *technique*[3]. Approximately, because an exhaustive knowledge cannot exist (but only the fragments of such a knowledge) even within a well-defined domain, and because the delimiting of domains in this way is never clear-cut.[4] Under this concept of 'rational activity' can be placed a large number of cases which, without belonging to technique in the strict sense, come close to it and which we shall henceforth include under this term. The repetitive activity of an assembly-line worker; solving a second-degree algebraic equation for someone who knows the general formula; deriving new mathematical theorems by means of the 'mechanized' formalism of Hilbert; many simple games, and so forth, are examples of technical activity in the broad sense.

What is essential in human activities can be grasped neither as reflex nor as technique. No human doing is non-conscious, and yet none could continue one second longer if a prior exhaustive knowledge were required, if a total clarification of its object and its mode of operation were necessary. This is obvious in the case of all the 'trivial' activities that make up daily life, both individual and collective. But this is also the case for more 'elevated' activities, with weightier consequences, those which directly involve other people's lives and those that aim at universal and lasting creations.

Raising a child (whether as parent or as teacher) can be done with greater or lesser consciousness and lucidity, but it is excluded by definition that this can be done on the basis of a total clarification of the child's being and of the pedagogical relationship. When a doctor, or better yet an analyst,[5] begins a treatment, do we think of asking him to put his patient into concepts first, to draw the diagrams of his conflictual structures and the *ne varietur* course of treatment? Here, as in the case of the pedagogue, we are dealing with something quite different from a provisional ignorance or a 'therapeutic' silence. The illness and the patient are not two separate things, one containing the other (anymore than the future of the child is something contained in the thing – child) of which we could define the essence and the reciprocal relationship, while awaiting a more thorough investigation. It is a mode of being of the patient, whose entire life, past as well as yet to come, is at issue and the meaning of this life cannot be fixed and closed off at a given moment since it continues and thus modifies past meanings. What is essential in this treatment, just as in education, corresponds to the very relationship that will be established between the patient and the doctor, or between the adult and the child, and to the evolution of this relationship, which depends on what each of them will *do*. We do not ask the teacher or the doctor for a complete theory of their activity, which, moreover, they would be incapable of supplying. But we should not, for all that, say that these are blind activities, that raising a child or treating a patient is a game of roulette. The requirements with which human doing confronts us are of a different order.[6]

The same thing is true for the other manifestations of human doing, even those in which others are not explicitly implicated, in which the 'isolated' subject undertakes a task or an 'impersonal' work. When an artist begins a work, and even when an author begins a theoretical book, he both does and does not know what he is going to say – even less does he know what that which he will say will actually *mean*. And it is no different for the most 'rational' activity of all, theoretical activity. We were saying earlier that the use of Hilbert's formalism for the relatively mechanical derivation of new theorems is a technical activity. However, the attempt to constitute this formalism in itself is absolutely not a technique, but instead a genuine doing, a conscious activity which can rationally assure neither its foundations nor its results. The proof of this, I dare say, lies in its grandiose failure.[7] More generally, if the application of 'proven' results and methods within this or that branch of mathematics can be assimilated to a technique, once mathematical research touches on the foundations or the ultimate consequences of the discipline, it reveals its essence as a doing which rests on no final certainty. The construction of mathematics is a project pursued by humanity for thousands of years; during the course of this elaboration the increasing rigorousness within the discipline has led *ipso facto* to a growing uncertainty as to the foundations and as to the meaning of this activity.[8] With respect to physics, this is not even a doing, but a sort of Western, where one surprising event after another creates an accelerating pace, astounding even the actors themselves who first set off the series of actions.[9]

Theory in itself is a doing, the always uncertain attempt to realize the project of clarifying the world.[10] And this is also true for that supreme or extreme form of theory – philosophy – the attempt to conceive of the world without knowing, either before or after the fact, whether the world is actually conceivable, or even just what conceiving of something exactly means. It is for this reason, moreover, that there is no question of 'going beyond philosophy by realizing it'. We 'go beyond' philosophy – that is to say, we do not forget it, even less despise it, but set it in place – when we understand that it is simply a project, one which is necessary yet uncertain as to its origin, its import and its fate; not exactly an adventure, perhaps, but also not a chess game, and certainly not the realization of the total transparence of the world for a subject and of the subject for itself. And if philosophy were to come and posit to a politics which aspired to be at once lucid and radical, the prior condition of total rigorousness demanding that this politics be wholly founded on reason, politics would be within its rights to answer: have you then no mirrors at home? Or does your activity consist in setting up standards for others which you are incapable of applying to yourself?

Finally, if particular techniques are 'rational activities', technique itself (we are using the term here in its restricted, ordinary sense) is absolutely not. Different techniques belong to technique, but technique itself is not technical. In its historical reality, technique is a project whose meaning remains uncertain, whose future is obscure, and whose end is undetermined, since, to be sure, the idea of making ourselves 'the masters and possessors of nature' is strictly meaningless.

To demand that the revolutionary project be founded on a complete theory is therefore to assimilate politics to a technique, and to posit its sphere of action – history – as the possible object of a finished and exhaustive knowledge. To invert this reasoning and conclude on the basis of the impossibility of this sort of knowledge that all lucid, revolutionary politics is impossible amounts, finally, to a wholesale rejection of all human activity and history as unsatisfactory according to a fictitious standard. Politics, however, is neither the concretization of an absolute Knowledge, nor a technique; neither is it the blind will of no one knows what. It belongs to another domain, that of doing and to the specific mode of doing called *praxis*.

Praxis and Project

We term praxis that doing in which the other or others are intended as autonomous beings considered as the essential agents of the development of their own autonomy. True politics, true pedagogy, true medicine, to the extent that these have ever existed, belong to praxis.

In praxis, there is something *to be done*, but what is *to be done* is something specific: it is precisely the development of the autonomy of the other or of others (this not being the case in relations that are purely personal, as in friendship or love, where autonomy is recognized but its development is not posited as a separate object, for these relations have no end outside of the relation itself). One could say that for praxis the autonomy of the other or of others is at once the end and the means; praxis is what intends the development of autonomy as its end and, for this end, uses autonomy as its means. This way of speaking is handy for it is easily comprehensible. But it is, strictly speaking, an abuse of language, and the terms 'end' and 'means' are absolutely incorrect in this context. Praxis cannot be circumscribed in a model of ends and means. The model of the end and of the means to attain this end belongs, precisely, in its proper usage, to technical activity, for the latter has to do with a real end, an end which is an end, a finished and definite end which can be posited as a necessary or probable result in view of which the choice of means amounts to a matter of more or less exact calculation. With respect to this end, the means have no internal relation, simply a relation of cause to effect.[11]

In praxis, however, the autonomy of others is not an end; it is, all word-play aside, a beginning, anything but an end. It is not finished; it cannot be defined in terms of a state or any particular characteristics. There is an internal relation between what is intended (the development of autonomy) and that through which it is intended (the exercise of this autonomy). These are two moments of a single process. Finally, although it evolves within a concrete context which conditions it and has to take into consideration the complex network of causal relations crisscrossing its terrain, praxis can never reduce the choice of its manner of operating to mere calculation, not that this would be too complicated, but because it would, by definition, allow the escape of the essential factor – autonomy.

To be sure, praxis is a conscious activity and can only exist as lucid activity, but it is something quite different from the application of prior knowledge (and cannot be justified by calling upon knowledge like this – which does not mean that it cannot justify itself). It is based on knowledge, but this knowledge is always fragmentary and provisional. It is fragmentary because there can be no exhaustive theory of humanity and of history; it is provisional because praxis itself constantly gives rise to new knowledge for *it makes the world speak a language that is at once singular and universal.* This is why the relations of praxis to theory, true theory correctly conceived, are infinitely tighter and more profound than those of any 'strictly rational' technique or practice; for the latter, theory is only a code of lifeless prescriptions which can never, in its manipulations, encounter meaning. The parallel development of psychoanalytic practice and theory by Freud, from 1886 until his death, probably provides the best illustration of this twofold relation. The theory cannot be given beforehand, because it constantly emerges out of the activity itself. The clarification and transformation of reality progress together in praxis, each conditioning the other. And this twofold progression is the justification of praxis. However, in the logical structure of the ensemble they form, activity precedes clarification; for praxis, the ultimate goal is not the clarification but the transformation of the given.[12]

We have spoken of fragmentary and provisional knowledge, and this may give the impression that praxis (and all doing) is essentially negative, a privation or a deficiency in relation to another situation which would be full and would possess an exhaustive theory or absolute Knowledge. This appearance, however, stems from our language, bound to a centuries old manner of treating problems, which consists in judging or thinking of what is actual after the pattern of what is fictional. If we were certain of being properly understood, if we did not have to take into consideration the tenacious prejudices and pre-suppositions holding sway even in the most critical of minds, we would simply say: praxis is based on an actual knowledge (one which, of course, is limited, provisional – as is everything actual) and we would not feel the need to add: being a lucid activity, it obviously cannot call upon the phantasy of an illusory absolute Knowledge. What grounds praxis is not a temporary deficiency in our knowledge, which could gradually be reduced. Even less is it the transformation of the present horizon of our knowledge into an absolute boundary.[13] The 'relative' lucidity of praxis is not a stopgap solution, better than nothing – this is so not only because something 'better' exists nowhere, but also because this is but another side to its positive substance: the very object of praxis is the new, and this cannot be reduced to the simply materialized tracing of a pre-established rational order; in other words, its object is the real as such and not a stable, limited, dead artifact.

This 'relative' lucidity also corresponds to another aspect of praxis which is just as essential: its subject, too, is constantly transformed on the basis of the experience in which it is engaged, which the subject *does* or *makes*, but which also *makes* the subject. 'Pedagogues are educated', 'the poem makes the poet.' And it is self-evident that a continuous modification results, both in form and in content, with respect to the *relation* between a subject and an object, which themselves cannot be defined once and for all.

What has, up to now, been called politics has almost always been a mixture in which the dominant component has been manipulation, treating people as things in terms of their properties and their supposed known reactions. What we call revolutionary politics is a praxis which takes as its object the organization and orientation of society as they foster the autonomy of all its members and which recognizes that this presupposes a radical transformation of society, which will be possible, in its turn, only through the autonomous activity of individuals.

It can readily be granted (after a brief inventory of a few phases of history) that a politics such as this has not existed up to now. How and why might it exist now? On what could it be based?

The answer to this question leads us to the discussion of the very content of the *revolutionary project*, which is, precisely, the reorganization and reorientation of society by means of the autonomous action of individuals.

The project is the element of praxis (and of all activity). It is a determined praxis, considered in its ties with the real, in the concrete definition of its objectives, in the specification of its mediations. It is the intention of transforming the real, guided by a representation of the meaning of this transformation, taking into consideration the actual conditions and inspiring an activity.

We must not confuse project and plan. The plan corresponds to the *technical* moment of an activity, when conditions, objectives and means can be and are 'exactly' determined, and when the mutual ordering of means and ends is based on a sufficient knowledge of the domain concerned. (It is apparent from this that the expression 'economic plan', despite its convenience in other respects, is, strictly speaking, an improper use of language.)

We must also distinguish between the project and the activity of an 'ethical subject' in traditional philosophy. The latter is guided – like the navigator by the North Star, following Kant's famous image – by the idea of morality, but at the same time remains at an infinite distance from this idea. There is thus a perpetual non-coincidence between the real activity of an ethical subject and the moral idea, even though they are related to one another. This relation, however, is equivocal, for the idea is at once an end and a non-end. An end, because it expresses, without excess or deficit, what should be; a non-end, because in principle there is no question that it be attained or realized. The project, however, regards its realization as an essential moment. If there is a gap between representation and realization, it is not one of principle, or rather it depends on categories other than the gap between 'idea' and 'reality': it refers to a new modification affecting representation as well as reality. The core of the project, in this respect, is a meaning and an orientation (a direction towards) which cannot be fixed in 'clear and distinct ideas' and which go beyond the representation of the project as it was fixed at any given moment.

When it is a matter of politics, the representation of the intended transformation, the definition of objectives, can take – and must necessarily take, under certain conditions – the form of a *programme*. The programme is a provisional concretization of the objectives of the project on certain points judged to be essential in given circumstances, in so far as their realization would lead to or would facilitate the realization of the project as a whole by its own inner dynamics. The programme is but a fragmentary and provisional figure of the project. Programmes come and go, the project remains. Like anything else, the programme can easily deteriorate and degenerate. The programme may be taken as an absolute; it may foster the alienation of people and their activities. This in itself proves nothing against the necessity of a programme.

Our topic here, however, is not the philosophy of practice as such, nor is it the elucidation of the concept of project for itself. We want to show the possibility and explicate the meaning of the revolutionary project as the project of transforming present society into a society organized and oriented towards fostering the autonomy of all, this transformation being accomplished by the autonomous action of human beings, such as they are produced by current society.[14]

This discussion, no more than any other, does not take place on a *tabula rasa*. What we say today is necessarily leaning on – and we might even say, if we were not careful: is sunk in – what has already been said for ages, by others and by ourselves. The conflicts that divide present society, the irrationality that predominates in it; the perpetual oscillation of individuals and the masses between struggle and apathy, the system's incapacity to deal with one or the other; the experience of past revolutions and, from our point of view, the ascending line that joins their apexes; the possibilities for the socialist organization of society and its modalities, to the extent that these can be defined at the present moment – all this is necessarily presupposed in what we are saying and it is not possible to go over it again here. For the moment, we should simply like to clarify the main questions opened up by the critique of Marxism and the rejection of its analysis of capitalism, its theory of history and its general philosophy. If there is no economic analysis which can show, in the form of an objective mechanism, both the grounds of the crisis of present society and the necessary shape of future society, what can serve as the bases of the revolutionary project in the actual situation and from where can we form any idea with regard to another society? Does not the critique of rationalism exclude the possibility of establishing a destructive and constructive 'revolutionary dynamics'? How can one posit a revolutionary project without wanting to grasp present society, and especially future society, as a totality and, moreover, as a rational totality, without succumbing to one of the pitfalls cited above? Once the guarantee of 'objective processes' has been eliminated, what remains? Once the guarantee of 'objective processes' has been eliminated, what remains? Why do we *want* revolution – and why would others want it? Why would they be capable of it? For does not the project of a socialist revolution presuppose the idea of a 'total man' to come, of an absolute subject, a notion we have denounced? Just what does autonomy mean, and to what extent can it be realized? Does this not blow the role of consciousness out of all proportion? Does it not make alienation a bad dream from which we are about to awaken, and prior history an unfortunate accident? Is there any sense in postulating a radical reversal; are we not pursuing the illusion of absolute novelty? Is there not behind all this another philosophy of history?

ii ROOTS OF THE REVOLUTIONARY PROJECT

Social Roots of the Revolutionary Project

There can be no complete theory of history, and the idea of the total rationality of history is absurd. However, neither can we say that history and society are *ir*rational in a positive sense. We have already tried to show that rational and non-rational are constantly intersecting in historical and social reality, and it is precisely this intersection which provides the condition for action.

Historical reality is not wholly and entirely rational. If it were, *doing* would never be a problem, for everything would have already been *said*. Doing implies that reality is not rational through and through. It also implies that it is not simply chaos, that it contains grooves, lines of force, veins, which mark out the possible, the feasible, indicate the probable and permit action to find points of anchorage in the given.

The mere existence of instituted societies suffices to demonstrate this. However, along with the 'reasons' for its stability, existing society also reveals, upon analysis, its cracks and the force lines of its crisis.

The discussion of the relation between the revolutionary project and reality must be shifted from the metaphysical terrain of the historical inevitability of socialism – or of the historical inevitability of non-socialism. To begin with, it must include a discussion of the possibility of transforming society in a particular direction.

We shall only begin this discussion here, restricting ourselves to two examples.[15]

In that fundamental social activity – *labour* – and in the *relations of production* in which this labour is performed, capitalist organization presents itself, since its origins, as dominated by a central conflict. The workers only half-way accept – perform, as it were, with only one hand – the tasks they are assigned. The workers cannot really participate in production, and yet cannot help but participate in it. Management cannot do otherwise than exclude the workers from production and, at the same time, it cannot exclude them from it. The conflict resulting from this – which is at once 'external', between directors and executants, and 'internalized', within each executant and each director – could fall away and become blurred if production were static and technique petrified, but economic expansion and technological upheaval keep it constantly alive.

The crisis of the capitalist enterprise presents a number of other aspects, and if one were to consider only the upper stages, one could perhaps speak simply of 'bureaucratic dysfunction'. But at the base, on the ground floor of the shops and offices, it is not a question of 'dysfunction', but of a conflict which is expressed in an incessant struggle, even when it is implicit and masked. Long before the revolutionaries, capitalist theoreticians and practicians discovered the existence and the gravity of this conflict and accurately described it, even if they stopped short, naturally, of the conclusions that could have been drawn from this analysis and if they remained bound to the idea of finding at any cost a 'solution' without upsetting the existing order.

This conflict, this struggle, display a logic and a dynamic, out of which three tendencies emerge:

- workers organize in informal groups and oppose a fragmentary 'counter-management of labour to the official management established by the employer,
- workers set out demands concerning the conditions and the organization of labour,
- during the phases of social crisis, workers openly and directly demand the control of production and attempt to realize this (Russia 1917–18, Catalogna 1936–7, Hungary 1956).[16]

These tendencies translate the same problem in different countries and in different phases. The analysis of the conditions of capitalist production show that they are not accidental but consubstantial with the most profound characteristics of this production. They cannot be amended or eliminated by partial reforms of the system, since they follow from the fundamental relation of capitalism, the division of the labour process into a moment of management and a moment of execution, each embodied in a different social pole. The sense they incarnate defines, beyond the framework of production, a type of antinomy, of struggle, *and* of the supersession of this antinomy, essential to the understanding of a great number of other phenomena of contemporary society. In short, these phenomena are interconnected, they are connected to the fundamental structure of capitalism, connected to the rest of social relations. And they express not only a conflict but a tendency towards a solution of this conflict through the realization of workers' management of production, which implies the elimination of bureaucracy. We therefore find in social reality itself a conflictual structure and the seeds of a solution.[17]

It is, therefore, a description and a critical analysis of what *is* which unearths, in this case, one of the roots of the revolutionary project. This description and this analysis are not even, truly speaking, 'our own' in any specific sense. Our theorizing only sets in place *what society itself expresses confusedly about itself at every level.* It is the capitalist leaders or bureaucrats who are constantly complaining about the opposition of the people; it is their own sociologists who analyse it, who exist in order to defuse it, and who most of the time confess that it is impossible. It is the workers who, once we begin to look closer, constantly combat the existing order of production, *even if they do not know they are doing it.* And, if we can be satisfied with ourselves for having 'predicted' the content of the Hungarian Revolution far in advance,[18] we did not, for all that, invent it (any more than in the case of Yugoslavia, where the problem is posed even if it is to a large extent mystified). Society itself speaks of its own crisis in a language which scarcely requires any interpretation.[19] One section of society, that which is most vitally concerned by the crisis and which, moreover, includes the vast majority of people, behaves in actual fact in a way which, at one and the same time, *constitutes* the crisis and shows a possible way out of it. And, under certain conditions, this section attacks the present organization, destroys it, and begins to replace it with another. In this other organization – in the management of production by the producers – it is impossible not to see the incarnation of autonomy in the fundamental domain of labour.

The questions that can legitimately be raised are therefore not: where do you see the crisis? where will you find a solution? The question is: is this solution – workers' management – really possible? Can it be realized durably? And, supposing that, considered 'in itself' it appears possible, does not workers' management imply much more than this management itself?

However closely, however deeply one may try to look at it, the management of a firm by those who work there presents no insurmountable problem. Quite the opposite, it reveals the possibility of doing away with an extraordinary number of problems which constantly hamper the functioning of the firms today, resulting in immense wastage and wear on human and material resources.[20] At the same time, however, it becomes clear that the problem of management goes far beyond the firm and its production and refers back to society as a whole, and that any solution to it implies a radical change in people's attitudes with respect to labour and the collectivity. We are therefore led to raise the questions of society as a totality, and of the responsibility of human beings – which we shall examine later.

The *economy* provides a second example which will allow us to clarify other aspects of the problem.

We have tried to show that there is not and that there cannot be a systematic and complete theory of the capitalist economy.[21] The attempt to establish such a theory runs up against the determining influence exerted on the economy by a factor not reducible to the economic, namely class struggle. It also runs up against the impossibility, at another level, of establishing a unit of measure of economic phenomena, which nevertheless are presented as magnitudes. This does not prevent the possibility of a knowledge of the economy, or of finding out certain facts and of stating some tendencies (with regard to which, of course, precise discussion is open). Concerning the industrialized countries, these facts and tendencies are, in our opinion:

- The productivity of labour is increasing at an accelerating pace. In any event, no limit to this growth can be seen.
- Despite the continuous rise in the standard of living, the problem of absorbing the fruits of this productivity is beginning to be posed in a virtual manner, in the form of the saturation of most traditional needs and in that of the latent underemployment of an increasing part of the labour force. Capitalism replies to these two phenomena by synthetically producing new needs, manipulating consumers, developing a mentality oriented towards 'status' and social rank tied to the level of consumption, and creating or maintaining outmoded or parasitic forms of employment. But it is by no means certain that these expedients will suffice for long. There are two apparent outcomes: turning the productive apparatus more and more towards the satisfaction of 'collective needs' (according to their capitalist definition and conception, to be sure), which seems hard to reconcile with the private economic mentality in the West and in the East (a politics such as this would imply a more rapid increase of 'taxes' than of wages). Or instead, introduce a more rapid reduction of labour time, which in the current social context would create enormous problems.[22] Either way, the base of the system's functioning, economic motivation and constraint, would suffer what would probably be an irreparable blow.[23] What is more, if these solutions are

'rational' from the point of view of the interests of capitalism as such, they are rarely so considered from the point of view of the specific interests of the dominant and influential capitalist and bureaucratic groups. To say that there is no absolute impossibility preventing capitalism from finding a way out of the situation that is being created today, does not mean that it is a sure thing capitalism will get out of it. The stubborn and up-to-now victorious resistance that the dominant groups in the United States oppose to the adoption of measures that would be beneficial to them – increase of public expenditure, the extension of 'aid' to underdeveloped countries, the reduction of labour time (which appears to them to be the height of extravagance, squandering funds, and sheer madness) – shows that an explosive crisis is as possible an evolution as is the pacific mutation of capitalism. This is all the more likely as this mutation would, at the present moment, put into question aspects of the social structure even more important than those concerned, in their time, by the New Deal, the introduction of economic controls, etc. Automation is progressing much more quickly than the decretinizing of American senators – although the latter might actually be speeded up by the very fact of a crisis. But whether it be through a crisis or through peaceful transformation, these problems will only be resolved by shaking the present social edifice to its very foundations.

• There is a tremendous potential waste (or possibilities lost) in the use of productive resources (despite 'full employment'), stemming from a number of factors, all of which are related to the nature of the system: the lack of participation by the workers in production; bureaucratic dysfunction on the level of the firm as well as on that of the economy; competition and monopolistic competition (artificial product differentiation, lack of standardization of products and machinery, secrecy surrounding inventions and manufacturing processes, advertising, intentional restrictions in production); the irrational nature of the distribution of the productive capacity among firms and branches, this distribution reflecting the past history of the economy as much as current needs; the protection of certain strata or sectors and the conservation of the *status quo*; the irrational nature of the geographical and professional distribution of the labour force; the impossibility of any rational planning with respect to investments as a result of ignorance of the present state of affairs as well as of avoidable uncertainties about the future (connected to the functioning of the 'market' or of the bureaucratic 'plan'); the radical impossibility of rational economic calculations (theoretically, if the price of one item of production contains an arbitrary element, all calculations throughout the system may thereby be jeopardized; now prices have only a very distant relation to costs, both in the West with its prevailing oligopolies and in the USSR where it is officially admitted that prices are essentially arbitrary); the use of a part of the product and of resources for ends that have a meaning only in relation to the system's class structure (cost of the controlling bureaucracy in the firm and elsewhere, army, police, and so on). It is by definition impossible to give a quantitative estimate of this wastage. Sociologists of labour have on occasion estimated at 50 per cent the loss in production due to the first factor we mentioned, undoubtedly the most important one, namely the fact that workers do not participate in production. If we were to advance an estimate, we would say that the current output of the United States must be of the order of one-fourth to one-fifth of that which could be attained by the elimination of the various above-mentioned factors [or that this output could be attained with one-fourth of the labour currently expended].

• Finally, an analysis of the possibilities which would result from making available to society, organized into councils of producers, economic knowledge and the existing techniques of information, communication and computation – the 'cybernation' of the global economy in the service of the collective self-management of human beings – shows that, however far we can see, not only is there no technical or economic obstacle to the establishing and the functioning of a socialist economy, but that this functioning would be, in its essential aspects, infinitely simpler and infinitely more rational – or: infinitely less irrational – than the functioning of the current economy, whether private or 'planned'.[24]

There is, therefore, in modern society an immense economic problem (which, ultimately, is the problem of 'overcoming the economy'), pregnant with an impending crisis. There are incalculable possibilities, which are currently being wasted which, if put into effect, would allow a general well-being, a rapid reduction of labour time to perhaps one half of what it is now, and the freeing of resources to satisfy needs that at the present moment are not even formulated. And there are positive solutions which, in a fragmentary, truncated, deformed manner are being proposed or introduced even now, and which, if they were applied radically and universally, would permit resolving this problem, realizing these possibilities, and bringing about an immense change in the life of humanity, by rapidly eliminating 'economic need'.

It is clear that the application of this solution would require a radical transformation of the social structure – and a transformation of people's attitude towards society. We therefore find ourselves once again face-to-face with the problems of totalization and responsibility, which we shall attempt to analyse later.

Revolution and Rationalization

The example of the economy allows us to see another essential aspect of the revolutionary problematic. A transformation in the direction indicated would mean an unprecedented *rationalization* of the economy. The metaphysical objection appears here, and here again, as a sophism: is a *complete* rationalization of the economy ever possible? The reply is: we do not care.

It is enough to know that a vast rationalization is possible and that it can only have a positive effect on people's lives. In the present economy we have a system that is only partially rational but which contains unlimited possibilities for rationalization. These possibilities can begin to be realized only at the price of a radical transformation of the economic system and of the vaster system in which it is embedded. Conversely, it is only in relation to this rationalization that such a radical transformation is conceivable.

The rationalization in question concerns not only the use of the economic system (allocate the output to the ends that are expressly desired by the collectivity). It also concerns the system's functioning and finally the possibility of the very knowledge of the system. On this final point we can see the difference between the contemplative attitude and praxis. The contemplative attitude confines itself to observing that the economy (both past and present) contains profoundly irrational elements, which forbid a complete knowledge of it. It finds therein the particular expression of a general truth, the irreducible opacity of the given, which obviously is just as valid for the future. This attitude will assert, as a result (and it has every right to do so on these grounds) that a totally transparent economy is impossible. From this, it could easily – should it be the slightest bit lacking in rigour – rush to the conclusion that it is not worth the bother of trying to change anything, or that all the possible changes, however desirable they may be, will never change anything essential but will instead remain on the same level of existence, since they can never accomplish the jump from the relative to the absolute.

The political attitude notes that the irrational character of the economy is not simply to be confused with the opacity of all being, that it is connected (not only from the human or social point of view but even from the purely analytical point of view) to a large extent to the entire present social structure which, to be sure, is by no means eternal or fatal. It asks to what degree this irrationality can be eliminated by a modification of this structure, and it concludes (in this it can, of course be mistaken, but this is a *concrete* question) that it can be eliminated to a considerable extent, so considerable that it would bring about an essential modification, a qualitative change: the possibility for people consciously to direct the economy, to make decisions in awareness of the problems – instead of submitting to the economy as is now the case.[25] Will this economy be totally transparent, rational through and through? Praxis will reply that this question is meaningless to it, that what matters to it is not speculating on the impossibility of the absolute but transforming the real in order to eliminate as much as possible all that is adverse to human beings. It does not concern itself with the possibility of moving from the 'relative' to the 'absolute', it observes that radical innovations have already taken place in history. It is not interested in complete rationality as a finished state but, as concerns the economy, in rationalization as the continuous process of realizing the conditions for autonomy. Praxis knows that this process has already crossed different stages and that it will cross more. After all, the discovery of fire or of America, the invention of the wheel, of metal-work, of democracy, of philosophy, of the Soviets, and certain other events in the history of humanity indeed took place *at a particular moment*, and have introduced a deep split between what went *before* and what came *after*.

Revolution and Social Totality

We have attempted to show, in relation to production and to labour, that the conflict displayed there contains at the same time the seeds of a possible solution in the form of the *workers' management* of production.

These seeds of a solution, both as a 'model' and through their implications, go far beyond the problem of production. This is self-evident *a priori*, since production is already much more than production. But it is helpful to show this concretely.

Workers' management goes beyond production when it is considered as a model: if workers' management is valid, it is because it suppresses a conflict by realizing a given mode of socialization, which would allow participation. Now the same type of conflict exists in other social spheres as well (in a sense, with the necessary transpositions, in all of them); the mode of socialization represented by workers' management appears here, too, in principle as a possible solution.

Workers' management goes beyond production through its implications: it cannot simply remain the workers' management of production in the narrow sense, at the cost of becoming a simulacrum. Its actual realization implies a practically total rearrangement of society, just as its consolidation, in the long run, implies another type of human personality. Another type of command of the economy and its organization, another type of power, another education and so forth, must, of necessity, accompany it.

In both cases we are led to pose the problem of the social totality. And we are also led to propose solutions which are presented as global solutions (a 'maximum programme'). Is this not to postulate that society forms potentially a rational whole, that nothing that may arise in another sector would render impossible what seems possible to us after an examination that is obviously partial, that what is emerging here can flower forth everywhere, and that we henceforth possess the key to this rational totality?

No. In posing the revolutionary project, in attributing to it the concrete form of a 'maximum programme', not only are we not claiming to exhaust the problems, not only do we know that we cannot exhaust them; rather we can and must indicate the problems that remain, tracing their outlines to the very limit of the unthinkable. We are aware and we must state that problems remain which we can only formulate; others we cannot even imagine; and still others which will have to be posed in different terms, currently inconceivable to us. We know that questions that cause us anguish now, because they are insoluble, may very well disappear by themselves, and that, on the contrary, replies that appear self-evident today may upon application reveal practically infinite degrees of difficulty. We also know that all this could possibly (but not necessarily) obliterate the sense of what we are saying now.

These considerations, however, cannot constitute the basis for object-ing to revolutionary praxis any more than to any kind of praxis or doing in general – except for someone who wills nothingness or who claims to stand on the ground of absolute knowledge and to judge everything from there. To do something, to do a book, to make a child, a revolution, or just doing as such, is projecting oneself into a future situation which is opened up on all sides to the unknown, which, therefore, one cannot possess beforehand in thought, but which one must necessarily assume to be defined in its aspects relevant to present decisions. This doing is lucid when it does not alienate itself to an already established image of this future situation, but modifies it as it goes along; which does not confuse intention and reality, the desirable and the probable, which does not lose itself in conjectures and specu-lations concerning aspects of the future irrelevant to what is to be done now, or beyond our control. But lucidity is also not giving up this image, for, if it did, 'not only would it not know where it is going', it would not even know where it *wants* to go (it is for this reason that the motto of all reformism: 'the goal is nothing, the movement is everything', is absurd; every movement is a movement *towards*; it is something else if, since there are no pre-assigned goals in history, all the definitions of goals prove to be provisional).

If the necessity and the impossibility of taking into consideration the totality of society could be opposed to revolutionary politics, they could and should be opposed to *every* sort of politics. For a reference to the whole of society is necessarily implied whenever there is a politics. The most narrowly reformist action must, if it is to be coherent and lucid (but what is essential to reformism in this respect is precisely the lack of coherence and lucidity) take into consideration the social whole. If it does not do so, it will see its reforms swept aside by the reaction of this totality which it has neglected, or a result completely different from the one it had intended. The same thing can be said with respect to purely conservative action. Completing an existing system, filling in the gaps in the system's defences, how can these actions fail to raise the question of whether the remedy is not worse than the illness, and in order to decide this, to look as far as possible into the ramifications of its effects, how can these actions dispense with the effort of aiming at the social totality, not only with respect to their intended end, the preservation of the global system, but also with respect to the possible consequences and to the coherence of the network of means that are employed? At the very most, this aim (and the knowledge it implies) can remain implicit. Revolutionary action differs in this regard only in that it attempts to make its own presuppositions explicit, as far as is possible.

The situation is the same outside of politics. Under the pretext that there is no satisfactory theory of the organism as a totality, nor any well-defined concept of health, would we dream of forbidding doctors from practising medicine? And during this practice, could any doctor worthy of the name abstain from taking this totality into account, as far as possible? And let no one say: society is not sick. Besides the fact that this is not certain, sickness or health is not what is at issue here. It is a question of practice, which can have as its field the sickness or the health of an individual, the functioning of a group or a society, but which constantly encounters the totality both as a certitude and as a problem – for its 'object' is given only as a totality and it is also as a totality that it slips out of grasp.

The speculative philosopher can protest against the 'lack of rigour' implied by these considerations touching on a totality that can never be grasped. But these very protests point to the greatest lack of rigour; for without this 'lack of rigour' the speculative philosopher could not survive a single instant. If the philosopher survives, it is only by allowing his or her right hand to be unaware of what the left hand is doing. It is because speculative philosophers divide their life into a theoretical activity including absolute criteria defining rigour – which, moreover, are never satisfied – and a simple living to which these criteria by no means apply, and for good reason, since they are inapplicable. The speculative philosopher is thus caught within an insoluble antinomy. But in fact, he actually generates this antinomy himself. The problems resulting for praxis from the attempt to take into account the totality are real ones in so far as they are concrete problems: but they are purely illusory when they are considered as absolute impossibilities. They arise only when one tries to gauge real activities after the mythical standards of a certain philosophical ideology, of a 'philosophy' which is simply the ideology of a certain philosophy.

The manner in which praxis *confronts* the totality and the manner in which speculative philosophy *claims* to *provide* itself with the totality are radically different.

If there is an activity that addresses itself to a 'subject' or to a lasting collectivity of subjects, this activity can exist only by being grounded in two ideas: the idea that it encounters, in its 'object', a unity that is not posited by the activity itself as a theoretical or a practical category but which exists first of all *for-itself* (whether clearly or dimly, implicitly or explicitly); and the idea that what is specific to this unity for-itself lies in the capacity to supersede every prior determination, to produce

the new, new forms and new contents (new in the manner of organization and in what is organized, the distinction between these being
relative, of course, and a matter of 'optics'). As concerns praxis, one
can sum up the situation by saying that it encounters the totality as an
open-ended unity in the process of making itself.

When the traditional speculative theory encounters the totality, it
has to postulate that it already possesses the latter. Otherwise, it has
to admit that it cannot fill the role it has assigned to itself. If 'truth is
not in the things but in the relations', and if, as is self-evident, relation
has no boundaries, then, necessarily, 'Truth is the Whole.' And if the
theory is to be true, it must possess everything, or else deny its own
claims and accept what, for it, is the supreme downfall, relativism and
scepticism. Possessing the whole in this way must be *actual* in the
philosophical as well as in the everyday sense: explicitly realized and
present at every instant.

For praxis, too, relation has no boundaries. But from this does not
follow any need to fix and to possess the totality of the system of
relations. The requirement of taking the totality into consideration is
always present for praxis, but praxis is not thereby held to come to the
end of this process, to complete it at any time. And this is so because
this totality is not, for it, a passive object of contemplation, whose
existence would hang in mid-air until such a time as it would be wholly
actualized by theory. This totality can, and does, constantly take itself
into consideration.

For speculative theory, the object does not exist if it is not complete
and the theory itself does not exist if it cannot complete its object.
Praxis, on the other hand, can exist only if its object, by its very nature,
surpasses all completion; praxis is a perpetually transformed relation
to the object. Praxis begins with the explicit acknowledgment of the
open character of its object and exists only to the extent that it acknowledges this. Its 'partial grasp' of the object is not a shortcoming it regrets
but something positively asserted and intended as such. For speculative
theory is only valid for that which, in one way or another, it has
managed to pack away and lock up in the strongboxes of its 'demonstrations'. Its dream – its phantasy – is the accumulation of a treasure
of everlasting truths. Inasmuch as the theory goes beyond this phantasy,
it becomes a true theory, the praxis of truth. For praxis, what is already
constituted as such is already dead once it has been constituted, what
has been acquired must, without exception, be reinserted within living
actuality in order to maintain its existence. However, it is not up to
praxis to assure this existence wholly by itself. Its object is not something inert, whose entire fate is to be assumed by praxis. The object
itself is active, it possesses tendencies, it is productive and it organizes
itself – for if it is not capacity for production and capacity for self-
organization, it is nothing. The speculative theory collapses, for it
assigns to itself the impossible task of taking the entire world on its
shoulders. But praxis does not have to carry its object in its arms while

acting on its object, and in the same stroke, it recognizes thereby that the object does actually exist for itself. There is no sense in showing an interest in a child or in a sick person, in a group or in a society, if one does not see in them first and foremost *life*, the capacity of being grounded in itself, self-production and self-organization.

Revolutionary politics consists in recognizing and making explicit the problems of society considered as a totality, but precisely because society is a totality, it acknowledges that society is something other than an inert mass in relation to its own problems. It observes that every society, in one way or another, has been able to deal with its own weight and its own complexity. And, on this level as well, it confronts the problem actively: cannot this problem, which it does not invent, a problem which, in any event, is constantly implied in social and political life, be confronted by humanity under different conditions? If it is a matter of managing social life, is there not at the present time an immense gap between needs and reality, between what is possible and what actually exists? Would not this society be in an infinitely better position to face up to itself if it did not condemn to immobility and to opposition nine-tenths of its own substance?

Revolutionary praxis is, therefore, not required to produce the complete and detailed model of the society it intends to establish; nor does it have to 'demonstrate' and provide an absolute guarantee that this society could solve all the problems that might ever arise. It is enough that it show that there is nothing inconsistent in what it proposes and that, as far as can be seen, its realization would greatly increase society's capacity to face up to its own problems.

The Subjective Roots of the Revolutionary Project

We sometimes hear it said that the idea of another society is presented as a project, but in fact is simply a projection of unacknowledged desires, an outer garment for motivations which remain hidden to those who possess them. In some people, it serves only as a vehicle for desire for power; in others, it simply marks the refusal of the reality principle, the phantasy of a world without conflict in which everyone would be reconciled with everyone else, and each person with himself, an infantile day-dream which would attempt to do away with the tragic side of human existence, running away in order to live at once in two different worlds, an imaginary compensation.

When the discussion takes this turn, it must first be recalled that we are all in the same boat. No one can be sure that what he says is unrelated to unconscious desires or unavowed motivations. When one hears 'psychoanalysts' of a particular tendency classify all revolutionaries in broad terms as 'neurotics', one can only congratulate oneself on not sharing their five-and-dime store 'health', and it would be only too easy to take apart the unconscious mechanism behind their conformism. More generally, those who believe they discover at the roots of the revolutionary project this or that unconscious desire, should simultaneously ask themselves what is the motive conveyed by their own critique and to what extent this critique is not a rationalization.

For us, however, this reversal is of slight interest. The question does indeed exist and even if no one were to raise it, whoever speaks of revolution should ask it to himself. Leave it up to the others to decide the amount of lucidity involved in their own positions; revolutionaries cannot impose limits on their desire for lucidity. Nor can they refuse the problem by saying: what counts are not unconscious motivations but the meaning and the objective value of ideas and acts; Robespierre's or Baudelaire's neurosis or madness were more fecund for humanity than the 'health' of a certain shopkeeper of the period. For revolution, as we conceive of it, precisely refuses to accept once and for all this split between motivation and result; it would be impossible in reality and incoherent in its meaning if it were carried by unconscious intentions unrelated to its articulated content. It would, then, simply reproduce once again previous history, and it would continue to be dominated by obscure motivations which, in the long run, would impose their own finality and their own logic.

The true dimension of this problem is the collective dimension. It is on the scale of the masses, who alone can realize a new society, that we must examine the birth of new motivations and new attitudes capable of carrying the revolutionary project to completion. This examination will be easier, however, if we first attempt to clarify what the desire and the motivations of a revolutionary might be.

What we can say about this is, by definition, highly subjective. It is similarly, also by definition, open to all the interpretations imaginable. If it can help someone see more clearly into another human being (even if it is only into the illusions and the errors of this human being) and through this into one's own self, it will not have been useless to attempt to say it.

I desire and I feel the need to live in a society *other* than the one surrounding me. Like most people, I can live in this one and adapt to it – at any rate, I do live in it. However critically I may try to look at myself, neither my capacity for adaptation, nor my assimilation of reality seems to me to be inferior to the sociological average. I am not asking for immortality, ubiquity or omniscience. I am not asking society to 'give me happiness'; I know that this is not a ration that can be handed out by City Hall or my neighbourhood Workers' Council and that, if this thing exists, I have to make it for myself, tailored to my own needs, as this has happened to me already and as this will probably happen to me again. In life, however, as it comes to me and to others, I run up against a lot of unacceptable things; I say that they are not inevitable and that they stem from the organization of society. I desire, and I ask, first of all that my work be meaningful, that I may approve what it is used for and the way in which it is done, that it allow me genuinely to expend myself, to make use of my faculties and at the same time ro enrich and develop myself. And I say that this is possible, with a different organization of society, possible for me and for everyone. I say that it would already be a basic change in this direction if I were allowed to decide, together with everyone else, what I had to do and, with my fellow workers, how to do it.

I should like, together with everyone else, to know what is going on in society, to control the extent and the quality of the information I receive. I ask to be able to participate directly in all the social decisions that may affect my existence, or the general course of the world in which I live. I do not accept the fact that my lot is decided, day after day, by people whose projects are hostile to me or simply unknown to me, and for whom we, that is I and everyone else, are only numbers in a general plan or pawns on a chess board, and that, ultimately, my life and my death are in the hands of people whom I know to be, necessarily, blind.

I know perfectly well that realizing another social organization, and the life it would imply, would by no means be simple, that difficult problems would arise at every step. But I prefer contending with real problems rather than with the consequences of de Gaulle's delirium, Johnson's schemes or Khrushchev's intrigues. Even if I and the others should fail along this path, I prefer failure in a meaningful attempt to a state that falls short of either failure or non-failure, and which is merely *ridiculous*.

I wish to be able to meet the other person as a being like myself and yet absolutely different, not like a number or a frog perched on another level (higher or lower, it matters little) of the hierarchy of revenues and powers. I wish to see the other, and for the other to see me, as another human being. I want our relationships to be something other than a field for the expression of aggressivity, our competition to remain within the limits of play, our conflicts – to the extent that they cannot be resolved or overcome – to concern real problems and real stakes, carrying with them the least amount of unconsciousness possible, and that they be as lightly loaded as possible with the imaginary. I want the other to be free, for my freedom *begins* where the other's freedom begins, and, all alone, I can at best be merely 'virtuous in misfortune'. I do not count on people changing into angels, nor on their souls becoming as pure as mountain lakes – which, moreover, I have always found deeply boring. But I know how much present culture aggravates and exasperates their difficulty to be and to be with others, and I see that it multiplies to infinity the obstacles placed in the way of their freedom.

I know, of course, that this desire cannot be realized today; nor even were the revolution to take place tomorrow, could it be fully realized in my lifetime. I know that one day people will live, for whom the problems that cause us the most anguish today will no longer even exist. This is my fate, which I have to assume and which I do assume.

But this cannot reduce me to despair or to catatonic ruminations. Possessing this desire, which indeed is mine, I can only work to realize it. And already in the choice of my main interest in life, in the work I devote to it, which for me is meaningful (even when I encounter, and accept, partial failure, delays, detours and tasks that have no sense in themselves), in the participation in a group of revolutionaries which is attempting to go beyond the reified and alienated relations of current society – I am in a position partially to realize this desire. If I had been born in a communist society, would happiness have been easier to attain – I really do not know, and at any rate can do nothing about it. I am not, under this pretext, going to spend my free time watching television or reading detective novels.

Does my attitude amount to denying the reality principle? But what is the content of this principle? Is it that work is necessary – or that it is necessary that work be meaningless, exploited, that it contradict the objectives for which it is allegedly done? Is this principle valid, *in this form*, for someone of independent means? Is it valid, *in this form*, for the natives of the Trobriand islands or Samoa? Is it still valid today for fishermen in a poor Mediterranean village? Up to what point does the reality principle reveal nature, and at what point does it begin to reveal society? Why not serfdom, slave galleys, concentration camps? Where does a philosophy get the right to tell me: here, on exactly this inch of existing institutions, I am going to show you the borderline between the phenomenon and the essence, between passing historical forms and the eternal being of society? I accept the reality principle, for I accept the necessity of work (as long, in any case, as it is real, for it is becoming less obvious every day) and the necessity of a social organization of work. But I do not accept the appeal to a false psychoanalysis and to a false metaphysics, which introduces the precise discussion of historical possibilities, gratuitous assertions about alleged impossibilities, about which this philosophy *knows nothing at all*.

Might my desire be infantile? But the infantile situation is that life is given to you and that the Law is given to you. In the infantile situation, life is given to you for nothing; and the Law is given to you without anything else, without anything more, without any possible discussion. What I want is just the opposite: I want to make my life and to give life if possible, and in any event to give something for my life. I want the Law not to be simply given, but for me to give it to myself at the same time. The person who remains constantly in the infantile situation is the conformist and the apolitical person, for they accept the Law without any discussion and do not want to participate in shaping it. Someone who lives in society without any will concerning the Law, without any political will, has merely replaced the private father with the anonymous social father. The infantile situation is first receiving without giving, and then doing or being in order to receive. What I want is a just exchange to begin with, passing beyond exchange afterwards. The infantile situation is the relation of duality, the phantasy of fusion – and in this sense it is the present society that constantly infantilizes everyone, by the imaginary fusion with unreal entities: leaders, nations, cosmonauts or idols. What I want is for society to cease to be a family, moreover a false one and even a grotesque one; I want it to acquire its peculiar dimension as a society, a network of relationships among autonomous adults.

Is my desire a desire for power? But what I want is the abolition of power in the current sense; I want the power of each and every one. For current power, other people are things, and all that I want goes against this. The person for whom others are things is himself a thing, and I do not want to be a thing either for myself or for others. I do not want others to be things, I would have no use for this. If I may exist for others, be recognized by them, I do not want this to be in terms of the possession of something external to me – power; nor to exist for them only in an imaginary realm. The recognition of others has value to me only inasmuch as I recognize them as well. Am I in danger of forgetting all this if ever events were to carry me close to 'power'? This seems more than improbable to me. If this were to happen, a battle would perhaps be lost but not the war, and am I to rule my entire life on the assumption that I might one day slip back into childhood?

Should I follow this chimera of wanting to eliminate the tragic side of human existence? It seems to me that instead I want to eliminate the melodramatic aspect, the false tragedy – the one in which catastrophe arrives without necessity, in which everything could have been otherwise if only the characters had known this or had done that. That people should die of hunger in India, while in America or in Europe governments penalize farmers who 'over'-produce – this is a macabre farce, this is Grand Guignol in which the cadavres and the suffering are real, but this is not tragedy, there is nothing ineluctable here. And if one day humanity perishes by hydrogen bombs, I refuse to call this a tragedy. I would call it stupidity. I would like an end to Guignol and to the transformation of people into puppets by other puppets who 'govern' them. When a neurotic repeats for the 14th time the same behaviour-pattern of failure, reproducing for himself and for those nearby the same type of misfortune, helping this person get out of such a situation is to rid his or her life of grotesque farce, not tragedy; it is to allow the person finally to see the real problems of life and the tragic element they may contain – which the neurosis served in part to express but especially to *mask*.

When one of Buddha's disciples came to tell him, after a long voyage in the West, that miraculous things, instruments, medications, methods of thinking and institutions had transformed people's lives since the time the Master had retreated into the mountains, Buddha stopped him after a few words. Have they wiped out sadness, sickness, old age and death? he asked. No, replied the disciple. Then, they might as well have kept still, thought the Master. And he plunged back into his contemplation, without bothering to show his disciple that he was no longer listening to him.

The Logic of the Revolutionary Project

The socialist revolution aims at transforming society through the autonomous action of people and at establishing a society organized to promote the autonomy of all its members. This is a *project*. It is not a theorem, the conclusion of a demonstration indicating what must unavoidably occur. The very idea of such a demonstration is absurd. But neither is it a utopia, an act of faith or an arbitrary wager.

The revolutionary project finds its roots and its supports in actual historical reality, in the *crisis* of established society and in the *challenge* put to it by the great majority of the people who live in it. This is not the crisis that Marxism believed it saw, the 'contradiction between the development of the productive forces and the continuance of the relations of capitalist production'. It consists in the fact that the social organization can attain the ends it sets for itself only by setting out means that contradict these ends, by creating demands it cannot satisfy, by positing criteria it is incapable of applying, norms it is obliged to transgress. It requires that people, as producers or as citizens, remain passive and restrict themselves to performing the task it has imposed on them. When it notices that this passivity is like a cancer within it, it encourages initiative and participation, only to discover that it cannot bear them, for they question the very essence of the existing order. Society must live with a double reality, distinguishing between an official version and a reality which are irreducibly opposed to one another. It does not suffer simply from an opposition between classes which would remain separate, outside one another; it is conflictual in itself, the yes and the no existing together as active intentions within the very core of its being, in the values it proclaims and denies, its manner of organizing and of disorganizing, in the extreme socialization and the extreme atomization of the society it creates. In the same way, the *protest* of which we were speaking is not merely the struggle of working people against exploitation, nor their political mobilization against the regime. Visible in the great open conflicts that mark the history of capitalism, it is constantly present, in an implicit and latent manner, in their work, in their daily life, in their mode of existence.

People sometimes say to us: you are inventing a crisis in society, you are labeling 'crisis' something that has always been there. You want, at all costs, to find a radical novelty in the nature or the intensity of current social conflicts, for this alone would permit you to claim that a radically new State is in the making. What you call the protest directed at the essence of social relations is something that has always existed as a result of the different and opposing interests of groups and classes. All societies, at any rate all historical societies, have been divided and this has only led them to produce other societies, divided as well.

We are in fact saying that a precise analysis shows that the deep-lying elements of the crisis of contemporary society are specific and *qualitatively unique*. There are, doubtless, naive pseudo-Marxists who, even today, are only able to appeal to class struggle and fill their mouths with it, forgetting that class struggle has been going on for thousands of years and that it can by no means supply, in itself, a basis for the socialist project. But there are also pseudo-objective – and just as naive – sociologists who, having learned to be suspicious of ethnocentric and 'epoch-centred' projections and to reject our tendency to consider our own epoch as something absolutely distinct, cannot go further, level off historical reality, and bury under a paper mountain of methodology the central problem of historical reflection, namely the specificity of each society as a specificity of meaning and of the dynamics proper to this meaning, the undeniable fact – even if it remains mys-terious – without which there would be no history, that certain societies introduce dimensions that did not exist before, the qualitatively new, in another than merely descriptive sense. It is of no interest to discuss these pseudo-philosophical arguments. Anyone who cannot see that between the Greek world and the Egyptian–Assyrian–Babylonian world, or even between the Medieval world and the world of the Renaissance, there is – despite the obvious continuities and cause and effect relations – *another* difference, another type, degree and sense of difference than between two trees or even two human individuals living in the same period – this person is missing an essential sense for the comprehension of things historical, and would be better off working in entomology or in botany.

Analysis shows a difference such as this between contemporary society and those preceding it, taken *globally*. This is precisely the result, first of all, of a rigorous sociological description which respects its object and makes it truly speak out, instead of squashing it under a cheap metaphysics asserting that everything finally amounts to the same thing. Consider the problem of labour: it is one thing when the slave or the serf rises up in opposition to his exploitation, that is to say refuses to make an additional effort or demands a greater share of the product, combats the orders of the master or the lord on the level, so to speak, of 'quantity'. It is something else again, something radically different, when the worker is forced to combat the orders of man-agement *in order to* be able to apply them, when not simply the quantity of labour or of the product but its content as well and the manner of doing it become the object of an incessant struggle – in short, when the labour process no longer gives rise to a conflict external to labour itself but has to be based on an *internal* contradiction, the simultaneous requirement of being excluded from and of participating in the organ-ization and the management of labour.

Consider, likewise, the problem of the family and of the structure of the personality. To be sure, the family organization has always contained a repressive principle, individuals have always been obliged to interiorize a conflict between their drives and the demands of a given social organization, every culture, whether archaic or historical, has always presented in its 'basic personality' a particular 'neurotic' tint. But what is radically different is that there is no longer any principle discernable at the base of the present organization or rather disorganization of the family, nor any integrated structure in the personality of contemporary human beings. It is, of course, stupid to think that the Florentines, the Romans, the Spartans, the Mundugumors or the Kwakiutl were 'healthy' and that our contemporaries are 'neurotic'. But it is hardly more intelligent to forget that the personality-type of the Spartan or of the Mundugumor, regardless of their 'neurotic' components, was *functionally adequate* to their society, that the individual felt adapted to it and could make it function in accordance with his own requirements and shape a new generation which would do likewise; whereas the 'neurosis' or 'neuroses' of people today appear, from a sociological point of view, as essentially phenomena of maladjustment, which not only are experienced subjectively as misfortune but moreover hamper the social functioning of individuals, preventing them from responding adequately to the demands of life as it is, and reproduced as an amplified maladjustment in the second generation. *The Spartan's 'neurosis' was what allowed him to be integrated into his society – the 'neurosis' of modern man is what prevents him from being integrated.* It is superficial to recall, for example, that homosexuality has existed in all human societies – and to forget that in every instance it has been socially defined: a marginal deviance that is tolerated, or despised, or sanctioned; a custom that is accorded a value, institutionalized, possessing a positive social function; a widespread vice; and that today it is – but just what is it, in fact? Or to say that different societies have been able to adjust to an immense variety of different roles for women – only to forget and to make others forget that current society is the first in which there is *no* definite role for women – and as a direct and immediate result, none for men either.

Consider, finally, the question of society's values. Whether explicit or implicit, there has been a system of values in every society – or even two systems, which were in conflict but which were present. No material coercion has ever been lastingly – that is to say, socially – effective, without this 'complement of justification'; no psychic repression has ever played a *social* role without this extension in broad daylight, an *exclusively* unconscious super-ego is not conceivable.[26] The existence of society has always presupposed that of rules of conduct, and the sanctions for these rules were neither simply unconscious nor simply material and legal, but always also included informal social sanctions, and meta-social 'sanctions' (metaphysical, religious sanctions and so forth, in short *imaginary* sanctions, but this in no way diminishes their importance). In the extremely rare cases in which these rules were openly transgressed, this was the act of a small minority (by part of the aristocracy in eighteenth-century France, for instance). Currently, rules and their sanctions are almost exclusively the province of the legal code, and unconscious formations no longer correspond to the rules, in the sociological sense, either because, as certain psychoanalysts have said, the super-ego is being considerably weakened,[27] or because the specifically social component (and hence function) of the super-ego is crumbling away in the pulverizing and mixing of situations and 'personality types' which intersect in modern society. Beyond legal sanctions, these rules, most of the time, have no extension of their justification in people's consciousness. But what is most important is not the weakening of sanctions surrounding rules and interdictions: it is the almost complete disappearance of positive rules and values. The life of a society cannot be based solely on a network of prohibitions, of negative orders. Individuals have always received from the society in which they lived positive injunctions, orientations, the representation of value-charged ends – at once formulated universally and 'embodied' in what was, for each epoch, its 'collective Ideal of the Self'. With respect to this, there exists in contemporary society no more than residues of prior phases which are becoming more motheaten every day, reduced to abstractions bearing no relation to life ('morality' or a 'humanitarian' attitude), or else we find flattened pseudo-values, whose realization is at the same time their self-denunciation (consumption as an end in itself, or fashion and the 'new').

People say to us: even admitting that there is a crisis of contemporary society, you cannot legitimately posit the project of a new society, for where could you draw the content for it, if not from your own head, your ideas, your desires – in short, from your subjective arbitrariness?

We answer: yes, if by that you mean that we cannot 'demonstrate' the necessity of the excellence of socialism, as one can 'demonstrate' Pythagoras' theorem. Or that we cannot show you socialism in the process of growing in an established society, as one can show a foal growing in the womb of the mare, you are doubtless correct, but at the same time you appear to be unaware that one is never dealing with this kind of self-evidence in any real activity, whether individual or collective, and that you yourself shove aside these requirements whenever you undertake anything. But if you mean that the revolutionary project merely conveys the subjective arbitrariness of a few individuals, this is because you have first chosen to forget, in defiance of the principles you defend elsewhere, the history of the past 50 years, and the fact that the problem of a different organization of society has constantly been posed, not by reformers or by ideologues, but by massive collective movements, which have changed the face of the world, even if they have failed with regard to their original intentions. Next, this is because you do not see that the crisis of which we are speaking is not simply a 'crisis in itself', this conflictual society is not a beam rotting with the ages, a machine that rusts or wears out. The crisis is due to the fact that it is at one and the same time a protest, it is the result of protest and constantly feeds this protest. Labour conflict, the destructuring of the personality, the collapse of standards and values are not and cannot be lived by people as mere facts or as external calamities, they also give rise to responses and to intentions, and the latter, while they complete the shaping of the crisis as a genuine crisis, go also beyond the crisis itself. To be sure, it is erroneous and mythologizing to want to find, in the 'negative' element of capitalism, a 'positive' element which would be symmetrically constituted in it, millimetre for millimetre – whether this be conceived in the objectivist style of some of Marx's formulations (when, for example, the 'negative' element of alienation is seen as depositing itself and becoming sedimented in the material infrastructure of technology and accumulated capital which contain – with their unavoidable human corollary, the proletariat – the necessary and sufficient conditions for socialism), in the subjectivist style of some Marxists (who see socialist society already constituted, so to speak, in the worker community of the factory and in the new type of human relations displayed there). The development of the productive forces as well as the evolution of human attitudes in capitalist society display meanings which are not simple, not simply contradictory in the sense of a naive dialectic which would proceed by the juxtaposition of contraries – meanings which, for lack of a better term, can be called ambiguous. However, the ambiguous, in the sense we are taking it here, is not the undetermined or the indefinite, it is not just anything whatsoever. The ambiguous is ambiguous only through the conjoining of several meanings capable of being specified, none of which, for the moment, predominates. In the crisis and in the protest of the forms of social life by our contemporaries, we find facts that are heavy with meaning – the wear of authority, the gradual draining of economic motivation, the lessening of the hold of the instituted imaginary, the non-acceptance of rules that are simply inherited or passed down – and these senses can only be organized around one or the other of two central meanings: either the progressive decomposition of the content of historical life, the gradual emergence of a new society which, ultimately, would be one where people were external to one another and to themselves, an overpopulated desert, a solitary crowd, not even an airconditioned nightmare but a general anaesthesia. Or, if we look instead to what appears in people's *work* as a tendency towards cooperation, the collective self-management of activities and responsibility, we can interpret the ensemble of these phenomena as the emergence in society of the *possibility* and the *demand* for autonomy.

People may still say to us: yours is only one reading, and you agree that it is not the only one possible. In the name of what do you read the facts this way, in the name of what do you claim that the future you envisage is possible and coherent, in the name of what, in particular, are you making this choice?

Our reading is not arbitrary, in a certain way it is only the interpretation of the discourse that contemporary society holds with respect to itself, the only perspective in which the crisis of business and of politics, the appearance of psychoanalysis as well as of psychosociology all become comprehensible. And we have tried to show that as far as we can see, the idea of a socialist society presents no impossibility, or incoherence. But our reading is also, indeed, the result of a choice: an interpretation of this nature and on this scale is possible, ultimately, only in relation to a project. We are affirming something which is not 'naturally' or geometrically imposed on us, we prefer one future to another – and even to any other.

Is this choice arbitrary? If you like, in the sense that every choice is. But of all historical choices, it seems to us the least arbitrary of any that have ever existed.

Why should we prefer a socialist future to any other? We are deciphering, or believe we can decipher, a meaning in actual history – the possibility and the demand for autonomy. But this meaning takes on its full weight only in relation to other considerations. This simple 'factual' datum is not enough, could not as such impose itself on our thinking. We do not approve of what contemporary history offers us, simply because it 'is' or because it 'tends to be'. Should we arrive at the conclusion that the most probable, even certain, tendency of contemporary history is the universal establishment of concentration camps, we would not deduce from this that we have to support them.[28] If we assert the tendency of contemporary society towards autonomy, if we want to work for its realization, this is because we are asserting autonomy as a mode of being of humans, that we are ascribing value to it, that we recognize it as our essential aspiration and as an aspiration that surpasses the peculiarities of our personal constitution, the only one that can be defended publicly with lucidity and coherence.

This, therefore, involves a twofold relation. The reasons why we are aiming at autonomy are and are not of this epoch. They are not because we would assert the value of autonomy regardless of the circumstances, and more profoundly, because we think that the aim of autonomy ineluctably tends to emerge wherever we find humans and history, that, like consciousness, the aim of autonomy is human destiny and that, present from the start, it constitutes history rather than being constituted by it.

These reasons, however, are also bound to our epoch, in so many ways that it would be pointless to state them. Not only because the links by which we and others arrive at this aim and at the ways of concretizing it are related to our epoch. But also because the content we may give to it, the way in which we think it can be embodied can be possible only today and presupposes all previous history, in more ways than we may suspect. In particular, the explicit social dimension that we are able to give to this aim today, the possibility of another form of society, the passage from an ethic to a politics of autonomy (which, without *suppressing* ethics, preserves it by superseding it) are clearly tied to the concrete phase of history that we are living.

Finally, one can ask: and why, then, do you think that this possibility is appearing just now? We say: if your 'why' is a concrete one, we have already replied to your question. The why is to be found in all the particular historical links which have led humanity where it is now, which have made capitalist society and its current phase this singularly unique epoch which we were trying to define above. But if your why is a metaphysical why, if it amounts to asking: what is the precise place of the current phase in a total dialectic of universal history, why should the possibility of socialism emerge at this precise moment in the plan of Creation, what is the relation that has been worked out between this originary constituent of history – autonomy – and the successive figures it assumes in time? – if this is what is meant, then we refuse to answer. Even if the question had a sense, it would be a purely speculative one, and we consider it absurd to suspend all doing and not-doing waiting for someone rigorously to work out this total dialectic, or to discover at the back of an old cupboard the plan of Creation. We are not going to fall back into a stupor simply because we do not possess absolute knowledge. However, we deny the legitimacy of the question, we deny that there is any sense in thinking in terms of total dialectic, of a plan of Creation, of an exhaustive clarification of the relation between what is founded *with* time and what is founded *in* time. History has given birth to a project, and this project we have taken as our own because in it we recognize our deepest aspirations, and we think that it is possible to realize it. We find ourselves here, at this precise place in time and space, among these people, with this horizon. Knowing that this horizon is not the only possible one does not prevent it from being ours and giving a shape to the landscape of our existence. All the rest, total history, from everywhere and from nowhere, is the work of an horizonless thought, which is only another name for non-thought.

iii AUTONOMY AND ALIENATION

The Sense of Autonomy – The Individual

If autonomy is at the centre of the objectives and at the crossroads of the paths of the revolutionary project, this term must be specified and clarified. We shall attempt to clarify it first on the level where it is easiest to grasp: in relation to the individual, and shall then move to the level which is of particular interest to us here, the collective level.

We shall try to understand what an autonomous individual is – and what an autonomous or unalienated society is.

Freud proposed as a maxim of psychoanalysis: 'Where Id was, Ego shall come to be' (*Wo Es war, soll Ich werden*).[29] *Ego* is here, as an initial approximation, consciousness in general. The *Id*, which properly speaking is the origin and the place of drives ('instincts'), must be taken in this context as representing the unconscious in the broadest sense. *Ego*, consciousness and will, must take the place of the dark forces which, 'in me', dominate, act for me – 'act me' as G. Groddeck said.[30] These forces are not simply – are not so much, but we shall return to this later – pure instincts, libido or death instinct. What is at issue is instead their interminable, phantasmatic and fantastic alchemy, and along with this, and in particular, the unconscious forces of formation and repression, the super-ego and the unconscious Self. It is necessary, straightaway, to interpret this sentence. Ego must take the place of Id – this can mean neither the suppression of drives, nor the elimination or the absorption of the unconscious. It is a matter of taking their place as an *agency of decision*. Autonomy would then be consciousness's rule over the unconscious. Without prejudice to the new depth dimension revealed by Freud,[31] this is the programme proposed by philosophical reflection on the individual for the past 25 centuries, at once the assumption and the outcome of ethics as it has been viewed by Plato and the Stoïcs, Spinoza or Kant. (It is of immense importance in itself, but not for this discussion, that Freud proposes an effective way to attain what, for philosophers, had remained an 'ideal' accessible through abstract knowledge).[32] If to autonomy, that is to self-legislation or self-regulation, one opposes heteronomy, that is legislation or regulation by another, then autonomy is my law opposed to the regulation by the unconscious, which is another law, the law of another, other than myself.

In what sense can we say that the regulation by the unconscious is the law of another? Of what other? Of a literal other, not of another, unknown 'Self' but of another *in* me. As Jacques Lacan says, 'The unconscious is the discourse of the Other'; it is to a great extent the depository of intentions, desires, investments, demands, expectations – significations to which the individual has been exposed from the moment of conception and even before, as these stem from those who engendered and raised him or her.[33] Autonomy then appears as: my discourse must take the place of the discourse of the Other, of a foreign discourse that is in me, ruling over me: speaking through myself. This clarification immediately indicates the *social* dimension of the problem (little matter that the Other in question at the start is the 'narrow' parental other; through a series of obvious connections, the parental couple finally refers to society as a whole and to its history).

What, however, is this discourse of the Other – no longer as to its origin but as to its quality? And up to what point can it be eliminated?

The essential characteristic of the discourse of the Other, from the point of view that interests us here, is its relation to the *imaginary*. It has to do with the fact that, ruled by this discourse, the subject takes himself or herself to be something he or she is not (or is not necessarily) and that for him or her, others and the entire world undergo a corresponding misrepresentation. The subject does not express himself or herself but is expressed by someone, and therefore exists as a part of another's world (certainly misrepresented in its turn). The subject is ruled by an imaginary, lived as even more real than the real, yet not known as such, precisely *because* it is not known as such.[34] What is essential to heteronomy – or to alienation in the general sense of the term – on the level of the individual, is the domination of an autonomized imaginary which has assumed the function of defining for the subject both reality and desire. The 'repression of drives' as such, the conflict between the 'pleasure principle' and the 'reality principle' do not constitute individual alienation, which is finally the almost unlimited reign of a principle of *de*-reality. The important conflict in this respect is not that between drives and reality (if this conflict sufficed as a pathogenic cause, there would never have been a single, even approximative resolution of the Oedipus complex from the beginning of time, and never would a man and a woman have walked upon the earth). The important conflict is that between drives and reality, on the one hand, and the imaginary development within the subject, on the other.[35]

The *Id* in Freud's adage therefore is to be understood as signifying essentially this function of the unconscious which invests imaginary reality, autonomizes it, and confers on it the power of decision – the content of this imaginary being related to the discourse of the Other ('repetition' but also amplified transformation of this discourse).

It is where this function of the unconscious was, and along with it the discourse of the Other which fuels it, that Ego is to come to be. This means that my discourse is to take the place of the discourse of the Other. But what is my discourse? What is a discourse that is mine?

A discourse that is mine is a discourse that has negated the discourse of the Other, that has negated it not necessarily in its content, but inasmuch as it is the discourse of the Other. In other words, a discourse that, by making clear both the origin and the sense of this discourse, has negated it or affirmed it in awareness of the state of affairs, by referring its sense to that which is constituted as the subject's own truth – as my own truth.

If in this interpretation Freud's adage were taken in an absolute sense, it would propose an inaccessible objective. Never will my discourse be wholly mine in the sense defined above. Obviously, I could never begin everything all over again, even if only to ratify what already happened. This is also because – and we shall return to this later – the notion of the subject's own truth is itself much more a problem than a solution.

This is just as true of the relation to the imaginary function of the unconscious. How can we conceive of a subject that would have entirely 'absorbed' the imaginative function, how could we dry up this spring in the depths of ourselves from which flow both alienating phantasies and free creation truer than truth, unreal deliria and surreal poems, this eternally new beginning and ground of all things, without which nothing would have a ground, how can we eliminate what is at the base of, or in any case what is inextricably bound up with what makes us human beings – our symbolic function, which presupposes our capacity to see and to think in a thing something which it is not?

Inasmuch as we do not want to make Freud's maxim a mere regulative idea defined in reference to an impossible state – and thus a new mystification – another sense had to be given to it. It must be understood as referring not to an attained state but to an active situation; not to an ideal person who has become a pure Ego once and for all, who would proffer a discourse all its own, who would never produce phantasies, but to a real person who would be unceasingly involved in the movement of taking up again what had been acquired, the discourse of the Other, who is capable of uncovering phantasies as phantasies and who, finally, never allows them to rule – unless he or she is so willing. This is not a simple 'tending towards', it is actually a situation, definable in terms of characteristics which mark a radical separation between it and the state of heteronomy. These characteristics do not consist in an 'awareness' achieved once and for all, but in *another relation* between the conscious and the unconscious, between lucidity and the function of the imaginary, in *another attitude* of the subject with respect to himself or herself, in a profound modification of the activity–passivity mix, of the sign under which this takes place, of the respective place of the two elements that compose it. How little it is a question in all this of a power grab by consciousness in the strict sense is shown in the fact that Freud's proposition can be completed by its inverse: 'Where Ego is, Id must spring forth' (*Wo Ich bin, soll Es auftauchen*). Desire, drives – whether it be Eros or Thanatos – this is me, too, and these have to be brought not only to consciousness but to expression and to existence.[36] An autonomous subject is one that knows itself to be justified in concluding: this is indeed true, and: this is indeed my desire.

Autonomy is therefore not a clarification without remainder nor is it the total elimination of the discourse of the Other unrecognized as such. It is the establishment of another relation between the discourse of the Other and the subject's discourse. The total elimination of the discourse of the Other unrecognized as such is an unhistorical state. The weight of the discourse of the Other unrecognized as such can be seen even in those who have made the most radical attempts to pursue the interrogation and the critique of tacit presuppositions to the end – whether this be Plato, Descartes, Kant, Marx or Freud himself. However, there are indeed those who – like Plato and Freud – never *gave up* this pursuit, and there are those who stopped and who, as a result, at times became alienated to their own discourse which became other. There is the continuous and continually actualizable possibility of regarding, objectifying, setting at a distance, detaching and finally transforming the discourse of the Other into the discourse of the subject.

But just what is this subject? This third term of Freud's sentence, which is to come where Id was, is certainly not the point-like ego of the 'I think'. It is not the subject as pure activity, possessing no constraints, no inertia, this will o' the wisp of subjectivist philosophers, this flame unencumbered by any physical support, ties or nourishment. This activity of the subject who is 'working on itself', encounters as its object the wealth of contents (the discourse of the Other) with which it has never finished. And, without this object, it simply *is* not at all. The subject is also activity, but this activity is acting on something, otherwise it is nothing. It is therefore codetermined by what it gives itself as an object. But this aspect of mutual 'inhering in' belonging to the subject and the object – intentionality, the fact that the subject exists only to the extent that it posits an object – is only an initial, relatively superficial determination, it is what carries the subject into the world, it is what continually puts the subject in the street. There is another determination, one that does not concern the orientation of the intentional fibres of the subject, but their very material, which carries the world into the subject and introduces the street into what the subject may take to be its own den. For the active subject, which is a *subject* of . . ., which convokes before itself, posits, objectifies, looks at and sets at a distance, what is it – is it a pure gaze, the naked capacity for evoking something, setting it at a distance, a spark outside of time, non-dimensionality? No, it is a gaze *and* the support for this gaze, thought *and* the support for this thought, it is activity *and* the acting body – the material body and the metaphorical body. A gaze in which there is not already something that has itself been looked at can see nothing; a thought in which there is not something that has been thought about can think of nothing.[37] What we have been calling *support* here is not simply the biological support; it is the fact that *content, no matter which, is always already present* and that it is not a residue, a scoria, something that encumbers or an indifferent material but the *efficient condition for the subject's activity*. This support, this content belongs neither simply to the subject nor simply to the other (or to the world). It is the produced and productive union of the self and the other (or of the world). In the subject *as subject* we find the non-subject, and all the traps it falls into have been dug out by subjectivist philosophy itself for having forgotten this fundamental truth. In the subject there is, to be sure, as one of its moments 'that which can never become an object', inalienable freedom, the always present possibility of redirecting the gaze, of abstracting from any particular content, of bracketing everything, including oneself, except inasmuch as the self is this capacity that springs forth as presence and absolute proximity at the very moment it places itself at a distance from itself.

However, this moment is abstract, empty; it never has and never will produce anything other than the silent and useless self-evidence of the *cogito sum*, the immediate certainty of existing as a thinking substance, which cannot legitimately express itself through language. For once even unpronounced speech makes a first opening, the world and others infiltrate from every direction, consciousness is overwhelmed by the torrent of meanings, which come, so to speak, not from the outside but from the inside. It is only through the world that one can think the world. Once thought is the thought of something, the content re-emerges, not only in what is to be thought but in that by means of which it is thought (*darin, wodurch es gedacht wird*). Without this content, in the place of the subject one would find no more than its ghost. And in this content, there is always to be found, directly or indirectly, the other and others. The other is just as fully present in the form as in the fact of discourse, as the demand for confrontation and for truth (which obviously does not mean that truth is confused with the agreement of opinions). Finally, and it is only apparently far-removed from our discussion to recall that the support for this union of the subject and the non-subject in the subject, the point of connection between the self and the other, is the body, that 'material' structure heavy with virtual meaning. The body, which is not alienation – this would be meaningless – but participation in the world and in sense, attachment and mobility, preconstitution of a universe of significations before any reflexive thought.

It is because it 'forgets' this concrete structure of the subject that traditional philosophy, the narcisissism of consciousness fascinated by its own naked forms, reduces to the level of the conditions of servitude both the other and corporeality. And it is because it wants to base itself on the pure freedom of a fictive subject that it condemns itself to rediscover the alienation of the actual subject as an insoluble problem. In the same way, wanting to base itself on exhaustive rationality, it must constantly run up against the impossible reality of an irreducibly irrational element. This is how it finally ends up being an irrational and alienated undertaking; all the more irrational as it seeks, digs out, and purifies unendingly the conditions for its rationality; all the more alienated as it unceasingly affirms its naked freedom, whereas this freedom is at once incontestable and useless.

The subject in question is, therefore, not the abstract moment of philosophical subjectivity; it is the actual subject traversed through and through by the world and by others. The Ego of autonomy is not the absolute Self, the monad cleaning and polishing its external–internal surface in order to eliminate the impurities resulting from contact with others. It is the active and lucid agency that constantly reorganizes its contents, through the help of these same contents, that produces by means of a material and in relation to needs and ideas, all of which are themselves mixtures of what it has already found there before it and what it has produced itself.

In this connection too, it cannot be a matter of entirely eliminating the discourse of the other – not only because this is an unending task, but because the other is in each case present in the activity that 'eliminates' him.[38] And this is why there can never exist any truth that would be the 'subject's own' in any absolute sense. The subject's own truth is always participation in a truth that surpasses him, a truth rooted in him and that finally roots him in society and in history, even as the subject realizes his autonomy.

The Social Dimension of Autonomy

We have spoken at length about the meaning of autonomy for the individual. This was because, first of all, it was necessary to distinguish clearly and forcefully between this concept and the old philosophical idea of abstract freedom, echoes of which can be found even in Marxism.

Next, this was because only this conception of autonomy and of the structure of the subject makes praxis, as we have defined it, possible and comprehensible.[39] In any other conception this 'action of one freedom on another freedom' remains a contradiction in terms, a perpetual impossibility, a mirage – or a miracle. Or else, it is confused with the conditions and the factors of heteronomy, since all that comes from the other concerns the 'contents of consciousness', 'psychology', is therefore on the order of a cause. Subjectivist idealism and psychologistic positivism ultimately meet in this view. In reality, however, it is because the autonomy of the other is not absolute fulguration and sheer spontaneity that I can aim at its development. It is because autonomy is not the pure and simple elimination of the discourse of the other but the elaboration of this discourse, in which the other is not an indifferent material but counts for the content of what is said, that an intersubjective action is actually possible and that it is not condemned to remain useless or to violate by its very existence what it posits as its principle. It is for this reason that there can be a politics of freedom and that we are not reduced to choosing between silence and manipulation, consoling ourselves with 'after all, the other will do whatever he wants with it'. It is for this reason that I am finally responsible for what I say (and for what I leave unsaid).[40]

The final reason for beginning with the autonomy of the individual is because autonomy, as we have defined it, leads directly to the political and social problem. The conception we have discussed shows both that one cannot want autonomy without wanting it for everyone and that its realization cannot be conceived of in its full scope except as a collective enterprise. If by this term we no longer mean the inalienable freedom of an abstract subject or the domination of a pure consciousness over an undifferentiated material, essentially 'the same' for all and for ever, a primary obstacle that freedom would have to overcome ('passions', 'inertia', etc.); if the problem of autonomy is that the subject meets in itself a sense that is not its own and that it must transform this sense in using it; if autonomy is the relation in which others are always present as the otherness *and* as the self-ness of the subject, then autonomy can be conceived of, even in philosophical terms, only as a social problem and as a social relation.

However, the term 'social' contains more than we have explicitated and immediately reveals a new dimension of the problem. Up to now we have directly referred to intersubjectivity, even if we have taken it in an unlimited sense – the relation of person to person, even if it is endlessly articulated. But this relation is located in a larger ensemble, which is *the social*, properly speaking.

In other words: the fact that the problem of autonomy immediately refers to, is even identified with, the problem of the relation of one subject to another – or to others; the fact that the other or others do not appear as external obstacles or as a malediction to be suffered – 'Hell is other people',[41] 'living with others is like being under an evil spell' – but instead as constituting the subject, the subject's problem and its possible solution; this fact recalls what, after all, was certain from the start for anyone who is not mystified by the ideology of a certain philosophy, namely that human existence is an existence with others and that whatever is said neglecting this presupposition is sheer nonsense (even when one strives painfully to bring 'the other' back, while 'the other' avenging himself for having been excluded at the outset from 'pure' subjectivity, refuses to allow anything of the kind). This existence with others, however, which appears in this way as an extended intersubjectivity, does not remain – and indeed is not from the start – mere intersubjectivity. It is social and historical existence and, to us, this is the essential dimension of the problem. In a way, the intersubjective is the material out of which the social is made but this material exists only as a part and a moment of the social, which it composes but which it also presupposes.

The *social-historical*[42] is neither the unending addition of intersubjective networks (although it is this *too*), nor, of course, is it their simple 'product'. The social–historical is the anonymous collective whole, the impersonal–human element that fills every given social formation but which also engulfs it, setting each society in the midst of others, inscribing them all within a continuity in which those who are no longer, those who are elsewhere and even those yet to be born are in a certain sense present. It is, on the one hand, given structures, 'materialized' institutions and works, whether these be material or not; and, on the other hand, *that which* structures, institutes, materializes. In short, it is the union *and* the tension of instituting society and of instituted society, of history made and of history in the making.

Instituted Heteronomy: Alienation as a Social Phenomenon

Beyond the individual unconscious and the intersubjective relation that is played out there, the conditions for alienation are to be found in the social world. Beyond the 'discourse of the other' lies that which gives it its unshiftable weight, limiting and rendering almost futile all individual autonomy.[43] This is manifested as a mass of conditions of privation and oppression, as a solidified global, material and institutional structure of the economy, of power and of ideology, as induction, mystification, manipulation and violence. No individual autonomy can overcome the consequences of this state of affairs, can cancel the effects on our life of the oppressive structure of the society in which we live.[44]

This is because alienation, social heteronomy, does not appear simply as the 'discourse of the other' – although the latter plays an essential role here as a determining factor and as a content of the unconscious and of consciousness of the mass of individuals. The other, however, disappears in collective anonymity, in the impersonal nature of the 'economic mechanisms of the market' or in the 'rationality of the Plan', of the law of a few presented as the law as such. And, along with this, what henceforth represents the other is no longer a discourse: it is a machine gun, a call to arms, a pay check and high-priced essential goods, a court decision and a prison. The 'other' is now 'embodied' elsewhere than in the individual unconscious – even if its presence by proxy[45] in the unconscious of all those concerned (the one holding the machine gun, the one for whom it is held, and the one at whom it is pointing) is the necessary condition for this embodiment. The opposite is also true; the fact that a few people possess the machine guns is without a doubt the condition for maintaining alienation, but on this level the question of the primacy of one condition or the other is meaningless, and what matters to us here is the properly social dimension.[46]

Alienation therefore appears as *instituted*, in any case as heavily conditioned by institutions (the word being taken here in its broadest sense, including in particular the structure of the real relations of production). And its relation to institutions appears twofold.

In the first place, institutions can be, and indeed actually are, alienating in their specific content. They are alienating to the extent that they express and sanction a class structure, more generally an antagonistic division of society and, concurrent with this, the power of one determined social category over the whole. They are alienating in a specific way as well for each of the classes or layers of a given society. In this way, the capitalist economy – production, distribution, market, etc. – is alienating inasmuch as it goes along with the division of society into proletariat and capitalists. The same thing holds in a specific manner for each of the two classes involved, for the proletariat, to be sure, but also for the capitalists. In the past, we corrected the simplistic Marxist view of capitalists as the mere toys of economic mechanisms,[47] but one must obviously be careful not to fall into the inverse error and dream of capitalists who are free in relation to 'their' institutions.

However, beyond this aspect and in a more general manner – for this is true also for societies which do not display an antagonistic division, as is the case in many archaic societies – there is an alienation of society, *irrespective of class*, with regard to its institutions. By this we do not mean the specific aspects that affect all classes 'equally' – the fact that even if the law serves the bourgeoisie, it binds it as well. We are instead thinking of the fact, of greater importance in its own right, that once an institution is established it seems to become autonomous, the fact that it possesses its own inertia and its own logic, that, in its continuance and in its effects, it outstrips its function, its 'ends', and its 'reasons for existing'. The apparent plain truths are turned upside-down: what could have been seen 'at the start' as an ensemble of institutions in the service of society becomes a society in the service of institutions.

'Communism' in its Mythical Sense

Surpassing alienation in these two forms was, as we know, one of the central ideas of Marxism. The proletarian revolution was, after a transitional period, to lead to the 'higher phase of communism' and this passage was to mark 'the end of the prehistory of humanity and the entry into its true history', 'the leap from the realm of necessity to the realm of freedom'. These ideas, however, remained vague,[48] and we shall not attempt here to present them systematically, nor to discuss them in detail. It is enough to recall that they involved, more or less explicitly, not only the abolition of classes but the elimination of the division of labour ('there will be no more painters, there will be men who paint'), a transformation of social institutions which is hard to distinguish, ultimately, from the idea of the total suppression of all institutions ('the fading away of the State', the elimination of all economic constraints) and, on the philosophical plane, the emergence of a 'total man' and of a humanity that henceforth 'would dominate its history'.

These ideas, despite their vague, remote, almost gratuitous character, not only translate a real problem, they unavoidably spring up along the path of revolutionary political reflection. In Marxism, it is indisputable that they conclude its philosophy of history, which without them would be indefinable. What we might regret is not that Marx and Engels spoke of them but that they did not say enough about them; not to give 'recipes for the socialist kitchens of the future', not to devote themselves to utopian definitions and descriptions of future society, but to attempt to circumscribe the meaning of future society in relation to present problems, and in particular in relation to the problem of alienation. Praxis cannot do away with the need to clarify the future it wants to bring about. No more than psychoanalysis can get rid of the problem of the *end* of the analysis, can revolutionary politics sidestep the question of its outcome and of the meaning of this outcome.

The exegesis and the polemics concerning a problem that up to now has remained vague are of slight importance to us. There are numerous elements of undeniable truth in Marx's intuitions concerning the surpassing of alienation: first of all, to be sure, the necessity of abolishing classes but also the idea of the transformation of institutions to such an extent that a vast difference would indeed separate them from what institutions have represented up to now in history. And all this both presupposes and leads to a radical change in the mode of existence of human beings – individually and collectively, the limits of which are difficult to imagine. These elements, however, have undergone – at times in Marx and Engels themselves and, at any rate, in Marxists – a shift towards an ill-defined mythology, that is finally mystifying and that feeds an equally mythological polemics or anti-mythology in the adversaries of revolution. A demarcation of these two mythologies, which moreover share a common base, is necessary in itself and will also allow us to make some progress in the positive comprehension of the problem.

If by communism ('higher phase') is meant a society in which all resistance, all depth, all opaqueness would be absent; a society that would be purely transparent to itself; in which everyone's desires would spontaneously harmonize with everybody else's, or, in order to harmonize would require merely an airborne dialogue which would never be weighted down by the gum of symbolism; a society that would discover, formulate and realize its collective will without having to pass through institutions, or in which institutions would never pose a problem – if this is what is meant, then we must clearly state that this is an incoherent reverie, an unreal and unrealizable state whose representation should be eliminated. This is a mythical formation, equivalent and analogous to that of absolute knowledge or of an individual whose 'consciousness' has absorbed his entire being.

No society will ever be totally transparent, first because the individuals that make it up will never be transparent to themselves, since there can be no question of eliminating the *unconscious*. Then, because the social element implies not only individual consciousnesses, nor even simply their mutual intersubjective inherencies, the relationships between persons, both conscious and unconscious, which could never be given in its entirety as a content to all, unless we were to introduce the double myth of an absolute knowledge possessed equally by all: the social implies something that can never be given as such. The social–historical dimension, as a dimension of the collective and the anonymous, initiates for each and every one of us a simultaneous relation of interiority and of exteriority, of participation and of exclusion, which can in no way be abolished or even 'controlled', in any definite sense of this term. The social is what is everyone and what is no one, what is never absent and almost never present as such, a non-being that is more real than any being, that in which we are wholly immersed yet which we can never apprehend 'in person'. The social is an indefinite dimension, even if it is walled in at every instant – a definite structure and at the same time one that changes, an objectifiable articulation of individual categories and that which, beyond all articulations, sustains their unity. It is what is given as the structure – indissociable form and content – of human ensembles, yet which goes beyond any given structure, an ungraspable productive element, an unformed forming element, something that is always more and always other. It is something that can be presented only in and through the *institution* but which is always infinitely more than the institution, since it is, paradoxically, both what fills in the institution, what is formed by it, what continually overdetermines its functioning, and what in the final analysis founds it: creates it, maintains it in existence, alters it, destroys it. There is the social as instituted, but this always presupposes the social as instituting. 'In ordinary times' the social is manifested in the institution, but this manifestation is at once true and, in a sense, fallacious – as in those moments in which the social as instituting bursts onto the stage and pulls up its sleeves to get to work, the moments of revolution. But this work aims at an immediate result, which is to provide itself once again with an institution in order to exist in a visible manner – and once this institution is set in place the social as instituting slips away, puts itself at a distance, is already somewhere else.[49]

Our relation to the social – and to the historical which is its unfolding in time – cannot be called a relation of dependence, for this would be meaningless. It is rather a relation of *inherence*, which as such is neither freedom nor alienation, but the ground upon which freedom and alienation can exist, and which solely the delirium of an absolute narcissism could wish to abolish, to deplore, or to see as a 'negative condition'. If one wants at all costs to find an analogue or a metaphor for this relation it will be found in our relationship to nature. This belonging to society and to history, infinitely obvious and infinitely obscure, this consubstantiality, partial identity, participation in something that surpasses us on every side, is not an alienation – no more than our spatial character, our corporal nature as 'natural' aspects of our existence that 'submit' us to the laws of physics, chemistry or biology. These are forms of alienation only in the phantasies of an ideology which refuses what is in the name of a desire directed at a mirage – the total possession or the absolute subject, which in fact has not yet learned to live or even to see, and so can see in being no more than intolerable privation and deficiency, to which it opposes (fictive) Being.

This ideology, which cannot accept inherence, finitude, limitation and lack cultivates the scorn for this all too green reality that it is unable to reach in two ways: by constructing a 'full' fiction and by an indifference with respect to what is and to what one can do with it. This is evident on the theoretical plan in the exorbitant requirement of recovering in its entirety the 'meaning' of history, past and to come. On the practical plane we see this in the no less exorbitant idea of humankind 'dominating its history' – the master and possessor of history, as it is about to, or so it sees, become the master and possessor of nature. These ideas, to the extent that they are found in Marxism, convey its dependency on traditional ideology, just as the symmetrical protests betraying the annoyance of those who, starting from the observation that history cannot be an object of possession or transformable into an absolute subject, conclude that alienation is perennial, thus betraying their dependence on traditional ideology *and* on Marxism. However, to term 'alienation' the inherence of individuals or of any given society in the social and in the historical that surpass them in every dimension, this is meaningful only from the perspective of 'man's Misery without God'.

Revolutionary praxis, because it is revolutionary and because it must dare beyond the possible, is 'realistic' in the truest sense and begins by accepting being in its profound determinations. For it, a subject that would loosen all of its inherent ties to history – even if this be by recovering 'the integral meaning of history' – and that would take a tangential line with respect to society – even if this be by exhaustively 'controlling' its relation to society – is not an autonomous subject, it is a psychotic subject. And *mutatis mutandis*, the same thing is true about every determined society, which, even if it be communist, can emerge, exist, define itself only against the backdrop of the social–historical, which itself is beyond every particular society and history and feeds them all. Revolutionary praxis knows not only that there is no question of recovering a unique 'meaning' of past history but that there is no question of 'controlling', in the accepted sense of this term, history to come, unless one is aiming to destroy the creative nature of history – fortunately, a hopeless endeavour. To recall, as a mere image, what we said about the sense of autonomy for the individual: we can no more eliminate or absorb the unconscious than we can eliminate or absorb the unlimited and unfathomable ground upon which every given society reposes.

Nor can there be any question of a society without institutions, regardless of the development of individuals, the progress of technology or economic abundance. None of these factors will ever do away with the innumerable problems that constantly arise from the collective existence of mankind. There is no way to do away with the necessity for arrangements and procedures that will permit discussion and choice – unless one posits a biological mutation in humanity, which would realize the immediate presence of each person in all the others and of all in each one (but science fiction writers have already seen that a state of universal telepathy would only lead to an immense, generalized confusion, producing only noise and not information). Nor can there be any question of a society that would completely coincide with its institutions, that would be exactly covered, without excess or deficit, by the institutional fabric and which, behind this fabric, would have no flesh on it, a society that would be a network of infinitely flat institutions. There will always be a distance between society as instituting and what is, at every moment, instituted – and this distance is not something negative or deficient; it is one of the expressions of the creative nature of history, what prevents it from fixing itself once and for all into the 'finally found form' of social relations and of human activities, what makes a society always contain *more* than what it presents. To wish to abolish this distance, in one way or another, is not to leap from prehistory to history or from necessity to freedom, it is to wish to leap into the immediate absolute, that is to say into nothingness. Just as an individual cannot grasp or provide himself with anything at all – neither the world nor himself – outside of the symbolic dimension, no society can provide itself with anything outside of this second-order symbolism represented by institutions. And, just as I cannot call my relation to language a form of alienation – a language in which I can both say everything and yet not just anything at all, with respect to which I am at once determined and free, in relation to which a corruption is possible but not inevitable – in the same way, there is no reason to call the relation between society and the institution a form of alienation. Alienation appears *in* this relation, but it *is* not this relation – just as error or delirium are possible only *in* language but *are* not language.

3

The Institution and the Imaginary
A First Approach

i THE INSTITUTION FROM THE
FUNCTIONAL–ECONOMIC POINT OF VIEW

Alienation is neither inherent in history nor the existence of the institution as such. Alienation, however, appears as a *modality* of the relation to the institution and, through its intermediary, as a modality of the relation to history. It is this modality that we must clarify and, in order to do this, we have to understand better what institutions are.

In historical societies, alienation appears to be embodied in the class structure and in the domination by a minority, but in fact it goes beyond these features. Superseding alienation obviously presupposes eliminating the domination of any particular class but goes beyond this aspect. (Not that classes can be eliminated while alienation remains, or the inverse; instead, classes will be effectively eliminated, or prevented from re-emerging, only in conjunction with the supersession of what constitutes alienation as such.) It goes beyond this aspect because alienation has existed in societies that did not present a class structure or even important social distinctions. Also because, in an alienated society, the dominant class is itself in a situation of alienation: its institutions are not related to it in a purely external and instrumental manner, as naive Marxists sometimes would have it; it cannot mystify the rest of society with its ideology without at the same time mystifying itself. Alienation appears first of all as the alienation of a society to its institutions, as the *autonomization* of institutions in relation to society. What becomes autonomous in this way, why and how? – this is what we must try to understand.

These observations lead us to question the current way of looking at institutions, which we shall call the functional–economic point of view.[1] By this we mean the view that both the existence of the institution and its characteristics (ideally, even in the slightest details) can be explained by the *function* the institution fulfils in society given the circumstances, by its role in the *overall economy* of social life[2]. It matters little from our point of view whether this functionality tends to be 'causalist' or 'finalist', nor is it of importance to us which process of emergence and survival is assumed with regard to institutions. Whether one says that people, having understood the necessity for a particular function to be filled, consciously created an adequate institution; or whether institutions, springing up 'haphazardly' but turning out to be functional, survived and allowed the society concerned to survive; or whether society, requiring that a particular function be filled, took hold of what happened to be there and attributed that function to it; or whether God, reason, the logic of history, have organized and continue to govern the societies and institutions that correspond to them – in all these cases the emphasis is placed on one and the same thing: functionality, the unbroken chain of means and ends or of causes and effects on the general level, the strict correspondence between the features belonging to the institution and the 'real' needs of the society considered; the accent is placed, in short, on the complete and uninterrupted circulation between a 'real' and a 'rational–functional' element.

We are not disputing the functionalist view inasmuch as it draws our attention to this obvious, yet crucial fact that institutions fill vital functions without which the existence of society is inconceivable. We are challenging it, however, inasmuch as it holds that institutions can be reduced to this and that they are perfectly comprehensible on the basis of this role.

To begin with, it is enough to recall that the negative counterpart to the view challenged indicates something incomprehensible for this view itself: the great number of cases where we observe in given societies functions that 'are not filled' (although they could be, at the given level of historical development), with consequences that may be minor or catastrophic for the society in question.[3]

We are challenging the functionalist view, in particular, because of the gap it presents just where its attention should be focused: what are the 'real needs' of a society, the needs institutions are there merely to serve?[4] Is it not obvious that, once we leave the company of higher apes, human groups provide themselves with needs that are not simply biological? The functionalist view can realize its programme only if it supplies itself with a criterion for the 'reality' of the needs of society. Where will it find this criterion? We know the needs of a living being, of a biological organism, and the functions that correspond to it; but this is because the biological organism is nothing but the sum of the functions it performs, the functions that make it living. A dog eats to live, but one could just as well say that it lives to eat: for it (and for the species, dog) living is nothing but eating, breathing, reproducing and so on. But this is meaningless with respect to a human being or to a society. A society can exist only if a series of functions are constantly performed (production, child-bearing and education, administrating the collectivity, resolving disputes and so forth), but it is not reduced to this, nor are its ways of dealing with its problems dictated to it once and for all by its 'nature'. It invents and defines for itself new ways of responding to its needs as well as it comes up with new needs. We shall return to this problem at length.

What will provide the starting point for our investigation is the manner of being in which the institution is given to us – namely, the symbolic.

ii THE INSTITUTION AND THE SYMBOLIC

Everything that is presented to us in the social–historical world is inextricably tied to the symbolic. Not that it is limited to this. Real acts, whether individual or collective ones – work, consumption, war, love, child-bearing – the innumerable material products without which no society could live even an instant, are not (not always, not directly) symbols. All of these, however, would be impossible outside of a symbolic network.

We first encounter the symbolic, of course, in language. But we also encounter it, to a different degree and in a different way, in institutions. Institutions cannot be reduced to the symbolic but they can exist only in the symbolic; they are impossible outside of a second-order symbolism; for each institution constitutes a particular symbolic network. A given economic organization, a system of law, an instituted power structure, a religion – all exist socially as sanctioned symbolic systems. These systems consist in relating symbols (signifiers) to signifieds (representations, orders, commands or inducements to do or not to do something, consequences for actions – significations in the loosest sense of the term)[5] and in validating them as such, that is to say in making this relation more or less obligatory for the society or the group concerned. A property title, a bill of sale is a symbol of the socially approved 'right' of the owner to undertake an unlimited number of operations with respect to the object of his ownership. A paycheque is the symbol of the wage earner's right to demand a given number of banknotes, which, in turn, are the symbol of their possessor's right to perform a variety of acts of purchasing, each of which will be symbolic in its turn. The work itself which is the basis for the paycheque, although it is eminently real both for its subject and in its results, is, of course, constantly bound up with symbolic operations (in the mind of the person working, in the instructions he receives, etc.). And it becomes a symbol itself when, after being reduced to hours and minutes multiplied by given coefficients, it enters into the accounting office's calculations of the paycheque or the company's 'operations account', or when, in the event of disputes, it fills the empty squares in the premises and conclusions of the legal syllogism that will settle matters. The decisions of economic planners are symbolic (both ironically and not). Court decisions are symbolic and their consequences are almost entirely so, including the hangman's act which, although eminently real, is also immediately symbolic at another level.

Any functionalist view is aware of and has to acknowledge the role of symbolism in social life.

Only rarely, however, does it acknowledge the importance of this – and then it tends to limit this importance. Either symbolism is seen as merely a neutral, surface covering, as an instrument that is perfectly adequate for expressing a pre-existing content, the 'true substance' of social relations, neither adding anything nor taking anything away. Or else a 'special logic' of symbolism is acknowledged, but this logic is viewed wholly as the insertion of the symbolic within the rational order, which imposes its own consequences whether these be intended or not.[6] Ultimately, in this view form is always dependent on substance, and the substance is 'real – rational'. But in reality this is not so, and this destroys the interpretive claims of functionalism.

Consider the institution that is so important in all societies, religion. It always contains (we shall not discuss here the limiting cases) a ritual. For example, the Mosaic religion. The definition of its cultic (in the broadest sense of the term) ritual contains an endless proliferation of details; this ritual, established with much greater detail and precision than the Law properly speaking,[7] stems directly from divine commandments, and because of this fact all its details are set on the same plane. What is it that determines the specificity of these details? Why are they all set on the same plane?

To the first question we can give only a series of partial replies. The details are determined in part by a reference to reality or to a given content (in a closed temple you need candelabra; a particular wood or metal is more precious in the culture considered and so worthy of being used – but even here the symbol and its entire problem of designation through direct metaphor or opposition is apparent: no diamond is precious enough for the Pope's tiara, yet Christ himself washed the feet of his Apostles). These details have a relation to content that is not functional but symbolic (whether in reality or in the religious imagination: the menorah has seven branches). Finally, details can be determined by the logical–rational implications or consequences of the preceding considerations.

These considerations, however, do not allow us to interpret a given ritual in a satisfactory, overall way. First of all, they always leave residuals; in the fourfold, intersecting network of the functional, the symbolical and their consequences, the gaps are more numerous than the points covered. Next, they assume that the symbolic relation is self-evident, whereas it poses immense problems: to begin with, the fact that the 'choice' of a symbol is never either absolutely inevitable, or merely haphazard. A symbol never imposes itself with a natural necessity, but neither does it ever lack *all* reference to reality (only in some branches of mathematics can we hope to find entirely 'conventional' symbols – and even here, a convention that has held over a period of time ceases to be a pure convention). Finally, nothing allows us to determine the *boundaries* of the symbolic in this matter. Sometimes, from the point of view of the ritual, the matter is indifferent, sometimes it is the form, and sometimes neither one: the matter of a particular object may be decided upon, but not that of all objects; it is the same in the case of form. A certain type of Byzantine church is in the form of a cross; we think we understand why (but we have to ask ourselves then why all Christian churches are not similar). The pattern of the cross, however, which could have been reproduced in the other segments and sub-segments of the architecture and in the decoration of the church, is not reproduced in this way. It is taken up again at certain levels but at other levels we find other patterns, and there are other entirely neutral levels, elements that simply serve as supports or for filling in. The choice of points that symbolism grabs hold of to give shape to and to 'sanctify' in the second degree the matter related to the sacred seems to a large extent (but not entirely) arbitrary. The boundary can lie almost anywhere: there is the bareness of Protestant churches and the jungle-like lushness of certain Hindu temples; and suddenly, just where symbolism seems to have invaded every square inch of matter, as in some Siamese pagodas, one sees that it has all at once lost its content and has become essentially mere decoration.[8]

In short, a ritual is not a rational affair – and this allows us to reply to the second question we were asking: why are all the details placed on the same plane? If a ritual were a rational matter, we could find the distinction between the essential and the secondary, the hierarchization characteristic of every rational network. But in a ritual there is no way of distinguishing, in accordance with any criteria based on content, between what counts more and what counts less. The fact that all the elements comprising a ritual are placed on the same plane with respect to their importance is precisely the indication of the non-rational character of its content. To say that sacredness does not contain different degrees is another way of stating the same thing: everything the sacred has taken hold of is equally sacred (and this is also true for the rituals of obsessional neuroses or perversions).

Functionalists, however, whether Marxist or not, are not much taken with religion, which they always treat as if it were, from a sociological point of view, a pseudo-structure, an epiphenomenon of epiphenomena. Consider, then, a serious institution, like law, directly related to the 'substance' of society, which is, we are told, the economy and which has nothing to do with ghosts, candlesticks and devotional objects but instead with the real and concrete social relations that are expressed in property, transactions and contracts. In law, one should be able to show that symbolism is in the service of content and can be otherwise only to the extent that rationality forces it. Let us also leave aside these crazy primitive peoples we are continually hearing about, where anyway, it is so hard to distinguish genuinely legal rules from the others. Let us instead take a tried and true historical society and reflect on it.

Thus, one will presumably say, there is a certain stage in the evolution of a historical society where the institution of private property necessarily appears, for the latter corresponds to the basic mode of production. Once private property is established, a series of rules has to be set: the owner's rights have to be defined, violations sanctioned, borderline cases decided (a tree grows on the boundary between two fields; to whom does the fruit belong?). To the extent that a given society develops economically, that exchanges increase, the free transmission of property (which at the beginning is by no means self-evident and is not necessarily accepted, in particular for real estate) has to be regulated, and the transaction that does this has to be formalized to make possible a verification that will minimize eventual disputes. Thus in the institution that remains an eternal monument to rationality, to economy and to functionality, the institutional equivalent of Euclidian geometry, I mean Roman law, over a period of ten centuries extending from the *Lex Duodecim Tabularum* to the Justinian code, this veritable, though well-ordered and well-trimmed forest of rules serving property, transactions and contracts was developed. And taking this system of law in its final form, one can show for every paragraph in the *Corpus* that the rule it holds either serves the functioning of the economy or is required by other rules that follow it.

One could show this – and yet nothing will have been shown that concerns our problem. Not only because, just when Roman law reaches this point, the reasons behind this functionality begin to slip away, as economic life suffers an increasing regression from the start of the third century AD; so that the Justinian code appears, with respect to patrimonial law, as a useless and largely redundant monument in relation to the actual situation of its epoch.[9] Not only because this sytem of law, forged in the Rome of the consuls and the Caesars, will paradoxically recover its functionality in many European countries after the Renaissance, and will remain the *Gemeines Recht* of capitalist Germany until 1900 (which is explained, up to a point, by its extreme 'rationality', hence universality). But in particular, by stressing the functionality of Roman law, one will sidestep the dominant characteristic of its evolution over ten centuries, which makes it a fascinating example of the type of relations between the institution and the 'underlying social reality': this evolution has been a long attempt, precisely, to *attain* this functionality starting from a state that was far from possessing any such thing. At the start Roman law is a rough set of rigid rules, in which the form overwhelms the content to a degree that far exceeds whatever would be justified by the requirements of any set of laws as a formal system. To cite only one example – although a central one – the will and the intentions of the parties entering into an agreement, which is the functional core of any transaction, plays for a long time only a minor role with respect to the law; what predominates is the *ritual*[10] of the transaction, the fact that certain words were uttered, certain gestures made. Only gradually is it admitted that the ritual can have legal effects only inasmuch as these are intended by the actual will of the parties concerned. However, the symmetrical corollary to this proposition, namely that the will of the parties can constitute obligations independently of the form its expression may take, the principle that is the very foundation of modern law of obligations and that truly expresses its functional character: *pacta sunt servanda*, this will never be acknowledged.[11] The lesson of Roman law, considered in its real historical evolution, is not the functional character of the law but the relative *independence* of formalism or of symbolism with respect to functionality at the outset, followed by the slow and never complete conquest of symbolism by functionality.

The idea that symbolism is perfectly 'neutral' or else – which amounts to the same thing – totally 'adequate' to the functioning of real processes is unacceptable and, strictly speaking, meaningless.

Symbolism can be neither neutral nor totally adequate, first of all because it cannot draw its signs from just anywhere, nor can it take just any signs whatever. This is obvious for the individual who always encounters a previously constituted language,[12] and who, if he endows a given word or expression with a 'private' and special meaning, cannot do so with unlimited freedom but must instead make use of what is 'already there'. This is also true, however, for society, although in a different way. In every instance society constitutes its symbolic order in an entirely different manner than the individual can. But this is not a 'free' constitution. It, too, must take its material from 'what is already there'. This is, first, nature – and since nature is not chaos, since natural objects are connected to one another, certain consequences ensue. For a society that knows the existence of this animal, the lion signifies strength. In the same stroke, the mane takes on a symbolic importance which it has probably never had for the Eskimos. But this is also history. Every symbolism is built on the ruins of earlier symbolic edifices and uses their materials – even if it is only to fill the foundations of new temples, as the Athenians did after the Persian wars. By its virtually unlimited natural and historical connections, the signifier always goes beyond a strict attachment to a precise signified and can lead to completely unexpected realms. The constitution of symbolism in real social and historical life has no relation to the 'closed' and 'transparent' definitions of symbols found in a work of mathematics (which, moreover, can never be closed up within itself).

A fine example, which concerns both the symbolism of language and that of institutions, is that of the 'Soviet of People's Commissars'. In his autobiography, Trotsky relates that when the Bolsheviks took power and formed a government, they had to find a name for it. The title of 'Ministers' and 'Council of Ministers' was highly unpleasant to Lenin because it recalled the bourgeois Ministers and their role. Trotsky suggested the terms 'people's commissars' and, for the government as a whole, 'the Soviet of people's commissars'. Lenin was thrilled by this – he found the expression 'terribly revolutionary' – and this name was adopted. A new language was being created and, so it was thought, new institutions along with it. But to what extent was all this new? The name was new; and there was, potentially at least, a new social content to express: the Soviets were there, and it was in agreement with the majority of them that the Bolsheviks 'had taken power' (which, for the moment, itself was only a name). But on the intermediary level, which was to prove decisive, that of the institution in its second-order symbolic nature, the embodiment of power in a closed, irremovable college, the summit of an *administrative* apparatus distinct from those who are *administrated* – on this level, in fact the *ministers* remained, cast in the mould already created by the kings of Western Europe since the end of the Middle Ages. Thus Lenin, whom events had forced to interrupt his work on *State and Revolution*, where he showed the uselessness and even the harm done by a government and an administration cut off from the organized masses, when he found himself confronting the void created by the revolution, and despite the presence of new institutions (the Soviets), was only able to return to the institutional form previously existing in history. He wanted nothing to do with the name 'Council of Ministers', but it was indeed a council of ministers that he wanted – and that, in the end, he got. (Of course, this is also true for the other Bolshevik leaders and for most of the party members.) The revolution was creating a new language, and had new things to say; but the leaders wanted to say the same old things with new words.

These symbols, these signifiers, even when it is a matter of language, and infinitely more so when it is a matter of institutions, are not totally subservient to the 'content' that they are supposed to convey for still another reason. This is because they belong to ideal structures that are peculiar to them, because they are placed within quasi-rational relations.[13] Society is constantly running up against the fact that any symbolic system must be handled coherently; whether it is or is not, a series of consequences necessarily follows, regardless of whether they were known and intended as such.

People often pretend to think that this symbolic logic, and the rational order that corresponds to it in part, pose no problems for the theory of history. In fact, they do, and these problems are almost intractable. A functionalist may consider it self-evident that, when a society provides itself with an institution, it gives itself at the same time, as something it can grasp, all the symbolical and rational relations that this institution carries or produces – or at any rate, that there can be no contradiction, no incoherence between the functional 'ends' of the institution and the effects of its actual functioning, that whenever a rule is set down, the coherence of each of its innumerable consequences with the set of all the other previously existing rules and with the ends that are consciously or 'objectively' sought is guaranteed. It is enough clearly to state this postulate to see how absurd it is; it signifies that absolute Spirit presides over the birth or the modification of every institution that appears in history (whether one imagines it to be present in the mind of those who create the institution or hidden in the nature of things changes nothing in this matter).[14]

The ideal of the economic–functional interpretation is that instituted rules must appear either as functional or as really or logically implied by functional rules. This real or logical implication, however, is not given straight away and is not automatically homogeneous to the symbolic logic of the system. The example of Roman law is there to show us that a society (marked by a strong predilection for juridical logic, as events have shown) took ten centuries to unveil these implications and to submit to them, in an approximative fashion, the symbolism of this system. The conquest of the symbolic logic of institutions and its gradual 'rationalization' are historical processes (and relatively recent ones). In the meantime, both a society's understanding of the logic of its institutions and its misunderstanding of them are factors that weigh heavily on its evolution (not to speak of their consequences on the actions of individuals, groups, classes and so on; half, so to speak, of the seriousness of the 1929 depression was due to the 'absurd' reactions of the leading groups). The evolution of this understanding is not itself open to a 'functional' interpretation. The very existence, and the wide audience, of Jacques Rueff[15] in 1965 defies all functional and even all rational explanation.[16]

Considered now 'in itself', the rational element of institutions which is unknown and unintended as such can aid the functional aspect; or it can be adverse to it. If it is violently and directly adverse to the functional aspect, the institution will immediately collapse (Law's paper money). But it can also be adverse to it in an insinuating, gradual and cumulative manner – and the conflict then appears only after a period of time. The 'normal' crises of overproduction found in classical capitalism belong essentially to this case.[17]

However, the most striking and the most significant case is that in which the rationality of the institutional system is, so to speak, 'indifferent' with respect to its functionality, which does not keep it from having real consequences. There are, of course, positive institutional rules that do not contradict the others but do not follow from them either; rules that are posited without our being able to say why they are established in preference to others that are just as compatible with the system.[18] But, in particular, there are a wide number of logical consequences following from the rules posited that were not made explicit at the outset and yet play a real role in social life. They thus contribute to 'shaping' social life in a way that was not required by the functional nature of social relations, one that does not directly contradict it but that can draw society into one of several different directions left undetermined by functionality, or even create effects that have a rebound effect on the latter (the stock market represents, in relation to industrial capitalism, essentially this sort of case).

This aspect is related to the important phenomenon we mentioned in connection with rituals: nothing allows us to determine a priori just where the boundary of symbolism lies, the point at which the symbolical overlaps with the functional. We can establish once and for all neither the general degree of symbolization, which varies with the culture,[19] nor the factors that decide the intensity with which a particular aspect of the life of a given society will be invested with symbolism.

We have tried to indicate the reasons why the idea that institutional symbolism is a 'neutral' or 'adequate' expression of functionality, of the 'substance' of underlying social relations is unacceptable. Actually, though, this idea is meaningless. It effectively postulates a substance which would be preconstituted in relation to institutions; it holds that social life has 'something to express' which is already completely real prior to the language in which it is to be expressed. It is impossible, however, to grasp a 'content' of social life that would be primary and that would then 'provide itself with' an expression in institutions independently of the latter. This 'content' (except as a partial and abstract moment, separated only after the fact) is definable only within a structure and this structure always contains the institution. The 'real social relations' concerned here are always *instituted*, not because they wear legal garb (in certain cases, they may very well not do so), but because they have been posited as universal, symbolized and sanctioned ways of doing things. This is also true, of course, and perhaps even more so, for 'infrastructures', the relations of production. The master–slave, serf–lord, proletariat–capitalist, wage-earner–bureaucracy relation is *already* an institution and cannot arise as a *social* relation without immediately becoming an institution.

In Marxism, there is an ambiguity about this due to the fact that the concept of institution (even if the word is not used) is not elucidated. Taken in the strict sense, institutions belong to the 'superstructure' and are held to be determined by the 'infrastructure'. This view is in itself untenable as we tried to show above. What is more, if one were to accept it, institutions would have to be seen as 'forms' serving and expressing a 'content' or a substance of social life, already structured before these institutions, for otherwise the determination of the latter by this content would be meaningless. This substance would be the 'infrastructure' which, as the word indicates, is already structured. But how could it be, if it is not instituted? If the 'economy', for example, determines the 'law', if the relations of production determine the forms of property, this means that the relations of production can be grasped as articulated relations and that they effectively are so even 'before' (logically and really) their juridical expression. However, the relations of production articulated on the social scale (not Robinson Crusoe's relation to Friday) signify *ipso facto* a network, one both real and symbolical, which is self-sanctioning – hence an institution.[20] Classes are already present in the relations of production, whether or not they are recognized by this 'second-order' institution, the law. This is what we tried to show elsewhere with respect to the bureaucracy and 'nationalized' property in the USSR.[21] The relation between the bureaucracy and the proletariat in the USSR is *instituted* as a productive, economic and social class relation, even if it is not institutionalized as such explicitly from a legal point of view (any more than the relation between the proletariat and the bourgeoisie has ever been, in any country). Consequently, the problem of institutional symbolism and its relative autonomy in relation to the functions of the institution is already apparent on the level of the relations of production. It is even more clearly apparent on the level of the economy in the strict sense, and already at this point a merely functionalist view is untenable. This analysis must not be confused with the critique some neo-Kantians, like R. Stammler, level against Marxism, based on the idea of the primacy of the 'form' of social life (this would be the law) over its 'matter' (the economy). This critique partakes of the same ambiguity as the Marxist view it attempts to combat. The economy can itself exist only as an institution, and this does not necessarily imply an independent 'judicial form'. As for the relation between the institution and the social life that unfolds there, it cannot be seen as relation between matter and form in the Kantian sense, and in any case not as one implying the 'anteriority' of one with respect to the other. It is a question of *moments* in a structure – which is never rigid and never identical from one society to another.[22]

Obviously, it cannot be said, on the other hand, that the institutional symbolism 'determines' the content of social life. What is involved here is a specific, *sui generis* relation, which is misunderstood and distorted when it is apprehended as pure causation or as a pure interconnection of meanings, as absolute freedom or as complete determination, as transparent rationality or as a sequence of raw facts.

Society does constitute its symbolism, but not with total freedom. Symbolism is bound up with nature, and it is bound up with history (with what is already there); finally, it partakes of rationality. As a result of this, links emerge between signifiers, relations between signifiers and signifieds, connections and consequences emerge which were neither intended nor foreseen. Not freely chosen, not imposed upon a given society, neither a neutral instrument nor a transparent medium, neither an impenetrable opacity nor an irreducible adversity, neither the master of society nor the flexible slave of functionality, not a direct and complete means of partaking of a rational order – symbolism determines the aspects of social life (and not merely those it was supposed to determine) while simultaneously being full of interstices and of degrees of freedom.

These characteristics of symbolism, however, even if they do indicate the *problem* that the symbolic nature of its institutions presents for society, do not constitute an insoluble problem, nor are they sufficient to account for the autonomization of institutions with respect to society. Although we do encounter an autonomization of symbolism in history, this is not an ultimate fact and cannot be explained by itself alone. There is an immediate use of the symbolic, in which the subject may let himself be dominated by the latter, but there is also a lucid or reflective use. Even if this second use can never be guaranteed a priori (no language can be constructed, not even an algorithm, in which all error would be 'mechanically' impossible), it is realized nonetheless and in this way shows the path and the possibility of another relation in which the symbolic is no longer autonomous and can be made adequate to the content. It is one thing to say that we cannot choose a language with absolute freedom, and that every language encroaches on what 'is to be said'. It is something else again to believe that we are fatally subject to language and that we can never say anything except what language makes us say. We can never get outside of language, but our mobility within language is limitless and allows us to question everything, including language itself and our relation to it.[23] It is no different in the case of institutional symbolism – except, of course, that there is an incomparably higher degree of complexity. None of the traits specific to symbolism ineluctably imposes the domination of an autonomous institutional symbolism on social life; nothing, in institutional symbolism itself, excludes its lucid use by society – if we understand again here that no institution can ever be conceived that forbids 'by its construction' or 'mechanically' the submission of society to its symbolism. In this regard, there is in our Greco-Western cultural cycle a real historical movement of the gradual conquest of symbolism in our relations with language as well as in our relations with institutions.[24] Even capitalist governments have learned to make use more or less correctly, in certain respects, of economic 'language' and symbolism, to say what they mean by credit, taxes and so on (the *content* of what they say is obviously something quite different). This, of course, does not imply that just any content can be expressed in any language. The musical thinking of *Tristan* could not be said in the language of the *Well Tempered Clavier*; the demonstration of even a simple mathematical theorem is not possible in everyday language. A new society will obviously create a new institutional symbolism, and the institutional symbolism of an autonomous society will have little relation with what we have known up to now.

Mastering the symbolism of institutions would, therefore, pose no problems that would be essentially different from those arising in the mastery of language (leaving aside for the moment its material 'encumberment' – classes, weapons, objects, etc.), if there were not something else involved. Any symbolism can be mastered, except inasmuch as it refers, ultimately, to what *is not* symbolic. For what goes beyond mere 'progress in rationality'; what allows institutional symbolism, not to deviate momentarily and then to be recovered again (as can be the case in lucid discourse as well) but to become autonomous;

what, finally, provides symbolism with its essential supplement, determining it and specifying it, does not belong to the symbolic.

iii THE SYMBOLIC AND THE IMAGINARY

The determinations of the symbolic, which we have just described, do not exhaust its substance. An essential, and, for our purposes, decisive component remains: the imaginary component of every symbol and of every symbolism, at whatever level they may be situated. Recall the common meaning of the term 'imaginary', which is sufficient for the moment: we speak of the 'imaginary' when we want to talk about something 'invented' – whether this refers to a 'sheer' invention ('a story entirely dreamed up'), or a slippage, a shift of meaning in which available symbols are invested with other significations than their 'normal' or canonical significations ('What are you imagining now?' says the woman to the man who is chiding her for a smile she exchanged with someone else). In both cases, it is assumed that the imaginary is separate from the real, whether it claims to take the latter's place (a lie) or makes no such claim (a novel).

The deep and obscure relations between the symbolic and the imaginary appear as soon as one reflects on the following fact: the imaginary has to use the symbolic not only to 'express' itself (this is self-evident), but to 'exist', to pass from the virtual to anything more than this. The most elaborate delirium, just as the most secret and vaguest phantasy, are composed of 'images', but these 'images' are there to represent something else and so have a symbolic function. But, conversely, symbolism too presupposes an imaginary capacity. For it presupposes the capacity to see in a thing what it is not, to see it other than it is. However, to the extent that the imaginary ultimately stems from the originary faculty of positing or presenting oneself with things and relations that do not exist, in the form of representation (things and relations that are not or have never been given in perception), we shall speak of a final or radical imaginary as the common root of the actual imaginary and of the symbolic.[25] This is, finally, the elementary and irreducible capacity of evoking images.[26]

The decisive grip the imaginary holds on the symbolic can be understood on the basis of the following consideration: symbolism assumes the capacity of positing a permanent connection between two terms in such a way that one 'represents' the other. It is only at very advanced stages in lucid rational thinking that these three elements (the signifier, the signified and their *sui generis* tie) are maintained as simultaneously united and distinct in a relation that is at once firm and flexible. In other words, the symbolic relation (whose 'proper' use presupposes the imaginary function *and* its mastery by the rational function) returns to, or rather remains from the start just where it arose, the rigid tie (most of the time, in the form of identification, participation or causation) between the signifier and the signified, the symbol and the thing, that is to say in the actual imaginary.

If we stated that the symbolic presupposes the radical imaginary and is based on it, this does not mean that the symbolic is, on the whole, only the actual imaginary with respect to its content. The symbolic includes, almost always, a 'real–rational' component: that which represents the real or is indispensible for thinking of it or acting on it. But this component is inextricably interwoven with the actual imaginary component – and this poses an essential problem for the theory of history as well as for politics.

In *Numbers* (15, 32–6) it is written that the Jews, upon finding a man who was working on the Sabbath – which was forbidden by the Law – brought him to Moses. The Law had set no penalty for this transgression, but the Lord manifested himself unto Moses, demanding that the man be stoned – and he was.

One cannot help but be struck by this case – as often happens when looking through the Mosaic Law – by the excessiveness of the penalty, by the absence of any necesary tie between the deed (the transgression) and its consequence (the content of the penalty). Stoning is not the only way to bring people to respect the Sabbath, the institution (the penalty) clearly exceeds what would be required by the rational connection of causes to effects, means to ends. If reason is, as Hegel said, an operation conforming to an end, did the Lord, in this instance, appear reasonable? But, one will say, the Lord himself is imaginary. Behind the Law – which is 'real', an actual social institution – sits the imaginary Lord, presented as its source and ultimate sanction. Is the imaginary existence of the Lord reasonable? It will be said that at one stage of the evolution of human societies, the institution of an imaginary possessing a greater reality than the real itself – God, or, more generally, a religious imaginary – 'conforms to the ends' of society, follows from real conditions, and fills an essential function. People will attempt to show, from a Marxist or Freudian perspective (these attitudes are not mutually exclusive, but complement one another) that such a society necessarily produces this imaginary – this 'illusion' as Freud said, speaking of religion – which it needs in order to function. These interpretations are valuable and true. But they encounter their limit in the following questions: Why must a society seek the complement necessary to its order in the *imaginary*? Why do we find, in every case, at the heart of this imaginary and in all of its expressions something that cannot be reduced to the functional, an original investment by society of the world and itself with meaning – meanings which are not 'dictated' by real factors since it is instead this meaning that attributes to these real factors a particular importance and a particular place in the universe constituted by a given society – a meaning that can be recognized in both the content and the style of its life (and which is not so far removed from what Hegel called 'the spirit of a people')? Why, of all the pastoral tribes that in the second millennium BC wandered in the desert between Thebes and Babylonia, did only one choose to dispatch to Heaven an unspeakable, strict and vindictive Father, to make him the one and only creator and the founder of the Law, and thus to introduce monotheism into history? And why, of all the peoples who founded cities in the Mediterranean basin, did only one decide that there was an impersonal law that ruled over the gods themselves, posited it as consubstantial to coherent discourse, and attempted to ground in this *logos* the relations between men, thereby inventing at one and the same time philosophy and democracy? How is it that, 3,000 years later, we are still bearing the consequences of these dreams of the Jews and the Greeks? Why and how did this imaginary, once it was posited, lead to specific conclusions that go beyond any functional 'motives' and at times even oppose them, consequences that survive long after the circumstances that gave rise to them, and that finally reveal the imaginary as an autonomous factor in social life?

Consider the institution of Mosaic religion. Like all religions, it is centred around an imaginary. And as a religion, it must establish rites; as an institution, it must surround itself with sanctions. But it can exist neither as a religion nor as an institution if, around the *central imaginary*, there is not also the proliferation of a *secondary imaginary*. God created the world in seven days (six plus one). Why *seven*? The number seven can be given a Freudian interpretation; it can also be related to any number of facts or customs. It nevertheless remains that this terrestrial determination (perhaps 'real' but probably already imaginary) exported to the Heavens is then re-imported in the form of the sanctification of the *week*. The seventh day now becomes the day of adoration of the Lord and obligatory rest. Innumerable consequences begin to flow from this. The first was the stoning of that poor wretch, who was collecting twigs in the desert on the Lord's day. Among the more recent consequences, we might mention the level of the rate of surplus-value,[27] the frequency curve of sexual intercourse in Christian societies showing a periodic maximum every seven days, and the mortal boredom of English Sundays.

Or consider, to use another example, the 'rites of passage', the ceremonies of 'confirmation', or 'initiation' that mark the entry of adolescents into adulthood, the ceremonies that play such an important role in the life of all archaic societies, noteworthy vestiges of which continue to be found in modern societies. In a given, specific context these ceremonies bring to light an important functional–economic component, and are bound up in a thousand different ways with the 'logic' of the life of the society considered (for the most part, an 'unconscious' logic, of course). The accession of a series of individuals to full rights has to be marked publicly and solemnly (in the absence of a public register, a prosaic functionalist would say), a 'certification' must be made, as it were, so that for the adolescent's psyche this crucial stage in development is marked by a feast and by a test. But around this core – one would be tempted to say, as for pearl oysters: around this impurity – crystallizes a sedimentation of innumerable rules, acts, rites, symbols, in short, components that arc full of magical and, more generally, imaginary elements, whose justification in relation to the functional core is more and more tenuous, and finally non-existent. The adolescents have to fast a certain number of days, eat only a particular type of food, prepared by a certain category of women, undergo a particular test, sleep in a given place or not sleep at all for a certain number of nights, wear certain ornaments and emblems, and so on.

Ethnologists, aided by Marxist, Freudian or other considerations, will attempt in each case to provide an interpretation of the ceremony in all its aspects. And they do all right – if they do it well. It is immediately apparent that the ceremony cannot be interpreted by reducing it directly to its functional aspect (no more than a neurosis can be interpreted by saying that it has to do with the subject's sex life); the function is just about the same everywhere, and so is incapable of explaining the unbelievable proliferation of details and of complications, which are almost always different. So the interpretation will contain a series of *indirect* reductions to other components, in which we again find a functional element *and* something else. (For example, the composition of the adolescents' meal or the category of women who prepare it will be related to the clan structure or to the tribe's food pattern, and these, in their turn, will be carried back to 'real' elements and also to totemic phenomena, to taboos concerning certain foods, etc.). These successive reductions sooner or later run up against a twofold limit: first, the ultimate elements are symbols, and the imaginary can neither be separated nor isolated from their constitution; second, the successive syntheses of these elements, the 'partial totalities' that make up the life and the structure of a society, the 'figures' that render society visible to itself (the clans, the ceremonies, the moments of religion, the forms of authority relations, etc.) possess an indivisible meaning, as if this meaning stemmed from an originary operation that posited it from the very outset – and this meaning, which henceforth is active as such, is situated at a level different from any functional determination.

This twofold action can be seen most easily in cultures that are most completely 'integrated', regardless of their mode of integration. It can be seen in totemism, where an 'elementary' symbol is at the same time a principle of world organization and the foundation for the tribe's existence. It can be seen in Greek culture, where religion (inseparable from the city and from the social and political organization) covers with its symbols every element of nature and of human activity *and* in the same stroke confers a global meaning upon the universe and the place of man in it.[28] It even appears in Western capitalist society, where, as we shall see, the 'disenchantment of the world' and the destruction of previous forms of the imaginary has, paradoxically, gone hand in hand with the constitution of a new imaginary, centred around the 'pseudo-rational', and involving both the 'ultimate constituents' of the world *and* its overall organization.

This discussion concerns what could be called the 'central imaginary' in every culture, whether this is situated on the level of elementary symbols or of global meaning. There is obviously in addition to this what could be termed the 'peripheral imaginary', of no less importance in its real effects, but which will not concern us here. It corresponds to a second or an nth imaginary development of symbols, to the successive layers of sedimentation. An icon is a symbolic object of an imaginary – but it is invested with another imaginary signification when the faithful scrape off the paint and drink it as a medication. A flag is a symbol with a rational function, a sign of recognition and for rallying round, which quickly becomes what one can and must die for, and what sends shivers down the spine of the patriots as they watch the military parade pass by.

The modern view of the institution, which reduces its signification to the functional aspect, is only partially correct. To the extent that it presents itself as *the* truth about the problem of the institution, it is only a projection. It projects onto the whole of history an idea taken not even from the actual reality of the institutions belonging to the Western capitalist world (which, despite the vast movement of rationalization, have never been and are still no more than partially functional), but from what this world *would like* its institutions to be. Even more recent views, which would like to see in the institution *only* the symbolic (and identify the latter with the rational) also represent merely a partial truth, and their generalization, too, includes a projection.

The ancient views on the 'divine' origin of institutions were, under their mythical cloak, much truer. When Sophocles[29] spoke of divine laws that were stronger and more lasting than those made by human hands (and here, as if by chance, this concerns the precise case of the prohibition of incest, which Oedipus has violated), he pointed to a source of the institution beyond the lucid consciousness of men as legislators. This same truth underlies the myth of the Law given to Moses by God – by a *pater absconditus*, by an invisible unnameable. Beyond the conscious activity of institutionalization, institutions have drawn their source from the *social imaginary*. This imaginary must be interwoven with the symbolic, otherwise society could not have 'come together'; and have linked up with the economic–functional component, otherwise it could not have survived. It can be placed, and it must be placed, in their service as well: there is, of course, a *function* of the institutional imaginary, although here, too, we observe that the effect of the imaginary *outstrips* its function; it is not the 'ultimate factor' (we are not looking for one anyway) – but without it any determination of both the symbolic and the functional, the specificity and the unity of the former, the orientation and the finality of the latter, remain incomplete and finally incomprehensible.

iv ALIENATION AND THE IMAGINARY

The institution is a socially sanctioned, symbolic network in which a functional component and an imaginary component are combined in variable proportions and relations. Alienation occurs when the imaginary moment in the institution becomes autonomous and predominates, which leads to the institution's becoming autonomous and predominating with respect to society. This becoming autonomous, or autonomization, of the institution is expressed and embodied in the material nature of social life, but it always presupposes at the same time that society lives its relations with its institutions in the mode of the imaginary, in other words, that it does not recognize in the imaginary of institutions something that is its own product.

Marx knew this. Marx knew that 'the Apollo of Delphi was in the life of the Greeks a power as real as any other'. When he spoke of the fetishism of merchandise and showed its importance for the actual functioning of the capitalist economy, he obviously went beyond a purely economic view and recognized the role of the imaginary.[30] When he stressed that the memory of past generations weighed heavily on the consciousness of the living, he pointed once more to this peculiar mode of the imaginary manifest in the past lives as present, where ghosts are more powerful than men of flesh and blood, where the dead clasp the living, as he liked to say. And when Lukács, in another context, says, returning to Engels, that the mystified consciousness of capitalists is the condition for the adequate functioning of the capitalist economy – in other words, that the laws can be realized only by 'using' the illusions of individuals – he again shows that one of the conditions of functionality lies in a specific imaginary.

This role of the imaginary, however, was seen by Marx to be a limited one, precisely a functional role, a 'non-economic' link in an 'economic' chain. This was because he thought he could reduce it to a temporary deficiency (a temporariness that stretched from prehistory to communism) in history seen as economy, to the technical immaturity of humanity. He was prepared to recognize the power of man's imaginary creations – supernatural or social – but this power was for him only the reflection of his real powerlessness. It would be overly schematic and uninteresting to say that for Marx alienation was merely another name for scarcity, but it is finally true to say that in his conception of history, as it is formulated in his later works, scarcity is the necessary and sufficient condition for alienation.[31]

We are unable to accept this conception for reasons we have expounded elsewhere:[32] briefly, this is because no level of technical development or economic abundance can be defined after which the division into classes or alienation would lose their *raisons d'être*; because an abundance that is technically accessible is today already hampered socially; because the 'needs' used to define a state of scarcity are by no means stable but represent a social–historical state.[33] But especially because it leaves out entirely the role of the imaginary, namely that it is at the root of alienation as well as of creation in history.

For creation, just as much as alienation, presupposes the capacity to grant oneself what is not (what is not given in perception, or what is not given in the symbolic links of previously constituted rational thought). And one cannot distinguish the imaginary at work in creation from 'pure and simple' imaginary by saying that the first 'anticipates' a reality not yet given, but then 'is verified' later. For it would first have to be explained how this 'anticipation' could occur without an imaginary and what would prevent the latter from ever going astray. Next, what is essential to creation is not 'discovery' but constituting the new: art does not discover, it constitutes; and the relation between what it constitutes and the 'real', an exceedingly complex relation to be sure, is not a relation of verification. And on the social plane, which is our main interest here, the emergence of new institutions and of new ways of living is not a 'discovery' either but an active constitution. The Athenians did not find democracy amidst the other wild flowers growing on the Pnyx, nor did the Parisian workers unearth the Commune when they dug up the boulevards. Nor did either of them 'discover' these institutions in the heaven of ideas, after inspecting all the forms of government, existing there from all eternity, placed in their well-ordered showcases. They invented something, which, to be sure, proved to be viable in particular circumstances, but which also, once it existed, changed these circumstances essentially – and which, moreover, 25 centuries or 100 years later, continues to be 'present in history. This 'verification' has nothing to do with the verification, by Magellan's circumnavigation, of the idea that the earth is round – an idea that also, at the start, offers something that is not in perception, but that refers to a *previously constituted* reality.[34]

When it is asserted that the imaginary plays a role with respect to the institution only because there are 'real' problems that people are not able to solve, this is to forget, on the one hand, that people manage to solve these real problems, precisely, to the extent that they do solve them, only *because* they are capable of the imaginary; and, on the other hand, that these real problems can be problems, can be constituted as *these* specific problems, presenting themselves to a particular epoch or a particular society as a task to be completed, only in relation to an imaginary central to the given epoch or society. This does not mean that these problems are invented out of nothing, that they spring up out of nowhere. But what for each society poses a problem in general (or emerges as such at a given level of specification and of con-cretization) is inseparable from its way of being in general, from the sense – a problematical sense, indeed – which it casts on the world and on its place in the world, a sense which as such is neither true nor false, neither verifiable nor falsifiable in reference to 'true' problems and their 'true' solution, except in a very specific acceptation, which we shall return to below.

When the history of an individual is involved, what sense is there in saying that his or her imaginary formations take on importance, play a role only because 'real' factors – the repression of drives, a trauma – have already created a conflict? The imaginary acts on a terrain where there is a repression of drives and it starts from one or numerous traumas; but the repression of drives is always present, and what is it that constitutes a trauma? Except for borderline cases, an event is traumatic only because it is 'lived as such' by the individual. This expression means here: because the individual ascribes a particular meaning to it, one that is not its 'canonical' meaning, or in any case one that is not necessarily imposed as such.[35]

In the same way, in the case of a society, the idea that its imaginary formations 'set themselves up in an independent empire in the clouds'[36] because the society in question is not able to solve its problems 'in reality' is true on a second level but not on the original level. For this is meaningful only if one can say just what *the* problem of society is, the problem it is temporarily unable to solve. It is impossible to answer this question, not because our investigations are not sufficiently advanced or because our knowledge is relative; it is impossible because the question is meaningless. There is nothing that is *the* problem of society. There is no 'thing' that men deeply want and that up to now they have been unable to attain because their technology was inadequate or even because society continued to be divided into classes. People themselves have been, individually and collectively, this willing, this need, this doing, which in each case has provided itself with a different object and, through this, another 'definition' of oneself.

To say that the imaginary emerges – or plays a role – only because man is incapable of solving his real problem presupposes that we know and that we can say what this real problem is, everywhere and at any time, and that it is, was and will be everywhere and always the same (for if this problem changes, we have to ask ourselves why, and we are led back to the preceding question). This presupposes that we know and that we can say what humanity *is* and what it *wants*, what it is *tending towards*, as we say (or think we are able to say) of objects.

Marxists always give a double answer to this question, a contradictory answer exhibiting a confusion and, ultimately, a bad faith that no 'dialectic' can mask:

Humanity is what is hungry.

Humanity is what strives for freedom – not freedom from hunger, but freedom as such; a freedom they would all agree has not and cannot have any determined 'object' in general.

Humanity is hungry, that is certain. But it hungers for what, and how? Half of its members are still hungry in a literal sense, and this hunger must be satisfied. But does humanity hunger for food alone? And in what way, then, does it differ from sponges or coral? Why is it that this hunger, once satisfied, always lets other questions, other demands appear? Why has the life of those social strata that have always been able to satisfy their hunger, or of entire societies that can do so today, not become free – or not return to vegetative existence? Why have not the satiation, the security and the copulation *ad libitum* in Scandinavian societies – but also, more and more, in all modern capitalist societies, (a billion individuals) given rise to autonomous individuals and collectivities? What is the *need* that these populations cannot satisfy? If the reply is that this need is kept continually unsatisfied by technical progress, which produces new objects, or by the existence of privileged groups who place before the eyes of the other groups other ways of satisfying it – then you will have conceded what I was trying to say: that this need does not contain in itself the definition of an object that could satisfy it, in the way that the need to breathe finds its object in the atmosphere, that instead it is born in history, that no specific need is *the* need of humanity. Humanity has hungered and does even now hunger for food, but it has also hungered for clothing and then for something other than last year's fashions; it has hungered for automobiles and for television; it has hungered for power and for saintliness; it has hungered for asceticism and for debauchery; it has hungered for mysticism and for rational knowledge; it has hungered for love and brotherhood but it has also hungered for its own cadavres, hungered for feasts and for tragedies, and now it appears to be hungering for the Moon and the planets. One would have to be a complete idiot to claim that all of these hungers were invented because humanity was not able to eat and copulate anough.

Man is not *this* need which contains its 'proper object' as its complement, a lock with its key (to be found or to be made). Man can exist only by defining himself in each case as an ensemble of needs and corresponding objects, but he always outstrips these definitions – and, if he outstrips them (not only as a permanent possibility but in the effectivity of the historical movement), this is because they spring out of him, because he invents them (not arbitrarily, to be sure, for there is always nature, the minimum of coherence required by rationality, and previous history), and hence because he *makes* them by making things and by making *himself*, and because no rational, natural or historical definition allows us to establish them once and for all. 'Man is that which is not what it is and is what it is not,' as Hegel has already said.

v SOCIAL IMAGINARY SIGNIFICATIONS

We have seen that institutions, and even more so the whole of social life, cannot be understood as a system that is purely functional, an integrated series of arrangements geared to satisfying the needs of society. For every interpretation of this type immediately leads to the question: functional in relation to what and to what end? This question has no answer within a functionalist perspective.[37] Institutions are certainly functional inasmuch as they must necessarily assure the survival of the society considered.[38] But what we call 'survival' has an entirely different content depending on the society in question. And, over and above this aspect, institutions are 'functional' in relation to ends that stem neither from functionality, nor from its contrary. A theocratic society, a society ordered essentially to allow groups of lords to make war interminably on each other, or, finally, a society like that of modern capitalism which creates a continuous flow of new 'needs' and exhausts itself in satisfying them, can be neither described nor understood *in their very functionality* except in relation to intentions, orientations, chains of significations, which not merely escape functionality but to which functionality is in large part subservient.

Nor can institutions be understood simply as symbolic networks.[39] Institutions do form a symbolic network but this network, by definition, refers to something other than symbolism. Every purely symbolical interpretation of institutions immediately opens the following questions: Why *this* system of symbols and not another? What are the *meanings* conveyed by the symbols, the system of signifieds to which the system of signifiers refers? Why and how do the symbolic networks become autonomous? One readily suspects that the answers to these questions are closely related.

(a) Understanding, as far as this is possible, the 'choice' a society makes of its symbolism demands that we go beyond formal or even 'structural' considerations. When one says about totemism that certain species of animals possess a totemic signification not because they are 'good to eat' but because they are 'good for thinking about',[40] an important truth is certainly revealed. But this must not blind us to the questions that come after: Why are these species 'better to think about' than others? Why is a given pair of oppositions chosen in preference to innumerable others offered by nature? Thought about by whom, when, how? In short, it must not serve to do away with the question of the content, to eliminate the reference to the signified. When a tribe holds that two clans are homologous with the pair: falcon–crow, the question immediately arises: why was this couple chosen out of all those that could connote a difference in kinship? And it is clear that this question arises with even greater insistance in historical societies.[42]

(b) Understanding, and even just grasping, the symbolism of a society is grasping the significations that it carries. These significations appear only as they are carried by signifying structures; but this does not mean that they can be reduced to these, that they result from them in a univocal manner, or, finally, that they are determined by them. When, in the Oedipus myth, a structure consisting of two pairs of oppositions is elicited,[43] a necessary condition (like the phonemic oppositions in language) for anything *being said* is probably posited. But what is said? Is it just anything at all – that is to say, nothing at all? Is it indifferent here that this structure, this multiple-staged organization of particular signifiers and signifieds finally transmits a global meaning or an articulated sense, the prohibition and the sanction of incest, and, through this very thing, the constitution of the human world as that order of coexistence in which the other is not simply the object of my desire but exists for himself or herself and entertains with a third party relations I am forbidden to enter into? When, again, a structural analysis reduces an entire series of archaic myths to the intention of signifying the passage from nature to culture by means of the opposition between the raw and the cooked,[44] is it not clear that the content signified in this way possesses a fundamental meaning: the question bearing on and the obsession with origins, form and part of the obsession with the identity, the being of the group that asks this question about itself? If this analysis is true, it signifies the following: Men ask themselves the question, what is the human world? – and they reply with a *myth*: the human world is one in which the things given in nature undergo a transformation (where we cook food, for instance); it is, finally, a rational response given in the imaginary through symbolic means. There exists a meaning that can never be given independently of *every* sign but which is something other than the opposition of signs, and which is not unavoidably related to *any particular signifying structure* since it is, as Shannon said, what is invariant when a message is translated from one code into another, and even, we might add, what allows us to define the identity (even if only partial) of messages in the same code but of different construction. It is impossible to hold that meaning is simply what results from the combination of signs.[45] One could just as well say that the combination of signs results from its meaning, for the world is not made up solely of people who interpret other people's discourses; if the former are to exist, the latter must first have spoken, and speaking is already choosing signs, hesitating, and correcting the signs already chosen – in relation to a meaning. The structuralist musicologist is an eminently respectable person, provided that he does not forget that he owes his existence (from an economic point of view, but also from an ontological one) to someone other than himself, who, before him, took the opposite path, namely to the creative musician who (consciously or unconsciously, little matter) posited and even selected these 'oppositions of signs', struck out certain notes on his score, enriched a certain chord, finally gave to the strings a phrase initially intended for the brass section, guided by a musical signification to be expressed (which, of course, is continually influenced throughout the composition by the signs available in the code used, in the musical language that the composer has adopted – although, finally, a great composer modifies this language himself and constitutes *en masse* his own signifiers). This is just as valid in the case of the mythologist or the structural anthropologist, except that here the creator is an entire society, and the reconstruction of codes is much more radical and more deeply hidden – in short, the constitution of signs in relation to meaning is an infinitely more complex matter. To consider meaning as a simple 'result' of the difference between signs, is to transform the conditions necessary for *reading* history into the conditions sufficient for its *existence*. And to be sure, the conditions for reading are already intrinsically the conditions for existence, since history exists only because men communicate and cooperate in a symbolic milieu. But this symbolism is itself *created*. History exists only in and through 'language' (all sorts of languages), but history gives itself this language, constitutes it and transforms it. To be unaware of this aspect of the question is to continue to consider the multiplicity of symbolic systems (and hence institutional systems) and their succession as blunt facts about which there is nothing to say (and nothing to be done), to eliminate the prime historical question concerning the genesis of meaning, the production of new systems of signifieds and signifiers. And, if this is true of the historical constitution of new symbolic systems, it is just as true of the use, at every instant, of an established and given symbolic system. Likewise, in this case, too, one cannot say absolutely either that the meaning 'results' from the opposition of signs, or the inverse; for this would be to bring in causal relations or, at any rate, rigorous bi-univocal correspondences that would mask and wipe out the most profound characteristic of the symbolic phenomenon, namely its relative indeterminacy. At the most elementary level, this indeterminacy is already clearly indicated by the phenomenon of the over-determination of symbols (several signifieds can be attached to the same signifier) – to which must be added the inverse phenomenon, which could be called the over-symbolization of meaning (the same signified is carried by several signifiers; in the same code there are equivalent messages; every language contains 'redundant features', and so on).

   The extremist tendencies of structuralism result from the fact that it has effectively given in to 'the utopian ideal of the day', which is not 'to construct a system of signs on a single level of articulation',[46] but *to eliminate sense* instead (and, in another form, to eliminate man). In this way, sense, to the extent that it cannot be identified with a combination of signs (or even with its necessary and univocal result) is reduced to an unconveyable interiority, to a 'certain savour'.[47] It thus appears that one is unable to conceive sense except in its most limited psychological and affective acceptation. But, the prohibition of incest is not a savour: it is a law, namely an institution that carries a meaning, a symbol, a myth and the stating of a rule that refers to a sense responsible for organizing an infinite number of human acts, an institution that raises a wall in the middle of the field of the possible, separating the licit and the illicit, creating value and rearranging the entire system of meanings, giving to consanguinity, for example, a content it did not possess 'before'. Nor is the difference between nature and culture the simple difference of savour between the raw and the cooked; it is a world of significations. (c) Finally, it is impossible to eliminate the question: How and why does the symbolic system of institutions become autonomous? How and why does the institutional structure, as soon as it is set in place, become a factor to which the actual life of society is subordinated and as if enslaved? To reply that it is in the nature of symbolism to become autonomous would be worse than an innocent tautology. This would amount to saying that it is in the nature of the subject to become alienated in the symbols he uses, and so to abolish all discourse, all dialogue, all truth, by positing that everything we say is carried by the automatic destiny of the symbolic chains.[48] And, in any case, we know that the autonomization of symbolism as such in social life is a secondary phenomenon. When religion stands as an ‚autonomous factor in front of society, religious symbols are independent and have value only because they embody religious meaning, their brilliance is borrowed – as shown by the fact that religion can cast meaning on new symbols, create new signifiers, and take hold of new regions to make sacred.[49]

We do not have to fall into the traps of symbolism for having acknowledged its importance. Discourse is not independent of symbolism, and this represents something other than a simple 'external condition': discourse is caught up in symbolism. This is not to say, however, that it is totally enslaved by it. And especially, what discourse intends is something other than symbolism: it is a *meaning*, which can be perceived, thought or imagined. And it is the modalities of this relation to meaning that will make it a discourse or a form of delirium (which can be grammatically, syntactically and lexically impeccable). The distinction, which we cannot avoid, between someone who, looking at the Eiffel Tower, says 'It's the Eiffel Tower' and someone who, in the same circumstances, says 'Look, here's Grandmother', can be found only in the relation between what is signified in their discourse and the canonical signified of the terms that are used and between the former and a core that is independent of all discourse and all symbolization. Meaning is this independent core that comes to expression (in this example, 'the real state of affairs').

We shall therefore posit that there are significations that are relatively independent of the signifiers that carry them and that they play a role in the choice and in the organization of these signifiers. These significations can correspond to the *perceived*, to the *rational* or to the *imaginary*. The close relations that practically always exist between these three poles must not make us lose sight of their specificity.

Consider God. Whatever points of support his representation may take in perceived reality, whatever his rational effectiveness may be as an organizing principle of the environing world for certain cultures, God is neither a signification of something real, nor a signification of something rational; nor is he a symbol of something else again. What is God – not as a theological concept and not as a philosopher's idea – but for we who are thinking about what he is for those who believe in God? They can evoke him, refer to him only with the help of symbols, even if this be simply the 'Name' – but for them and for us, too, when we are considering this historical phenomenon constituted by God and those who believe in God, he infinitely surpasses this 'Name'; he *is* something other. God is neither the name of God nor the images a people may give of him, nor anything of the sort. Carried by, pointed at by all these symbols, he is, in every religion, that which makes these symbols religious symbols – a central *signification*, the organization of signifiers and signifieds into a system, that which supports the intersecting unity of both those components and which also permits the extension, multiplication and modification of this signification. And this signification, which is neither something perceived (real) nor something thought (rational), is an imaginary signification.

Or consider the phenomenon that Marx called reification, in more general terms, the 'dehumanization' of individuals of the exploited classes in certain historical phases: a slave is seen as *animal vocale*, the worker as a 'cog in the machine' or as mere merchandise. Little does it matter here that this assimilation can never be realized totally, that the human reality of slaves or of workers puts it into question, etc.[50] What is the nature of this signification – which, we must recall, far from being simply a concept or a representation, is an operative signification, with weighty historical and social consequences? A slave is not an animal, a worker is not a thing; but reification is neither a false perception of reality nor a logical error. And neither can it be seen as a 'dialectical moment' in the totalized history of the advent of the truth of human essence, in which this essence would radically negate itself first in order then to realize itself positively. Reification is an imaginary meaning (there is no need to stress that the social imaginary, as we understand it, is more real than the 'real'). From a strictly symbolic, or 'linguistic', point of view, it appears as a shift of meaning, as a combination of metaphor and metonymy. The slave can 'be' an animal only metaphorically, and this metaphor, like every metaphor, is based on a metonymy, the part being taken for the whole with respect to the animal as well as to the slave, and the pseudo-identity of partial properties being extended to the whole of the objects considered. This shift of meaning, however, which is after all the indefinitely repeated operation of symbolism, the fact that one signified slips under another, is simply one way of describing what occurs; it accounts for neither the genesis nor the mode of being of the phenomenon concerned. Reification – in the case of slavery or in that of the proletariat – involves the establishment of a new *operative signification*, the grasp of one category of men by another category as assimilable, in all practical respects, to animals or to things. This is an *imaginary creation*; it cannot be accounted for by reality, by rationality, or by the laws of symbolism (it is something else again to say that this creation cannot 'violate' the laws of the real, the rational and the symbolic; it has no need to be clarified in concepts or in representations in order to exist; it is operative in the practice and in the doing of the society considered as a meaning that organizes human behaviour and social relations, independently of its existence 'for the consciousness' of that society. The slave is seen metaphorically as an animal, the worker as merchandise in actual social practice long before the Roman jurists, Aristotle or Marx.

What compounds the problem, and what probably explains why it was seen for so long from a partial perspective and why, even today, in anthropology as well as in psychoanalysis we observe such great difficulty in distinguishing the various registers of the action of the symbolic and of the imaginary, are not simply the 'realist' and 'rationalist' prejudices (a curious mixture of these can be found in the most extreme tendencies of contemporary 'structuralism') which prevent investigators from recognizing the role of the imaginary. The main reason is that, in the case of the imaginary, the signified to which the signifier refers is almost impossible to grasp as such, and, by definition, its 'mode of being' is a mode of non-being. On the register of the 'external' or 'internal' perceived (real), the distinct physical existence of the signifier and the signified is immediate: no one would confuse the word 'tree' with a real tree, the words 'anger' or 'sadness' with the corresponding effects. On the level of the rational, the distinction is no less clear: we know that the word (the 'term') that designates a concept is one thing and the concept itself is something else again. But in the case of the imaginary things are not so simple. To be sure, on an initial level, we can also distinguish here the words and what they designate, the signifiers and the signifieds. 'Centaur' is a word that refers to an imaginary being distinct from this word, a being that can be 'defined' by words (by this trait it resembles a pseudo-concept) or represented by images (by this trait it resembles a pseudo-object of perception).[51] But even this easy and superficial example (the imaginary Centaur is only a recombination of pieces taken from real beings) is not exhausted by these considerations, because, for the culture that experienced the mythological reality of the Centaurs, their being was something other than the verbal description or the sculpted representation that could be given of them. But how are we to get a hold of this final a-reality? In a certain sense, like the 'thing-in-itself', it offers itself only on the basis of its consequences, its results, its derivatives. How can we grasp God, as an imaginary signification, except on the basis of the shadows (*Abschattungen*) projected onto the effective social action of a people – but, at the same time, how could we overlook that, just like the thing perceived, he is the condition for the possibility of an inexhaustible series of such shadows, but, unlike the thing perceived, he is never given 'in person'?

Consider a subject who lives a scene in the imaginary, abandons himself to a daydream or accompanies with phantasies an actually experienced scene. The scene consists of 'images' in the broadest sense of the term. These images are made of the very material out of which symbols can be made; are they symbols? In the explicit consciousness of the subject, no; they do not stand for something else, they are 'lived' for themselves. But this does not exhaust the question. They can represent something else, an unconscious fantasy – and this is how they are generally seen by psychoanalysts. The image is therefore a symbol here – but of what? In order to know, one must enter the labyrinths of the symbolic elaboration of the imaginary in the unconscious. What is at the end of it? Something that is not there to *represent* something else; something that is instead the operative condition for every subsequent representation, but that already itself exists in the mode of representation: the fundamental phantasy of the subject, his or her nuclear (and not 'primitive') scene, where that which constitutes the subject in his or her singularity exists; the organizing–organized schema that provides its own image and exists not in symbolization but in the imaginary presentification that is already for the subject an embodied and operative signification, the initial grasp and the first, overall constitution of an articulated, relational system positing, separating and uniting the 'inside' and the 'outside', the sketch of gesture and the sketch of perception, the division into archetypal roles and the originary ascription of a role to the subject as such, positive and negative valuation, the source of subsequent symbolic significance, the origin of privileged and specific investments of the subject, something at once structuring and structured. On the level of the individual, the production of this fundamental phantasy stems from what we have termed the radical imaginary (or the radical imagination); this phantasy itself exists both in the mode of the actual imaginary (of the imagined) and is a first signification and core of subsequent significations.

It is doubtful that this fundamental phantasy can be grasped directly; at the most, it can be reconstructed on the basis of its manifestations because it does appear as the ground of the possibility and the unity of everything that makes up the singularity of the subject other than as a purely combinatory singularity, as the sum of all that which, in the life of the subject, goes beyond his or her reality and history, the final condition for the fact that a reality and a history *do happen to* the subject.

When we are concerned with society – which, obviously, is not to be transformed into a 'subject' in either the literal or metaphorical sense – we encounter the same difficulty, but compounded. For here we do have indeed, starting with the imaginary that abounds immediately on the surface of social life, the possibility of penetrating the labyrinth of the symbolization of the imaginary. And by pursuing the analysis further, we do arrive at significations that are not there *in order to* represent something else, that are like the final articulations the society in question has imposed on the world, on itself, and on its needs, the organizing patterns that are the conditions for the representability of everything that the society can give to itself. Of their very nature, however, these patterns do not themselves exist in the form of a representation one could, as a result of analyses, put one's finger on. One cannot talk in this case of 'images', however vague and indefinite the sense ascribed to this term. God is perhaps, for each of the faithful, an 'image' – which can even be a 'precise' representation – but God, as an imaginary social signification, is neither the 'sum', nor the 'common part', nor the 'average' of these images; it is rather their condition of possibility and what makes these images images 'of God'. And the imaginary core of the phenomenon of reification is not an 'image' for anyone. The imaginary social significations do not exist strictly speaking in the mode of representation; they are of another nature, for which it is of no use to seek an analogy in the other spheres of our experience. Compared to individual imaginary significations, they are infinitely larger than a phantasy (the pattern underlying what is designated as the Jewish, Greek or Western 'image of the world' is of infinite extension) and they have no precise place of existence (if indeed the individual unconscious can be called a precise place of existence). They can be grasped only indirectly and obliquely: as the gap, at once obvious and impossible to delimit precisely, between a first term – the life and the actual organization of a society – and a second term, likewise impossible to define – this same life and organization conceived of in a strictly 'functional-rational' manner; as a 'coherent deformation' of the system of subjects, objects and their relations; as the curvature specific to every social space; as the invisible cement holding together this endless collection of real, rational and symbolic odds and ends that constitute every society, and as the principle that selects and shapes the bits and pieces that will be accepted there. Imaginary social significations – at any rate, those that are truly primary – *denote* nothing at all, and they *connote* just about everything. It is for this reason that they are so often confused with their symbols, not just by the peoples that use them but also by the scientists who analyse them, and who, as a result, come to consider that their signifiers only signify themselves (since they refer to nothing real, nothing rational that one could *point to*), and to ascribe to these signifiers as such, to symbolism considered in itself, a role and an effectiveness infinitely superior to those they certainly possess.

Would it not, however, be possible to 'reduce' this social imaginary to the individual imaginary – which would, in the same stroke, provide a *denotable* content for its signifiers? Could we not say, for instance, that God derives from the individual unconscious and that God signifies, quite precisely, an essential phantasmatic moment of this unconscious, the imaginary father? It seems to us that reductions such as these – like the one Freud attempted for religion, like those one could attempt for the imaginary significations of our own culture – contain an important element of truth but do not exhaust the question. It is incontestable that an imaginary signification must find points of support in the individual's unconscious; but this is not a sufficient condition, and one might even legitimately wonder whether it is a condition or a result. The individual and the individual's psyche seem in certain respects, especially to us, the people of today, to possess an eminent 'reality', which the social supposedly would lack. But in other respects this concept is illusory, 'the individual is an abstraction'; the fact that the social–historical field can never be grasped in itself but only in its 'effects' does not prove that it possesses a diminished reality; rather, the opposite is likely to be true. The weight of a body conveys a property of this body but also of the surrounding gravitational field, which is perceptible only through 'mixed' effects of this sort. And what belongs to the body in queston as 'its own', its mass in the classical conception, would not be, in accordance with certain modern cosmological conceptions, a 'property' of the body but the expression of the action on this body of all the other bodies in the universe (Mach's principle); in short, a property of 'coexistence' that emerges on the level of the whole. The fact that, in the human world, we encounter something that is at once more than and less than a 'substance' – the individual, the subject, the for-itself – should not diminish in our eyes the reality of the 'field'. Concretely, by positing, as in the Freudian interpretation of religion, the existence of a 'place to be filled' in the individual unconscious, and by accepting its reading of the processes that produce the necessity of religious sublimation, it nevertheless remains that the individual cannot fill this place by means of his own productions but only by using signifiers which are not freely at his command. What the individual can produce are private phantasies, not institutions. The junction sometimes occurs, in a way that can even be situated and dated, in the founders of religions and in certain other 'exceptional individuals', whose private phantasy comes at the right time and place to fill the unconscious hole in others and possesses enough functional and rational 'coherence' in order to prove itself viable once it has been symbolized and sanctioned – that is to say, institutionalized. This observation does not, however, solve the problem in the 'psychological' sense, not only because these cases are so rare, but because even here the irreducibility of the social is readily apparent. In order for this junction between the tendencies of the unconscious of many individuals to occur, for the discourse of the prophet not to remain a personal hallucination or the credo of an ephemeral sect, favourable social conditions must first have shaped, over an indefinite area, the unconscious of many individuals and have prepared them for these 'good tidings'. And the prophet, too, works in and through the institution; even if he overthrows it, he leans on it. All the religions whose genesis we know are transformations of earlier religions, or else contain a large syncretic component. Alone, the myth or origin, formulated by Freud in *Totem and Taboo*, escapes these considerations in part; this is because it is a myth, but also because it refers to a hybrid – and, actually, an incoherent – state. The instituted is already there, the primitive horde itself is not a fact of nature; neither the castration of male children nor the preservation of the last-born can be considered as the result of biological 'instinct' (to what end and how would it then have 'disappeared'?) but already convey the full action of the imaginary, without which, moreover, the submission of the descendants is inconceivable, and the murder of the father is not the inaugural act of society but a reply to castration (and what is the latter if not an anticipated parrying?), just as the community of brothers, as an institution, succeeding the absolute power of the father, is a revolution rather than initial institution. What is not yet present in the 'primitive horde' is that the institution, present in all of its components, is not symbolized as such.

Outside of the mythical postulation about origins, it remains that any attempt exhaustively to derive social meanings from the individual psyche appears doomed to failure due to the impossibility of isolating this psyche from a social continuum which cannot exist unless it is always already instituted. And if an imaginary social signification is to exist, there must be collectively available signifiers but, above all, there must be signifieds that do not exist in the same mode as individual signifieds (as perceived, thought or imagined by a given subject).

Functionality borrows its meaning from outside itself; symbolism necessarily refers to something that is not symbolical and that is not simply real or rational either. This element – which gives a specific orientation to every institutional system, which overdetermines the choice and the connections of symbolic networks, which is the creation of each historical period, its singular manner of living, of seeing and of conducting its own existence, its world, and its relations with this world, this originary structuring component, this central signifying-signified, the source of that which presents itself in every instance as an indisputable and undisputed meaning, the basis for articulating what does matter and what does not, the origin of the surplus of being of the objects of practical, affective and intellectual investment, whether individual or collective – is nothing other than the *imaginary* of the society or of the period considered.

No society can exist that does not organize the production of its material life and its reproduction as a society. However, none of these organizations is or can be inescapably dictated by natural laws or by rational considerations. In what appears here as a margin of indeterminacy we find what is essential from the point of view of *history* (where what is important is certainly not that humans have always eaten or produced children but, to begin with, that they have done so in an infinite variety of ways – namely, that the total world given to a particular society is *grasped* in a way that is determined practically, affectively and mentally, that an articulated meaning is imposed on it, that distinctions are made concerning what does or does not possess value (in all the senses of the word 'value', from the strictly economic to the strictly speculative), and what should and should not be done.[52]

This structuration, to be sure, leans on corporality, inasmuch as the world given to the senses is already necessarily an articulated world, and also inasmuch as corporality is itself already need and therefore material objects and human objects, food and sexual coupling are already inscribed within this need; inasmuch, thus, as a relation to objects and to other humans, hence an initial 'definition' of the subject as need and as the relation to what can fill this need, is already contained in biological existence. However, this universal premise, everywhere and always the same, is absolutely incapable of accounting for either the variations in or the evolution of the forms of social life.

vi　THE ROLE OF IMAGINARY SIGNIFICATIONS

History is impossible and inconceivable outside of the *productive* or *creative imagination*, outside of what we have called the *radical imaginary* as this is manifested indissolubly in both historical *doing* and in the constitution, before any explicit rationality, of a universe of *significations*.[53] If it includes the dimension that idealist philosophers called freedom, and which is more appropriately termed indeterminacy (which, presupposed by what we have defined as autonomy, is not to be confused with the latter), this is because this *doing* posits and provides for itself something other than what simply is, and because in it dwell *significations* that are neither the reflection of what is perceived, nor the mere extension and sublimation of animal tendencies, nor the strictly rational development of what is given.

The social world is, in every instance, constituted and articulated as a function of such a system of significations, and these significations *exist*, once they have been constituted, in the mode of what we called the *actual imaginary* (or the *imagined*). It is only relative to these significations that we can understand the 'choice' of symbolism made by every society, and in particular the choice of its institutional symbolism, as well as the ends to which it subordinates 'functionality'. Incontestably caught up in the constraints of the real and the rational, always inserted in an historical continuum and, consequently, codetermined by what was already there and cannot be freely manipulated, the production of these significations cannot be exhaustibly reduced to one of these factors or to all of them together. This cannot be done because none of these factors can fill the role of these significations, none can 'answer' the questions that they 'answer'.

Every society up to now has attempted to give an answer to a few fundamental questions: Who are we as a collectivity? What are we for one another? Where and in what are we? What do we want; what do we desire; what are we lacking? Society must define its 'identity', its articulation, the world, its relations to the world and to the objects it contains, its needs and its desires. Without the 'answer' to these 'questions', without these 'definitions', there can be no human world, no society, no culture – for everything would be an undifferentiated chaos. The role of imaginary significations is to provide an answer to these questions, an answer that, obviously, neither 'reality', nor 'rationality' can provide (except in a specific sense, one we shall return to later).

Of course, when we speak of 'questions', 'answers', and 'definitions', we are speaking metaphorically. These are not questions and answers that are posed explicitly, and the definitions are not ones given in language. The questions are not even raised prior to the answers. Society constitutes itself by producing a *de facto* answer to these questions in its life, in its activity. It is in the *doing* of each collectivity that the answer to these questions appears as an embodied meaning; this social doing allows itself to be understood only as a reply to the questions that it implicitly poses itself.

When Marxism believes it shows that these questions and the corresponding answers belong to that part of the ideological 'superstructure' occupied by religion or philosophy, and that, actually, they are only the distorted and refracted reflection of real conditions and of human social activity, it is partially correct to the extent that it is concerned with explicit theorizing and that this theorizing is indeed (although not entirely) sublimation and ideological distortion, and, finally, that the authentic meaning of a society is to be sought first and foremost in its actual life and activity. But it is mistaken when it thinks that this life and this activity can be grasped outside of a meaning that they carry, or that this meaning is 'self-evident' (that it is, for instance, the 'satisfying of needs'). The life and the activity of societies are, precisely, the positing, the definition of this meaning; human labour (in both the narrowest and the broadest sense) indicates in all of its aspects – in its objects, its ends, its modalities, its instruments – a specific manner of grasping the world, of defining itself as need, of positing itself in relation to other human beings. Without all of this (and not merely because it presupposes the prior mental representation of the results, as Marx says) it would not effectively be distinguishable from the activity of bees, to which one could add a 'prior representation of the result' without changing matters in any respect. Man is an unconsciously philosophical animal, who has posed the questions of philosophy in actual fact long before philosophy existed as explicit reflection; and he is a poetic animal, who has provided answers to these questions in the imaginary.

Here are a few preliminary indications on the role of the imaginary social significations in the areas mentioned above.

First, the being of the group and of the collectivity: every human being defines himself or herself and is defined for others in relation to an 'us'. But this 'us', this group, this society – what is it, who is it? It is, first of all, a symbol, the insignias of existence that every tribe, every city, every society has always ascribed to itself. Above all, it is, of course, a name. But this name, at once conventional and arbitrary, is it so conventional and arbitrary? This signifier refers to *two* signifieds, which it indissolubly unites. It designates the collectivity in question, but it does not designate it as pure extension; it designates it at the same time as intension, as something, a quality or a property. We are leopards. We are macaws. We are the Sons of Heaven. We are the children of Abraham, the chosen people whom God will make triumph over his enemies. We are the Hellenes – the people of light. We call ourselves, or others call us, German, Frank, Teutsch, Slav. We are the children of God, who suffered for us. If this name were a symbol with a strictly rational function, it would be a pure sign, denoting simply those who belong to a particular collectivity, itself designated by reference to unambiguous external characteristics ('the inhabitants of the 20th Arrondissement in Paris'). But this is true only of the administrative divisions of modern society. For the historical collectivities of the past, we observe that unlike this, the *name* was not restricted to *denoting* them but at the same time *connoted* them as well – and this connotation refers to a signified that is not and cannot be either real or rational, but imaginary (regardless of the specific content or the particular nature of this imaginary).

However, at the same time or beyond the name, in totems, in the gods of the city, in the spatial and temporal extension of the person of the King, the institution is constituted, grows heavier and materializes, that *posits* the collectivity as existing, as a substance defined and enduring beyond its perishable molecules, and that replies to the question of its being and its identity by referring them to the symbols that unite it to *another* 'reality'.

The nation (and in this connection, one would have better liked a Marxist other than Stalin to explain, over and above the accidents of its historical constitution, its *real functions* since the triumph of industrial capitalism) plays today this role, fills this function of identification by means of the threefold imaginary reference to a 'common history' – threefold, because this history is sheer past, because it is not really common, and, finally, because what is known of it and what serves as the basis for this collectivizing identification in people's consciousnesses is largely mythical. This imaginary characteristic of the nation nonetheless proves more solid than any other reality, as two world wars and the survival of nationalism have shown. Today's 'Marxists', who believe they have done away with all of this by simply saying 'nationalism is a mystification' are obviously mystifying themselves. That nationalism is a mystification – this is certain. That a mystification has effects so massively and terribly real, that it proves itelf to be much stronger than any 'real' forces (including even the instinct of self-preservation) which 'should have' pushed the proletariat to fraternization long ago, this is the problem. To say: 'The proof that nationalism was a simple mystification, *and hence something unreal*, lies in the fact that it will be dissolved on the day of world revolution', is not only to sell the bearskin before we catch the bear, it is to say: 'You who have lived from 1900 to 1965 and to who knows when, and you, the millions who died in the two wars, and all the others who suffered in them and who profess your solidarity with the dead – all of you, you are *in*-existent, you have always been in-existent with respect to true history; all you have lived was your hallucination, the shadows of a dream, this was not history. True history was the invisible potentiality that *will be*, and that, behind your back, was preparing the end of your illusions.' And this discourse is incoherent because it denies the reality of the history in which it participates (a discourse is certainly not a form of the movement of the productive forces) and because it calls upon unreal men using unreal means to bring about a real revolution.

In the same way, every society defines and develops an image of the natural world, of the universe in which it lives, attempting in every instance to make of it a signifying whole, in which a place has to be made not only for the natural objects and beings important for the life of the collectivity, but also for the collectivity itself, establishing, finally, a certain 'world-order'. This image, this more or less structured vision of the whole of available human experience, makes use in each case of the rational lines of what is given, but arranges them according to and subordinates them to significations which themselves do not belong to the rational order (nor, moreover, to a positive irrational order) but to the imaginary. This is just as self-evident in the beliefs of archaic societies[54] as in the religious conceptions of historical societies; and even the extreme 'rationalism' of modern societies does not completely escape this perspective.

World-image and self-image are obviously always related.[55] Their unity, however, is in its turn borne by the definition each society gives of its needs, as this is inscribed in its activity, its actual social doing. The self-image a society gives itself includes as an essential moment the choice of objects and acts, etc., embodying that which, for it, has meaning and value. Society defines itself as something whose existence (a 'valued' existence, an existence 'worth living') can be endangered by the absence or scarcity of these things and, correlatively, as the activity aiming at making these things exist in sufficient quantity and in an adequate fashion (these things can, in certain cases, be wholly immaterial, like 'saintliness').

We have always known (at least since Herodotus) that need, whether it be nutritional, sexual or other, becomes a social need only in relation to a cultural development. But most often people stubbornly refuse to draw the consequences that follow from this fact, which, as we have already stated, refutes any functionalist interpretation of history as a 'final interpretation' (since, far from being final, it remains suspended in the air because of its inability to reply to the question: what is it that defines the needs of a society?). It is also clear that no 'rationalist' interpretation is sufficient to account for this cultural development. We know of no society in which food, dress and dwellings obey strictly 'utilitarian' or 'rational' considerations. We know of no culture in which there are not 'inferior' foods, and we would be surprised if any had ever existed (outside of 'catastrophic' or marginal cases, like the Australian aborigines described in *Captain Grant's Children*).[56]

How does this elaboration take place? This is a vast problem, and any 'simple' answer that would fail to include the complex interaction of a great number of factors (natural environment, technical possibilities, the 'historical' state, the play of symbolism, etc.) would be despairingly naive. It is easy to see, however, that what *constitutes* human need (as distinct from animal need) lies in investing the object with a value that exceeds, for example, its simple inscription in the 'instinctual' opposition, nutritive–non-nutritive (which 'holds' for animals as well) and which establishes within the nutritive the distinction between the edible and the non-edible, which creates *food* in the cultural sense and arranges foods within a hierarchy, classifying them into 'better foods' and foods that are 'not as good' (in the sense of cultural value not in that of subjective tastes). This cultural sampling among available foods and the corresponding hierarchization, structuring, etc. are leaning on natural givens, but they do not stem from them. It is *social* need that creates scarcity as social scarcity, and not the opposite.[57] It is neither the availability of snails and frogs nor their scarcity that makes them for contemporary, nearby and related cultures, in one instance a gourmet's delight and in the other a sure cause of vomiting. One has only to draw up the catalogue of everything that humans can eat, and actually have eaten (not feeling any the worse for it) in different periods and in different societies, to see that what is edible for humans far exceeds what each culture has taken as its food, and that what has determined this choice has not been simply natural availability and technical possibilities. This is even more clearly apparent when one examines needs other than food. This choice is carried by a system of imaginary significations that value or devalue, structure and hierarchize an intersecting ensemble of objects and corresponding lacks; and it is here that one can read, more easily than anywhere else, what is just as uncertain as it is incontestable – the *orientation* of a society.

Along with this ensemble of objects, constituted correlatively with needs and of the same nature, a structure or an articulation of society is also defined, as is seen in totemism ('true' or 'so-called'), where the function of a particular clan, for example, is to 'bring into being' for the others its eponymous type. In this 'stage', or better, variety, the social articulation is homologous with the distinction between objects, sometimes the forces of nature, that a particular society has posited as relevant. When objects are posited as secondary with respect to the abstract moments of the social activities that produce them – which doubtless presupposes an advanced evolution of these activities as *technique*, a growth in the size of the communtiy, etc. – these activities themselves provide the foundation for an articulation of the society, no longer into clans but now into castes.

The appearance of the antagonistic division of society into *classes*, in the Marxist sense of the term, is, to be sure, the major fact behind the birth and evolution of historical societies. Yet, we have to acknowledge that it continues to be shrouded in deep mystery.

The Marxists who believe that Marxism accounts for the birth, the function and the *raison d'être* of classes are at a level of understanding on a par with Christians who believe that the Bible accounts for the creation and the *raison d'être* of the world. The alleged Marxist 'explanation' of classes is, in fact, reduced to two schemata, each of which is unsatisfactory and which, when taken together, are heterogeneous. The first[58] consists in positing at the origin of evolution a state of almost absolute scarcity, where, incapable of producing any sort of surplus, society cannot maintain an exploiting group (the productivity per person and per year is barely equal to the biological minimum, so that no one can be exploited without sooner or later dying of starvation). At the end of the evolution there is, as we know, a state of absolute abundance where exploitation would have no reason to exist, for each person's needs could be completely satisfied. Between the two lies known history, the phase of relative scarcity, where the productivity of labour is sufficiently high to allow the constitution of a surplus, which serves (only in part!) to maintain the exploiting class.

This reasoning collapses whichever of its parts is put to the test. Admitting that at a given moment the exploiting classes did become possible, why did they then become *necessary*? Why was the apparent surplus not gradually and imperceptibly reabsorbed in the increasing well-being (or a less acute 'misery') of the tribe as a whole? Why did it not become an integral part of the definition of the 'minimum' for the collectivity in question.[59] Have cases in which the exploited classes were reduced to a biological minimum ever existed, except as marginal cases? Can a 'biological minimum' even be defined, and outside of meaningless conditions, have we ever encountered a human collectivity that was concerned only with its food? Was there not, during the paleolithic and the neolithic periods, a progress, on reflection nothing short of incredible, in the productivity of labour and, doubtless, also of the standard of living, without our being able to speak in this regard of 'classes' in the true sense of the term? Is there not behind all this something like the image of people waiting for the moment when the rise in production will reach the level 'permitting' exploitation, in order, then, to rush against each other, and establish themselves as victors and masters, vanquished and slaves? And does not this image itself correspond in particular to the imaginary of the capitalist nineteenth century, and how can it be reconciled with the descriptions of the Iroquois and the Germans, so full of humanity and nobility, whom Engels discusses with such lengthy complacency?

The second schema consists in connecting together, not the existence of the classes as such to a general state of the economy (to the existence of a 'surplus' that remains insufficient) but each precise form of social division to a given stage of technology. 'To the hand-mill corresponds the feudal society, to the steam-mill the capitalist society.' However, if the existence of a relation between the technology of every society and its division into classes cannot be denied without absurdity, it is something quite different to ground the latter in the former. How can we ascribe to an agricultural technique that has remained practically the same from the end of the neolithic period to our own day (in most countries) social relations that extend from hypothetical, yet probably, primitive agrarian communities to the free farmers in nineteenth-century United States, passing by way of the small independent farmers of the first Greece and the first Rome, by way of the colonate, Medieval serfdom, and so on? To say that the great hydraulic works conditioned or favoured the existence of a proto-bureaucracy in Egypt, Mesopotamia, China, etc., is one thing; to carry back to these hydraulic installations, constant through time and space, the extreme variations from one country to another and in the history of each country, the historical life and the forms of social division, is something else again. The four millennia of Egyptian history are not reducible to four thousand seasonal floodings of the Nile, nor to the different ways used to control them. How can the existence of feudal lords be reduced to the specificity of the productive techniques of the period, when these lords stand, by definition, outside of all production?

When Marxist interpretations go beyond simple schemata, when they deal with the concrete material of an historical situation, then they give up the claim, in the best of cases, to put their finger on *the* factor that has produced *this* division of society into classes, then they try to provide themselves, as a means of explanation, with the totality of the situation concerned considered as an *historical* situation, that is one that, for its explanation, refers back to what was already present. This is what Marx did felicitously, when he described certain aspects or phases of the genesis of capitalism.[60] We must recognize, however, what this means for the problem of history in general as well as for the more specific problem of the classes. There is no longer a general explanation of history but an explanation of history in terms of history, moving back little by little, attempting to take account of all of the factors, but always running up against facts, 'raw' facts, both as the emergence of a new signification that cannot be reduced to what already exists and as the predetermination of all that is given in the situation by previously existing significations and structures, that, 'in the final analysis', lead back to the raw fact of their birth, hidden in an unfathomable origin.

This is not to say that all the factors are on the same level, nor that theorizing about history is useless or of no interest. This is, rather, to stress the limits of this theorizing. For not only are we dealing in history with something that has already commenced, where what is already constituted in its facticity and in its specificity cannot be treated as a mere 'concomitant variation' that could be abstracted from, but also and especially, the historical exists in every instance only within a structuration carried by significations whose genesis escapes us as a comprehensible process, for it stems from the radical imaginary.

We can describe, explain and even 'understand' how and why the classes *perpetuate themselves* in current society. But we cannot say much about the way in which these classes are born, or rather in which they were born. For every explanation of this type takes the emerging classes in a society that is already divided into classes, and where the *signification* of 'class' was already available. Once born, the classes have shaped all subsequent historical evolution. Once we have entered into the cycle of wealth and poverty, of power and submission, once society has been established, not on the basis of differences between human categories (which have probably always existed) but on *non-symmetrical* differences, all that follows is 'explained'; but this 'once' is the whole problem.

We can see what it is in the mechanisms of present-day society that sustains the existence of classes and constantly reproduces them. The bureaucratic organization is self-catalytic, self-multiplying, and the way it shapes the whole of social life can be seen. But where does it come from? In Western societies, it is the result of sprawling growth of the classic capitalist enterprise (Marx's 'great industry') which refers, in its turn, to manufacturing, etc. and, ultimately, to bourgeois craftsmen on the one hand and to 'primitive accumulation' on the other. We are positively sure that it was in these regions of Western Europe, beginning in the eleventh century, that, first, the bourgeoisie was born (and, as a class, born truly *ex nihilo*), and, then, capitalism. The birth of the bourgeoisie, however, is the birth of a class only because it emerges in a society that is already divided into classes (here, as is apparent, we are using the word in its most general sense, making no distinction between feudal 'estates', economic 'classes', and so on), in a milieu in which the nucleic acids carrying *this* information, the significations of 'class', are everywhere present. They are present in private property which was developing here over thousands of years, in the hierarchical structure of feudal society, and so forth. It is not in the specific features of the burgeoning bourgeoisie (an 'egalitarian' organization of craftsmen is perfectly conceivable) but in the general structure of feudal society that the necessity for this new level to posit itself as a particular category in opposition to the rest of society is inscribed: the bourgeoisie is born into a world which can conceive of and carry out its internal distinctions only as an ordering into 'classes'. Is it enough to go back as far as the fall of the Roman Empire? Certainly not. This did not create a *tabula rasa*, and the Germans, whatever their previous social organization may have been, were without the shadow of a doubt 'contaminated' by the social structures they encountered.

We must continue to move back further until we plunge into the darkness that covers the passage from the neolithic to proto-history. In what was probably a period of no more than 2–3,000 years, in the Near and Middle East in any case, we find the transition from the most advanced neolithic villages with no apparent trace of social division to the first Sumerian cities, where, from the beginning of the fourth millennium before Jesus Christ, the basic elements of every well organized society exist all together and in a practically completed form: priests, slaves, police, prostitutes. The die is already cast, and we do not know *how* or *why* this occurred.

Will we know one day? Will more extensive excavations enable us to understand the mystery of the birth of the classes? We confess we do not see how archeological finds will enable us to *understand* that, starting at a certain 'moment', people saw one another and acted with respect to one another not as allies to help one another, rivals to surpass, enemies to exterminate or even to eat, but as *objects to possess*. Since the content of this vision and this action is perfectly arbitrary, we cannot see in what its explanation or its understand might consist. How could we constitute what is the *constituting* element of historical societies? How are we to understand this originary positing, which is the condition for understanding the subsequent development? We must be given, we must already possess this initial signification; one individual can be a 'quasi-object' for another, a quasi-object not in a relation between two people, in a private relationship, but in the anonymity of society (in the slave market, in the industrial cities and the factories over a long period of the history of capitalism) to be able to understand history for the past 6,000 years. We are able to understand this state of 'quasi-object' today because this signification is available to us, because we are born within *this* history. But it would be illusory to think that we could *produce* it and to reproduce its emergence in our understanding. Men gave rise to the possibility of slavery: this was a *creation* of history (Engels said of this, uncynically, that it was the condition for great progress). More exactly, one fraction of humanity gave rise to this possibility *against* the others who, without ceasing to combat it in a thousand ways, also participated in it in a thousand ways. The *institution* of slavery marks the emergence of a new imaginary signification, a new way for society to live, to see itself and to conduct itself as articulated in an antagonistic and unsymmetrical manner, a signification that is immediately symbolized and sanctioned by rules.[61]

This signification is closely connected to the other major imaginary significations of society, in particular the definition of its needs and its image of the world. We shall not examine here the problem that this relation poses.

The impossibility of understanding the origin of the classes does not, however, leave us unarmed before the problem of the existence of the classes as a current and practical problem – any more than in psychoanalysis the impossibility of reaching an 'origin' prevents us from understanding in the *actual* (both in the sense of current and in that of active, in act) what is in question; it does not keep us from relativizing, setting loose and desacralizing the significations constituting the subject as a sick subject. There comes a time when the subject, not because he has discovered the primitive scene or detected penis envy in his grandmother, but through his struggle in his actual life and as a result of repetition, unearths the central signifier of his neurosis and finally looks at it in its contingency, its poverty and its *insignificance*. In the same way, for people living today, the question is not to understand how the transition from the neolithic clans to the markedly divided cities of Akkad was made. It is to understand – and this obviously means, here more than anywhere else, to act – the contingency, the poverty and the insignificance of this 'signifier' of historical societies, the division into masters and slaves, into dominators and dominated.

The questioning of this signification represented by the division of society into classes, the decanting of this imaginary, in fact begins very early in history, since almost at the same time as the classes appear class *struggle* also appears and, with it, the primordial phenomenon that opens a new phase in the existence of societies: challenges, the opposition within society itself. What, up to then, was the immediate reabsorption of the collectivity in its institutions, the simple submission of humans to their imaginary creations, a unity that was only marginally disturbed by deviance or infractions, now becomes a torn and con-flictual totality, and society challenges itself. What is internal to society becomes external to it, and this, in so far as it signifies the self-relativization of society, placing at a distance and criticizing (in facts and in actions) what is established, marks the initial emergence of autonomy, the first crack in the imaginary [the instituted imaginary].

It is certain that this struggle begins, continues for a long time, and almost always slips back into ambiguity. And how could this be otherwise? The oppressed, who struggle against the division of society into classes, struggle mainly against their own oppression; in a thousand ways they continue to depend on the imaginary that they combat in one of its forms, and often what they aim at is merely a permutation of roles in the same scenario. But very early too the oppressed class responds by denying as a whole the social imaginary that is oppressing it and by opposing to it the reality of an essential equality among individuals, even if it clothes this assertion in mythical robes:

Wenn Adam grub und Eva spann
Wo war denn da der Edelmann?
(When Adam toiled and Eve spun
Who was then the gentleman?)

sang the German peasants in the sixteenth century, as they burned the nobles' castles.

This questioning of the social imaginary has taken a new dimension since the birth of the modern proletariat. We shall return to this at length.

vii   THE IMAGINARY IN THE MODERN WORLD

The modern world presents itself, on the surface, as that which has pushed, and tends to push, rationalization to its limit, and because of this, it allows itself to despise – or to consider with respectful curiosity – the bizarre customs, inventions and imaginary representations of previous societies. Paradoxically, however, despite or rather due to this extreme 'rationalization', the life of the modern world is just as dependent on the imaginary as any archaic or historical culture.

What is presented as the rationality of modern society is simply a matter of *form*, externally necessary connections, the perpetual dominance of the syllogism. But in the syllogisms of modern life the premises borrow their content from the imaginary; and the prevalence of the syllogism as such, the obsession with 'rationality' unconnected with anything else constitutes a second-order imaginary. Modern pseudo-rationality is one of the historical forms of the imaginary; it is arbitrary in its ultimate ends to the extent that these ends themselves stem from no reason, and it is arbitrary when it posits itself as an end, intending nothing but a formal and empty 'rationalization'. In this aspect of its existence, the modern world is in the throes of a systematic delirium; the most directly perceptible and most imminently threatening form of this delirium lies in the autonomization of uncontrolled technical development, which is 'in the service' of no definite end.

The economy in the broadest sense (from production to consumption) passes for the most perfect expression of the rationality of capitalism and of modern societies. But it is the economy that exhibits most strikingly the domination of the imaginary at every level – precisely because it claims to be entirely and exhaustively rational.

This is visibly so with respect to the definition of the *needs* the economy is supposed to serve. More than in any other society, the 'arbitrary', non-natural, non-functional character of the social definition of needs is apparent in modern society, precisely because of its productive development, of its wealth that allows it to go beyond the satisfaction of 'basic needs' (this often has, as its no less significant counterpart, the result that the satisfaction of these basic needs is sacrificed to the satisfaction of 'gratuitous' needs). More than any other society, too, modern society permits us to see the historical manufacturing of needs that are produced every day before our own eyes. The description of this state of affairs was done many years ago; these analyses should be considerably sharpened, but it is not our intention to return to them here. Let us recall simply the gradually increasing place accorded to the purchase of objects corresponding to 'artificial' needs in the expenditures of consumers, or the replacement, serving no 'functional' purpose, of objects that are still useful,[62] simply because they are no longer fashionable or do not include this or that 'improvement', often only an illusory one.

It is useless to present this situation exclusively as a 'replacement response', as the offer of substitutes for other needs, 'real' needs, that present society does not satisfy. For, by admitting that these needs exist and that they can be defined, it is all the more striking that their reality can be totally hidden behind a 'pseudo-reality' (a pseudo-reality co-extensive, we recall, with the essential features of modern industry). It is equally useless to wish to eliminate the problem by restricting it to the aspect of the manipulation of society by the dominant strata and by referring to the 'functional' side of this continuous creation of new needs, as the condition for the expansion (that is to say, the survival) of modern industry. For not only are the dominant strata themselves dominated by this imaginary, which they do not freely create; not only are its effects manifested just where there is no necessity for the system to manufacture a demand ensuring its expansion (for example, in the industrialized countries of the East, where the invasion of modern consumption occurs long before there is any saturation of the markets). What is especially noticeable in this example is that this functional element is conditioned on the imaginary: the modern capitalist economy can exist only to the extent that it answers the needs it manufactures itself.

The domination of the imaginary is just as clear as regards the place of individuals at all the levels of the productive and economic structure. This alleged rational organization displays – as we know and has long been asserted, although no one took it seriously except unserious people like poets and novelists – all the characteristics of a systematic delirium. In the case of the worker, the employee or even the 'executive', replacing the person by an ensemble of partial features selected arbitrarily in terms of an arbitrary system of ends and in reference to a pseudo-conceptualization that is just as arbitrary, and treating him in practice in precisely this way, conveys a prevalence of the imaginary, which, regardless of its 'efficacy' in the system, differs in no respect from that of the most 'foreign' archaic society. To treat a person as a thing or as a purely mechanical system is not less but *more* imaginary than claiming to see him as an owl; it represents an even greater plunge into the imaginary. For not only is the *real* kinship between a man and an owl incomparably greater than it is with a machine, but also no primitive society ever applied the consequences of its assimilations of people with things as radically as modern industry does with its metaphor of the human automaton. Archaic societies always seem to preserve a certain duplicity in their assimilations, but modern society takes them, in its practice, strictly literally in the most naive fashion. There is no essential difference with respect to the type of mental operations or even to the deep psychic attitudes, between a Taylorian engineer or an industrial psychologist, on the one hand, who isolates gestures, measures coefficients, decomposes the person into wholly invented 'factors' and then recasts the person as a secondary object, and a fetishist who experiences pleasure at the sight of a high-heeled shoe or asks a woman to imitate a lamppost. In both cases we see at work that particular form of the imaginary, the subject's identification with an object. The difference is that the fetishist lives in a private world and his phantasy has no effects beyond the partner who wishes to participate in it, but the capitalist fetishism of the 'effective gesture', or of the individual defined by tests, determines the real life of the social world.[63]

We recalled above the sketch Marx gave of the role of the imaginary in the capitalist economy, speaking of the 'fetishistic character of merchandise'. This sketch should be expanded by an analysis of the imaginary in the institutional structure that, increasingly, alongside of and beyond the 'market', is assuming the central role in modern society: the bureaucratic organization. The bureaucratic universe is permeated through and through with the imaginary. Ordinarily, we pay no attention to it – or only to joke about it – because we see only the excesses in it, an abuse of the routine or 'errors', in short, exclusively negative determinations. But there is indeed a system of 'positive' imaginary significations that articulate the bureaucratic universe, a system that can be reconstructed on the basis of fragments and indications offered by instructions about the organizations of production and of labour, the very model of this organization, the objectives it sets for itself, the typical behaviour of the bureaucracy, etc. This system, has, moreover, evolved through time. The essential features of bureaucracies in the past, like the reference to 'precedent', the will to abolish novelty as such, and to unify the flow of time, have been replaced by the systematic anticipation of the future; the phantasy of the organization as a well-oiled machine gives way to the phantasy of the organization as a self-reforming, self-expanding machine. Likewise, the vision of man in the bureaucratic universe tends to evolve: there is, in the 'advanced' sectors of the bureaucratic organization, a shift from the image of the automaton, the partial machine, to the image of the 'personality well integrated into the group', paralleling the shift noted by American sociologists (notably Reisman and Whyte) from an emphasis on 'productivity' to an emphasis on being 'well-adjusted'. The 'analytical' and reifying pseudo-rationality tends to give way to a 'totalizing' and 'socializing' pseudo-rationality that is no less imaginary. Although it acts as an important indicator of the cracks in the bureaucratic system, and ultimately of its crisis, this evolution does not alter its central significations. People, mere nodal points in the network of messages, exist and have worth only in relation to the rank and the position they occupy in the hierarchical scale. The essential characteristic of the world lies in the fact that it can be reduced to a system of formal rules, including those that enable one to 'calculate' the future. Reality exists only to the extent that it is recorded; ultimately, truth is nothing and the document alone is true. And here we find what seems to us to be the *specific* feature, and the most profound one, belonging to the modern imaginary, full of consequences but also full of promises. This imaginary has no *flesh of its own*, it borrows its substance from something else, it is the investment of phantasy, the ascription of value, the autonomization of elements that in themselves do not stem from the imaginary: the limited rationality of the understanding and the symbolical. The bureaucratic world makes rationality autonomous in one of its partial moments, that of the understanding, which is concerned only with whether or not the partial connections are correct and is unaware of questions concerning the foundation, the totality, ends, and the relation between reason and man, reason and the world (this is why we called its 'rationality' a pseudo-rationality); and it lives, essentially, in a universe of symbols that, most of the time, neither represent the real nor are necessary to conceive of it or manipulate it. Thus, it materializes the extreme autonomization of pure symbolism.

This autonomization, the strength of its grip on social reality to the point of dislocating it, and the degree of alienation the dominant stratum itself is in return subject to are visible in their extreme forms in the bureaucratic economies of Eastern Europe, especially before 1956, when the Polish economists had to invent the term 'Moon economy' to describe the situation in their country. Although it usually does not reach these limits, the Western economy, nevertheless, displays the same essential features.

This example should not confuse us about what we mean by imaginary. When the bureaucracy persists in wanting to build a subway in a city – Budapest – where this is physically impossible; or when it falsely declares to the population that the production plan has been realized while continuing to act, to take decisions and to make commitments, resulting in the sheer loss of real resources, as if it actually had been, then the two senses of the term 'imaginary', the most common and superficial and the most profound sense, come together, and there is nothing we can do about it. But what matters in particular is obviously the second sense, the one that can be seen at work when a modern economy functions effectively and really, in accordance with its own criteria, when it is not stifled by the second-order outgrowths of its own symbolism. For it is here that the pseudo-rational character of its 'rationality' clearly stands out: everything is actually subordinated to effectiveness – but effective for whom, in view of what, and in order to do what? Economic growth is realized; but this is the growth of what, for whom, at what cost, and to arrive at what? A partial *moment* of the economic system (not even the quantitative moment, but one part of the quantitative moment concerning *certain* goods and services) is set up as the sovereign moment of the economy; and, represented by this partial moment, the economy, itself a moment of social life, is set up as the sovereign instance of society.

It is precisely because the modern social imaginary has no *flesh of its own*, it is because it borrows its substance from the rational, from one moment of the rational which it thus transforms into a pseudo-rational, that it is doomed to crisis and to erosion and that modern society contains within it the 'objective' possibility of a transformation of what up to now has been the role of the imaginary in history. But before going into this problem, we must consider more closely the relation between the imaginary and the rational.

viii   THE IMAGINARY AND THE RATIONAL

It is impossible to understand what human history has been or what it is now outside of the category of the imaginary. No other category permits us to reflect on these questions: What is it that posits the *finality* without which the functionality of social institutions and processes would remain indeterminate? What is it that, amidst the infinity of possible symbolic structures, specifies *one* symbolic system, establishes the prevalent canonical relations, orients in *one* of the innumerable possible directions all the metaphors and metonymies that are abstractly conceivable? We cannot understand a society outside of a unifying factor that provides a signified content and weaves it with the symbolic structures. This factor is not simple 'reality'; every society has constituted *its* reality (we are not bothering to specify here that this constitution is never completely arbitrary). Nor is it the 'rational', as the most summary inspection of history suffices to show, for if it were, history would not have been genuinely history but the instantaneous access to a rational order, or, at most, a pure progress in rationality. Although history indisputably *contains* progress in rationality – we shall return to this – it cannot be *reduced* to this. A *meaning* appears here from the very start, one that is not a meaning of the *real* (referring to what is perceived), one that is neither strictly rational nor positively *ir*rational, neither true nor false and yet that does belong to the order of *signification* and that is the imaginary creation proper to history, that in and through which history constitutes itself to begin with.

We do not need, therefore, to 'explain' how and why the imaginary, the imaginary social significations and the institutions that incarnate them, become autonomous. How could they not become autonomous, since they are what was already present 'at the start', what, in a certain sense, is always present 'at the start'? In truth, the very expression 'become autonomous' is visibly inadequate in this respect; we are not dealing with an element that is first subordinate and then 'separates itself off' and becomes autonomous in a second stage (whether real or logical) but *with the element that constitutes history as such*. If there is something that poses a problem, it is instead the emergence of the rational in history and, in particular, its 'separation', its constitution as a relatively autonomous moment.

If this is the case, then an immense problem arises already on the level of the distinction between concepts. How are we to distinguish between the imaginary significations and the rational significations in history? We defined above the rational–symbolic as that which represents the real or else is indispensible for conceiving of it or acting on it. But represents it *for whom*? Conceives of it *how*? Acts on it in what context? *What* reality is in question? What is the definition of the real implied here? Is it not clear that we are running the risk of introducing surreptitiously *one* rationality (our own) and making it play the role of rationality *as such*?

When, in considering a culture of another time or another place, we call a particular element of its world view, or this view itself, imaginary, what is our reference point? When we find ourselves not before a 'transformation' of the earth into a divinity, but before an originary identity, in a given culture, of the Earth-Mother goddess, an identity that for this culture is inextricably bound up with its general manner of seeing, thinking of, acting on and experiencing the world, is it not impossible simply to call this identity 'imaginary' and to stop at that? If the rational–symbolic is what represents reality, or what is indispensable for thinking of it or acting upon it, is it not obvious that this role is also held, in all societies, by imaginary significations? Does not what is 'real' for every society include as inseparable from it this imaginary component, both with respect to nature and, especially, with respect to the human world? What is 'real' in nature cannot be grasped outside of a categorial framework, outside of organizing principles of sensible data, and these are never – not even in our society – simply equivalent, displaying neither excess nor defect, to the table of categories as worked out by logicians (which, moreover, is itself continually reworked). And as to what is 'real' in the human world, it is not only as a possible object of knowledge but immanently, in its being in-itself and for-itself, that it is categorized by the social structuring and the imaginary this signifies. Relations between individuals and groups, behaviour, motivations are not simply *incomprehensible* for us, they are *impossible in themselves* outside of this imaginary. A 'primitive' who would want to act not taking into account distinctions between clans, a Hindu of the past who would decide to ignore the existence of the castes, would most likely be mad – or would soon become so.

In speaking of the imaginary, we must therefore be careful not to impute to the society considered a capacity for absolute rationality, which, present from the outset, would then have been shoved aside or covered over by the imaginary. When an individual, growing up in our culture, running up against a reality structured in a precise manner, subject to constant social control, 'decides' or 'chooses' to see in each person he encounters a potential aggressor and develops a persecution delirium, we can label his perception of others not only 'objectively' or socially imaginary – in reference to established norms – but subjectively imaginary, in the sense that the person 'could have' constructed a correct view of the world. The strong influence of the imaginary function in the development of this individual requires a separate explanation, inasmuch as other kinds of development were possible and actually took place in the case of the vast majority of people. In a certain way we *impute* madness to our madmen, not only in the sense that it is theirs, but that they *could have* done otherwise. But who could say of the Greeks that they were well aware, or should have been, that the gods did not exist and that their mythical universe is a 'deviation' with respect to a serious view of the world, a deviation that has to be explained as such? This serious view – or what is alleged to be so – is quite simply our own view.

These remarks are not inspired by an agnostic or relativist attitude. We know that the gods do not exist, that people cannot 'be' crows, and we cannot forget this on purpose when we study a society of the past or of another geographical area. But we encounter here, at a deeper and more difficult level, the same paradox, the same antinomy of the retroactive application of categories, of 'backwards projection' of our own manner of apprehending the world, as we mentioned above in connection with Marxism, an antinomy we have already said to be constitutive of historical knowledge. We observed at that time that the Marxist schema of the 'determination' of social life and of its various spheres – of power, for example – cannot be maintained for most precapitalist societies because this schema presupposes an autonomization of these spheres that exists fully only in capitalist society. In a case as close to us in time and in space as feudal society, for example (and in the present bureaucratic societies of Eastern Europe) power relations and economic relations are so structured that the idea of the 'determination' of the first by the second is meaningless. In a much more radical way, the attempt to distinguish clearly between the functional, the imaginary, the symbolic and the rational in order to articulate their relations, in the case of societies other than those of the West in the past two centuries (and a few moments in the history of Greece and Rome) runs up against the impossibility of giving any rigorous content to this distinction, one that is truly meaningful for these societies and one that has a genuine hold on them. If divine powers or 'totemic' classifications are, for an ancient or archaic society, categorial principles for organizing the natural and social world, as they undeniably are, what does it mean, from an operative point of view (that is to say, for the understanding and the 'explanation' of these societies) to say that these principles belong to the imaginary to the extent that they are opposed to the rational? It is thanks to *this* imaginary that the world of the Greeks or the Aranda is not chaos but an ordered plurality, that diversity is organized without being crushed; due to it, value and non-value emerge, the line of demarcation between 'true' and 'false', between what is permitted and what is prohibited is drawn – without which no society could exist even one second.[64] This imaginary does not merely hold the function of the rational, it is already a form of the latter and contains it in an initial and infinitely fertile indistinction; in it, one can start to distinguish the elements presupposed by our own rationality.[65]

So it would be not incorrect but, properly speaking, meaningless to want to apprehend the entire history of humanity in terms of the pair of categories, imaginary–rational, which has its complete sense only for us. And yet – this is the paradox – we cannot avoid doing this. We are no more able, when we speak of the feudal domain, to pretend to forget the concept of economy, or to avoid categorizing as economic, phenomena that were not so for people of the period, than we can claim to be unaware of the distinction between the rational and the imaginary in speaking of a society in which it has no meaning or not the same content as for us.[66] Our considerations on history must necessarily assume this antinomy. The historian or the ethnologist is obliged to try to understand the universe of the Babylonians or the Bororos, both their natural and their social world, as they lived it and, in attempting to explain it, to refrain from introducing into it determinations that did not exist for this culture (consciously or unconsciously). But one cannot stop here. The ethnologist who has so thoroughly assimilated the Bororos' view of the world that he or she can no longer see the world any other way, is no longer an ethnologist but a Bororo – and the Bororos are not ethnologists. The ethnologist's *raison d'être* is not to be assimilated to the Bororos but to explain to the Parisians, the Londoners and the New Yorkers in 1965 the other humanity represented by the Bororos. And thus he can do so only through *language*, in the deepest sense of the term, through the categorial system of the Parisians, the Londoners and so forth. Now these languages are not 'equivalent codes' – precisely because in their structuring imaginary significations play a central role.[67]

This is why the Western project of constituting a total history, the exhaustive understanding and explanation of societies of other times and other places is necessarily rooted in failure, if it is taken as a speculative project. The Western manner of conceiving of history is based on the idea that what was once a meaning for-itself, a meaning of their society for the Assyrians can become without remainder and without deficit, a meaning for us. But this is obviously impossible, and thereby the *speculative* project of total history becomes impossible. History is always history as it is for us – this does not mean that we can truncate it however we may wish or naively submit it to our projections, since what interests us in history is precisely our authentic *otherness*, other human possibilities in their absolute singularity. As absolute, however, this singularity necessarily suppresses itself when we attempt to grasp it, just as in microphysics, when the position of a particle is established, it 'disappears' as a definite momentum.

And yet, what appears to speculative reason as an insurmountable antinomy undergoes a change of sense when we bring the consideration of history back into *our* project of the theoretical elucidation of the world, and in particular of the human world, when we see in it a part of our effort to interpret the world *in order to* change it – not by subordinating truth to the party line but by explicitly establishing the articulated unity between elucidation and action, between theory and practice, in order to give our life its full reality as autonomous activity, that is as lucid, creative activity. For then the ultimate point of junction of these two projects – understanding and changing – can in every instance be found only in the living present of history which would not be an historical present if it did not supersede itself in the direction of a future that *is to be made by us*. The fact that we can understand the other times and other places of humanity only in terms of our own categories – a fact which, in turn, bounces back upon these categories, relativizes them, and helps us to surmount our enslavement to our own forms of the imaginary and even of rationality – does not simply translate the conditions for all historical knowledge and its rooting, but manifests that any elucidation we may attempt is finally an *interested* one, it is *for us* in the strong sense, for we are not here to say what is but to make be what is not (saying what is belongs to this as one of its moments).

Our project of elucidating past forms of humanity's existence takes on its full sense only as a moment of the project of elucidating our existence, which, in its turn, is inseparable from our current *doing*. We are already, whatever we may do, involved in changing this existence, with respect to which our sole choice is between suffering and acting, between confusion and lucidity. Some may deplore the fact that this unavoidably leads us to reinterpret and recreate the past, denouncing in this a 'spiritual cannibalism, worse than the other kind'. We can do no more about this than they can, any more than we can prevent our food from containing, in constantly increasing proportion, the elements that made up the bodies of our ancestors for 30,000 generations.

II
The Social Imaginary and the Institution

4

The Social–Historical

Our aim in this chapter is to elucidate the question of society and that of history, questions that can be understood only when they are taken as one and the same: the question of the social–historical. Inherited ways of thinking can make only fragmentary contributions to this elucidation. Perhaps this contribution is mostly negative, marking out the limits of a mode of thought and exposing its impossibilities.

This assertion may seem surprising, considering the quantity and the quality of what, at least since Plato and especially over the past centuries, has been provided by reflection in this domain. However, the essential part of this reflection – except for germinal asides, lightning strokes quickly dying out, moments of the intractable presence of the aporia – has been spent not in opening and broadening the question, but in covering it over as soon as it was uncovered, in reducing it as soon as it emerged. The same mechanism and the same motivations are to be found in this covering over and this reduction as in the covering over and the reduction of the question of the imagination and the imaginary – and for the same profound reasons.

On the one hand, the inherited way of thinking has never been able to separate out the true object of this question and to consider it for itself. This object has almost always been split into a society, related to something other than itself and, generally, to a norm, end, or *telos* grounded in something else, and a history, considered as something that happens to this society, as a disturbance in relation to a given norm or as an organic or dialectical development towards this norm, end, or *telos*. In this way, the object in question, the being proper to the social–historical, is constantly shifted towards something other than itself and absorbed in it. The most profound views, those that are truest with respect to the social–historical, those that have taught us the most and without which we would still be babbling incoherently, these are still implicitly governed by an elsewhere – and this also belongs to the essence and the history of thought; it is in the direction of this elsewhere that these views attempt to orient what they say about the social–historical. What rules *a tergo* the reflection inherited concerning society and history, that in spite of which it discovers what it does manage to discover, is, for example, the place of society and of history in the divine economy of creation or in the infinite life of reason; or the possibility they have of encouraging or hampering the individual's fulfilment as an ethical subject; or their standing as the final avatar of natural beings; or the relation of social matter and its corruption or historical instability (its being indefinite – undetermined, the *apeiron*, determined by its privation of determinability; its character of always becoming, *aei gignomenon*) to the form and the norm of the determined and stable political city, implying the subordination of the study of the first to the requirements of the latter, hence to the right form of the right city, even if one must then deny its very possibility.[1]

In this way, too, representation, imagination and imaginary have never been seen for themselves but always in relation to something else – to sensation, intellection, perception or reality – submitted to the normativity incorporated in the inherited ontology, brought within the viewpoint of true and false, instrumentalized within a function, means judged according to their possible contribution to the accomplishment of the end that is truth or access to true being, the being of being (*ontos on*).

In this way, finally, there has not been the slightest concern with knowing what *doing* means, what the being of doing is and what it is that doing brings into being, so obsessed have people been with these questions alone: what is it to do good or to do evil? Doing has not been thought because no one has attempted to think of anything other than two particular moments of doing, the ethical moment and the technical moment. And even these moments have not been truly thought, since that of which they are the moments was never thought and since their very substance had been eliminated from the outset when doing as making-be was ignored, and when it was subordinated to its partial determinations, which are the products of doing but were presented as absolutes, reigning from an elsewhere, good and evil (of which the efficient and the inefficient are derivatives).

Moreover, the reflection on history and society has always been situated on the terrain and within the boundaries of inherited logic and ontology – and how could it have been otherwise? Society and history cannot be the objects of reflection if they are not. But what are they, how are they, in what sense are they? The classical rule enjoins: do not multiply beings unnecessarily. At a deeper level lies another rule: do not multiply the meanings of being; being must have a single meaning.[2] This meaning, determined from start to finish as determinacy – *peras* in the Greeks, *Bestimmtheit* in Hegel – already in itself excluded the possibility of recognizing a type of being that essentially escapes determinacy, like the social–historical or the imaginary. Consequently, whether or not it recognized it, whether or not it intended it, and even in the instances when it may have explicitly intended the opposite, inherited thought has necessarily been led to reduce the social–historical to the elementary types of being that it knew or thought it knew – having constructed them and hence determined them – from somewhere else, making the social–historical a variant, a combination or a synthesis of the corresponding beings: thing, subject, idea or concept. Consequently also, society and history found themselves subordinated to the logical operations and functions that were already established and were considered to be conceivable by means of the categories used in fact to grasp a few entities, themselves particular but posited by philosophy as universal.

These are but two aspects of the same movement, two indissociable effects of imposing the inherited logic–ontology on the social–historical. If the social–historical is conceivable by means of the categories that are valid for other beings, then it cannot help but be homogeneous with them; its mode of being poses no particular question, and it allows itself to be absorbed within total being. Reciprocally, if being means being determined, then society and history exist only to the extent that their place within the total order of being (as the result of causes, as means to an end, or as a moment in a process), their internal order, and the necessary relation between the two are determined; these orders, relations and necessities take the form of categories, that is to say, of determinations of all that can be inasmuch as it can be (thought). The best that can be obtained this way is the Hegelian–Marxist view of society and of history: the sum and sequence of actions (whether conscious or not) of a multiplicity of subjects, determined by necessary relations, and by means of which a system of ideas is embodied in an ensemble of things (or reflects it). Whatever in actual history appears as irreducibly in excess or in deficit in relation to this schema becomes scoria, illusion, contingence, chance – in short, unintelligible; this is not scandalous in itself, but it should be so for a philosophy for which the unintelligible is only another name for the impossible.

However, if we decide to consider the social–historical for itself; if we understand that it is to be questioned and reflected upon on the basis of itself alone; if we refuse to eliminate the questions it poses by attributing to it from the start determinations we know or believe we know and that come from other sources – then we observe that it shatters our inherited logic and ontology. For we see that it does not fall under traditional categories – except in a nominal and empty manner – but instead it makes us recognize the narrow limits of their validity, permits us to glimpse a new and different logic and, above all, radically to alter the meaning of: being.

i   POSSIBLE TYPES OF TRADITIONAL RESPONSES

The question: what is the social–historical? joins together the two
questions that tradition and convention generally separate, that of
society and that of history.[3] A brief study of the *status* of traditional
responses will be facilitated by formulating the core of these two
questions in a more specific way.

What is society? In particular, what constitutes the unity and identity
(*ecceity*) of a society, or what holds a society together?

What is history? In particular, how and why is there temporal alteration in a society; in what way is this an alteration; does something
new emerge in history, and what does it signify?

The meaning and the unity of these questions can be further clarified
if we ask ourselves: in what way and why are there many societies and
not just one; in what way and why are there differences between
societies? If we were to reply that the differences between societies,
and their histories, are merely apparent, the question would still remain,
just as before: why then do we find this appearance, why does the
identical appear as different?[4]

The countless replies given since the start of reflection on these two
questions can be grouped under two basic types and their various
mixtures.

The first type of reply is the physicalist type, which reduces, directly
or indirectly, immediately or in the final analysis, society and history
to nature. This nature is, first of all, human biological nature; it matters
little whether this is seen to be reducible, in its turn, to a simple
physical mechanism, or whether it is held to go beyond the latter, for
example, a generic being (*Gattungswesen*) for the young Marx, a Hegelian concept[5] representing a later stage in the logical–ontological development of *phusis* characterizing the Aristotelian living thing, the aspect/
species (*eidos*) that reproduces itself without ever changing. Functionalism is the purest and most typical exemplar of this point of view:
it takes human needs as fixed and explains social organization as the
ensemble of functions intended to satisfy these needs. This explanation,
as we saw above, explains nothing at all. A host of activities in every
society fill no specific function in the functionalist sense. And, what is
more, the very question that matters, that concerning differences
between societies, is eliminated or covered over by platitudes. The
alleged explanation is left hanging in mid-air for lack of a stable point
to which it could relate the functions that social organization is supposed
to serve. This stable point can be supplied only by postulating an
identity of human needs in all societies and in all historical periods, an
identity contradicted by the most superficial look at history. One is
then forced to resort to the fiction of an inalterable core of abstract
needs, that would receive from place to place different specifications

or varying modes of satisfaction, and to platitudes or tautologies in order to account for this difference and variability. The essential fact is thereby covered over: human needs, to the extent that they are social and not simply biological, are inseparable from their objects, and both these needs and their objects are in every instance instituted by the society considered. The same is true with respect to the impostures propagated nowadays, ever since 'desire' has been the fashion; society is, in fact, reduced to desire and to its repression, without any effort to explain the difference between the objects and the forms of desire, without expressing any surprise at the strange division into desire and the desire for the repression of desire which is, according to them, supposed to characterize most societies, the possibility for this division and the reasons for its appearance.

The second type is the logicist type, which takes on different forms depending on the acceptation of the radical *log-* in this term. When the logic in question ultimately amounts (irrespective of its surface complications) to arranging a finite number of black and white pebbles in a predetermined number of boxes following a few simple rules (for example, no more than n pebbles of the same colour in the same line or column), we have the most impoverished form of logicism–structuralism. The same logical operation, repeated a certain number of times, is thereby held to account for the totality of human history and for the different forms of society; the latter would then be no more than different possible combinations of a finite number of the same discrete elements. This elementary combinatorics – which mobilizes the same intellectual faculties as those used in constructing magic squares or doing crossword puzzles – must, in every instance, unquestionably take for granted both the finite set of elements on which the operations are performed and the oppositions or differences it postulates between them. However, even in phonology – of which structuralism is but an abusive extrapolation – one cannot take as a basis the *natural* givenness of a finite set of discrete elements – here, the phonemes or distinctive features that can be uttered and perceived by man; as Plato already knew,[6] sounds that are uttered and perceived are undetermined, *apeiron*, and *peras*, determination, the simultaneous positing of phonemes and their relevant differences is an institution of language, and of each specific language. This institution and its differences – the difference between French phonology and English phonology, for example – phonology accepts as a fact and is not obliged to question. As a positive and limited form of knowledge, it can leave the question of the origin of its object dormant. How could one proceed in the same way when the question of society and of history is, essentially, a question of the nature and the origin of differences? Structuralism's naivete in this respect is disarming. It has nothing to say about the sets of elements it manipulates, about the reasons for their being-thus, or about their modifications in time. Masculine and feminine, north and south, high and low, dry and wet, seem self-evident to structuralism, simply found there by humans, stones of meaning scattered on the Earth since the origins, in a being-thus which is at once completely natural and totally meaningful, among which each society selects a few (following the results of a game of chance)[7] provided that it can choose elements only by pairs of opposites and that the choice of certain pairs leads to or excludes the choice of others. As if social organization could be reduced to a finite sequence of yes/ no, and as if, wherever a yes/no is involved, the terms it implies were themselves given from somewhere else and from all time – whereas they are, as terms and as these particular terms, the creation of the society concerned.

Or else, at the opposite end and in its richest form, the logic employed claims to stir all the figures of the material and spiritual universe. Accepting no limit, it wants to and has to bring everything into play, into relation with everything else, into complete determinacy and exhaustive reciprocal determination. It must then generate them, some on the basis of others, and all on the basis of the same first or last element, as its necessary figures or moments, necessarily unfolding in a necessary order, of which the logic itself must necessarily be a part as a reflecting on, reflecting back, repetition or apex. No matter whether this element is termed reason, as in Hegelianism, matter or nature, as in the canonical version of Marxism (matter or nature that, in principle, are reducible to rational determinations). We have already indicated in the first part of this book a few of the countless and interminable aporias to which this conception leads.

Thus, the question of the unity and identity of society and of any particular society is carried back to the assertion of a given unity and identity of an ensemble of living organisms; or of a hyper-organism containing its own needs and functions; or of a natural–logical group of elements; or of a system of rational determinations. Of society as such in all this, there remains nothing; nothing that might be the being proper to society, nothing that manifests a mode of being any different from what we already know from elsewhere. Nor does there remain much of history, of the temporal alteration produced in and through society. Faced with the question of history, physicalism naturally becomes causalism, that is the elimination of the question. For the question of history is the question of the emergence of radical otherness or of the absolutely new (even the assertion of the contrary would attest to this, for neither amoebae nor galaxies talk in order to say that everything is eternally the same). And causality is always the negation of otherness, the positing of a double identity: an identity in the repetition of the same causes producing the same effects; an ultimate identity of the cause and the effect since each necessarily belongs to the other, or both to the same.[8] It is therefore not by chance that the very element in and through which the social–historical unfolds, namely, significations, is neglected or else transformed into a mere epiphenomenon, a redundant accompaniment to what is supposed really to be happening. How, indeed, could one signification be the cause of another signification, and how could they be the effects of non-significations?

Precisely the same elimination of the question of history is brought about by the form that logicism takes, becoming in the face of history, rationalistic finalism. For, if logicism sees in significations the element of history, it is incapable of considering these significations other than as rational (this, of course, does not imply that it must posit them as conscious for the agents of history). But rational significations can and must be deduced or produced on the basis of other rational significations. Their unfolding is then no more than a spreading out, and the new is, in every instance, constructed through *identitary* operations[9] (even if they are termed dialectical) by means of what was already there; the totality of the process is only the exposing of the necessarily realized virtualities inherent in a primordial principle, present from all time and for all time. Historical time thus becomes a simple abstract medium of successive coexistence or a mere receptacle of the dialectical chains. True time, the time of radical otherness, an otherness that can neither be deduced nor produced, has to be abolished, and no reason other than contingent reason can explain why the totality of past and future history is not, in principle, deducible. The end of history annoys Hegel's commentators because it seems absurd to them to situate it in 1830; this displays insufficient knowledge of the necessities of the philosopher's thought, for which this end had already occurred before the beginning of history. For history cannot be Reason if it does not have a *raison d'être* that is its end (*telos*), that is just as necessarily fixed for it (from all time) as the paths of its progress. This is simply another way of saying that time is abolished as it is in every true teleology; since, for every complete and necessary teleology, everything is controlled from the end, and the end is posited and determined already at the start of the process, positing and determining the means that will make it appear as accomplished. Time is then only a pseudonym for the order of positing and of the reciprocal generation of the terms of the process, or, as actual time is a mere external condition that has nothing to do with the process itself. I have already indicated, above and in other texts,[10] that canonical Marxism represents an attempt to glue back together the causalist and the finalist view.

Let us note that beyond the contingent incapacity of the exponents of structuralism to confront the problem of history (apart from denying, more or less explicitly, that such a problem exists), nothing would prevent positing the fiction of a structure of history in its temporal unfolding; or, rather, that the postulate of a structure such as this would be required by a structuralist conception that desired to be self-consistent. Actually, structuralism cannot be taken seriously as a general conception as long as it does not venture to affirm that the different social structures it claims to describe are themselves simply elements of a hyper- or metastructure that would constitute total history. And, since this would amount to bringing history to a close, as far as ideas are concerned – speaking of structures means nothing unless all the elements and their relations can be determined once and for all – and to placing oneself in the spot of absolute knowledge,[11] structuralism cannot be taken seriously in this either.

It is not these conceptions as such, that truly matter, nor their critique, and even less the critique of their authors. With important authors, conceptions are never pure, their use in contact with the material they are attempting to think about reveals something other than what they explicitly think, and the results are infinitely richer than their programmatic theses. A great author, by definition, thinks beyond his means. He is great to the extent that he thinks something other than what has already been thought, and his means are the result of what has already been thought, which continually encroaches on what he does think, if only because he cannot wipe away all that he has received and place himself before a *tabula rasa*, even when he is under the illusion that he can. The contradictions that are always present in a great author bear witness to this fact; I am speaking of true, blunt, irreducible contradictions, which it is just as stupid to think cancel by themselves the author's contribution as it is useless to try to dissolve or to recuperate at successive and ever deeper levels of interpretation.

The most pregnant, the richest form that these contradictions may take is that which results from the impossibility simply to think together and with the same means what the author discovers – which is, in the important cases, another region of what is, another mode and another sense of: being – and what was already known. Nothing guarantees in advance the coherence or, more precisely, the identity (immediate or mediated) of the mode of being belonging to the objects of a new region, hence of the logic and the ontology that a new region requires, and of the logic and the ontology already developed somewhere else; even less, that this coherence will be of the same order and type as that existing within known regions. In particular, the regions considered here – the radical imaginary and the social–historical – imply a profound questioning of the received significations of being as determinacy and of logic as determination. To the extent that the resulting conflict is perceived by the author, it tends to be resolved by subordinating the new object to the significations and determinations already acquired, leading to the concealment of what has been discovered, the occultation of what has been revealed, its marginalization, the impossibility of thematizing it, its denaturing through its resorption into a system to which it remains alien, its transformation into the form of an intractable aporia.

Thus, Aristotle discovers the imagination philosophically – *phantasia* – but what he says about it thematically, when he treats it *ex professo* (fixing the imagination in its alleged place, between sensation, of which it would be a reproduction, and intellection, thereby governing for 25 centuries what everyone thinks about it) is of little consequence next to what he has truly to say about it, which he says elsewhere, and which he has no way of reconciling with what he thinks about *phusis*, the soul, thinking and being. Thus, too, Kant, repeating the same move three times (in the two editions of the *Critique of Pure Reason* and in the *Critique of Judgement*) discovers and conceals the role of what he calls the transcendental imagination. Thus Hegel, and Marx incomparably more, can say what they have to say that is fundamental about society and history only by transgressing what they think they know about what being and thinking mean and finally reduce it, forcing it to enter into a system that cannot contain it. Thus, finally, Freud who unveils the unconscious, affirms its mode of being to be incompatible with diurnal logic and ontology and yet never manages to conceive of it, up to the end, except by calling upon all the machinery of the psychical apparatus, agencies, places, forces, causes and ends in order to manage to conceal its indetermination as radical imagination.

The reproduction of these situations with features that are essentially analogous, considering the depth and the audacity of minds such as these, shows that fundamental factors are involved here. The inherited logic-ontology is solidly anchored in the very institution of social–historical life; it is rooted in the unavoidable necessities of this institution, and it is, in a sense, the development and the branching out of these necessities. Its core is the *identitary* or *ensemblist* logic, and it is this logic that rules sovereignly and ineluctably over the two institutions without which no social life can exist: the institution of the *legein*, the ineffaceable component of language and of social representation, and the institution of *teukhein*, the ineffaceable component of social doing.[12] The fact that social life has been able to exist shows that this identitary or ensemblist logic has a grip on what there is – not only on the natural world in which society emerges but on society itself, which cannot represent things and represent itself, speak and speak (of) itself, make things and make itself without at the same time employing this identitary or ensemblist logic, which can establish institutions and institute itself only by instituting *legein* and *teukhein* as well.

This logic – and the ontology that is homologous to it – far from exhausting what there is and its mode of being, touches only the first stratum; but at the same time, its internal exigency is to cover over or to exhaust every possible stratum. The problematic sketched out above is simply the concrete realization, in the areas of the imaginary and of the social–historical, of this antinomy. Physicalism and logicism, causalism and finalism are only ways of extending the exigencies and the basic patterns of identitary logic to society and to history. For identitary logic is the logic of determination, which particularizes itself, depending on the case, as a cause and effect relation, as means and end or as the logic of implication.

It can operate only by positing these relations as relations between the elements of a set (in the sense that these terms have in contemporary mathematics, but that is already at work from the start of the institution of *legein* and *teukhein*). This is what is essential and not the fact that it defines the mode of being of these elements as that of physical entities or logical terms. Because, for it, just as for the ontology that follows from it, to be means to be determined, and it is only starting from this assertion that the oppositions develop concerning what truly is, that is to say, what is truly, solidly and fully *determined*. From this point of view, not only is the opposition between materialism and spiritualism secondary; but secondary, too, is the opposition between Hegel and Gorgias, for example, between absolute knowledge and absolute non-knowledge. Both do, in fact, share a common conception of being, the first positing being as infinite self-determination, and the core of the arguments of the second (like all the sceptical and nihilist arguments ever uttered) when he wants to demonstrate that nothing is, and that if something is, it is not knowable, amounting to this: nothing is really determinable, the requirement of determination will forever remain empty and unsatisfied, for every determination is contradictory (hence indetermination), which is meaningful only on the basis of the tacit criterion: if something did exist, it would be determined.

Any discussion of the inherited concepts of society and history is, therefore, inseparable from bringing to light their logical and ontological foundations, just as their critique can only be the critique of these foundations and the elucidation of the social–historical as a domain irreducible to inherited logic and ontology. The typology of the answers to the question of society and history sketched out above is important inasmuch as these types of answers are the only ones possible on the basis of this logic-ontology. They concretize the ways in which inherited thought can conceive of coexistence and succession, posit the being, the being-thus, and the *raison d'être* (the why) of coexistence and succession.

ii   SOCIETY AND THE SCHEMATA OF COEXISTENCE

Society presents itself immediately as the coexistence of a host of terms or entities of different orders. What is available to inherited thinking in order to think of coexistence and of the mode of being-together of a variety of terms?

Either this coexistence, this being-together of a manifold, is considered to be a real system, whatever its complexity. There must then be the possibility of actually decomposing (whether in reality or ideally and abstractly) the system into well defined sub-systems, into parts, and, finally, into elements taken temporarily or definitively as ultimate. These elements, clearly distinct and well defined, must be amenable to univocal definition. They must be connected together by relations of causal determination, linear or cyclical (reciprocal), categorical or probabilist – relations which themselves are amenable to univocal definition; and relations of the same type must hold between parts, subsystems, and so on, of the global system. It results from this, too, that there must be a possibility of recomposing (whether in reality or ideally and abstractly), without surplus nor defect, the system starting with these elements and relations, considered alone to possess ultimate reality. – Or, the being-together of the manifold can be that of a logical system (in the broad sense, including mathematics). In this case as well, ultimate elements must be posited that are clearly distinct and well-defined, amenable to univocal definition, and, with them, univocal relations between these elements.

In both cases, ensemblist–identitary logic is used. In both cases, society is thought of as an ensemble of distinct and well-defined elements, referring to one another by means of well-determined relations. To the extent that – and we shall return to this at length – society is something quite different from a set or a hierarchy of sets, there is no way that anything essential about it can be thought along this line. But also, the question arises immediately: what are the elements and the relations with respect to which society, considered as coexistence-composition, would be the (real or ideal–abstract) system, and which ones are they? The difficulty or the refusal to recognize the mode of being proper to the social–historical necessarily means that, whatever the concomitant reservations, qualifications, restrictions or modalizations may be, these elements and relations will, in the final analysis, be those whose being and mode of being have already been recognized elsewhere, and hence both will ultimately be determined in other ways and from elsewhere. Such are the relations of causation, finality or logical implication. Such are also the elements to which inherited thought, for deep-seated reasons, was led at a very early stage to ascribe an ultimate substantiality and consistence: individuals, things, ideas or concepts.

Thus, for example, every society immediately presents itself as a collection of individuals. This immediate appearance is rapidly challenged by serious thinkers. But is it really challenged? For centuries one hears it affirmed that man does not exist as man outside of the city: 'Robinsonades'[13] and social contracts are condemned and the irreducibility of the social to the individual is proclaimed. But when we take a closer look, we see not only that nothing is said concerning what it is that would remain irreducible but that, in fact, this irreducible something is in reality reduced: society repeatedly reappears as determined by the individual considered the efficient or the final cause, the social as constructible or composable with the individual. This was already the situation in Aristotle, for whom 'the city is first according to nature' in relation to the individual man, but for whom as well the being of the city is determined by its end, and this end is the well-being of the individual man.[14] But this is also the situation in Marx:

'the real basis' of society that 'conditions' all the rest is 'the set of the relations of production', which are 'determined, necessary, independent on the will' of men. But *what* are these relations of production? They are 'relations between persons mediated by things'. And by what are they 'determined? By the 'state of the productive forces' – that is to say, by another aspect of the relation of persons to things, an aspect that is mediated, at the same time as it is determined, by concepts, those that are embodied in the technical know-how of each period.[15] Despite unassimilable and explosive formulations, the same is true with respect to Freud, to the extent that he does consider the social dimension: it is the *psyche*, with its corporeal anchor, its confrontation with a natural *ananké*, its internal conflicts and its phylogenetic history, that must account for the whole of the human world.[16]

But how could we think of society as the coexistence or the composition of elements that are held to pre-exist or that are supposed to be determined – really, logically, or teleologically – from elsewhere, when these so-called elements do exist as such and are only what they are in and through society? One could not compose a society – if this expression were meaningful – except with individuals, who themselves would already have to be social, who would already contain the social within themselves. Nor would it be possible to use here the schema that seems to apply, more or less, in other domains, namely the idea that properties emerge on the level of a totality that do not exist or that are meaningless on the level of the components – what physicists call cooperative or collective phenomena,[17] corresponding to the well-known theme of the transformation of quantity into quality. There is no sense in considering that language, production, social rules would be additional properties that would emerge if a sufficient number of individuals were juxtaposed; these individuals would not just be different, but inexistent and inconceivable outside of or prior to these collective properties – without their being, for all that, reducible to the latter.

Society is not a thing, not a subject, and not an idea – nor is it a collection or system of subjects, things and ideas. This observation seems quite banal to those who are quick to forget to ask themselves how and why one can then speak of a society and of this particular one. For in conventional language and in the logic it contains, '*a*' and '*this*' apply only to what we are able to name, and we are able to name only things, subjects, concepts and their collections or unions, relations, attributes, states and so on. However, the unity of a society, like its *ecceity* – the fact that it is this particular society and not some other one – cannot be analysed into relations between subjects mediated by things, since every relation between subjects is a social relation between social subjects, every relation to things is a social relation to social objects, and since subjects, things and relations are what they are and such as they are here only because they are instituted in the way they are by the society concerned (or by society in general). The fact that some men can kill and die for gold, while others do not, has nothing to do with the chemical element *Au*, or with the DNA properties of each group; and what is one to say when people kill or die for Christ and for Allah?

These difficulties are resolved merely in words when a collective consciousness or a collective unconscious is invoked, illegitimate metaphors, terms for which the only possible signified is the very problem discussed here. And they are also resolved merely in words when one simply affirms the existence of a social totality, of society as a whole, different from its parts, superseding them and determining them. For, if no more than this is said, one cannot help but slip back toward the only schema available to inherited thought for conceiving of a whole that is not a system *partes extra partes*: the schema of the organism. A schema that, despite the rhetorical precautions that are taken, in fact returns more often than is thought, and even today, in discussions on society. But, to speak of an organism, whether literally or figuratively, or of a hyperorganism, is to speak of a system of interdependent functions determined by an end; and this end is the conservation and the reproduction of the same, the affirmation of the permanence across time and accidents of the essence, *eidos* (aspect/species).[18] What would the same be which is conserved and reproduced here? And what would be the stable and determined functions controlled by this conservation–reproduction?

It is only in appearance and in the most superficial fashion that the various sectors or domains in which social activities unfold – economics, law, politics, religion, etc. could be identified or made to correspond with these functions. It is useful, outside of any critique of functionalism, of organicism or of other similar conceptions, to take a closer look at the question raised by the relation between these sectors or domains and the organization or the overall life of society. For, here again, we have a type of coexistence between a whole and its parts, even a type of existence of these parts, that cannot be apprehended within the framework of inherited thought. There is obviously no question of constituting society starting with an economy, a law or a religion that would be its components, each possessing an independent existence, whose union would bring about the appearance of a society (with or without additional new properties). The economy, for example, is conceivable and can exist only as social economy, the economy of a society and of this particular society. The problem, however, extends much further than these self-evident facts (the implications of which, going far beyond the question of society, have yet to be drawn). No available schema permits us truly to grasp the relations between the economy, law, politics and religion, on the one hand, and society, on the other; nor does it permit us to grasp the relations between these sectors themselves. For – and this precedes any discussion of content, any critique, for example, of the causal determination of the alleged superstructure by the alleged infrastructure – every known schema of relation presupposes that the schema of separation is applicable in the field considered and permits the constitution of the entities (whether real or abstract) that are placed into relation. This is not the case here, for the domains of social activity are not genuinely separable – I mean, not even ideally – they are so only in a nominal and empty sense. And this carries us back to a much deeper level of questioning: nothing in inherited thought allows us to say what these are or in what manner they exist as particular entities. They are certainly not abstract aspects, correlative to the place chosen to observe the object or to the categories used to grasp it. And this is so, first, because these places and categories exist only starting from and in relation to a particular social–historical institution – possessing no special privileges – that has brought them into existence in and through a particular social reality. If the theoretician distinguishes between a religious aspect and a legal aspect in the activities of a given traditional or archaic society which itself, does not distinguish between them, this is not due to the progress of knowledge or to the purification and the refinement of reason but to the fact that the society in which the theoretician lives has, for a long period of time, instituted in its own reality legal categories and religious categories as relatively distinct. He then extrapolates these categories and the distinction between them to the past, without, in general, questioning the legitimacy of this extrapolation, and tacitly postulating that the distinctions established in his own society correspond to the essence of every society and express its true articulation.

But neither can we consider these sectors of social life as coordinated partial systems – like the circulatory, respiratory, digestive and nervous systems of an organism – since we can, and often do, encounter the predominance or relative autonomy of one or another of these sectors in a given social organization.

What, then, are these sectors? We see already that, if we are to begin to think seriously about this question, we have to take full consideration of this massive, irreducible fact which remains, in reality, unassimilable for traditional thought: there is no articulation of social life that is given once and for all, neither on the surface nor at a greater depth, neither really nor abstractly. This articulation, whether with respect to the parts it posits or to the relations established between these parts and between the parts and the whole, is in every instance the creation of the society in question. And this creation is an onto-logical genesis, the positing of an *eidos*: for what is posited in this way, established, instituted each time, although it is always carried by the concrete materiality of acts and things, goes beyond this concrete materiality and any particular *this*, and is a *type* permitting the indefinite reproduction of its instances, which can exist in general and as what they are only as instances of this type. A specific tool (*teukhos*) – knife, adze, hammer, wheel, boat – is such a type, a created *eidos*. So, too, is a word (*lexis*), as are marriage, purchase and sale, enterprise, temple, school, book, inheritance, election, painting. At a different, and yet not entirely separate, level, the self-articulation of each society and the sectors or domains in and through which it exists displays this as well. Society establishes itself as a mode and a type of coexistence: as a mode and type of coexistence in general, with no analogue or precedent in another region of being and as *this* particular mode and type of coexistence, the specific creation of the society considered. (In the same way, as we shall see, it establishes itself as a mode and type of succession, that is as a social–historical temporality). Thus, the articulation of society into technique, economy, law, politics, religion, art, etc. which seems self-evident to us, is only one mode of social institution, particular to a series of societies to which our own belongs. We know perfectly well, for example, that only in recent times do the economy and law appear as explicitly posited moments of social organization; that religion and art considered as separate domains are, on the scale of history, quite recent creations; that the type (and not just the content) of the relation between productive labour and other social activities displays, throughout history and across different societies, vast modifications. The organization of society deploys itself in each case in a different way, not only inasmuch as it posits different moments, sectors or domains in and through which it exists, but inasmuch as it brings into being a type of relation between these moments that can be new and even that is always new in a non-trivial sense.[19] Neither the former nor the latter can be inductively inferred from the forms of social life observed up to now, deduced *a priori* by theoretical reflection, or thought within a logical framework that is given once and for all.

Reflecting on society refers us thus to two limits of inherited thought, limits that, in truth, are but the single limit characteristic of identitary logic and ontology. There is no way, within this limit, to conceive of the self-deployment of an entity as the positing of new terms of an articulation and of new relations between these terms, hence as the positing of a new organization, of a new form, of another *eidos*. For there is no way within the logic-ontology of the same, of repetition, of the forever intemporal (*aei*) to think of a creation, a genesis that is not a mere becoming, generation and corruption, engendering of the same by the same as a different exemplar of the same type, but is instead the emergence of otherness, ontological genesis, that brings about beings as *eidos*, and as the *ousia* of *eidos*, another manner and another type of being and of being-a-being. And it may be that this self-evidence is actually blinding; it may be that it is, at most, recognizable but not thinkable. This question, however, will possibly be resolved only when it has been recognized, perceived, experienced, when it is no longer denied or covered over by the veil of tautology.

There is no way, within this limit, to think of society as coexistence or as the unity of a manifold. For reflection on society places us before a requirement, one we can never satisfy by means of inherited logic: the requirement that we consider terms that are not discrete, separate, individualizable entities (entities that can be posited in this way only temporarily, as markers), in other words, terms that are not elements of a whole, and that are not reducible to such elements; relations between these terms, relations that themselves are neither separable nor definable in any univocal way; finally, the pair, terms/relations, as it presents itself in each instance at a given level, as impossible to grasp at this level independently of the others. What is in question here is not a greater logical complexity, that could be handled by increasing the traditional logical operations, but an unprecedented logical–ontological situation.

This situation is unprecedented from an ontological point of view: *what* the social is, and the way in which it is, has no analogue anywhere else. It therefore forces us to reconsider the sense of: being, or else to shed light on another, previously unknown, side of this sense. By this very fact, we once again see that what has been termed 'ontological difference', the distinction between the question of being and the question of beings, is impossible to maintain or, to say the same thing another way, simply exposes the limit of inherited thought. Briefly speaking, traditional ontology has been no more than the surreptitious positing of the mode of being of these particular categories of beings on which its gaze has been riveted as the meaning of: being. It is from these categories, as well as from – practically the same thing – the necessities of language as *legein* (as an ensemblist–identitary instrument) that traditional ontology has drawn the meaning of: being as being determined. This has not prevented it from always envisaging other types of being, but it has always led it to characterize them as being-less (*hetton on*, in opposition to being-more, *mallon on*), by which it has always meant to say this and only this: less determined or less determinable.

This situation is also unprecedented from the point of view of logic – an aspect that is inseparable from the preceding one, since, despite the apparently strange – but in reality natural – alliance between Heidegger and the positivists on this point, there is no thought of being that is not also a logos of being, an ordered and self-ordered, hence logical logos, just as there is no logic without a presumption of being (even if only as being in and through language). We cannot think of the social, as coexistence, by means of inherited logic, and this means: we cannot think of it as the unity of a plurality in the usual sense of these terms; we cannot think of it as a determinable ensemble of clearly distinct and well-defined elements. We have to think of it as a *magma*, and even as a *magma* of *magmas* – by which I mean not chaos but the mode of organization belonging to a non-ensemblist diversity, exemplified by society, the imaginary or the unconscious.[20] In order to speak of it, which we can do only in the existing social language, we unavoidably call upon the terms of ensemblist *legein*, such as one and many, part and whole, composition and inclusion. These terms, however, function here only as markers, not as genuine categories. For there are no transregional categories: the rule of connection dictated by a category is empty if that which is to be connected in this way is not taken into account. This is merely another way of saying that being is always only the being of beings, and that each region of beings unveils another sense of: being.

iii HISTORY AND THE SCHEMATA OF SUCCESSION

History presents itself immediately as succession. What is available to inherited thought to think of a succession? The schemata of causality, of finality or of logical consequence. These schemata presuppose that what is to be grasped or thought by their means can, essentially, be reduced to an ensemble. One must be able to separate elements or discrete entities, clearly distinct and definite, in order to be able to say that *a* is the cause of *b*, that *x* is the means of *y*, or that *q* is a logical consequence of *p*.

Inherited thought is therefore unable to grasp a succession in the social, except on the condition that it has made the latter an ensemble or is in the process of doing so; we have just seen, and we shall see again at length, that this is impossible. It amounts to the same thing to say that it can think of *succession* only from the point of view of *identity*. Causality, finality and implication are merely amplified and unfolded forms of an enriched identity; they aim at positing differences as merely apparent and at finding, at another level, the same to which these differences belong. It is of no importance in the present context whether the same is understood as an entity or as a law. To be sure, the question of knowing how and why the same is given as or appears in and through difference remains the central aporia in inherited thought in all its forms, in the most ancient ontology or in the most modern positive science. This aporia follows from the fact that it has been decided that the same exists and, what is more, that in an ultimate sense, the same alone exists. It is easy to see that this proposition goes hand in hand with another, namely that *what* exists is fully determined from and in all time, an 'in all time' that can be rigorously thought only as an intemporal *aei*, which may or may not be translated into an omnitemporal always.

It is self-evident and well known that logical implication is an elaborated identity, that the conclusion is simply a disimplication of what is already in the premises (analyticity). But the same thing is true with respect to the frameworks of causality and finality. Cause and effect belong to the same; if we can separate and determine a set of causes, it goes with the set of its effects, neither of these two sets can exist without the other, and they, therefore, both partake of the same, are the parts of a single set.[21] Likewise for what concerns means and ends. Likewise, finally, if we consider not entities but laws, whether causal or final: a law exists only in and through the same, it is the essential and internal identity to which the external difference of phenomena refers, without which this difference could not exist. Or: this differing exteriority of phenomena as such must ideally be carried back to the identical interiority of a law.

Causes go with effects, means go with ends. This *going with* is explicitly present at least since the Aristotelian definition of the syllogism: 'a discourse in which, some things being posited, another thing ... necessarily goes with them (*ex anankēs sumbainei*), by reason of the being of the former.' *Sumbainein*, to walk together, to go with, *comitari* (*cum-eo*); *sumbēbēkos*, translated by *accidens* in Latin, actually means what *goes with*, which one can and should translate by *comitant*. *Sumbainein*, *sumbēbēkos* most often designate for Aristotle what is found to go with, what has externally coincided with– the accident; but they also designate, in the opposite sense, what essentially and necessarily goes with something else.[22] In his definition of the syllogism, Aristotle obviously can leave no room for ambiguity: conclusion and premises *ex anankēs sumbainei*, necessarily go with one another, ineluctably walk together.

However, what necessarily goes with something else, what is it if not a part of that other thing, or else together with it, a part of the same other thing? How and why do the legs and the body of an animal go together if not because they belong to one and the same animal?

If what follows necessarily goes with that which it follows, succession is at best only a subjective manner of inspecting the total thing, the actual counterpart of which in the thing is, and is only, an order of coexistence. In truth, the conclusion is given together with the premises; the Philosophy of mind together with the Science of logic; and the expansion of the universe together with the initial hyperdense state and the laws governing physical being. If succession is determined or necessary, it is given as soon as are given its law and its first term; it is itself but an order of being-together. Time is then simply a relation of order that nothing permits us to distinguish intrinsically from other relations of order, for example, from a spatial arrangement or from the relation of 'greater or lesser'. And, to the extent that the terms are necessarily *taken up* in this order, they are no more than 'parts' of the One-Whole and *co*-exist as parts of One-Same. In the intemporal always, there can be, at most, an order of coexistences but not an order of successions; and in the omnitemporal always of determination, the order of succession is simply a variant of the order of coexistence, for succession can and must be reduced to a particular type of coexistence.[23]

However, just as society cannot be thought of within any of the traditional schemes of coexistence, so history cannot be thought of within any of the traditional frameworks of succession. For what is given in and through history is not the determined sequence of the determined but the emergence of radical otherness, immanent creation, non-trivial novelty. This is manifested by the existence of history *in toto* as well as by the appearance of new societies (of new *types* of society) and the incessant transformation of each society. And it is only on the basis of this radical otherness or creation that we can truly think of temporality and time, of the excellent and eminent actuality which we find in history. For, either time is nothing, a strange psychological illusion masking the essential intemporality of a relation of order; or else time is the very manifestation of the fact that something other than what exists is bringing itself into being, and bringing itself into being as new or as other and not simply as a consequence or as a different exemplar of the same.

It may be helpful to stop here and consider a confusion that seems to have been spreading for some time. The emergence of the new appears with a special intensity at times of upheaval, of catastrophic or great events that mark and punctuate the existence of societies often termed 'historical' in a restricted sense of the term. Authors sometimes express themselves as though historicity belongs only to this category of societies, to which could be opposed 'cold' societies – where change would be marginal or simply non-existent, the essence of their life unfolding as stability and repetition – as well as societies 'without history', in particular so-called archaic societies, where not only do repetition and absence of change seem self-evident but another mode of relating to their own past and future seems to prevail, making them radically different from so-called 'historical' societies. These distinctions are not false and do, indeed, point to something important. They would become fallacious if we were to forget that to which they refer: different *modes* of historicity and not the presence of history here as opposed to the absence of history there. Different modes of the actual institution of social–historical time by different societies, in other words different modalities according to which different societies represent and make their incessant self-alteration – even if, in the extreme case, they deny it or, rather, attempt to deny it. To be sure, this makes a difference not only with respect to the pace or the rhythm of this self-alteration but also with respect to its content. It does not, for all that, prevent it from existing.

Thus, the extraordinary stability of living conditions, rules and representations that characterizes the existence of European peasants over a period of centuries (and, in a sense, all peasants from the neolithic age to the twentieth century) cannot but strike us when it is opposed to the stage of the theatre of 'history', as it is commonly called, constantly shaken by the sound and fury of wars, discoveries, the movement of representations and ideas, changes of government and regimes. And yet, important segments of this peasantry pass, in the space of a few decades, from a universe of papism and witchcraft to the Reformation. The question posed by this passage – and by every passage – is obviously not eliminated, or even reduced by a hair's breadth, by the illusion of the alleged – and unrealizable – division *ad infinitum* of the gap that separates the before and the after (a division that merely multiplies the problem *ad infinitum*). To underscore just one aspect of the problem: the Reformation implies an upheaval in the psychic organization of the individuals concerned, who are obliged to pass from a state in which everything is tied to the representation of the Absolute, the Law, the Master in and through the visible organization of the Church and its flesh and blood officials, to a state in which there is, for the individual, no conceivable intermediary between himself and transcendence other than the Text, which he interprets at his own risk. We must, nevertheless, insert this upheaval within the apparently stable and repetitive self-reproduction of the preceding stage: Catholic fathers and mothers, in a cold society, produced sons and daughters ready to become Protestants. The fact that this took place in the space of one generation or of ten changes absolutely nothing here. It is obviously the illusion of the historian – our illusion, necessary to all of us – to measure eternity on the basis of his own life expectancy and to consider that whatever does not change for three centuries is 'stable'. But change the scale of time, and the stars in the heaven will step to a dizzy dance.

The same is true for archaic societies, even if it is infinitely more difficult, for obvious reasons, to illustrate by its apparent consequences the implacable and incessant self-alteration that unfolds in their depths.[24] The 'static', 'repetitive', 'anhistorical' or 'atemporal' character of this class of societies is simply their way of instituting their own particular historical temporality.

It is impossible, however, to manage without a discussion of the question of time in general. For, on the one hand, this is where all the threads that inherited thought uses to weave its denial of history and of creation stem from and the place to which they return – the denial of genuine time as that in which and through which otherness exists, in the name of being interpreted as determined and determined in the always: *aei*. On the other hand, it is possible, on the question of time, to attempt an initial elucidation of the infinitely complex relations entertained by: society's reception of a 'natural datum' and what could be termed, to borrow an expression from Freud, the *Anlehnung*, the leaning of the social–historical institution on the natural stratum; this institution itself as the simultaneous and indissociable institution of identitary relations and of non-identitary significations; finally, the philosophical problematic that emerges, at a particular moment, in society and the philosophical negation/affirmation of the social–historical world of significations.

iv THE PHILOSOPHICAL INSTITUTION OF TIME

Every society exists by instituting the world as its world, or its world as the world, and by instituting itself as part of this world. In this institution, of the world and of society by society, the institution of time is always an essential component. But do we know why time is instituted as separate from space as well as, in particular, from *what* is produced in it?

The man of commonsense shrugs his shoulders at this philosophical hairsplitting: *there is* time, humans see themselves grow, change, die; they observe the sun and the stars as they rise and set, and so on. We know this as well as he does. But why is it, then, that these indubitable humans have posited and represented to themselves throughout the course of history in such indubitably different manners what so indubitably 'there is'? Why have they conceived of it as open or closed, suspended between the two fixed terms of Creation and Parousia, or infinite, as the time of progress or the time of fallenness, as absolutely homogeneous or qualitatively differentiated? All of this is just representative nonsense, replies the commonsense man, and the progress of science is gradually freeing us from it, we know more and more what time is. As usual, the commonsense man refers all the more readily to science as he is ignorant of it. He must be brought – something he generally refuses to do – to meet the physicist of today, who will tell him that he at any rate does not know *what* time is, whether it is truly distinct from space and how it is so, whether it is infinite or finite, open or cyclical, whether it corresponds to something that is separable from the observer or only to a necessary manner in which the observer inspects a manifold.

It is, in fact, clear that once we begin to question it, the possibility of distinguishing absolutely between 'time', a 'space' and 'what' is encountered there, becomes highly problematical. And it is superfluous to recall that this discussion runs from one end of the history of philosophy, and even of scientific thought, to the other; the last 50 years have witnessed the pulverization of certainties in this respect just as in many others. There is multiplicity – or, as Kant says, the manifold; there is, therefore, difference or otherness (these terms are used provisionally here as equivalent, but later we shall be led to distinguish between them and to set them in radical opposition). Why, then, is this difference or otherness always posited, by the subject and society, as given *in* a first medium, 'space', and also *in* a second medium, 'time', *and* as separable from that in which it is?

To measure the depth and the implications of this question, we should return at length to the first great philosophical text in which 'space', 'time' and 'what' exists were explicitly thematized and discussed in terms of their relations, and in which all the almost insurmountable necessities that will govern philosophical thought down to the present are already apparent: Plato's *Timaeus*. This cannot be done here.[25] Instead, we must simply indicate a few aspects in which the *impossibility* for inherited thought truly to think of time, a time essentially different from space, makes itself apparent. To begin with, there is neither time nor space in what Plato gives himself – gives to the Demiurge – to construct the world. There is the always being (*aei on*) and the always becoming (*aei gignomenon*). 'Always' is here, Plato explicitly states, a monstrous abuse of language: it is not omnitemporality, but atemporality, which is clearly posited as the impossibility, the inconceivability of movement and change (*akinēton*). What is the privilege accorded to, or what is simply proper to, the essence of the always being – what is the essence of the essence? The always being is always in accordance with the same determinations (*aei kata tauta*); this means that atemporally, and in all respects, it is determined identically, determined in accordance with the same. The always becoming does not become with or in time – there is not 'yet' any time in which it could become, change. This apparent absurdity is a self-evident necessity: the always becoming, *genesis* as such or what we must dare to call the *eidos* of *genesis*, absolute and pure becoming-ness, is that which is 'never' in accordance with the same determinations, that which is 'always' in accordance with other determinations. And, since 'always' and 'never' do not and cannot have a temporal sense here, this means: that which, 'at every (logical) moment and in every relation', maintains contradictory determinations, which amounts to saying it has no determination whatsoever in any respect. At this stage, the always becoming signifies: the totally non-determined.

This is not the case with actual genesis, with becoming in the world, the mingling of becoming *aei* – of the indefinite, *apeiron* Plato will say in the *Philebus* – and of being *aei* – of the determined, *peras* – which is always subject to forms, to rational relations 'as far as this is possible',[26] to partial determinations. And it is among these partial determinations that the time of the world is to be counted: if it is akin to genesis by reason of its mobility (which, once again, actually means: *indetermination*), by reason of its global inalterability, by its cyclical repetition (for it is *essentially* cyclical), hence by its quasi-self-identity it figures-images eternity/atemporality, the mark of which it imprints on the world, on actual becoming, here, too, within the limits of the possible: 'the moving image of eternity . . . this image eternal but moving according to number, while eternity itself rests in unity.'[27] Time is the image or figure of non-time; in a sense, once it goes beyond its astonishment, the aporia, and wants to *say* something about it, philosophy (and science) never basically speaks about time in any other way.

Time is what is, what permits or realizes the return of the same: whether this return is conceived of as the unalterable cyclicity of becoming (as in ancient cosmologies but also in certain solutions of the equations of general relativity) or simply as repetition in and through causal determination, changes nothing essential about it. In what way are cycles that are repeated other? They cannot be said to be other to the extent that they are in 'another time', since time is only *in* each of these cycles, it is but a 'local property', just as it is 'irreversible' (my death in this cycle *precedes* my birth in the next cycle).

In what way also can an essential difference be established between time and 'space'? Not only does time – *this* time – presuppose 'space' as a circle, as an image as such (an image can exist only in the gap and the spacing and the unity of what is spaced), and as an image *of* – hence, *in* a relation *to* that of which it is the image; but time *is* space to the extent that nothing allows us to distinguish the mode of co-belonging of its parts or moments from the mode of co-belonging of the parts or points of space.

For what is space? People were led to believe that Plato had said all he had to say when, suddenly, after a longer development and after the world has been made,[28] he stops, retraces his steps and says that everything has to be begun all over again, the division reconsidered from a higher level, and that, in addition to always being and always becoming, a third term must be posited: *chora*, 'space', 'what' *receives* 'what' is-becomes, that 'in which' exists everything that is, on Earth or in Heaven, and which is neither intelligible, like always-being, nor sensible, like becoming, 'a third incorruptible kind that we grasp as in a dream', 'a sort of invisible and formless *eidos*'. *Eidos*, that is to say a form/aspect, hence a formless form, an invisible aspect: 'tangible, outside of any sensation, to a bastard reflection' – sensible insensible, unthinkable thought. *Aporotaton*, superlatively intractable: we do not feel space, Plato says, and yet we touch it (*hapton*); we touch it, not with our hands but with a bastard reflection. This bastard reflection is addressed to something that partakes of the intelligible, that is incorruptible, and that is an absolute necessity – based on a vision 'as in a dream'. *Aporotaton*, indeed – and all the more so as it *must* be separated from what is found 'there' and from what takes place 'there' and at the same time this separation *cannot* really be made.[29]

Let us open a triple parentheses here. First, this separability-inseparability of the Receptacle (*dechomenon*)[30] and of 'what' is there shows up again in contemporary physics, with general relativity: energy-matter '*is*' the local curvature of space-time and, moreover, the global properties of space-time 'depend' on the quantity of the energy-matter that it 'contains'. Second, it is impossible to avoid a comparison between Plato's *chora*, visible as in a dream, partaking of the sensible and the intelligible but being neither one nor the other, formless form – and what Kant will call the pure forms of the intuition, space and time. But Kant will believe that these forms can be separated not only from any particular content but from any content *whatsoever*; he will believe he can supply a space and a time containing *nothing* at all (not even pure figures), that is a space and a time as the pure possibility of the self-difference of identity, or the pure production of difference out of nothing – which, in fact, as we shall see in a moment, leads to the impossibility of a genuine distinction between space and time. It is in this way that Kant, following Aristotle, posits that we represent time by means of pure non-time, that is, by means of a line; Hegel will continue along this same path.[31] This separation – the separation of temporality and of *what* is by making temporality be: <u>*otherness* – produced by an analytic abstraction, one that is reflexive and secondary, is in fact impossible</u>. Third, the usefulness of the following considerations will be more easily perceived if the idea that guides them is stated here and now. There is no essential time, no time that is irreducible to any sort of 'spatiality', no time that is any more than a simple referential aid in getting our markings, unless and to the very extent to which there is an emergence of radical otherness, that is absolute creation – that is to say, to the extent to which *what* emerges is not *in* what exists, not even 'logically' or as an already constituted 'potentiality', to the extent that it is not the actualization of pre-determined possibilities (the distinction between power and act is only the most subtle and most profound manner of suppressing time), hence, to the extent that time is not simply and not only in-determination but the springing forth of determinations or, better yet, of *other eidē*-images-figures-forms. Time is the self-alteration of what is, which is only to the extent that it is *to-be*. For this reason, any separation between time and what is reveals itself to be reflexive, analytical, secondary – identitary. And it is as this time, the time of otherness and alteration (*altération-altérité*), that we have to think of history.

Plato posits a *chora*, a 'space', as separable–inseparable from what unfolds 'there'. This *chora*, itself an *eidos*, being always, incorruptible, other than the genesis it 'receives' is referred by Plato here only to sensible becoming, to actual genesis, to what is 'in' the world. But how can one keep from generalizing and radicalizing this idea? Plato himself is ambiguous in this regard: 'we ... say of all being (*to on apan*) that it must of necessity be somewhere (*pou*), be in some place (*en tini topō*) and occupy a space (*choran tina*), but that what is neither in heaven nor in earth has no existence.'[32] The Heaven is here, of course, the world; but *all being* must be 'somewhere'. Does 'all being' thereby exclude what truly is, the always-being? Plato speaks in other dialogues of the 'supra-celestial place' (*hyperouranios topos*) *where* Ideas are. Are these poetical metaphors, as will be said since Aristotle? But there is no intelligible, no *eidos*, that is without a *relation to* ..., as the *Sophist* has shown. Being an *eidos* necessarily implies being 'with', 'before ...', 'opposed to ...' some other *eidos*; and the *topos*, the place, whether it be celestial, supra-celestial or 'ideal' is in this respect, and is only this, being-in-a-relation-to ..., being *syn-*: 'space' and 'place', the *chora* and the *topos*, these are the *co-* in the order of coexistences, if we wish to speak like Leibniz, and this order itself. Can there be intelligibility except in and through the order of coexistence? A 'space', a 'dimensionality', is necessary if the *eide* are to be able to be together, at once, *ama* – and they have to be able to exist in this way for they cannot exist without one another, for they exist only *in* and through this relation. The *topos* is necessarily implied as soon as there is more than One – regardless of the nature, substance or consistency (sensible, intelligible, or other) of this 'more'. The *topos* or *chora* is the first possibility of the Plural. (And, to be sure, the pure thought of the One must exclude the *topos*: Parmenides). In this sense, it is what allows the identity of the different (and, as we shall see in a moment, the difference of the identical) since it founds the final co-belonging of all that is different, irrespective of their differences: to differ (*dia-phero*) is to *displace*, to *trans-port*; to differ is still to relate to ..., to-be-placed, to-be-posited or to-be-taken (depending on the school) *together*, hence in the unity of a spacing or a gap.

If there were no *place*, no *topos*, how could what is different exist? Could it exist in and through the 'order of succession'? But, as the terms of a succession are, by definition, not *com*possible, there could be no difference. More precisely, difference could then exist only to the extent that 'somewhere' – in the inspection of a 'retentional spectator' or in the In-Itself of the 'ideal' preservation of the past – the Plural, which would have been set-posited-taken only *in* (once again) the succession, would have been *com*-posited, *com*-prehended, *zu-sammengesetzt*. Pure succession has never been thought, and could never be, except as a modality of the *co*existence of the terms of a series. A *topos* is still – is always – required here, for the *topos* is that very thing, whether there is identity of the different, co-belonging of the Plural, the holding-together of spacing – all of this is always there (stated) when the different, the Plural, the spacing is (stated). And, of course, conversely, 'time' as the 'order of succession' *seems* to be required – and, in this referential aspect is required *only* – in order to permit the identical to differ from itself: the 'same' thing is never exactly the same, even when it has suffered no 'alteration', for the very reason that it is *in* another time. But in what way is this other time *other*? Strictly speaking, here we are still in the 'dream' of which Plato spoke. We cannot think of time if we do not rid ourselves of a certain way – the inherited way – of thinking of being, that is to say, of positing being as determinacy. It is absolutely not true that time is necessary 'to prevent everything from happening all at once', since, if everything is already given (even ideally), if everything is in a sense 'acquired' somewhere, everything *can* happen 'all at once' – and perhaps 'at this very moment' everything is happening all at once, but simply *somewhere else*; and, especially: everything has already happened all at once, from time immemorial, outside of time. It is fatal to the inherited referential thinking that there is no real *place* for time or that time cannot really *take place* (= exist) precisely because we must look for a place for time, an ontologically determined place in the determinacy of what is, hence that time is but a mode of place. No literature on 'temporality' or on the 'epochality of Being' can change this, as long as being is thought of within the same horizon of determinacy and of the atemporal always, as an indubitable *self*, *selbst*, that is to say, once again and always as Plato thought of it: *auto*, *aei kata tauta*.

If time is not the self-generation of absolute otherness, if it is not ontological creation, if it is not that by reason of which the other, and not simply the identical, exists in the necessarily external form of difference – if time is not all this, then time is *superfluous*, mere repetition in cyclicity or the simple illusion of a 'finite mind', at any rate, no more than the modalisation, carrying no special privilege, of a primordial *chora* of which space, too, would be simply another modalization. More than superfluous, it is harmful, so to speak (and this has often been repeated). For the idea that A, subsisting in absolute self-identity, is no longer 'entirely' identical with itself simply because it exists 'in another time', either is pure non-sense (and this has always been the source of countless immediate and insoluble paradoxes in identitary thought); or else it acquires its apparent sense only through relating – by means of the 'in' of 'in another time' – A *to* something that coexists with it *in another* relation (of whatever type) from that *in* an 'initial time' (for example, a clock whose hands are in another *position*). However, all these *ins* as well as the comparison (*com-parution*, *con*-gruence) implied in this way between the *situation*, as the language so aptly calls it, of 'after' and the situation of 'before', have already *placed* all these considerations within the ideal *chora*, which makes them possible and permits them, perhaps, to be 'true' by treating their logical and temporal *co*existence as a necessary *co*existence – that is as the absolute determinacy of their reciprocal determinations.

It serves no purpose to criticize the 'spatialization' of time, its 'reduction to extension', if one maintains the traditional determinations of being – that is being as determinacy. For, once being has been thought of as determinacy, it has also, necessarily, been thought of as atemporality. All temporality, henceforth, can be but a secondary and derived modality; the only question that then remains (and continues to torture philosophy throughout its history) is the possibility of different determinations that do not annihilate identity, hence the Plural. And if the latter is to be (thinkable), it is necessary and sufficient that a *chora* or primordial Spacing exist, in and through which *what* exists as determined can be determined (it is a matter of strict indifference that *what* exists be *eidos*, *ousia* or 'matter', etc.). In its most 'elementary', most abstract, and barest form, this possibility is contained in pure 'space', which is nothing other than this miracle: points x and y are different without *anything* differentiating them except 'their place'. This possibility of the coexistence of the different, and of the order that it implies, are required, however, everywhere. If memories are, in any sense, acquired – then memory is a *place*, a *topos* in which a multitude of memories can *co*exist without one driving out or destroying another (as, moreover, it incontestably is *as well*). And the fact that this *topos* cannot be measured with a yardstick no more prevents it from being this very thing than the impossibility of measuring the distances and the proximity of mathematical propositions prevents them from being-together in this *chora*, in this *topos* of mathematics that they generate by being 'true' – that is to say, by maintaining among themselves an 'order of determined and necessary coexistence', that we read 'subjectively' as an order of succession of proofs.[33]

Time can exist only if there is an emergence of what is other, of what is in no way *given with* what is, what does not *go together* with it. Time is the emergence of *other* figures. The points of a line are not *other*; they are *different* by means of *what they are not* – their place. To present the line as a figure of time is to confuse (spatial) difference and (temporal) otherness. The points of a line are fallaciously posited as other and not simply as different, because I already construe time as that in which the inspecting or the drawing of a line occurs. This implies that I have already fully available to me what it is that distinguishes a 'temporal' line from a 'spatial' line. But this possibility is an illusion, unless time as such has been given to me, and it is given to me by *otherness*, by the fact that the *other* does appear. There is no 'pure' time, separable from what is brought into being through time as it makes time be. More precisely: the 'pure' schema of time is the schema of the essential alteration of a figure, the schema that presentifies the breaking up and the suppression of one figure through the emergence of a(nother) figure. As such, it is independent of any particular figure, but not of any figure *whatsoever*. Time as the 'dimension' of the radical imaginary (hence, as a dimension of the radical imagination of the subject as subject as well as of the social–historical imaginary) is the emergence of other figures (and, in particular, of 'images' for the subject, of social–historical *eide*, imaginary social institutions and meanings for society). It is the otherness-alteration of figures and, originally and in its core, it is this alone. – These figures are other not depending on what they *are not* (their 'place' *in* time) but depending on *what* they *are*; they are other inasmuch as they shatter determinacy, inasmuch as they cannot themselves be determined, to the extent that they are determined, on the basis of determinations that are 'external' to them or that come from *somewhere else*.

Now, this determination as external or as coming from somewhere else is known as difference. In this sense, a 'pure' space is, from a reflexive and analytical point of view, a necessity for thought and for its most elementary operations. To think, we must be able to grasp the same as different and vice versa; we must be able, for example, to *iterate* or *repeat*, to retain as plural and as different the absolutely self-identical that 'repeats' itself. This is the possibility that 'pure' space provides, the possibility for the 'same' point to be different if it is placed *somewhere else*; and in this sense, reflexively, space exists prior to the figure as its *a priori* condition. There is nothing like this in the case of time, which would be *nothing* if it were the mere possibility of iteration of the identical. An 'empty' space is a logical and physical *problem*; an 'empty' time is an absurdity – or else, it is simply a certain name given for no particular reason to a spatial dimension. What would time be if only the same existed? If I 'extend' a square or a circle on a plane into an infinite parallelepiped or cylinder, and, then, reiterate them interminably in an additional dimension, I obtain, precisely, no more than an additional spatial dimension; what I am doing is still geometry. In the same way, if I were to stretch out the 'sphere of the world' into a fourth dimension, I would still be working on the geometry of a hypersphere in R^4. Even physics cannot be content with this.

'Pure' space is the possibility of difference in so far as it is the condition of the repetition of the same as different, that is to say, as *iteration* – atemporal repetition, in the *forever, aei*, of spatiality or of coexistence, or of composition. In its most basic form, it is what allows the possibility of granting (or of 'seeing') that points x and y are at once the same (in that nothing intrinsic to them distinguishes them) and different (in and through their spacing). As such, it is 'logically' (and not 'psychologically') presupposed by logic and mathematics, because it is already presupposed by the most elementary *legein*. If the *sign* is to exist, the different must be identical and the identical must be different or capable of differentiating itself, multiplying itself, making itself plural without ceasing to be the same. *a* and *a* are the same independently of where they may appear on the page. And *a* is not a sign – letter or phoneme – if it cannot be made plural, be iterated, and if it cannot become 'different' (take on different 'values') while remaining the same and simply being in another 'position': the two '1's of the figure '11' acquire their difference in sameness due to their *place*.

Space is the possibility of the difference of the same from the same, without which there is nothing at all. If what is (thought) must be (thought) in the form of the difference of the same from the same, it is necessary, and sufficient, that space or primordial spacing exist. Every 'rigorously' logical – that is to say, identitary, or, tautological – system is, as such and if it could be only this, essentially 'spatial'. If mathematics could be wholly formalized and closed upon itself – which they essentially cannot be – they would be exactly this. For, if I have 'space', one point, and the operator 'iteration' (with the network of the identitary operators it implies or condenses), then I can posit a point: '.', and two points '..', which means that I have a binary alphabet in which I can *write* everything (Bourbaki's *Elements of Mathematics* as well as the *Orestia*, the *Phenomenology of Mind* or *The Interpretation of Dreams*). And if mathematics were simply the ordered manipulation of signs, capable of being closed upon itself, statements and demonstrations would be only arrangements of different order iterations of this 'single' sign: '.'; and the 'rules' determining what is a 'well-formed formula' and a 'demonstration' would, in fact, be simply the 'accepted' or 'chosen forms' of the spatial arrangement of points or, if you prefer, they would possess a rigorous representation in these forms. Nothing else is said when it is held that the 'verification' of an entirely formalized text amounts to an inspection of this text, ensuring that signs of the appropriate form are found at the appropriate places, which boils down to observing the congruence of figures in space, through a work which is 'somewhat mechanical'.[34]

And it is still this primordial 'space' that is in question when physical being is thought of as rationalizable. It is to it that Democritus implicitly refers when he thinks he is able to create the world with atoms and the void: perceived differences are construed as different arrangements of atoms which themselves are indistinguishable except for their position. And it is again to this 'space' that Plato refers when he posits that the difference between 'elements' *is* the difference between regular polyhedra; or Western physics, from classical mechanics to the contemporary research into quarks.

v TIME AND CREATION

To be sure, time – in the sense we give to the term here, time as otherness-alteration – does imply space, since it is the emergence of other *figures* and since figures, that is the Plural as it is ordered or minimally *formed*, presuppose spacing. However, to say that figures are *other* (and not simply different) has a sense only if figure B can in no way derive from a different arrangement of figure A – as a circle, ellipse, hyperbole or parabola derive from one another and so are the *same* points *arranged* differently – in other words, only if no identitary law, or group of laws, is sufficient to produce B starting from A. Or, if one likes: what I call *other* are figures of this type and of this type only; figures not of this nature I call different. And so I say that the circle is different from the ellipse but that the *Divine Comedy* is other than the *Odyssey*, and capitalist society is *other* than feudal society.

To say that figure B is other than figure A means then, in the first place that it cannot be deduced, produced or constructed on the basis of what is 'in' A, whether implicitly or explicitly, or on the basis of what is posited, mediately or immediately, 'with' A. This is to say that, when I have drawn out of A all the presuppositions, implications and consequences that it requires or leads to (in the sense in which *practically all* of mathematics is directly or indirectly implied by 1, 2, 3 ...), made explicit all the laws to which it refers and which determine A in its fact-of-being and in its being-thus, I could never on the basis of all this construct, deduce or produce B. It amounts to the same to say that, inasmuch as and to the very extent to which B is determined, its determinations cannot themselves be determined on the basis of A's determinations, that they are, then, *other* determinations; or that the being of B does not derive from the being of A, that as being (both as a fact of being as well as as a being-thus which itself is *other*, the two being indissociable) it comes from *nothing* and out of *nowhere*, that it does not have a *provenance* but is an *advent*, that it is *creation*.

Long before the principle of conservation was formulated by Western physics (or the idea of 'spontaneous generation' refuted in biology) philosophy had posited that creation is impossible, that a being can be thought only as *proceeding* from a being – this provenance being material, certainly, but *in particular* 'formal', eidetic, essential (logical–ontological). Thus thinking what is necessarily becomes: moving back to its origin or its principle.[35] Conversely, if thinking is moving backwards in this way, and if this movement is not to remain suspended in mid-air, it has to stop somewhere, *ananke stenai*; this stopping point is, then, inevitably the *eidos* (or the system or hierarchy of *eide*) as an a priori that is both logical and ontological, and as such necessarily implies the thought of *aei*, of the atemporal always or of atemporality, hence also of complete determinacy in all possible respects (this will become the *explicit* definition of 'being' in Kant). Far from allowing a creation or any essential alteration, an ontological genesis (which, under these conditions, is more than inconceivable, it is a contradiction in terms), temporality can then be no more than a downfall, or an imperfect imitation of eternity (Plato), at best the relative indetermination of corporeal beings in so far as they are possessed of *matter* (that is, of *apeiron*, the indefinite), or of *power* (*dunamis*, as incompletion, the possibility of being differently, and so a deficiency of being, that is, of *eidos*) or of *movement*, the three terms being rigorously equivalent here since each implies the other two.[36]

Creation, within the framework of inherited thought, is impossible. Creation in theology is obviously merely a pseudo-creation; it is producing or manufacturing. One may discuss endlessly whether 'eternal truths' are obligatory for God or not. The fact is that a God who would never obey *any* 'eternal truth' in any respect whatsoever (for example, that he is in so far as he is, that in so far as he is he is necessarily *such* as he is, that is to say, God; that it is impossible even for him not to be or not to be God, or to be something other than God or to possess an attribute that would be excluded by his essence, etc.) is strictly and superlatively unthinkable, it can only be a mystical and ineffable representation. The 'created' world is necessarily created, if only as the necessary effect of the necessary essence of God and, as the act and product of God, it is necessarily such as it is in its being-thus.[37] Creation itself is predetermined and entirely determined starting from the elsewhere and the atemporal always of God; it takes place once and for all, once and for always (this is why predestination, sin, salvation, grace – regardless of the interpretation they are given and regardless of whether or not they are accepted or refused, have to remain mysteries of faith beyond the limits of so-called rational theology). Continued creation signifies nothing more within this referential than the indispensable support that the only true being-a-being, God, constantly grants to created beings in order to maintain them in this minor mode of being which is theirs and which they owe to him; the created world cannot sustain itself in being, it is not ontologically autarchic, its back leans upon the sole being which 'lacks nothing for its existence'.

The seriousness and the scope of this question are such as to force us to dig deeper while remaining within the limits of our preoccupations. What are we to say about the passages in which Plato affirms, in contrast to what he says elsewhere and to the position we ascribe to all of traditional ontology, that there is creation (*poiēsis*) and that this is the 'cause of the passage from non-being to being', that which 'leads a former non-being to a subsequent beingness (*ousia*)'?[38] We reply that they can only be understood and interpreted correctly if we consider what is meant here by this passage, this 'leading to', wherefrom it begins and to what it leads. Now the context leaves no doubt about this. Plato notes that we unduly restrict the terms 'creator' and 'creation' (*poiētēs, poiēsis*) to what is but a part of 'poietics' (the one that concerns 'music and metre'), whereas any work belonging to an art (*technē*) is, properly speaking, poietic and the artisans that perform it are all 'creators' – *poiētai*. But in what does this work consist and what is a *technē*? By what token is an artisan actually an artisan and, as such, a 'creator'? To the extent that he gives a shapeless piece of matter its form, its *eidos* (and here we can use, indifferently, either Plato's or Aristotle's language, for Aristotle does no more than make Plato's thought more precise, pushing it to its limit). It is this *eidos*, this form that makes of wood a table, of bronze a statue, and of earth a vase. Now bronze *is* bronze regardless of its form. But the statue is a statue only due to its form; its being-a-statue, its essence, *is* its *eidos*. So, to say that someone creates the statue (ontologically) is meaningful only if we say (which is true, at least for the sculptor who is not copying any other sculptor) that someone creates the *eidos* of the statue, that what is created *is* the *eidos*. The statue is *brought into being* as a statue and as this particular statue only if its *eidos* is invented, imagined, posited out of nothing. If we imprint upon a mass of bronze an *eidos* that is already given, we are merely repeating what essentially, as an essence – *eidos* – was already there, we are creating nothing, we are imitating, we are *producing*. Conversely, if we 'make' *another eidos*, we are doing more than 'producing', we are *creating*. The wheel revolving around an axis is an absolute ontological creation. It is a greater creation, it weighs, ontologically, more than a new galaxy that would arise tomorrow evening out of nothing between the Milky Way and Andromeda. For *there are already* millions of galaxies – but the person who invented the wheel, or a written sign, was imitating and repeating *nothing* at all.

Now, this creation of the *eidos* in and through social–historical doing, presupposing the existence of the artisan, for example, the fact that the artisan can be an artisan only by *creating* an *eidos* or by imitating an *eidos created* by another artisan (or, in another area, the fact that the institution of the *polis* neither imitates nor repeats anything but is the creation of an *eidos*) suffers a total eclipse, is excluded from consideration in inherited thought from the time of Plato and Aristotle and, following them, by all of Western philosophy.[39] For it would break the determinacy of being and the idea of being as determinacy which must necessarily be construed as immutability, the inalterability of *eidē* as a totality, a system and a hierarchy, closed upon themselves and already given, excluding the possibility of introducing into them *other eidē* while leaving intact those that are already found there; for which others could these be and where would they come from? To see the situation clearly there is no need to discuss the origin of the *eidos* that the terrestrial artisan contemplates, imitates and reproduces. We have only to consider the paradigm of the artisan, the one with respect to whom every artisan is but a pale imitation, the Demiurge himself, as he 'creates', that is to say, actually, as he fabricates or *produces* the world. In the *Timaeus*, he is called, precisely, a demiurge (maker, producer, artisan) as well as a poet (creator). In truth, however, he is by no means a poet: he 'looks at' his model (paradigm) and fashions the world after this model; the world 'is necessarily an image of something' (*anankē tonde ton kosmon eikona tinos einai*);[40] explaining the world is therefore to distinguish bewen the image and its paradigm.[41] This paradigm is the eternal, intelligible, perfect (*pantelei*),[42] Living being. The creation of the world by the Demiurge is not creation, *is not* a passage from non-being to being, it is governed by a pre-existing paradigm, predetermined by the *eidos* that it imitates, repeats, reproduces. And in complete consistency with this view, the *Sophist* will state that 'the products of nature, as they are called, are works of divine art' (*theia technē*).[43] The 'creation' of the world does indeed involve a *technē*, precisely in the sense that it *imitates* a model. Aristotle pushing Plato's thought to its limit, found himself on the borderline of Western and Greek thought, or even beyond it, and some of his statements concerning *technē* can be interpreted as putting into question the entire edifice; basically, however, he will say nothing different. The creative art *par excellence*, the one that, as Plato noted, had ended up monopolizing the term '*poiesis*', poetry and tragedy, will be defined by him too as *imitation*.[44]

One would be hard put to explicate and enumerate the consequences of this fundamental position. In a sense, almost everything that is thought in the West today, including its most apparently 'subversive' discourses, follow from this position, are tied to it, are meaningful only in relation to it. The example that is most important to us is provided by the occultation of the imaginary and of the social–historical, always governed by the denial of creation, by the necessity to reduce history, at any cost, to repetition and to present this repetition itself as determinacy from a physical, logical or ontological 'elsewhere'. In this way, Heidegger and 'Marxists' meet curiously (in appearance) in the theme of 'production' – the sense of which, clearly, (*pro-ducere, hervor-bringen*, placing before, making come before) can only be, precisely, the one implied and required by Heideggerian ontology: the 'disclosure', the placing-before of what remained hidden but, of course, was already there. Where, then, was the piano hidden during the Neolithic age? It was inside the possibilities of Being; this means that its essence was 'already there'. In the same way, Kant termed the imagination 'productive' – productive and not creative. This corresponds perfectly to the role he had necessarily to assign to it: always to produce the *same* forms, forms that are valid only in so far as they perform *determined* functions in and for knowledge of given data. In the same way, finally, owing to the necessities of this frame of reference and in an interminable *Comedy of Errors*, 'materialism' is regularly overturned into 'idealism' and 'idealism' into 'materialism'. I have already abundantly illustrated the first proposition; here is an illustration of the second one. Why, in Kant and in Heidegger[45] (and, in fact, in all of philosophy) is man a 'finite being'? (Let us leave aside the strangeness of this expression, obviously meaningless – for man is not a number, and I do not know what finite means outside of mathematics or the mathematizable – and which can acquire meaning only in reference and in opposition to the theological phantasy and its translation into a philosophical thesis on God's infinity). Man is a 'finite being' not by reason of the 'banalities' represented by his mortality, his 'spatio-temporal' anchoring, etc.; philosophically speaking, in brief, man is a 'finite being' *because he can create nothing*. But create what? Create a milligramme of matter – that is what is actually in question. When man creates institutions, poems, music, tools, languages – or monstrosities, concentration camps, etc. – he creates Nothing (and even, as we shall see, later, less than Nothing). To be sure, all these things are *eide*; hence, man creates *eidos*. However, this idea is *unthinkable* within the inherited frame of reference. *Eidos* is *akineton*, true forms are immutable, incorruptible, unengenderable. How could anyone create them? At best, the forms created by man are *productions*, fabrications out of ... and in accordance with a given form and norm. So man does not create *eide*; and, possessing no 'intuitive understanding', as Kant says, he cannot provide himself in sensible intuition what he thinks or represents to himself (imagines), he does not make *sensible* (that is, actual matter) *what* he thinks or imagines *simply* by thinking it or imagining it. Man's finiteness means this and only this: that he cannot make an electron exist out of nothing. All the rest, which he makes exist out of nothing, does not count; the standard of being, for these non-materialist philosophers, is a speck of matter.

Let us return to the question of otherness and to another of its aspects, one of even greater importance. To say that figure B is other than figure A, in the sense given to this term here, is to say that, from A to B, there is *essential indetermination*. This obviously does not mean that the indetermination is total, that everything that is determinable in B must be other than everything that is determinable in A. There can be and, in fact, there always is a persistence or a subsistence of certain determinations. The 'reification' of these determinations and the accompanying assertion that the persisting and subsisting determinations are always and necessarily the 'principal', 'essential' deter-

minations is the metaphysical thesis of the essence-substance, of *ousia*,
the philosophical translation and purification in the identitary frame of
reference of the social–historical institution of the 'thing' in the most
general sense.

Acknowledging this essential indetermination creates insurmountable
difficulties for identitary logic and ontology. For it implies not only the
questioning of the schema of the necessary succession of events 'in'
time (causation) but also that of the group of central logical ontological
determinations (categories) as closed, certain, sufficient – not to mention the impossibility of any 'deduction' of the categories. This is so,
in any event, if the categories are posited as having to ensure an actual
grasp of what exists and not simply as a catalogue of the minimal
requirements of discourse as an instrument for marking; in other words,
if the categories are considered as the necessary and universal forms
of thinking of what is (or of its constitution) and not as grammatical
forms.[46] For, if time is truly otherness-alteration, it is out of the question
that, at any given moment, the group of essential determinations of
what exists can be considered as closed – and even more so that we
can say precisely why these determinations are such as they are. On
the other hand, it becomes imperative that we take account of the
other, equally decisive, aspect of the question, an aspect that is just as
necessarily ignored and hidden in the inherited logic and ontology: the
historicity of thinking and of knowledgeable action. Time, the emergence of other figures and hence of other determinations, is
logical-ontological genesis; thinking of what exists as temporal demands
thinking of it as giving rise to other modes of being (and of thinking).
History itself and the unfolding of history provide a blinding illustration
of this. The emergence of history reduces to nothingness, strictly speaking, everything that has ever been said about being and the necessities
of thinking of it; for *what* history *is is not*, if we restrict ourselves to
what may have been thought up to now concerning the sense of: being.
Thus, it is a life or death necessity for inherited thought to eliminate,
in one way or another, history as such – just as it must eliminate
society, the imagination and the imaginary. What the greatest thinkers
may have said that was truthful and fecund was always said *despite*
what they thought of as being and as thinkable, not because of what
they thought or in agreement with it. And, to be sure, it is in this
despite that their greatness is expressed, now as ever.

The inherited philosophical institution of time is, therefore, the institution of time as *identitary*; it is the institution of time as a super-
numerary spatial dimension – and, beyond this, a jungle of 'residual'
aporias. This founds the common institution of time – until the moment,
as is the case today, when scientific activity itself shakes it to its core.
This philosophical institution of time is, itself, the product and the
result of the logical–ontological purification of the social–historical
institution of time in *one* of its dimensions, that of *legein* and of

marking, once this dimension has been entirely delivered over to the requirements of *legein* pushed to their limit, that is to the requirements of ensemblist–identitary logic.

This identitary time is the homogeneous and neutral medium of 'successive coexistence', which is coexistence itself for the Gaze (*Theoria*) that examines the latter spread out before it. Here, traditional ontology, mathematics and classical mechanics (even physics) meet absolutely. In this identitary time exists the identitary present – and, reciprocally, identitary time is but the innumerable (and *numbered*) repetition of identitary presents, always identical *as such* and different *only* by their 'place', as Aristotle so admirably stated: 'The "now" (*nun*) in one sense is the same, in another it is not the same. In so far as it is in succession (in another and in another, *en allô kai allô*), it is different (*heteron*) ... but its substratum (in so far as the present is what it is, *o pote on*) is an identity (the same, *to auto*); 'In so far then as the "now" is a boundary (determination, *peras*), it is not time, but an attribute of it (*alla sumbebeken*).'[47] This identitary time is indispensable if there is to be identitary determination. The identitary present provides the instrument for all determinacy; it permits the *ama*, the 'at once', copresence and cobelonging, both 'objective' and 'subjective'. To assert the principle of identity, I need the *nun*, the absolute present: A cannot be different from A *at the same moment* and in the same relation, as will be interminably repeated. *At this moment* A is indeed A and fully A and nothing but A. And, in order to say this, I must be present and close to A at the same time I say it and at the same time A is as I say it is.[48]

However, time that is not reduced to the necessities of bearings and of *legein*, true time, the time of otherness-alteration is a time of bursting, emerging, creating. The *present*, the *nun* is here explosion, split, rupture – the rupture of what is as such. This present exists as originating, as immanent transcendence, as source, as the surging forth of ontological genesis. What is contained *in* this present is not contained *there*, for it is burst asunder as a determined 'place' in which something determined could simply stand, as the copresence of compatible determinations. Social–historical time – time that *is* the social–historical itself – allows us to apprehend the most pregnant, the most striking form of this time. The social–historical present gives us a blinding and paroxystic illustration of this present each time instituting society irrupts within instituted society, each time society as instituted is self-destructed by society as instituting, that is to say each time another instituted society is self-created. But just because we are attempting to clarify what we mean by this example, the reader must not be led to think that only cataclysmic irruptions make up historical time, that there is an historical present only at the time of a catastrophe or a revolution. Even when, in appearance, a society is merely 'preserving itself', it never ceases to alter itself.

vi   THE SOCIAL INSTITUTION OF TIME

All these questions re-emerge when we consider the social institution of time. It seems obvious to us that society's institution of the world necessarily contains, as one of its 'components' or 'dimensions', an institution of time. But it is also obvious that this very self-evidence is inseparable from our experience of life within an instituted temporality. How can we move outside of this experience? We can try to test its limits, and this we continuously do in the 'empirical' direction (time considered a 'natural datum'), in the 'psychological' direction (time as an experienced self-evidence), and in the 'transcendental' or 'onto-logical' direction (time as the condition for a subject's experience – or as a dimension, element, horizon or whatever of being). This testing, however, is always problematic for banal and long-recognized reasons. For example, we never have access to primordially 'natural' data but always to data that have already been elaborated. To be sure, no elaboration of X would be possible if X were not capable of being elaborated, did not carry within it a certain organization. But all that we can assert with respect to this organization is that it 'lends' itself to a certain type of elaboration (namely, a particular manner of instituting the world, a naive one or a scientific one), *up to a certain point* – and it is this 'up to a certain point' (or in certain respects, or *as to ...*, *quatenus*) that poses a question to us.

Consider, for example, the essential datum, at once naive and scientific, the core of our experience of time and an ingredient in every social institution, that finds its counterpart and its support in the 'natural' fact of the *irreversibility* of the succession of events or phenomena. Here is an indubitable datum, verified every second by each one of us with respect to every possible type of experience. It would, of course, be absurd to say that the irreversibility of time is instituted, in the sense that it would be possible for a society not to take account of it; it is not instituted purely and simply any more than men, animals or stars are instituted purely and simply. The irreversibility of time belongs to the first natural stratum of which every institution of society must (under penalty of death) take account. However, just as for everything that belongs to this stratum, it is immediately evident that social–historical development has to take account of it *in a certain way* and not 'absolutely'. This amounts to saying that in its *being-thus*, in the case of each society, the irreversibility of time is, nevertheless, instituted. In fact, whether in an archaic society or in Western science in its most advanced form, all that the development must absolutely account for is a *local* irreversibility. Beyond this, it may, as is the case in a wide number of known cultures and scientific or philosophical cosmologies, place this local irreversibility within a time that, taken as a whole, is cyclical (in which death precedes the birth that follows it), posit it as an illusion, consider it as a mere 'probability', even though an extremely likely one, or say that this is simply one obligatory way of grasping the multiple, related more to the characteristics of the 'observer' than to what is 'observed' (this, of course, refers to a presumed indubitable being-thus of the 'observer' himself and so places us once again before the same question, formed in a different manner).

Now, just as the social-being of the social is not manifested in the properties of human beings as sexual, living things but in the being-thus of men and women and in the difference between the sexes as it is instituted, in the same way, what characterizes a society is not the obligatory recognition of the local irreversibility of time, which is trivial and the same everywhere, but the manner in which this local irreversibility is instituted and taken into consideration in the representation and the activity of society. And this is indissociable from the imaginary significations of this society in general and, more particularly, of the total imaginary time in which this locally irreversible time is immersed. The possibility (or impossibility) of metempsychosis will be based on this recovery of the 'natural' datum of irreversibility in the social institution of time – the return of the ancestor in the newborn, the existence and the power of magic and its limits, the possibility of miracles, the view – that of the 'civilized' West for over 2,000 years – that this irreversible time is but a minute parenthesis in an eternity, whose irruption in *this* time, always imminent, will abolish it. How can all of this be deduced or induced from the 'natural' datum of the irreducibility of time?

What can we say now if we want to test the limits of the arbitrary character of the social–historical institution of time from a philosophical – 'transcendental' or 'ontological' – point of view? Almost nothing, rigorously speaking: for nothing in a transcendental philosophy provides any way of thinking of a *plurality* of subjects, except as an empirical contingency (which, moreover, even as such remains unassimilable, if these other, empirical men are themselves to be consciousnesses – as is demonstrated by the irreducible impossibility of the *alter ego* in Husserl's philosophy, as long as it remains self-consistent). Let us assume that this contingency becomes actual. *It happens*, then, that there is a plurality of subjects, of consciousnesses. Each of these organizes its experience, its *Erfahrung*, necessarily in accordance with the pure forms of space and time and with the categories (or its vision of essences, *Wesenschau*); and, by means of a judgement that is only probable and never necessary, since it contains empirical elements, consciousness postulates that the speaking phenomena that it encounters are the empirical supports of other consciousnesses. It then recognizes an essential (probable) identity between itself and the latter as consciousnesses, namely as powers capable of organizing experience, but not an identity of *experiences*, since experience also contains that which comes from the 'receptivity of impressions' and since every judgement about the essential similitude (the term 'identity' would be meaningless here) of the 'impressions' received by one consciousness and by another would be empirical to the second degree (would have to go through the empirical study of the psychophysiology of the subjects, etc.). What then guarantees the coherence, even if it be only approximative, of these various experiences and of their form, to the extent that they are all submitted to time in general, to space in general, and to the same categories – but in their full and concrete being-thus? Certainly not the identity or the similarity of the 'datum' since, in this perspective, the datum as such = X, this is all that we can say about it. Is there a pre-established monadological harmony?[49] Or, rather, before any social contract, did the consciousnesses conclude an ontological contract (the obvious presupposition of the first contract) obliging them to recognize in one another the fact that each is a subject of experience, not only *formally* but *materially* compatible with one another? And how are they able to know if the contract is respected by each one of them? Whatever the reply may be, the only conclusion that we can draw from this with respect to the social–historical institution is that, at best, this institution must include, in one way or another, something in which the *formal* compatibility of the experiences of subjects can be presentified or embodied, in so far as these experiences are submitted to the *form* of time. In other words, all that remains is this triviality: there must be a social institution of a common or collective marking of time.

Let us start again, further back, or further forward, one knows that it is the same thing.

In being, in having-to-be, the social–historical element emerges, itself a rupture of being and an 'instance' of the appearance of otherness. The social–historical is radical imaginary, namely the incessant originating of otherness that figures, and figures itself, is in figuring and in figuring itself, giving itself as a figure and figuring itself to the second degree ('reflexively').

The social–historical is positing of figures and the relation between and to these figures. It contains its own temporality as creation; as creation, it is also temporality, and as *this* creation, it is also *this* temporality, social–historical temporality as such, and the specific temporality that each society *is* in each instance, in the mode of temporal being that it causes to be by existing. This temporality is both scanned by the institution's positing *and* fixed in it, frozen in it, inverting itself into the negation and denial of temporality. The social historical is perpetual flux of self-alteration – and can only exist by providing itself with 'stable' figures by which it makes itself visible, visible to and for itself as well, in its impersonal reflexivity, which is also a dimension of its mode of being; the primordial 'stable' figure is here the institution.

The social–historical emerges in what is not social or historical – in the pre-social, or the natural. The emergence of otherness is already inscribed in pre-social, or natural, temporality. This term implies a being-thus in itself, at once undisputable and indescribable, of the first, 'physical' and 'biological', stratum, which every society not only presupposes but from which it can never be absolutely separated–distinguished–abstracted, by which, in a sense, it is permeated through and through, which it necessarily 'receives' but 'takes over' arbitrarily, otherwise, in and through its institution. The indissociability of this necessary reception and this arbitrary taking over is designated here by the term 'leaning on' – the institution's leaning on the first natural stratum.

Now it is clear that the social–historical institution of temporality is not, and cannot be, a repetition or an extension of natural temporality – any more than the social–historical institution of identity, for example, can be the repetition or the extension of a natural identity. What is natural identity? *There is* something like a natural identity, there is an enigmatic and irrepressible sense, which is at once impossible to explicate and yet without which we could not take a single step, in which we can say that the men of the Neolithic age lived on the same Earth as we do, that as men they were the same as us, and so on. But identity exists fully and purely only as instituted, in and through the social–historical institution of identity and of the identical. The enigmatic character of the natural identity of men, for instance, is, and is enigmatic, only by means of the indubitable identity of the word 'man' regardless of who states it or of the moment when it is stated. Identity is instituted as the nuclear framework of social *legein*. If it is said that, here too, it is never 'actual' or 'real', this simply confirms what I am maintaining: identity is instituted as the *rule* and *norm* of identity, as the first norm and form without which nothing could be of society, in society, for society. The institution is always the institution of the norm, as well. 'The Earth was the same Earth two hundred million years ago' – this expression is at once indubitable and indefensible. However, to return to a classroom example, Pythagoras's theorem is the *same*, whether in Samos 25 centuries ago or in Paris today. Little matter in what context it is taken by those who are thinking it, or even whether it is 'actually' the same: it *has to* be, I can think-speak only by positing this condition, I must posit it at the very moment that I want to show that it is absurd and in order to show this. It is not only that the social–historical institution alone can 'state', 'formulate', 'explicitate' the idea, the schema, the actuality of identity: the social–historical institution alone *brings* identity *into being*, for the first time in the history of the world, by bringing into being the identical as rigorously identical. In this sense, 'full' identity exists if and only if it is instituted. The identity brought into being by society is Other than the 'identity' that we can (and must) postulate in nature: society brings identity into being in a mode of being that is impossible and inconceivable elsewhere. It is not only – for this is secondary – that identity is 'posited' by the institution as a decree proclaiming that the identical has to be. It is, rather, that the institution itself can exist only as a norm of identity, the identity of the institution with itself, for it can exist only by being itself *what* it decrees as having to be: *the identity of the norm with itself which is posited by the norm so that there can be a norm of self-identity.* In the same way, 'there are laws' is the *law* that is presupposed by every set of laws, and it can be a law if and only if there indeed are laws. Or again: 'the law must be obeyed' is the first law, without which there would be no law – and which is not a law, since it is empty if laws do not exist.

In an analogous and profoundly more complex manner, the question of the relation between the social–historical institution of time and natural temporality arises. For, 'before' being the explicit institution of time – the positing of markings and measurements, the constitution of an identitary time immersed in a magma of imaginary significations, itself instituted as an imaginary time – society is itself the institution of an 'implicit' temporality that it brings into being by existing and that, through its existence, in turn, brings society into being. And this institution is impossible, both formally and materially, without an explicit institution of time. Society in general, and each society in particular, is 'first' the institution of an implicit temporality; it exists 'first' as self-alteration and as a specific mode of this self-alteration. We are not saying: each society has its own way of living time, but: each society *is* also a way of making time and of bringing it into existence, which means: a way of making itself be, of bringing itself into existence as society. And this bringing into being of social–historical time, which is also society's bringing itself into being as temporality, is not reducible to the explicit institution of social–historical time, while being impossible without the latter. The social–historical *is* this temporality, in each case specific, which is instituted as the global institution of society and not made explicit as such. The time that each society brings into being and which, in turn, makes society exist, is its own particular mode of historical temporality that it unfolds by existing and by which it unfolds itself as an historical society, without necessarily knowing this or representing this to itself in such a way. It would not even be enough to say that the description or analysis of a society is inseparable from the description of its temporality; the description and analysis of a society *is* obviously the description and analysis of its institutions. And among these, the first one is that which institutes it as being, as being-society and *this particular* society, namely the institution of its own temporality.

We can illustrate what has just been stated by briefly evoking two more or less familiar examples.

What is capitalism? An innumerable host of things, facts, events, acts, ideas, representations, machines, institutions, significations, results – that we can, somehow or other, carry back to a few institutions and to a few nuclear or germinal significations. These institutions and these significations, however, are – would have been – effectively impossible outside of the actual temporality established by capitalism, outside of this particular mode of society's self-alteration that irrupts with, in and through capitalism and that, finally, in a sense *is* capitalism. One could say that capitalism brings into being this actual historical temporality, but one could just as well say that capitalism can exist only *in* and *through*, only *as* an actual temporality such as this. This temporality is not *explicitly* instituted as such, even less is it thought or represented (except, perhaps, in an unconscious manner). For the explicit institution of time in capitalism, as identitary time or the time of marking, is that of a measurable, homogeneous, uniform and wholly arithmetizable flux. And, as an imaginary time or a time of signification, typical capitalist time is an 'infinite' time represented as a time of indefinite progress, unlimited growth, accumulation, rationalization, time of the conquest of nature, of the always closer approximation of a total, exact knowledge, of the realization of the phantasy of omnipotence. The present state of the planet attests to the fact that these are not just empty words, that these imaginary significations are more 'real' than any reality. Capitalist society exists in and through this explicit institution of its identitary time and of its imaginary time, the two being, moreover, obviously indissociable. But this is not the actual temporality of capitalism, *what* capitalism *brings into being* as temporality, by means of which it *is what* it is. And this actual temporality is not 'simple' or 'homogeneous'. On one level of its actuality, capitalist time is the time of incessant rupture, of recurrent catastrophes, of revolutions, of perpetually being torn away from what already exists, so admirably perceived and described by Marx, both in itself and in its opposition to the time of traditional societies. On another level of its actuality, capitalist time is the time of accumulation, of universal linearization, of digestion-assimilation, of making the dynamic static, of the effective suppression of otherness, of immobility in perpetual 'change', of the tradition of the new, of the shift from 'ever more' to 'more of the same', of the destruction of signification, of powerlessness at the heart of power, of a power that empties iteslf out as it extends over a wider range. And these two levels are also indissociable, each existing in the other and through the other, and it is in and through their imbrication and their conflict that capitalism is capitalism.[50] Note the otherness that separates capitalism's actual temporality from that of most archaic societies. First, in the explicit institution of time made by these societies, the relation between identitary time (the time of marking, calendar time) and the time of signification (imaginary time) is not the same, the connection between them is much closer (the markings themselves have a signification and are what they are in relation to the latter; the seasons are not simply 'functional' seasons, etc.). Next, the relation between the explicitly instituted time and the society's actual temporality is different, or at least seems different to us; we do not observe between the two the same split, the same degree or same type of split. The explicit institution of time in an archaic society is not in reality, or not essentially, that of a homogeneous flux in which something grows unceasingly (as it is in capitalism) but much more like a cycle of repetitions, punctuated by the recurrence of natural events, full of imaginary significations, or that of important rituals. As such, it is much closer to the actual temporality of this society, such as we are capable of understanding it, which, for its part, is comparable to rhythmical beats – to the extent that external 'accidents' do not happen to disturb or modify the flow – behind which its self-alteration continues silently, just as each night the true celestial pole shifts an imperceptible distance.

As our second example, we take Thucydides' description, through the mouths of the Corinthian envoys to Sparta, of a few aspects of the actual temporality of Sparta and of Athens, as they contrast with one another: 'The Athenians are addicted to innovation, and their designs are characterized by swiftness alike in conception and execution; you (the Lacedaemonians) have a genius for keeping what you have got, accompanied by a total want of invention, and when forced to act you never go far enough. Again, they are adventurous beyond their power, and daring beyond their judgement, and in danger they are sanguine; your wont is to attempt less than is justified by your power, to mistrust even what is sanctioned by your judgement, and to fancy that from danger there is no release. Further, there is promptitude on their side against procrastination on yours; they are never at home, you are never from it: for they hope by their absence to extend their acquisitions, you fear by your advance to endanger what you have left behind. They are swift to follow up a success, and slow to recoil from a reverse. Their bodies they spend ungrudgingly in their country's cause; their intelligence they jealously husband to be employed in her service. A scheme unexecuted is with them a positive loss, a successful enterprise a comparative failure. The deficiency created by the miscarriage of an undertaking is soon filled up by fresh hopes; for they alone are enabled to call a thing hoped for a thing got, by the speed with which they act upon their resolutions. Thus they toil on in trouble and danger all the days of their life, with little opportunity for enjoying, being ever engaged in getting: their only idea of a holiday is to do what the occasion demands, and to them laborious occupation is less of a misfortune than the peace of a quiet life. To describe their character in a word, one might truly say that they were born into the world to take no rest themselves and to give none to others.'[51]

This passage could be commented on at great length. Let us simply note that there clearly appears here the actual temporality of a society viewed in its mode of *doing*, and that this is perceived in its deep relation to the *signification* of the past and of what is to come, and this, in turn, is inseparable from the *signification* of 'reality' (what already exists, or has already been acquired, is nothing in relation to what is to be or to be acquired), or, what amounts to the same thing, in its relation to the ultimate foundations of what is of *value* and what is of no *value*. And, let us note that, for this to be the case, it is by no means necessary that the Athenians modify anything in their *explicit* institution of time, either identitary or imaginary, the institution that, except for a few details, they share with the other Greeks. For this to be the case, it is necessary, and sufficient, that they do just what they do, that they institute themselves as fifth-century Athens, by bringing into being this mode of doing, this mode of being a city, which, moreover, they tend to try to impose on everyone else, by leaving no one alone, by obliging all the others to do as they do against them or else to disappear. And this is *also* at issue in the Peloponesian War, from which Athens will emerge as the vanquished, while Athenian temporality will continue victorious for many centuries – and perhaps even to our own day.

vii IDENTITARY TIME AND IMAGINARY TIME

If we now consider the time explicitly instituted by each society, we are obliged to distinguish between two different yet obligatory dimensions of this institution, the identitary dimension and the properly imaginary dimension. The time that is instituted as identitary is time as the time of mark-makings, as time-marking and time of markings. Instituted time as imaginary (socially imaginary, we mean) is the time of signification, or significant time (a distinction that by no means implies a separation of what we are distinguishing).

Instituted time considered as identitary or as the time of markings is that related to the measurement of time or to imposing a measure on time and as such entails its segmentation into 'identical' or ideally (and impossibly) 'congruent' parts. This is calendar time, with its 'numerical' divisions, for the most part leaning on the periodical phenomena of the natural stratum (day, lunar month, seasons, year), and then refined by means of logical–scientific developments, but always in reference to spatial phenomena. Even this leaning on the natural stratum is not absolutely determining, in the first place for well-known 'natural' reasons, namely that the great natural periodicities do not have, in respect of one another, simple numerical relations (there is not a whole number of days or of lunar months in a solar or sidereal year, these two years do not strictly coincide, etc.). But also for reasons that have to do with the society considered. The Mayas' extraordinary astronomical knowledge, for example (which enabled them, as it seems, to predict the helioc risings of Venus with an error of one day in 6,000 years) did not prevent them from using, at the same time, ritual 'years' of 260 days. In the same way, the Moslem calendar with its lunar months and its 'short' years in relation to solar years did not take advantage of the knowledge already available in the cultural sphere at the time it was established.

Instituted time considered as the time of signification, as significant time or imaginary (social) time maintains with identitary time a relation of reciprocal inherence or of circular implication that always exists between the two dimensions of any social institution: the identitary–ensemblist dimension and the dimension of signification. Identitary time is 'time' only because it is referred to the imaginary time that gives it its signification of 'time'; and imaginary time would itself be undefinable, impossible to situate, ungraspable – it would be *nothing* without identitary time. In this way, for example, the articulations of imaginary time parallel or lend depth to the numerical points of reference of calendar time. What takes place there is not a simple repeated event, but the essential manifestation of the world-order, as this is instituted by the society in question, of the forces that animate it, of the privileged moments of social activity – whether this concerns work, ritual, feasts, politics. This is obviously the case for the cardinal moments of the daily cycle (dawn, dusk, noon, midnight), for the seasons, and often for the years themselves, placed under the sign of a particular signification. It is unnecessary to recall that, before the contemporary period, no society ever considered the start of spring or the beginning of the summer as mere bench marks in the passage of the year, or even as functional signals for the beginning of a given 'productive' activity, but instead as always interwoven with a complex of mythical or religious significations; and even contemporary society has not yet managed to live time as simply calendar time.

It is also in imaginary time that the *boundaries* of time, on the one hand, and the *periods* of time, on the other, are posited. The boundaries of time illustrate the *logical* necessity of the institution of time *as* imaginary. The idea of an origin and an end of time as well as the idea of the absence of any such origin or end both lack content or natural, logical, scientific or even philosophical signification. But one or the other must be posited in the social institution of the world; this time 'in' which society lives *must* either be suspended between a beginning and an end or else be 'infinite'. In both cases, this positing is necessarily and purely imaginary, lacking any natural or logical support. Thus, there is a 'date' of the creation of the world or simply a 'moment' of the creation of the world, or repeating cycles, an 'end' of the world that is awaited and that requires that we prepare for it, or an 'indefinite future', etc. As for the periodization of time, it is obviously nothing but a part of the magma of imaginary significations of the society considered: Christian and Moslem eras, 'ages' (golden, silver or bronze), eons, great Mayan cycles, etc. This periodization can play an essential role in the imaginary institution of the world for the society in question. Thus, for Christians there is an absolute, qualitative difference between the time of the Old Testament and that of the New Testament, the Incarnation marks an essential division in the history of the world between the boundaries of Creation and of Parousia, the eternal destiny of a man would be radically different depending on whether he lived before or after the Incarnation, whilst none of it is of his own doing.

Finally, for every society there is what might be called the *quality* of time as such, what time is 'brewing' or 'preparing', what it is 'pregnant' with: the time of Exile for the Jews in the Diaspora, the time of trial and of hope for Christians, the time of 'progress' for Westerners. This quality is correlative to the magma of instituted imaginary significations; it may appear to be 'derived' from the latter, but it would be more correct to say, risking an improper use of language, that it is the essential *'affect'* of the society considered. The quality of time as such shows that instituted time can never be reduced to its purely identitary, calendar and measurable time. Even in the Western societies of modern capitalism, where the attempt at this reduction has been carried the farthest, not only does a quality of the temporal flux subsist, and massively so, but this very reduction of time to purely and solely measurable time is but one manifestation among others of this society's imaginary and the instrument of its 'materialization'. Time *must* be *only* this, no more – a pure, homogeneous, neutral medium or the parameter *t* of a family of exponential functions, if there is to be, as economists say, a 'rate of discounting the future', if everything is to appear as measurable and calculable, if the central imaginary signification of this society: pseudo-rationalization, is to be able to appear to possess minimal coherence in accordance with its own norms. This example simply illustrates, in the case of time, a general proposition: an instituted time that would be purely identitary is impossible because an instituted world that would be purely identitary is impossible, because the separation of the ensemblist organization of the social world from imaginary social meanings is impossible.

All that has just been stated refers first of all, explicitly, to the *time of social representing* – of which represented time as such is but an aspect or a moment. Time must be instituted (both as identitary and as imaginary) for social representing to be possible, the time in and through which this representing exists and which this representing makes exist. This time, however, is inseparable from the *time of social doing*: the time that must be instituted for social doing to be possible, the time in and through which this doing exists, the time that this doing makes exist. This time is based on markings from the calendar of identitary time, but it could also be said that these markings are posited primordially and essentially in so far as they permit the instrumentation of doing – *teukhein*.

Here again, to be sure, there is leaning on the natural level, as is obvious in natural labour or in war. After carefully setting in place all the available calendar markings, the historian makes apparent this leaning-on: 'The thirty years' truce which was entered into after the conquest of Euboea lasted fourteen years. In the fifteenth, in the forty-eighth year of the priestess-ship of Chrysis at Argos, in the ephorate of Aenesias at Sparta, in the last month but two of the archonship of

Pythodorus at Athens, and six months after the battle of Potidaea, just at the beginning of the spring, a Theban force a little over three hundred strong ... about the first watch of the night, made an armed entry into Plataea, a town of Boeotia in alliance with Athens.'[52]

The natural leaning-on appears as a potential injunction, the gathering together of all the favourable or unfavourable conditions for doing, but it is and comes to be as it is only in correlation with doing and with a particular doing. Here again one can see the irreducibility of time to a merely calendar time, since even if it is a leaning on nature, the time of doing presents itself and exists as internally differentiated, organized, unhomogeneous, inseparable from *what* is done in it. 'There is a time for birth, a time for dying ... a time for war and a time for peace ...'[53] But this leaning on nature not only does not exhaust the time of doing (the time of sowing and the time of harvesting are 'self-evident', but not the auspicious and inauspicious days and years); the time of doing would not be a time of doing and would not even be a time at all, if it did not contain the critical moment, the singularity which does not exist 'objectively' and which will become so only by means of and for the appropriate doing, its occurrence as such and the point of its realization on the calendar being neither certain nor predictable (whether this concerns primitive hunting or the moment of interpretation in a psycho-analysis). In short, this is what the Hippocratic writings call *kairos*, in terms of which they define time: *chronos estin en ô kairos, kairos d'en ô chronos ou polus*, 'time is that in which there is *kairos* (propitious instant and critical interval, the opportunity to take a decision) and *kairos* is that in which there is not much time.' A much more essential definition certainly, than the one that sees in time no more than the interminable addition of point-like, identical 'nows': time is, say the Hippocratic writings, only as that in which there is occasion and oppor-tunity for acting.

The time of doing must thus be instituted so as to contain singularities that are not determinable in advance, as the possibility of the appearing of what is irregular, of accidents, of events, of the rupture of repetition. It must, in its institution, preserve or make room for the emergence of otherness as intrinsically possible (not as the possibility of miracles or of acts of magic). For this very reason, the time of doing is necessarily much closer to true temporality than the time of social representation is or can be.

Indeed, the social institution of imaginary time as the time of social representation always tends to cover over, to conceal and to deny tempor-ality as otherness-alteration. From this point of view, it makes absolutely no difference whether time is represented as cyclical, as linear and infinite, or as an enigmatic illusion appended to transcendence. To the anguished question it raises, to the certainty of its uncertainty: 'I contemplate the task that God gives mankind to labour at. All that he does is apt for its time; but though he has permitted man to consider time in its wholeness,

man cannot comprehend the work of God from beginning to end,' Ecclesiastes replies by affirming the nihilistic character of time: 'I know that
what God does he does consistently. To this nothing can be added, from
this nothing taken away ... What is, already was, what is to be has already
been ...'[54]

Thus, everything happens as if the time of social doing, which is
basically irregular, uneven, changing, had always to be, in the imaginary, swallowed up by a denial of time through the eternal return of the
same, its representation as wearing away and as corruption, its flat-
tening out in the indifference of simply quantitative difference, its
annulation in the face of Eternity. Everything occurs as if the ground
where the creativity of society is manifested in the most tangible way,
the ground on which it acts, brings into existence and makes itelf exist
in bringing into existence, had to be covered over by an imaginary
creation arranged in such a way as to allow society to conceal what it
is to itself. Everything occurs as if society had to negate itself as society,
conceal its being as society by negating the temporality that is first and
foremost its own temporality, the time of otherness-alteration that it
brings into existence and that, in turn, makes it exist as society. To say
the same thing in another way: everything happens as if society were
unable to recognize itelf as making itself, as instituting itself, as self-
instituting.

This denial, this concealment can be understood and interpreted on
several different levels and in several ways, which, far from con-
tradicting one another or being mutually exclusive, converge. It corresponds, first, to the needs of the psychic economy of the subjects as
social individuals. Forcibly stripping them of their monadic madness,
of their originary representation-desire-affect of atemporality, of un-
otherness, and then of all-powerfulness, imposing on them, by instituting them as social individuals, the recognition of the other, difference, limitation and death, society holds out for them, in one form or
another, a compensation in terms of this ultimate denial of time and
of otherness. Obliging them to take their place, whether they like it or
not within the flux of time as instituted, (or run the risk of psychosis),
society offers subjects at the same time the means by which to defend
themselves by neutralizing time, representing it as flowing always along
the same banks, carrying along the same forms, taking with it what
was and prefiguring what is to come. This denial expresses also, just
as profoundly, the very logic of logic, an essential necessity of
identitary–ensemblist logic, rooted in the very existence of language,
of *legein*, of the postulate of atemporality that *legein* brings into being
and incarnates. The transition from these necessities to the necessities
of philosophy, of ontology, is almost immediate. For the hunter of the
Paleolithic age, 'yesterday, there was a bear in the forest' must be true
even today, and tomorrow, as a statement about yesterday. For the
philosopher 'p is true' is meaningless if it does not mean 'p is always
true', 'p is true independently of time'; 'the truth of p does not depend

on time'. And what is more important than truth? What is there *other* than truth? Being has always signified being truly and being true has always signified being. How, then, could what truly is be truly dependent on time; how could it be 'in' time; how, finally, could time be truly since what is truly is other than time, for if it were not other than time and without relation to time, it would not be? For, either its determinations would change with time in an indeterminate way, and it would not truly be, or it would only exist in a lesser mode of being; or else, its determinations would change in a determinate way – and time would not exist. By this very fact we see, finally, that the denial of time displays a necessity inherent in the institution as such. Born in, through and as the rupture of time, a manifestation of the self-alteration of society as instituting society, the institution in the profound sense of the term can exist only by posing itself as outside of time, by refusing to be altered by time, by posing the norm of its immutable identity and by posing itself as this norm of immutable identity, without which it would not exist. To say that the institution can foresee, control and manage its own change is still to say that it institutes this change as its unchanging state in relation to itself, that it claims to control time, that it refuses to be altered as an institution.

Thus we can understand, interpret the covering over of otherness, the denial of time, society's ignorance of its own social–historical being in so far as these are grounded in the very institution of society such *as we know it*, namely, such as it has up to now instituted itself. It amounts to the same thing to say that we interpret them as expressions of society's alienation with respect to itself, as manifestations of its heteronomy (*heteros*, the other, in this case – no one, *outis*), of its manner of instituting itself which contains the refusal to see that *it* institutes itself. Refusal: some would say, the impossibility of essence or ontological structure. We do not say this. The discourse that, in this domain, claims to determine non-trivial, essential impossibilities is the very one we refuse and that we have tried, in the preceding pages, to refute. For it continues to place the essence or the being of society in an *aei*, in an intemporal always in which, in the same stroke, the person who is speaking places himself as well. What we do know is that the denial of time and of otherness (which, in actual fact, is unceasingly translated into the continuous self-destruction of creativity in society and in human beings themselves) is itself an institution, a dimension and a mode of the institution of society as it has existed up to now. It is therefore arbitrary in the same way as any institution is – and is so up to a point that no theoretical discourse can establish in advance. For in this field, trivialities aside, the words 'impossible' and 'unavoidable' have no meaning. To what extent and on what condition can individuals accept themselves as mortals without any instituted imaginary compensation? To what extent can thinking hold together the requirements of identitary logic rooted in *legein* and the requirements of what exists, and which is certainly not identitary, without annihilating itself in simple incoherence? To what extent, finally and even more importantly, can society truly recognize in its institution its own self-creation, recognize itself as instituting, can it institute itself explicitly and overcome the self-perpetuation of what is instituted by showing itself to be capable of taking a new look at it and transforming it in accordance with its own requirements and not following the inertia of the already-instituted, of recognizing *itself* as the source of its own otherness – these are questions – *the* question of revolution – that do not go beyond the bounds of theory but are placed from the start on another terrain. If what we are saying has any meaning at all, this terrain is the very one of the creativity of history. And the latter has already brought about comparable ruptures. For example, the break that, 25 centuries ago, through the simultaneous and consubstantial institution of democracy and philosophy, inaugurated the explicit questioning by society of its own instituted imaginary.

viii LACK OF DISTINCTION BETWEEN THE SOCIAL AND THE HISTORICAL: ABSTRACTIONS OF SYNCHRONY AND OF DIACHRONY

It is, therefore, impossible to maintain an intrinsic distinction between the social and the historical, even if it is a matter of affirming that historicity is the 'essential attribute' of society or that society is the 'essential presupposition' of history. Statements such as these are, in truth, at once insufficient and redundant. It is not that every society is necessarily 'in' time or that a history necessarily 'affects' every society. The social *is* this very thing – self-alteration, and it is nothing if it is not this. The social makes itself and can make itself only as history; the social makes itself as temporality; and it makes itself in every instance as a specific mode of actual temporality, it is instituted implicitly as a singular quality of temporality. In the same way, it is not that history 'presupposes' society or that that of which there is a history is always a society in a descriptive sense. The historical *is* this very thing – the self-alteration of this specific mode of 'coexistence' that is the social as such; outside of this, it is nothing. The historical makes itself and can do so only as social; the historical is, in an exemplary and pre-eminent manner, the emergence of the institution and the emergence of *another* institution. Of course, here again, it is difficult to undo the force of language and tradition, as we are obliged to use these terms as separate in order to assert that they are not distinct. This does not matter for anyone who knows how to think and to remember; what is more, the distinction can even be useful, with this condition in mind, for it allows us to discuss in succession what we cannot dispense ourselves from conceiving transitorily as 'aspects' of one and the same object.

This becomes harmful, however, when the bloodless abstractions of 'synchrony' and of 'diachrony' are set up as absolutes. This fashion of the past few decades is but another way of concealing the social–historical. For, here, synchrony is intrinsically diachronized and diachronizing, just as diachrony is intrinsically synchronizing and synchronized. Saussure was justified in his time in stressing, in reaction to a pseudo-historicism in the linguistic domain, the impossibility of understanding anything at all about language by the mere description of phonological or semantic evolution, by the etymology of words or by changes in grammatical forms, emphasizing as he did the necessity of conceiving of language as a system that, at each moment, must function and functions effectively, independently of its past. Since then, however, the distinction between the synchronic and the diachronic view has been transformed into an absolute opposition and the synchronic point of view has been held to be the only legitimate one, diachronic considerations being regarded with condescendance, relegated to the descriptive level, and excluded from 'scientific' status. In fact, once again, this was a way of eliminating time. We know that the 'structuralists' distinguished themselves in their use of this rhetoric, which allowed them to mask the void that with them takes the place of any reflection on history. History itself thus becomes the mere juxtaposition of different 'structures' (or, in other domains, of *episteme*), spread out longitudinally, each being essentially atemporal. Why then are there several structures that 'follow' one another? Because they are subjected, as someone has written, to 'erosion'. Structures, it would seem, wear themselves away by being used. Curious property of time, allowing it – without being anything, without positing anything, without making anything exist – to erode what is. The savage mind is still among us.

It is, nevertheless, clear that the idea that the same object can be considered from the point of view of instantaneous cross-sections, on the one hand, and from that of its becoming, on the other hand, without these views ever communicating at any moment, is patently absurd. And the question of the relations between the 'system' and its 'becoming' is already posed in an unavoidable fashion in domains that are 'simpler' or more readily 'formalizable' than the social–historical domain; it is posed there as the question of the very possibility of this distinction, once one goes beyond superficial descriptions. This is already the situation in contemporary physics, in particular, in cosmology, where the distinction between 'structure' and 'becoming' seems increasingly obscure, since the structure of the universe entails a history – in the optic of general relativity – or *is* its history – in that of the steady-state theory. This is also the situation in biology, where the system is a *living* system by means of its capacity for 'evolving', both on the ontogenetic and on the phylogenetic level and as a global biosystem. If the system were *only* the capacity to preserve its 'state' and its 'flux', homeostasis and homeorhesis, there would never have been such a thing as a living being and if, by some miracle, there had been one, it would have been the *only* one. The living thing possesses as an intrinsic property not simply its capacity for development but for evolving, for organizing itself in a different way; its organization is this very capacity for transforming an accident or a disturbance into a new organization.

There is, however, another way as well, and another degree – other than the minor, secondary and always provisional one – in which the impossibility of distinguishing between synchrony and diachrony appears in the social–historical domain. The clearest example of this is provided, precisely, by language itself, considered in its essential aspect, namely in its relation to signification. For it is an essential property of language *as a system* that it is not exactly equivalent to its synchronic state, that it is not reducible to a closed totality of fixed, determined, available significations but instead always contains *something more*, eminent and constantly immanent, and is always synchronically *open* to a transformation of significations. A word is a word, 'has' a signification or refers to a signification if and only if it can acquire others, refer to other significations,[55] otherwise it would not be a word, but, at best, the symbol of a mathematical concept. (Actually, it would not even be this for even in mathematics the situation is different; π 'was' to begin with the ratio of the circumference to the diameter of the circle, it 'is' now a host of other things as well.) As a system, a language is unthinkable as pure synchrony; language exists only in as much as its own continuous transformation draws its resources from itself, as it is 'at any given moment'. It is only in this way, for instance, that language makes possible, through 'acquired' means, another discourse, only in this way does it allow an uncommon use of the common, serving to generate originality in what, apparently and really, is found everywhere – only in this way can it always recover its virginity intact in its universal prostitution.

Language must already contain the possibility of producing new abstract–material 'terms' in the form of words; it must possess 'lexical productivity'. This aspect is of little interest to us here, however, for it concerns language as a *code*. A code is a system of signs whose terms and their relations are fixed and given once and for all, in bi-univocal correspondence with another system. It remains a ('free') code if, to it, are related specific operations of generating new terms starting from a fixed and given 'base' (family of elements).[56] The abstract–material part of language (the system of 'signifiers') is a *code* or, better, a hierarchy of codes; as such, it is subject to ensemblist–identitary logic, its 'lexical productivity' is (almost) determined and determinable – it is, in fact, no more than *production*. But language is also *langue* to the extent that it refers to significations. Now significations do not lend themselves to algebraic formulation; there is no algebra of significations for there are no elements or atoms of signification, no determined operations governing a 'production' of significations out of any such elements or atoms (except partially, in domains that lend themselves to set theory and to the extent that this set theory concerns only one stratum of the object: in biological classification or taxonomy, for example). However, the possibility of the emergence of other significations is immanent in language and permanent as long as language is living. The absurdity of the 'strictly synchronic' and structural point of view is plainly apparent here. If the linguistic signifieds form a 'system' and if, as structuralism claims, each signified is rigorously nothing but the ensemble of its relations (differences) to all of the others, it follows that, just as the entire universe would collapse if a single particle of matter were destroyed (Leibniz), so the French language is no longer the *same* (the same 'synchronic system') if *a single* signified is modified. So, the 'synchronic state' of the French language, that is this language itself, changes, for example, between 1905 and 1922, every time that Proust completes a sentence. Since at the same time Saint-John Perse, Apollinaire, Gide, Bergson, Valéry and so many others are also writing – each of whom would not be a writer if he did not imprint on a good number of the 'signifieds' entering into his text an alteration that is his own but that henceforth belongs to the significations of the words in the language – *what* is then the 'synchronic state' of French as a language, as it refers to significations, during this period? It is not even a legitimate abstraction, it is a sheer incoherent fiction, constructed on the total misunderstanding of what a language is.

If there has ever been, even once in the entire history of humanity, a single new idea, a single original discourse, this is sufficient to prove what we are saying here: language itself, considered 'synchronically' was essentially open to 'diachrony', it contained the possibility of its own transformation and 'actively' supplied the partial means for this. This transformation is irreducible to 'operations' on elements of signification that would be already available. The way in which it instruments itself in and through what is linguistically established and supports itself on what is in order to make be what is other, to make emerge what is new, has to be explored and reflected upon for itself and on the basis of what is proper to it; it is original and has no model or analogy elsewhere.

Inversely, it is obviously an essential property of language as well, as history, to produce as a modification of its 'state' that which can always be integrated within a 'state', to be able to alter itself while continuing to function efficiently, constantly to transform the uncommon into the common, the original into the established, to be continual acquisition or elimination, and, in this, to perpetuate its capacity to be itself. Language, in its relation to significations, shows us how instituting society is constantly at work and also, in this particular case, how this work, which exists only as instituted, does not hamper the continued instituting activity of society. It is essential that language remain the same while not remaining the same, and vice versa. There would be no language, no society, no history, nothing if an ordinary Frenchman of today were not able to understand *Le Rouge et le noir*, or even

Saint-Simon's *Mémoires*, as well as an innovative text of an original writer. To forget this is to forget the other fundamental function of language – assuring every society's access to its own past.

What language shows us, concerning the impossibility of distinguishing absolutely between a synchronic dimension and a diachronic dimension, a social dimension and an historical dimension, is just as clearly marked on the level of global considerations. The social 'space' and all that it 'contains' are such as they are only through their constitutive opening up to temporality. Nothing, in any society whatsoever (however archaic, however cold it may be), exists that is not at one and the same time the inconceivable presence of what is no longer and the just as inconceivable imminence of what is not yet. However rigid, however repetitive the cycles of its activities and rites may be, the most narrowly present life of a society always unfolds in the explicit and implicit reference to the past, as in the expectation and the preparation of what is 'socially certain' but also in the certainty of uncertainty and in the face of the virtuality of unexpected and unforeseeable otherness. The actual existence of the social is always internally dislocated or, as some would say, constituted in itself by what is outside itself. It is the effective presence of the 'past' in tradition and in what is established (far beyond what in tradition and in the established is in each case known, explicated, taken into account); just as it is the effective presence of the 'future' in anticipation, uncertainty, undertaking (far beyond, here again, what can be taken into account, foreseen, included within a margin of probability). And that in and through which the social figures itself and makes itself be – the institution – is what it is in so far as, grounded in what was left behind, it is designed to make possible the reception of what lies ahead, since the institution is nothing if it is not form, rule and condition of what is not yet, an attempt that is always successful, and always impossible, to posit the 'present' of society as surpassing it in both directions and to allow to coexist there both the past and the future.

This is an incomparable situation, one that is conceivable in no other sphere and on no other basis than its own. We cannot separate here – except in the most external way, obliged by the linear nature of discourse – a 'space', a 'time' and 'that which' unfolds there. The social–historical 'dimensionality' is not a 'framework' *in* which the social–historical is spread out and in which it unfolds; it is itself the mode of self-unfolding *of the* social–historical. For the social–historical is, or comes into existence as, a figure, hence as spacing, *and* as the otherness-alteration of the figure, temporality. The 'space-time' (the R^4) *in* which we 'situate' all 'reality' and social–historical 'reality' itself when we posit it as mere exteriority, is itself a product of the social–historical institution and, beyond this, an unending enigma. The historical 'present' is only superficially the 'origin of the coordinates' – it is so only through the necessary postulations of identitary logic. It cannot be the origin of the coordinates, for it is not, except by the most violent of abstractions, 'point-like'. As has already been stated in the first part of this book, it includes within it 'all those who have existed and all who are yet to be born'; it is worked from within by the 'past' and the 'future' that 'dislocate it at the same time that they fix it'. The 'instantaneous cross-section' of social–historical life (the hypersurface $t =$ constant) is a simple means, in some respects convenient, in other, more important ways, fallacious, to situate and classify what one is speaking about. None of the 'points' that comprise it can for one second be considered separately from the arrow, from the temporal orientation and polarization that co-constitute it and without which it is nothing. And none of its essential 'spatial fibers' can be considered independently of the others. Even today, one can write a modern treatise on optics or thermodynamics, after having postulated once and for all a few propositions borrowed from basic physics – although we know that light and heat are only 'aspects' of the physical being. But one cannot write a work on economics, by condensing the 'rest' of social life to a few hypotheses *ne varietur* that provide the 'institutional framework' and the 'exogenous data'; everything that has been written in this way amounts more or less to exercises in elementary algebra without any actual content. I can always project a volume onto a plane, a figure onto an axis, the operation leaves me with some result in my hands; I cannot project social–historical life onto one of its 'axes', for the operation leaves me with *nothing*.

5

The Social–Historical Institution
Legein and *Teukhein*

Causation, finality, motivation, reflex, function, structure are simply pen names or *noms de guerre* assumed by necessary and sufficient reason. The latter, an offspring of reason as such, has become its exclusive representative, at the end of an evolution and following an interpretation whose roots lie deep within the institution of the social–historical. This interpretation, coextensive with inherited logic (in the broadest sense of the term 'logic'), is at the same time consubstantial to the ontology corresponding to this logic. Likewise, the central thesis of this ontology, as it conceives of and posits being as being-determined, beingness as determinacy, consists in the elaboration and the totalizing extension of the requirements of this logic. For the past 25 centuries, Greco-Western thinking has constituted, developed, amplified and refined itself on the basis of this thesis: being is being something determined (*einai ti*), speaking is saying something determined (*ti legein*). And, of course, speaking the truth is determining speaking and what is said by the determinations of being or else determining being by the determinations of speaking, and, finally, observing that both are but one and the same. This evolution, instigated by the requirements of one dimension of speaking and amounting to the domination or the autonomization of this dimension, was neither accidental nor inexorable; it corresponded to the institution by the West of thinking as Reason.

i IDENTITARY LOGIC AND SETS

I call the logic described above identitary logic and also, aware of the anachronism and the stretching of words involved here, set-theoretical logic, for reasons that will soon be apparent. The privilege it bears stems from the fact that it constitutes an essential and inexpungible dimension not only of language but of all life and all social activity. In addition, it is found in the very discourse that intends to circumscribe it, to relativize it, to question it. So that we, too, following so many others, shall be obliged to use its resources – as, of course, we have continually done up to now – in order to say that they are not equal to the task of thinking what is to be thought or of doing what is to be done.

The most advanced and the richest achievement of identitary logic is the development of mathematics. It is doubtless here that the main reason for the fascination that mathematics has exerted on philosophy, from Pythagoras and Plato to Husserl, is to be sought. It amounts to the same thing to say that mathematics has always seemed to offer the only available and effectively complete model of a true demonstration, namely a sufficient determination of what is said in its necessity. This achievement returns, today, to its starting point, envelops it or, better, coincides with it, since logic now becomes formalizable and must be formalized, that is to say mathematized: so-called formal logic becomes algebra of propositions, calculus of predicates, etc. This forms a circle, which it would be superficial to term vicious. For not only is this circle inevitable, circularity is in a profound sense the ultimate essence of this logic. Only local circles can be said to be vicious; the totality of a system, however, necessarily forms a circle (the diameter of which can, to be sure, dilate, apparently without limit). For every linear or open logical order (a hypothetical–deductive order, for example) leaves open the question of the justification or the necessity of its starting point, implying, therefore, that this is external to the discourse at hand and that it is posited from somewhere else. But this positing cannot be external to *every* discourse, it has to be taken in hand and justified in and through discourse. Ultimately, the justification of the initial thesis lies in the totality of its consequences, which in this way found what founds them. Acknowledged since Plato and Aristotle, the situation described here is made explicit and universal in the culmination of Western logic-ontology, the Hegelian system, which is necessarily cyclical.[1]

Mathematics is obviously interminable, not only with respect to the proliferation of its results but also in terms of the substance of its ideas. In its case, no more than in others, we cannot think that its construction has been completed in the past 50 years; instead, this construction has exploded. But we have seen a considerable unification of mathematics at the same time as an important elucidation of questions related to its foundation. Both outcomes are essentially tied to the constitution and to the development of the theory of ensembles, set-theory, which today provides the language and the basic tools for all branches of mathematics, and for this reason, constitutes the first part of mathematics.[2]

The logical rudiments of set-theory are important in this respect for, regardless of what may happen in the future from the perspective of mathematics, they condense, clarify, and exemplify in a pure manner what, all the while, was underlying identitary logic, and what, long

before this logic was sketched out, constituted an essential and unexpungible dimension of all activity and all social life. These rudiments,
indeed, posit and constitute explicitly both the type of logic, in its
greatest generality, required by identitary logic and the relations necessary and almost sufficient for this logic to function unhampered and
without limit; the type of object and the relations are posited and
constituted by one another, each depending on the other, inseparably.
And this type of object and these relations are also implied in every
institution of society and, eminently, in the institution of language.

The 'naive' definition of the set, given by Cantor,[3] was: 'A set is a
collection into a whole of definite and distinct objects of our intuition
or of our thought. These objects are called the elements of the set.' It
is not despite, but because of, its undefined and undefinable terms,
its circularities and its naive formulations (which rapidly led mathematicians to eliminate it and to replace it with this or that other
group of axioms) that this alleged definition is fundamental. It displays
precisely the undefinable, if not circular, character of the initial terms
of set theory (and of all logic or mathematics); it shows that this theory
is posited straight away or that it presupposes its own positing, that it
can be constituted only by presupposing that it has already been constituted. This essential characteristic, which I call the objective reflexivity of set-theory and of identitary logic (and which characterizes every
originary institution) is hidden or covered over by the later elaborations.
But also, Cantor's definition admirably condenses the fundamental and
essential operations of *legein*. Implicitly or explicitly, it posits the
objects and the relations that have to be constituted by the operations
of *legein* and the condition for these operations to take place.

Legein: distinguish-choose-posit-assemble-count-speak; at once the
condition and the creation of society, the condition created by what it
itself conditions. If society is to exist, if a language is to be established
and if it is to function, if a thoughtful practice is to develop, if people
are to be able to relate to one another other than through phantasies,
then, in one way or another, on a certain level, on a certain layer or
stratum of social doing and representing, everything must be made
consequent with what Cantor's definition implies. To see this, it is
enough to consider what is at stake in this definition, its consubstantiality to identitary logic as well as to what is always posited
through and in language.

In order to speak of a set or an ensemble, or to think of one, we
must be able to distinguish-choose-posit-assemble-count-say objects.
The nature of these objects is of little matter, universality is here – just
as the potential and actual universality of language – absolute: these
objects can belong to the sphere of perception or internal or external
sensation, to thought in the narrow sense or to representation in the
broadest sense of this term. These objects must be able to be posited
as defined, in the sense of a decisory–practical definition, and as
distinct. One must then be able to posit by distinguishing – or be able

to act as though one could distinguish – and be able to posit by defining – or to speak as if one were able to define, namely in such a way that what is intended is also, by means of speaking, sufficiently and adequately designated to the intention of other people.

One must, therefore, have available the schema of separation and its essential product, which is always already presupposed in the operation of the schema of separation: the term of the element. How could one separate two objects, if not on the basis of features or terms – ultimately, a single term, the point separating a segment into two – already posed as separate? The schema of separation, or of discreteness, is not only irreducible; its application presupposes that it has already been applied. But to posit a term or an element as distinct and definite implies, at the very least, that it is posited in its pure self-identity and in its pure difference with respect to everything that is not itself. Identity and difference – alleged to be constructed at much later stages of formalized mathematics, as special cases of the relation of equivalence and its negation – are, in fact, posited from the outset as soon as mathematics, or *legein*, begins.

To speak of an ensemble or to think of an ensemble, 'to collect into a whole' distinct and definite objects, also signifies, of course, that a schema of union is available.[4] Distinct objects must be able to be posited as being assembled into a whole, which is itself a distinct and definite object of a higher type. Or we must be able to speak as if we could collect into a whole this manifold of objects. The application of this schema itself presupposes that it has already been applied before it is able to be applied: that each of the terms collected together in this way to form a whole has already been implicitly posited as collected together into this whole which it itself is, that the diversity of features defining it and distinguishing it (little matter if it is numerically reduced to unity) has been united in order to posit–form–be *this* very object. As a collection into a whole, the ensemble is the self-identical unity of differences; what distinguishes the ensemble from the element is that the positing of the ensemble as a self-identical unity does not abolish the difference of the elements that compose it but coexists with it or is superimposed on it – while the internal differences belonging to the element are provisionally abolished in positing it, or are considered to be irrelevant or indifferent.

It is self-evident that the schemata of separation and of unification make possible the schema of decomposition, allowing us to find in a given whole wholes of a lesser type or the distinct and definite elements out of which it was made up. More generally, it is obvious that the schemata of separation and of union mutually imply and presuppose one another. But in addition: to say that a given ensemble is an ensemble of elements, or is itself an element, an object posited *as* an object, or else *as* a collection of objects implies that we have available to use the basic schema of *as for* (*pros ti*, quatenus) or *as* ... (*ê*).

Last but by no means least: separation and union make use of the basic operation of *legein* (imply it and are implied by it), designation, which presupposes the possibility of individuation and of gathering together pure *this*(es) (*tode ti*) as such.

Another series of consequences results from Cantor's definition. If one whole can be unified, another whole can always be formed as well (for example, by applying the schemata of separation and of union in the first whole, in other words, by taking way a part from a given ensemble). Then the elements out of which the first whole was assembled no longer differ from the elements of the second whole solely *as* elements, but also *as* they are included in the second whole and not in the first. Henceforth, to their pure designation as they are in themselves is added their belonging to this or that whole (ensemble), namely, a property, attribute or predicate that they share in common. Inversely, if a given predicate is ascribed in any way (*pôs, irgendwie*), it allows the elements it affects to be placed together. Without entering here into the discussions that this question has once again provoked in the past few decades, for they are not relevant for what we want to consider, ensemblist logic implies that one, in fact, has available the operational equivalence, property $\equiv$ ensemble (set) or predicate $\equiv$ class: a set defines a property of its elements (belonging to this set), a predicate defines a set (formed by the elements for which it is valid). It amounts to the same thing to say that Cantor's definition implies the construction of the pair subject–predicate, not simply in general but in particular: to say that X is a set is to say, in the naive version, that there exists x belonging to X or, in modern versions, that there exists Y to which X belongs; it is, therefore, to say that something is predicable *as to* its belonging to ....

Finally, as our last example, all of the above being simply a series of illustrations: if separation and union are repeated, there is a possibility of forming new sets on the basis of already given sets. Inversely, this possibility requires the possibility of repeating the operations of separation and union. It therefore requires the fundamental schema of iteration – which is, moreover, already present in positing a set (this and this and this ... are elements of the set) and which, as we shall see, is an essential schema of *legein*. However, the iteration of separation or of union in the case of given sets produces a hierarchy, in which the schema of order is concretized – a schema which is, as we shall see in the case of *legein*, already at work in the possibility of all the operations of which we have spoken. Now a hierarchy of ensembles, for reasons stated above, is *ipso facto* a hierarchy of predicates. In other words, this possibility already contains within it the whole of classical syllogistics. The construction of the pair essence–accident is an immediate upshot. To say that, for an element x in so far as it belongs to the set X, a given predicate is essential, is to say that this predicate defines the act X, or necessarily follows from those that define it (for example, because X was posited as included in set Y, characterized by this predicate). To say that, for the same element x in so far as it belongs to the set X, a different predicate is accidental, is to say that this predicate defines only some parts of X. Humanity and mortality belong to the essence of Socrates, the colour of his skin and his size to his accidents. Also: to say that a property *p* has a meaning in relation to the set X, is to say that there exists a non-empty part of X defined by this property, or that there exists at least one element *x* belonging to X such that *p* (*x*) is true. Now to say that *x* is determined with respect to *p* signifies being able to say whether *p* (*x*) is true or false; and to say that *x* as an element of the set X is completely determined means that it is determined with respect to all the properties, or all the predicates, that have a meaning relative to X, or else that all the parts of X to which *x* does or does not belong can be defined. The philosophical implications of this innocent tautology are considerable. Indeed, it *seems* obvious that if an element *x* belonging to a set X is given, that in the same stroke all the *parts* of X to which *x* does or does not belong are unambiguously determined. In other words: all the *possible* predicates of *x* are thereby immediately affirmed or denied. In still other words: to say that a thing is is to say that it is determined as to all its possible predicates (Kant).

It is obvious that identitary logic is presupposed by set theory: identity and difference are present in Cantor's definition, just as the principle of the excluded middle (without this an element's belonging to a set would be undetermined). But it is just as obvious that identitary logic can be employed, or simply formulated, if and only if there are, if indeed there exist sets in the Cantorian sense. Propositional logic, for instance, posits a set of elements *p*, *q* ... that are distinct and definite (and individual – neither the 'content' nor the sub-elements of a proposition are taken into consideration), with respect to which two predicates (true and false) and a certain number of operations (or relations) are defined. This is entirely independent of the fact that contemporary logic is formalized: ensemblization is already at work not only in the Aristotelian *Organon*, but long before this, as soon as society and language exist. In the same way, it is of no matter, from the point of view we are interested in here, whether the Cantorian definition is criticized as naive and replaced by other more refined definitions in a more advanced formalism; all these formalizations presuppose the validity of the Cantorian definition to the extent that they always presuppose signs posited as distinct and definite elements, united into a whole, the set of signs of the theory in question. Every set theory presupposes identitary logic, and every formalizable logic presupposes the possibility of ensemblizing the signs with which it operates. This amounts to saying that all these formalizations involve the application of *legein*, which is ensemblizing and identitary. The mutual inherence of identitary logic and of set-theory (or of formal and formalizable mathematics) is simply the expression of the fact that they are both elaborations and explicitations of what is already at work in and through *legein*.

I said that identitary logic can be formulated if and only if there are, if there exist sets in the Cantorian sense; *a fortiori*, then, it can be put to use only on this condition. One might think that 'there are', 'there exist' are here no more than strict references to the possibility of pure designation. But if this were the case, this designation would, precisely, remain pure, that is the designation of nothing, an empty designation, a non-designation. To say that identitary logic can be formulated and put to use therefore amounts to saying that there actually are sets, that sets *actually* exist. But at the same time, too, sets exist only in and through identitary logic, only in and through *legein*. In this sense, identitary logic, like *legein*, is equivalent to an ontological decision concerning what is and the manner in which it exists: what is is such that sets exist (things and identitary relations). A decision that is at the same time the expression of a creation, of an ontological genesis: sets, these sets and the *eidos* of the set are henceforth posited instituted and as such exist in a new region of being. We cannot think of this creation without a relation *sui generis* of partial support on what was there before; the ensemblization instituted by *legein* finds a partial basis in the fact that what it finds before it is in part ensemblizable. This relation *sui generis* of partial support is the leaning of society on the first stratum, or natural stratum, of the given.

ii THE SOCIAL INSTITUTION OF ENSEMBLES

It is self-evident that the very existence of society, as anonymous and collective doing/representing, is impossible (or, at any rate, inconceivable for us) without the institution of the *legein* (of the ability to distinguish-choose-posit-assemble-count-speak) and the application of the identitary–ensemblist logic incorporated in the latter. Social doing/representing always presupposes and refers to distinct and definite objects that can be collected together to form wholes, which can be composed and decomposed, and which are definable in terms of determined properties, serving in turn as the basis for the definition of these properties. This is true of a society's institution regardless of the type or content of the global and detailed organization of itself and of its world; it is true regardless of the explicit form of thought that accompanies it, and however inaccessible the imaginary significations underlying this organization. A visible object may possess invisible properties; a stone or an animal may be a god; a child may be the reincarnation of an ancestor or this very ancestor in person. It may be that these attributes, properties, relations, forms of being are lived, spoken, thought and enacted in sincerity, duplicity or (in our eyes) utter confusion. But whatever the case, it is always and absolutely necessary that each and every cow belong to the category 'cow', that it not be a bull (or not in just any way) and that it give birth, with practically absolute certainty, to calves. Likewise, it is necessary that the ensemble of huts form a *particular* village, *this* village, *our* village, the one to which we *belong* and to which do not belong the people of the other village, or those of any other village. It is always and absolutely necessary that knives cut, that water flows and fires burn. Society is not a set, neither a structure nor a hierarchy of sets (or structures); it is a magma and a magma of magmas. But there is an indispensable dimension of social doing/representing, of all life and of all social organization, of the institution of society, which is, and can only be, congruent with identitary or ensemblist logic, for it is posited, or simply 'is' in and through this logic.

To be sure, it would be a critical mistake, a murder of the object – the structuralist murder – to claim that this logic exhausts the life, or even the logic, of a society. We would have to give up thinking to dismiss the question: how and why a society distinguishes, chooses, posits, assembles, counts and speaks in certain terms and not others, in one way and not in another. We would have to act, consequently, as though the ensembles of elements posited by different societies were given once and for all, were self-evident, or corresponded to the self-organization of the given, at once indubitable and fully grasped by the person who is speaking (whereas even the terms 'masculine/feminine', as social not as biological terms, are socially instituted and are variable from place to place). In all these cases, we remain wholly and naively prisoner not only to ensemblist logic but to a specific material content of this logic, as it is socially instituted, that of the society and the period of the investigator.

These naive notions should not keep us from observing that the institution of society is always, at the same time, necessarily the institution of the *legein*, in and through which the identitary–ensemblist logic is deployed. Why this is so is the question that will always seize us but that we shall never truly be able to seize firmly. For we could neither think nor speak if we were to abandon identitary logic entirely. We can question it only by using it; bring it into doubt only by confirming it in part. This 'why' is, in fact, the 'why' of the *legein*, and, hence, the 'why' of language as well (for language cannot be reduced to the *legein* but is impossible without the latter, without, here again, our ever being able to say why), to which we can only reply in and through language. This excludes our being able to formulate it as a theory, but does not prevent us from elucidating it, in the sense given here to this term.

Saying all this amounts to saying that the ontological decision referred to above is well founded in part; or that the ontological creation represented by the institution of society is leaning on a stratum of what is already there, and this signifies that it finds in it partial support and stimulation. To say that every known society was able to exist by instituting an identitary logic is to say that there exists a layer or a stratum of what is, of what is given or actually manifests itself, that is amenable to an ensemblist organization. In this, the first natural stratum, what exists always lends itself interminably to an analysis that constitutes in it distinct and definite elements, elements that can always be grouped into specifiable sets, always possessing sufficient properties to be definable as classes, conforming to the principle of identity and of the excluded middle, and classifiable in terms of hierarchies, permitting the juxtaposition or unambiguous interconnection of hierarchies. This stratum has a formidable representative in the person of the living being, vegetal or animal, with which society deals from its inception, immediately and ineluctably, and which immediately comprises its own matter. *Anthropos anthropon genna*, Aristotle tirelessly repeats: it is a human being who engenders a human being and it is a human being that is engendered by a human being; then there are, in themselves, species, individuals as specimens of a genus, the different as it partakes of the same. Not only stable properties, sufficient decisory characteristics, are intrinsically necessary for the existence of the living being and of the human being who lives and lives on the former, but also the living being presents itself as already realizing in-itself and for-itself an Aristotelian ensemblization-hierarchization, grouped of itself into genera and species that are completely definable in terms of the union, intersection or disjunction of properties or attributes.

iii THE LEANING OF SOCIETY ON NATURE

How are we to understand the leaning of the first natural stratum on the ensemblizable dimension? Men and women live in society; they can be unambiguously classified (biologically) as male and female. They give birth to boys and girls who are, always and everywhere, incapable of surviving unless they are cared for by adults for a rather long period of time. All of this results neither from the legislation of transcendental consciousness nor from the institution of society. The ensembles of males and females, or children who have not yet reached a sufficient degree of biological maturation are, considered strictly as such, given in nature, as are, with certainty or extreme probability, the attributes affecting them. The institution of society is always *obliged* to take into account this division of the collectivity (considered as a set of heads) into two subsets, male and female. But they are taken into account in and through a transformation of the *natural fact* of being-male and being-female into an *imaginary social signification* of being-man and being-woman which refers to the magma of all the imaginary significations of the society considered. Neither this transformation itself nor the specific tenor of the signification in question can be deduced, produced or derived on the basis of the natural fact, which is always and everywhere the same. This natural fact puts stops or limits on the institution of society, but the consideration of these limits results in mere trivialities. When, as is the case, a certain archaic society compels the men, for weeks after the birth of a child, to mimic the woman in childbirth and to take her place, one may triumphantly point to the fact that men can never actually be obliged to give birth. But in order to know this, there is no need to study society, we could have simply looked at a herd of goats. What is important to us is, obviously, how and why a society obliges its men to mimic the situation of the other sex and what this signifies. In the same way, no society institutes men and women in such a way that they are, for one another, absolutely undesirable. But to say that a minimal heterosexual desire must be tolerated by the institution of society, under pain of the rapid extinction of the collectivity in question, still says nothing about the unending alchemy of desire that we observe in history – and this is what is important to us.[5] Likewise, a natural fact can provide support or stimulus for a particular institution of signification, but an abyss separates this support or stimulus from a necessary and sufficient condition. Supports and stimuli are taken into account in one case, ignored in another, cancelled out or directed uphill in a third but, everywhere they are recovered, transformed, transubstantiated by their insertion in the network of imaginary social significations. We have only to think of what becomes, in different societies, of the natural facts of the human male's superior physical strength or of female menstruation.

What is meant by this leaning on the natural stratum can perhaps better be illustrated by considering the difference between adults and children. Here, not only is the signification of being a child instituted in each case in a different manner and with a different tenor – not only is this signification seldom unitary – but the institution can do practically anything it likes with the supports and stimuli it finds in the natural facts of maturation. The only natural invariant here amounts to the distressing commonplace that someone has to care for the child (the infant, the pupil) for a certain period of time. It is false, logically and factually, that this person must be the mother or the biological family. Those who care for the child may be adults or, after awhile, older children; these people may or may not have blood or familial ties. The successive changes in the status of children can be related to stages in their biological maturation or to criteria or tests that are instituted arbitrarily. Their sexual activities may be repressed, tolerated, ignored, encouraged or solemnly instituted. Children may participate in the work of the collectivity at an early age or only long after they are physically capable; they may contract marriage long after they are sexually mature, before this, or even at birth; and so on.

In these cases the leaning of the institution on the natural stratum which is, so to speak, internal to society, appears and actually is vague and remote. It is almost non-existent when we consider the tenor of the instituted imaginary significations as such. But at the same time, it cannot be eliminated, not only as the (trivial) physical and biological condition for the existence of society, but more especially as the logical support, the point of anchorage of the actual ensemblization implied by the institution of society, fixing the terms of marking without which imaginary significations would have no points of reference. Irrespective of the tenor of the imaginary social signification of being-a-child, its articulations and its ramifications, in each instance we must know *who* is a child, to what class he belongs, and so on. Whether the passage from one class to another depends on official registers, entry into high school, the participation in a particular initiation rite or the start of menstruation – social *legein* has to be able to fix, in a univocal manner, the referential and marking terms so that the elements of the instituted classes can be distinguished and reassembled in actions and in discourse, that is to say, so that they can be designated unambiguously. This possibility exists only because the first natural stratum is ensemblizable – because individual events can be separated out from the flux of becoming and focused on, because the natural periodicity of certain phenomena provides a support for the ensemblist and measurable marking of instituted time, and so forth.

The situation is essentially analogous in the case of the leaning of the social–historical institution on nature considered so to speak as external to society. (The expressions 'internal' and 'external' to society are, needless to say, gross abuses of language.) One could say that society encounters from the outset an initial natural stratum – the very one from which humanity emerges – which is not only ensemblizable but already ensemblized in itself: living species, varieties of soil, minerals, the Sun, the Moon, and the stars did not wait to be stated or instituted in order to be distinct and definite, to possess stable properties and to form classes. But from what point of view are they distinct and definite; in what respect do they possess stable properties; in whose eyes do they form classes? The illusory self-evidence of a given, assignable organization of nature which society would have only to take up, be it in the form of the progressive conquest of the logic of this organization, of the arbitrary appropriation of elements in this organization forming a system or a structure, or of the determination by nature itself (including the nature of man) of what is to be taken up in this way, this illusory self-evidence shared by innumerable authors from Marx to Lévi-Strauss that can only be based, on close examination, on a most peculiar idea: the first human is held to have been at once a pure animal and a nineteenth-century man of science suffering from partial and temporary amnesia.

Why a nineteenth-century man of science? Because the representation of nature underlying the discussions on the relations between nature and society, or nature and culture, the idea of a given, assignable organization of nature (and one that is essentially, that is ontologically, simple) which society could take up part by part or progressively, is simply the incoherent fantasy of a certain stage of Western science. How then did the Neanderthals reconcile the general theory of relativity and quantum theory? – But when we speak of nature we are thinking of those aspects of nature that are relevant for human existence. – Which human's existence? And relevant in relation to what? Are petroleum deposits or the fusion of hydrogen relevant for humans? And the naming of flowers or the stars? And the properties of vibrating columns of air, are they relevant for humans?

There is only one point of view from which one could actually attempt to grasp the aspects of nature that are, *ne varietur*, relevant for humans, and to grasp them within the framework of an identitary logic. This is the point of view that considers humans as pure animals or as merely living beings.

Living beings may, in fact, be described as identitary automata,[6] although this definition is certainly insufficient. Living beings may thus be said to possess an initial transforming filter by means of which part of the events deemed 'objective' are transformed into events *for* the living being or as *information* for it. Living things also possess a second transforming filter that differentiates within the set of this information a sub-set of relevant data and a sub-set of irrelevant data, or noise. Beyond this, they may be said to possess a series of mechanisms that elaborates the elements of relevant information, endowing them with, for example, weights, values, univocal 'interpretations', and promoting, in turn, the activation of response mechanisms ('programs'). (For any given type of living being catastrophic events represent the limit of relevant events, beyond which it has no response program). Thus, for terrestrial beings radio waves do not exist: they are not elements belonging to the ensemble of information defined for and by these automata; whereas, sun rays do exist for the majority of these beings, but they are one thing for plants and quite another for sea turtles. It is probable that a good part of the sensorial information received by higher animals is of no relevance.[7] The configuration of the starry sky (outside of the Sun, the Moon and exceptional phenomena) is probably not relevant for the mammals that perceive it.

It can then be said that the living being constitutes part of the 'objective' world *for* itself, that it establishes within this part a division between relevant and irrelevant sub-sets, that within the first it makes new subdivisions, defining classes of events according to their properties, that it 'recognizes' a given event as an individual instance of a given class, and that it responds, depending on the set of other relevant data available to it and on their elaboration, in accordance with fixed programs that can, of course, be extremely complex.[8]

If we adopt this description and this language (which, we must remember, have no absolute privilege but merely express our identitary logic at a certain stage of its explicitation and application), we can say that living beings exist by ensemblizing parts of the world (distinguishing therein elements possessing stable properties, and usable as instances of classes, and so on). Here again we are obliged to say (tautologically) that, if this is possible, it is because what exists is, at a certain level, ensemblizable. At no time, however, can we say that what exists is actually only a single, well-ordered hierarchy of ensembles. We know nothing of the sort (and we are rather forced to believe that this is not so). We can simply say that, as we understand it today, the living being comes into existence as establishing ensembles and as establishing itself in and through ensembles. A rabbit and a dog are for one another instances of a class defined by stable properties, sufficiently determined 'things'. But what is a 'thing' in general? Here sociologists as well as biologists forget most often not only their philosophy but even their physics. For according to physics, what 'there is' (*today*) is a dance of electrons or other elementary particles, or force fields, local torsions of space-time, and so on. Within this, living beings constitute 'things' and are themselves constituted as 'things'. They produce translations for themselves of a minute number of characteristics of what exists, translations that are what they are and precisely as they are due to the nature of the transforming filters that make them. What exists for the living being – and this includes humans – as a thing or a stable property is so only as the result of the coarseness (or the refinement) of its transforming filter and its 'temporal setting'. With a different 'temporal setting' the configuration of the Earth's mountains and continents might be just as changeable for a living being as the shape of clouds on a windy day; just as, perhaps, what we perceive as the expansion of the universe is simply the diastole of the heart of an animal in which we live as parasites. And what 'things' would we see if the differentiating powers of our retina were those of an electron microscope? To be sure, all of this brings us back once again to the properties of what exists, to the fact that it is presented, throughout its successive strata, as organizable, and, finally, that it is not just anything nor does it exist in just any manner. But this also suggests that what appears as organized is inseparable from what organizes it. We can seemingly stretch this circle without limit but we cannot step outside it.

Thus, to speak of nature as a given organization, as a system of ensembles, as subject to a certain particularization of identitary logic (for example, the particularization that 'sees' physical existence as 'material things' instead of 'seeing' it as local torsions of space-time) is to speak of humans as pure animals or as simple living beings, for whom there is an established 'universe of discourse', homologous to the organization of the ensemble of mechanisms constituting them as a living being and as this particular one. Conversely, it is only in as much as we speak of humans as pure animals or as simple living beings that we can say that there must be for them a set and stable organization of nature, an ensemblist categorization or classification of what is given to them – or of what they constitute – as living beings. And it could not even be said that humans could ignore or transgress this stable organization only at the risk of endangering their own existence as living beings; by definition, there is absolutely no question of them ignoring or transgressing it – any more than any living being can ignore or transgress what is for it the organization of nature corresponding to its own organization.

This set and stable organization of a part of the world homologous to the organization of humans as simple living beings (forming, of course, two complementary parts of the same system for a meta-observer, that is for a human as he attempts to theorize it) is what I call the first natural stratum on which the institution of society is leaning and which it can neither simply disregard nor force as it wills.

To say that the institution of society *leans on* the organization of the first natural stratum means that it does not reproduce or reflect this organization, is not *determined* by it in any way. Instead, society finds in it a series of conditions, supports and stimuli, stops and obstacles. To use the language of the preceding pages, society, like any automaton, defines its own universe of discourse. And to the extent that society is not simply the human species as a mere living or animal being, this universe of discourse is necessarily different from that of the animal, man. What is more, each society is an automaton of a different type, since (or in so far as) each establishes a different universe of discourse, since each institution of society establishes what, for the society in question, is and is not, what is relevant and what is not, the weight, the value, the 'translation' of what is relevant – and the 'response' that corresponds to this.

If, however, we take a closer look at the terms just used, we observe that the metaphor of the automaton is practically empty here, or that, more precisely, society is not an identitary or ensemblist automaton, however complex one would suppose this automaton to be. This is already evident in the fact that the weight, value, 'translation' of the relevant information and the 'response' to these are not set for a given society in any univocal (or finitely multivocal) fashion. But it will be helpful to show this starting from a more elementary consideration.

An identitary automaton implies the division of the objective world (of the world for a meta-observer, that is someone who can consider both the automaton and its world as objects) into a part that exists for the automaton and a part that does not exist for it; and, within the first part, there is a further division into a sub-set of relevant information and another of irrelevant information or 'noise'. These partitions, however, have strikingly different meanings for society considered as society (and not as a herd of bipeds).

In the first place, for society there *exist* entities that correspond to no organization (whether identitary or not) of the natural stratum; to cite a few obvious examples, spirits, gods, myths and so on do *exist* for society. And what *does not exist* for society is not always, and not necessarily, pure non-being, absolute non-being, that which could never enter into the universe of discourse, even if it is only to be denied. Quite the opposite, the being of non-being, or non-being as such, always exists for society; into its universe of discourse enter entities whose being is or has to be negated, positions that must be asserted by means of explicit negations or that are presented only to be negated. The possibility of 'this does not exist' or of 'it is not like that' is always explicitly posed in the institution of society.

In the second place, for society as such there is no irrelevant information; the irrelevant exists only as a limiting case of the relevant. In other words, for society, there is no 'noise' *qua* noise; 'noise' always exists as something and at its limit is explicitly posed as noise or as irrelevant information. This takes us, by way of a seemingly minor route, to the very heart of the question of the social: everything that is, in one way or another, grasped or perceived by society has to *signify* something, has to be endowed with signification, and what is more, it is always already grasped in and through the possibility of signification, and it is only as a result of this possibility that it can finally be defined as devoid of signification, insignificant or absurd. It is clear that the absurd can appear – even, and especially, when it is irreducible – only on the basis of the absolute requirement of signification.

For an identitary automaton (or, for what amounts to the same thing, for a completely formalized calculus) to say that a term *is* means that it has a recognizable form that is determined and predetermined (it is an instance of a given *eidos*). And to say that a term 'has a meaning' (actually an abuse of language) is to say that this form determines the entry of this term into a determined and predetermined syntax of operations. (Of course, what is not or has no meaning *for* the automaton can act *on* it and, even, partly or totally destroy it.)

For a society, to say that a term *is* means that it signifies (is a signification, is posited as a signification, is tied to a signification). Once it *is*, it *always* has meaning, in the narrow sense indicated above, that is it can always enter into a syntax or can constitute a syntax in which to enter. The institution of society is the institution of a world of significations – which is obviously a creation as such, and a specific one in each case.

Within this world an important place must always be found for the first natural stratum, whose being and being-thus (for humans as living beings) is the condition for the existence of society. But at the same time, this stratum is never, and could never be, taken up simply as such. What belongs to it is taken up in and through the magma of significations instituted by society, and in this way it is transubstantiated or ontologically altered. It is altered in its mode of being inasmuch as it exists and exists only by reason of its investment by signification. It is also altered in its mode of organization and cannot help but be altered in this way. For not only is the mode of organization of the world of significations not the ensemblist mode of organization of the first natural stratum, but also, from the moment that everything has to signify something, this ensemblist organization does not, as such, answer the question of signification, and ceases to be an organization, even an ensemblist one.

That the ensemblist organization does not answer to the question of signification is indicated quite clearly by the fact that formalist conceptions, whether mathematical, linguistic or ethnological, are forced to deny that a question of signification exists. It is not difficult to see that

that the ensemblist organization ceases to be an organization at all once the requirement of signification appears, for this organization, considered as it presents itself immediately, is an organization (and is coherent) only in certain respects and from a certain point of view – that of animal-man, precisely in so far as from this point of view the question of signification does not arise. Assume, for example, that the regularity of the given obliterates or excludes the question of signification – which is, by the way, absolutely untrue and nothing more than the naive projection of modern scientism: observing or establishing a regularity still raises the question of the significance of this regularity; all societies account for the regularities they observe or construct an interpretation of them; and it remains to be seen just what is meant by regularity, what objects it has to include, and how far the regularity must go. – Now, the existence of such a regularity is as much granted as it is denied by the first natural stratum: game becomes scarce, the rains are late, the child is stillborn, there is an eclipse of the Moon – what do these various events signify? It would be even false to say that the ensemblist organization of the first natural stratum, as it is 'naturally' given, is incomplete, deficient or lacunary. If we take the point of view of animal-man, this organization is neither complete nor incomplete; it simply is what it is, and, as it is, it is necessary and sufficient (after the fact) for the existence of animal-man, homologous and consubstantial to this existence. But if we take the point of view of signification, that of society from its first day forward, natural ensemblist organization as such is almost non-existent. And if we ascribe to signification the (abusive) meaning of coherence or regularity, the natural organization is more than lacunary, even fragmentary; the part that would seem to be irregular or incoherent is no less extensive, no less important than that which seems to be regular and coherent. To be sure, the latter not only conditions the biological existence of society but provides that which the institution, and in particular the ensemblist identitary dimension of this institution is leaning on. An enormous distance, however, separates this observation from the idea that society's creation of a world of significations exists only to fill up a few gaps in a rational (that is, identitary–ensemblistic) organization that is already given in itself with nature or as a sort of substitute that will be gradually reduced with the progressive discovery of this supposedly rational organization. We can now break this widespread idea (imaginary significations considered as substitutes or compensations) down into its constituents: the Western scientist, obsessed by these two phantasies: first, that the world has a rational organization (in fact, he knows nothing about it), and second, that his science is about to disclose this organization fully or almost (while it produces more riddles than it solves), transports these phantasies 10,000 years in the past or 10,000 kilometres away, and interprets the representations of the savages as attempts to fill up the holes that they *should have* discovered in the organization of *their* world, *if* they had been possessed

by *his* phantasies. Now, here is a tautology worth
the organization of the natural stratum appear as l
organization only once it has been decided that th
nation is a *rational* one, or that the only true (
identitary–ensemblist organization. But this decision
recent social–historical institution. And this is why ar
is also naively ethnocentric: the idea that mythical the
classificatory, hence reducible to the rudiments of
(imaginary significations like flavours, will-o'-the-w   , or illusions
shared by noble savages and bad ethnologists). To paraphrase the
father of this idea:[9] to say that savages classify is a truism (for otherwise
they would not speak) but to say that essentially they do nothing but
classify is an absurdity. What may appear to the contemporary Western
scientist as lacunae in the organization of the natural stratum, lacunae
that should help to stimulate rational investigations aimed at filling
them, actually appear as lacunae of this sort only on the basis of the
institution of unlimited interrogation within the horizon of identitary
logic. The given is logically or rationally incomplete only when completeness has been posited as logical or rational completeness. But the
idea that everything must answer the requirement of logical or rational
completeness (*logon didonai*, to give an account of and a reason for,
Hegel's 'all that is real is rational') is simply a particular avatar of the
idea that everything must answer the requirement of signification – if,
that is, we can term 'idea' that which is the condition for every idea.
The institution of society is at once the institution of this requirement
and of the response that is supplied in each case. To be sure, a tension
can always appear between the requirement and the response; this is
part of the very question of history in the sense of the self-alteration
of society. Nevertheless, for the vast majority of known societies, that
is, mythical societies, the given does not appear as *logically* incomplete,
not because they have classified everything that is classifiable, nor
because their classifications are logically watertight and complete, but
because this is not their criterion. Even more, the given does not
appear to them to be incomplete in any way whatsoever, for the
mythical response to the question of signification is one that *saturates*
everything with meaning, something the logical or rational response
can never do (this is why it is irresistibly drawn towards the myth of
rational completeness, of the integral rationality of the given, and of
being as determinacy).

iv *LEGEIN* AND LANGUAGE AS CODE

The social–historical institution is that in and through which the social
imaginary manifests itself and brings itself into being. This institution
is the institution of a magma of significations, imaginary social sig-

ations. The participable representative support of these sig-
nications – to which, of course, they are not reducible and which can
be direct or indirect – consists of images or figures, in the broadest
sense of the term: phonemes, words, bank currency, jinns, statues,
churches, tools, uniforms, body paintings, numerical figures, border-
posts, centaurs, cassocks, lictors, musical scores – but also the totality
of what is perceived in nature, that is or could be named by the society
in question. Compositions of images or figures can be in turn, and
often are, themselves images and figures *and* thus also new supports
for significations. The social imaginary is, primordially, the creation of
significations and the creation of the images and figures that support
these significations. The relation between a signification and its supports
(images or figures) is the only precise sense that can be attached to the
term 'symbolic' – and this is the sense in which we are using the term
here.[10]

A large part of the significations of a society – those that are, or can
be made, explicit – are also instituted, directly or indirectly, through
its language. At the same time, however, the ensemblization or the
identitary organization of the world instituted by society occurs through
legein (distinguishing-choosing-positing-assembling-counting-speaking).
Legein is the ensemblist–ensemblizing dimension of social representing/
saying, just as *teukein* (assembling-adjusting-making-constructing) is the
ensemblist–ensemblizing dimension of social doing. Both lean on the
identitary aspect of the first natural stratum but both are already, as such,
social institutions, primordial institutions instrumental for every institution
(which does not imply any temporal or logical anteriority).

Language is in and through two indissociable dimensions or components. Language is *langue* to the extent that it signifies, that is to
say, to the extent that it refers to a magma of significations. Language
is a *code* to the extent that it organizes and organizes itself in an
identitary manner, that is to say, to the extent that it is a system of
ensembles (or of ensemblizable relations), or, in other terms, to the
extent that it is *legein*.

The ensemblizing of the world instituted by society is not simply
performed *by language as a code, that is as legein*, as an instrument
acting on what is external to it. Instead, it is incarnated and realized
in language itself; it is presentified in *legein* as a product of its own
operation. And it is only in and through this ensemblizing that language
can also be a code.[11]

Language is always necessarily also a code; it always establishes terms
(ensemblist elements) and practically univocal relations (ensemblist or
ensemblizable relations) between terms. Language always includes and
institutes a univocal or identitary dimension. It exists only by instituting
an identitary dimension and by instituting itself within this dimension.
Language, as a code, is also instituted as a system of ensembles and
of ensemblist (or ensemblizable) relations, that is to say, as a system
of mappings, in the mathematical sense, of one ensemble on another.

Contemporary linguistics is almost exclusively concerned with this sole aspect of language.

Such is the situation of language in its abstract–material being-there, as a representative support, a hierarchy of sets of images or figures or as a system of signifiers at different levels. If a language is to exist, the sound continuum has to be cut up into intervals, each of which corresponds to a single phoneme. The being of the phoneme, as it was defined by Troubetzkoy and Jakobson, is an abstract–material being. A phoneme is an entity – image or figure – that is abstract and, within the limits defining it, independent of its concrete material realization and the inevitable and indefinite variations affecting it, but not independent of all material realization whatsoever. A phoneme is a form, an *eidos*, that makes sound phenomena identical (or indiscernible) when they actually are not and by definition cannot be physically identical. (The discussion of whether or not phonemes can be analysed into distinctive features is not relevant to us here.) The same thing is true if we shift from phonemes to graphical supports. The phonological system of a language (and, more generally, any semiotic system) is therefore the institution of discrete terms, or distinct and well-defined elements. It includes simultaneously the ensemblization of the sound continuum, the definition of a finite ensemble of phonemes, and the mapping (in the mathematical sense) of the former into the latter. Then, by means of ensemblist operations, new sets and determined hierarchies of sets (morphemes, grammatical classes, syntactical types, the lexicon) are constructed, between which ensemblist or ensemblizable relations are posited. In this way, at every instant there is a finite and definite ensemble of possible 'words' in a language, which itself is a sub-set of a finite Cartesian power of the set of phonemes or, in simpler terms, the result of a finite combinatorics of the elements of the set of phonemes, certain combinations being excluded. Grammatical categories represent a partition of the set of words; syntactical types, a combinatory system of the elements of the parts defined by this partition, and so on. These definitions, operations and relations are in each case specific to and characteristic of the language in question. Language is able to ensemblize the world only because it is itself a system of ensembles and of ensemblist relations, only because it institutes itself as a system of this sort. In its abstract–material being-there as a code or a system of signifying codes, language is the first and the only genuine ensemble that has ever existed, the only 'real' and not simply 'formal' ensemble; every other set not only presupposes it logically, but is able to be constituted solely on the basis of the same type of operations. Every identitary logic (and, ultimately, every ontology) is but the activation of identitary operations instituted in and through *legein*, in and through language considered as a code.

   These operations are presupposed by the whole of formalized mathematics and are both necessary and sufficient conditions for its constitution as formalized mathematics (which should not for one minute be mistaken for mathematics as such). To the extent – by principle, as we know, incomplete – that formalized mathematics manages to realize its programme, it is indeed a set of formal elements, that is, abstract–material elements (signs: images or figures) which are instituted as such (and are generally supplied by being exhibited or shown, whether actually or virtually). The laws or rules of composition of these signs are just the definitions of the combinations that are permitted or forbidden, and those that are permitted, the 'words', being here well-formed statements or formulas. And the laws or rules of composition (concatenation) of the formulas – that is, a new division of their combinations into those that are permitted and those that are forbidden – define a syntax. The final result is a formalized mathematical 'discourse'. This construction is possible at each stage only on the basis of the operations of ensemblist or identitary logic which it presupposes, not naively, as is often stated, but in a manner that is unavoidable and not amenable to inspection. So it would seem that the venerable author of the beautiful 'Introduction' to the *Elements of Mathematics*, is somewhat lacking in rigour when he writes: 'It goes without saying that the description of formalized language is done in ordinary language, like the description of the rules of chess; we shall not enter into a discussion of the psychological or metaphysical problems raised by the question of the validity of the use of ordinary language in such circumstances (for example, the possibility of recognizing that a letter of the alphabet is 'the same' in two different places on the same page, etc.).' The problems at issue here are neither psychological nor metaphysical, nor could they even be termed logical since they are consubstantial to the possibility (and the actuality) of logic and of any logic whatsoever. It is not a question here of the 'validity of the use of common language in these circumstances' considered from the perspective of the material use of the results or products of language, but of the insurpassable necessity of using, instituting the same operations, the same *types* of operations as those used and instituted by language considered as a code. Whether or not he has to 'describe' to someone what he is doing, the mathematician can do mathematics – and books of mathematics can exist as such – only starting from the decision that the innumerable occurrences of something, of a term or *quid* indicated in one way or another (but always as an image or a figure, always including a representative support) *belong to the same*, that despite differences in the place and time they appear, in the spot they appear on the page, their typographical form or the particular handwriting that shapes them, and even their context (not always yet without insurmountable ambiguity), they are but the representatives of a class that has *one* canonical abstract–material representative, which is *the* sign '*x*', *the* sign '=' or *the* sign '1'. This sign must be distinct and definite, capable of being multiplied indefinitely without ceasing to be one, self-identical and different from all the others, all of its occurrences referring to the same even though they are obviously different, and by essence such that it can enter into combinations with other signs. Segregating, within what is given as naturally open to inspection, an ensemble of signs from everything that is not a sign, imposing on the ensemble of signs a family of relations of equivalence that make an '*x*' and a '*y*' exist as signs (that is, posing all the '*x*'s that might be encountered as equivalent *modulo* one of these relations), allowing the possibility of forming higher-order signs through the combination of elementary signs – all these operations are themselves already ensemblist and ensemblizing operations without which set theory, the *theory* of ensembles (whether naive or not) cannot even commence. And it is useless to try to hide this situation by the empty positing – empty because it cannot be realized – of a hierarchy of metalanguages, necessarily infinite, whose construction would only reproduce this situation at every stage, making it increasingly complex.

We know that even in the case of formalized mathematics, aside from the questions we have just discussed, ensemblization cannot achieve the completion and the logical closure of the systems constituted, unless these systems are trivial, that is to say, finite (as are those that structuralists deal with in various social and historical disciplines). A formalized system that is rich enough to contain the arithmetic of whole numbers – the most impoverished form of infinity – necessarily includes undecidable propositions, that is to say, contains something that is undetermined and undeterminable. The arithmetic of whole numbers appears as the spoil-sport here, in so far as it presentifies a denumerable infinity, that is the simple, *indefinite* iteration of the same – an expression perfectly comprehensible and significant for everyone, and at the same time, properly speaking, *undefinable*, and undefinable to a degree other than the undefinability of the elementary terms and relations of a formalized theory. For what is implied here is the reference to the ascertained potentiality of an operation that cannot be performed,[13] hence something that breaches the absolute determinacy required by identitary logic. The fact that this breach has been filled in each case by *ad hoc* measures taken by mathematicians attests, in particular, to their creative imagination and shows that, even in this extreme case, formal mathematics, the automatism of the ordered manipulation of signs, when left to itself, produces mere trivialities in the domain of the finite and incoherences in that of the infinite. This is even more striking when we consider the substance of mathematics. The fact that all the propositions of a given branch of mathematics can be reduced to a small number of axioms and deduced from them by means of a small number of schemata, substitution rules and deductive criteria,[14] hides the equally – if not more – important fact that all the 'axioms' that could 'freely' be chosen are not of the same fecundity or interest, far from it. It is the mathematician's creative imagination that posits rich and germinal mathematical ideas without necessarily being in a position to found them or justify them as such;[15] the history of every branch of mathematics is marked by the discovery of demonstration procedures that are specific yet powerful, typical and irreducible to formal and general deductive schemata (from Archimedes' method of exhaustion or Fermat's infinite descent to Cantor's diagonal method or Gödel's factoring of sentences), and these are the true tools of living mathematics. Formal mathematics is but the *caput mortuum* of mathematics as already constituted, it is not living mathematics in the making. If this were not the case, mathematics would be no more than a simple *semeiotechnique*, that is to say, approximately the equivalent of what today is pompously called 'semiotics', and would exhibit the same depressing poverty as the latter.

It remains, nonetheless, that mathematics (and, more generally, everything that we can conceive of as a formal system), within the limits sketched out above, is wholly subject to ensemblist or identitary logic. The same is obviously true with respect to topology, which has recently become fashionable in the most unexpected places, due perhaps to the excessive attention paid to the signifier at the expense of the signified. Topology can provide striking metaphors or, in certain cases, allow the construction of models less rigid than those of other branches of mathematics. Doing topology, however, is basically no different than doing arithmetic: from a fundamental perspective, in both cases the logical operations and the mode of being of the object are the same.

Language's being-a-code is not confined to its abstract–material aspect; it also extends to its signifying aspect. Language necessarily includes also the ensemblist–identitary dimension with regard to its signifieds – in other words, significations are also constituted, in part, as a code (this has helped to lead astray structuralist semanticists). This is immediately obvious when we consider the significations implied in the operations of designation (or nomination): the great majority of words in any language represent a coding, the institution of a set of elements or terms that are distinct and defined within the perceivable, or in other words, the establishment within this realm of entities or properties that are separate, fixed and stable, and, simultaneously, the institution of a set of linguistic terms (words or sentences), and the establishment of a bi-univocal correspondence between these two ensembles. These are, actually, three aspects of a single operation. It is of no matter, in *this* respect, (although the same is not at all true in others) that the elements defined in the domain of the perceivable correspond to 'things' (trees), to 'processes' (running) or to 'states' (the weather is good), to 'individuals' (Pierre, Olympus) or to classes (dog). It is also unimportant whether the correspondence fails to be perfectly bi-univocal, that is to say, some ambiguities remain 'locally' (as a result of synonymy, homonymy or difficulties in clearly distinguishing classes of objects: mountain/hill, for example), provided that the univocity is 'sufficient for usage' (*pros tēn chreian ikanōs*), as Aristotle stated in another context, or better, provided that this ambiguity can be removed through a *finite* number of additional operations.[16] It is evident that the ensemblization of the world (implied in counting out a herd of goats just as much as in sending a man to the Moon) is consubstantial to the institution of language as a code of significations and that the former operates in and through the latter. It is just as evident that the vast majority of the significations that can be termed 'rational' ('concepts') are constructed by refining and developing the elements of this code of significations, involving exclusively operations of identitary–ensemblist logic (for example, the taxonomy of living beings).

But, what is more, the identitary–ensemblist dimension is present in all significations, including those that have no relation to the real or the rational. For anyone who is not caught up in contemporary ideology, for anyone who has ever reflected on the being of signification, this affirmation may seem paradoxical, and even absurd. For a signification, any signification, including those that do refer to the real or the rational – dog, circle – is essentially indefinite and undetermined; when we take into consideration the full being of signification, ensemblist–identitary logic has no real hold on it. To say that signification belongs to ... or can be divided up into ..., if these terms are not to be taken as the most awkward of metaphors, makes no more sense than to say that a signification is blue or yellow, carries a negative or positive electric charge.[17] Grasped in their fulness, significations are not elements and do not compose sets; the world of significations is a magma. And yet, signification is such, it can enter the very discourse that is attempting to state what we wish to say here, only inasmuch as in one of its aspects, in one of its strata, it can be grasped as something distinct and definite, for otherwise we could never know what we were talking about. I can use words like 'vague', 'fuzzy', 'approximately' only on the implicit assumption that they nevertheless define well-determined modalities or properties, and that the neighbourhood described by 'approximately', the class of vague or fuzzy *things* is posited unambiguously, with borderlines that are sufficiently clear.

What is a signification? We can describe it only as an indefinite skein of interminable *referrals* to *something other* than (than what would appear to be stated directly). These other things can be both significations and non-significations – that to which significations relate or refer. The lexicon of the significations of a language does not revolve around itself, is not closed in upon itself, as has flatly been stated. What is closed in upon itself, fictively, is the code, the lexicon of ensemblist–identitary signifieds, each of which can take on one or more sufficient definitions. But the lexicon of significations is always open; for the full signification of a word is everything that can be socially stated, thought, represented or done on the basis of this word.[18] In other words, it can never be assigned determined limits, a *peras*. To be sure, this skein of referrals, in which each leads to what, in turn, is the source of new referrals, is far from being an undifferentiated chaos. In this magma, there are flows that are denser, nodal points, clearer or darker areas, bits of rock caught in the whole. But the magma never ceases to move, to swell and to subside, to liquify what was solid and to solidify what was almost inexistent. And it is because the magma is such, that man can move himself and create in and through language, that he is not pinned down once and forever by the set and univocal signified of the words he uses – in other words, that language is language. And yet, not only this definition but the thing itself would be impossible if the ensemblist–identitary dimension were not present as well. For *this* signification must be *this* skein and not another, and *these* referrals must be referrals from … to …, relations that are provisionally posited as stable between terms transitorily posited as fixed. A signification is nothing 'in itself', it is only a gigantic loan – and yet it has to be *this* particular loan; it is, one might say, entirely outside of itself – but it is *this signification* that is outside of itself.

Signification necessarily escapes the determinations of identitary– ensemblist logic. And yet, even in this case, we observe the partial grasp of this logic and its necessities. We shall return to this later (chapter 7).

v ASPECTS OF *LEGEIN*

The central operation of *legein* is *designation*. Already 'this is called …' fully involves the entire bundle of operators that we normally think of as separate and separable.

What is first implied here, and in full operation, is the *sign* (and the plurality of signs) and all that it brings into existence. (*Sign* is used here in its commonly accepted sense and not in that given to it by Saussure.) It is implied as a concrete instance, as a material realization separate from all the rest, posited as distinct and definite: 'this is called x' presupposes that x (spoken or written word, ideogram, or other) has been constituted as a 'separate object' outside the Heraclitean flux. It is implied at the same time as a formal *eidos*: x is not a sign unless it is a type or a form; it is only by virtue of this type or form that every concrete x that could be encountered is itself a sign. Finally, it is implied as the relation *sui generis* of the concrete instance and of the formal *eidos* that constitutes the sign. The different graphic or phonetic forms of x are not related to the *eidos* of x as the concrete dog to the species dog or to the concept of dog. If x possesses a sufficiently well-defined form, it 'exhausts' x as an *eidos*; it does not differ 'in itself' from any other x, it can differ from another x only by reason of its position; it is identical with all xs without being them, and not by reason of being a different instance of the same concept, since x is not a 'concept'. It is identical with them as a *figure*, and this identity is analogous to universality or, better, to the *generical* character of the figure (*the* triangle in every triangle) without in any way being assimilable to it. All the 'accidental' properties that the sign may possess are not relevant; it is enough that its concrete instances be similarly 'sufficient for usage' (*pros tēn chreian ikanōs*) and this usage is the usage of the sign as a sign (whilst one can go wrong in a geometrical construction concerning a triangle because one necessarily draws *a* particular triangle – isosceles, scalene – and particular attention must be paid to this fact). *x* is or is *not x*, it is or is not recognizable as *x*; if it is, it is a canonical representative of an indefinite class, it is absolutely equivalent as a sign to every possible *x*. In positing a sign, the social imaginary, for the first time in the unfolding of the universe, brings *identity* into existence, an identity that does not, and cannot, exist anywhere else. It *institutes identity* and does this in and through the *figures*.

What is next implied here is the 'object' (both in the form of the sign and in that of which the sign is a sign) understood as 'thing', 'property', and so on. Henceforth, the object appears, and is posited, as a definite unity of what is indefinite (not necessarily a multiplicity), as separable–separate, as freely detachable from everything else and capable of being reintegrated into the latter, as belonging to a class or an ensemble, and as a representative of this class, which is confused neither with other members of the class nor with the class as such. Finally, it is apprehended as *index sui*, as self-indicating, representing *itself*, and subsisting through all of its 'parts', 'manifestations', 'qualities' which are not immediately apparent or which may only appear at a later moment. In this way identity is instituted as full or substantial, not as the identity between this and that but as self-identity as selfhood, *autotēs*, *Selbstheit*.

Lastly, what is implied here is the *signitive* relation, the relation between the sign and the object as absolutely specific, unanalysable and unconstructable, which posits and takes both terms together as cobelonging, although between them there is no real or logical relation of any sort (which is a tautology, for real and logical relations can exist only on the basis of and by means of this signitive relation). This relation brings its two terms into existence immediately as universal or, better, generic terms. It is universalizing or productive of generic terms because, at the same time that it posits these two terms, it posits two 'classes' and cannot help but do so. There can never exist an 'atomic' sign or object: the 'atomic' object, like the 'point-like event', is an abstract elaboration belonging to a later stage of the development of *legein* as logical–scientific. The signitive relation is, in every instance, singular in itself ('... is called ...' is a unique relation between two classes and does not exist if it is not unique) *and* a universalizable core (for if one relation of designation is available, then the possibility of designation becomes available everywhere).

From this moment on, what is posited are two concrete entities as separable–separate, two *eidos*, and concrete entities as representatives of the corresponding *eidos*, in a specific relation of one concrete entity to another which is at the same time a relation of one *eidos* to another and a plurality of interweaving re-presentation relations. *This* dog represents dogs *as such* but can also be used to make the word 'dog' comprehensible to someone who does not know it – and the appearance of this word, whether uttered or written, can designate this dog, every dog and dogs in general.

What is involved in the signitive relation is *quid pro quo*, something for something else or in the place of something else, re-presentation (*Vertretung*), which, as we shall see, 'implies' or 'entails' logical categories but cannot be constructed on the basis of these categories, since it is presupposed by every use of categories. This re-presentation is quite obviously an institution. This was seen, clearly and profoundly, by Democritus, who demonstrated by means of arguments, to which almost nothing has been added since, that language is instituted and is not 'natural', not only to the extent that the sign is conventional or arbitrary – the fact that *what* on one side of the Rhine is called *boeuf* is called *Ochs* on the other side – but to the extent that this 'what' is itself instituted. Hot and cold exist only through the institution (*nomō*), Democritus states, not the 'words' hot and cold, and not their relation to some given and indubitable 'hot' and 'cold', but hot and cold *themselves as such*.[19] It is not simply *that* sign or *each* particular sign that is 'arbitrary' (quite the opposite: the arbitrary is limited and finally problematical in the case of each sign taken individually) but the sign-relation as such, *legein* as such and taken as a whole.

But what is also put into play by the signitive relation is a concrete, material–sensuous figure (usually audible or visible) which is a sign only inasmuch as it exists as sensuous without matter for the members of the society in question, beyond the concrete existence of any particular individual. Sensuous without matter: this is precisely Aristotle's definition of the *phantasma*, the phantasy, the 'image'.[20] What appears to be an indefinite multiplicity of concrete instances (words that are actually uttered or written, and so on) is held together only because the indefinite multiplicity of sensuous figures without matter, *phantasmata*, sensuous, generic representations ('acoustic images' for example) of individuals (this multiplicity is twice indefinite: an indefinite multiplicity for each individual and an indefinite multiplicity of individuals) is, in its turn, held together by *the* sensuous, immaterial figure constituted by *the* sign as such and by *this* sign for everybody within a given social sphere, by what we are obliged to call the social–historical *phantasma*, 'social representation' (representation for no one and for everyone, the indefinite 'all') of the word and of a given word in its abstract–material existence, entirely independent of its relation to signification. This social *phantasma* cannot be reduced to the schemata in terms of which one has always tried to think of the imagination and the imaginary, without in fact thinking of them. It is patently not a fainter repetition, a reproduction, the partial retention of something given, an imitation or anything of the sort. It is a creation, the positing (institution) by the social imaginary of a figure or group of figures that are not real, which *makes* concrete figures (materializations, particular instances of the 'word-image') *exist* as *what* they are: word-figures, signs (and not noises or marks). Imaginary: an unmotivated creation that exists only in and through posing images. Social: inconceivable as the work or the product of an individual or a host of individuals (the individual *is* a social institution), underivable from the psyche in itself as such.

The sign, as social *phantasma*, creates at the same time the possibility of its representation (*Vorstellung*) and of its reproduction by anyone placed within the social sphere in question. It thereby entails the quasi-certainty of this reproduction due to the individual's social shaping, shaping for which this social *phantasma* is the basic means. The sign can exist, however, only if the possibility of its representation *for* individuals is secured and, at the same time, if its recovery and incessant reproduction *by* individuals is categorically certain. This implies not only that the individual speaks in and through representation but that he is capable of speaking only to the extent that representation is excentring and self-otherness: to speak, to be in signs, is literally to see in what is what is absolutely not there. Not just 'empirically' or 'psychologically', but at all levels, and not just once, but ten thousand times ten thousand times, thinking, whether philosophical or other, mathematics, the simple manipulation of an algorithm – all of these presuppose representation, imagination and, finally, the social imaginary and the institution of *legein*.

It is important to insist on the irreducibility of the signitive relation. A sign can be a sign of 'this' only if 'this' has been adequately delimited and 'identified', which is never the case unless a sign or a group of signs has been associated with 'this'. 'This' can begin to be delimited and 'identified' only by becoming an *index of itself* – hence by being already 'contaminated' by the signitive operation. The 'this' of designation, the 'object' designated ceases to be an absolute immediate (or, what amounts to the same thing, it never was outside of the reflexive abstraction claiming to be situated outside of language and before *legein*). It is hollowed out from within or it opens up, by acquiring a depth, by making possible all the subsequent ascriptions or determinations that will take it as a referent. Moreover, it splits itself, or multiplies itself indefinitely, becoming the representative of itself in the open series of its occurrences. In this way, the 'object', *that which* is designated is at one and the same time more and less than 'itself' – and, as it is posited in and through *legein*, it is what it is, a distinct and definite element that can be taken up again indefinitely in the operations of identitary–ensemblist logic. If something is to be a sign, it must be delimited and 'identified' as a sign and and *this* particular sign. The institution of the sign is immediate institution of the class of signs, and every sign is, as such, the indicator of the existence of signs as such (and, of course, of everything that this implies). In a sense, a sign has to indicate itself as a sign, indicate itself to someone for any sign to exist, indicate all other signs, and be indicated, in turn, by them as a sign. This could never be the case of *one* sign in isolation – there is always necessarily a class of signs forming a 'system' (*code*). This is why it is an abuse of language to speak of 'natural signs' (smoke and fire, for instance). Here, as in other cases, certain signitive relations may, initially, lean on the concomitance (*sumbainein*) of two 'natural' occurrences; an abyss separates this from the institution of a system of signs. Likewise, information theory is of no assistance to us in this domain; the most it can provide is the trivial condition holding that figures or occurrences that are 'naturally' too frequent can never function as signs for they are continually in danger of blending in with what surrounds them, that is, of being taken for 'objects'. At any rate, this is already entailed by the signitive relation, for the sign can never be an 'object' (except as a sign-object); and sign-objects must be posited as a class of pseudo-objects apart from the objects they designate. They, therefore, have to be *created* as sign-objects (forms, types, *eidos* of signs forming a system). The improbable or exceptional object or event is an *omen*, a 'natural sign' – it is not a sign. The sign system must indicate itself as a sign system – and this short-circuits any attempt to construct a 'metalanguage' in order to account for this operation.

In particular, however, it is the signitive *relation* that is irreducible and impossible to construct. To be sure, it can be said that '*x* designates *y*' puts into play all the categories by means of which *x* and *y* are constituted as 'objects', as *these particular objects* and as 'objects in a relation'. But this is to say almost nothing. In '*x* (sign) designates *y* (object')', *x*, precisely, is *not* constituted as an object, it is posited as sign, as non object, where the categories constitutive of the object are not relevant for it. Other basic operators, which we shall discuss shortly, enter into play here – just as they do in positing the 'object' *y* as an object of designation. 'Designating' is not a relation that has a place in inherited logic and ontology; it is neither a category corresponding to a form of judgement or to a level of being, nor can it be constructed logically, since it is presupposed by every logical construction. Designation (re-presentation, *Vertretung*), *quid pro quo*, is original institution.

What, to abstract–reflexive thinking, can appear as the simple use, in *legein*, of 'constitutive' categories (one, several, substance) or of 'reflexive concepts' (identity, difference, form, matter) in fact presupposes ('really' and 'logically') something quite different from 'categories' and 'concepts': it presupposes a bundle of operative schemata that are not 'logical functions', that exist as operating figures or figurations, none of which can function unless the *results* of its own functioning and of that of all the others are already present (thereby excluding any possibility of 'constructing' them). The same thing can be said concerning the operating schemata of *teukhein* and this can be extended to the relations between *legein* and *teukhein*. *Legein* exists only if *teukhein* and its results are already available. *Legein* is a *teuxis* ('making') and a *teukhos* or a *tukton* (tool, well-made instrument).

Teukhein is a *lexis* (a well-articulated 'saying') and a *lekton* (a result of this 'saying' and this very 'saying' as a possibility). What is manifested here in this way is a decisive aspect of instituting as such and of original institution, which we could attempt to express – poorly – by saying that the institution 'presupposes *itself*, that it can exist only by acting as if it had already existed fully)and as if it had, indefinitely, to go on existing). The social imaginary exists as social–historical doing/representing; as such, it institutes and is obliged to institute the 'instrumental condition' for its social–historical existence, which are doing/representing as identitary or ensemblist, in other words, *teukhein* and *legein*. This institution itself, however, the institution of the 'instrumental conditions' of doing and representing, is still itself a doing and a representing – a 'making be' as presentation, a figuring and a figure; the institution of *legein* and of *teukhein* as such is still a *legein-teukhein*.

This situation can be illustrated by the example of some of the main operative schemata of *legein* (which are the same as the essential ones for *teukhein*).

The signitive relation involves circular implication or, better, is in a relation of reciprocal inherence with the operating schema of discretion-separation.[21] Sign and object must obviously be separated from everything else and from one another. The latter separation suffices to distinguish, immediately and radically, *legein* from alleged 'genetic language' or 'computer language'. For in these cases, 'sign' and 'object' are really and logically the *same*: what has been improperly presented as a 'sign' *is* an object and *acts as* one; here one can speak of a 'sign' only through naive anthropomorphism, only by forgetting that the alleged 'sign' functions solely as an object, that it acts by means of effective causality. The stereochemical properties of the molecule cause, in the most banal way (banal in *this* respect), a given association with another molecule or the 'production' of a given product. The situation is the same, both really and logically, in a computer, only the 'support system' of causality is different.

The signitive relation also implies the operative schema of union: uniting what belongs to the sign, uniting what belongs to the object, by which both exist as *this* sign and *this* object. But it also implies another type of union, which makes the pair, sign-object, exist, this sign being the sign *of* this object, and the object being assigned *to* this sign. The circular implication, or the reciprocal inherence, of separation and union is immediately self-evident: one can only unite by separating (what is united from the rest), one can separate only by uniting (putting back together what has been separated from the rest).[22]

The operative schema of union is actually twofold – and seems immediately to bring about another schema, as a result of which it is twofold. Uniting can also be said to be co-belonging: the 'object' dog implies the co-belonging of certain aspects, properties, parts, and so on; the sign (spoken or written) 'dog' implies the co-belonging of phonemes, letters and so on. This co-belonging, however, is neither absolute nor indifferent: it is co-belonging (or uniting) *with respect to* ... (*qua, pros ti, quatenus*); and, in the same way, every separation is separation qua ..., *with respect to* ... This *with respect to* ... is itself an irreducible operative schema that cannot be constructed. Now the signitive relation as such circularly implies the operative schema *with respect to* ... in a number of ways. At the same time, however, it is itself an operative schema that cannot be reduced to the schema of uniting-separation with respect to ... but instead is 'required' by the latter. For the signitive schema as such ('*x* designates *y*') obviously poses a co-belonging of *x* and *y*, but as a specific, signitive co-belonging: the object and the sign (a given object and 'its' sign) belong together *as* (*with respect to* ...) the sign of this object and the object of this sign; they belong together by reason of the signitive relation and *as regards* this relation. And it is only because this co-belonging of the sign and the object (posited by the signitive relation) exists that there can be a co-belonging of the 'parts' of the object and of the 'parts' of the sign. We can never reflect enough on this self-evidence: the word 'dog' and the dog belong together – in an entirely different way than the dog's paws and head belong together. Without the first co-belonging, the second *does not exist* – does not exist in and for *legein*, language, thought, does not exist 'for us'. Far from the signitive relation being able to be 'constructed' or 'composed' on the basis of separation–union with respect to ..., it is the latter that presupposes the former or, better, implies it in a circular manner. *This* can be separated-united because 'this' designates it. And, once these operative schemata are 'available' as embodied in operating products, their operation can be repeatedly used to 'manufacture' other instances of *this* and 'this'.

This co-belonging, which can be termed signitive co-belonging to distinguish it from 'objective' or 'real' co-belonging, obviously cannot exist without (for it circularly implies) the operative schema of the *rule*: *x must* be used to designate *y* and not *z*, y *must* be designated by *x* and not by *t*. This *must* (*Sollen*) is a sheer fact: its violation, as such, entails no logical contradiction, no ethical transgression, no aesthetic ugliness. (For the *individual* who violates it, accidentally or systematically, there may be 'real sanctions' – but that is another matter.) It cannot be 'founded' on anything other than itself. Not only can no particular signitive relation be 'founded' (it can, at most, be partially 'explained' or 'justified' on a *second* level) but the signitive relation as such and the rule that it implies circularly can themselves be founded only on the necessities of *legein*: there must be an approximately univocal rule of designation if *legein* is to exist, and there must be *legein* if a rule such as this is to exist.

Let us stress this fact: nothing in all of inherited logic and ontology enables us to conceive of *what* this signitive co-belonging is and *how* it is (just as nothing enables us to conceive of *what* the institution is and *how* it is). It is obviously neither a 'logical relation' nor a 'real relation', it can be neither of these. If one, improperly, makes the 'object' a concept, it is placed in relation by signitive co-belonging with something that is not a concept – the sign. Hence, this is not a 'logical relation'. Nor could one present it as a 'real relation' – except by referring to actual individual representations: here, the 'word-image' and the 'object-image' stick together (and one would have to consider the individual's history in order to explain how and why this is so). This presentation, however, is untenable on many counts. Signitive co-belonging is, of course, instrumented in individual representations but by no means can it be said to be *there* as such: what is *there* in each case is, for each individual, the interminable series of *particular* realizations of the object, the sign, and their relation ('association'). Nothing in this tells us whether or not, in what way or why this relation (or 'association') differs from any sort of association between 'images'. The relating (referral) of representations in and through the individual representative flux is, to be sure, the necessary basis for all language – but it does not account for language. Speaking is not associating in general, nor forming a concatenation of 'word-images'; it is connecting together and reproducing signs, as signs of ..., in accordance with certain rules – in particular, the rule implied in signitive co-belonging. And I cannot think of these rules as a descriptive abstraction extracted from the actual use of speech in a given collectivity, since this speech exists as such only by means of these rules. Particular realizations of the object-sign relation by each individual can exist only because signitive co-belonging and rules themselves exist as social, as instituted – that is to say, as non 'real', as without any particular place or outside of any place ('real' or 'logical'). This is also the reason why we are unable to represent this co-belonging directly to ourselves as a signitive co-belonging. I can trace as much as I like the words 'tree' and *arbor* in the drawing of a tree or provide myself with a figure of them, or repeat them endlessly while looking at a real tree, yet I can never represent to myself the co-belonging of the word and of the thing as such, nor intend it for itself, I am unable even to think of *it* except in an oblique way. Now this is never the case when we are considering the simple association of representations: however puzzling, however improbable, however disparate, however incomprehensible the linking together of two actual events or memories in my representation may be, this linking together or this association is given to me 'in person' as a coincidence, a similitude, or the inclusion of a 'part' in a 'whole', and so on, along with its 'terms' when it is presented to me. The connection is given as an actual part of that which is connected and this is unrelated to the fact that I can endlessly question why and how this is so. The connection of representations is an actual 'part' of the representative flux, whereas signitive co-belonging cannot be so. Or, to use Kantian language: *every* connection or relation (whether of thoughts or representations) is a connection or relation of 'images' or of schemata which is itself supported, presentified, figured by a schema of a higher order. Now no schema can be conceived of or constructed that would account for the signitive relation (or that could 'figure' it) as such, already for this simple reason that nothing in the *Critique of Pure Reason*, and nothing in all of philosophy from its beginnings up to the present, allows us, gives us the right to establish any difference between an ellipse and the letter O, between a line segment and the letter I. The letter O (and this applies to all letters and can be directly transposed to phonemes) *is* not and cannot be for Kant or for any other philosopher; it is *not even* Nothing. it is obviously neither a 'thing' nor a 'concept'. Nor does it partake of Nothing: it is not a being of reason; not privative nothingness, nor negative nothingness; and it is not an imaginary being, *ens imaginarium*, for as such O is an ellipse, not a letter. The most rigorous, the most exigent philosophy perhaps written to date, thinks in and through a language that it renders infinitely more unthinkable than negative nothingness, one that cannot even be posited as negating itself as a contradictory concept: language, from this perspective, does not even exist sufficiently for one to be able to say that it does not exist, as can be said of the squared circle.

This is only one consequence of the *egological* position of inherited thought and of the concealment of the social imaginary, of the social–historical implied by it. O and I are less than Nothing – for O and I are institutions, ('instituted elements'), historically created figures, forms-*eidē*. Concealment of the social imaginary: the sign *qua* sign can exist only as an instituted figure, a form-norm, a creation of the social imaginary. But what is more, signitive co-belonging can exist only as an institution, as an operative schema, as the figuration of figures in a manner that is, as such, unrepresentable in the egological field and literally unthinkable as such. Lastly, as we have already stated and as is quite obvious, inasmuch as this co-belonging is and has always to be instrumented by the representation of individuals, it implies as its counterpart in the individual psyche the essential property of radical imagination (which traditional philosophy touches on only to the extent that it leads to the true and the false): not 'imagining what is not' but imagining/figuring one thing by means of another thing, being able to 'see' in what is what is not there, presenting or presentifying one thing by another thing.

The signitive relation circularly implies the operative schema of value, or of *being worth*, as it serves two different functions: *standing for* ... in the sense of being valued as ..., having the same value as ..., *wie*; and *serving for* ... in the sense of serving a given end, *um* ... *zu*. These two functions can subsequently be distinguished and specified as 'exchange value' and 'use value' in different areas. The signitive relation implies, on the one hand, the schema of *standing for* ..., being valued as ... as a schema of equivalence in a number of different forms. The generic character of the figure or image (of the sign or the object) becomes here primary universality and the creation of classes (of ensembles). Occurrences of the 'same sign' are equivalent regardless of their 'concrete' differences (graphics, pronunciation or position); instances of the 'same object' are equivalent to the extent that they correspond to the 'same sign'. Let us recall that the class is created along with the object; the object *is* a class, even if it is singular – there are no proper names. *This* dog *is* the class of its indefinite occurrences, and these occurrences of the 'same dog' are posited as equivalent *with respect to* ... (or, as amounts to the same thing, this dog is 'the same' dog only on the basis of the schema of equivalence operating on its different occurrences). Equivalence is an historical creation, leaning on data given in the first natural stratum (the biological 'species' dog, *this* dog as an 'individual' organism). Let us consider more specifically what equivalence implies in the case of signs. In *legein* all the occurrences of a sign, if and only if they can be apprehended as occurrences of *this* sign have the same value at a given level (and *with respect to* ...). They can, therefore, be exchanged for one another, replaced by one another, substituted for one another. This capacity for substitution functions on all levels of *legein*: it founds the 'associative' (Saussure) or 'para-digmatic' (Hjelmslev) relation, which we prefer to call the substitutive relation. Equivalence appears as absolute equivalence or perfect sub-stitutibility between all the material realizations of a sign provided that these are at least minimally discernable; it appears as relative equiv-alence or limited substitutibility in the 'paradigmatic' relation in the strict sense.

Moreover, the signitive relation implies the schema of *serving for* ..., being valued as ... (*valoir pour* ...). There is no *legein* with a single sign: there is a system of signs at different levels (it is not our purpose to discuss here whether or not 'double articulation' is a necessary character of language). At each level signs function by means of their *combination* (this is what Saussure called the syntagmatic relation). This would not be a combination of signs, but simply the manifestation of separation/union at iterated levels, if the operative schema of *serving for* ... did not enter in here. Each sign is characterized by its possible use, in other words, by the possible combinations in which it may enter. As such, the 'use value' of a sign is its combinatory value (just as its 'exchange value' is its substitutibility). Thus in French, the 'phoneme' *n* has a null 'use value' between two consonants. Each sign, therefore, possesses potential indices of *serving for* ... or 'use values'. If we consider the *legein*, (in other words, language as a *code*, as an identitary–ensemblist system), these indices are, in principle, definite and finite in number. The possible uses of a phoneme, the syntagmas in which a word can enter are determined, definite and *finite* in number.[23] However, if we consider language as *langue*, that is beyond its identitary–ensemblist dimension, and if we refer words and sentences to *significations*, the possible uses of a word or a sentence are not rigorously circumscribed nor are they absolutely determined; they are neither finite nor infinite – they are *indefinite*, for a particular use of a word, for instance, can be the basis for a *new* and *different* meaning, one not given directly with the language and the *code*. On the level of language, of the relation between language and meaning, *standing for* ... and *serving for* ..., equivalence and potential use, the capacity for substitution and combination can no longer be determined in an identitary manner.

The indissociability of the two forms of the operative schema of value, the reciprocal inherence of standing for ... and of serving for ..., is already evident if we consider the signitive relation. For, with respect to *legein*, this relation posits both a certain 'equivalence' of the sign and the object and a certain 'use' of the sign and the object in in the particular combination that constitutes the signitive relation. More generally: as soon as the *legein* is instituted, the operative schema of value (or *being worth* ...) is instituted as well, for there is a separation between the abstract-material basis of *legein* from everything else, positing that a given ensemble of occurrences are not 'natural events' but have the *value* of signs: they all *stand for* ..., they are equivalent in so far as they are signs and not events, and they all *serve for* ..., can be used for designation. This double, criss-crossing operation is repeated on the successive levels of the *legein*. Every sign or combination of signs serves (or does not serve) for ... its insertion in a combination of signs through its possibility of making (something) be ... starting from ... in a manner appropriate to ... and in view of ...; it is immediately evident here that the *legein is* a *teukein*. Every sign has a value inasmuch as it can be 'used' in accordance with a set of conditions, and used 'well or poorly'. But what does 'well or poorly' mean here? This is value in its other form – the form of equivalence. What was, abstractly speaking, on the level of the singular sign its index of *value as* a sign – what institutes it as a sign and distinguishes it from a natural occurrence – is now carried to a higher level, where a combination of signs *has value as* (stands for) a sign and where only certain combinations have value as signs and not others. What does it mean to say that a phoneme *serves for* a particular combination with certain other phonemes? It means that this combination is a word and, *as a word*, *has the value of* any other word. 'I he cupboard,' a linguist would say, is not an English sentence – it does not have the value of a sentence, does not stand for a sentence – 'I', 'he', 'cupboard' do not *serve for* this combination = this combination does not *stand for* a combination (sentence) = this 'sentence' does not *serve for* a possible entry in a discourse.[24] At the opposite end of the functioning characteristic of *legein*, the impossibility of distinguishing the two forms of value appears in the unending enigma of its relation to the referents of the *legein*, to *what* is said. How can discourse *serve* to say what is, if, in a sense, it does not *stand for* what is (little matter whether this standing for ..., this equivalence in the general sense given to the term here, is called strict identity, adequation, correspondence or reflection)? To say something is to speak truly, to say what is *as* it is. What does

as signify here if not an equivalence? And how is an equivalence
possible between a series of words and a group of facts or things – if
not *as an institution*?[25]

The operating schemata of value are also decisive for the relations
between the institution of *legein* and individuals. To begin with, *legein*
implies, and *brings it about* that every individual has the same value as
any other individual in the collectivity considered, with respect to
legein: stands for any other, serves for the collective utilization of
legein.[26] And the institution of *legein*, inseparable from the institution
of the individual as a social individual, implies that this institution is
the imposition of the equivalence of signs and of combinations of signs
for all (in the indefinite sense) individuals within a given sphere of
legein. Equivalence signifies the equivalence and not the identity of
that which, in each individual, 'corresponds' to the sign. To assert such
an identity would obviously be meaningless, since that to which a sign
corresponds for an individual is inseparable from the representative/
affective/intentional flux which that individual *is*; representations corresponding to the same signs for different individuals are themselves
incomparable. This incomparability is obviously merely another way of
saying that each individual actually *is* this singular, representative flux.
Now the existence of the individual as a social individual and his
'functioning' in and through *legein* implies and requires 'positively' that
he *be* a singular, representative flux such as this; for, if he were not,
he would be no more than a talking machine – that is to say, nothing
at all. Philosophy most often considers this positive and essential condition for social–historical life a psychological scoria, since it is obliged,
from its egological and identitary perspective, to assert that language
implies and requires the rigorous *identity* of 'that which' in each individual corresponds to the same linguistic expression. However, since
legein can exist only as an unseparable dimension of language, and
since language would not exist if individuals did not function as they
do and 'with' all that they are, this assertion of a rigorous identity,
across all individuals, of that which is 'essential' in linguistic expression
is not only empty but amounts to the destruction of language. This
destruction – which is obviously 'contradictory', striking out philosophy
itself, which, unaware, is directed towards it – is, moreover, gratuitous
and useless. If social communication (and, for that matter, thought) is
to exist, it is necessary and sufficient that there be an equivalence *with
respect to legein* (and also, *with respect to teukhein*) of 'that which' in
each individual, corresponds to the social sign and that this equivalence
mediate the access to significations.[27]

The operating schema of equivalence, of *standing for____*, circularly
implies that of *iteration* and even makes it possible, since to iterate is
to repeat the same as different or to posit the different as the same
with respect to ... And it is at the same time itself made possible by

the latter, since it could never function without this repetition of the same as different and of the different as same.

Likewise, there is a circular implication between the schema of *serving for* ..., which cannot be concretized outside of combinatory arrangements, and the operating schema of *order* in general. Combination – the combination of signs – implies, in fact, that the value of a term depends on its 'place' in a grouping where the order is pertinent.[28] This is possible, therefore, only through the use of the schema of order, and quite precisely, of well-ordering (the successor of a term, if it exists, is always unique and well-determined). Conversely, the schema of well-ordering can never be *realized* (operating in and through its figuration) without a combinatory arrangement. More generally, the schema of well-ordering circularly implies *legein* and *teukhein*, for it implies that discrete terms are given, whereas terms such as these 'exist' for the first time only in and through *legein* and *teukhein*. There can be no 'well-ordering' in the individual representative flux, or in any 'natural' given before (or without) the operation of the schemata of separation and reunion. Conversely, there can be neither *legein* nor *teukhein* without a relation of well-ordering.[29] We can simply evoke here the deep-rooted relation that exists between the requirements posited by the schema of well-ordering – in other words, the 'discrete succession' of *legein* – and the institution of a punctual 'consciousness' in the individual, on the one hand, and the 'linear' character of explicitly instituted, identitary time, on the other. Finally, it is immediately evident that the schemata of iteration and of well-ordering circularly imply one another – and this refers back to the circular implication of the two forms of the schema of *value*.

By means of these schemata – or of schemata *such as these*: the preceding discussion is illustrative, not exhaustive – by means of their carrying over, iteration, composition, functioning in terms of reciprocal inherence, a hierarchy is instituted in and through *legein*. What is instituted is a hierarchy or, better, a more or less hierarchical network of signs and combinations of signs or various orders, corresponding to an identitary pseudo-world, *coded* by these signs and formed by distinct and definite 'objects' and by the distinct and definite 'relations' between these 'objects'. In this hierarchized network, and the corresponding parts in the identitary pseudo-world, particular domains are established, of course, in each of which the schemata of separation/union, with respect to ..., standing for ... and serving for ..., schemata of order and iteration, etc., function by receiving and by giving rise to particular specifications. (Thus, the rules of pertinence can exist only by possessing in every instance a 'content' that is specific and relative to the domain in question.) This establishment, that of the identitary dimension of doing and of social representing, is inseparable from the network of institutions in the broad sense of the term, in and through which this doing and this representing unfold. Thus, the institution of law is the institution of legal 'objects' and 'relations' – it cannot exist unless it is a specific institution of legal *legein*; but the state of affairs is no different in the case of magic, religion or even art.

vi *LEGEIN*, DETERMINACY, UNDERSTANDING

After this discussion, it is perhaps easier to see for what reason and in what respect inherited logic-ontology is so deeply rooted in *legein* and in its requirements; why logic-ontology is, in a central sense, simply the interminable elaboration of *legein* and the effort to extend it without limit, so that it can absorb within itself even that which 'denies' it. Determinacy sovereignly reigns in, through, and for *legein*: all that can be/all that can have value is only that which is distinct and definite (to be sure, in a sense of these terms which is itself undefinable), that which is necessarily and sufficiently separated/united with respect to ..., that which is always in a well-ordering, that which is indifferent *with respect to* time and *with respect to* matter, or that whose matter interminably lends itelf to determination (namely, to being *said*), that whose modes of value – possible equivalences and possible uses – are fixed, given, unambiguous. What is the limit of these requirements, of their fulfilment without remainder? '... *everything which exists* is *completely determined* ... not only ... one of every pair of *given* contradictory predicates, but...one of all possible predicates must always belong to a thing ...'[30] Being, in *legein*, is being-determined. In this expression, it is enough to omit the clause 'in *legein*' and to qualify the term 'determined' (entirely determined, less determined, etc.) to encompass all of inherited ontology. And, in *legein* as in ontology existence and value cannot be distinguished, they signify the same thing: being a sign is having the value of a sign, standing for a sign – but also being an object is having the value of, standing for an object. A collection of objects is or is not itself an object if it stands for an object – if it has been posited by *legein* as an object. The dream I had last night, the battle of Cannes, the nucleus of the Andromeda nebula, and Cromwell's kidney *exist*; they are, for better or for worse, 'objects'. But their collection does not *exist*; for it does not constitute, in any respect, an 'object' in *legein* (or at any level of *legein*) – it does not *stand for* an object. *Legein* is and makes (things) be by making them *stand for* ..., by giving them value.

By an inversion, which is only paradoxical in appearance, philosophy, the elaboration and extension of *legein*, of its norms and its requirements, is then led to conceal, to veil, to cover over the *legein* itself and its own relation to the *legein*. Not taking into account, being unable for deep-rooted reasons to take into account – not being able *to give an account of or a reason for, logon didonai* – the nuclear and basic schema of *legein*, of the signitive relation, philosophy can only, in the canonical case, act as though it could have direct access to that of which it speaks (whether it be things, ideas or the subject), that is to say, as though it could either completely eliminate *legein*, treat it as a totally transparent optical medium or a perfectly neutral instrument, or, finally 'correct' it without remainder or fully absorb it within a purified logic that would be entirely independent of it. This is still true when philosophy 'criticizes language', this critique always being made in reference to another mode of access to what is, one that is perfectly adequate and postulated as capable of being effected (Plato in the *Seventh Letter* or Husserl in the *Logical Investigations* and elsewhere) or as impossible to accomplish (sceptics in general). And this is, obviously, even truer when language is taken *in toto* as 'rational' and the 'being-there of Spirit'; the process throughout which Reason and Knowledge appear (*phainontai*: Phenomenology) in and through language is simply the side we see of the atemporal, 'dialectical' – tautological process in and through which Reason must *necessarily* and in a *determined* manner posit itself as language, that is to say, deposit itself in language and state itself through language. This 'not taking into account' because one cannot *account for* is evident in every philosophy that situates itself in the perspective of a 'foundation' or a 'deduction', since a perspective such as this is nothing other than the search for an origin that would display its own necessity as at once intelligible and expressible, in relation to which the institution of *saying* would, then, be external and indifferent. Reciprocally, it is an insurmountable necessity for a philosophy situated in this perspective to conceal the end point that the institution of *legein* constitutes for its work – since philosophy knows only the contingent and the necessary, and *legein*, which is neither 'contingent' nor 'necessary', is that on the basis of which alone necessity and contingency can have any meaning at all. But at the same time, it is impossible *to give* an account of or a reason for, hence to take into account, the signitive relation as such – as irreducible, inconstructable, non-deducible – for a philosophy for which there is a cyclical, logical order, like the Hegelian dialectic, since in this order an equivalence or a generalized transformability holds together all the moments of the circuit, where nothing is ever encountered that is 'irreducible'.

All this, of course, is just another way of saying that *legein* is a primordial institution, and that at this level identitary logic *cannot* seize hold of the institution, since the institution is neither necessary nor contingent, since its emergence is not determined but is that on the basis of which, in which and by means of which alone something determined exists. Recognizing the signitive relation, the *quid pro quo*, representing (*vertreten*) as essential and irreducible, is recognizing the 'arbitrary' (instituted) character of this re-presenting; the consequence is abolishing determinacy as an ultimate norm.

We alluded earlier to the fact that *legein* involves an essential part of reflexive categories and concepts, but that it cannot itself be 'constructed' on the basis of these. The *understanding* is implied in *legein*:

it cannot be separated from the latter; it presupposes *legein* at the same time as it is presupposed by it – but it is presupposed by *legein as one of its parts, indissociable from the rest*. There is 'more' in *legein* than in the understanding, the latter being only one part of the institution of *legein*, arbitrarily (and fallaciously) separated from the latter and considered in itself starting from and in relation to a specific social–historical institution. To have *legein* at one's command is to have understanding at one's command, but having understanding 'at one's command' is not yet having *legein* at one's command – and having understanding 'at one's command' without *legein* is having nothing at one's command. The institution of *legein* is from the start the (implicit) institution of understanding *and* of something else – of the signitive relation which is, in truth, unanalysable and without which nothing is possible. *Legein* implies the signitive relation which understanding cannot construct or produce. We indeed saw that the essential operative schema of the signitive relation, the *quid pro quo*, re-presentation (*Vertretung*), or the presentation of A by means of not A or other than A, is not and cannot be a logical or ontological category or the product of these categories. But at the same time, the implementation of these categories, their correct use, is *impossible* outside of the signitive relation and, in particular, outside of the *quid pro quo* schema. And this is so because there is no thinking subject, no thought without language. And also, because (from an intrinsical 'transcendental' point of view), if the object is to exist, to be thinkable or to be constituted, it must be maintained as a 'self-index', it must re-present 'itself' throughout the (logical) 'moments' of its being, of its being-thought or being-constituted. The constitution of the object already requires an initial 'genericization/symbolization' of the object (of that which is *not yet* an object) in relation to 'itself'. Likewise, no object 'is' (constituted) if it is not caught up in relations of causation and reciprocal action, which imply other objects, gradually extending to include the totality of phenomena. Either this totality is present each time 'in person' whenever I think of an object – which is absurd, or it is there without being there, and, in particular, it is re-presented there; something that is not it is posited for it and as it, 'in its place'.[31]

The understanding is instituted, for it is simply 'part' of *legein*. Let us examine another aspect of this implication. The understanding is 'the faculty of binding according to rules' (Kant) and there are no rules outside of the institution. Rules imply the institution. The possibility of rules is created by and posited along with the institution. The category is a rule of connection of that which is given; *unity* signifies the order (the injunction) to think of that which is given from the viewpoint of the 'one'; *substance*, the order to think of the 'permanent', the 'enduring', the 'persisting' – or 'that which cannot be the predicate of some other thing', and so forth. Of course, these orders are such only to the extent that they have this *value* – and they never have value, in their concrete implementation, except *with respect to* .... It is always only *with respect to* ... that any sort of thing is, for example, *one*. Of course, it is true, too, that categories are the operative schemata of both *legein* and teukhein, and, like all operative schemata, they are themselves the 'results' of a *teukhein*; thinking in accordance with categories is making (something) be ... starting from ... in a manner appropriate to ... and in view of .... Making connections in accordance with a rule is obviously a *legein* as well as a *teukhein*.

vii ASPECTS OF *TEUKHEIN*

Teukhein signifies: assembling-adjusting-fabricating-constructing. It is, therefore, making (something) be as ... starting from ... in a manner appropriate to ... and in view of .... What has been called *techne*, a word that derives from *teukhein* and that has given the term *technique*, is but a particular manifestation of *teukhein* and concerns only secondary and derivative aspects of it.[32] For example, 'before' there can be any question of 'technique' of any sort, the social imaginary must assemble-adjust-fabricate-construct *itself* as society and as this society, it must make *itself* be as society and as this society, starting with itself and with what 'is there', in a manner appropriate to and in view of being a society and this particular society. *Teukhein* is implied in instituting, just as *legein* is.

The essential operative schemata for *legein* are, with one exception, directly and immediately the same as those for *teukhein*. For assembling-adjusting-fabricating-constructing, the following must be available: separation and union, the *with respect to* ..., value as *standing for* ... and as *serving for* ..., hence, equivalence and possible use, iteration and order. It would be useless, and even senseless, to debate whether *legein* borrows its schemata from *teukhein* or the other way around (whether 'speech' precedes the 'tool' or the opposite). For it is easy to see that *legein* and *teukhein* refer to one another and circularly imply one another. It is not a question of an external conditioning – for example, the fact that technique, as social, requires that men cooperate with one another and, in order to do this, that they speak – but of an essential interconnection of *legein* and *teukhein*. *Teukhein* intrinsically implies *legein*, *is* in a sense a *legein*, for it operates and is able to exist only by distinguishing-choosing-assembling-positing-counting. *Teukhein* separates 'elements', fixes them as such, orders them, combines them, unites them into totalities and organized hierarchies of totalities within the field of doing. And in this field, it operates under the aegis of determinacy and as actual determination and the condition for all determination. – Conversely, *legein* intrinsically implies *teukhein*, *is* in a sense a *teukhein*. For it assembles-adjusts-fabricates-constructs the 'abstract–material' elements of language along with all of the 'objects' and 'relations' corresponding to them. The fabrication of language as a *code* is a work of *teukhein*; it is making (something) be ... starting from ... in a manner appropriate to ... and in view of .... *Legein* is not *legein* if it is not an organized totality of efficacious operations with a 'material' basis. *Teukhein* is not *teukhein* if it is not the positing of distinct and definite elements involved in functional relations (in both the ordinary and mathematical sense of the word 'function').

Let us illustrate this identity of the essential operative schemata of *legein* and *teukhein* in the example of the operative schema of *value*. It is self-evident that every technique is based on the schema of *serving for* ... (and, of course, with *respect to* ...). A given object, tool, act or gesture enter into it in so far as it is appropriate to ... in view of ..., that is to say, in so far as it has a 'use value' in, through and for a given combination. But also, and this comes before any 'standardization' of products and instruments, technique exists as social (and not as the unique and accidental utilization of a 'natural' object) only by means of the property of *standing for* ..., as equivalence, the possibility of repetition. A given tool or product has the *same* use as another, it can be reproduced, it has or can have equivalents, and it is a tool in the first place in so far as it is its own equivalent on the various occasions of its use. Creating a tool is creating an *eidos*, a form, whose concrete instances or exemplaries *have the same value* as instances of this *eidos*, which allows its own indefinite reproduction. And these tools *stand for* tools to the extent that they *serve for* doing what it is they permit to be done.

This is not only a matter of material tools. The 'fabrication' of individuals by society, the imposition on somato-psychic subjects in the course of their socialization not only of *legein* but also of all the codifiable attitudes, postures, gestures, practices, comportments and know-how is obviously a *teukhein*, by means of which society makes these subjects exist as social individuals, starting from somato-psychic givens, in a manner appropriate to life, to their life in this society and in view of the place that they will have in it. In this way, social individuals are made, as standing for individuals and as serving for certain social 'roles', 'functions' and 'places'. More generally, instituting as such is always a form of *teukhein* and implies the schema of value as this operates in *teukhein*. For every institution is also an assembling together in view of ...; and in this the instituted terms always function in relation to one another and all of them in relation to the institution, and so stand for the terms of this institution and serve for the institution as such, possess value by reason of their insertion in instituted combinations. Individuals, objects, procedures, which are posited as 'terms' or 'elements' in and by a specific institution, each possess a 'use value' with respect to ..., in relation to the network that is instituted in this way. Thus, as sexed, as capable of copulating and as fecund, every human being 'serves for' copulating and 'stands for' any other individual of the same sex. As a possible husband or wife, however, men and women are ascribed 'use value' indices relative to the institution of marriage, a 'use value' that is created by this institution, outstripping infinitely its biological basis (one has only to consider what marriage presupposes, entails and signifies, always and everywhere) and not even depending on it entirely (impotency or sterility neither rigorously forbid nor necessarily dissolve marriage). But, at the same time, the institution is immediately the positing of the *same* values, of relations of equivalence, since the institution can exist only by massively creating classes of substitutability defined in relation to individuals, acts, and objects: classes of marriage and of kinship, substitutability of individuals with respect to the 'functions' and 'roles' they perform, replaceability of objects, etc.

One central operative schema of *legein* does not appear in *teukhein* as such: the signitive relation in the strict sense. One central operative schema of *teukhein* does not appear in *legein* as such: the relation of *finality* or of *instrumentality*, referring that which is to that which is not *and* at the same time, could be. Here, the *quid pro quo* is no longer something *in place of* something else but something *in view of* something else ('means' and 'end', 'instrument' and 'product' or 'result'). This relation far exceeds the bare *serving for* ...: the tool, of course, *serves for* ... – but *for making something be* that *is not*. Its 'use value' is much more than the value of its *use* – for it is the value of *production* or of *transformation*. In this way *teukhein* constitutes, and constitutes itself, in and through a universality that has a different character than that of *legein*. The 'tool' is created as a form, as an *eidos*, not only to the extent that it is actually reproducible or repeatable in the form of other examples of the 'same' tool, not only to the extent, then, that it repeats itself in its possible successive utilizations; even if it were one of a kind and were only used once, it is an *eidos* to the extent that it is not a mere 'thing' but 'ideally' posited as an element in a relation of finality, as *the* 'means' that enables or should enable bringing it about that .... Now *that which* the 'means' *will be able* to bring about *is* not, does not yet exist when the 'means' is posited, taken, fabricated as a means. The 'tool' is what it is starting from what *it* is not and from *that which* is not, starting from that which it *can* bring into being, make be (*faire être*).

By this we see that the relation of finality circularly implies the schema of possibility, of being able to make (something) be, of being able to be. There would be no finality, hence no *teukhein*, no society if that which is not were not able to be, or if that which is could never also be in some other way. The schema of possibility establishes *ipso facto* the division into the possible and the impossible (the *necessary* is obviously simply another name for the impossible: something is necessary if its non-existence is impossible, and something is impossible if its non-existence is necessary). It is in than through the interweaving of the possible and the impossible that society as a whole and every society in particular constitutes the 'real' and its own 'real'. Reality is not only, as has been repeated since Dilthey, 'that which resists'; it is just as much, and indissociably, that which can be transformed, that which permits *making* (and *teukhein*) as making be something other than that which exists or making be in some other way that which exists in a particular way. Reality is that in which the do-able and the undo-able reside. In this way, making or doing and *teukhein* establish, by means of the institution of reality, a new division in addition to being/not being, value/non-value which are established by *legein*: that of possible/ impossible, do-able/undo-able. It immediately follows from this that 'reality' is socially instituted, not only as reality in general, but as a specific reality, as the reality of *this particular* society. In this way the fecunding of a woman by a spirit is do-able – and hence real – for certain societies and undo-able, hence unreal, in our own.

Let us underscore this point: the distinction possible/impossible is *secondary* and *derivative* in *legein* as such, that is as a *code*. When *legein* states the possible and the impossible, it states what *teukhein* has posited and brought into being. As a *code*, *legein* tends towards the bipartition: obligatory/impossible.[33] For the reasons stated above, this is not a true bipartition (the impossible is that which, mandatorily, must not be or be stated) but an *exclusion*, the exclusion from the universe of *legein* of that which does not conform to its laws. But the division that is established by *teukhein* into possible/impossible is a genuine bipartition, on the basis of which the 'real' exists as divided. Society and individuals thus live and function each time within the obligatory representation of the absolute existence of preconstituted 'possibles' and 'impossibles', in other words, within the imaginary positing of a reality inside of which the boundary between the 'possible' and the 'impossible' would be rigorously traced out once and for all – since the beginning of time. The possible itself is thus posited as *determined* (that which is, in each case, possible and that which is not is definite and distinct). In the same way, the means, instruments, procedures and ways of doing things that transform the possible into the actual or the effective (whether it is a question of tools, incantations, ceremonies, magic actions, etc.) are also posited as *determined*. In so doing, *teukhein* extends determinacy over the entire range of the representable and relives it by thickening it, positing that even that which does not 'exist' is *determined* with respect to its power-to-be or by the absence of this power. And *teukhein* also posits itself as *determining* the *determined* manners according to which that which can be but is not can be brought to be. It also circularly implies the determined relation in succession as indissociably efficient causation and final causation (it is hardly necessary to recall the interminable philosophical extensions of this indissociability).

The 'end', 'result', 'product' in view of which the means, tool, instrument or act is posited or simply is, does not exist 'effectively' at the moment when this positing is made. It exists as an *aim*, an intention, and this intention can exist socially only as an *eidos*, form or type, an instituted figure representing that which is, possibly, going to exist. The 'product' has to exist in and through the actual social imaginary before it can and in order to be 'real'. The counterpart in the individual is the imagination as the representation of that which, possibly, will be, in other words, the power-to-posit as capable-of-being that which is not. 'The result in which labour culminates ideally pre-exists in the imagination of the labourer,' Marx wrote, repeating once and again here what Aristotle stated in a much more general manner concerning the practical or deliberative imagination (*phantasia bouleutike*).[34] It is clear, however, that, if we are speaking strictly of 'labour' or even of 'teukhein' as such, this 'imagination' simply brings into being for the individual as a particular representation a representation of the socially instituted *eidos* (as a product to manufacture, using a particular method, etc.). The creative role of the radical imagination of subjects lies elsewhere: it is their contribution to the positing of forms-types/*eide* other than those that already exist and are in force for the society, an essential, inexpungible contribution, but one that always presupposes the instituted social field and the means that it supplies, and that effectively becomes a contribution (something other than daydreams, whimsy, delirium) only to the extent that it is taken up again on the social level in the form of the modification of the institution or the positing of another institution. The conditions for its being taken up in this way, not simply the 'formal' ones but the 'material' ones as well, extend infinitely beyond what can be provided by the individual imagination.

Just as *legein* incarnates and brings into being the ensemblist–identitary dimension of language and, more generally, of social representing, so *teukhein* incarnates and brings into being the ensemblist–identitary dimension of social doing (or activity). And, just as in the case of language the ensemblist–identitary dimension, through which language exists as a *code*, is impossible without and indissociable from its dimension of signification, through which language exists as *langue*; in the same way, *teukhein*, as ensemblist–identitary is inseparable from the imaginary dimension of *doing* and of the magma of social imaginary significations which social doing brings into being and through which this doing exists as social doing. The parallel runs deep and extends a long way. *Legein*, as strictly ensemblist–identitary, becomes at the limit the incoherent and untenable fiction of the pure formal system closed up on itself. *Teukhein*, as strictly ensemblist–identitary, becomes in the same way the incoherent and untenable fiction of technique for the sake of technique. But, of course, every *teukhein* and every technique are always *for the sake of* something other than themselves and remain dependent on ends that do not result from their own intrinsic determinations. Whereas, for example, technique might appear as an 'end in itself', as it tends to appear in modern capitalist society, *this* positing of technique as an end in itself is not something that technique, as such, could posit; this positing is imaginary. Technique *stands* today *for* the pure social delirium presentifying the phantasy of omnipotence, a delirium which *is* in large part the 'reality' and the 'rationality' (with, but even more without quotation marks) of modern capitalism. More generally in time, and more particularly with respect to the 'aspects' of social activities, every 'productive' technique is such only by reference to the particular 'ends' that determine it and that it, in turn, determines (by circular implication) – that is, social *needs*, needs that are always defined in terms of the imaginary and that could not be defined any other way. (The *only* thing that is not defined by the imaginary in human needs for the past three million years is an approximate number of calories per day, including an approximately given qualitative composition.) Without returning to what was stated in the first part of this book concerning technique and need, I should simply like to underscore the circular implication which exists between them and which, here again, makes *teukhein* and imaginary significations inseparable not only 'at their extremities' but *in medias res*: a need can be posited as a social need (and not as a dream or the Promised Land) only to the extent that *that which* could satisfy it appears in and through social *teukhein* as realizable, even if only virtually. Likewise, the positing of social needs orients and determines, constantly and internally, in innumerable ways, the concrete modalities and manners of instrumenting of *teukhein*. Then, too, from the other end, every *teukhein* and every technique 'presuppose' or have as their starting point the positing, the absolute creation, in and through the social imaginary, of figures and schemata – 'things', 'objects' as they are separated–united as means in view of ... – which institute the world as a world in which a *teukhein* is possible, and which is itself a product of *teukhein* as the inexpungible 'means' of every institution.

Let us illustrate this situation by one final example. We discussed above the operative schema of *value* as it appears in *teukhein* in both its forms, as serving for ... and as standing for ...; we recalled, in particular, that the institution always exists through the massive creation of classes of equivalence (or of substitution – for example, classes of equivalence between social individuals (marriage or kinship groups, clans, castes, 'states', classes in the strict sense of the term, etc.). The identitary dimension is forcefully in play here, as *legein* as well as *teukhein*. However, not only does *that which*, in each case, 'defines' the classes of equivalences between individuals also refer these to imaginary significations (from the most superficial to the ultimate sense of the term 'imaginary'), but the network of classes instituted in this way can itself exist only by being referred finally to terms that are explicitly posited as singular, unique, irreplaceable, the foundation or source of the instituted equivalences: the founding hero, territory, holy city, charismatic leader – as well as, correlatively, that mysterious and ungraspable entity that constitutes society considered in itself, the indefinite, anonymous, collective, open '*us*', not only an indeterminate number of individuals but a coexistence and succession that are instituted and instituted *in a given way*, in this unique, irreplaceable, privileged way. These two singularities can be distinct: thus, Christians define themselves as defined by Christ, by reference to Christ – and this is not a question of the definition that actual Christians 'freely' give of themselves and of Christ, but of the *positing* in and through which, from the social–historical point of view, they exist as Christians and Christ, as the imaginary pole of this instituted collectivity, exists as Christ (and not as a pure fiction, a given empirical individual or the leader of an obscure sect in Galilee). They can also merge together: France, from this point of view, is nothing other (as the 'French nation' or as the subject of the 'history of France') than 'a certain idea of France', as has been stated, without reading the deep truth of the expression, which signifies quite the opposite of a certain (sure) idea of France.[35] The instituted network can exist only by referring to, or by positing singular entities such as these which figure-presentify social imaginary significations.

Like *legein, teukhein* exhibits the unconstructibility, non-deducibility, non-productibility, self-presupposition which I have termed *objective reflexivity*. The operation of the essential schemata of *legein* presupposes that these schemata have already operated before operating and in order to be able to operate: how are we to separate, if we do not have available to us a separating feature, itself separable and separated? In the same way, *teukhein* is always based on a *teukhos* or a *tukton*, a 'tool' that is already there; fabrication presupposes that something is already fabricated, the means of production is always itself a product.Every *teukhein* implies that something has *already* been assembled-adjusted as ... in a manner appropriate to ... and in view of ... (ultimately, this applies even to the body of the one who *teukhei*, who assembles-adjusts in view of ..., a body which, then, is no longer simply a 'natural body'). Technique institutes itself or, better, is proto-institution, its operation presupposes that it has already operated, the conditions for its operation contain straightaway the results of this operation. Every effort to 'deduce' or 'produce' these results on the basis of certain conditions fails, for these conditions can be such only if they contain certain results, only if they are in part produced. It is this aspect which, in an ideological and mystified form, returns in the arguments of bourgeois political economy concerning the nature of 'capital' as an 'original, primary, irreducible factor' of production. This is also why there is never any such thing as 'simple labour' in the sense of the simple movement of animal-human or in that of the simple 'expenditure of nervous and muscular energy' by his organism. Even the 'labour' of oxen or horses is not 'simple', for it implies the immense expenditure and transformation by means of which neolithic societies fabricated oxen and horses (and so many other living species) as tools in the most general sense. The distinction between 'simple labour' and 'qualified labour' is relative and secondary; 'simple labour' presupposes the huge 'qualification' (and the corresponding 'investment') by means of which every society in its own, specific way and with varying results, transforms the soma-psyche into a social individual, that is to say, into what is also a tool fabricated in a manner appropriate to ... in view of .... The social individual is always at the same time a fabricated tool, whose fabrication presupposes that other tools of the same type already exist and are in operation.

Thus, technique, *teukhein* must already be available in order to be invented – just as language must already be available in order to be established. There is nothing surprising in the fact that both of these are so often presented in myths as possessing an other than human or super-human origin, and this is still what Aeschylus says in affirming that all *technai* come to mortals from Prometheus, after having been the exclusive possession of the gods;[36] one can say that a given man invented a particular *techne*, but it seems absurd to say that one man or men in general invented *techne as such*, and indeed it is absurd, since accounting for this invention would require that we go back 'beyond' it, while continuing to presuppose it. To be sure, in this case more than in that of the question of the 'birth of language', the slow and long evolution of the most primitive tools creates the impression of an imperceptible transition, in which the institution of *teukhein* could be dissolved as an alteration that moves from animal man (or the 'society' of proto-hominids) to society; eoliths have been preserved, but 'proto-words', if ever there were any such things, not. The problem, and the criterion, however, is the same in both cases. The question is not to know whether society 'begins' with the Cro-Magnon, the Neanderthal, the Zinjanthropus or before them – since this question is meaningless unless we know what society *is*, or, if you prefer, unless we have 'defined' what we mean by society. For us, there is society only where there is institution, and technique or, more generally, *teukhein* is the ensemblist–identitary dimension of doing as socially instituted. Hominids can use dead branches or stones accidentally or 'instinctively' – and this utilization can support the passage to technique; but technique exists when the dead branch or the pebble no longer appears in a random or simply 'natural' context but when it is distinguished-separated-sought after-assembled in order to make (something) exist ... in a manner appropriate to ... and in view of ...; in other words, when they are posited as effective, enduring and typical means in the schema of finality. As strange as this way of speaking may appear, this signifies that the pebble is *instituted* as a tool, that it *stands for* a tool because it *serves for* such and such a use (the realization of a given end), that it is immediately a *type* or an *eidos*, etc.; and, more concretely, that the pebble itself is already produced as a means of production. Looking for and keeping pebbles that are simply heavier or sharper than others is already the production of tools, or a *teukhein*. The pebble preserved in view of ..., without immediate utilization and without any biological process that would take care of 'storing' it (as glucose is stored in the organism) is produced to the extent that it is simply preserved. Preserving the pebble is already 'fabrication', which presupposes that other fabrication – the search for or the choice of the pebble in question. And this fabrication refers to the transformation – hence the production – of man's own body in a manner appropriate to ... and in view of ..., that is to say, as a body capable of using the pebble itself as a rudimentary tool. This transformation is impossible, however, without the pebble itself and could never have occurred – it could not have been 'chosen', 'looked for', or 'preserved' – unless at the same time the appropriate pebbles were chosen, looked for and preserved. One cannot become a pianist without a piano, just as a piano is useless unless one is a pianist. If, as Leroi-Gourhan states, the tool 'simply attests to the externalization of an effective gesture',[37] this gesture is, or became, effective only by bringing the tool into being. The gesture becomes effective only because the pebble becomes a tool, and vice versa. Both have to be posited together, neither of them can be the 'means' unless the other is already available, as the product of a transformation appropriate to ... in view of ..., however slight and 'gradual' this transformation may be considered. And both of these – effective gesture and tool – can exist as they do only by being caught up in unanalysable schemata of finality, of instrumentation – and of *possibility*.

There is no doubt, from the viewpoint of our positive knowledge, that the *tooling up* of the Eolithic man over an extremely long period, must have been a gradual process, just as coming to a standing position or the development of the brain and of the hand, processes it probably paralleled. Nor is there any question that during a very long phase the 'seeds' of what was to become technique were able, haphazardly, to appear, disappear, reappear and finally impose themselves. This could be called a neo-Darwinian process, by means of which random changes imposed themselves by the competitive advantage they conferred on their owners – except for the fact that in a neo-Darwinian process these changes are preserved genetically. In the case discussed, they can be preserved only in and through their *institution*, by the creation of the institution in general, as the *fixation* of the random and the optional into the systematic and the obligatory as well as the *conservation and transmission* of what has been fixed in this way, and; finally, as the possibility of *variation* and *alteration* (in turn fixable and transmissible) depending in no way on the 'biological substratum' and affecting it in no way.

viii   HISTORICITY OF *LEGEIN* AND *TEUKHEIN*

Just as in the case of *legein*, we can conceive of *teukhein* only as an institution, with all that the institution presupposes and entails: the fixation and the diffusion of the 'product' and of the mode of operating throughout the collectivity; the unique and at any rate unanalysable 'properties' which result in the fact that the 'product' and mode of operation can be *participated in* by individuals in general and that they, in turn, render the individuals capable of participating in them; the capacity of the collectivity to 'recognize' them as such, to fix them, preserve them and transmit them, vary them and alter them. All of this implies immediately a mode of being characteristic of this collectivity which can no longer be conceived of as natural, which must be *instituted* – and so one which already implies *legein* and *teukhein* as indispensible *for* the institution of society itself, since this institution cannot exist unless 'things', 'individuals', 'objects', 'signs', 'tools' have been separated, united, designated, assembled, fabricated in a manner appropriate to and in view of the being of the society. Society must make *itself* and state *itself* in order to make or state anything. Making itself and stating itself are the work of the radical imaginary considered as society instituting itself. But neither can be realized without reference to signification, without bringing into being a magma of social imaginary significations. For society cannot institute itself without instituting itself *as* 'something' and this 'something' is necessarily already an imaginary signification (and the *apex* of the magma of imaginary significations) for it *can* be nothing else. Already in this, *legein* and *teukhein* are found to be immerged in the magma of significations.

Legein and *teukhein* as such are absolute creations of the social–historical. To be sure, in a certain sense we also find them in life. The living being is living only to the extent that it distinguishes-chooses-assembles-adjusts-transforms in a manner appropriate to ... and in view of .... [38] But this *legein-teukhein* of the living being differs *toto caelo* from the social–historical *legein-teukhein*. Here there is neither signitive relation nor relation of finality in any genuine sense (the anticipated positing of what is not in the *eidos*). The *legein-teukhein* of living being *is* the living being itself, which as such is nothing outside of this – nothing 'really' and nothing 'ideally'. In the case of living beings, both are fixed, fixed upon an unchangeable substratum which fixes them, determines them as *these* means subservient to *these* ends. Finally, and most importantly, for the living being as such, whatever is not taken into account in the organization of its *legein-teukhein* does not exist at all, or else exists only as noise or as catastrophe.

The social–historical institution of *legein* and *teukhein*, however, is potentially the means of an unlimited opening onto what, at the start, was not taken into account in its organization. In each case, caught up in the 'closed' world that each society organizes and institutes, and as instruments of this closing, they provide, at the same time, the resources that allow breaking open what has been closed, altering society and the world. And this is so because the capacity for extension and transformation of the domains covered by *legein* and *teukhein* is 'incorporated' in the very organization of *legein* and *teukhein*. Having at one's command the schema of signitive relation is having it at one's command everywhere and with respect to anything that might 'present'

itself as 'real', 'rational' or 'imaginary'. It is being able to name everything that can be 'shown' or 'signified'. And having available the other
schemata that organize *legein* is always being able to group things
together in another way, to define new classes or properties, to refine
or modify the lexical–semantic grid applied to the given. Having *teukhein* at our disposal is to possess the schemata of the possible and the
feasible, of the end as the *eidos* of that which is not and yet conditions
that which is (is done) now, of the means ('tool') as product, hence as
a result of what had previously existed as an inexistant *eidos* and as
simply possible, which might not have existed – or have existed in
another way, by means of some *other* activity. To be sure, the two
cases are not symmetrical, in so far as it may seem that the totality of
the possibilities of a language as *legein* are given straightaway as soon
as language simply exists; in so far also as the mode of organization of
the abstract–material base of the language seems to have reached from
the start (or at a very early date, or as far back as we can see) a state
of equilibrium and of adequation such that there is no 'progress' as
regards the possibilities of *legein*. This is not true of *teukhein*, at least
not for the techniques of material production, where only the most
abstract 'conditions of possibility' are posited at the start, and where
there is, as we know, a fantastic 'progress' over the past million years
or so. We shall return to this difference shortly; it does not affect
the essential import of what we were saying: *legein* and *teukhein* are
intrinsically extensible and transformable.

It is in this way that they are at once compatible with history and
themselves open to the possibility of a history. They are compatible
with history, for they can serve as instruments in the successive creations
of the radical imaginary and of the radical imagination, whether these
are manifested as clear breaks or as 'unnoticeable' alterations. They
provide new and different significations with the support for their
institution. This implies that *legein* and *teukhein* are themselves open
to the possibility of a history, that they alter themselves. What is altered
is, of course, the tenor or the consistency of *legein* and *teukhein*, which
is specific in each case: the specific nature of their mode of operation,
their privileged fields, their 'products' – all of these are, in fact, indissociable. This specific tenor and consistency is, in turn, inseparable
from the magma of imaginary significations whose social–historical
institution it serves to instrument. Thus, the history of social–historical
doing is at the same time the history of *teukhein* as well, the latter acting
as its support and its inexpungible dimension; 'productive technique',
material tools in the strict sense, is simply one part of this history,
possessing no special privilege. By far the most important manifestation
of *teukhein* in this history is the assembling-adjusting-constructing that
is manifested in the institution itself: the village or the city, the 'Asiatic'
monarchy, the city-state, the modern State are also the products of
teukhein, gigantic tools or instruments. Lewis Mumford's mega-
machine,[39] the organized armies of workers or slaves used by 'Asiatic'

monarchies are themselves the results and the means of social *teukhein*, means of production which are themselves produced. So, too, are all the *technē*, in the broadest sense of the term: productive or sexual techniques, magical or political techniques, the organization of men or of discourse, of the body or the intelligence, of artistic expression or of warfare. This is true, too, of the *technē* that brings into being the most effective tool ever made by society: the social individual. But it is also true that the history of social *representing* and *saying*, of all that in the creation of significations, of participable representations, of ideas can be manifested in language – all this is at the same time a history of *legein*. Of course, in this case, as we indicated above, we observe the existence of an historical invariant which we do not know how to 'explain': the history of language and of particular languages affects and alters concrete languages, including their 'abstract–material' base which is in each case specific, but not the general nature of its organization. There is a phonological, grammatical, syntactical, semantic evolution, but language as *legein* functions everywhere by positing phonemes, combining them into morphemes or lexemes, grouping the latter into grammatical classes, organizing the elements of these classes in accordance with syntactical rules. But beyond this invariance of its abstract mode of operation, *legein* is at once subject to historical alteration and an active instrument for this alteration. What is particularly important in this respect is its semantic history. And this is so, not so much to the extent that it conveys changes in the 'lexical–semantic' grid of the given, whether 'real', 'natural' or 'identitary rational' (the 'naming' of the various polygons is more or less self-evident; likewise, archaic biological taxonomy is, in *this* respect, despite the immense and admirable effort that it represented, a 'trivial' operation: one can always separate by means of observation and name two different species of bird if one has a 'rudimentary' language at one's disposal); but, mainly, to the extent that global organizations of the world that are, in each case, different and new imaginary significations are made to exist socially by being 'embodied' directly or indirectly in the terms of language, of being symbolized. The proof of the existence of God for a given society is the existence in its language of the word 'God'. Leaving aside the invariance of the general type of organization of *legein* mentioned above, there is, to be sure, a vast history of *legein* as *legein* in the broadest sense, which, considered cursorily from our contemporary perspective, appears as a 'progressive' evolution just as important as that of productive technique in the narrow sense (and, in a way, this is self-evident since all *teukhein* is at the same time a *legein*, and since technique is a kind of logic). The history which makes knowledge pass from 'one, two, three, many' to the theory of distributions, from the classification of living species in the surrounding biotope to molecular biology, from recognizing the movements of the heavens to contemporary cosmology is but a vast deployment of distinguishing-choosing-assembling-positing-counting-saying under the requirements of identitary logic and of determinacy, that is to say an interminable extension of the fields of *legein*, a limitless proliferation of the products of its operation, an extraordinary refinement of its specific methods. Here is not the place to speak of this. Let us simply note that, when we examine it closely we observe that the operation of *legein* and of identitary logic has, in this respect, in each case displayed a strong dependence on the imaginary organization of the world instituted by society, which has fixed its objects, its orientation, its interests and its ends. The successive upheavals which can be observed in the 'rational knowledge' of societies known to us have always been conditioned by upheavals in the global imaginary representation of the world (and of nature and of the ends of knowledge itself) – the most recent one, occurring in the West a few centuries ago, created the particular imaginary representation whereby all that is is 'rational' (and, in particular, mathematizable), that which is to be known, is exhaustible *de jure*, and the end of knowledge is the mastery and the possession of nature.

6

The Social–Historical Institution
Individuals and Things

We have to posit that whatever exists, in any domain, *lends itself* to an identitary–ensemblist organization and is *not* thoroughly or ultimately *congruent* to the latter. It never ceases to lend itself to this organization, does not lend itself in an empty manner but offers a partially effective grasp, so that it is impossible to think of this organization as a sheer construction, as imputable solely to the 'awesome power of understanding', to borrow Hegel's expression. We can construe what is as an ensemble only because what is is capable of being so construed; we can categorize it only because it is categorizable. However, any ensemblizing, and categorizing, any organization that we establish/ discover there proves sooner or later to be partial, lacunary, fragmentary, insufficient – and even, more importantly, intrinsically deficient, problematic and finally incoherent.

This situation – which has nothing to do with the fallacious idea of the 'asymptotic progress of knowledge', anymore than with the platitudes proffered about 'epistemological breaks' – is abundantly illustrated, as I have attempted to show elsewhere, by the history of the pre-eminently 'exact' science – physics.[1]

The questions and the aporias with which contemporary physics struggles refer to a mode of being underlying the physical entity, a mode that cannot be grasped by means of identitary logic. Even if we manage to settle them – as might be expected – at the price of new theoretical upheavals, the certainty would still remain not only that these new solutions would sooner or later generate new enigmas, but, moreover, that their relation to the old ones would continue to be untreatable by means of logic and identitary ontology – as is untreatable by these means the relation between Newtonian physics and relativity.

The situation becomes incomparably more acute when we leave the physical universe. We have attempted to show above that the central categories and determinations of identitary logic collapse at the contact of the social–historical – and this permits us to understand why the latter has never actually been conceived of in its own right by tradition. We have also seen, and we shall see this in even greater detail, that, implied by the world of significations and by our relation to this world, these categories and determinations let the mode of being of this world slip out of their grasp. We find the same situation in the domain we are now about to consider: that of the social–historical institution of the individual (and, correlatively, of perception and of things), that is, the transformation of the psychical monad into the social individual for whom there exist other individuals, objects, a world, a society, institutions – things none of which, originally, has meaning or existence for the psyche. This will lead us to a discussion of the question of the psyche, which, in truth, is inseparable from the question of the social–historical, two expressions of the radical imagination – here, as radical imagination; there, as social imaginary. The discussion will be conducted starting from the Freudian conception, which we are not about to improve upon or overhaul, but to clarify in another way, on the basis of the two themes that have proven, and not by chance, to be blind-spots for it: the social–historical institution and the psyche as radical imagination – that is to say, essentially, as the emergence of representations or as representative flux not subject to determinacy.[2]

i THE MODE OF BEING OF THE UNCONSCIOUS

The unconscious, Freud wrote, is unaware of time and of contradiction. This dizzying thought, amplified and made even more insistent by Freud's entire work, has been almost entirely neglected – when it has not been made to say the opposite of what it states, by transforming the psychical apparatus into a real machinery or by reducing it to a logical structure. The unconscious constitutes a 'place' where (identitary) time – as determined by and as itself determining an ordered succession – does not exist, where contraries do not exclude one-another; more precisely, where there can be no question of contradictory terms and which, itself, is not really a place since place implies order and distinction. Of the essential stuff of the unconscious, the representation, we can say practically nothing, if we confine ourselves to our customary logic. We are already doing violence to it when, in speaking of the unconscious (and even of consciousness) we speak of representation separating it from the unconscious affect and intention, which is impossible both *de jure* and *de facto*.[3] The unconscious exists only as an indissociably representative/affective/intentional flux. But let us suppose this separation to be effectuable and already effected, and let us halt at representation as such. How could we fail to see that it escapes the most elementary logical schemata, that it slips past them on all sides, that it can never be subjected to any of the requirements of determinacy?

Consider, for example, Freud's dream: 'My friend R is my uncle, he wears a long yellow beard ...'. Does this dream form *one* representation or *several*, and *how many*? What sort of thing is it of which we cannot say, even *with respect to* ..., whether it is one or many? Or consider the analysis of 'little Hans'; what is, *for* little Hans, the representation of his father, of the horse, of his phobia and the relation between them? We are fooling ourselves, in the last case, when, carried away by the habit of interpretation, the necessity of translating the givens of the unconscious in linguistic terms and in the relations forged in and through language, we posit *the* representation of the father and its re-presentation or 'symbolization' by the animal of the phobia as a clear and distinct relation, a simple *quid pro quo*, the positing of one thing for another thing. To be sure, if we do not return to this world of interpretation and of the translation into waking language, we would be able to say nothing at all. But the actual situation is not really similar to what we do when we speak about it – as anyone who has ever dreamed will know. What is more, you do not even have to dream to see this. Mélanie Klein's little Richard says: 'Mama *is* the fish *and* the big fish above';[4] he is not saying that *x* is (for) *y*, he is saying that *y is* at once *x* and *z*.

It has been suggested recently that Freud's displacement and condensation be replaced by metonymy and metaphor. This terminology, which assimilates the operations of the unconscious to *secondary* modes of functioning belonging to waking language,[5] flattens out Freud's brilliant discovery and conceals ever more deeply the treasures of the sixth chapter of the *Interpretation of Dreams*. Actually, the opposite could have been affirmed: that metaphor, metonymy and the other tropes of waking language borrow something from the operations of the unconscious, without being able to reproduce their abundance and richness. But the unconscious had, at all costs, to be submitted to the structure alleged to be already established by linguistics. Just as, in speaking of infantile sexuality, one almost irresistibly takes the point of view of the adult, imputing by implication to the child an experience he does not have and using this to describe his sexual being, while totally deforming it, in the same way, the mode of being and the organization of the unconscious are translated into a logical language by inventing discrete signifiers subject to rule-governed substitutions which some have even dared to call algebraic. What the unconscious gives us and forces us to think of, however, which no language – and no algebra – could ever enable us to conceive of, is radically different. It *is not* the fact that a definite and distinct *a*, through a network of relations however complex, yet themselves definite and determined, comes to take the place of a *b*, just as definite and distinct; this is simply imputing to the unconscious the point of view of the awakened state, partly inevitable if we wish to speak of it but totally absurd if it is taken seriously over and beyond the necessities of *legein*. The dream: 'My friend R. is my uncle' *does not say*: 'there exists an *x*, *x* = my friend R., and there exists a *y*, *y* = my uncle, and, given the laws of the unconscious, $x = y$ and $x \neq y$.' The dream gives the unconscious representation as it *is*, in what we are obliged to call, when speaking of it, its fusion, its indistinction – which, for all that, do not result in sheer chaos. And this is not the result of operations coming afterward, blurring figures that were originally separate, clear and distinct; instead it results from the being of the psyche which *is* the genesis of representations, in which, perhaps in this case, 'my friend R.' is formed starting from and in relation to 'my uncle' – but in general, at any rate, all 'separate' representations that waking logic necessarily distinguishes are certainly formed starting from and in relation to a minute number of archaic representations which *were* the world for the psyche, which have been separated during the long work of the formation of the individual *for the ends of awake existence* and which in turn refer us back to the enigma of an original representing-representation. What causes a problem here is not this fusion and lack of distinction, even less is it the contradictions that are implied for waking logic – or better yet, for identitary logic for all that is awake is far from identitary. Instead the problem lies in this separation and its very possibility, the origin of the schema of discreteness and its partial hold on what is. Once we find ourselves within it, it is not so much the imaginary–representative magma of the unconscious that is the inexhaustible source of astonishment, but rather the schema of discreteness, the idea of identity, the relative effectiveness of the separation.

Representation – whether unconscious or conscious – is, in fact, unanalysable (without thereby being simple). Every decomposition into elements is here a provisional artifact, every positing of separating-unifying schemata an awkward attempt to recover a being with an indefinite number of dimensions by means of a few scraps that have been ripped out of it. Representation has no borders, and any separation that is introduced into it can never be held to be pertinent – or rather, it will always be certain to be non-pertinent in some essential aspect. What exists there refers back to what does not exist there, or to what calls for it; but it does not call for it under the auspices of a determined and formulable rule, as a theorem calls for its consequences, even if these are infinite, a number its successors, a cause its effects, even if these are innumerable. The abyss that separates the indefiniteness of representation from the highest order of mathematical infinity is still greater than that separating mathematical infinity from an ordinary number. It is an abyss of being, not a difference in cardinality. That which is not in a representation can still be there, and there is no limit to this, no *peras*.

This is also the reason why – or rather: this is only another way of saying that – the actual, essential 'relation' between representations, what is called association, is not a *relation*, properly speaking; it is neither a relating of terms external to one another, nor the logical disimplication of what would have meaning only by being taken together. So-called 'free' association, such as one attempts to induce it in psychoanalysis – and which, obviously, is neither free nor not free – is the partial unveiling of aspects of a co-belonging, of which we shall never be able to say whether it pre-exists its formulation or whether it is created by the latter – and indeed this question is irrelevant. The association is the thread drawn between two summits of an immersed mountain chain, a thread disappearing in the crevices of oceanic depths. But summits and crevices are not ordered; nothing here establishes a necessary before and after, and we never know whether a summit will not appear to be a crevice or vice versa, nor even whether we should be speaking of appearing or of being transformed. If one wanted to use mathematical terms, one would have to say, not only that it is impossible to represent the associative links – or any other relation between representations – as the positing of biunivocal relations between distinct and definite terms, but also that it is even impossible to call a 'correspondence', in the sense given to this term in set-theory, of relation of several/several. For not only would this correspondence be virtually the correspondence between every family of elements and every other, but, in particular, *that which* enters into this correspondence is constantly redefined, remodeled, refigured, its manner of entering into relation is altered, and this alteration itself, and not merely its product, becomes one of the terms to be considered.

What representation gives us is 'inconsistent multiplicity' to borrow Cantor's term: a type of being which not only is both one and many, but for which these determinations are neither decisive nor indifferent. To be sure, the 'aspects' under which we grasp all that exists as one and as many are never more than transitory, points of support for the advance of discourse, as are, moreover, all the terms and the fixed points of *legein*. But these 'aspects' can in other cases – in that, for example, of the physical entity – be determined 'sufficiently as to use' and need, and the relations constructed on these points of support present a remarkable stability; the obligatory and the impossible, even if they are not determined exhaustively, are found almost everywhere. There is no such thing in representation: here, the obligatory is trivial and empty, and the impossible exists barely at all. The 'relation', which is constantly altered in the actual unfolding of what is in question here can bring close to each other any and all 'terms', or can hold them separate indefinitely. So that neighbourhoods are not determined here or are constantly redetermined, and, to use a topological metaphor, almost every point is at once arbitrarily close and arbitrarily far from every other point.

To be sure we do *speak* of representation – how could we not speak of it? And what we say about it is not entirely useless. We do so by using fragments of it that we fix, fragments that play the role of terms of marking, to which we attach terms of language, so that we can know approximately 'what we are talking about'. We would be lost, however, if we were to forget that these terms cannot bear the full weight of the ensemblist and identitary operations, even less that of 'exact' scientific constructions. We use these terms, as a galloping horse uses the ground beneath it; it is not the ground but the gallop that counts. The fact that the ground and the tracks exist is the condition and the consequence of the race; but it is the race that we want to grasp. From the tracks of the horseshoes we can then reconstruct the horse's direction, and perhaps have an idea of its speed and of the weight of the rider; but we cannot know who he was, what he had in mind, or whether he was racing to his love or to his death.

But does not interpretation restore a logic and an order to unconscious representations and does it not aim at determining their meaning? And does not the Freudian theory, notably the metapsychology, refer all the time to a psychical apparatus constituted in a particular way and not in some other way, to places, forces and entities borrowed from the identitary logic of the real and from its constructions in other domains?

One wonders, first how and why the being of dreams, or, more generally, of unconscious representation, could be *eliminated* by its being-interpreted (or being interpretable). Would the being of madness as madness be eliminated if it could be interpreted, even if it were interpreted completely? (By eliminated, of course, I do not mean actually eliminated by curing the madness – but eliminated ontologically). Is the mode of being, the level of being and the being-thus of delirium or hallucination cancelled out by the postulate that the *content* of the delirium or the hallucination is interpretable? Is the being-colour of a colour cancelled out by the equations of physics? As much as the colour is an equation, to the same extent the dream is the meaning of the dream. There is an almost imperceptible shift here – so great is the force of inherited logic-ontology, as it insinuates itself everywhere – but a decisive one; it is just as serious as that which, from the birth of scientific thinking and up to the time of Freud approximately, refused to consider the meaning of dreams. Because the dream did not present itself as a meaning articulated in accordance with the canons of identitary logic, it was relegated to the scoria of psychical functioning. Once interpretation discovers a meaning-equivalent for it, it becomes an ontological scoria; an absolute Nothingness, a *nichtiges Nichts*. Supposedly, it would be entirely dissolved by its reduction to its meaning – and by the explanation of the reasons for which *this* meaning presents itself as *this* representation.

And why is it, then, that meaning in general presents itself in the psyche and is able to do so *only as* a representation? How is it that any interpretation or reduction of the imaginary in terms of the real–rational could eliminate the *fact of being-there* (the *Das-sein*) of the imaginary and its specific *mode of being* (the *Was-sein*)?

This alleged reduction, however, is an incoherent fiction. The true interpretation of the dream is a specific enterprise, in a singular practico-poetic context – that of analysis. The correspondences established by the analysis between the representation and its meaning are valid only within the context of the analysis; they are neither generalizable nor transportable; they are not even *verifiable* in the usual acceptation of this term.[6] This does not mean that they are arbitrary, that they can be simply anything at all; but their meaning can be constantly reconsidered – and in an analysis worthy of the name, it always is, in principle; meaning exists only for the analysed subject, an enigmatic subject *par excellence*, an unknown subject – neither the patient as he is nor the patient as he ought to be according to some pre-established norm, but the patient as he is and will continue to make himself in and through the analytic process. Meanings are interminable, as is their interpretation, as the analysis would be if it were *only* a question of interpretation. For if in the analysis it were essentially a matter of establishing meaning-equivalents, *every* analysis would be strictly speaking interminable, death alone would come not to complete it but to interrupt it.

Freud wrote: 'There is at least one spot in every dream at which it is unplumbable – a navel, as it were, that is its point of contact with the unknown'. And also: 'the question whether it is possible to interpret every dream (*zur Deutung gebracht werden kann*), must be answered in the negative.' Why? In the 20 or so lines that follow, Freud, in a surprising logical layout actually replies to two different questions, and does so in heterogeneous ways. He explicitly formulates only one of them: can *every* dream be interpreted? No, there exist uninterpretable dreams; in sum, this depends on the 'relations of strength' between 'internal resistances' and what consciousness can mobilize on behalf of interpretation. – Then, he replies to a question which he does not formulate explicitly: Are there dreams that can be *completely* interpreted? Freud begins by saying that, even in dreams that are the most completely interpreted, one must *frequently* leave a part obscure, and he concludes by affirming that the *in*completeness of the interpretation is a universal and essential necessity.

> There is often a passage in even the most thoroughly interpreted dream which has to be left obscure; this is because we become aware during the work of interpretation that at that point there is a tangle of dream-thoughts which cannot be unravelled and which moreover adds nothing to our knowledge of the content of the dream. This is the dream's navel, the spot where it reaches down into the unknown. The dream-thoughts to which we are led by interpretation have to, in an entirely universal manner [or: must indeed compulsorily ..., *müssen je ganz allgemein ...*], remain without any definite endings; they are bound to branch out in every direction into the intricate network of our world of thought. It is at some point where this meshwork is particularly close that the dream-wish grows up, like a mushroom out of its mycelium.[7]

The dream wish, which in Freud's conception provides the sense of the dream, '(grows up) at some point where this meshwork is particularly close'; the 'dream's navel' is 'a tangle of dream-thoughts which cannot be unravelled'. The densest, the richest place, the most important place of the dream is 'unplumbable'; the exploration of its central point cannot reach a conclusion – not because we are not intelligent enough, not because we are not spending enough time on it, not because we encounter overwhelming resistances – but due to the very nature of the thing itself: because the dream thoughts *müssen ganz allgemein* remain without a conclusion. *Müssen ganz allgemein*, there is no stronger form of expression in German: *müssen* expresses absolutely insurmountable necessity, *ganz* (totally) reinforces *allgemein* (universally). '(They) branch out in every direction into the intricate network of our world of thought': they are magmas in a magma. The meaning of the dream, to follow Freud faithfully, cannot be fully established, determined, because it is by its essence 'without a conclusion' (*ohne Abschluss*): interminable, undetermined, *apeiron*, indefinite (not infinite: the infinite is definite and determined). The meaning of the dream as the dream wish is the condensation of what is ungraspable, the articulation of what cannot be articulated. The meaning of the dream as this is provided by interpretation is what completes, determines and brings to a conclusion 'thoughts' which, of themselves, cannot come to a conclusion. These thoughts are formulated by interpretation and translated into the language of judgements and intentions; but they are, inseparably, representations/intentions/effects. This inseparability is also *sui generis*.

And this meaning established by the interpretation, in what does it consist? In the really important cases, it consists in formulating several meaning segments that are contradictory for waking language, incompatible wishes, the ambivalence of affects, the same images belonging to series that should exclude one another or cancel one another out. What it restores as a meaning is not actually one – or is impossible following the rules of identitary logic. One is then forced to put some order in this intolerable situation and the schema of separation enters into operation. The unconscious is in fact transformed – and this transformation begins with and is brought to completion by Freud himself – into a multiplicity of consciousnesses opposing one another; 'contradiction' then becomes the conflict of agencies, to each of which are imputed, in the mode of clear and distinct *cogitos*, particular and well-defined aims, the capacity for its own pleasure/unpleasure, an independent, coherent, effective rational instrumentation. In this way, the confusion-indistinction-indetermination in and through which the unconscious and more generally, the psyche, including consciousness as well exist, are held to be simply the interference produced by the coexistence, the composition of several discourses, which have only to be distinguished in order to show that each is entirely coherent in itself, in the service of a distinct psychical person, who knows what it wants and how to obtain it, and always would obtain it if it were not for the opposition of the other psychical agencies. Of course, this description is not a mere fiction, or even a construction; it corresponds not only to the necessities of language and intelligibility, at least what we are in the habit of calling in this way, but to aspects of the thing itself. However, this description is far from exhausting its object and even misses what is essential in it; besides, it does not settle the question in contention here. In any case, it does not settle it for Freud, since it does not prevent him from discovering, for example, what he termed the splitting of the ego (*Ichspaltung*), namely the fact that the *same* agency, the unconscious ego, can operate under incompatible injunctions (not to speak of the conscious ego, which could not survive a single minute if its right hand ceased to ignore what its innumerable left hands are doing); nor did it prevent him from obliterating the very concepts of pleasure/unpleasure as distinctly opposite terms by writing 'The Economic Problem of Masochism'. The same thing can be said about Mélanie Klein's work: the ambivalence of affects, incompatible properties of representations, the conflicts of desires are in fact posited as original and essential characterisics of the psyche, in its indivisibility, despite efforts to reduce them by decomposing them and imputing them to partially independent systems.

The a-logic of the unconscious is therefore something quite different from the juxtaposition of several different exemplars of the same logic. The unconscious does not belong to the domain of identitary logic and determination. A product and continuing manifestation of the radical imagination, its mode of being is that of a *magma*.

ii THE QUESTION OF THE ORIGIN OF REPRESENTATION

The essential part of Freud's work consisted, perhaps, in the discovery of the imaginary element in the psyche – in revealing the most profound dimensions of what I am calling here the radical imagination. But one could just as well say that a large part of his work aims at, or ineluctably leads to, reducing, covering over or concealing anew this very role. In the positivist atmosphere surrounding him, and which influenced him profoundly and definitively – behind which, obviously, lies traditional metaphysics, determined-being, causes that have become forces, ends that have become 'principles' – Freud began by seeking 'real' factors that would account for the history of the psyche, its organization, and, finally, even its being. We are familiar with his initial belief in the positive reality of the event corresponding to the traumatic memory of neurotics; then, the reversal of this opinion brought about by the impossibility of believing in the 'reality' of the vast number of the seduction scenes of a child by an adult recounted by patients; the search for the primal scene as a real event, finally abandoned but only regretfully and over strong resistance, in the case of the *Wolf-man*; and, finally, when ontogenesis was unable to deliver real material as the necessary and sufficient support, if not the cause, of phantasy, the recourse (how paradoxical and how intrinsically contradictory!) to phylogenesis in the theoretical hope of a 'positive' verification of his theses on the psyche.

The essential role of the imagination, although it is neither recognized or even named, in fact appears in Freud by means of the central importance of phantasy in the psyche and the *relative* independence and autonomy of phantasizing. Phantasizing is discovered as an unexpungible component of deep psychic life. But how was one to account for its relation to the other components of this life, of the origin of its content, and of the source of its power?

The drive (*Trieb*) can be manifested in the psyche only by means of a representation; the psyche submits the drive to the obligation of a delegation through representation (*Vorstellungsrepräsentanz des Triebes*); also, undoubtedly, to that of the 'delegation through affect', but this is a different problem. What is the origin of this representation, and what can its content be, in particular: why is it *this specific* content?

Paradoxes arise as soon as we approach these questions.

Representation can be formed only in and through the psyche; this assertion, moreover, is redundant for the psyche *is* that very thing, the emergence of representations accompanied by an affect and inserted into an intentional process. This representation, Freud explicitly affirms, can be formed only on the instructions of the drive – which at the start, however, has no representative (delegate) in the psyche and so finds itself condemned to silence. An initial bridge must be postulated between the 'soul' and the 'body'; the first representative core must be found to be constituted, to conform to, or better to relate to the demands of the drive as the mediation between the soul and the body before any canonical procedure of mediation has been established. To be sure, we can say that the first delegation of the drive in the psyche is the affect, in particular that of displeasure. But we can find nothing in an affect, whether of pleasure or of unpleasure, that could account for the form or the content of a representation; at most the affect could induce the 'finality' or the 'orientation' of the representative process. It is therefore necessary to postulate (even if this is only implicitly) that the psyche is the capacity to produce an 'initial' representation, the capacity of putting into image or making an image (*Bildung* and *Einbildung*). This may appear self-evident. But this image-making must at the same time relate to a drive, at a time when nothing ensures this relation. This may well be the point of condensation and accumulation for all the mysteries of the 'bonding' between the soul and the body.

Where does the psyche get the elements – the material *and* the organization – for this representation? The paradoxes we encounter here are by no means proper to Freud alone; they have a venerable tradition in philosophy. If the psyche produces everything out of itself, if it is sheer and total production of its own representations with respect to their form (organization) and to their content, we can wonder how and why it should ever meet anything other than itself and its own products. And, if we say that it borrows the elements of representation from the 'real', then we are advancing an assertion that is meaningless (how can one borrow something from someone that he does not possess? The real cannot be at one and the same time real and the real representation of the real in the real); we are also obliterating what will be a constant vector in Freudian thought: the 'impression' (*Eindruck*, to use the Kantian term), that by means of which the 'real' announces itself in the psyche, becomes an element in the representation only in relation to a psychical elaboration that can produce, depending on the subject and the moment, the most divergent and most unexpected results. The 'gradualist' attempt to solve the problem is here, just as it is everywhere else, simply a way of sidestepping it: impressions are held to be elaborated, at each stage, in a 'richer' and more 'developed' manner, in relation to the totality of previous 'experience'. But already the 'first stage' of the constitution of this experience presupposes the psyche's capacity to organize into an *experience*, however rudimentary, what would otherwise remain a chaos of internal and external impressions. There is no doubt that this capacity of organization undergoes a vast development in and through the history of the subject; but how could it undergo this if it were not, at some minimal yet essential degree, already present at the start? The very postulate of the gradualist thesis, namely that this capacity is refined in relation to and through the feedback of its 'products', presupposes an initial producer of an initial product.

There is no possibility of understanding the problematic of representation if we seek the origin of representation outside of representation itself. The psyche is, to be sure, 'the receptivity of impressions', the capacity of being-affected-by ...; but it is also, and more importantly (for without this the receptivity of impressions would produce nothing) the emergence of representation as an irreducible and unique mode of being and as the organization of something in and through its figuration, its 'being put into images'. The psyche is a *forming*, which exists in and through *what* it forms and *how* it forms; it is *Bildung* and *Einbildung* – formation and imagination – it is the radical imagination that makes a 'first' representation arise out of a nothingness of representation, that is to say, *out of nothing*.

Psychical life can exist only if the psyche is this original capacity to make representations arise, and, 'at the start', a 'first' representation which must, in a certain manner, contain within itself the possibility of organizing all representations – something that is formed and forming, a figure that would be the seed of the schemata of figuration; hence, in as embryonic a form as one may like, the organizing elements of the psychical world that will later develop, with decisive additions coming from outside but which are, nevertheless, received and elaborated in accordance with the requirements posited by the original representation.

This necessity, which is inherent in the Freudian problematic, is not made explicit there. It is even covered over due to the deep motivations that prevented Freud from thematizing the question of the imagination as such. Contained potentially within his thought, it is in fact hidden in Freud and in many of his successors by a second problematic, that of phantasies and of derived imaginary formations.

It is obviously in phantasy and in similar formations that the imagination in action presents itself to observation and clinical study. And if we concentrate on the analysis and interpretation of phantasies provided by clinical material, we shall always, by definition, be dealing with derived products; the constitution of these products involves the entire range of psychical functions. We would then see in phantasmatization (and in the imagination) no more than late modes of operation which could never be understood in their *raison d'être*, their organization and their content except through recourse to other functions and factors. Thus Freud will write that phantasying (*phantasieren*) is reduced to what occurs 'after the reality principle has been established' and that, before this, there is simply 'whatever was thought of (wished for) [that is to say, the represented] was simply presented in a hallucinatory manner': 'With the introduction of the reality principle one species of thought-activity was split off; it was kept free from reality-testing and remained subordinate to the pleasure principle alone. This activity is *phantasying*, which begins already in children's play, and later, continued as *day-dreaming*, abandons dependence on real objects.' Before this phase, when the state of psychic tranquility is disturbed by the demands of internal needs, 'whatever was thought of (wished for) was simply presented in a hallucinatory manner, just as still happens today with our dream-thoughts every night.' 'Thought' signifies here, as so often in Freud, 'represented'.[8] This shift is possible only if one neglects to investigate further into the signification of this 'hallucinatory manner' and its dream equivalence. It may, however, be explained, if not justified, in terms of the apparent and paradoxical reference to the 'real' implied by the term 'hallucination': both in general and in the cases cited by Freud, the hallucination borrows its elements from the 'real', and the primary hallucination *par excellence* is, for Freud, the one that palliates the absence of the mother's breast, by positing its image as 'real'. This is the model – that is, the model of the product of the imagination which, under the pressure of drive (or even of need, as Freud says in the text quoted above) covers over a 'deficiency' with the reproduction of the representation (posed as equivalent to perception) of a scene of satisfaction which has an antecedent in 'real' perception – that has always been used subsequently to conceive of the question of the phantasy, however 'primal' it may have been termed, and of the imagination. One might, nonetheless, have wondered just what is and of what is made the 'state of psychical tranquility' to which Freud refers, and what is the representation that accompanies it. For if this is a *psychical* state, it also necessarily exists as a *representation*;

its breaking apart by 'internal need' is the calling into question of this representation and, in being restored with the help of an activity of representation (whether hallucinatory or not), the aim of the psyche must betray the *statu quo ante* to which it wishes to return.

The exploration of this primal level, assuredly more than difficult, has not yet been attempted; instead it has been avoided by means of various types of reference to the 'real'. In this way, even Mélanie Klein, who has, nevertheless, accorded a central importance to phantasmatic formations, when she qualifies as 'good' or 'bad' objects, . . . 'imagos, which are a phantastically distorted picture of the real objects upon which they are based, [and which] become installed not only in the outside world but, by the process of incorporation, also within the ego,'[9] finally makes of phantasies, as J. Laplanche and J.B. Pontalis note,[10] false perceptions – leaving entirely open not only the question of the 'origin of the error' but, more especially, the origin of its *systematic* character and, in particular, its *organizing* function. In this way, the 'realism' that is aimed at leads to an antinomy: the psyche is posited as the capacity to deform, phantasmatically and systematically, what is offered to it by the perception of the real – hence, the capacity to produce out of nothing something that possesses a meaning for it (whether it finds an incitement in the presence or in the absence of 'something' is of no importance in this respect). Likewise, what Susan Isaacs[11] has to say about this appears to misconstrue, by postulating an organization of the drive 'prior to phantasy', what Freud had clearly formulated concerning 'delegation through representation'.

The difficulties encountered by J. Laplanche and J.B. Pontalis[12] in their effort to move back to a primal phantasy are of a different nature. They do obtain a series of important results; the recognition of the organizing ('structuring', in their terminology) character of the phantasy, the clear distinction between the primal phantasy and the others, the connection between the phantasy and the 'time of auto-eroticism'; but they do not succeed in drawing a rigorous distinction between what could be termed the ensemble of 'constituted' phantasies and the 'constituting' phantasy-phantasmatization. To do this, it would be necessary to radicalize the separation between Freud's formulations (by far the most numerous) which refer to the secondary phantasmatic activity (unconscious or even conscious; as Laplanche and Pontalis are correct in noting, day-dreaming maintains a deep tie to the phantasy properly speaking) and those which refer to the final presuppositions of psychical activity and its primal mode of being. It is clear, for example, that when Freud spoke[13] of 'phantasies being produced by an unconscious combination of things experienced and of things heard,' he was thinking of late formations. Less apparent, this is still most certainly the case when he speaks of 'primal phantasies' (*Ur-phantasien*).[14] Whatever archaic traces may still be visible in these phantasies – or in the phantasy of 'a child being beaten' – the secondary and composite character of the scenarios, which borrow their representative elements from an experience which itself is in an advanced and differentiated state, is evident. How could we qualify this staging as the receptive structure to everything that may come along in the psychical apparatus of a given subject, when it presupposes a vast series of well-developed psychical events? How could we see in it the source of significance, when it includes in the conditions of its possibility an advanced articulation of 'real' elements *as* signifiers? The *trace* of the archaic in the phantasy 'a child is being beaten' is, in fact, this decisive trait, which Laplanche and Pontalis deserve the credit for bringing out, yet without thematizing it or sufficiently exploiting it: the impossibility of attaching the subject to *any one* of the places of the phantasy. And this is so not only because, depending on the moment and the circumstances, the 'place' of the subject can be identified with this or that term (even with a non-substantive) of the scenario, or, even, find itself 'in the very syntax of the sequence in question';[15] but because the unconscious intention is the global situation staged by the phantasy *in the fundamental modality of the lack of distinction between the subject and the non-subject.* It amounts to the same thing to say that *every phantasy containing a multiplicity of 'distinct' representative elements is, by definition, secondary*: the presence of elements such as this in the form of 'distinctions' is the irrecusable mark of an elaboration – yet it bears the trace of the originary state of the psyche inasmuch as the latter aims at coinciding with the total scene, for its originary state, the 'first' representation, *is* the 'total scene'. In the same way, Freud's *Ur-phantasien*[16] – castration, seduction, primal scene – cannot be taken as genuinely originary phantasies, as they presuppose an advanced articulation and organization of 'contents', 'characters', and their 'acts' – although here as well the archaic trace remains visible in the permutability translating the intention, the aim of the psyche.

The role of this archaic trace is fundamental: it is this permutability that assures at once the being-thus of the organization of the phantasy and, especially, its *significance* for the subject. The phantasy can borrow from 'experience' whatever you like except, here again, what experience cannot lend to it since it does not possess it: that organization full of significance or primary meaning for the subject, a meaning that is not to be found in the 'nature' of the elements organized but in the mode of organization in so far as the latter, through its permutability, presentifies and figures, in and through 'distinction', an indistinction or essential 'reunification'. Laplanche and Pontalis speak in this regard of a 'structural bond'. In what way do we progress in our understanding of a connection by referring it to a binding principle? And, in particular: why would this binding principle manifest itself and act differently in the primary process than elsewhere?

If, as Laplanche and Pontalis correctly remind us, 'far from seeking to base the phantasy on drives, Freud instead made the play of drive forces depend on prior phantasmatic structures,'[17] then one must admit that originary phantasmatization, what I term the radical imagination, pre-exists and presides over every organization of drives, even the most primitive one, that it is the condition for the drive to attain psychical existence, that the drive borrows 'at the start' its 'delegation by representation', its *Vorstellungsrepräsentanz* from a backdrop of primal representation (*Ur-vorstellung*). But, if this is the case, then it is not sufficient to say that 'the emergence of the phantasy ... (can be found) by tying it to the appearance of auto-eroticism.'[18] For what is generally meant by auto-eroticism, what Freud is referring to in the *Three Essays*,[19] anyway, is still a secondary formation, presupposing the child's capacity 'to form a total idea of the person to whom the organ that is giving him satisfaction belongs' and the 'loss of the object', tied to a manifest corporeal activity. There is, however, something quite different, something at an infinitesimal and infinite distance from the latter, which Freud later in the context of the theory of narcissism brought to light and which he never gave up. This is what could be called originary auto-eroticism or primary narcissism, the fact that the 'first object of the libido is the undifferentiated Id-Ego', that 'to begin with, the child does not distinguish between the breast and its own body; when the breast has to be separated from the body and shifted to the "outside" ..., it carries with it as an "object" a part of the original narcissistic libidinal cathexis.'[20] So it is not the case that one 'must assume a reflexive form (seeing oneself) in the drives that, according to Freud, would be primordial.'[21] Rather, the 'reflexive' form – an improper term, as we shall see – of the libido *is*, if we follow Freud, its primordial form. This originary narcissistic cathexis or investment is necessarily *representation* as well (otherwise it would not be psychical) and it can then be nothing other than a 'representation' (unimaginable and unrepresentable for us) of the *Self*. If, as Laplanche and Pontalis aptly remark, one must 'look for this primordial degree precisely where the subject no longer situates itself in the various terms of phantasy,' this is for the simple reason that the originary psychical subject *is this* primordial 'phantasy': at once the representation and the investment of a Self that is All. This is why the subject is not this or that thing *in* the phantasy – nor will it be this or that in the unconscious phantasies that will occur later, inasmuch as these fully obey the rules of the primary process.

This same difficulty in distinguishing, among the various formations as they offer themselves, mixed together on the level of phenomena, the different strata of their constitution and that to which each stratum refers as a mode of being and a mode of organization, reappears when we consider social imaginary significations. Freud will thus speak of 'wish-compensating phantasies' in connection with cultural formations such as religion, art, and so on.[22] More generally speaking, the psychoanalytic conception of social phenomena will tend to assimilate them to compensations, coverings, defences, etc.; this is correct at a certain level or in relation to a certain order of these formations. But these compensations, coverings or defences have meaning and the capacity to exist only on the basis of the institution of society, as the already signifying condition of every developed signification, which could borrow neither its mode of being nor its content from any source outside itself, which is a 'response' to the requirement for signification posited by the social–historical, a response which must *also* provide for the possibility and the actuality of meaning for the social individuals that it institutes and produces.

Forgetting this difference imposes a confusion on the conceptions which – just as popular interpretations stretching back to times immemorial[23] – attempt to construe imaginary formations as a 'response' to a situation (of the subject or of society) which would already clearly be defined outside of any imaginary component, on the basis of 'real' (or 'structural') givens. When they do not aim at interpreting the *content* of *secondary* and *derived* formations, these conceptions can exist only by covering over essential questions. First of all, even when it is a question of secondary formations, why is it that the prevalent mode of response by the subject (or by society) is situated in the imaginary, and how can an imaginary formation 'respond' to a real need or to a 'structural' necessity – namely, a logical one? Next, how can the 'triggering' situation, however it may be defined, come to *signify* something for the subject (or for society) in a way that will provoke or induce a 'response'? Finally, where does the subject (or society) get the elements of this response? These conceptions are the only ones to be represented in contemporary psychoanalytic literature – just as in sociological literature the homologous ones are almost the only ones to be found. The various versions all share a common postulate: the whole psychical elaboration, regardless of the elements it 'borrows' right and left and the laws governing it, finds its starting point in the necessity for the subject to fill in, cover over, stitch up a void, a lack, a gap which is considered consubstantial to the subject itself. Little matter the way in which this gap is defined: as the insurmountable refusal of the unconscious to give up Oedipal desire (this obviously refers to relatively late formations and posits the gap as conditioned by an 'outside', a division corresponding to the split into consciousness and the unconscious); as a difference between the satisfaction sought and the satisfaction obtained; the quest for an initial lost object which, by definition, can never reach its conclusion; the split implied in the very structure of the subject. In all these cases, the function imputed to the imaginary is that of replacing, patching together, covering over what is necessarily a gaping hole, a split, a lack in the subject's being.

How is it, then, that this lack comes into being as a *lack for a subject*? The subject, it is said, is this very thing – desire; and desire is sustained only by the lack of its object.

This apparently innocent tautology, however, that one can only desire in as much as one does not possess something,[24] becomes here the instrument of a paralogism. Desire is sustained only by the lack of a *desired* object. How can we speak of an object that is lacking if the psyche has not first posited this object as desirable? How can an object be desirable if it has not been invested (cathected), and how can it be invested if it has never been 'present' in any way? Desire is certainly always the desire of a missing object (or one that could be missing) but the missing object is constituted as such by the relation to desire. Lack as such, whether 'real' or otherwise, constitutes nothing at all, and every subject bathes in a non-denumerable infinity of 'lacks'. One should therefore posit at least the following connection: the subject emerges by positing itself as desiring a given object, which is to say, by positing at the same time a given object as desirable for it. The subject would then constitute itself as a desiring subject by constituting in the same stroke the object as a desirable object. But can we simply stop here and consider this moment as the 'first' one, as inaugurating the subject? Only if we renounce asking the essential question: under what conditions can an object be constituted by the psyche as an object of desire (aside from the trivial condition that it must be 'lacking')? In other words, under what conditions can a lack, a loss or a difference *exist* for the psyche – and be that very thing, lack, loss, difference? More than this: under what conditions can this lack, loss or difference be, in every instance, *other*, be 'constituted' in another way by this or that other subject?

It is futile to attempt to reduce these conditions to characteristics of the 'object' as such, or to characteristics of the subject as a living being, correlative and coordinated to the former. The 'missing object' – which is typically and generally speaking, the breast – is the same everywhere and always. It is also the same, for instance, for all mammals; but if certain 'desiring machines' are calves, all calves are not 'desiring machines'. The correlation, coordination and preadequation of the 'object' to the subject as a living being refers, of course, to something that the subject as a living being cannot be unaware of or neglect, and grants to certain objects are given an important privilege; this translates the subject's insertion in an organization that already exists, posited before him and independently of him. This organization, however, is that of the first natural stratum, and all this concerns the subject as a simple living being, that is as animal human being. This insertion of the subject as a living being and of certain objects in a chain that translates the biological–corporeal reality of the subject, which *is* this very reality says nothing yet, as such, about the psychical world. Obviously, what the psyche brings into being is not dictated by this biological–corporeal reality, for then it would always and everywhere be the same; nor is this done in 'absolute freedom' in relation to this reality, which can neither be ignored nor manipulated in any totally arbitrary way (even this affirmation has to be made with certain reservations: an anorexic infant *makes* himself die, his psyche is stronger than his biological regulatory system).

It is this original and irreducible relation of the psyche to the biological–corporeal reality of the subject that is intended by the Freudian idea of *anaclisis* (*Anlehnung*),[25] which contains much more than simply positing these two extreme and abstract limits: that psychical working out is neither dictated by biological organization nor absolutely free with respect to it. What the idea of *anaclisis*, of leaning on, states is: in the first place, there can be no oral instinct without mouth and breast, no anal instinct without an anus – *and* the existence of the mouth and the breast, or of the anus, still says nothing about the oral instinct in general, the anal instinct in general, about what becomes of them in a given culture, even less, what becomes of them in a given individual. But *more importantly*, in the second place: the existence of the mouth and breast, or of the anus, is not a mere 'external condition', without which there would be no oral or anal instinct, or more generally, no psychical functioning as we know it – in the same way as it is clear that without oxygen in the atmosphere or the circulatory system there would be no psyche, no phantasies or sublimation. Oxygen contributes nothing to phantasies, it 'allows them to exist'. The mouth-breast, or the anus, have to be 'taken into account' by the psyche and, what is more, they support and induce. Support and induce what, exactly? Here again, the radical powerlessness of traditional thought, of inherited logic-ontology, is evident as soon as we move outside of the areas in relation to which this thought has been developed. Mouth and breast, like the anus and faeces, like the penis or vagina are neither causes nor means, and certainly not 'signifiers' in some univocal relation to a signified which would always and everywhere be the same, *nor even* the *same* for the *same* subject. We must learn to think otherwise; we have to understand that the idea of anaclisis, of leaning on, is just as original and irreducible as the idea of cause or the idea of symbolizing. The privileged somatic data will always be taken up again by the psyche, psychical working out will have to 'take them into account', they will leave their mark on it – but which mark and in what manner cannot be reflected in the identitary frame of reference of determinacy. For the creativity of the psyche enters in here as radical imagination, as the emergence of representation (phantasying) and the alteration of representation, thereby rendering absurd the idea that the breast or the anus are the 'cause' of a phantasy as well as the idea that the oral or the anal can be assigned once and for all to a universal and complete determination-determinacy.

In this way, too, the 'lack' of the object – which is obviously only another aspect of the being of the object itself – is an *anaclisis*, psychical creation. If there is to be a lack for the psyche, the psyche must be that which *makes* something *be* – representation – *and* the psyche may make something exist as 'lacking': this implies that it can at one and the same time posit as existing that which is not, hence that the psyche can presentify-figure it, and that it can figure it in relation to another figure, in which it is caught up: the figure or the representation 'of itself' (an abuse of language) as that in which 'nothing is lacking'. It is when Freud speaks of the breast as 'hallucinated' by the infant that we are relatively close to the psychical imagination, to the radical imagination – not when one speaks of the 'specular', which is no more than a derivative of the vulgar ontology of 'reflection'. If it can be said that *after a given moment* the 'object' acquires its signification (of *object*) in relation to its disappearance or its loss, in other words, because it is found *not to go without saying* (*weil sie so häufig vom Kind vermisst wird*, 'because the child so often finds it [the breast] absent', Freud says), nevertheless, we must question what this discovery presupposes and implies. For this fact – that it does not go without saying that there are things which do not go without saying – *itself does not go without saying*. The 'discovery' of the breast as absent – and this occurs in a psychical formation which itself is undeniably 'secondary', riddled with distinctions and articulations – is made only in relation to and on the basis of the requirement that nothing is to be absent, nothing is to be lacking; it is only in this way that something can be posited as 'missing', as not being where it ought to be. This necessarily refers back to an originary mode of being of the psyche, as representing-representation to which nothing is 'missing', to an aim-intention-tendency of figuring-presentifying (itself) in and through representation which is *always realized*. To this we have certainly to associate an originary 'affect', these distinctions themselves (of representation, intention and affect) being simply ways of describing, in our secondary and waking language, something that precedes their possibility. At the originary level, not only can there not be any distinction between representation, intention and affect; there cannot be any 'missing object' and any 'desire', for 'desire' is always fulfilled – 'realized' before it is able to be articulated as 'desire'. The sort of 'desire' which has been drummed into our ears in the past few years, concerns the citizen as he walks down the street. At the level of the originary unconscious, to say that there is an intention, an aim, a 'desire' is to say *ipso facto* that there is a representation which *is* this intention as something realized, in the *sole* reality which exists and which counts from the psychical point of view: that in which only 'images' and 'figures' can and do exist. The indelible marks of this are manifested in 'hallucinatory satisfaction' as well as, in a second stage, in the organization of the phantasy.

iii PSYCHICAL REALITY

We must now thoroughly interrogate Freud's formulations: that there 'exists in the unconscious no index of reality', and that it is 'impossible to distinguish (there) truth from a fiction invested with an affect.'[26] What they state is not that there is in the unconscious a truth and a fiction from which the tags have been removed; nor do they state that it is hard to find a torch with which to pick them out in the darkness that engulfs them. The element of existence belonging to the unconscious is unrelated to truth or non-truth, radically different from these determinations, it belongs to another region of being. As unconscious, the radical imagination brings itself into being, makes be that which exists nowhere else and which, for us, is the condition for anything at all to be able to exist. It is this non-being – non-being, following diurnal canons – which Freud calls 'psychical reality'.

This psychical reality is made up essentially of representations. Nothing can exist for the psyche except in the mode of representation – as shown by the expression 'ideational representative of drives' (*Vorstellungsrepräsentanz des Triebes*) and many other formulations made by Freud. 'The thought process ... has been formed on the basis of representations.'[27] It is belatedly, and then only partially, that 'thought processes' are connected to, conveyed by and mediated through 'word representations', which form part of the mnemetic traces of the preconscious and which, for Freud, *never* belong to the unconscious properly speaking, in which there are only 'images of things'. And it is only when a thought process is the object of hypercathexis, and hence an 'object of perception' (in the broadest sense of the term), that 'we think that we are thinking the truth.'

If Freud so often speaks, even with respect to the unconscious, of 'thought process' rather than of 'representation process' or of just 'representing', this is because he is considering above all the *putting into relation* or the *connection* (if one wishes to recall Kant) of representations and is interested in particular with this relation or connection in so far as it conforms to certain 'laws', or 'rules', or 'principles'. These laws or rules which guide the emergence and the relation of representations can be summed up in terms of two postulates. In the psyche, nothing is gratuitous; putting into relation takes place as the realization of an unconscious intention. In the psyche, nothing is indifferent (the indifferent would not be evoked there); putting into relation is necessarily accompanied by an *affective charge*. Once again, this successive separation and presentation of 'different moments' is simply a necessity imposed by language. Unconscious 'thought processes' exist only in the indistinction of these 'moments' from one another. This is what is expressed by Freud when he speaks of the 'unlimited reign of the pleasure principle' in the primary processes. The unconscious psyche is therefore the representative process in which the emergence and interrelation of representations is 'regulated'/guided by the pleasure principle. The question of psychical reality in its original being is thus a question of the origin of representation, the origin of relation, the origin of the pleasure principle as an intention aiming at an affect.

In order to clarify this question, let us start with some considerations relating to much later stages in the evolution of the psyche, and in particular to the secondary and conscious formations of a 'normal' adult. We can, and we commonly do, distinguish with respect to the origin of representations a 'real origin' (the actual or retained presence of an internal or external 'perception'), an 'ideal or rational origin' (a mixture of complexes formed of word-representations and of deposits of earlier rational elaborations), and, finally, an 'imaginary origin' in the common and secondary sense of the term (the emergence of representations that are not dictated by the 'real' or the 'rational', and which often but not always are analogous to or repeat real or ideal elements). – Correspondingly, we can also distinguish with respect to the 'rules' or 'laws' of the interrelation of representations: in the first instance, the dominance of reality–testing; in the second, the dominance of rationality-testing (intention of conforming to ..., transformation or control in accordance with the rules of implication, inference, coherence, etc.); in the third, the dominance (only partial, in the secondary and derivative processes in question here) of the pleasure principle (which is manifested here in the form of *wish compensation*).

Little matter that even at this stage these distinctions possess but a partial and relative validity. What is important to our purposes is that they have *no meaning* at all in relation to the unconscious and that when we consider the unconscious, the 'moments' which are distinguished in this way are resorbed into 'psychical reality' and its mode of being – that is, into the radical imagination. In the unconscious there is no index of reality, no index of truth – this means that there is not and cannot be either 'reality-testing' or 'rationality-testing'; there is no representation of words as *words* that would convey some sort of rationality; there is not, and cannot be, any symbolism, anything symbolic. What can exist as 'perception', in the absence of an index of reality or reality-testing, can only be simply 'perception', that is, *self*-representation – not as the representation of an 'inside' distinct from and in opposition to an 'outside', but the representation, prior to this distinction, of *everything* (as) *self*, of *self* (as) *everything*, the words in parentheses serving to indicate the powerlessness of our waking thought to express this 'state'.

This 'resorption' within psychical reality of the elements that we commonly distinguish, the original indistinguishability of these 'elements' ultimately leads, then, to a representation of *'everything* (as) *self*', the sole *reality* for the psyche. This representation is automatically and entirely under the dominion of the pleasure principle. It is what comes before desire, since an 'object' which does not exist cannot be lacking and since what exists is what has to exist.[28] It always provides desire with its impossible aim, that of a state in which the presence of the 'object' and the satisfaction of desire are assured by their very construction, to the extent that the 'subject' and the 'object' of desire overlap with neither excess nor defect, coincide automatically. The entire 'psychical energy' of the subject can have a relation of cathexis with – can invest – nothing else at this stage than this 'self-all' which is the subject; it can only be absolute, primary, narcissistic libido or, better, 'autistic' libido – that is to say, that which excludes the reflexive element implied in narcissism, even if this is 'primary': not taking 'oneself' *as* 'object', moving outside the self in order to return to it, but remaining immediately alongside the self or in the self. This representation is, finally, in its senseless character, the matrix and the prototype of that which, for the subject, will always be *meaning*: indestructible holding-together, aiming at itself and grounded on itself, the unlimited source of pleasure to which nothing is lacking and which leaves nothing to be desired.

iv   THE MONADIC CORE OF THE PRIMAL SUBJECT

In its first 'state' and its first 'organization' – diametrically opposed to all that we understand by 'state' and 'organization' – the subject, if indeed there is a subject, can only refer to itself; a distinction with respect to itself and the rest is not and cannot be posited. To the extent that we can speak in this context of a 'world' of the 'subject', this world is at one and the same time self, proto-subject and proto-world, as they mutually and fully overlap. Here, there is no way of separating representation and 'perception' or 'sensation'. The maternal breast or what takes its place, is a part without being a distinct part, of what will later become the 'own body' and which is, obviously, not yet a 'body'. The libido circulating between the *infans* and the breast is a libido of auto-cathexis. It is preferable not to speak of 'narcissism' in this regard, not even of 'primary' narcissism, for this refers to a libido fixed upon itself to the *exclusion* of all the rest, whereas what is in question here is a totalitarian *inclusion*. Instead we should use Bleuler's term of *autism* which was explicitly approved by Freud in the same context and with respect to the very same problem.[29] This autism is '*undivided*': not the autism of representation, of the affect and of the intention as separate, but a single affect which *is* immediately (self-) representation and the intention of the atemporal permanence of this 'state'. In this immediate identity of what will later become a series of 'moments', an identity in which totality is a simple unity, in which difference has not yet emerged, being is being in this circle, and being is immediately 'meaning': an intention completed before any formulation and before any gap between a 'state' and an 'aim', as it is immediately the 'existence' of the subject for the subject. Not only the subject and the object but the 'copula' which joins them are all the same: not 'A is B', but 'I = am = id' and 'am = I = am' and 'id = am = id', along with all the other possible combinations.

This absurd description contains nothing more than the 'absurdities' of the Freudian description of the unconscious, when the latter is actually taken seriously and shorn of its positivist or structuralist coverings with which it was so quickly coated – so as to make it 'acceptable'. Let us try once again to show the necessity for this.

When we read: 'The phantasy, however, is not the object of desire, it is a scene. In the phantasy, indeed, the subject is not aiming at the object or its sign. It figures itself to be caught up in the sequence of images. It does not represent the desired object to itself, but instead it is represented as participating in the scene without thereby, in the forms closest to the primal phantasy, our being able to ascribe to it any particular place',[30] in this description, which is exact except for one thing, is it difficult to see the characteristics of the state from which the phantasy stems and which *it attempts to reproduce*? To say that we are unable to assign a place to the subject would seem to lend itself to two interpretations. One could say that the subject is 'caught up', in the strong sense, in the sequence of images: that is, the images *catch it*, the subject representing itself originarily as being caught, subjected, alienated in a scene in which it is no more than an element at the disposal of the 'play's director'. But this interpretation, unless it is a matter of secondary formations (and even, in this case, the inevitable exchange of roles would exclude this way of looking at things), is unable to account for the fact that it is impossible to assign *one* place to the subject in its phantasy; the alienating representation would, precisely, require this fixity, this subjugation of the subject. Now it is not only that, as soon as we take a close look, we can no longer say who is beating and who being beaten, nor even that it is the desire of the whipped that guides the whipping hand. The subject is not now here and now there; it is more than the totality of the characters and the organization of the scene, *it is the scene*. Now the 'subject' is not a 'scene' in diurnal reality nor even in secondary unconscious formations. The subject *is* the scene of the phantasy (at once its elements, organization, 'director', and stage and scene in the strict sense) *because* the subject *has been* this undifferentiated monadic 'state'. The phantasy ineluctably refers back, as to its origin, to a 'state' in which the subject is everywhere, in which everything, *including the mode of coexistence*, is *only* subject. In this sense, one could just as well say that the phantasy is the 'object of desire' as the 'fulfilment of desire' – and, in fact, it is impossible in this case to state one without stating the other. There is no sense in making a distinction here between the object of desire, its fulfilment and the scene. Once we leave the field of secondary formations, the idea of the object of desire, in psychoanalysis, appears clearly as a realist residue. What desire aims at is not an 'object' but that 'state', that 'scene' which, when we can grasp it (and we can do so, by definition, only in its derivative and secondary forms) implies not simply a 'subject' and 'objects' but a certain *relation* between them (of course, this is always made specific in one way or another in forms that are accessible to us and which bear the profound marks of the entire previous history of the subject) – and it is in this *relation* that the *meaning* of the phantasy is to be found for the subject ('objects' being always contingent and replaceable).

The expressions 'object of desire' and 'desire of a desire' are shattered fragments, and as such without much significance, of the formula *desire of a state*, a state which the phantasy-scene attempts to reproduce as best it can with the means available to it, and in which the object of desire just as the desire of the other are submitted to the subject *to the point of being united with it*. To the fracture of its world, of itself, as that which was experienced at one stage, the breaking-in performed by the separate object and by the other, the subject responds by reconstituting interminably in phantasies this initial world, if not in its now inaccessible untouched unity, at least in its characteristics of closure, mastery, simultaneity and the absolute congruence between intention, representation and affect. The alienation of the subject with respect to the desire of the other is a second moment; the first moment is the (psychical) realization of the alienation of the other with respect to the subject, through the subjugation and total appropriation in the phantasy. And this first moment refers us back to a zero moment, where the other and the object are not 'alienated' to the subject but exist, in so far as they do exist, only *as* the subject, expropriated from their existence before having acquired it.

Desire is indestructible, Freud wrote after Sophocles and Plato, and one may wonder why. The only possible reply is that, in its essential form, it is unrealizable. But what, in desire, is unrealizable? It is to be feared that too often what is aimed at behind these assertions is, once again, the citizen walking in the street – who is full of unrealizable desires, and even of unsatisfied needs, all of which are respectable, important and decisive. But this is not what is at issue in the psychoanalytical perspective. *In psychical reality all desires are not fulfillable, they are always fulfilled.* How could the Oedipal desire be said to be unrealizable, when it is constantly realized by every Oedipal dream?

The sole unfulfillable (and for this reason indestructible) desire for the psyche is the one which aims, not at what could never be presented in the real, but at what could never be given, as such, *in representation* – that is to say, in psychical reality. What is missing and will always be missing is the unrepresentable element of an initial 'state', that which is before separation and differentiation, a proto-representation which the psyche is no longer capable of producing, which has always served as a magnet for the psychical field as the presentification of an indissociable unity of figure, meaning and pleasure. This initial desire is radically irreducible not because *what* it aims at does not find in reality an object that embodies it, or in language words that state it, but because it cannot find in the psyche itself an image in which to depict itself. Once the psyche has suffered the break up of its monadic 'state' imposed upon it by the 'object', the other and its own body, it is forever thrown off-centre in relation to itself, oriented in terms of that which it is no longer, which is no longer and can no longer be. *The psyche is its own lost object*. The reduction of all that will henceforth appear as irremediably separated and differentiated to a single world, at once subject to and at the absolute disposal of the subject, is impossible, even as a pure phantasmatic representation. But this aim will continue to reign in the fullest, rawest, most savage and intractable manner over the unconscious processes, and this will make, to a degree much stronger than any type of repression, out of this 'state' that which can never truly be brought to speech, because its 'meaning' lies in an elsewhere, lost forever. This loss of self, this split in relation to the self, is the first work imposed on the psyche by the fact of its being included in the world – and it can happen that the psyche refuses to perform it.

In this initial, radically imaginary positing of the subject one finds the first 'identification', more precisely, the pre-identification presupposed by every identification. The identifications which are usually considered and which are indeed 'the precipitation of the cathexes of abandoned objects', obviously imply that the two 'terms' that they put into relation are themselves already posited in some way– certainly not 'logically' – as 'self-identical'. The *Ich bin die Brust* (I am the breast) in Freud[31] can have, and effectively does have, two significations which have to be articulated in terms of their relation and in time. 'I am the breast' can mean, and will also mean later, that the lost or abandoned object is introjected in the mode of identification. But in an earlier time, and on a deeper level, the statement signifies the simple, unmediated identity of the subject and the breast – as is indicated by Freud's statements according to which the object (what *will become* an 'object') is not seen first of all as separate or different from the self. Before being the breast transitively, the subject *is* the breast intransitively, and this being is also the being of the breast as indistinguishable from the subject. Every 'transitive' or 'attributive' identification of whatever kind (A is B, *I* am *that* object) is the transformation and working through of a primary identity which could be termed an *autistic identification* or *idemization*. Here, the 'terms' which, in language, we call I, mouth, breast, milk, oral sensation, proprioceptive sensation, pleasure, being, all – *are* absolutely the *same* without being 'reduced' to one another; they are identical in a non-attributive and non-predicative manner.

The subsequent, ascertainable evolution of the subject is the history, starting from a breaking point, of a series of creations of representations as differentiated and as different, the history of a representative/affective/intentional flux which ceases only with the death of the subject, which unfolds according to the rhythm of successive upheavals and in-depth reworkings of psychical organization – the 'mature' subject embodies also the stratified and intercommunicating deposits of this flux – and which is essentially the history of the psyche's socialization, in other words, of the creation, by means of the *teukhein* and the doing of others, of a social individual. This history, however, at all of its stages carries the traces of its point of origin, of an initial state in which subject, world, affect, intention, connection, meaning are the same. The social individual, as society produces him, is inconceivable 'without the unconscious'; the institution of society, which is indissociable from the institution of the social individual, is the imposition on the psyche of an organization which is essentially heterogeneous with it – but it too, in its turn, *'leans on'* the being of the psyche (and here again the term 'leaning on' takes on a different content) and must, unavoidably, 'take it into account'.

This being of the psyche is governed at one of its poles by the primal unconscious, which is the monadic core of the psyche and which has never been repressed but instead rendered impossible – unrepresentable – from the moment a world of diversity and of displeasure has been set up and which, unrepresentable in person, is presentified and figured in and through the very modalities of the deepest psychical processes. It is first necessary that a certain reality, as other than the subject, be established in order for the pleasure principle to undergo the torsion-transformation which will separate off from it a reality principle; for reality-testing to become possible; for that which does not conform to representation to be announced and impose itself upon the psyche; and for repression, which as such is nothing but a consequence of avoiding unpleasure – hence a manifestation of the reality principle in the broad sense[32] – to be able to begin. Repression is the second task imposed on the psyche by reason of its inclusion in the world. The dynamic unconscious in the usual sense of the term, or the whole of what Freud calls the primary processes, will gradually be peopled with all of the creations of the psyche that have been repressed, and its organization will undergo numerous reworkings. But it will always be dominated by that which formed the psyche's initial core, the psychical monad, which, absent as such from the unconscious, will mark everything that occurs there with its seal. It is this desire, master of all desires, of total unification, of the abolition of difference and of distance, manifested above all as being unware of difference and distance, which, in the field of the unconscious, arranges all the representations that emerge in the direction of its own lines of force. If the unconscious is unaware of time and contradiction, this is also because, crouched in the darkest part of this cave, the monster of unifying madness reigns there as lord and master. If we must say, not that desire can never be fulfilled, but quite the opposite, that in the unconscious desire is fulfilled *ipso facto* as soon as it arises, fulfilled on the only level that matters – that of unconscious representation; if the subject *is* the phantasmatic scene; if nothing there limits the 'magical omnipotence' of thought, this is because all of these are the effects and the remainders of an initial 'state' in which the object was but a segment of the self, immediately connected to the subject or part of the unitary subjective circuit, capable of being modified at will by an indefinitely and infinitely plastic hallucination. It is this constitutive remanence which makes possible the presentation by means of contraries, identity through contiguity, condensation or displacement, and finally the entire logic and rhetoric of phantasy, of dream and of madness, which is perpetuated in and through the functioning of diurnal language itself, and which remains entirely to be thought, as nothing essential has been said about it since the creative explosion of *The Interpretation of Dreams*.

It is also in this mode of originary being of the psyche that we find the first matrix of meaning, the operating–operated schema of bringing into relation or connection, the presentification of something which, in so far as it simply is, satisfies the requirement that it posits by its being. It is here that the subject once was 'in person' the prototype for the connection it will always continue to search for, against all odds. The demand for universal cognitive connection, or more generally, upon transposition to the social level, the demand for universal signification, for the adequation between world and desire, between desire and knowledge, between the conclusions of knowledge and the aims of desire, finds one of its inexhaustible well-springs here as well. It is not hard to recognise one of the origins of reason in this madness of inclusion-expansion, of plurality as unity, of the ultimate 'simplicity' of the given. The proto-meaning realizes by itself, just where meaning obviously cannot yet exist, total meaning, the universal and unbroken bringing into relation which will tend to wish to encompass even that which denies it (and transform, for instance, death into eternal life). If the madness of this stage is transformed into reason in the adult, this is, to be sure, through the social institution which is imposed on the individual, but also because, although it has had to give up immediate satisfaction, it continues to hold the intention of this relation, of total and universal connection. Man is not a rational animal, as the old commonplace affirms. Nor is he a sick animal.[33] Man is a mad animal (who begins by being mad) and who, for this reason as well, becomes or can become rational. The sperm of reason is also contained in the complete madness of the initial autism. An essential dimension of religion – this goes without saying – but also an essential dimension of philosophy and of science derive from this. One does not put reason where it should be, and, what is even more serious, one cannot reach a reasonable attitude with respect to reason, that is, rather than being faithful to reason one betrays it, if one refuses to see in it something other than, of course, but *also*, an avatar of the madness of unification. Whether it is the philosopher or the scientist, the final and dominant intention – to find, across difference and otherness, manifestations of the *same* (regardless of the name given to it, even if this be 'being' as such) which would dwell, entirely similar to itself, in phenomenal diversity – is based on the same schema of a final, that is to say, a primary unity, a schema, indissociably, of presentification, operation and valuation. The rational use of the form of the One, which allows access to a world which exists only as one *and* as the *other* than one, almost always tends to be transformed into the rational–imaginary use of the Idea of the One, which swallows up Relation by positing it as a pseudonym of Belonging, which, ultimately, would simply be a form of Identity. In this way, relation becomes the relation of being to itself, and the signs of truth and of illusion come to be, in a certain way, permuted: the existence of relations in the strong sense, which imply irreducible otherness, falls on the side of illusion, whereas Being is held to include relation only as reflected, not as truly actual. It is, certainly, of fundamental importance that philosophy recognized at an early stage the impossibility of this intention and genuinely assumed castration by affirming that this intention had to be abandoned;[34] the fact that what was recognized in this way has been periodically and regularly concealed, forgotten, cancelled out shows the force of the motivations in play here – as much as the incoercible 'natural' tendency of identitary logic.

v   THE BREAK-UP OF THE MONAD AND THE TRIADIC PHASE

The process of the social institution of the individual, that is to say, the socialization of the psyche, is indissociable from the process of psychogenesis or *idiogenesis*, and from a sociogenesis or *koinogenesis*. This is the history of the psyche in the course of which the psyche alters itself and opens itself to the social–historical world, depending, too, on its own work and its own creativity; and also, the history of society's imposition on the psyche of a mode of being which the psyche can never generate out of itself and which produces-creates the social individual. The common result of these two histories is the emergence of the social individual as the always impossible and always realized coexistence of a private world (*kosmos idios*) and of a common or public world. How is it that things, individuals, a world, a society come to be *for* a psyche which is in no way 'predestinated by nature' for them (and which, in its final strata refuses them, and is even *unaware* of them up to the end): this is the question – to be sure, it is inexhaustible and insoluble – that I propose to discuss once again here.

The psychical monad is a forming–formed, it is formation and figuration of itself, figuration figuring itself, starting from nothing. It is, to be sure, an 'aspect' of the living body or, if one prefers, it *is* this body as forming/self-forming, as figuring/self-figuring *for* itself. Perhaps no one will ever be able to add anything to what Aristotle said about the psyche as existing *only* as 'form' or 'entelechy' of the body – on the condition that these terms be separated out from the metaphysics in and through which they were posited and that we understand that the psyche is a form in so far as it is forming, that the 'entelechy' in question here is something entirely different from the predetermined predestination in view of an end, a definite *telos*, that this 'entelechy' is the radical imagination, *phantasia* subjected to no given end but the creation of its ends, that the living body is the human living body in so far as it represents and represents itself, that it puts things and itself into 'images' far beyond what would be required or implied by its 'nature' as a living being. For the living human body, that is to say, originally, for the psychical monad, all external calls, all external or internal 'sensorial stimulations', all 'impressions' become *representations*, that is to say, they are 'put into images', and emerge as figures. This emergence of figures, however, is not 'determined' by the sensorial either in the fact of its being or in its being-thus (ultimately, it is impossible to assign any meaning at all to the idea of such a 'determination'). The psyche's representative flux continues whether or not there is any 'outside stimulation'; it unceasingly makes *itself* and the 'primary processes' continue to unfold whether we are eating or sleeping, whether we are working or making love. This emergence of figures occurs first (and, in a sense, always) under the rule of the figuring-figure of 'everything = self', where 'activity' and 'passivity' are indistinguishable, just as are 'inside' and 'outside'. Berkeley's *esse ist percipi* (the being of things is their being perceived), Bergson's 'my body extends out to the stars' are always and absolutely true for the psyche, and they never entirely cease to be so for the individual in the waking state. In a sense, the psyche never does anything other than to dilate the sphere which it is, which it figures as itself, all the while figuring itself as occupying the centre of this sphere.

The great enigma here as everywhere, and which will always remain so, is the emergence of *separation*. A separation which will lead, for the individual, to setting up a private world and a public or common world, which are distinct and yet interdependent. What we know and can state is that separation exists in so far as it is created and instituted by society; it is, as we have seen, the essential operative schema, the producer-product of the institution of *legein* and *teukhein*. Imposing socialization on the psyche is essentially imposing separation on it. For the psychical monad, this amounts to a violent break, forced by its 'relation' to others, more precisely, by the invasion of others as others, by means of which a 'reality' is constituted for the subject, a reality which is at once independent, malleable and participable, and the dehiscence (never fully realized) between the 'psychical' and the 'somatic'. Just as much as the irresistible tendency of the psychical monad to close in upon itself, this break is equally constitutive of what the individual will be.[35] If the new-born infant becomes a social individual this is to the extent to which it suffers this break while at the same time managing to survive it – and this, mysteriously, almost always happens. In fact, when one considers this process closely, one is struck much more by the exceedingly small number of its failures than by their existence.

The relation to the other and to others (a relation which is always and at the same time 'a source of pleasure' and 'satisfying' as well as 'a source of unpleasure' and 'disturbing') is imposed through a series of breaks inflicted on the psychical monad by means of which the social individual is constructed as divided between the monadic pole, which always tends to lock everything up and to short-circuit it in order to carry it back to an impossible monadic 'state' and, failing to do so, to its substitutes, hallucinatory satisfaction and phantasizing – and, on the other hand, the series of successive constructions by means of which the psyche has in each case succeeded more or less in integrating (that is to say, it has represented, affectively invested and connected by means of tending towards or through an intention) whatever was imposed on it. The successive 'formations' of the subject which must all, to a gradually increasing extent, take into account both the separation and the diversity imposed on the psyche and which exist only as attempts to hold this diversity together (a diversity which itself becomes ever more diverse) represent the various levels of integration as this occurs under the aegis of the unitary principle translating the magnetic attraction over the entire psychical field by the monadic pole. As already stated, this pole as such is unrepresentable – but, at the same time, we are reading its effects when we observe, at all stages of psychical life, the tendency towards unification, the immediate or mediate reign of the pleasure principle, the magical omnipotence of thought, the requirement for meaning. And this is also what the social institution of the individual 'takes into account' when it assures the individual a *singular identity*, posits him as 'someone' recognized by others, provides, even and especially if this is on the level of the imaginary, satisfactions for him, presents to him a world in which everything can be referred to a signification.

The break up of the psychical monad, to be sure, leans on somatic needs; but it simply leans on these. Somatic needs 'explain' nothing; hunger announces itself to the psyche and cannot be 'ignored' by it – but it is neither a necessary nor a sufficient condition. Stuffing a newborn or watching him day and night to give him the breast or the bottle as soon as he awakes will perhaps make him a psychotic child, but never a calf with a human face. The canonical 'response' to need is hallucination and phantasmatic satisfaction; it occurs in and through imagination, and in an undetermined manner. To be sure, the imagination does not provide calories and if nothing else were to take place, the infant would die – as indeed he does die as a result of his imagination and despite the food he is offered, if he is anorexic. And, each time that 'real satisfaction' appears, it is represented as the manifestation, confirmation, restoration of the initial unity of the subject. Hunger is normally appeased when the breast, or whatever takes the place of the breast, is offered and made available. The availability of the breast simply re-establishes, to begin, the monadic state; it can be 'lived' at this period only in terms of the representations and the schemata available to the subject – and this is the only one available. The breast can only be apprehended as the self: I am the breast, *Ich bin die Brust*, in the pristine sense. What takes place, on the somatic level, as the appeasement of need is understood by the psyche – in the normal case – in its own language as restoring the unity and the proto-affect indissociable from it. This is what, henceforth, will form the core of *pleasure*. The psychical equivalent, the 'delegation through representation' of the somatic process of need and of its satisfaction will be a restoration of unity; this is where the psyche will seek its pleasure to begin with – and, in a certain way, in the unconscious it will eternally seek its pleasure there. At this stage of the *effective* omnipotence of the psyche, it will be capable of reproducing this pleasure all alone, by reproducing the corresponding representation, hallucinating or phantasizing the breast.

Correlatively, unpleasure is the break up of the autistic monad. Hunger is certainly – or can be – what it leans on; but the absent breast does not, and *cannot* have the meaning of the *cause* of hunger, a meaning which simply does not and cannot exist at this stage. The absent breast is the negation of meaning or a negative meaning, in so far as it is the break-up of the monadic closure – in so far as it is a hole in the subjective sphere, the *ablation* of an essential part of the subject (from this doubtless comes the intensity of oral anguish, the most difficult to master of all, as the questioning of the subject's first identity). In their initial form, otherness, reality, the negation of meaning or negative meaning are simply the *unpleasure* presentified by this ablation of the breast which the psychical monad undergoes. The absence of the breast is unpleasure in so far as it is the tearing apart of the autistic world. It is because the first schema is perpetuated as the condition and presentification of all signification, it is because everything is always lived by the psyche in terms of the indistinguishability of I-world-sense – pleasure, that the absence of the breast can become a *figure*, more precisely: a constitutive component of the 'object' in its alternation with the latter's 'presence'. A border of virtual non-being begins to take shape at the boundary of representation; the polar opposition of yes/no, of reality and negation, of the possible and the actual find here their first subjective seeds, and the figure-ground schema begins to be posited as the general articulation of a 'consciousness' and a 'perception' in their embryonic state.

However, from the perspective of the psyche, pleasure excludes unpleasure, identity excludes otherness. Consequently, 'because the child so often finds it absent', the breast 'has to be ... shifted to the "outside".'[36] Let us say rather that an 'outside' is *created* so that the psyche can cast off into it whatever it does not want, *whatever there is no room for in the psyche*, non-sense or negative meaning, the breast as absent, the bad breast. It is obvious that this constitution of an embryonic object is possible only in and through the simultaneous constitution of an 'external space'. The psyche invents-figures an outside in order to place the breast of unpleasure there. What will subsequently become 'world' and 'object' is literally a *projection*, which in its origin is the expulsion of unpleasure (and it will keep this character in all the mechanisms related to this archaic state, in particular in psychosis). At the same time, the other side of the breast, the present or gratifying breast, continues to submit to the schema of inclusion. The latter, however, can no longer be completely unaware of the relative otherness of the object; it can no longer be pure and simple identity. Supported on the first sketch of the articulation of self and non-self, it becomes *introjection* and incorporation. 'I am the breast' thus takes on its second sense, in which predication is possessive or attributive *to the self*.

The imaginary creations of projection and introjection are equivalent to the first sketch of the boundary inside/outside, as already stated; they also go along with the polarity of value (good/bad). Here too begins to take shape a relative articulation of the three 'moments' of psychical processes, representation, affect, intention; for only in this way can an intention be directed towards a positive affect and deflected away from a negative affect, by being coordinated with the corresponding representations which begin to be distinguished as 'opposing'. Here, finally, an initial division of the autistic libido is outlined, which has a positive relation of cathexis with the subject and the good breast and a negative one with the 'outside' and the bad breast that is to be found there.

This is not yet, however, the constitution of a *real* object, that is one that escapes the grasp of the subject. This real object can appear only once the good breast and the bad breast begin to coincide for the subject, once the two imaginary entities appear as connected to a third entity which is the ground of both of them without being identical with either of them. It is more than likely, as Freud stated, that this constituting of the object as real can only be achieved at the moment when the fact that the object 'belongs' to a 'person' is actually apprehended. In other words, the object can never be constituted except as a *partial* object – hence, it is constituted as real only at the moment when it is truly 'lost', in so far as it is placed once and for all within the power of someone else. Doubtless, too, the other is posited as such only once it can be posited as the one who disposes of the object.

The two distinct and opposing quasi-objects of the preceding phase, the good and the bad breast, become the same to the extent that they are posited as depending on the *same* person. This immediately signifies that the other, who actually disposes of this now unified object which, nevertheless, joins together two opposing qualities, is grasped straight away under a double sign. Carrying the bad object, he is hated; carrying the good object, he is loved. The other is constituted necessarily in ambivalence – in other words, the ambivalence affecting the other (and, hereditarily, everything which will succeed the other as an object of cathexis for the psyche) which can never be eliminated, is the co-product of the imaginary moments which presided over its constitution. Even more decisive is the projective constitution of the other on the basis of the schema of all-powerfulness. It seems to me that no one has drawn all of the consequences that ensue from the omnipotence the infant imputes to the other, all that it implies concerning the schemata available to the psyche at the moment when the first other is constituted for the psyche. The subject can grasp the other only by means of the sole schema available then and always to it, since it draws this out of itself – the schema of omnipotence. The image of the other constituted in this way is, therefore, the projection of the subject's 'own image' for itself. One might say that the other is actually omnipotent at this stage with respect to the only thing that matters, namely the breast, and that for the child, it is of no importance that the other cannot fly or countervene the second principle of thermodynamics. This is obvious and entirely beside the point: where did the infant get a signification of omnipotence, and the capacity to endow it in addition with this overwhelming excess in relation to all that is real? The fact that this signification leans on the actual relation that develops around the breast does not contradict, but rather reinforces what I have said about it. Imaginary omnipotence with respect to the breast, which the infant imputed first to himself, and would have liked to continue to impute to himself afterwards, he is finally forced to place somewhere else, in another; this means, first and foremost that *he can constitute another only by projecting onto the latter his own imaginary schema of omnipotence*.

The fundamental pattern of the phantasy, as the essentially triadic schema which always includes the subject, the object and the other, is henceforth established. This evidently occurs under the domination of earlier requirements and schemata – although it includes the possible circulation of omnipotence among the 'terms' which are put on stage. The phantasy *subjects* the terms it puts on stage by submitting them to the initial requirement for total meaning, for the reciprocal inherence of what henceforth has been separated, for the unobstructed circulation of the affect. The cement that holds the elements of the phantasy's triadic schema together is the experience of meaning as *co-presence*, the basic characteristic of the monadic phase.

What results from the radically imaginary and projective positing of the other as all-powerful for the subsequent life of the subject, and what is constantly translated into the content of social imaginary significations or what finds its equivalent there can be readily enough understood for us to underscore it here. It is important, however, to stress, even at the risk of being tiresome, the sovereign character of the radical imagination during all of these stages. The subject can begin to sketch out the elements of the real, the object and the human other, only starting with and under the exclusive control of its own imaginary schemata. Scarcely has he grasped a bit of 'reality' when he must metamorphosize it to make it agree with the irreality which alone has meaning for him. Despite this, the importance of the triadic stage for the formation of the subject is critical. Passing by way of the triadic schema – subject, other, object – is almost mandatory under pain of death. This is the reason why an absolute psychosis – that is to say, wholly autistic – is practically unobservable, why all of psychoanalytic experience, including that relating to psychosis, feeds on what stems from this triadic stage or comes after it, and is sometimes theorized as though it were the only one – why, in any event, it can certainly not go back beyond it except through constructions or reconstructions, such as the one attempted here.[37]

The passage by way of the triadic phase represents a sketch of the psyche's socialization, to the extent that the psyche gives up omnipotence; this socialization is, however, entirely relative, since omnipotence is simply thrown off onto the other and since, even here, the psyche keeps this imaginary other within its grasp, by making him do what it wishes in phantasy. (The religious extensions of this situation are too obvious for us to dwell on them). Even 'reality', as the unavoidable imposition of the other's presence/absence and of the other's disposing of the object is constituted as the manifestation of the imaginary omnipotence of the other. As such, it is obviously not 'reality'.

It happens, however, that this other is himself already a social individual, who speaks, speaks to the child and speaks *of himself*, that both in his words and in his behaviour, his corporeal manner of being and of doing, of touching, of taking and handling the child, he embodies, presentifies, figures the world instituted by society and refers to this world in an indefinite diversity of ways. The other speaks: he designates *himself* and signifies *himself*; he designates and signifies the *child; he designates and signifies to* the child 'objects' and 'relations' between 'objects'. This is still far from enough to constitute the other as real or to constitute reality; but this already gives rise to a new series of decisive modifications in the world of being of the psyche and in the mode of being of that which 'is' *for* the psyche. If the other continues to be essentially imaginary, if all its manifestations can be grasped and interpreted by the subject only through its own phantasmatic schema, the other is also an outside agency that may or may not comply with the demands of the subject, may love or remain indifferent, promise, forbid, give, take away, scold, embrace, punish in a way that the subject construes as related to its own 'attitudes', that is to say, essentially, as related to its own representations, affects and intentions. In this way, for instance, the wishes of destruction, unexpressed and inexpressible, which inevitably accompany the ambivalence affecting the other for the subject, provoke in the imaginary the fear of reprisal by the omnipotent other (and obviously, omniscient as well) which will be the core of unconscious guilt. The subject creates in this way, by projection, a schema of action and reaction, the 'reflexive' character of which is obvious (the effect turned back upon the cause, the wish for the destruction of the other can lead to the destruction of the subject by the other), and makes the other the first and necessary embodiment

of a *cause* separate from the subject and the support of the 'if ..., then
...'.

The phase which then sets in, through the parade of 'partial objects'
and the successive modifications of 'central' representations and the
subject's relations of cathexis which characterize this phase, leaves, as
Freud has shown, profound and indelible imprints on both what will
later become the 'real' individual and on the unconscious, where the
partial objects that are successively abandoned and the corresponding
phantasmatic figurations are maintained. The subject remains here
under the dependence of the other, onto whom he projects the indivisible union of power and 'knowledge', of representation and meaning,
of desire and the fulfilment of desire which he loses as he gradually
becomes 'conscious'. The intersecting of projections and introjections
continues in increasing complexity and amplitude. Identification takes
on now its second meaning; it ceases to be autistic identification to
become transitive identification, the identification *with* something or
someone (generally both at once). In it, simultaneously alternate or
coexist as distinct yet indissociable, the positing of the subject as being
the other (which, once again, is but the projection of the subject in its
omnipotence) and the positing of the subject as being the object posited
(by the subject) as the object of the desire of the other. Auto-eroticism
is no longer the immediate closed circuit of the libido relating to itself;
it now takes on a secondary and articulated character in and through
phantasmatic formations where the other is figured as such and as
desiring.[38] The differentiation of the single originary principle of
pleasure reaches a new stage. The pleasure principle splits into two:
the pleasure principle in the strong sense, which falls on the side of
the unconscious and continues to satisfy itself in the imaginary activity
over which it reigns; and the principle of avoiding displeasure, increasingly tied to the actions and reactions of the other and of their 'effects'
on the subject. Actions, reactions, effects are always constructed in
and through the subject's imagination, not only in that the other is
always imaginary but in that they imply the imaginary imputation to
the other of 'pleasures' and 'unpleasures' 'caused' by the subject's
imaginary states, and to which the other is held to react this or that
way.

We have just mentioned the 'conscious' and the 'unconscious'. Actually, setting up the other in his position of omnipotence is at the same
time the setting up of an interiorized agency of repression and the
origin of this agency. As the master of pleasure and unpleasure, the
other is the origin and imaginary source of a 'must' and 'must not', of
the seed of a norm. This introjection – return to the source of the
imaginary representation of the subject projected 'outside' and weighed
down by its separation as well as by its leaning on an 'independent'
person – the introjection of a figure that intimidates or forbids, is the
setting up of an 'archaic' super-ego, certainly a pre-Oedipal super-ego,
whose explanation in terms of phylogenesis is at once superfluous and

useless. In this way, an unconscious in the dynamic sense of the term and a genuine repression are set up: the repression not of that which *cannot* be expressed because it cannot be represented but the repression of that which *must* not be expressed *because* it has been represented and *continues* to be so.

vi   THE CONSTITUTION OF REALITY

All of this is still a far cry from the constitution of a 'reality' and of the subject as a separate individual, correlative to a reality separate from him-self and independent of the power of an imaginary other. It happens, once again, that this other speaks. But this is not enough. This language – felt, understood, and soon reproduced by the child – is, to be sure, the indispensible condition for a 'perception' to begin to arise, for 'objects' to be separate from representation and from one another, for them to acquire, or to be coupled with, the irreality that makes up their 'reality' to the extent that they are assigned to a sign and to a signification which 'assemble them together' each in itself, perpetuate them, make them the basis for relations, and so forth. But these are no more than pseudo-objects in a pseudo-world as long as the other continues to be omnipotent. These pseudo-objects and this pseudo-world continue to depend on the other not only to the extent that they exist but, even more importantly, as *that which* they are. The access to signs and then to 'significations' – which are not yet genuine significations, and we shall soon see why – is as yet nothing with respect to the constitution of reality and of the individual. As such, it begins by plunging the subject even more deeply, if this is possible, into irreality *to the extent that this signification remains within the power of the other*, as it always is at the start and remains so for a long time, to the extent that it is the other who has use of it and establishes it, to the extent that being and non-being, relation and non-relation, good and bad are what the other says they are. As long as between the child and the other there is *only* language – and even though this language can exist in the other only by means of its social institution and as conveying potentially the entire being of the social – the other cannot be stripped of his imaginary position, nor can the pseudo-world that he sustains be transformed into a true world, a common or public world. Now the language between the child and the person who takes care of the child starts by being a 'private language' – a private use of language; it is even necessarily set up at the start as a 'private language', just as two psychotic children can set up a highly perfected private language between themselves. And the 'significations' it conveys and the pseudo-world to which it refers are just as private.

The other can be stripped of his imaginary omnipotence only in so far as he is stripped of his power over 'significations'. Being stripped in this way can be the work neither of language as such nor of 'reality' as such through their own power (as is clearly shown in the thousands of really and logically airtight and irrefutable discourses proffered every day by paranoiacs as well as, from another point of view, by the great majority of social and religious systems). The other can become 'real' – and so make 'objects' and the world 'real' – only if he is stripped of his omnipotence, that is, if he is limited. And he cannot be limited in and through 'reality', since 'reality' never is anything other than the signification ascribed to it – and, for the child, this signification is ascribed, precisely, by the other.[39] The other can be stripped only if he strips *himself*, if he signifies *himself* as not being the source and the master of signification (and of values, norms, and so on). For this, it is neither necessary nor sufficient that he be able to indicate, designate a 'real' third person (the father, in the case of the mother) – if this third person is simply the other of the other, source and master of signification in his turn, if omnipotence is, then, simply shifted onto another support. It is necessary, and sufficient, that the other be able to signify to the child that *no one* among all those he might encounter is the source and absolute master of signification. In other terms, it is necessary and sufficient that the child be referred to the *institution* of signification and to signification as instituted and not depending on any particular person. In this sense, a mother surviving with her child on a desert island after a shipwreck can, should the case arise, socialize the child and make for him or for her a genuine world – and a 'real' family in Paris can have a perfectly psychotic effect on its children. For, of course, the father is a father only if he refers himself to society and to its institution, only if he signifies to the child that he is one father among others, that he is so only to the extent that he desires to be in a place which he himself does not have the power to create, and if in this he figures and presentifies for the child what explicitly goes infinitely beyond him – an anonymous and indefinite collectivity of individuals who coexist in and through the institution and who continue forward and backward in time. Only the institution of society, proceeding from the social imaginary, can limit the radical imagination of the psyche and bring into being for it a reality by bringing into being a society. Only the institution of society can bring the psyche out of its originary monadic madness, and what could well exist – and, at times, actually does – as a madness of two, three, or more. And this implies the 'hereditary' fabrication of individuals as social individuals – and this also means: individuals who are able and who want to continue the fabrication of social individuals.

It is here, beyond all socio-cultural relativity, that the profound signification of the Oedipus complex resides.[40] For in the Oedipal situation the child must confront a state of affairs which can no longer be imaginarily manipulated at will: the other (the mother) at once strips herself of her omnipotence by referring herself to a third party, signifies to the child that her own desire has another object outside of him and that she herself is the object of another's desire, the father. This situation cannot be grasped by the child as manipulable (despite his interminable efforts to do so), as contingent (despite his innumerable wishes that it go away, by the death of the father, for instance), or as a raw, meaningless fact: it is full of a signification which expresses itself, and in and through this signification a nuclear world is posited which is a world of subjects, in which the subject has found his origin and from which he is, in a sense, excluded. And, of this signification, no one is master: the father and the mother are such as they are through the institution of the parental couple, *which is not at their disposal*. As such, the encounter with the Oedipal situation sets before the child the unavoidable fact of the institution as the ground of signification and vice versa, and forces him to recognize the other and human others as subjects of autonomous desires, which can interrelate with one another independently of him to the point of excluding him from this circuit. This absolutely unmasterable situation is, as a result, always equivalent to a 'castration'. As a result, too, it refers the subject definitively to real–rational chains, completes the constitution of the 'reality ego' (*Real-Ich*) and establishes the bar of repression in its more or less definitive form. Over and beyond the proto-meaning which will always continue to dominate the unconscious, it opens for the subject the access to meaning as open meaning and to signification properly speaking, as the virtually interminable putting into relation, mediated by the absolute other of the psyche, of representation, of intention and of affect: the real or rational *fact* conveyed by the institution. This situation establishes the subject's models and identifying markings in the usual sense of the term – and it does so by completing the conditions of possibility of the processes of sublimation, which I shall return to later.

These inexpungible socializing functions or operations have been realized in a series of cultures, our own included, by means of a particular institution (although it has presented a wide variety of forms), that of the patriarchal family. The fact that this institution, profoundly in crisis today, can or should be modified or abolished is not a question we have to discuss here.[41] It is obvious, and has long been recognized, that Freud's analysis and its extension by Lacan appear to be, and effectively are tied to this form of 'familial' institution (the institution which assures the reproduction of individuals as social individuals), and, in particular, to the patriarchal family, presented abusively as a meta-cultural and trans-historical necessity.[42] But what is important lies elsewhere. Unless one believes – which appears more and more clearly between the lines in contemporary pseudo-'subversive' confusionism – that the human new-born is predestined by its nature, by Good Nature, the Mother of us all, or by God, our Good Father; or by the Holy Spirit speaking through the mouth of the latest fashionable prophet, for a social existence which matures within the child with the years, just as his members grow and his weight increases; unless one dreams that he is, genetically or in some other, unknown way, preorganized to constitute (or 'reflect') a reality coherent together with that of all the others and referred to the same significations, to recognize spontaneously the other and his autonomy, recognize oneself as an individual, never to have any desires but those accorded by some pre-existing harmony with the desires of others, able to exist in a wholly non-instituted collectivity or able, from birth (or, more precisely, from conception) freely to negotiate his entry into instituted society; in short, unless one is completely unaware of what the psyche is or what society is, it is impossible to fail to recognize that the social individual does not grow like a plant, but is created-fabricated by society, and that this occurs *always* by means of a violent break-up of what is the first state of the psyche and its requirements. And this will *always* be the task of a social institution in one form or another. The form and the orientation of this institution can and must change; *what* it creates-fabricates – the social individual in his mode of being, his references, his comportments – also can and must change, otherwise a social revolution is impossible or is condemned in short order to slip back into the 'old medley'. But the new-born will *always* have to be torn out of *his* world, without asking him for an opinion he cannot give, and forced – under pain of psychosis – to renounce his imaginary omnipotence, to recognize the desire of others as equally legitimate with his own, and taught that he cannot make the words of the language signify whatever he may want them to,[43] made able to enter the world as such, the social world and the world of significations as everyone's world and as no one's world. It is impossible to see how those who care for the new-born could ever help but become the supports of an imaginary pseudo-world in which they would incarnate the figures of omnipotence, nor how they could help him move out of it without presentifying-figuring for him, in one way or another, the existence of a desire to which he *must* not have access – for without this the other could never be for the child the subject of an autonomous desire, nor the child himself be such a subject. This is the true signification of the Oedipal situation, for which, *in this respect*, the embodiment in the patriarchal family is *at once* exemplary and accidental. We are justified in imagining everything with respect to the transformation of social institutions; but not the incoherent fiction holding that the psyche's entry into society could occur *gratuitously*. The individual is not the fruit of nature, not even a tropical one, but a social creation and institution.

vii SUBLIMATION AND THE SOCIALIZATION OF THE PSYCHE

'Sublimation' is nothing other than the psychogenetic or idiogenetic aspect of socialization, or the socialization of the psyche considered as a psychical process. This process can only take place by means of essential conditions which are rigorously external to it; it is the taking up again by the psyche of forms, *eide*, which are socially instituted and of the significations which they convey, or, in other words, the appropriation of the social by the psyche through the constitution of an interface between the private world and the public or common world.

Freud wrote at a late stage: 'If one were to yield to a first impression, one would say that sublimation is a vicissitude which has been forced upon instincts entirely by civilization. But it would be wiser to reflect upon this a little longer'.[44] To say that sublimation has been forced upon instincts by civilization, when it is obvious that 'civilization' – that is to say any form whatsoever of instituted society, and already language – can exist if and only if there is sublimation, shows the irreducibility of the social–historical to the psychical as well as the inverse irreducibility. In the same way – and despite other more superficial formulations[45] – the irreducible character of the social is implicitly recognized in this passage from *Totem and Taboo*:

> The asocial nature of neurosis has its genetic origin in their most fundamental purpose, which is to take flight from an unsatisfying reality into a more pleasurable world of phantasy. The real world, which is avoided in this way by neurotics, is under the sway of human society and of the institutions collectively created by it. To turn away from reality is at the same time to withdraw from the community of man.[46]

This is as much as to say that, for man, there is no reality outside of that over which society and its institutions 'reign', that there is never any reality other than socially instituted reality, and this this has to be taken into account by efforts to define the content of the 'reality principle' – that is, the referent of the term 'reality' – which is undetermined in Freudian theory and which has too often been identified – and to begin with, by Freud himself – with a 'natural reality' assumed to be simple and indubitable.

From the point of view we are concerned with here, sublimation is the process by means of which the psyche is forced to replace its 'own' or 'private objects' of cathexis (including its own 'image' for itself) by objects which exist and which have worth in and through their social institution, and out of these to create for itself 'causes', 'means' or 'supports' of pleasure. This obviously implies, on the one hand, the psyche itself as imagination, namely as the possibility of positing this for that, this in the place of that (*quid pro quo*); on the other hand, this implies the social–historical as the social imaginary, namely as the positing, in and through the institution, of forms and significations which the psyche as such is absolutely incapable of bringing into existence. Access to language in the full sense of the term (as public language) and access to *doing* as social activity are cardinal instances of this.

What is therefore at issue in sublimation, as we understand it here, is neither simply nor necessarily the 'desexualization' of drives, but the establishing of a non-empty intersection between the private world and the public world, conforming 'sufficiently as to usage' to the requirements posited by the institution of society as this is specified in each case. This implies, generally, a conversion or a shift of aim for drives, but always and essentially a shift of *object* in the broadest sense of the term. What was the 'object' of the preceding phases must be taken by the psyche in another mode of being and in other relations – thus it is henceforth *another* object, because it has another signification, even if it is 'the same' physically and even if, for the psyche, this separation is never truly realized and the 'successive layers of lava'[47] corresponding to the successive formations of the object are not only shot through with volcanic openings but are almost never entirely solidified (and this refers to what we said above concerning the magma-like nature of representation). This aspect – the alteration of the object – is masked in the usual presentations of sublimation, when, for instance, it is said to concern only a change of aim for the drives, the replacement of sexual satisfaction by a non-sexual satisfaction.[48] The 'object' of the drive cannot be conceived of apart from its 'aim', any more than it can be separated from the network of relations in and through which it is posited as an 'object' and as *this* particular 'object'. The 'sublimation of homosexuality' in the social relations between individuals does not so much signify, or simply signify, that one gives up the sexual satisfaction that others could provide, but that these others are henceforth not simply sexual 'objects' but social individuals.[49]

The transformation of the mother as sexual object into the tender mother is not simply the conversion of the aim of the drive but a modification of the object of the drive: the tender mother is not and cannot be the mother as sexual object, for she can only be a tender mother (for the subject) in so far as she is a socially instituted mother, referred to a host of relations and significations which go infinitely beyond her and exist only as socially instituted meanings. She is the same mother for the doctor or the zoologist; she is not the same mother for what concerns us here. And to the very extent to which these successive and *other* mothers – the all-powerful mother of the triadic phase, the Oedipal mother, the tender mother – coexist for the psyche and refer to one another, we can again see in this example what *the* representation of the mother as a magma is for a subject. To hold the contrary would be to hold that representation (or the 'object') is for the psyche no more than a coat-hanger on which are placed, one after the other, affects, intentions, different relations and significations, each of which leads an independent existence and which, all together, leave intact their common 'support'.

It is this change of object which results in the fact that, for the subject, 'objects' no longer exist, but instead things and individuals; no longer 'private signs and words' but a public language. For this reason too it is not possible to say that sublimation and repression are two fates of drives which mutually exclude one another. In fact, the successive repressions which occur when the conscious/unconscious split is established correspond to so many moments in the process of sublimation. These repressions are, indeed, impossible without concomitant changes – even if these are embryonic – in the aim and in the object of the drives. The infant must cathect (invest) the sight or the prehension of objects other than the breast, just as he must cathect (invest) speech, otherwise he would not talk. To be sure, at the start these relations of cathexis are fully (or, better, directly) 'erotic'; this in no way changes the fact that the aim sought by the infant's babbling is no longer that sought by sucking. And, of course, the erotization of the objects of cathexis never entirely disappears. The subject never wholly abandons the positions it has once occupied (cathected, invested, *besetz*); this is also its history. These positions, however, subsist, 'normally', only as *mostly* unconscious. Repression and sublimation are not fates of the drives which mutually exclude one another, but ways of distributing the energy of cathexis among ancient representations and new and altered representations/significations. The sublimation which makes the Oedipal mother a tender mother not only does not prevent but *always* accompanies the persistence of the mother as a repressed erotic object. Likewise, the components of the anal drive are always at the same time sublimated and repressed – and the anal zone, in function of its maintained erogeneity, will often be the object of an excessive counter-cathexis in the so-called 'normal' individual in many cultures. The 'normality' of the individual for a given society depends also, and mostly, on the relation between repression and sublimation and its modalities.

There is no need for us to enter here into an examination of the 'topical' and 'economic' modifications implied in the final phase of the psyche's socialization. Let us simply note that once a 'reality ego' (*Real-Ich*) and its 'synthetic functions' – to use Freud's terminology – appear, that is to say, once the social individual, as we understand this term, is definitively constructed, the intention, the tending-towards, the 'desire' of the psyche themselves undergo an essential alteration in their mode of being. Intention becomes the intention of modification in the real and of the real – and this will henceforth support the action of the individual in all its forms. This modification of intention is indissociable from a 'conversion of the aim' of drives (more generally, of psychical activity) which amounts to the emergence of a new form of pleasure or of a new form of satisfaction. Pleasure began by being the proto-pleasure of the psychical monad, the immediate presence of satisfaction, not distinct from representation; pleasure became erotic as well in a more restricted sense of the term once a differentiated representation (even if it is rudimentary) of the 'body' appears, making it, through the mediation of the other, the preferred ground of satisfaction. For the social individual, a third pleasure then appears (one which is not necessarily always conscious): the individual can and must be able to find pleasure in modifying the 'state of affairs' outside of himself or in the perception of such a 'state of affairs'. The 'nature' of these affairs matters little – on the understanding, of course, that these are social affairs. Whatever components of the earlier stages may continue to be present, the social individual is someone who can take pleasure in making an object, in talking with others, in hearing a story or a song, in looking at a painting, in demonstrating a theorem or in acquiring knowledge – and also, in learning that others have a 'good opinion' of him and even in thinking that he has 'acted well'. This transformation of the 'source' as well as of the 'character' of pleasure, which in itself is one of the most astonishing of all the things with which the psyche confronts us, doubtless involves a host of processes and points of support.[50] How could we fail to observe that the possibility of this lies in a certain *state of the representation* – namely the fact that in all of the cases we have mentioned, it is representation as such which procures satisfaction?

One can thus say, paradoxically, that the subject, at the end of its socialization process finds itself close to its original situation in which representation was, in itself as such, pleasure. The difference is that then it had this representation 'at its disposal', whereas now it is mediated by a 'state of affairs' which is not at the subject's disposal. The social individual cannot be constituted 'objectively' except through the reference to things and to other social individuals, which he is ontologically incapable of creating himself for these can exist only in and through the institution. And he is constituted 'subjectively' in so far as he has managed to make them things and individuals *for himself* – that is to say, to invest positively the results of the institution of society.

This 'recovery' by the individual of the network constituted by other individuals and by things obviously implies as well that he himself finds a place in this network and that he fits into it. Considered in its psychogenetic aspect, this is nothing but the constitution of the final 'identification model' for the individual. At one of its poles, this model is a social imaginary signification which concretizes and articulates the institution of the individual by the society in question (the hunter, the warrior, the craftsman, the *mater familias*, the starlette, the militant, the inventor, and so on). Mediated by the individual's own history, it possesses a second pole in the singularity of the individual's creative imagination. Thus, the individual may, at times, exceed to a greater or lesser degree, the 'model' which is proposed by society (and generally imposed so as to be 'sufficient as to usage') and so become, if he finds himself in turn to be socially accepted and valued, the source and origin of an alteration of the institution of the social individual in his specific content. However, through this 'identification model', what is invested is still also *always* an 'image' of the individual for himself, mediated by the 'image' which he imagines he is giving to the others.[51] This implies that other social individuals are cathected by the subject and preserve a share in the role of masters of signification. But also, the fact that the individual conforms to his own image of himself is part of this image and of the very being of the individual, impossible without the image, and can prove – indeed does typically and overwhelmingly prove – to be more important than corporeal wholeness or life itself, which are frequently sacrificed in order to maintain the wholeness of the image – for without this, humans would no longer be humans. The absolute relation of cathexis of the closed self-representation of the originary psychical monad is found to be at once maintained and radically altered as the indispensible importance for the individual of the wholeness of his image, of his self-representation, the final support for him of all meaning and all signification.

viii   THE SOCIAL–HISTORICAL CONTENT OF SUBLIMATION

The psychogenetic perspective, by itself, is therefore radically incapable of accounting for the formation of the social individual, of the psyche's process of socialization. This is a truism which the vast majority of psychoanalysts – beginning with Freud himself – persist in ignoring. What is behind this obstinance, and the concealment of the social–historical which goes hand-in-hand with it, is the tenacious illusion that it is possible to reduce the psychical to the biological (or, more recently, to 'structure' and to logic), which is itself governed by the will to eliminate the imaginary, both as social imaginary and as the radical imaginary of the psyche – that is to say, as the unmasterable origin, which is perpetually at work, of history in general and of the history of the individual psyche; unmasterable in its actuality, unmasterable by thought. In this way, the same corporeal constitution, the same sexuality, the same Eros and Thanatos, the same oral, anal, genital drives always and everywhere at work, are held to produce, depending on unknown minor and external accidents, sometimes polyg-amy, sometimes monogamy, sometimes boomerangs and sometimes atomic bombs, sometimes a God-King and sometimes a people's assembly, sometimes shamans and sometimes psychoanalysts, some-times the glorification and official consecration of masculine homosexu-ality and sometimes the destruction of Sodom by heaven-sent fire. In the name of the scientific and rigorous mind, one ends up once again with this scientific monstrosity as a consequence: constant factors prod-uce variable effects. At most, one might then add – and this costs nothing – to this rather peculiar animal one more 'instinct', a drive for knowledge, and endow this 'drive' with a curious and singular property, which would distinguish it from all others – and this costs nothing either – that of 'progressing' by itself in its intrinsic results as well as in the modifications it is capable of introducing into 'reality'. But here, too, 'hypotheses' which cost nothing – like the phylogenetic hypotheses to which Freud so often resorts – are of no benefit either. Gratuitous, they are useless as well.

In this way, the 'oral' and the 'genital' seem to be self-evident as consequences of the biological constitution of the human being, as well as as conditions for the preservation of the individual and of the species. But this is, to be sure, infinitely removed from *what* human oral and genital characters *are* in general, even further removed from what they are, *in other ways*, in different societies, and, in conclusion, *in other ways*, too, in different individuals in the same culture. But even this semblance of biological 'necessity' collapses when we consider the anal drive. For, obviously, there is no way to ascribe, directly or indirectly, to the biological functions of elimination the weight of the constitution of an 'anal drive'. The anal drive *as such* and as a *drive* is a pure social–historical creation. It has nothing to do with the function of elimination (why, then, is there no respiratory drive?) nor even with a particular 'sensitivity' (or erogeneity) of the anal zone, as this can, in a sense, be observed in certain mammals. Nothing necessitated or even truly induced, in this case, from a biological or corporeal point of view, its transformation into a privileged field of subjective experience and of cathexis of such decisive importance for the psychical and social life of the individual. There is an anal drive only due to the fact, not that the anal zone is erotogenic 'by itself' but this erogenicity is fixed and maintained because the faeces are posited as a significant object in the relations between the child and the mother. And they are posited as such only because around the faeces and 'cleanliness' are tied (or more precisely, *can* be tied depending on the institution of society, highly variable in this respect) a series of significations which are *totally* arbitrary from a biological point of view. It is contradictory to conceive of a society in which people would not, at least in some minimal way, cathect heterosexual genitality. But it is by no means contradictory to conceive of a society in which people would defecate and urinate wherever they happened to be and when they felt the need to. Faeces are an object which exists only through its social–historical creation as an object. Animal-man does not produce faeces, he eliminates excrement. And beyond or before this aspect, the erogenic character of the anal zone (as privileged in the general erogenicity of the entire corporeal surface) is totally incomprehensible outside of the alchemy of the psychical imagination, capable of making this orifice and what comes out of it the supports for the most astonishing and widely varying representations.

One can thus pretend to provide oneself with an 'oral drive' or a 'genitality' as more or less self-evident; but one cannot do the same thing with the anal drive. But neither can one supply oneself with an anal drive in general and attempt to reduce the 'sublimation' of it to social–historical products and institutions as different as work and order, money and painting. For not only is this sublimation impossible if its objects are not offered and presented to it from somewhere else, and they are presented in this way only by being socially created and *instituted*. But this sublimation is in each case *such as it is*, in each case specific – otherwise there would be no psyche, no drive, no psychoanalysis – through the institution of society which renders *obligatory* for the innumerable individuals of society *particular* objects of sublimation to the exclusion of others, and these objects are caught up in relations with one another which not only give them their signification but make the life of society possible as a relatively coherent and organized life. This is precisely the *very opposite* of the 'variability' or the 'vicariousness' of the objects of drives as this was posited by Freud,[52] which has a meaning only in the field of the individual, narrowly considered. Society can exist only to the extent that the objects of sublimation are at once typical, categorized, *and* mutually complementary; in the same way as, correspondingly, the identificatory roles socially presented to individuals have to be both typical *and* complementary. The pole of identification 'lord', for instance, proposed to the son of a lord in the feudal period, would be purely empty in its *psychical* functioning (or would only produce strange psychotics) unless parallel to this the society proposed and *imposed* upon innumerable other children the pole of identification and the significations making them serfs for the rest of their lives.

Let us illustrate this situation with one more example. A psychoanalytic interpretation should be able to account for what enables an individual to assume, more or less, his actual situation, which, to be sure, is always a social situation. There can be no capitalist society unless capitalists and proletarians are reproduced daily in millions of instances by social functioning, where this functioning produced, scarcely a century before, only semi-feudal lords and peasants. The psychogenetic processes that enable individuals to assume the situations of capitalists and proletarians have a critical importance, they form one of the conditions for the existence of the capitalist system – something Marxists generally forget, by wanting to reduce them to an epiphenomenon, an automatic concomitant to the 'mode of production'. These processes are irreducible to purely social processes; but at the same time they logically and effectively presuppose them, since what is in question here is forming the individual as capitalist or proletarian, and not as lord, patrician or Amon-Râ priest. Nothing in the psyche as such can produce *these* significations, the *world* of significations without which they are nothing, the *mode of being* of these significations as instituted. No 'constitutive' component, aberration of formation, vicariousness of the object of drives or the perversity of parents could predispose, in Athens or in Rome, a child to become President of General Motors; no such component can predispose a child, in Paris or New York, to become a pharaoh or a shaman – except to the extent that it would make him psychotic and that the content of the delirium can make use of historically available significations. 'Naive self-evidence': but *why*? And in particular, why is psychoanalytic discourse so often obliged to act as though the 'self-evidence' did not exist?

Let us look a bit closer at the capitalist as an individual. It is not enough simply to recall that, for this type of individual to exist, the subject has to relate to another, to others and to 'reality'. What 'reality'? Symmetrical to the stubborn denial of the imaginary and consubstantial to it is the equally stubborn and general denial by psychoanalysis of the historical character of reality which is never anything but social reality, and the emptiness of psychoanalytic discourses when they are asked to state which reality is in question and what makes it a reality. For someone who lives in capitalist society reality is what is posited by the institution of capitalism as constituting reality – and this is what counts and is pertinent from the psychoanalytic point of view, not universal gravitational force or the structure of the atomic nucleus. This reality is, in this case, that of a host of second-level institutions, of socially categorized individuals (capitalists and proletarians), of machines, and so forth – social–historical creations held together by the common reference to a magma of imaginary social significations which are those of capitalism, and by means of this common reference these significations actually *do exist* and exist as *what* they are both in general and for each individual. This reality as a social–historical creation includes within it, and would be impossible without, the social construction of individuals who *are* capitalists. This construction, in its turn, requires much more than, for instance, the anal drive and its 'sublimation' in the strict sense. To say that money corresponds to a sublimation of faeces from the psychogenetic point of view *presupposes* that money exists as a social institution (and this does not go without saying nor is it a purely external accident) *and* as a condition for sublimation, practically obligatory in a given type of society (for without this, a society such as this could never exist, nor could the individuals who are born there survive). There is much more, however, for capitalism implies something much more specific than the intensive investment of money or even ownership in general – both from a social–historical and from a psychoanalytic perspective. As a psychical formation, a capitalist in the proper meaning of the term is not a hoarder, a usurer or someone who accumulates land-holdings – neither a Grandet nor a Jérôme Nicolas Séchard.[53] He belongs to another universe, sociologically as well as psychoanalytically speaking. Being a capitalist, as were the individuals who incarnated the birth, propagation and triumph of industrial capitalism for the past centuries in Western Europe, is investing not money or ownership in general but machines and enterprises, and investing in a specific way. Being a capitalist does not consist in the relation to the machine as such: those who invent machines or have a passion for them are not, or are only accidentally, capitalists. Nor the controlling relation in a collectivity, the relation to power as such: a capitalist is not, generally, a minister or a bishop. Nor the relation to some sort of 'rationality' or 'rationalization' as such: a capitalist is not a mathematician, a scientist or a philosopher. Being a capitalist is investing this specific object, which can exist only as a social institution: the enterprise as the complex arrangement of men and machines, implying an indefinite number of other institutions and processes outside of the enterprise itself; *and* it is investing the latter as the support and instrumentation of a specific subjective phantasmatic formation, that of an entity continuously expanding and proliferating, tending towards continual self-aggrandizement and submerged in a nutritive solution, a 'market' in which anonymous, social supply and demand are to be created and exploited. All this would be *no more than* phantasy or the component of a delirium *if it did not happen* that this entity is also something which can be realized socially, and actually already is realized. And it also happens that this capitalist would not exist, that his 'sublimation' would simply be a form of psychosis, if, for instance, at the same moment the 'sublimation' of other individuals did not push them to invent machines, to constitute exact sciences, to reform religion or to work at establishing national States, not as phantasmatic elements but as components of the institution of society.

ix THE INDIVIDUAL AND REPRESENTATION IN GENERAL

The social institution of the individual must make a world exist for the psyche as a public and common world. It cannot absorb the psyche into society. Society and psyche are inseparable and irreducible one to the other. The countless correspondences and correlations that can be observed – a few of these were mentioned above – between, for instance, certain important features of social imaginary significations and the tendencies or requirements proper to the socialization of the psyche can never lead us to believe that one group can be deduced or produced on the basis of the other – in the first place because their *mode of being* is radically other.

Considering things from the perspective of the institution of society, we can say that the latter must allow – or is not able not to allow – the individual the possibility of finding and of bringing into existence for himself a meaning in the instituted social signification. But it must also allow him – and whatever it does cannot help but allow him – a private world, not only as a minimum circle of 'autonomous' activity (as we know, this circle can be reduced to a very narrow area) but also as a world of representation (and of affect and intention), in which the individual will always be his own centre.

It amounts to the same thing to say that the institution of society can never absorb the psyche in so far as it is radical imagination – and that, moreover, this is a positive condition of the existence and the functioning of society. The constitution of the social individual does not and cannot abolish the psyche's creativity, its perpetual alteration,

the representative flux as the continuous emergence of other representations. And this leads us to consider once again the question of
representation in general.

From the point of view we are concerned with here, nothing distinguishes unconscious representation from the banal, conscious representations in which we are constantly submerged, or rather, which in a
sense we are, with respect to the fact of their being or to their mode
of being. If the latter is considered for itself and without preconceptions;
if we manage to strip it of its covering of ensemblist–identitary organization; if we can allow ourselves, even the slightest bit, to undertake a
destructuration of the orthodox social vision constantly imposed on us;
if the *époché*, the effort to bracket prior judgement with respect to
what gives itself to us as it gives itself, is aimed not simply and not so
much at a thesis about its being or non-being but at its mode of being,
its logical organization, the features that make it be as it is, each of us
can perceive that he has a direct and immediate access to what escapes
identitary logic.

An individual's representations at every instant and throughout his
entire life – or, better, the representative (-affective-intentional) flux
that an individual *is*, are first and foremost a magma. They are not a
set of definite and distinct elements and yet they are absolutely not
pure and simple chaos. A *particular* representation can be extracted
from it or marked out there – but this operation is obviously transitory
in relation to the thing itself (and even essentially pragmatic and
utilitarian), and the result, as such, is neither true nor false, neither
correct nor incorrect. A fragment, aspect or moment of the representative flux is made to exist – by means of *legein* – as provisionally
separated from the rest, *with respect to* ... and for a given end and, in
order to do this, it is generally attached to a particular linguistic term.

There is no need to repeat or to transpose here what has already
been said about unconscious representation. We were asking: how
many representations are there in a dream? We might just as well ask:
how many representations are there in a representation? What is the
representation, for instance, of dog, of house, of the sea or of my
friend C.? How many distinct and definite terms do they include; what
is essential there and what is secondary; what is the subject and what
are the attributes? If someone talks to me of a dog, for example, I
think of or I represent to myself – I give myself an image, a figure, I
figure to myself – dog as no particular dog – not a basset or a German
Shepherd or a terrier or a mongrel – but which just as well could be
a particular one without bothering me or preventing me from talking
about dogs; I can imagine a muzzle, a head and ears, paws and a furry
body, or none of that, or a specific dog with particular clarity. None
of this prevents me from 'recognizing' – from representing to myself,
imagining or providing myself a figure of – a dog in a breed of animal
unknown to me, of a strange kind, all the while saying to myself, 'What
a strange dog.' It is only if I am acting, theoretically or practically, as

a zoologist, and in the case where a doubt, a virtual or actual question arises, that I make up a list of relevant and decisive features of being-a-dog to decide whether a given animal is or is not a dog. It is only in the context of a mathematical discussion on the rigorousness of a demonstration that I ask myself whether the triangle I am imagining to myself, or drawing on the blackboard, is isosceles or scalene, and if what I say about it depends on these particularities. Otherwise, I have no problem representing-figuring-imagining the triangle which is always in my representation-figure-image *one* particular triangle with specific features without necessarily being this one and yet without these features being indifferent, although they are not clearly posited as being either relevant or accidental.

All of these examples are taken from a particular region of representation, perceptual representation (or the 'ordered' representation of the triangle) in which the weight of identitary–ensemblist logic is especially great. This can create – and interminably does create in inherited thinking – the illusion that what is undetermined in representation is deficient in relation to the supposed (postulated) perfect determination of 'things', due to insufficient attention, to the incomplete, but always capable of being completed and rectified, exercise of our logical faculties, etc. It would be only too easy to pursue this illusion, and the conception it belongs to, onto its own terrain and up to its frontiers to grant it complete attention, the most penetrating logical faculties, the entire universe of mathematics and the most powerful tools, and then to put the question to it: very well, now tell us if what you 'see' there is a wave or a particle, both at once, sometimes one and sometimes the other while staying the same – and how is all this possible? In order to have a perception of 'things' as determined, we must pay attention to them – but not too much; we must take them seriously – but not too seriously. We must pay attention to them and take them seriously just within the limits our social–historical institution sets for us as conscious individuals acting in and through *legein* and *teukhein*. The social–historical institution of the 'thing' and its perception is homologous to the social–historical institution of the *individual*, not simply because a 'thing' and a *particular* thing can exist only for individuals but also because the individual, as such, is a cardinal 'thing', necessarily instituted as such *also* by every society.[54] If the limits of attention and seriousness are overstepped, what was the full and apparently determined being of the 'thing' suddenly becomes a hole in being, an undetermined enigma slipping away on all sides, fascination, sinking-away, philosophical signification, poem or starting point for an interminable series of scientific explorations, attitudes which do not necessarily concord with one another.

Let us consider representation as such, the representative flux which constantly presents itself to us or which, in a sense, we ourselves are; let us attempt to rid it of the 'perception of things' and of all that has been said about the reflection, the imitation, the receptivity of

impressions and the spontaneity of concepts, the unveiling of beings in
the clearing of Being, and so forth. Let us close our eyes, plug our
ears and let ourselves go in memory, in daydreams, in nothing at all.
Nothing at all: this is not possible.[55] *There is* – and it matters not a
whit whether *what* there is 'is' or 'is not', whether it is 'real' or 'not
real' – the uninterrupted surging forth of a representative flux, of
images and figures of all kinds (visual, acoustic, verbal and so on)
which present themselves or jostle one another, stay awhile or flit by,
enter into one another or move away without ever being resolved, fuse
together or decompose, attaching to one another while continually
disappearing. Outside of dreamless sleep, there is always an image in
the most general, the most indefinite sense of the term; there is always
representation.

What interests us here is not the fact of being of the representation
(this certainly poses interminable questions, which do not concern the
fact that there is representation, but the sense of: being) but its mode
of being; not its mode of being for someone but its mode of being in
itself. Concerning this mode of being, there is no need to go on and
on about it: it is perfectly clear, to the extent that it is totally mysterious
and impossible to grasp by all the means available to inherited logic,
to identitary–ensemblist logic. We could repeat here all that was stated
above concerning unconscious representation. Representation is neither
one nor many, and its determinations are neither essential nor indifferent to it. It contains or presents or allows us to see relations of
belonging, of inclusion, and so on, but these relations are undetermined
or constantly redetermined; the respective positions or functions of the
'terms' that may be discerned there are fluid and constantly redefined.
All that can be said in general about its organization can be reduced
to this practically empty condition: there is always figure and ground
(but the figure can *itself* become ground and the ground, figure, as
we know). It would perhaps be preferable to say: there is always
differentiation or heterogeneity or minimal otherness. This otherness,
however, as concrete otherness makes itself other than itself, and we
can say almost nothing in general about its supports, from which it is
inseparable in each case. We depend on these supports when we apply
to representation the schema of separation or of discretion; but this
application is always, in an unlimited number of ways, artificial. The
representation of a man's head is never really separate from the man,
and if I imagine a head that is literally cut off and severed from the
trunk, it can still carry along with it the vague body of an indefinite
person. Assuming that this separation has been made, different sorts
of relations between these segmented representations can exist, but the
only one that is always found is the relation of *referral* (*renvoi*): every
representation refers to other representations (what in psychology is
termed 'association' is but one particular case of this). Refers to them:
generates them or is capable of making them arise. How is this, on the
basis of what, supported on what and tending towards what? Nothing

universal can be said about this. In particular, it is impossible to determine the class of *b*s to which *a* refers, to establish the totality of terms which maintain a relation of referral with any other.[56]

To be sure, the representative flux also appears to be subjected to the relation of temporal succession – and so, to a relation of order and even of total order. But once we go beyond the context of the social–historical institution of time as identitary–ensemblist time, the time of marking definite and distinct events, we cannot avoid the question: is the representative flux subjected to a relation of temporal succession, or do we find here the self-generation of the representative flux as the emergence of otherness which *is* as well the continued creation of time or the time of continued creation? What Kant called time as the pure form of intuition – that is to say, the pure representation of succession, 'pure' meaning here: independent of any 'term', whether or not this term is empirical, in which one would inspect the succession from one to another, the succession from nothing to nothing or from same to same, the generation of the same as different – is this really possible or does it not presuppose, is it not inseparable from the emergence of otherness as it is figured, as the emergence of *another* figure? This question has already been discussed above in a more general context, and there is no point in repeating what was said there. It is enough to recall that the emergence of otherness, as representative flux, is always both temporalization and spatialization, since what exists is never an indivisible point but instead an image or a figure implying at once spacings, gaps, extensions, differentiations. Here it is obvious, as has been known for a long time, that the linearity of time is simply the result of the conscious grasp of representations, their projection (in the geometrical sense) onto the unidimensional axis of speech, which itself is required by the 'one-some-thing-distinct-and-definite-at-a-time' implied by identitary *legein*.

To the extent, then, to which the determinations and the relations of ensemblist logic appear in this context, they do not, even minimally, occupy the same role or function as in the areas where this logic actually does have a grasp of its object. Essentially stripped of their relevance, they constitute nothing in the object, reveal nothing of it, they make nothing in it intelligible. All they do is to enable us to talk about it and, with this restriction, enable us to conceive of it. In this sense, of course, we cannot do without these determinations and relations, and in this sense, too, they cannot help but impinge on what we can say. The paradox – or better, the antinomy – which results from this (and which must have been long apparent to the reader and may, perhaps, have proved an irritation to him or to her, since we are continually writing things like 'two representations are not two representations, a representation that contains another does not contain it,' since we too must constantly proceed by argumentation) cannot be eliminated by means of identitary logic. But at the same time, an antinomy in the strong sense of the term exists only from the point of view of this logic.

We have to learn, and continually relearn, to live and to think along two circuits which constantly lead back to one another, which interconnect everywhere and continuously but which are neither identical nor reducible to one another and which, moreover, cannot be deduced from one another: these circuits are those of identitary logic and of thinking. When it is a matter of representation, the means of ensemblist–identitary logic do little more than allow us to speak of it. They function here basically as terms and means for *marking out*. They allow us to posit, in a transitory and external way, what we are speaking of or 'what we are referring to', and the aspect under which it is referred to. The impression is then created that 'what we are referring to' is thus caught up in the network of the customary ensemblist–identitary relations; but this impression is illusory. In contrast to what occurs in the areas where identitary logic is, to varying degrees, relevant, here there is no genuine grasp on the object, outside of the possibility of marking it out and talking about it.

It might be said that already in itself the expression 'what we are referring to' implies not only an entire logic but an entire ontology as well. This is precisely what I am saying – adding that this ontology is not the *whole* of ontology and that this is the place where the almost imperceptible shift takes place. We cannot decide up to what point we are obliged to accept and to assume for ourselves the ontology carried by language or rather by its unexpungible dimension of *legein*, solely on the basis of the fact that we cannot for one second dream of a thought without language or outside of language. This decision must be taken after reflection on *what* we are thinking and on its mode of being. And the fact that we are able to do this also results from language's not being simply *legein* but also relating just as much to the magma of significations.

In the expression 'what we are referring to', the 'referring to' is not univocal. If what we are referring to is a dog, for instance, a 'real' dog, then 'referring to' has a particular signification. Independently of the interminably enigmatic character of the fact of being-a-dog, of the indefinite nature of the different ways in which a dog or the dog can be taken, and the points of view from which it can be considered, the expression immediately posits and fixes its 'objective' correlate as stable, observable by all, placed with certainty in a host of determined relations and attributions, which are not only specific but categorial and, finally, ontological. A dog as dog is *actually one*, the *qua* ... in terms of which it is *one* despite its millions of cells and so forth, is essential. Its interminable exchanges with the universe do not keep it from being this well-defined border *with respect to* another essential aspect, by reason of which it is a living thing. It is excluded that the dog simply dissolve, that it be replaced by a theorem, a melody, or anything other than a continuation of itself, that it contain other dogs (except embryos, if it is a pregnant female) or that it be a part of other dogs. *Being* and *one* have the same meaning, Aristotle used to say.

Referring to *a* dog is immediately situating it in terms of a host of determinations, positing it as or recognizing in it an ontological thickness which is essentially defined, relating to an already actualized coagulation (although this is always incomplete), to something that is *already done* and stated as *already done*. Here, we can clearly see why the 'thing' in general was almost fatally destined to become the logical and ontological prototype.

However, if we refer to a simple representation – a memory, a dream or even 'my' representation of the dog 'at this moment' – the expression 'refer to' has an entirely different signification. It entails, by reason of its own qualities, almost nothing at all – outside of a first term of marking, an initial point of support upon which to begin to speak and to think. Saying 'this representation ...' commits us to nothing and entails nothing (other than empty commonplaces) with respect to what is in question. This expression is infinitely slight; there is no essential *with respect to* ... here, no categorial organization mobilized *ipso facto* by the expression. The latter imposes practically nothing at all and at the same time excludes almost nothing; it has no content and no function other than provisionally identifying something fluid and fleeting, out of which stem an indefinite number and direction of vectors, and of which only one thing is categorically certain: that it will dissolve or burst apart to leave in its stead something totally other than 'itself'. That to which we are related here is a concreteness or a coagulation *yet to be* realized, something that is not made but that *makes itself* by making itself as *something else*. And we see again here why this region – and the mode of being proper to it – has never been taken into account by inherited philosophy, why it became, and continues to be, the object of a stubborn denial, why the logic and ontology of being as determinacy have always felt, and rightly so, mortally threatened by representation, imagination and the imaginary.

Again and again: we have just written 'identify'; we say that representation, the representative flux, makes 'itself': 'itself' – who or what is this? The problematic I wish to bring to light reappears once again here. For, at the same time, everything slips away from us and we are reduced to silence, even 'internally', if *this* representation is not indeed *this* representation, and hence: identical to itself and different from any other. And we are irremediably lost if we take these terms as full determinations bearing on the things themselves and if we forget that the being of representation is nothing other than this perpetual and omnidirectional flight – temporal and spatial – outside of itself (where the term 'itself' reiterates once again the same problematic and so on, indefinitely), that representation does not lend itself to the ensemblist–identitary grasp of *legein* except in the most external and empty fashion, and that, finally, *legein* itself could neither exist nor function if it were not itself also rooted in representation.

To say that everything lends itself to ensemblist–identitary logic and to its determinations – the logic and the determinations of *legein* – from the moment it can be *said* is a tautology – the tautology of which the major part of the history of philosophy stands as the interminable, rich and fecund development. This tautology becomes deceptive as soon as the difference is rubbed out between those domains in which identitary logic is more or less fully operative and those in which it operates simply as a means of taking markings, unavoidable yet external, formal and nearly empty. And this too can be said only by using the terms and relations forged in and through *legein*. But if it can be said it is because we can think beyond *legein* and even think the limits of *legein* which appear in *legein* only as indeterminations and as raw contradictions, provoked by *legein* itself and which, in accordance with its own rules should cancel it out, leaving *nothing* remaining. If we take the requirements of *legein* seriously, *legein* destroys itself: everything must be defined – but there are, obviously, and necessarily, undefinable first terms and so all that follows is undefinable as well and hence *is nothing*; everything must be determined – but everything is not, the undecidable exists, and if one were to take formalism and the identitary requirement completely seriously, one would have to say that the totality of mathematics is null and void (except the operations on finite sets). Long before Gödel, the founder of logic himself knew this perfectly well: of the first and final terms there is *nous*, and not logos. The logical use of logic requires something other than logic: *nous*, the grasp of thought. Outside of this, *legein* is at once empty and suspended in mid-air; for *legein* cannot be closed in upon itself by remaining what it is and by conforming to its own rules.

This empty character of identitary logic when it is separated from thought has been masked for centuries by the will o'the wisp of the *concept*, which creates the illusion of the possibility of a discourse at once identitary and full. This rock of traditional logic-ontology falls to dust, however, as soon as it is touched; this pure representative of a full logic is but a conglomeration of marking terms and significations. Whether the term of concept is given the restrictive acceptation of a decisory definition, whether one speaks of the systematic ensemble of true judgements referring to the same object or whether it is qualified as a determined extension and comprehension, the same aporias arise, the same enigmas appear. A decisory definition is, to be sure, simply a marking term which has been broadened and made explicit (formed by a group of such terms), which refers to the totality of language (if the explicitation of the terms comprising it is asked for), which can be decisory while being totally 'external' to what is in question and which, at the same time, is never decisory except in a given context and for certain people. To say that a systematic ensemble of judgements refers to the same object obviously raises immediately the question: what is an *object*? and under what conditions is it the *same*? This question receives a certain response, one which itself is interminably enigmatic, only within a certain metaphysics, the metaphysics of substance-essence, *ousia*. Aristotle knew this perfectly well: definition, he said, is discourse that signifies *to ti ên einai*, that which it was to be, *tou ti esti kai tês ousias*, which concerns *that which is* and the essence.[57] Judgement (*apophainesthai*) in so far as it states something *about something* (*ti kata tinos*) presupposes not only the logical but the ontological assured and determined positing of *ousia*, the essence-substance of *that about which* one speaks. This assurance and this determination *preceding all logic* are, moreover, secured for thought, for *nous*, by its very essence: '... for the *nous* is true, not always, but when it thinks that which is according to that which it was to be, not when it thinks something *of* something (*ti kata tinos*).[58] *Nous* can be mistaken in assertion, in judgement – but it is always assured access to the essence. Just as seeing is never mistaken, Aristotle continues, about the proper object of seeing (*idion*) – this is white – although it can be mistaken about the attribution – this white object is a man – so *nous* can be mistaken about attributions, but not about what could be termed its own, proper object: the essence. If this point is not secured, if this anchoring does not exist, then all attributions simply float on the ocean of discourse. *This* metaphysics – the metaphysics *at once* of essences and of thought – is necessarily implied whenever we speak seriously of concepts.[59] Along with this are implied its numerous aporias and the supplementary means it provides for itself in order to deal with them. What are we to do, for instance, with the distinction between the extension and the comprehension of a concept, apparently so clear-cut? In the name of what can a true judgement concerning one or more members of the class corresponding to the extension of the concept be excluded from the comprehension of the concept? In order to exclude it, the distinction would have to be introduced between essence and 'accidents', power and act, essential and accidental possibilities, and so on. The fact that Socrates did exist does not concern the comprehension of the concept of man. Is this so certain? Does the fact that philosophers have existed concern this comprehension or not? And beginning *when*? Does the power to philosophize belong to the essence of man or is it a *sumbebēkos*, an accidental property? 'All men by nature (*physei*) desire to know.' The power to philosophize and the actualizing of this power are then part of man's *ousia*. Since when? From all time, in all time and for all time. For *ousia* is *ti ên einai*, that which it was to be, that which it was from all time and for all time destined to be. If we want the concept in its fullest sense, then we must also desire this metaphysics, this ontology, without which it is nothing. And desire its consequences as well: for instance, *essentially*, with respect to its essence, everything has been determined from all time; whatever is not so determined is – by definition – no more than an accident. Hegel never said anything more than this.[60]

There is no concept which is logical and full. The full concept is merely the counterpart in identitary logic to substance-essence, the central position of identitary ontology. If we move away from this position, as we are forced to do, the concept of concept becomes empty – and useless. There are marking terms which, by growing broader and becoming enriched in discourse, become decisory definitions; these are always transitory and eminently relative. And there are significations which also lend themselves – although not always and not always essentially – to a logical elaboration, which is essentially interminable.

Representation is radical imagination. The representative flux is, makes itself, as self-alteration, the incessant emergence of the other in and through the positing (*Vor-stellung*) of images or figures, an imaging which unfolds, brings into being and constantly actualizes what appears retrospectively, to reflective analysis, as the pre-existing conditions of its possibility: temporalization, spatialization, differentiation, alteration. (The unconscious is unaware of logical and 'real' time, not of time as such: dreams take place in dream-time or unfold a dream-time). There is no thought without representation; thinking is always necessarily putting representations into motion, in certain directions and according to certain rules (directions and rules which are not necessarily mastered): figures, schemata, word-images – and this is not accidental, not an external condition, not a leaning-on, but the very element of thinking. To deny it would be to affirm the incoherent fictions of a thought without language, a transcendental language or language as condition external to thinking. All consciousness is consciousness of .... But representation is not necessarily representation of ... (something which would be external to representation). Obviously, some representations are: for example, perceptive representations, called perceptions, the putting-into-images of ... (something about which nothing can be said except in and through another representation). Here, it will be forever impossible absolutely to separate what comes from *that which is put into images* and *what puts* into images, the radical imagination, the representative flux. In the same way, representation (*Vorstellung*) is not re-presentation (*Vertretung*); it is not there for something else or in place of something else, to re-present it a second time. What, then, did the characteristic and fundamental chord of *Tristan* re-present when it welled up in Wagner's mind?

x THE PREJUDICE OF PERCEPTION AND THE PRIVILEGE OF 'THINGS'

Why has representation always been thought of – if indeed it ever has truly been thought – in relation to what it is not in order immediately to be reduced to confused thinking, an imitative and defective hotchpotch which, through a sufficient and adequate effort of attention, could be restored as thought, pure intuition or perception? Or, why has it been considered a projection screen which, unfortunately, separates the 'subject' and the 'thing'; or even, by the decrees of a recent 'ontological' mode, suppressed outright, denounced as a fabrication of these miserable modern times, intended fraudulently to mask our forgetting of being? Why has it always been taken for what it is not? Because it could be grasped in no other way by inherited thought, because traditional logic and ontology have no grasp on it. The problem of representation is nothing other than the problem of radical imagination in its most basic manifestation; the concealment of both stems from the same deep-lying factors.

For representation calls into question, and strictly speaking destroys, both the thesis on being which underlies Greco-Western philosophy from beginning to end, according to which being is considered as determinacy and its essential consequences, being as one, being as sameness, as the same for all, hence being as common – *koinon* – and the type of logical organization consubstantial, homologous to this thesis. What is given in and through representation considered for itself fails to conform to the most basic logical schemata. Inherited thought has always shunned this, with embarrassment and horror; for – just as it could see in dreams no more than the scoria of psychical functioning – it could find in representation merely the absence or the scrambling of the schemata without which it cannot exist. In this way one can explain the apparent paradox constituted by the violent critique and the vehement denunciation of the word and the fact of representation, at the very moment when psychoanalytic theory set it back at the centre of the life of the subject and strongly brought out its a-logical characteristics – whether this critique was made by philosophers such as Heidegger, who sought to ignore psychoanalysis (and sexuality, and along with these, society, power and politics) or, more comically, by others who adhere to psychoanalysis or refer to it. The paradox is merely apparent for, much more than the moral order of society, what psychoanalysis put so profoundly into question – moreover, without being aware of this itself – was its logical and ontological order.

In the same way, representation had to be criticized or reduced in order to save being, since being means being-determined, being one, being the same, being the same for all, being common – and since representation as such was unaware of these norms or transgresses them. To accept representation in the first place as irreducible would be to reduce being and the world to dust, cry with one voice idealists, realists and sceptics, in order, then, to conclude, some of them, that representation does not exist or else that it can be reduced to something else, while others hold that a common world does not exist or that nothing can be said about it. As if at all costs it had to be asserted that *what* each of us hears, sees, thinks or sees while listening to the *Mass in B minor does not exist* in order to save the being of the *Mass in B minor* or to make it 'intelligible'. The being of the *Mass*, however, consists in this *as well*, the power of bringing into being the irreducible other for all of those who hear it, interminably, as long as there are these humans and this music. As for making the being of the *Mass* or of the world intelligible, in the accepted sense of this word, the effort has, fortunately, proved to be futile.

So representation has never been considered for itself but has always been carried back to the point of view of the question: what does it provide with respect to truth? what is its contribution to the constitution of knowledge? to what extent does it allow an access to being (always posited implicitly, therefore, as an *elsewhere* and *solely elsewhere*, a single elsewhere, unique, one and common)? And thus it has always been seen as a reflection or a copy (generally an imperfect one), an image of ..., which is not perfectly clear and distinct, a screen between consciousness and the thing or the world, *doxa*, and finally a source of error and the siren of non-being. Its minute being originates in what representation is not; its own organization, in so far as one must, at all costs, be constructed for it, is always conceived of on the basis of two other *constructa*: the 'subject' and the 'thing'. It then becomes a set and stable 'spectacle', a painting hung 'within' the subject, a defective tracing of the 'thing', a weakened and retained perception.

Representation, however, is not a painting hung within the subject decked out with various kinds of *trompe-l'œil*, or else itself an immense *trompe-l'œil*; it is not a bad photograph of the 'spectacle of the world' which the subject clutches to his heart and can never mislay. Representation is perpetual presentation, the incessant flux in and through which anything can be given. It does not belong *to* the subject, it *is*, to begin with, the subject. It is that by reason of which we are in the light even when we close our eyes, that by reason of which we are light in the darkness, that by which *the dream itself is light.* It is that by which, even if we 'are thinking about nothing', this thick and continuous flow which we ourselves are always exists, that by which we are present to ourselves only by being present to something other than ourselves even when no 'thing' is 'present', that by which our presence to ourselves can never exist except as the presence of that which is not simply ourselves. Representation is precisely that by which this 'us' can never be closed up within itself, that by which it overflows on all sides, constantly makes itself other than it 'is', posits itself in and through the positing of figures and exceeds every given figure. Stupidly assimilated to an alleged self-immanence of 'psychological consciousness', the representative flux makes the radical imagination visible, precisely, as immanent transcendence, as the passage to the other, as the impossibility for what 'is' to 'be' without bringing what is other into being – in short, it makes visible the artificial and manufactured character of the opposition between the immanent and the transcendent considered to be assured and absolute. As radical imagination, we are that which 'makes itself immanent' by positing a figure and that which 'transcends itself' by destroying this figure and by bringing into existence another figure. Representation is not tracing out the spectacle of the world, it is that in and through which at a given moment a world arises. It is not something that provides impoverished 'images' of 'things' but that of which certain segments take on the weight of an 'index of reality' and become 'stabilized', as well as they might, without this stabilization ever being assured once and for all, as 'perceptions of things'. To hold the contrary is to hold that one is personally in possession of the separation of the 'real' and the imaginary as fixed and indubitable and of the standard of its application in all circumstances – an assertion which does not merit one second's discussion. The cut-ups which in the representative flux produce 'images' alleged to be clearly separated – this is what the philosopher generally thinks of when he speaks of 'representation of ...' – leans, to be sure, on the 'forms', 'figures', 'singularities', 'differences', 'levels', 'pregnancies' which emerge in the representative flux, which this flux brings into being through its being; but these cut-ups constitute, at any rate, subsequent and secondary operation. The representative flux contains or, better, *creates* the supports and the seeds of this – otherwise, neither *legein* nor thought would be possible – but it is not the confused postcomposition of this operation.

In the concealment of representation and of imagination, the exclusive or, at any rate, the dominant preoccupation with 'things' and hence with perception, that is to say the *fetishism of reality*, have obviously played an essential role. Representation and imagination have been viewed – this has been the case, even if the terms were not pronounced, as soon as *doxa* was considered as opposed to *alētheia* – solely in opposition to the positing of a separate, distinct and determined entity, being as substance-essence, definite and independent, *by itself*; this positing, to begin with, is obviously that of 'things', co-originary with the institution of *legein* and *teukhein*, and hence co-originary with the institution of society. The 'thing' and the 'individual', the individual as 'thing' and as the one for whom there are indubitably 'things' are, to begin with, precisely that – dimensions of the institution of society.

The exorbitant ontological privilege granted to the *res* (*extensa* and *cogitans*, each always involving the other) translates the continued subordination of philosophy to the demands of the social–historical institution of *legein* and *teukhein*. There results from this a focusing on things and on perception – totally independent of the words employed; I am speaking of the underlying, imaginary *schema* – setting up the former as the generic type of being and the latter as the model of every relation to being.[61]

There is no essential change in this respect when the schema of perception is replaced by that of constitution. In the former, the thing is there, already given, I relate to it passively, even if my 'cooperation' is required; this cooperation is ontologically passive, it is governed and ruled by the 'thing' which is *what* it is, and, further off, by being itself, speaking in and through us, seeing in and through us, and doubtless also perceiving in and through us. And of course, just as in traditional theodicy we must not raise the question: why did God need to create man and the world, so in Heideggerian ontodicy, we must not raise the question: why can being speak, see and perceive only through our procuration? – In the second framework, I (as constituting conscious-ness) constitute or construct things by means of those 'functions', those universal types of operation and activity of the mind called the categories, freely modeling the amorphous clay provided to me by the receptivity of impressions; the thing is my synthesis (which itself means composition). In both cases, the schemata or rather: *the* schema of activity/passivity is sovereign. Now the secondary and reflexive charac-ter of this schema, the fact that it belongs to constructive constructions, to the conditions of production produced in and through *legein* and *teukhein* are obvious. Activity/passivity are modes in which socially–historically instituted individuals and things are related to one another. The schema of activity/passivity which has dominated the history of philosophy possesses no originary character, no privilege and no universal relevance. For example, it has no hold on the representa-tive flux: *there is* the emergence of representation; to say that I make it or suffer it is meaningless in the general case.

This focusing has been possible only by reason of – or has entailed – the covering over of another path, in a sense an unavoidable covering-over in relation to which perception and things are secondary and subsequent (which, to be sure, does not mean that they are deducible or constructible). On this path we observe that perception and things are not given at the outset but, psycho-genetically, *emerge* in the history of the subject, that there is a representative flux independent of perception and indubitably prior to the latter. This banal fact has always been truncated in its signification by the will to see in the history of the subject no more than the conditions that will enable it to reach the canonical state of a conscious subject perceiving correctly and normally real, distinct and definite things. As if there were no more to see and to think of in the infant and in the child than the imperfect adult. Certainly, the child *will become* an adult; but the fact that in the new-born there is always the possibility of an opening up to a world, of that enigmatic break which produces a double decentring of the representa-tive flux – one which is never complete – referring it to an 'ego' and to an 'outside', changes nothing as to the secondary and subsequent character of perception and of things, and as to the discontinuity they introduce in this flux and the impossibility of their ever becoming separate from it. We know that this break can be more or less of a failure, as is shown by various forms of early infant psychosis; but we also know that, for inherited ontology, pathological being is always *less* than 'normal' being, it is but a fraction of being (since in it are found simply fragments, debris of the essence, of *physis*, of that which makes being be by being *what* it is). Being has always, of course, also meant: the value and norm of being.

This emerging of perception and of things in the history of the subject can never be thought of solely from the psychogenetic perspective – or, more generally, from the *idiogenetic* perspective, as production, creation, maturation, discovery of or by *a* proper, singular (*idion*) subject. And yet it has almost always been considered from this perspective, whether by psychology (and even by psychoanalysis) or by philosophy, in its insurmountable egology; and this has been the case whether this emerging has been seen as a genesis or as given all at once, as reception or as constitution. The emergence of perception and of things can be thought of only from a sociogenetic or *koinogenetic* (*koinos*, common, shared) perspective. For not only is it in and through the institution of society that individuals, things and world exist (if they exist also for bacteria, it is up to the biologists to say so, on the condition that they say it without using language). But each society is *this particular* institution, bringing into being *this* particular magma of social imaginary significations and not some other one, in *this particular* way and not in any other, by means of a given socialization of the psyche and not some other. Each society brings it into being in the very materiality of the acts and sensorial dispositions of the subjects, in their vision, their hearing, their touch, even in the formation it imposes on their *corporeal imagination* (gestual, proprioceptive). Throwing a boomerang, dancing like the Africans, singing the flamenco are neither instinctive nor transcultural. ('Body techniques' are a special case of the corporeal imagination, more precisely, the part that can be codified). It also does this in particular through its language. It is not possible to think of a *perception*, in the full sense of the term, outside of language; this possibility would imply that, strictly speaking, no 'logical' function, no signification and no reflexivity intervene in the formation of 'things' (or, what amounts to the same thing, that they are all already in 'things'). It is just as impossible to think of a perception outside of the subject's *doing*, even if this is minimal. As in the case of language, *legein*, the language-code dimension of language is not separable from *langue*, its signifying dimension, once again in the case of doing, *teukhein*, the strictly functional dimension is not separable from social activity, from the significations in which the reciprocal activities of individuals are caught up. The conditions for and the organization of representing and doing as we participate in them can only be, and are, socially instituted.

The existence of a transcultural pole of the institution of the things – leaning, to be sure, on the natural stratum, both internal and external, as this stratum would already be articulated in part for animal-humans – still says nothing about *what* a thing is and what things are for a given society, any more than the existence of a transcultural pole of the individual says anything about *what* an individual is and *how* the individual is for a particular society. How great is the courage of the philosopher, the sociologist or the biologist – a courage we cannot claim for ourselves – who affirms the identity of the perception of things, in so far as it is the perception of things, for a man for whom nothing exists that is not inhabited, animated, intentional and for another man for whom things are most often and above all inert instruments, objects of possession or means of existing in the eyes of others; or who believes he possesses the means of separating rigorously a core of relations which man entertains with things and with the world, a core which would be always self-identical, from 'imaginary' branchings (which in this connection can only mean thoroughly fictive) which would surround it in this or that culture. But, since this sort of separation is not possible, we are unable to think of an individual perception essentially independent of the social institution of the individual, of the thing, of the world. And, conversely, we are able to think of this institution in the fact of its being, in its mode of being, and as *what* it is in each case, only as the creation of the social imaginary, which it is impossible to deduce or to construct on the basis of the presumed canonical perception of a world and of things deemed eternal by a man, himself eternal. We know of no opening up to the world which is not that of a social–historical individual, opening up to a *particular* institution of the world and relating to *particular* things. The psyche doubtless contains as potentiality its opening up to the world – we cannot conceive of it any other way, yet this is simply a tautology – but this opening is actualized only by means of the break imposed upon the psyche by its constitution as a social–historical individual. This 'actualization' is much more than the actualizing of preconstituted possibilities in the *physis* of the psyche, for if this were so, the psyche would always in every case be one and *the same*.

These considerations are not intended to juxtapose and to oppose a factual genesis to an order which would be *de jure*, a psychology and a sociology of the individual, the things and the world to their logic and their ontology, the empirical to the transcendental. Taken as absolute and as ultimate, these distinctions are practically meaningless; they hold only relatively and *with respect to* ... . All alleged transcendental foundations are in the end obliged to call upon a fact, and a raw fact at that: whether this is experience for Kant or the *Lebenswelt* for Husserl. Reciprocally, the idea of a science of facts which would not imply an ontology has never amounted to more than an incoherent phantasy of certain scientists; an incoherent phantasy which, as such and in terms of its content, already expresses a particular and particularly incoherent metaphysics.

Language, for instance, is not a factual but a logical, or, if you wish, transcendental, presupposition of full perception. What is in question here, however, is never a language in general, or the faculty of a speaking-being in general, but acceding to a determined language. And it is *de jure* and not *de facto* that no pure or transcendental language exists, the idea of such a language being in itself contradictory, not just once but many times over. So to say that a subject has access to a world (or that being-there encounters beings within the horizon of being) is to say, transcendentally and ontologically, that it exists in and through a *particular* language. (Whence, of course, the almost irresistible temptation for the philosopher who wants to be entirely self-consistent to say that every fact, including the *fact* of one particular language, German for instance, is *de jure*: Hegel). In this way, too, concerning the relation of things and of the world to the representative flux, we heavily underscored above that things and the world are, in each case, social–historical institutions, namely, in this respect, the creations of the social imaginary. But also, things and world exist only inasmuch as the psyche exists – and this also means, inasmuch as the subject is not reducible to its social–historical institution, inasmuch as it is always something other and more than its social definition of the individual, for otherwise it would be but a robot or a zombie. So that psychology (by which, to be sure, I do not mean the observation of rats in labyrinths) is the logical–transcendental condition for all ontology, for all reflection on things and the world, on beings and being. A world and things (and a logic) are possible only to the extent that there is a psyche and the madness of the psyche. There is no perception if there is no representative flux which, in a sense, is independent of perception. A subject that would have *only* perception would have *no* perception: it would be completely swallowed up by 'things', flattened up against them, crushed against the world, incapable of shifting its gaze and so just as incapable of fixing it on the world. And this is not, as has been flatly stated in connection with the imagination and the imaginary, a simple capacity for denying or negating that which is given. Without even speaking here of what is essential (that is, of the imagination as it radically forms, not *Einbildungskraft* but *Bildungskraft*, as that which puts into images and gives form) this implies and requires 'positively' that what 'is given' is always at the same time caught up in that which 'is not given', in an undefinable host of shadows which, far from constituting that which simply 'could not exist' each have a peculiar tenor other than *that which* is seen. There are 'things', that is, 'outside' depth and thickness, only because there is also thickness and depth 'inside'; there are fixity and resistance 'outside' only because there are also flexibility and fluidity 'inside'; just as there is mobility 'outside' only because there is also persistence 'inside'. There is perception only because there is also representative flux. From this point of view as well, the imaginary – as the social imaginary and as the imagination of the psyche – is the logical and ontological condition of the 'real'.

xi   REPRESENTATION AND THOUGHT

The imaginary is equally, to be sure, a condition for all thought – from the flattest, from quasi-non-thinking reduced to the almost mechanical manipulation of signs, if this were possible, to the richest and most profound. I shall return elsewhere to this question, the concealment of which, as already stated, has governed the entire history of philosophy. 'Logically' there is no thought without figures, schemata, images, word-images. As was discussed at length above, the operative schemata of discretion, order, coexistence, and succession cannot be constructed logically: every logical construction presupposes them. At once produced by social *legein* and presupposed by the latter, these schemata also emerge in another way as modalities of representation and in order to function must also be based upon the latter. Neither in social *legein* nor in psychical representation can these schemata exist and operate if they are not carried by figures/images, posited arbitrarily, in an unmotivated manner by the imaginary and the imagination. I might mention in passing that in this lies the profound, albeit incomplete truth (because it is egological and neglects the social dimension and language) of Kant's Transcendental Aesthetic and his doctrine of schematism, which has never been questioned, as has been affirmed for over a century, by non-Euclidean geometries or the generalization of the notion of number. For what Kant was intending under the title of pure intuition and the schemata of transcendental imagination (whose connection with a particular stage of knowledge proves, here, to be accidental) was the non-deducible, inconstructible root presupposed by every construction or deduction, as also the non-inducible, non-inferable root presupposed by every induction or empirical inference, of imaginary *mathesis*: that which can only be described as indissociably aestheticological but which precedes in fact all aesthetics and all logic, all *aisthesis* and all *logos*. This root is the possibility implied in and through representation of making the most basic schemata emerge and of providing a figure for them, that is, *presentifying* them, thus making possible even the first 'logical' operations and allowing the separation within the representative flux of an ensemble of objects, capable of being determined with respect to their consistency and their reciprocal relations and, to begin with, with respect to their respective *place* in a 'space' and in a 'time'. The fact that this 'space' and this 'time' are here no more than specifications of a receptacle in general, and the fact that Kant thought of them as independent not only of any particular content of the representative flux but of any content *whatsoever* of this flux – which he terms the a priori – whereas they can exist and be what they are only in and through the otherness that emerges from this, the continuous creation of other figures, the unfolding of the works of the radical imagination, the fact that space and time can then appear as 'pure' only for a *second-order* reflexive separation – all this should be clear after what was stated above concerning the philosophical institution of time. It must simply be added that all this would serve no purpose and that the radical imagination could never become thought if the schemata and the figures that it brings into being simply continued to be caught up in the indefinite character of the representative flux, if they were not 'fixed' and 'stabilized' in material–abstract 'supports' (material in so far as a determined *this or that*, abstract in so far as holding beyond a determined *this* or *that*) namely, briefly speaking, as a *sign*. Language is not merely an instrument of communication between different consciousnesses; it is the ground of consciousness's communication with itself – which is as much as to say, simply of consciousness. Even a solipsistic thought, if we were to call upon this incoherent fiction, could not be without language. But language implies signs – and hence implies fixed and stable 'things' – non-things (things which are taken as non-things, namely as signs), and both aspects of this operation imply *legein* as a social–historical institution, which shows, once again, the impossibility of thinking of thought in an egological perspective, and finally of thinking of being while neglecting the social.

Psychogenetic or idiogenetic and sociogenetic or koinogenetic perspectives are at once irreducible to one another and inseparable, constantly leading from one to another; they cannot be eliminated, we cannot think of the subject, things or the world by setting them aside or by forgetting them. At the same time, however, we do think of *the* subject, society *as such*, *the* thing, *the* world – or try to – and, in one way or another, we constantly say in as complete a manner as possible that they *exist*, just as the institution, the juridical code, merchandise, the *Art of the Fugue*, dreams, hallucinations as hallucinations *exist*. What is more, we are truly capable of thinking only to the extent that, rooted in our social–historical institution and in the social–historical institution of thinking, penetrated through and through by them, we intend beyond this institution a truth which, although it owes almost everything to the latter, owes it almost nothing at all and which would be ruled by something other than the simple necessities of coherent discourse, the figures of the world and the things posited by our society and carried by our representation, the social imaginary significations which make them exist as they do and exist together. We are capable of thinking only by positing together these indubitable and undemonstratable statements: there is a world, there is a psyche, there is society, there is signification. And this path is the path of philosophy and of the only true science, thoughtful science.

Now to say that philosophy is – as it most obviously is – a social–historical institution does not cancel it out as philosophy. To say that it is only in and through the institution of society that there is an opening up to the world does not block this opening – in a sense it even widens it. It only blocks it for traditional ontology, whose diplopia was signaled by Merleau-Ponty, although it must be added that this ontology was more particularly afflicted with congenital hemianopsia. One could see the world only on the condition of ceasing to see representation – or vice versa. How could there be *a* world if there was an innumerable plurality of incomparable representative flux? How could the world be common (*kosmos koinos*) if each of us had his own private world (*kosmos idios*)? *Hence*, there is no representation – the dominant position in the philosophical Empire; or there is no world, for the sceptical barbarians beyond the gates of the Empire. As if one could resolve a problem by doing away with half of the terms that caused the problem. There would be no question of the world as a common world, and *no question would arise at all*, if there was not an indefinite number of private worlds. Just as there would be no question of truth, *alētheia*, without the indefinite number of opinions, *doxai*. It is *because* there is a common world *and* private worlds that there is a world and the question of the world can arise. I do not have to do away with representation in order to recognize the world, any more than the inverse. If philosophy were actually obliged to affirm that in order to save the being of the world the being of representation had to be suppressed, one would have to point out that there is a perfect symmetry and hence identical presuppositions – between this position – and that in which the being of representation can be saved only by suppressing the being of the world, which is one possible definition of psychosis. Nor do I have to do away with the difference between societies – manifested above all by the fact that each society institutes and organizes *its* world, as its *kosmos idios*, and accepts that of others when it encounters it only by including it in its own, reabsorbing it, digesting it in one way or another – in order to recognize that in·and through their different, particular worlds, and only in this way, is a world created or does it exist as a world.

Both paths, then, are essential, inexpungible, irreducible and indissociable. The path which, starting with idiogenesis and koinogenesis, shows the rootedness of things, perception, the world, logic, thought at once in the representative magma of the psyche and in the social–historical institution; the path which shows, therefore, that thing, world, individual, thought, signification are institutions and sedimentations of institutions, which must also at the same time be carried by the subjects' representative flux in order to exist and to operate; the path which shows that from the moment one thinks-talks, there is no 'before' that one can think-talk, that it is only from within these successive institutions and starting from them that we are able to think-talk – so that there is never any possibility of a *tabula rasa*, no generalized doubt or first foundation, and that the search for the conditions of speech and thought can never be radical since it can never abstract from them nor put them into question except by confirming them. And the path that tirelessly returns to all these points in order to question them in another way, which juxtaposes the *there is* in the expression: there is representation and at the *there is* in there is a thing, and which, in and through the differences and the kinds of otherness of private worlds and social–historical worlds, attempts to sight *one* world signification and *one* world, attempts to test its institution and every given institution and, in the most favourable cases, leads only to the point at which a new institution begins to crystallize, but also, at times, to the starting point for another interminable path which will question the institution in a new way.

Each of these paths leads to the other at every point; each is everywhere dense in the other. And their relation cannot be termed antinomy, complementarity or circularity; it is what it is, it is its own model, conceivable on the basis of itself. It is the mode of being of thought as historical thought and as thoughtful *doing*.

7

Social Imaginary Significations

Recognizing that identitary or ensemblist logic has a hold only on one stratum of what is and that thoughtful doing is unavoidably led to go beyond this stratum brings us to the question: can we go further than simply acknowledging the limits of identitary logic and of the ontology which is consubstantial to it, go beyond merely negative ontology and open up a path (or several paths) in order to think what is without confining ourselves to saying how it is not to be thought?

This immense question goes far beyond the bounds and the goal of this work. However, what has already been stated here concerning the social–historical and the imaginary, significations and representation, enables and obliges us to clarify it by means of some preliminary considerations.

i THE MAGMAS

The present philosophical and scientific situation, the direct conse-quence of cognitive activity over the past three-quarters of a century, urgently requires a reflection on the mode of being and on the logic of the organization of those new objects, elementary particles and the cosmic field, the auto-organization of living organisms, the unconscious or the social–historical, which, each in a different yet no less certain manner, all radically question inherited logic and ontology.

Knowledge of these objects has been possible only by means of the creation of new significations or matrices of signification which are certainly, to the extent that they prove fruitful, specific in each of the cases considered. Or, if you like, this knowledge has brought to light other modes of being and other modes of organization than those known formerly. Part of what I am trying to say is that it is useless to argue over which of these formulations is the 'truest' – for, ultimately, the question is not simply undecidable, it is meaningless.

The question then arises of knowing whether these significations, or these organizations, present common features or entertain among themselves relations that can be explored, and which ones; and in this way we hope to clarify with greater precision the relation which they maintain in each case with traditional logic. It is clear that any attempt to reflect on this question must be conscious of the fact that it is related to *this* stage of thoughtful doing, the one we are passing through, and so related to the strata of what is correlative to this stage, just as we must keep in mind the essential *regionality* of significations (and categories)[1] and refrain from giving in to the temptations of universalization or naive unification. It is not because quanta phenomena, on the one hand, and the unconscious, on the other, go beyond the framework of identitary logic that they can necessarily be reflected upon within the framework of *a single* new logic. It is also clear that if one – or more – new logic were able to be constituted, its relation to identitary logic could not, in its turn, be thought of within the inherited framework. For it could not simply be added onto identitary logic, nor be considered a generalization or a supersession of the latter. It could only maintain with identitary or ensemblist logic a paradoxical relation *sui generis*, since, for example, it would have to use distinct and definite terms – as we are continually doing here – to say that what is, what allows itself to be thought of or to be stated *is* not, in a particular region or stratum, organized in itself in accordance with the modes of the distinct and the definite. For this new logic would have to make use of the identitary in order to bring to light and to clarify the non-identitary – and, to the extent that this is possible within the decisive limits mentioned above, it has to make use of the non-identitary in order to elucidate, partially, the blossoming of the identitary. (It is not because Hegel employs identitary terms – otherwise, how could he *speak*? – but because he operates essentially with the schema or hyper-category of *determinacy* that the 'dialectic' is but a variant of identitary logic).

What we know of the regions mentioned above, and in fact what has always been known,[2] leads us to say: what is, in any region whatsoever, can be thought of neither as disordered chaos upon which theoretical consciousness – or culture in general or each culture in its own way – imposes, and alone imposes, an order which translates simply its own legislation or its arbitrariness; nor as a set of clearly separated things, well-situated in a world which is perfectly organized in itself, or (what amounts to the same thing) as a system of essences, regardless of its complexity.

What is, is not and cannot be, absolutely disordered chaos – a term to which, moreover, no signification can be assigned: a random ensemble still represents *as* random a formidable organization, the description of which fills the volumes expounding the theory of probabilities. If this were the case, it could not lend itself to any organization or it would lend itself to all; in both cases, all coherent discourse and all action would be impossible. If the empiricist–skeptical thesis is taken absolutely and radically, it reduces everything to dust, including the expectation of the one who states it that the other, or he himself, comprehends what he says, understands what he pronounces or even exists. If it is taken relatively, one is obliged to concede probabilities to phenomena or, like Hume, habits in the subject, hence already to deny the idea of absolute chaos. When critical philosophy (Kant) refuses, in an initial stage, the idea of any organization in what presents itself, outside of that imposed on it by thought, it does so because it posits that an organization such as this would never possess necessity (namely, true determinacy), the sole necessity being by definition (tautologically, identitarily) that which follows from the very necessities of the act of thinking. In this way, the necessary forms of organization of that which is given can be nothing other than the necessary forms by which the one to whom 'something = X' is given thinks of it (categories). Critical philosophy, however, must encounter in its later stages the fact that nothing in thought itself guarantees that what is given is such that the categories have an effective hold on it – in other words, it encounters the fact that the alleged chaos of sensations is nevertheless organiz*able* and, moreover, that the world is not merely filled with possible supports for the category of substance, that it is not simply organiz*able* but already in a certain manner organiz*ed* (that there are stars, trees, dogs, etc.), for without this the legislation of consciousness would be without any object. What could one do with the category of causality if it were certain that *every* sequence of phenomena observed once would *never* be produced again? The idea of an absolutely formless matter is unthinkable, for it amounts to an absolute indifference of matter with respect to the form 'imposed' on it, which would entail that the imposition of various forms on matter would be equally indifferent among themselves ('the art of carpentry could embody itself in flutes,' Aristotle would say),[3] and nothing in relation to experience could be either true or false. Critical philosophy must then acknowledge a correspondence between consciousness and the being-thus of the world, which it terms a 'lucky chance' (*glücklicher Zufall*;[4] recall that we started with the necessary idea of necessity) but for which it will seek and will secure a transcendent guarantee – which, one immediately realizes, actually overdetermined everything from the start. God, in fact, is not only and not so much a postulate of practical reason entailing cosmological consequences (if God had wanted a chaotic world, how could we ever act ethically?); he is above all, although between the lines and despite refutations of the proofs of his 'existence', more than a postulate of theoretical reason: as a 'transcendental ideal' not only does he govern the use of reason (which governs the use of understanding), but as alone fully determined, he alone fully determines the sense of: being.

Neither is what is given an ensemble or a hierarchy of ensembles, an essence or system of essences. This has been sufficiently demonstrated by what we said above in relation to the social–historical, the imaginary, significations, language and representation (which bring into being thoughtful doing); the situation of contemporary physics shows this as well.[5] What is given is not congruent to ensemblist logic, to the organization of the *legein*. One of its strata, the first natural stratum, lends itself in part to this organization; but once *logical* interrogation arises and widens its scope, this organization proves to be all the more fragmentary, lacunary, incomplete. What we then encounter beyond the first natural stratum still appears to be organizable, but it also appears already to be organized in a way that forces us to modify our 'categories' – without allowing us to say whether we extract them from it or impose them on it. And not only does each new layer or stratum appear sooner or later in its turn as lacunary, but the relations among these layers or strata of what is given – terms which, to be sure, must not be substantialized or reified – are neither chaotic (there is a certain passage from quantum microphysics to so-called classical physics) nor submitted to identitary logic (from the point of view of the latter they are full of paradoxes and aporias). In another way, we have also seen that within language itself the relations between code and language are themselves neither chaotic nor identitary; and in yet another way, this is also true of the relations between 'private worlds' and a 'common world' in society.

What we seek to understand is the mode of being of what gives itself before identitary or ensemblist logic is imposed; what gives itself in this way in this mode of being, we are calling a *magma*. It is obviously not a question of giving a formal definition of it in received language or in any language whatsoever. The following statement, however, may not be unhelpful:

A magma is that from which one can extract (or in which one can construct) an indefinite number of ensemblist organizations but which can never be reconstituted (ideally) by a (finite or infinite) ensemblist composition of these organizations.

To say that what is given permits us to extract from it (or to construct in it) ensemblist organizations amounts to saying that one can always fix marking terms (whether simple or complex) in what gives itself. Knowing whether one wants to treat these terms as elements of a set, in the full sense of the term, and whether they can accommodate fruitful ensemblist operations is a matter that concerns the object one is considering as well as what one wishes to do with it (theoretically or practically). Everything is always ensemblizable (that is to say, tautologically, everything that can be falls under the rules of saying in so far as it is said); but beyond certain limits or outside of certain domains everything is so only trivially (one can always count the typographical signs in a book, weigh the statues in the Louvre, which would be most important if they were to be moved, or transform the Amerindian myths into one another after having posited that they are each composed of a small number of discrete elements), incompletely (mathematics taken *in toto*) or antinomically (contemporary physics). The entanglement of what can be ensemblized in a relevant manner and what cannot be except in an empty manner or not at all can reach degrees of complexity which are almost unimaginable (to wit, the relation between mathematics and economics).

Let us try then, by means of an accumulation of contradictory metaphors, to give an intuitive description of what we mean by magma (the best intuitive support the reader can present to himself is to think of 'all the significations of the English language' or 'all the representations of his life'). We have to think of a multiplicity which is not one in the received sense of the term but which we mark out as such, and which is not a multiplicity in the sense that we could actually or virtually enumerate what it 'contains' but in which we could mark out in each case terms which are not absolutely jumbled together. Or, we might think of an indefinite number of terms, which may possible change, assembled together by an optionally transitive pre-relation (referral); or of the holding-together of distinct–indistinct components of a manifold; or, again, of an indefinitely blurred bundle of conjunctive fabrics, made up of different cloths and yet homogeneous, everywhere studded with virtual and evanescent singularities. And we have to think of the operations of identitary logic as simultaneous, multiple dissections which transform or actualize these virtual singularities, these components, these terms into distinct and definite elements, solidifying the pre-relation of referral into relation *as such*, organizing the holding-together, the being-in, the being-on, the being-proximate into a system of determined and determining relations (identity, difference, belonging, inclusion), differentiating what they distinguish in this way into 'entities' and 'properties', using this differentiation to constitute 'sets' and 'classes'.

We are positing that everything that can actually be given – representation, nature, signification – is according to the mode of being of the *magma*, that the social–historical institution of the world, of things and individuals, considered as the institution of *legein* and *teukhein*, is always the institution of identitary logic as well and hence the imposition of an ensemblist organization on an initial stratum of the given which unceasingly lends itself to this. But we are also positing that it is never and can never be *simply* that – that it is always at the same time necessarily the institution of a magma of social imaginary significations, and, finally, that the relation between *legein* and *teukhein* and, the magma of social imaginary significations cannot be thought in terms of the identitary and ensemblist grid – any more than the relations between *legein* and representation, *legein* and nature or between representation and signification, or representation and world, or 'conscious' and 'unconscious'.

ii SIGNIFICATIONS IN LANGUAGE

We now turn to the question of social imaginary significations in the widest and most familiar domain: that of significations in language. Signification is here the co-belonging of a term and of that to which it *refers*, by degrees, whether directly or indirectly. It is a bundle of referrals starting from and surrounding a term. In this way a word refers to its canonical linguistic signifieds, whether they be 'proper' or 'figurative' and to each of them in the mode of identitary designation. These signifieds are those which a complete dictionary or thesaurus records for a 'state' of the language considered as given; a dictionary such as this can exist only for a finite and definite corpus of linguistic expressions, hence only for a dead language. As was already indicated above, the continuous possibility of the emergence of linguistic signifieds *other* than those already recorded for a given 'synchronic' state of the language is constitutive of a living language. The bundle of such referrals is therefore *open*. But the word also refers to its referent or referents. Now this referent is never an absolute and separate singularity; it is neither simple nor autarchic – even if it be *ousia*. There are no 'proper names'. Strictly considered, the famous *singularia nominantur, sed universalia significantur* is meaningless. A universal is 'named' in identitary designation (thus 'unity' is 'named' *unité, Einheit, hen,* etc.) and a 'singular' is 'signified' by its name, since this name would not be a name if it did not automatically cover the indefinite character of the 'moments' and the 'aspects' of what it 'designates'. The 'name of the individual' – person, thing, place or anything else – refers to the interminable ocean of what that individual *is*. It is its name only inasmuch as it refers virtually to the totality of the manifestations of that individual throughout its existence, both the actual and the possible ones ('Pierre would never do that'), and under all the aspects that it might present, in so far as it conveys this multidimensional tube with indefinite borders and it becomes imbricated, through all of its fibres, with all that exists elsewhere. The only abstractly constructable absolute singularity, the 'concrete' here-and-now (not the *form* of the here-and-now which is obviously, as Hegel indicated, an abstract universal) can be constructed as a singularity only in so far as it is 'simple' or 'indivisible' – not in so far as it is 'separate' and 'autarchic'. It can be constructed (and said) only by means of a formidable accumulation of abstractions, each of which mobilizes an indefinite number of referrals to something other than it (think only about what is required to 'give meaning' to the expression: the observation was made at 12 o'clock 21′7″ on November 23, 1974 at x degrees North latitude and y degrees East longitude with respect of a given meridian). Therefore, just as, beyond the identitary postulation of designation – of the identitary use of meaning – the referent is itself and in itself essentially indefinite, undeterminable and open, so the bundle of referrals is equally open for the same reason. I am not saying that linguistic signification is never *anything but* the referent, but that signification is never separable from the referent, and that it also includes the referral to the referent. We shall see, in connection with the primary or central imaginary significations, that it is quite possible that a signification need not possess any 'referent' genuinely differenciable in any particular respect from the signification itself. Finally, we cannot, in considering language, abstract from the fact that signification – to be sure, in another manner – refers to the representations of individuals, whether actual or virtual, which it gives rise to, induces, permits or models. Without this relation, there is no language; the indefinite and undetermined permeability between individuals' worlds of representation and linguistic signifieds is the condition for existence, functioning and alteration in the case of the former as well as the latter.

All this does not mean that we have reduced all that is.to being simply signification, or that we have dissolved signification into everything that is and each signification into all the others. We are not saying that the signification of each and every term is *all* of language – as some have not failed to hold and as, in truth, they would be forced to hold in a logical (structuralist) perspective.[6] More generally, consider the alternative: on the one hand, each linguistic term signifies a determined 'object' which can be displayed in an unambiguous showing (or 'thought') without anything else being presupposed or entailed; or, on the other hand, a linguistic term never signifies anything but 'its' (?) difference with respect to the others, 'what' the others do not signify. Both alternatives are untenable and merely demonstrate the impasse resulting from a 'logical' approach to language. Either signification is not determinable nor determined in an identitary manner, and then it is nothing; or, it is something and then it is determinable and determined, hence it is the univocal relation between this 'word' and this 'thing' or this 'idea', each unambiguously determinable. Or else it is the pure relation of relations, each of which is determined as the negation of all the others (there is no point in adding that the 'determination' here is utterly empty).

This alternative, however, is purely fictitious. As a magma, the significations of a language are not the elements of an ensemble subject to determinacy as their mode and their criterion of being. A signification is indefinitely determin*able* (and the 'indefinitely' is obviously essential) without thereby being determin*ed*. It can always be marked out, provisionally assigned as an identitary element to an identitary relation with another identitary element (this is the case in designation), and as such be 'a something' as the starting point for an open series of successive determinations. These determinations, however, in principle never exhaust it. What is more, they can, and always do, force us to reconsider the initial 'something' and lead us to posit it as 'something else', overturning by this very fact, or in order to bring it about, the relations by means of which the initial determination had been made.

It is certain that operations such as these would be impossible for a computer and it is probable that a linguist, as linguist, would get lost in them; the fact is that an illiterate fisherman almost never does get lost. Precisely in so far as they are a magma, significations are something entirely different from chaos. What we are describing as the bundle of referrals of each signification is obviously not just anything whatsoever, any more than is anything whatsoever that to which a referral leads in every instance or the particular manner in which it leads to it. *Table* does not lead in the same way to *manners* and to *logarithms*. It is this other way which becomes the *with respect to* ... in identitary development and purification, which aims at grasping and fixing the moving and undetermined being of signification by transforming it into a finite, definite and determined assembly of determined and univocal relations between each term and several others.

This being of signification, long perceived by philosophers and grammarians, has been inadequately described, and in fact concealed, by the distinctions between proper and figurative meaning, central signification and semantic aura, denotation and connotation. What these distinctions are actually aimed at, without being able to formulate it, is the difference between the identitary–ensemblist aspect of the signified and the full signification. And under the hold of identitary logic and the ontology that is homologous to it, they explicitly posit the ensemblist–identitary element as proper, central, the denotation of something which is assured in itself. But there is no proper meaning, it is impossible to grasp and to enclose a meaning in its properness (proper-ty); there is simply an identitary *use* of meaning. There is no denotation opposed to connotation. The idea of denotation necessarily implies an ontology of substance-essence, of *ousia*, of a being which in itself is definite and distinct outside of language, complete and closed in on itself, to which the word would be addressed, clearly: an ontology of the *thing*, whether real or ideal, to which could be opposed the *comitants*, accompaniments (*sumbebekota*) which have come to it objectively or the accidents which have come to the word in its linguistic utilization. Little matter whether this ontology has an 'idealist' (as in Frege) or 'realist' coloration. To say that 'the victor of Austerlitz' and 'the prisoner of Saint-Helena' have the same denotation (or *Bedeutung*): Napoleon, and different connotations (or *Sinn*) is to slide over the fact that the first two expressions have indeed different *denotations*, (to stick to this terminology) since the first designates Napoleon *as* (this) or designates a particular property of Napoleon or Napoleon as he was the subject of a given act, and the second designates him *as* (that) or designates another particular property or attribute of Napoleon or Napoleon as having suffered a given thing. To this one cannot oppose 'Napoleon' in a purely denotative sense except by positing that there exists absolutely separately, beyond, under or above any attribution, property, essential or accidental accompaniment, something, an *ousia*, which *is* Napoleon – that is to say, by positing that it is possible to speak outside of any *with respect to* ..., to speak *absolutely*. Now this is not a description or analysis of language but a most peculiar metaphysics; an irresistible metaphysics, to be sure, induced by the identitary use of language and its substantialist–essentialist extension but one which has not, for all that, to be accepted blindly. The one who carried this metaphysics to its limit – Aristotle – spent his life formulating, deepening, discussing the aporias which arise from positing *ousia*; contemporary logicians and linguists often seem not even to suspect them.

What is a 'figure of speech', a trope, and what is the proper meaning? What, from antiquity, have been termed tropes are merely particular tropes or second-order tropes. *Every expression is essentially tropic.* Even when it is used in its so-called 'proper meaning' or with its 'cardinal signification', a word is still utilized in a tropic sense. There is no 'proper meaning'; there is simply– but always and unavoidably, even in the most subtle or far-fetched metaphors or allegories – an identitary marking out, a point in a network of identitary markings, which is itself caught up in the magma of significations and related to the magma of what is. Is there an attribution which is not metonymical? To say that there could be one would be to say that attributions or predications exist which are not *with respect to* ..., that there exist absolute attributions or predications. But what could an absolute attribution be? Ultimately, it could only be the attribution of *ousia* to *ousia*, namely absolute tautology, the empty form of self-identity. '*x* is *x*': does this mean anything other than '*x* is', and is being a predicate? There is apparently no figure of speech in my saying 'This vase is blue'; and yet it is evident that the term 'vase' is used here as its own metonymy, *pars pro toto*, [and, in fact, *totum pro parte*][7] since what the sentence is aiming at is not *the* vase but its surface. 'The dog is sleeping': this sentence is so simple and yet it opens up into an abyss as soon as one thinks about it a little. 'Last night, I had a dream' is simply an accumulation of 'abuses of language': *I*, if it is not taken as a simple marking term, is but a mist masking an abyss; one does not have a dream as one has a child, a record-player, the measles or a mistress; and what does *a* dream mean, in what sense and when is a dream *one*? Hence, the sentence *is not* an accumulation of abuses of language – for *all language is the abuse of language*; there is no use of language as language which is the proper use.

Obviously, the 'analysis' of these expressions can always be made; it is always, in principle, incomplete and interminable, To say that it could be complete, is to say that absolute knowledge exists; we shall return to this. What matters here is that it is not by means of these 'analyses' that language operates. Everyone knows 'what is meant' by the dog is sleeping, this vase is blue, I had a dream – and knows this without making, or being in a position to undertake this so-called 'analysis'. And these expressions function in language as univocal 'sufficiently as to usage'. This is because the identitary–ensemblist dimension of language is always present. How is it present? In the most basic declarative statement – the dog is sleeping, this vase is blue – the terms convey an intention of signification as provisionally simple and undecomposable, on the one hand, and as composable in a *determined* relation (or a finite number of relations), on the other. The statement posits at the same time a *with respect to* ... specific to it, without making it explicit or being able to do so (the explicitation would be endless), in a transitory closure. But this closure is full of pores for the identitary–ensemblist dimension can never really be isolated and never actually is; it is isolated, ideally, only within a completely formalized system, hence within that which is no longer a language.

Let us open a parenthesis here. Rigorously speaking, there is no break in continuity between the most blatant sophisms, those closest to the stupidest pun in the Platonic dialogue which contains the worst of them, namely the *Euthydemus*, and the final aporias of the *Parmenides*, the *Sophist*, the *Metaphysics* or the Hegelian system. These sophisms are such only through the implacable use of identitary logic, the demand that a term have, in each case, one and only one meaning, that the *with respect to* ... implicit in every statement be made perfectly and completely explicit. How can one say that Socrates seated and Socrates standing are one and the same Socrates, since it is blindingly clear that *it is not* the same Socrates? Do being-seating and standing partake of the meaning or of the being of Socrates? If they do not, then what is Socrates seated and Socrates standing? If they do, there is then in a corresponding manner two meanings of Socrates – and two Socrates. And obviously, there are an infinite, and more precisely an indefinite, number of them. If the handsome Clinias is not wise, making him wise is making him other than he is; it is thus doing away with him as he is now, destroying his being as being-thus and making him be as another being-thus: 'you want him to be destroyed, it seems,' Dionysodorus emphatically states.[8] 'Confusing the quality with the object itself and with the existence of the object', note the commentators. Is there then an object without any quality? Is being-alive a quality of the object, or is it the object itself? At any rate, it cannot be the object itself, since other objects are alive as well. Then, it is a quality in the most general sense; but then life is one of Socrates' qualities? But, following Aristotle, we would all say that the corpse is no longer Socrates, except through an abuse of language. Is being separable from being thus? And up to what point? To say that a thing is, is to say that it is completely determined with respect to all possible predicates, Kant affirmed. Clinias being a man, and wise/not wise being possible predicates of man, Clinias is truly only if he is determined with respect to wisdom and non-wisdom. Obviously, Clinias wise is *determined otherwise* than Clinias not-wise. *Is he other* for all that? He is other *with respect to* ...; and he is not other, he is the same – the same *with respect to what*? With respect to *eidos*, with respect to *ousia*. But what is *eidos*, what is *ousia*? The *Metaphysics* is an immense effort to reply to this question, one that does not really come off. Plato and Aristotle spend a good part of their life in reconsidering, explicitating, developing, rectifying the *with respect to ...* (*pros ti*), that is to say, in struggling to save discourse in relation to its own demand for determinacy, which is unsurpassable but which also, when taken absolutely, results in the destruction of discourse. At the end of this struggle – which will require positing and opposing being always and always becoming, power and act, essence and comitant, accompaniment – Plato will be led to agree that even Being '*is not* myriads upon myriads of things', that the other *is* as *non-being*, and that one must in each case consider *with respect to what* (*ekeinê kai kat' ekeino*) the same is other and the other is same.[9] In the same way, Aristotle, recognizing the unavoidable poly-semy (*pollachos legomenon*) of the ultimate vocables of language: being, one; and agreeing that the explicit operations of identitary logic are conditioned, at both ends, by that which cannot be made explicit in and through this logic – 'for both the first terms and the last are objects of intuitive reason (*nous*) and not of argument (logos)'[10] – will affirm that we cannot resist those who, in discourse, seek only viol-ence.[11] Not physical violence, to be sure, but the violence of discourse: the exclusive and pitiless use of identitary logic, which *is* an essential requirement of discourse as soon as the question of determinacy and coherence has been posited – that is, in fact, from the very first day of language – and which inevitably destroys discourse itself, for it can never be satisfied there. In a sense, the true ground of grand sophistic is the same as the true ground of inherited philosophy: the requirement of tautology; recall, in this regard, that in modern logic truth is termed tautology.[12] Sophistic posits this requirement bluntly and arrogantly in order to show that it cannot be satisfied; philosophy posits it scrupu-lously and attempts to satisfy it. This is what makes Aristotle say that the sophist and the philosopher differ only by an ethical choice (*proairesis*): one can do philosophy only by seeking communication in truth, in one and the same coherent discourse.[13] All the 'refutations' of sophistic and of scepticism that have ever existed have consisted simply in showing that sophistic destroys *itself* as coherent discourse, that it *can* destroy the idea of coherent discourse, but does this by destroying itself *as coherent discourse*. All these refutations, then, are valid only for someone for whom the idea of coherent discourse is itself valid and are of no avail against those for whom discourse is only play or warfare – whether they live in fifth-century Athens or in today's Paris.

The identitary–ensemblist dimension, we stated above, can never genu-inely be isolated and never actually is. Aiming at isolating it perfectly is aiming at destroying language (just as wishing to neglect or eliminate this dimension would be an attempt to destroy language). Being in language is accepting to be in signification. It is accepting the fact that there is no determined response to the question: what is Socrates and who is Socrates? It is admitting that Socrates–somato-psychical Heraclitean flux, dance of electrons and of representations, caught up, any way you look at him, in an indefinite number of other flux and other dances – as a name (mistakenly termed 'proper') covers both a marking term 'sufficient as to use' *and* a signification which refers to an indefinite number of other significations as well as to an indefinite number of aspects of what is. Speaking is being simultaneously in both dimensions. Even in those cases where language appears as operating exclusively in the identitary dimension – purely as an instrument of practical cooperation, for example – where the functioning of signifieds seems perfectly to be governed by a code, the passage from one dimension of language to the other is always possible and continually imminent – otherwise this functioning would cease. For this functioning must always be capable of rectification both in relation to what is and in relation to speech, and this rectification can never be merely the passage from one identitary sub-set to another; instead it once again involves significations.

We are still at an infinite distance from this very thing when we think that the idea of 'contextual dependence' replies to the question of the being of signification. The idea – which anyhow is obvious – says something only as long as it remains vague: what in each case orients the exploration of the signification of a term or a sentence, what sheds light in a privileged manner on an aspect of it has to do with the context – it being understood that this context itself can and often does (*de jure*, always) see its virtual contribution to the clarification of the term considered modified by the appearance of the term itself. In the first place, however, this context (even if we limit ourselves to the strictly linguistic context) cannot be rigorously defined, or defined in a univocal fashion. At best, one might compare it to a family of neighbourhoods which covers an immense part of the language considered. Strictly speaking, the linguistic context of a sentence is the totality of the language in which it is stated, and its non-linguistic context, the entire universe. The question arising in this way is not resolved nor could it be, except in trivial cases, by a 'contextual function' inscribed in language as a code; it is resolved in each case by human doing in language – by speech. In the second place, we cannot fail to consider the fact that the sentence or the term create their own particular context. Consider for example the sentence matrix: '*x* was mistaken'. 'Pierre was mistaken' creates, for instance, a context relative to a discussion in a café yesterday. 'Parmenides was mistaken' creates as its context the entire history of philosophy. Finally, no rigorous sense can be given to the expression 'contextual dependence', nor can one claim to reply to the question of signification by means of it, unless language were a code in the definite sense of a system of determined identitary relations. To say, then, that the signification of a term depends not only on the term itself but on its context amounts to replacing $f(x) = a$ by $f(x,C) = b$ (C being a group of letters, possibly ordered, representing the 'context'). This in itself is a platitude which could only impress those who believe that a world of difference separates a function of one variable from a function of several variables. But this platitude is at the same time an absurdity. To say that there is a mapping of the set of words on the set of significations, or that there is a mapping of the *n*th Cartesian power of the set of words on the set of significations, presupposes, in both cases, that *there is* a set of significations (that significations form a set) and that it is indeed a matter of mapping (that the value of a given group of terms is determined, unique and always the same). Now both presuppositions are metaphysical and arbitrary. At most, they correspond to partial operative postulates (holding for certain limited uses of language), postulates which constantly find themselves close to the vanishing point. They hold only for the identitary use of meaning, that is to say, they hold to the extent that someone, in speaking, repeats strictly what has already been said and which remains reproducible *ne varietur* – namely, that which is set within language as a code of univocal designations. However, to affirm that these two presuppositions cover the totality of the aspects and the functioning of language amounts to affirming that everything that has ever been said is never anything other than the strict repetition of what has already been said; hence, that everything that can be said in a language has already been defined and determined in and through this language from the first instant of its institution, and for all time. It then follows, since there are several languages, and since in each of them one can speak of the others and describe them in a satisfactory manner, that each language contains in itself, from the start, the actual possibility of all the other languages that have ever existed or will ever exist, at any rate as concerns the significations they carry. For indeed, in this case, either *logos*, *omen*, *wirklich* could never find an equivalent, whether exact or approximative, in English nor be understood to any degree at all; or they merely represent particular combinations of the same elements of signification which are combined differently in English. The first hypothesis being patently false, it results that all languages would be perfectly translatable into one another, all being referred to the same ultimate elements or atoms of signification, combined differently by each. There would then be not even equivalence or isomorphism but absolute identity of the set of significations to which all languages refer. This amounts to saying that all that can ever be said was already expressible as soon as the first language came into existence and that, ideally, it has already been posited, always and in this 'always'. We see once again here the consubstantiality of identitary logic to the ontology of intemporal determinacy and of *aei*, and, of course, along with this the complete and blind subordination of 'positive' linguistics to a particular metaphysics. The idea of the possibility of a complete analysis of linguistic expressions is equivalent to positing that absolute knowledge exists.

To be sure, this view is shown to be untenable not only by the existence of different languages and their mutual irreducibility (which does not mean incommunicability) or the existence of a history of each language and of the significations to which it refers, but also by the manner of being of significations in and through language. A language is language only inasmuch as new significations, or new aspects of a signification, always can and constantly do emerge in it. As was stated above, this is not a 'diachronic' aspect but an essential property of language as a 'synchronic' totality. A language is such only inasmuch as it offers speakers the possibility of *taking their bearings* in and through what they say *in order to move within it*, to base themselves on the same in order to create the other, to use the code of designations in order to make other significations appear or other aspects of significations apparently already given. The pseudo-'mappings' of the set of words and of sentences onto the pseudo-'set' of significations are never more than means of describing the identitary dimension of language. And it is only in relation to the latter that the idea of contextual dependence, taken rigorously, can have a meaning.

There is thus a logical and a real inseparability of these two aspects of signification, *peras* and *apeiron*, definiteness-determinacy-distinctness-limitation and indefiniteness-indeterminacy-indistinctness-unlimitedness. It is essential that language always provide the possibility of treating the meanings it conveys as an ensemble formed by terms which are determined, rigorously circumscribable, each identical to itself and distinct from all the others, separable and separate. And it is equally essential that it always provide the possibility of new terms emerging, that the relations between existing terms be redefined, and so that the existing terms, inseparable from their relations, also be redefined. This possibility, in its turn, rests on the fact that the relations between previously given terms are inexhaustible and undetermined, as are the terms themselves, since at no time could the positing of a new signification be represented as an external addition, leaving intact what was already present. Beyond any set which could be extracted from it or constructed out of it, significations are not a set; their mode of being is other, it is that of a magma.

iii SOCIAL IMAGINARY SIGNIFICATIONS AND 'REALITY'

We discussed at length above the relation of society to what I termed the first natural stratum, a relation designated by the Freudian term 'leaning on' (*Anlehnung*). Society's doing and representing/saying are neither dictated by an indubitable, in-itself, being-thus of the natural stratum nor are they 'absolutely free' in relation to the latter – this is self-evident. But, as we have attempted to show, already in psychoanalysis the idea of leaning-on says much more, and something quite different than the positing of these two far-off and abstract limits.

The situation is even richer and more complex – indeed, qualitatively other – when we consider the way the institution leans on the first natural stratum. The world of significations instituted in each case by society is obviously neither a copy or a tracing ('reflection') of a 'real' world, nor is it without any relation to a certain being-thus of nature. The fact that the latter must be 'taken into account' in society's institution of the world, that it supports and induces it, can appear as a truism; this truism contains what has appeared at once as the truth and the necessary fallacy of identitary–ensemblist logic. Here again, one can ask: nature supports and induces society's organization of the world – what does it support and induce, and how? It does not induce as a cause (we would then have a constant cause producing variable effects), as a simple means (means of what?), nor as a 'symbol' (symbol of what and for whom?). And that *in* which it induces, the institution of society and the correlative world of significations, emerges as the *other* with respect to nature, as the creation of the social imaginary.

Just as in the 'passage from the somatic to the psychical', we find the emergence of another level and another mode of being, and nothing exists as psychical which is not representation; so in the 'passage from the natural to the social', we find the emergence of another level and another mode of being, and nothing exists as social–historical which is not signification, caught up in and referred to an instituted world of significations. The organization of this world leans on certain aspects of the first natural stratum, where it finds points of support, incitements, inductions. However, not only is it never purely and simply the repetition or reproduction of this stratum; it cannot even be described as a partial and selecting 'sampling' of it. What is 'sampled' is so only in relation to and on the basis of an organization of the world posited by society; it is so only by being *formed* and *transformed* in and through social institution; and, finally but most importantly, this formation–transformation is *actual*, figured–presentified in and through modifications of the 'sensible world': so that, finally, *the very thing* which is leaned on is *altered* by society by the very fact of this leaning on – which has strictly no equivalent in the psychical world. For the institution of the world of significations as a social–historical world is *ipso facto* 'inscription' and 'incarnation' in the 'sensible world' starting from which the latter is historically transformed in its being-thus.

To be sure, there is still an ultimate condition of possibility for this transformation which resides in a decisive aspect of the being-thus of the natural world to which we have already alluded. 'Natural reality' is not only what resists and cannot be manipulated; it is *just as much* what lends itself to transformation, what allows itself to be altered 'conditionally' depending *at once* on its 'open interstices' *and* on its 'regularity'. And both of these moments are essential. Natural 'reality' *is* undetermined to an essential degree for social activity; one can move things around in it and move oneself, transport things and change places oneself, cut and assemble. There is even indetermination on the macroscopic scale – there is movement, the capacity of being other, 'matter' or 'power' in the Aristotelian sense of the term. *And* this indetermination goes along with a determination, with relatively fixed and stable properties, and necessary or probable relations: if … then, the condition for making what is be otherwise. The resistance and malleability which are indissociable from the 'natural given' and the manner in which both are manifested, permit the actual instrumentation of *teukhein* and of social doing in general. But the level on which, in each case, the resistance and malleability of the 'natural given' are manifested, and the way in which both are manifested, depend on social doing and on *teukhein*. So that this ultimate condition of possibility becomes in an abstract sense: society is always dealing with the 'natural given' as at once resistant and malleable; but *what* is resistant and malleable, and the manner in which it is so, is such only in correlation with the social world considered in each case. The fact that the fusion of hydrogen is possible – and very difficult to realize – has a meaning for contemporary society and for no other; the fact that a certain type of wood is excellent for making bows has almost no meaning for this same society, although it was of capital importance for human life over thousands of years.

We can no longer speak of 'leaning on' when we consider the relation of social imaginary significations and the institution of society to the stratum of 'reality' which is no longer natural but social, between the former and what can be termed the 'abstract materiality' of society itself, 'things', objects or individuals which society brings into being by making them – *teukhein* – at once as concrete entities and as copies or instances of an *eidos* created (imagined, invented, instituted) by society. It was found necessary to affirm that social facts are not things. In truth, what is to be said is that social things are not 'things': they are social things and *these particular* things only inasmuch as they 'incarnate' or, better, figure and presentify, social significations. Social things are what they are depending on the significations they figure, immediately or mediately, directly or indirectly. Marx himself was already aware of this and showed it admirably in describing 'the fetish character of merchandise': except that, for him, this 'fantasmagoria', this 'hieroglyphic' character was imposed on things only in the capitalist mode of production (or, more generally, the merchant mode) and as the consequence of a 'logic' following from this mode of production. We shall return to this shortly. Reciprocally, social imaginary significations exist in and through 'things' – objects and individuals – which presentify and figure them, directly or indirectly, immediately or mediately. They can exist only through their 'incarnation', their 'inscription', their presentation and figuration in and through a network of individuals and objects, which they 'inform' – these are at once concrete entities and instances or copies of types, of *eide* – individuals and objects which exist in general and are as they are only through these significations. This relation *sui generis* to social individuals and things makes of them social imaginary significations and forbids our confusing them with significations in general, even less our treating them as fictions, pure and simple. To say that social imaginary significations are instituted, or to say that the institution of society is the institution of a world of social imaginary significations, also means that these significations are presentified and figured in and through the actuality of the individuals, acts and objects that they 'inform'. The institution of society is what it is and as it is to the extent that it 'materializes' a magma of social imaginary significations, in reference to which individuals and objects alone can be grasped and even simply exist. Nor can this magma be spoken of in isolation from the individuals and the objects that it brings into being. What we have here are not significations that would be 'freely detachable' from any material support, purely ideal poles; rather, it is in and through the being and the being-thus of this 'support' that these significations exist and are such as they are.

Marx wrote: 'A machine is no more, in itself, capital than gold is, in itself, money.' Here again, just as when he spoke of the fetishism of merchandise, what he was aiming at without naming it in this way, was what we are calling social imaginary signification. To say that gold in itself is not money may appear superficially as trite but it immediately leads to the question of the institution of society and of this institution as essentially historical. For gold to become money, it is not enough that it possess the 'natural' qualities listed in the manuals of political economy which 'predestine' it for this role; it requires that particular social–historical development which, starting from the appearance of embryonic forms of exchange, leads to the institution of a 'general equivalent' (this, anyway, is Marx's conception, which we shall not discuss here for itself). For a machine to become capital, it has to be placed within the network of socio-economic relations which capitalism institutes. It is in and through this insertion that the machine acquires its signification – capital – which does not 'depend' on the machine as such (nor on the existence of a sufficient number of machines, quantity being transformed into quality, etc.), but on the socio-economic 'system', on the 'mode of production' in which this machine is placed; the same 'ensemble' of machines would no longer be 'capital' the day following a socialist revolution – just as the 'productive capacities' of men would no longer be 'labour power' the day following this revolution.

Let us note in passing that, once again here, the antinomic character of Marx's thought is apparent. If the 'state of productive forces', technical evolution, unambiguously *determines* the organization of the relations of production and, through this, the social system as a whole – if 'feudal society corresponds to a hand mill and capitalist society to a steam-mill' – then the machine, in the narrow sense of the term, and this type of machine, *determines* the appearance of capitalist society, *and* in this society, the machine cannot help but be 'capital'. It is not so 'immediately'; but this immediate is, like any immediate, no more than an abstraction, the being of the machine is fully what it is only when all the mediations have been effected and when their results, turning back upon the immediate, have completely determined it to its depths. In this sense, the machine *is* indeed capital – in opposition to gold, in which being-money is, from this point of view, something much more external and accidental. It is not the same thing to say that the machine brings capitalism into being, even if this is 'in the final analysis', and to say that it is capitalism that makes out of these machines – in themselves neutral and simply means – *capital*.

Now Marx says both things at once – sometimes one and sometimes the other – and this expresses his imprisonment in inherited ontology. As a 'materialist', he wants to determine capitalism by the machine; as an 'Hegelian', he knows that the machine is what it is, takes its meaning (its being) only through its immersion in Totality – here, the social system which confers a 'signification' on it. And, obviously, both positions are untenable. The machine, even reduced to its technical-being, cannot be thought of as neutral, except in an accidental manner. The machines in question during the capitalist period are indeed 'intrinsically' capitalist machines. The machines that we are familiar with are not 'neutral' objects which capitalism uses for capitalist ends, 'diverting' them (as technicians and scientists so often naively imagine) from their purely technical character, but which could also be used for other social 'ends'. They are in a thousand different ways, most of them already in themselves but, in any event, all of them logically and really, impossible outside of the technological *system* that they form, as the 'incarnation', 'inscription', presentation and figuration of the essential significations of capitalism. In the same way, when, like Marx, one speaks of the relations of production as 'relations between persons mediated by things', one is in danger of making these relations appear to be something external or added onto 'persons' and to 'things', which would be, moreover, ideally definable outside of their insertion in these 'relations', which could themselves be 'modified' while leaving 'persons' and 'things' unaffected. This is not even a danger, it is a certainty, as is shown by the fact that neither Marx nor the Marxist movement has ever conceived of anything other than of 'placing (capitalist) technique in the service of socialism', modifying the 'relations of production' (soon identified, and not by chance, with the legal forms of property), without ever considering that the abolition of capitalism was inconceivable without an upheaval in existing technology. Except at limit-points set at infinity, there exist no 'persons' or 'things', which, in addition to their attributes, properties, and intrinsic characteristics, would acquire additional qualities due to the fact that they happen to be immersed in a capitalist or other social system. 'Relations between persons mediated by things' can be capitalist relations, for instance, if and only if they are mediated by specific 'things', which one must venture to call capitalist things (or feudal things, or Aztec things). On the other hand, however, things such as these are not 'sufficient' for the emergence of these relations; they *determine* nothing. Capitalist machines, as such and in themselves, 'taken separately' (as they have to be taken if we are to speak of relations of causation or of determination) are not even sufficient to induce capitalist relations, if individuals which are 'capitalist individuals' (contradictorily and conflictually) are not given at the same time; one proof of this lies in the enormous difficulty capitalism has in penetrating 'precapitalist' societies. This difficulty is not one of importing machines; or 'capital', nor the difficulty of providing 'technical training' in vocational schools. It is the difficulty and even the impossibility of producing from one day to the next, or in the space of a few years, 'capitalist people' (as capitalists, properly speaking, and as proletarians) – that is to say, of socially *fabricating* individuals for whom what does and does not count, what does and does not have a signification, for whom the signification of a given thing or a given act are henceforth defined, posited and instituted in another way than in their traditional society. Men for whom space and time are organized, internally articulated and imaginarily represented in a different manner; men whose own body is not merely subjected to other, external disciplines but caught up in another relation to the world, capable of touching, grasping, manipulating other objects and in other ways; men for whom the relations between individuals are overturned, traditional collectivities and communities crushed, attachments and corresponding loyalties destroyed; men for whom, finally, an eventual economic 'surplus', should there be one, is destined not to be spent for prestige, distributed among the members of the extended family or clan, used for a pilgrimage or hoarded, but *accumulated*. But fabricating individuals in this way, a *teukhein* of this sort, is nothing other than fabricating them in reference to the social imaginary significations of capitalism and on the condition of these significations; it is nothing other than imposing on these societies the capitalist institution of the world – without which the machines which are imported in such great numbers are just as 'useless' and ridiculous as the big snow-plough given by the Russians as aid to Guinea and long exhibited in Conakry.

In the same way, in the place where the institution of capitalism emerged for the first time – in Western Europe – it has been, indistinguishably, an alteration of individuals, things, social relations and 'institutions' in the second sense of this term; it has been the creation of a capitalist humankind, of a capitalist technique, of capitalist relations of production, all of which are inconceivable and impossible without one another and all of which presentify and figure the capitalist institution of the world and the social imaginary significations that it carries. This means that the specific organization of the 'natural' and social world made by Western capitalism, its original *legein* and *teukhein* in their mode of operation, in their means and in their results, the 'social reality' which they bring into being as the indivisibility of the actual and the possible, are at once 'instrument' and 'expression', the figuration and the presentation of a core of social imaginary significations in reference to which, for this society, things, individuals, representations and ideas *are* or *are not, do* or *do not have value.*

iv SOCIAL IMAGINARY SIGNIFICATIONS AND THE INSTITUTION OF THE WORLD

The institution of society is in each case the institution of a magma of social imaginary significations, which we can and must call a *world* of significations. For it is one and the same thing to say that society institutes the world in each case as its world or its world as the world, and to say that it institutes a world of significations, that it institutes itself in instituting the world of significations that is its own, in correlation to which, alone, a world can and does exist for it. The radical break, the alteration represented by the emergence of the social–historical in pre-social nature is the positing of signification and of a world of significations. Society brings into being a world of significations and itself exists in reference to such a world. Correlatively, nothing can exist for society if it is not related to the world of significations; everything that appears is immediately caught up in this world – and can even come to appear only by being caught up in this world. Society exists in positing the requirement of signification as universal and as total, and in positing its world of significations as what can satisfy this requirement. And it is only in correlation with this world of significations as it is instituted in each case that we can reflect on the question raised above: what is the 'unity' and the 'identity', that is to say the *ecceity* of a society, and what is it that holds a society together? What holds a society together is the holding-together of its world of significations. What permits us to think of it in its *ecceity*, as *this particular* society and not another, is the particularity or specificity of its world of significations as the institution of *this* magma of social imaginary significations, organized in a particular way and not otherwise. It immediately becomes obvious that a given society is not and cannot be a distinct and definite object, nor can it be a system of this sort of objects – since this is not the mode of being of significations. Likewise, we can never reflect in the identitary frame of reference on questions such as: From what point on is a society, in its self-alteration, no longer *that particular* society? Or, under what conditions can contemporary and 'related' collectivities be said to be segments of the 'same' society or to constitute several different societies? Athens, Corinth, Sparta are neither mere segments of ancient Greek society, nor instances of the 'concept' of the Greek city any more than they are societies other than ancient Greek society. The very *mode* of co-belonging of Greek cities to ancient Greek society is part of the proper and original institution of this society – just as the mode of co-belonging of national States to a kind of world society under modern capitalism is part of the institution of modern capitalism. In both cases, this mode includes the possibility and the actuality of particular institutions and of particular significations related to this or that collectivity. – In the same way, it is out of the question that we could think of the relation between republican Rome and imperial Rome or that of a change in a few attributes or qualities, leaving a substratum, a substance-Rome unaltered, or as an absolute break, or, again, as that of an 'influence' of the first on the second across time, by means of the transmission of a heritage. In and through this passage, it is Roman society that is altered. It is just as impossible to fail to recognize, through this passage, the maintenance and the preservation of an innumerable host of institutions as to fail to see the essential alteration of the significations which these institutions carry, bring into being and by means of which these institutions themselves *are*.

Why does society institute itself in instituting a world of significations, why is the emergence of the social–historical the emergence of signification and of signification as instituted – why, finally, *is there* signification? These questions have no more meaning than the question: why is there something rather than nothing? We are not replying to these questions (it is not apparent how there could ever be a 'reply' which would not *ipso facto* be a reiteration of the question), we are simply attempting to clarify the situation in which we find ourselves and which, globally, cannot be examined, when we observe that society exists only in so far as it institutes itself and as it is instituted, and that institution is inconceivable without signification. We have written at length above concerning this circular implication, in connection with language, *legein* and *teukhein*. The institution of society is the institution of social doing and of social representing/saying. In both of these aspects, it includes as an ineffaceable part of itself an identitary–ensemblist dimension which is manifested in *legein* and in *teukhein*. *Teukhein* is the identitary dimension (which can be termed functional or instrumental) of social doing; *legein* is the identitary dimension of social representing/saying which presents itself in particular in language inasmuch as language is also always necessarily a *code*. But we have also seen at great length that language cannot simply be a code, that it includes as an ineffaceable part of itself a signitive dimension as well, related to the magma of significations, that it is always *language (langue)* as well. This is because a formal system cannot be closed up within itself – or, if you prefer, because nothing starting *from* or residing *within* an identitary system permits the production of such a system in general, allows it to refer to anything other than to itself, or decides anything about its concrete, peculiar tenor or organization. Or again: language must say the world, and nothing in the code allows positing a world or deciding *what* this world will be. – Likewise, social doing cannot be simply *teukhein* or technique. The acts and objects which are posited in and through the schema of finality, in the instrumental and functional dimension of doing, cannot be defined and grasped on the basis of sheer instrumentality or functionality. They are what they are and in the way that they are through the global orientation of social doing, an orientation which is but one aspect on the world of imaginary significations of the society considered. And, in this case too, the instrumental or functional dimension of doing (*teukhein* and technique) and its signitive dimension are indissociable. It is not only that it would be absurd to consider *teukhein* and technique as purely neutral instruments, capable of serving any sort of ends. It is just as impossible to think of them as a 'consequence' of the ends and the significations posited by society, to see in them the conclusion to a syllogism for which the orientation of doing would provide the premises. Society does not, 'first', posit ends and significations on the basis of which it would then deliberate as to the techniques most suited to serving and embodying these. Ends and significations are posited together in and through technique and *teukhein* – just as significations are posited in and through *legein*. In a sense, the tools and instruments of a society *are* significations; they are the 'materialization' of the imaginary significations of that society in the identitary and functional dimension. An assembly line is (and can only exist as) the 'materialization' of a host of imaginary significations central to capitalism.

Up to now we have considered significations mostly in terms of their so to speak immediate or intrinsic relation to *legein* and *teukhein*. It was important to show and to illustrate, in both of these cases, the circular implication of the identitary and of the signitive dimensions. A word is a word inasmuch as it relates, indissociably, to an identitary *designated* and conveys a signification of language (*langue*). A tool or instrument is always at one and the same time defined in an identitary manner in the functional relations of a partial or local finality *and* caught up in the magma of social doing. Signification can therefore appear as *attached to* ... 'something' which would exist separately, independently, prior to signification, even if one is prepared to acknowledge that this 'something' – natural being, manufactured material object, logical or rational entity – can exist *for* society only by being 'invested' with a signification. I hope that what has been said up to now will persuade the reader that this view is more than just insufficient, that it is fallacious. There is more to it than this, however. This view offers an appearance of plausibility only with respect to what could be called second-order or derived significations. It has no meaning whatsoever in the case of the central or primary imaginary significations of a society; for these *create* objects *ex nihilo*, they organize the world (as the world 'external' to society, as the social world, and as the mutual inherence of each of them). Thus – to take an example which, although a facile one, is, nevertheless, decisive – *God* is not a signification 'attached to something': to what thing? The word *God* has no referent other than the signification God, as it is posited in each case by the society in question. The 'referent' which would be the individual representations of God (or of gods) is *created* through the creation and institution of that central imaginary signification which is God. The signification God at once creates an object of individual representations and is the central element in the organization of the world for a monotheistic society, since God is posited at the same time as the source of being and as the pre-eminent being, as the norm and the origin of the Law, as the ultimate foundation of all value and as the pole in relation to which all social doing is oriented, since it is in reference to God that there is a *separation* into a sacred region and a profane region, and that a host of social activities are instituted and objects created which have no other *'raison d'être'*. It is only in a secondary, derived and, finally, uninteresting sense that, once there is an institution of God and of religion, religious significations can be said to be attached as well to objects or acts which have, or might have had, a social existence 'independent' of these. The situation is essentially the same in other forms of 'belief' (polytheistic, 'animist', 'fetishist'); demonstrating this would require a detailed analysis which cannot be undertaken here. Likewise, for example, the 'economy' and the 'economic' are central social imaginary significations which do not 'refer' *to* something but on the basis of which a host of things are socially represented, reflected, acted upon and made *as* economic. This has *nothing to do* with the theorist's 'abstraction' which separates an economic 'aspect' out of social processes in order better to study it. The theorist could separate nothing out in this area unless, at a certain moment and in certain societies, the economic signification had not emerged and was not implicitly instituted, first, as important and, then, as central and decisive. This is not the empirical condition but the logical and ontological condition for the theorist's 'abstraction'. This economic signification is 'cashed' or converted, on the one hand, into a host of significations referred to 'concrete' objects (the goods prod-uced, the instruments of production, etc.) and, on the other, into a multiplicity of 'abstract' yet socially effective and active significations (thus, in the capitalist economy, capital, stock, labour, wages, revenues, profit and interest are 'abstract' significations, thematized and made explicit as such by and for the participants; their being-explicit is the actual condition for this society's operation). But what is it that holds all of these significations together and makes them *economic* signifi-cations? All the attempts to give trans-historical replies to this question lead to fallacies. Thus, when one states, as do academic economists, that an economy exists whenever unlimited ends are confronted with limited means – which concerns technique as well, touching, for exam-ple agronomy as much as spatial navigation – and neglects the fact that the idea of 'unlimited ends' can germinate only in the head of an economist of the capitalist period; or when one speaks of 'exchanges' between the members of society, which has led to the still flourishing confusions over the exchange of things, of women and of words; or, finally, when one speaks of the production and reproduction of the material life of society, as if one knew what a 'material life' of society separable from the rest might actually be, as if this very idea of a separate 'material life' were not itself one of the most typical and most clearly historically dated products of the capitalist period. We have already stressed the fact that the *separation* of the economic sphere from the rest of social activities, its constitution as an 'autonomous' and, finally, predominant domain, is itself an historical product which appears only in certain societies and in relation to a complex development. However, to ascertain the historicity of this phenomenon by no means dispenses us from asking ourselves in what it consists; quite the opposite. What do we mean when we say that in certain societies the economy 'separates itself off' from the rest? This can mean, certainly, neither a 'real' separation nor a logical construction of the theorist aimed at making the phenomena more intelligible. What is involved here is the emergence of a central signification which reorganizes, redetermines, and reforms a host of previously available social significations, thereby altering them, conditioning the constitution of other significations, entailing analogous lateral effects throughout practically the totality of the social significations of the system considered. And, of course, all of this by no means concerns 'disembodied' significations; this goes hand in hand with, and is impossible without, transformations in the *activities* and the *values* of the society in question, as well as actual transformations in social individuals and objects, without there ever being any question of a logical or real priority of one of these aspects over the others. The economic cannot be constituted and instituted as a central social signification if it is not embodied, figured, presentified, instrumented in and through actual social activities – nor can these activities become economic activities or acquire a predominantly economic aspect without the emergence of the economic signification and the alteration of the entire magma of social significations which it implies and entails. The two are, in turn, inseparable from the transformation of the social system of values, both globally and specifically. This emergence of the economic signification with these decisive characterstics in the actual history is in large part independent of its becoming explicit for its participants, and even more so from its theoretical thematization. Xenophone's *Economics* or that attributed to Aristotle precede the appearance of capitalism by 20 centuries, and Antoine de Montchrestien at the beginning of the seventeenth century wrote the eponymous work for the new reality and the new 'science'. This theoretical thematization, as shown by the preceding examples, is, however, neither the result of nor the condition for the institution of economic signification as central by capitalism. This institution operates implicitly, is intended as such by no one, is realized through the pursuit of an undetermined number of particular ends, which are present and can be represented only in the social sphere, coordinated for the participants with partial significations, both 'concrete' and 'abstract', which subsequently prove to be overdetermined by this central significcation, in the process of being instituted. The latter thus allows itself to be grasped, after the fact, as the non-real condition of the real coexistence of social phenomena. The non-real yet eminently actual (*wirklich*) since it is actualizing (*wirkend*).

This analysis could be undertaken in the case of all the central social imaginary significations – whether this be the family, the law or the State; for, before rushing on to define these terms as referring to 'institutions' in the second-order and usual sense of the term, we must first ask ourselves how, through what means and on what basis a given group of facts, acts, etc. can be posited by a society as 'legal', for instance.

Central significations are not significations 'of' something – nor are they, except in a second-order sense, significations 'attached' or 'related' to something. They constitute that which, for a given society, brings into being the co-belonging of objects, acts and individuals which, in appearance, are most heterogeneous. They have no 'referent'; they institute a mode of being of things and of individuals which relate to them. In themselves, they are not necessarily explicit for the society that institutes them. They are presentified–figured through the totality of the explicit institutions of society and the organization of the world as such and of the social world which these institutions serve to instrument. They condition and orient social doing and representing, in and through which they continue as they are themselves altered.

v   THE MODE OF BEING OF SOCIAL IMAGINARY SIGNIFICATIONS

Social imaginary significations place us in the presence of a mode of being which is primary, originary, irreducible, one which we must, again here, reflect upon in terms of itself without submitting it in advance to the logical–ontological schemata already available elsewhere.

What has already been stated in this connection sufficiently shows that social imaginary significations cannot be thought of on the basis of an alleged relation to a 'subject' which would 'carry' them or 'intend' them. They are not the noemata of a noesis – except in a secondary and inessential way. If one wanted at all costs to use these terms, they would have to be considered not only as noemata without noesis, but as that which, for the individuals of a society, makes it possible that noemata and noesis can be there; and this, not in the manner that the 'object' makes its intending possible but in the manner that language makes speech possible. For these significations are that by reason of which 'subjects' exist as subjects and as *these particular* subjects. The fact that reflection can always attempt to intend them explicitly as such, posit them as noemata of a noesis, is second and secondary, and the condition for the possibility of a reflection such as this (ultimately, problematical and, at any rate, historically recent) continues to lie in social imaginary significations.

Nor could we think of social imaginary significations on the basis of their 'relation' to 'objects' as their referents. For it is in and through these significations that 'objects' and the relation of 'reference' as well are made possible. The 'object' as referent is always co-constituted by the corresponding social imaginary signification – the individual object as well as objectivity as such. What is most important is that central or primary significations are without any referent whatsoever or, if you like, are their own referent. There is no referent for God, the divinities, religious or mythological figures or entities in general – outside of these figures themselves as significations. Nor is there a referent for the significations: citizen, justice, commodity, money, capital, etc., other than these significations themselves. To say that an object or a class of objects are commodities is not to say anything about these objects as such but about the manner in which a society treats (can treat) this object or class of objects, about the manner of being of these objects for that society. It is to say that this society has instituted the signification commodity – as such and in and through a network of derived significations – that it has instituted individual behaviour and material systems which give being to objects, and these particular objects, as 'commodities'.

In this way, too, a 'thing' is an imaginary signification (with, obviously, a widely variable content) instituted by all known societies. This institution involves, as has already been stated above, the essential operative schemata of *legein* (separation/union identity, 'continuity', etc.), namely the operative figures of the social imaginary, but it also *always involves other imaginary* components. For any society whatsoever 'things' are, for instance, *either* animate *in toto or else* in part inanimate. Now even if this assertion may seem scandalous, *both* of these positions are imaginary ones. Positing 'things' as inanimate is *never* the simple 'negation' of their being 'animate', it is always the positing of something else: created by God for us, pure inert material forms to exercise our mastery and possession of nature, etc. The instituted signification of 'thing' in a given society is what makes possible 'perceived things' or perceptual representations (as representations carrying with them an index of 'independence') for the individuals of that society, and which defines in each case *which* entities are 'things' and *what* they are. This is not to be confused with the philosophical 'concept' (or category) of the same name, which, by the way, has no assignable meaning if not the enigma of 'substance'.

It is clear that social imaginary significations cannot be related to a 'subject' constructed explicitly in order to 'carry' them – whether this is called 'group consciousness', 'collective unconscious' or whatever. These terms were forged and the corresponding pseudo-entities constructed by exporting them illegitimately from other spheres, or tracing them after other entities, by reason of the inability to come to terms with the mode of being specific to significations. In this sense too, the terms 'collective representation' or 'social representation' by means of which certain sociologists have attempted, correctly although insufficiently, to sight an aspect of what we are attempting to reflect on in this way, are themselves unsuitable and are in danger of generating confusion.

More generally, the world of instituted significations cannot be reduced to actual individual representations or to their 'common', 'average' or 'typical part'. Significations *are* obviously not *what* individuals represent to themselves, consciously or unconsciously, or *what* they think. They are that by means of which and on the basis of which individuals are formed as social individuals, capable of participating in social doing and representing/saying, capable of representing, acting, thinking in a compatible, coherent, convergent manner, even if this be in the form of conflict (the most violent conflict that can tear a society apart still presupposes an indefinite number of things that are 'common' and 'participatory'). This entails – and, to be sure, even requires – that part of the social imaginary significations has an actual 'equivalent' in the individuals (in their conscious or unconscious representation, their behaviour, etc.) and that the others can be 'translated' into them, either directly or indirectly, proximately or distantly. But this is something quite different from their 'actual presence' or their existing 'in person' in the representation of individuals. No individual, in order to be a social individual, has any need to 'represent to himself' the totality of the institution of society or the significations that it carries, nor indeed could do so. And this poses, precisely, an immense problem which cannot be examined here, that of the necessary *complementarity* of the types of individuals instituted in and through the articulation of society, and hence also that of the *complementarity* of the 'equivalents' or the 'translations' of the social imaginary significations actually present in the representations of individuals. Nothing has yet been stated when it is said that individuals learn or take on social 'roles', that they are induced, led or conditioned to play them. There would be no roles if there were not a play; how could there be any roles, if the ensemble of roles did not form one play? What play, and who wrote it? It is possible that at times people drape themselves in Roman tunics to play the bourgeois revolution – or that a general wants to play Joan of Arc in twentieth-century dress; but how is it that, in real history, it is never Zerlina who replies to Agamemnon and that Brutus never has Monsieur Perrichon for his friend and confidant? There is no serf without a lord, and vice versa; there is no serf who does not have a certain representation of the lord in general, of his lord and of the relation of serfdom; there is no lord who does not have a certain representation of serfs in

general, of his serfs and of the relation of serfdom. These representations are and must necessarily be different and complementary –
and without this complementarity, there is no feudal society. This
complementarity can exist only through instituted signification (it is an
aspect of this signification or belongs to it). The instituted signification
(here, the relation of serfdom) is not the 'sum' of these complementary
significations; it is because this signification is instituted that these
representations exist (those of the serf, the lord, the relation of serfdom,
for the serf and for the lord) and that they are complementary.

This compatibility and, above all, essential complementarity of the
representations of individuals, without which both the representations
and the individuals would be nothing at all, illustrates what I said about
social significations as conditions for the representable and the do-able
and points up the impasses awaiting any attempt to 'explain' the social
on the basis of the individual, any attempt to reduce society to psychology, whether this be in terms of a 'positivist', behaviourist or even
psychoanalytic orientation.

Finally, social imaginary significations are not to be confused with the
various types of signification or sense (*Sinn*) starting from which Max
Weber was attempting to think of society.[14] They are assuredly not the
'subjectively intended sense' (*subjektiv gemeinte Sinn*), a side or aspect
of the signification intended as such by the social individual and hence,
in a sense, 'present' for him – and not an 'average' sense or the
'common part' of senses subjectively intended either. Social imaginary
significations are that by reason of which these concrete or 'average'
subjective intentions are made possible. Already for this reason there
is no confusing them with 'ideal–typical significations' or 'ideal types',
constructions of the theorist aimed at helping him to understand social
phenomena. For 'ideal types' are the product of a reflection on society
– which presupposes that society *is* and that concordant and complementary subjective intentions are possible and actual there; whereas
social imaginary significations are 'immanent' to the society considered
in each case. In reality, the 'ideal–typical sense' of which Max Weber
speaks is but the means he provides for himself to sight and then to
reconstruct actual social significations – which his methodology and
epistemology, strongly influenced by neo-Kantianism, prevent him from
recognizing as such: what would, what could, an *actual sense* be, if it
is not sense *for* a subject or else sense in and through a theoretical
construction? We have been led to establish that there can be no sense
for a subject, unless, in actuality, there is sense for no one, unless there
is social signification and the institution of this signification. To say
that, for this reason as well, this sense is never 'directly' accessible to
us when we reflect upon society and that we can only attempt to
'reproduce' it or to 'construct' it, is of little matter. Constructivism is
only a word, unless it asserts that all constructions are of equal worth
– something Max Weber would certainly never have affirmed. To say

that a particular construction is *preferable* to some other one implies that it maintains a certain relation to that which is in question. This is precisely what is expressed by the fact, for instance, that it is impossible actually to construct ideal–typical significations as correlative to one or to several 'phenomena' or 'aspects' of society. The latter are in each case what they are and as they are only through their immersion in society as a whole – consequently, they refer to one another, and all to the magma of significations that underlies and orients the institution of the society considered. This is manifested, once again, by the *complementarity* – not simply of the representations of individuals but of the *types* of individuals, objects and acts which a given society brings into being. The 'ideal type' of Roman citizen refers *from within* to the 'ideal type' of Roman woman, of religion and of law as these existed in Rome, etc. – and it is not the theoretical construction that can ever assure this intrinsic holding-together, this outside-itself immanent to each of these significations. This is also expressed by the essential *historicity* of significations: apparently similar 'institutions' can be radically other, since, immersed in another society, they are caught up in other significations. To cite one massive and clear example, referring to an 'ideal type' of bureaucracy in general cannot help but mask the critical differences between Chinese imperial bureaucracy, for instance, and the bureaucracy of modern capitalism. What these two types of bureaucracy may have in common – or what they may have in common with other types – stems from a conceptualization *about* bureaucracies in general, which, to be sure, in its turn reveals important aspects of the social–historical institution and poses the vast problem of the 'universal' and the 'transcultural' in this institution – which we cannot examine here. This problem, however, is merely *designated*, not worked out, by the concept of 'ideal type' and of 'ideal–typical sense'.

The world of social significations is to be thought of not as an irreal copy of a real world; not as formed by that which is 'expressible' in individual representations – or as what is to be postulated as the 'objective correlate' (*entgegen-stehend*) of subjective noesis; not, finally, as a system of relations which would be added onto subjects and objects which themselves are given fully and which would modify, in this or that historical context, their properties, effects or behaviour. We are to think of the world of social significations as the primary, inaugural, irreducible positing of the social–historical and of the social imaginary as it manifests itself in each case in a given society; a positing which is presentified and figured in and through the institution, as the institution of the world and of society itself. It is this institution of significations – always instrumented in the institutions of *legein* and *teukhein* – which, for each society, posits what is and what is not, what has worth and what does not, and *how*, in what way is or is not, does or does not have worth that which can actually be or have worth. This is what establishes the conditions and the common orientations of the do-able and the representable, and in this holds together, in advance and by construction, so to speak, the indefinite and essentially *open* multitude of individuals, acts, objects, functions, institutions in the second-order and customary sense of the term, which in each case, concretely, constitutes a society.

We therefore have to think of a mode of being belonging to this world – to these worlds – of significations in its specificity and its originality, without 'substantializing' them, even metaphorically, or transforming them into 'subjects' of another order (by saying, for instance, that 'myths reflect upon one another').[15] Likewise, when we speak of the social–historical and of the social imaginary, the difficulty is not to invent new words for what is at issue here, but instead to understand that what these words are aiming at is not categorizable by means of the grammatical categories (and behind these, logical and ontological categories) in accordance with which we are in the habit of thinking. The difficulty lies in understanding that when we speak of the social–historical, for instance, we are not intending a substantive, an adjective, nor a substantified adjective; in understanding that the social imaginary is not a substance, not a quality, not an action or a passion; that social imaginary significations are not representations, not figures or forms, not concepts.

vi RADICAL IMAGINARY, INSTITUTING SOCIETY, INSTITUTED SOCIETY

Within the having-to-be the radical imaginary emerges as otherness and as the perpetual orientation of otherness, which figures and figures itself, exists in figuring and in figuring itself, the creation of 'images' which are what they are and as they are as figurations or presentifications of significations or meanings.

The radical imaginary exists as the social–historical and as psyche/soma. As social–historical, it is an open stream of the anonymous collective; as psyche/soma, it is representative/affective/intentional flux. That which in the social–historical is positing, creating, bringing into being we call social imaginary in the primary sense of the term, or instituting society. That which in the psyche/soma is positing, creating, bringing-into-being for the psyche/soma, we call radical imagination.

The social imaginary or instituting society exists in and through the positing-creating of social imaginary significations and of the institution; of the institution as the 'presentification' of these significations, and of these significations as instituted. The radical imagination exists in and through the positing-creating of figures as the presentification of meaning and of meaning as always figured/represented. The institution of society by instituting society leans on the first natural stratum of the given – and is always found (down to an unfathomable point of origin) in a relation of reception/alteration with what had already been instituted. The position of meaningful figures or of figured meaning by radical imagination leans on the being-thus of the subject as a living being, and is always found (down to an unfathomable point of origin) in a relation of what had already been represented by and for the psyche.

The institution of society is each time the institution of a magma of significations, possible only through its instrumentation in two basic institutions, which bring into being an identitary–ensemblist organization of what exists for society. The instrumental institution of *legein* is the institution of the identitary–ensemblist conditions for social representing/saying. The instrumental institution of *teukhein* is the institution of the identitary–ensemblist conditions for social doing. The two institutions mutually imply one another, they intrinsically inhere in one another, and each is impossible without the other. Both are 'objectively reflexive', both presuppose themselves and can operate only if the products of this operation are already available. Both are 'everywhere' dense, in social doing and social representing/saying: as near as one may like to any signification, any representation or social act, one will always find an indefinite number of ensemblist–identitary elements. Both are absolute creations of the social imaginary; one can think of them as 'sampled out' of the magma of instituted significations, on the condition of not forgetting that it is only through *legein* and *teukhein* that this magma can exist and be for the society considered.

In and through *legein* and *teukhein* the global institution of society is instrumented, the figurating–presentifying of the magma of significations which this institution brings each time into being. This institution is each time the institution of the world, as the world of and for that society, and as the organization–articulation of the society itself. It supplies the content, the organization and the orientation of social doing and representing/saying. It includes as non-eliminable, as a creation of society, the institution of the social individual, through this *teukhein* and this particular doing represented by the socialization of psyche/soma. By this means, society brings into being individuals for whom there is perception, speech and reflection, individuals who are indefinitely self-reproducible as social individuals, for each of whom there is always both a private world and a public world, and whose life in society *is*, in a sense, the life and the functioning of society as instituted society.

The creation of instituting society, as instituted society, is each time a common world – *kosmos koinos*: the positing of individuals, of their types, relations and activities; but also the positing of things, their types, relations and signification – all of which are caught up each time in receptacles and frames of reference instituted as common, which make them exist together. This institution is the institution of a world in the sense that it can and must enclose everything, that, through and in it, everything must in principle, be sayable and representable and that everything must be totally caught up in the network of significations, everything must have meaning. The manner in which everything, each time, has meaning, and the meaning it has is rooted in the core of the imaginary significations of the society considered. But this overlapping is never guaranteed: what escapes it, at times almost indifferent, can be and is of the utmost seriousness. What escapes it is the enigma of the world as such, which stands behind the common social world, as having-to-be, that is to say, an inexhaustable supply of otherness, and as an irreducible challenge to every established signification. What escapes it as well is the very being of society as instituting, that is to say, ultimately, society as the source and origin of otherness or perpetual self-alteration.

The institution of the common world is necessarily each time the institution of that which is and is not, does and does not have worth, of what is and is not do-able, both 'outside' the society (in relation to 'nature') and 'within' it. As such, it must also necessarily be 'presence' for society of non-being, of the false, the fictive, of the merely possible but not actual. 'Reality' for a given society is constituted through the synergy of all these schemata of significance.

Reality, language, values, needs and labour in each society specify, in each case, in their particular mode of being, the organization of the world and of the social world related to the social imaginary significations instituted by the society in question. These significations are also presentified–figured in the internal articulation of society – inasmuch as the collectivity can be instituted as distributed into categories of individuals, divided in a purely symmetrical manner or split asymmetrically in and through an internal conflict; in the organization of relations between the sexes and the reproduction of social individuals; in the institution of the forms and sectors specific to doing and to social activities. Here belongs also the mode in which society refers to itself and to its own past, present and future; and the mode of being of other societies for it.

This specifying occurs through a host of second-order institutions and imaginary significations; second, not in the sense that they are minor or simply derived, but that they are always held together by the institution of significations central to the society considered. The latter cannot exist without the former; there is no relation of priority between them, and in general relations such as these have no meaning on the level in question here. The enterprise is a second-order institution of capitalism – without which there would be no capitalism.

In and through the totality of these second-order institutions the functioning of society as instituted society is assured and continued – which implies also a proliferation of institutions (and of significations) that are truly secondary and derived (this is what is usually referred to when someone speaks of an institution).

As instituting as well as as instituted, society is intrinsically history – namely, self-alteration. Instituted society is not opposed to instituting society as a lifeless product to an activity which brought it into being; it represents the relative and transitory fixity/stability of the instituted forms–figures in and through which the radical imaginary can alone exist and make itself exist as social–historical. The perpetual self-alteration of society is its very being, which is manifested by the positing of relatively fixed and stable forms-figures and through the shattering of these forms-figures which can never be anything other than the positing–creating of other forms-figures. Each society also brings into being its own mode of self-alteration, which can also be called its temporality – that is to say, it also brings itself into being *as* a mode of being. History is ontological genesis not as the production of different tokens of the essence of society but as the creation, in and through each society, of another *type* (form-figure–aspect-sense: *eidos*) of being-society which is in the same stroke the creation of new *types* of social–historical entities (objects, individuals, ideas, institutions, etc.) on all levels and on levels which are themselves posited-created by a given society.

Even as instituted, society can exist only as perpetual self-alteration. For it can be instituted only as the institution of a world of significations, which exclude self-identity and exist only through their essential possibility of being-other; and it is instituted through the constitution of social individuals, who are as they are and can function as they do only to the extent that their socialization *informs* the manifestations of their radical imagination but does not destroy it. It is true that, as such, the institution that is posited in each case can exist only as a norm of self-identity, as inertia and as a mechanism of self-perpetuation; but, equally true, that of which there should be self-identity, the instituted signification, can exist only by altering itself, and alters itself through doing and social representing/saying. In this way, the norm itself alters itself through the alteration of that of which it should be the norm of identity, awaiting the moment it will be shattered by the explicit positing of another norm.

Society is, therefore, always the self-institution of the social–historical. But this self-institution generally is not known as such (which has led people to believe that it cannot be known as such). The alienation of heteronomy of society is self-alienation; the concealment of the being of society as self-institution in its own eyes, covering over its essential temporality. This self-alienation – sustained by the responses that have been supplied by history up to now to the requirements of psychical functioning, by the tendency proper to the institution, and by the practically incoercible domination of identitary logic-ontology – is manifested in the social representation (itself instituted in each case) of an extra-social origin of the institution of society (an origin ascribed to supernatural beings, God, nature, reason, necessity, the laws of history or the being-thus of Being). From this point of view, an essential part of inherited thought is but the rationalization of this heteronomy of society and, as such, one of its manifestations. Its replies to the question of the world and of history and even, when it is kept open, its questioning are always situated on a ground where the radical imaginary as social–historical and as radical imagination, indetermination as creation, temporality as essential self-alteration are excluded. Borne most of the time by the phantasy of mastery as the exhaustive determination of being in and by theory, inherited thought abandons it only to sink into the melancholia of impotence or to posit itself as determined from an elsewhere, consoling itself by saying that it is being that is speaking in it and through it. Founded from the start on the concealment of doing and of bringing into being, inherited thought suffers the *nemesis* of this concealment by being condemned to be unaware of its own nature as *thoughtful doing*, itself a manifestation and a mode of being of the social–historical.

To be sure, the self-alienation or heteronomy of society is not 'mere representation' or the society's incapacity to represent itself in some other way than as instituted on the basis of and by an elsewhere. It is embodied, strongly and weightily materialized in the concrete institution of society, incorporated in its conflictual division, carried and mediated by its entire organization, interminably reproduced in and through social functioning, the being-thus of social objects, activities and individuals. Thus also its supersession – which we are aiming at *because we will it* and because we know that others will it as well, not because such are the laws of history, the interests of the proletariat or the destiny of being – the bringing about of a history in which society not only knows itself, but *makes itself* as explicitly self-instituting, implies a radical destruction of the known institution of society, in its most unsuspected nooks and crannies, which can exist only as positing/ creating not only new institutions but a new *mode* of instituting and a new relation of society and of individuals to the institution. As far as our eyes can see, nothing allows us to affirm that a self-transformation of history such as this is impossible; no place – except the fictive and finally incoherent non-place of identitary logic-ontology – exists where the one who would assert this could possibly stand. The self-transformation of society concerns social doing – and so also politics, in the profound sense of the term – the doing of men and women in society, and nothing else. Of this, thoughtful doing, and political thinking – society's thinking as making *itself* – is one essential component.

Notes

PREFACE

1 *Socialisme ou Barbarie*, nos. 36–40. As with my other texts from *Socialisme ou Barbarie* which have been republished in the 10/18 collection, 'Marxism and Revolutionary Theory' is reprinted here unchanged, except for the correction of printing errors, a few *lapsus calami* or obscurities and, when necessary, the updating of certain references. Additions are indicated by square brackets. To the original footnotes I have added some new notes, indicated by an asterisk.

1 MARXISM: A PROVISIONAL ASSESSMENT

1 Dating back from 1964, the year this text was written [Ed.].
2 By historical reality we, of course, do not mean particular events and facts separated from the rest but the dominant tendencies of the evolution, together with all the necessary interpretations.
3 Marx, 'Eleventh Thesis on Feuerbach', in Marx and Engels, *Selected Works* (London: Lawrence and Wishart, 1968) p. 30.
4 'Universal history is the Last Judgement.' Despite its theological overtones, this is Hegel's most radically atheistic idea: there is no transcendence, no recourse against what happens here, we *are* definitively what we become, what we will have become.
5 As we 'know', the need to destroy every State apparatus set apart from the masses on the first day of revolution is the central thesis of *State and Revolution*.
6 See below, chapter 2.
7 Cf. *In Defense of Marxism*, (London: New Park Publications, 1966).
8 'What is orthodox Marxism?', in *History and Class-Consciousness*, translated by Rodney Livingstone (Cambridge, Mass.: MIT Press, 1971) pp. 1–26. C. Wright Mills also appears to adopt this viewpoint. See *The Marxists* (Harmondsworth: Penguin, 1962) pp. 98 and 129.
9 The classic example of this shift is obviously the passage from Kant to Hegel, by way of Fichte and Schelling. The problematic is the same, however, in the later works of Plato or in the neo-Kantians, from Rickert to Lask.
10 To be sure, the positions must not simply be reversed. Neither logically nor historically can physical categories be considered merely the result of material (even less a 'reflection' of it). A revolution in the domain of categories can lead to the grasp of a material previously undefined (as with Galileo). Furthermore, an advance in experimentation can 'force' a new material to appear. Ultimately there is a twofold relation, but there is certainly no independence of the categories in relation to content.
11 'The Changing Function of Historical Materialism', in *History and Class Consciousness*, pp. 223–55.
12 One passage among a thousand: 'The monopoly of capitalism becomes a fetter upon the mode of production, which has sprung up and flourished along with, and under it. Centralisation of the means of production and socialisation of labour at last reach

a point where they become incompatible with their capitalist integument. Thus integument is burst asunder. The knell of capitalist private property sounds. The expropriators are expropriated.' *Capital*, 1, p. 763 (New York: International Publishers, 1967).

13 On the critique of Marx's economic theory, see 'Le Movement révolutionaire sous le capitalisme moderne', in *Socialisme ou Barbarie*, Dec. 1960, no. 31, pp. 68–81; now in *Capitalisme moderne et révolution*, Paris, ed. 10/18, 1978, vol. 2, pp. 20–105; English edition by the University of Minnesota Press forthcoming as *Cornelius Castoriadis: Political and Social Writings*, 2 volumes.

14 Cf. Marx's own terms, defining his 'standpoint': '... *the evolution of the economic formation of society is viewed as a process of natural history* ...' (*Capital*, 1, p. 10 (author's italics).

15 See 'Le Movement révolutionnaire sous le capitalisme moderne', in *Socialisme ou Barbarie* (April 1961) no. 32 (now in *Capitalisme moderne et révolution*, pp. 105–19). See also 'Sur le contenu du socialisme, III', in *L'Expérience du mouvement ouvrier, 2: Prolétariat et organisation*, Paris, 10/18 collection, 1973, p. 9ff.

16 Karl Marx, *Contribution to the Critique of Political Economy*, translated by S. W. Ryzanskaya (New York: International Publishers, 1970) p. 21.

17 See, for example, the first part ('Bourgeois and Proletarians') of the *Communist Manifesto*, in *Selected Works*, pp. 35–46.

18 Leon Trotsky, *The Defence of Terrorism: Terrorism and Communism* (London: Allen and Unwin, 1935) p. 17. It must be recalled that, until very recently, Stalinists, Trotskyites and 'far-left' purists were practically in agreement for purposes of denying, camouflaging or minimizing under any pretext the continuation of the development of production after 1945. Even now, a 'Marxist's' natural reply is, 'Ah, but that's due to the production of arms.'

19 '... it is always necessary to distinguish between the material transformation of the economic conditions of production, which can be determined with the precision of natural science, and the legal political ...' Marx, Preface to *A Contribution to the Critique of Political Economy*, p. 21, (author's italics). [Also: 'Darwin has interested us in the history of Nature's Technology, i.e., in the formation of the organs of plants and animals, which organs serve as instruments of production for sustaining life. Does not the history of the productive organs of man, of organs that are the material basis of all social organisation, deserve equal attention? And would not such a history be easier to compile, since, as Vico says, human history differs from natural history in this, that we have made the former, but not the latter? Technology discloses man's code of dealing with nature, the process of production by which he sustains his life, and thereby also lays bare the mode of formation of his social relations, and of the mental conceptions that flow from them.' *Capital*, 1, p. 372, note 3.]

20 See 'Sur le contenu du socialisme', in *Socialism ou Barbarie*, no. 22, July 1957, pp. 14–21. (now in *Le Contenu du Socialisme*, Paris, 10/18 collection, 1979, pp. 126–37).

21* See also my article 'Technique' in the *Encyclopaedia Universalis*, vol. 15, pp. 803–9, Paris, 1973. (now in *Crossroads in the Labyrinth*, trans. Kate Soper and Martin H. Ryle, The Harvester Press and MIT Press, pp. 229–59).

21 Letter to Joseph Bloch, 21 September 1890. [In fact Engels' concession remains 'merely verbal': 'Among all of them, it is the economic conditions which are finally the determinant ones. Political conditions, etc., however, even the tradition which haunts men's minds, also play a role, although not a decisive one.' And again: 'Thus history up to today unfolds as a natural process and is subjected as well, in substance, to the same laws of motion as nature.']

23 'Immediately' is taken here not in the chronological but in the logical sense: without mediation, without the need to pass by way of another signification.

24* The central position of the 'relations of production' in social life is a creation of the bourgeoisie and an element in the historical institution of capitalism. See 'La Question de l'histoire du mouvement ouvrier' in *L'Expérience du mouvement ouvrier*, 1, pp. 57–66.

25 This is clearly seen by Lukács in 'The Changing Function of Historical Materialism', pp. 223–55.

26 Obviously, no culture can train people to walk on their heads or to fast eternally. Within these limits, however, we meet in history all the types of training we could ever imagine.

27 This is what Sartre does in the *Critique of Dialectical Reason*, for instance (London: New Left Books, 1976) p. 217.

28 See Ruth Benedict, *Patterns of Culture*, (London, RKP, 1952). [Demonstrating the impossibility of projecting retroactively the motivations and the economic categories of capitalism onto other societies, in particular 'archaic' ones, is one of the most important contributions of certain currents of contemporary 'economic anthropology'.]

29 See Margaret Mead et al., *Cultural Patterns and Technical Change*, UNESCO, 1953.

30* It is clear that in these cases the distribution of productive resources (land and human beings) is determined at the outset, and subsequently modified, by the play of factors which are basically not 'economic' ones.

31 See Margaret Mead, *Male and Female* and *Sex and Temperament in Three Primitive Societies* (London: RKP, 1952).

32 In English in the original [Ed.].

33 See also on this problem, 'La Question de l'histoire du mouvement ouvrier'. Here is what Engels had to say about it in his Preface to the third German edition (1885) of the *Eighteenth Brumaire*: 'It was precisely Marx who had first discovered the great law of motion of history, the law according to which all historical struggles, whether they proceed in the political, religious, philosophical or some other ideological domain, are in fact only the more or less clear expression of struggles of social classes, and that the existence and thereby the collisions, too, between these classes are in turn conditioned by the degree of development of their economic position, by the mode of their production and of their exchange determined by it. This law, which has the same significance for history as the law of the transformation of energy has for natural science – this law gave him here, too, the key to an understanding of the history of the Second French Republic.' In *Selected Works*, p. 96.

34 Rigorously speaking, one would have to say: in all their details, period. Determinism makes no sense unless it is a thoroughgoing determinism, even the tone of voice of the fascist demagogue or of the workers' tribune should follow from the laws of the system. To the extent to which this is possible, determinism conceals itself behind the distinction between the 'important' and the 'secondary'. Clemenceau added a certain personal style to the politics of French imperialism but with or without this style, these politics would have remained in any event the 'same' in their important aspects, in their essence. In this way, reality is divided into a main stratum, in which causal connections can and must be established before and after the event considered, and a secondary stratum, in which these connections do not exist or are not important. Thus determinism can be realized only by dividing the world up once more; only conceptually does it intend a unified world, in its application it is, in fact, obliged to postulate an 'undetermined' part of reality.

35 French politician of the Fourth Republic [Ed.].

36 It intervenes only at the limits – historical and logical – of the system: capitalism does not arise organically through the simple operation of the economic laws of market production; what is necessary is the primitive accumulation which constitutes a violent break with the old system. Nor does capitalism cede its place to socialism without the workers' revolution. All of this changes nothing, however, in what we are saying here, for it must be added that these active interventions of classes in history are themselves predetermined, introducing nothing that is unpredictable in principle.

37 See 'Le Mouvement révolutionnaire sous le capitalisme moderne' in *Socialisme ou Barbarie*, no. 31; and *Capitalisme moderne et révolution*.

38 'The matter is not what this or that proletarian, or even the proletariat as a whole, *represents* to himself at a given moment as a goal. The matter is instead *what* the

proletariat *is* and what, corresponding to its *being* it will be historically forced to do' as Marx states in a well-known sentence in *The Holy Family*.

39 This is also true, despite appearances, for Lukács. For example, when he writes, '(the proletariat) ... can be transformed and liberated only by its own actions ... The objective (economic) evolution could only give the proletariat the opportunity and necessity to change society. Any transformation can only come about as the product of the – free – action of the proletariat itself' ('Reification and the Consciousness of the Proletariat', in *History and Class Consciousness*, pp. 208–9), one must not forget that the entire dialectic of history that is exposed by him holds only on the condition that the proletariat accomplishes this free action.

40 French economist (b. 1903) [Ed.].

41 In the terms of Kantian philosophy: the subject's corporeality is a transcendental condition for the possibility of a science of nature and, consequently, all that is implied by this corporeality.

42 See for example his critique of the abstractions of bourgeois economists in *Introduction to a Critique of Political Economy*, which was published along with the *Contribution to the Critique of Political Economy*, in an edition by N. I. Stone (New York: International Library Publishing Co.: 1904).

43 To be reflected on seriously and profoundly. With naive authors, there is no paradox, nothing but the sheer platitude of projections or of a relativism, both uncritical.

44 The necessity of such an infinity and the necessity of its contrary, is one of the impossibilities of Hegelianism and, in fact, of the entire dialectic taken as a system. We shall return to this later.

45 Lukács, in *History and Class Consciousness*, developed this view with the greatest rigour and depth.

46 See 'The Changing Function of Historical Materialism', in *History and Class Consciousness*, pp. 223–55.

47* Written for the English translation of the preceding part of this text (*History and Revolution*, published by *Solidarity*, London, August 1971).

48 Published by Kautsky in the *Neue Zeit* in 1903; ed. N. I. Stone as 'Introduction to a Critique of Political Economy' (New York: International Library Publishing Co.: 1904).

49 Entirely false and not 'an approximation improved upon by later theories'. The idea of 'successive approximations', of an accumulation of scientific truths is progressist nonsense of the nineteenth century, which continues in large measure to dominate the consciousness of scientists.

50 See above, note 34.

51 See, for example, Margaret Mead's studies in *Male and Female* or in *Sex and Temperament in Three Primitive Societies*.

52 Hence, simply referring to an infinite series of causation does not resolve the problem. [Coherence cannot be explained as the product of a series of processes of causation, for an explanation like this presupposes coherence at the *origin* of the potentialities of the *ensemble* of these processes *as such*. Likewise, the coherence of the developed living organism cannot be explained by simply referring to the development of tissues and organs and their interaction; one must go all the way back to the coherence already posited of the potentialities of the *germen*.]

53 Of course, this is not an absolute truth; there are also 'bad laws', which are incoherent or which themselves destroy the ends they are intended to serve. This phenomenon appears, moreover, curiously limited to modern societies. But this observation does not alter what we were saying, in its essential features: it remains, instead, an extreme variant of the production of coherent social rules.

54 We are not saying 'of society *as such*', we are not discussing the metaphysical problem of origins.

55 This discussion can, obviously, be pursued endlessly. What can be said, above all, is that the revolution would not have taken the form of the seizure of power by the Bolchevik party, that it would have consisted in a repetition of the Commune. The content of considerations like these may seem pointless. The fact that they cannot

be avoided shows that history cannot be thought of, even retrospectively, outside of the categories of the *possible* and of *the accident which is more than an accident*.

56 See the texts collected in *La Société bureaucratique*, 1 and 2 (10/18, 1973) and 'Le Rôle de l'idéologie bolchévique dans la naissance de la bureaucratie', in *L'Expérience du mouvement ouvrier*, 2: *Prolétariat et organisation* (10/18, 1974;, p. 385ff. (English edition by the University of Minnesota Press forthcoming).

57 What Kant, in the *Critique of Judgement*, called 'a happy chance'.

58 We know that Alexander had taken Achilles 'for his model'.

59 *History and Class Consciousness*, p. 146.

60 Castoriadis is referring here to knowledge as a reflected image, as he takes this to be a standard expression in Marxist theory of knowledge [Ed.].

61 Elements of this type of 'subjectivist' dialectic can be found in Marx's early writings and they form the substance of Lukács' thought. We shall return to this later.

62 Except, up to a certain point, by Lukács (in *History and Class-Consciousness*). It is, moreover, striking that when he wrote the essays contained in this book, Lukács was unaware of some of the most important of Marx's early manuscripts (in particular the 1844 manuscript, known as the *Economic and Philosophic Manuscripts*, and *The German Ideology*) which were published only in 1925 and 1931. [This fact has already been noted by L. Goldmann and others.]

63 In the afterword to the second German edition of *Capital*, Marx quotes, calling it 'generous', the description of what is taken to be 'actually [his] method', in the *European Messenger* of St. Petersburg, which asserted in particular: 'Marx treats the social movement as a process of natural history, governed by laws not only independent of human will, consciousness and intelligence, but rather, on the contrary, determining that will, consciousness and intelligence.' *Capital*, 1, p. 18.

64 This comparison is made a number of times by Engels. We obviously do not want to say that the importance of Darwin in the history of science, or even in the history of ideas in general, is to be underestimated.

65 This is the idea expressed by Engels on numerous occasions, in particular in *Against Dühring*. An idea which covers a strange and shamefaced crypto-Kantianism, in open contradiction to the entire 'dialectic'.

66 Lukács has correctly shown that practice as it is understood by Engels, that is as 'the behaviour of industry and scientific experimentation' is 'contemplation at its purest' (*History and Class Consciousness*, p. 132). However, just as Noah's sons covered their father's nakedness, so Lukács allows us to understand implicitly that this is a personal error by Engels, who is held on this point to have been unfaithful to the true spirit of Marx. Now what Marx – even the young Marx – thought was by no means different from this: 'The question whether objective truth can be attributed to human thinking is not a question of theory but is a *practical* question. In practice man must prove the truth, that is, the reality and power, the this-sidedness of his thinking. The dispute over the reality or non-reality of thinking which is isolated from practice is a purely *scholastic* question' ('Second Thesis on Feuerbach', in *Selected Works*, p. 28). Obviously, in this text it is not exclusively or essentially a question of historical *praxis* in Lukács's sense but of 'practice' in general, including that of experimentation and of industry, as is shown elsewhere in other passages of the early writings. Not only does this practice remain within the category of contemplation, as Lukács reminds us, but it can never be a verification of thought in general, a 'demonstration of the reality of thinking'. It never brings us into contact with anything but *another phenomenon*, it is incapable of allowing us to go beyond the Kantian problematic.

67 Text included in the Conclusions to *Capital* in the French edn., la Pléiade, II, pp. 1487–8.

68 Correlatively, it ceases to be so only when it slows the development of these forces. This idea returns repeatedly in the writings of the great classical authors of Marxism (beginning with Marx himself), not to speak of those who ride on their coat-tails. What becomes of it today [1967], when we observe that for the past 25 years, capitalism has developed the productive forces more than had occurred in the past

40 centuries? How can a *Marxist* speak today of a revolutionary perspective while remaining Marxist and hence affirming at the same time that 'No social order is ever destroyed before all the productive forces for which it is sufficient have been developed' (Marx, Preface to *A Contribution to the Critique of Political Economy*, p. 21)? Neither Nikita Khrushchev nor 'leftists' of whatever sort have ever bothered to explain this.

69 We obviously do not want to say that the bourgeoisie was never 'progressive', nor that the development of the productive forces is reactionary or of no interest. We are saying that between these two things the relationship is not simple and that one cannot merely make a direct correspondence between the 'progressive' nature of a regime and its capacity to advance the productive forces, as Marxism does.

70 Trotsky, *Terrorism and Communism*, p. 174.

71 To be sure, slogans can be mistaken, for the leaders were mistaken in their evaluation of the situation, and in particular in estimating the level of consciousness and combativity of the workers. But this does not modify the logic of the problem: workers always appear as a variable of uncertain value in the equation the leaders have to solve.

72 We can see how foreign this conception is to Marxists by the fact that for the 'purists' among them real history is seen implicitly as if it had 'derailed' after 1939, or even after 1923, since it has not run along the rails laid down by theory. The fact that theory might just have well jumped the tracks at a considerably earlier period never crosses their minds.

73 The young Hegel was aware of this when, after having criticized Fichte's philosophy and shown that its essence was identical with that of religion to the extent that both express 'absolute separation', he concluded by saying that 'this (philosophical or religious) attitude would be nobler and worthier if it turned out that union with time cannot help but be vile and infamous' (*Systemfragment*, 1800).

74 See *L'expérience du mouvement ouvrier*, 1 and 2.

75 S. Freud, 'Notes upon a Case of Obsessional Neurosis', *Standard Edition*, trans. James Strachey (London: The Hogarth Press, 1961) 10, pp. 244–5; *Gesammelte Werke* (Frankfurt am Main: S. Fischer Verlag, 1968) VIII, p. 460. [These editions will hereafter be cited as *S.E.* and *G.W.*, respectively].

76 This was in fact the spirit and the practice of the young Hegel's dialectic – in works unknown to Marx – a spirit which, in this case too, disappeared when the dialectic was converted into a system. *The Phenomenology of Mind* (1806–7) marks the moment of this passage.

77 Engels, *Ludwig Feuerbach*, (New York: International Publishers, 1941) p. 15. This work is actually quite late (1888) but this does not prevent us from finding a host of elements continuing the original inspiration of Marxism, just as we do in many of the works of Marx's later years.

78 *The German Ideology* (1845–6) is full of these.

79 Once again, we are not saying that Marxist theory is the necessary and sufficient condition for bureaucratization, that the degeneration of the worker's movement is 'due' to Marx's erroneous conceptions. Both of these factors express, each at its own level, the determining influence of traditional culture which survives in the revolutionary movement. Ideology, however, also plays a specific role, and to this extent Marxism has served bureaucracy – and can no longer serve us.

80 In order to show that our critique of the Marxist *system* was 'existentialist', an *agrégé* in philosophy mobilized his recollections of oral examinations and tried to confront us with this quote from Kierkegaard: '... Being a system and being closed correspond to one another, but existence is just the opposite ... Existence is itself a system – for God – but can never be one for an existing mind.' It is unfortunate that Engels was never chosen for the agrégation programme. Our Marxist philosopher might then have been lucky enough to hit upon the following quote: 'With all philosophers it is precisely the "system" which is perishable; and for the simple reason that it springs from an imperishable desire of the human mind – the desire to overcome all contradictions.' (*Ludwig Feuerbach*, p. 15.) [The *agrégé* in question was Jean-François Lyotard. He still is.]

81 The empirical, yet necessary, expression of this fact is found in the unbelievable incapacity shared by all shades of Marxists for decades to renew their thinking in contact with living history, in the continuing hostility with which they have received what is best and most revolutionary in modern culture, whether this be psychoanalysis, contemporary physics or art. Trotsky is the sole exception in this respect, and just how atypical he is can be seen in the opposite example of one of the most productive and original Marxists, G. Lukács, who remained, with respect to art, the worthy heir to the great classical tradition of European 'humanism', a 'cultured man', basically conservative and foreign to modern 'chaos' and to the forms that emerge there.

82 We are obviously taking 'experience' in the broadest possible sense – in the sense, for example, in which Hegel could think that his philosophy expressed the total experience of humanity, not only theoretical experience but practical, political, artistic, etc. as well.

83 When we speak of completed theory, we obviously do not mean the *form* of the theory; little matter whether one can find in it a 'complete' systematic exposition (in fact, one can in the case of Marxism), or whether the advocates of the theory protest and affirm that they do not want to constitute a new system. What does matter is the tenor of the ideas, and these, in historical materialism, irrevocably set the structure and the content of the history of humanity. The Preface to the *Contribution to the Critique of Political Economy* (1859) already formulates completely, despite its brevity, a theory of history, one as full and as tightly closed as an egg.

2 THEORY AND REVOLUTIONARY PROJECT

1 We are speaking here, to be sure, of activities that go beyond the body of a subject and substantially modify the external world. The 'biological' functions of the human organism are obviously another matter, including an infinite number of 'reflexive' or non-conscious activities. One has to admit that discussing them cannot shed light on the problem of the relations of knowing and doing in history.

2 It is enough that it be decidable in terms of probabilities; what we are saying does not presuppose a complete, deterministic knowledge of the area considered.

3 Technique, that is, to the extent that it is applied to *objects*. Technique in the more general sense as this is commonly used today – 'military technique', 'political technique', etc. and more generally, the activities that Max Weber included under the term *Zweckrational* – does not enter into our definition, even though it is related to people, for reasons that will be explained in the text.

4 It is not a matter of exhaustive knowledge in the absolute. The engineer who builds a bridge or a dam does not need to know the nuclear structure of matter; it is enough for him to know statics, the theory of elasticity, the resistance of the materials, and so on. It is not knowledge of matter as such that concerns him but knowledge of the factors that can have a practical importance. This does exist in the vast majority of cases; but the surprises (and catastrophes) that occur from time to time show the limits of this knowledge. Precise replies are possible to a great number of questions, but not to *all* of them. To be sure, we are leaving aside here the other – essential – limit of the rationality of technique, namely the fact that technique can never account for the ends it serves.

5 Better yet, because in large part today's medicine is practised in a trivial and fragmentary manner, the doctor trying to act almost as a 'technician'.

6* I have attempted to clarify this idea in relation to psychoanalysis, defined as a practico-poetic activity, in 'Epilégomènes à une théorie de l'âme que l'on a pu présenter comme science', in *l'Inconscient*, no. 8 (Paris, October 1968), pp. 47–87. Now translated as 'Epilegomena to a Theory of the Soul which has been presented as a Science' by Kate Soper and Martin H. Ryle in *Crossroads in the Labyrinth*, (Cambridge, Mass.: MIT Press, 1984) pp. 3–45.

7 This attempt failed once it was demonstrated that it is impossible to demonstrate the

non-contradiction of systems constituted in this way and that undecidable propositions can appear in them (Gödel, 1931).

8 This uncertainty was far less for the Greeks, since the 'rational' foundation of mathematical rigour was, for them, of a nature which is clearly 'irrational' for us (the divine essence of numbers or the natural character of space as the receptacle of the cosmos). The uncertainty is much greater for the moderns, where the attempt to establish this rigour conclusively ends up shattering the idea that there can be a rational foundation to mathematics. It is not futile in this regard to remind those who maintain a nostalgia for absolute certainties of the tragic fate of Hilbert's efforts, who proclaimed that his programme was to 'eliminate from the world once and for all the questions of foundation' (*'die Grundlagenfragen ein für allemal aus der Welt zu schaffen'*), *thereby setting off an investigation which would show, and even demonstrate, that the question of foundations will always exist in this world as an insoluble question.* Once more, hubris provoked nemesis.

9* For a justification of these ideas, see 'Le Monde morcelé' (*Textures*, nos. 4–5, 1972, pp. 3–40) and 'Science moderne et interrogation philosophique' (*Encyclopaedia Universalis – Organum*, vol. XVII, pp. 43–73). (English translation in *Crossroads in the Labyrinth*, pp. 145–226).

10 The moment of elucidation is always necessarily contained in doing. It does not result from this, however, that doing and theory are symmetrical at every level, each encompassing the other. Doing constitutes the human universe to which theory belongs as a part. Humanity is involved in a multiform conscious activity, it *defines itself as* doing (which contains the elucidation in the context of and in relation to doing as a necessary but not sovereign moment). Theory as such is a specific doing, it emerges once the moment of elucidation becomes a project for itself. In this sense one can say that there is actually a 'primacy of practical reason'. One can conceive of, and indeed there existed for millennia, a humanity without theory; but there cannot exist a humanity without doing.

11 'Are my profession and my children ends or means or both? They are nothing of the sort, certainly not means for my life, which loses itself in them instead of using them; and they are much more than ends, since an end is *what* one wants, and since I want my profession and my children without measuring in advance where this will lead me, which will be far beyond what I can know of them. Not that I dedicate myself to something I do not know – I see them with the kind of precision that belongs to existing things, I recognize them among all others without completely knowing of what they are made. Our concrete decisions do not aim at closed meanings.' This text by Marleau-Ponty (*The Adventures of the Dialectic*, translated by Joseph Bien (Evanston: Northwestern University Press, 1973, p. 127) implicitly contains the closest definition, to my knowledge, given up to now of praxis.

12 In an experimental science or an observational science, it may seem that 'activity' precedes elucidation as well; but it precedes the latter only in time not in logical order. One undertakes an experiment in order to elucidate, and not the other way around. And the activity of the experimenter is transforming only in a superficial or formal sense: it is not aimed at transforming its object as such and, if it does modify the object, this is only to make another, more 'deeply hidden' level appear as 'identical' or as 'constant'. ['Invariants' are the obsession of science.]

13 Assuming that one day physics can attain an 'exhaustive knowledge' of its object (an assumption which, anyhow, is absurd), this would in no way affect what we are saying about historical praxis.

14 This means: a revolution of the working masses eliminating the domination of any particular stratum over the whole of society and establishing the power of workers' councils over all aspects of social life. On the *programme* making the objectives of this revolution concrete in current historical circumstances, see in no. 22 of *Socialisme ou Barbarie* (July 1957) 'Sur le contenu du socialisme, II', now in *Le Contenu du Socialisme*.

15 Once again, our discussion here can only take up a very small part of this question and we must refer here to various texts published previously in *Socialisme ou Barbarie* on these matters.

16 When we speak of logic and dynamics, this obviously concerns *historical* logic and dynamics. On the analysis of informal struggle in production, see D. Mothé, 'L'Usine et la gestion ouvrière', *Socialisme ou Barbarie*, no. 22 (July 1957), reprinted in *Journal d'un ouvrier*, (Paris: Éditions de Minuit, 1959) and my text 'Sur le contenu du socialisme, III, *Socialisme ou Barbarie*, no. 23 (January 1958), reprinted in *L'Expérience du mouvement ouvrier*, 2). On 'workers' management' demands see 'Les Grèves sauvages dans l'industrie automobile américaine', 'Les Grèves des dockers anglais' and 'Les Grèves de l'automation en Angleterre', *Socialisme ou Barbarie*, nos. 18 and 19 (reprinted in *L'Expérience du mouvement ouvrier*, 2); on the Hungarian workers' councils and their demands, see all of the texts on the Hungarian Revolution published in no. 20 of *Socialisme ou Barbarie* and Pannonicus, 'Les Conseils ouvriers de la révolution hongroise', *Socialisme ou Barbarie*, no. 21. Let us recall, moreover, that a continuous dialectic appears in this struggle: just as the means used by management against the workers can be taken by the latter and used against management itself, so management is able to recover the positions held by the workers and, ultimately, even make use of their informal organization. Each of these types of assimilation, however, gives rise in the end to a response on another level.

17 Finicky sociologists can be found who will protest: how can one include under the same signification data coming from domains as diverse as investigations in industrial sociology, strikes at Standard in England and at General Motors in the United States, and the Hungarian Revolution? This breaks all methodological rules. The same hypersensitive critics fall into trances, however, when they see Freud compare 'the return of the repressed' in a patient in the course of an analysis and in the entire Jewish people ten centuries after the alleged 'murder' of Moses.

18 By affirming since 1948 that the experience of bureaucratization henceforth made the workers' management of production the central demand of all revolution (*Socialisme ou Barbarie*, no. 1, reprinted in *La Société bureaucratique*, 1, pp. 139–83).

19 I have, for my part, taken up again the analyses of industrial sociology and, assisted by concrete information contributed by workers who constantly live this conflict, have attempted to clarify its signification and to bring out the conclusions to be drawn from it. For this, I have recently been reproached, by reformed Marxists like Lucien Sebag, for 'partiality' (*Marxisme et structuralisme*, Paris: Payot, 1964) p. 130: I am supposed to have committed the sin of 'admitting that the *truth of the enterprise* is concretely given to certain of its members, namely the workers.' In other words: ascertaining that a war exists; that both adversaries agree on its existence, on the way it unfolds, on its modalities and even on its causes, this is deemed to be a partial (in both senses of the term) point of view. One can then only wonder what, for Lucien Sebag, would not be partial in this sense: might this be the point of view of university professors or 'researchers' who themselves would, perhaps, belong to no social sub-group? Or does he mean that one can never say anything about society, but then why does he bother to write? On this level, a revolutionary theorist has no need to postulate that the 'truth of the enterprise' is given to certain of its members; once it is analysed, the discourse of capitalists says nothing else; from top to bottom, society expresses its crisis. The problem begins when one wants to know what one is to *do* with this crisis (and this overdetermines, ultimately, theoretical analyses; then indeed one can only place oneself in the perspective of a particular group (since society is divided), but then the question is no longer 'the truth of the enterprise' (or of society) as it is but the 'truth' of that which is to be done by this group *against* another. At this moment one actually does take sides, but this is the case for everyone, including the philosopher who, by holding forth on the impossibility of taking sides, actually does take sides in favour of what is and so in favour of certain people. Moreover, Sebag mixes up two different considerations in his critique: the difficulty of which we have just spoken and which is held to result from the fact that the 'Marxist sociologist' attempts to express a 'global signification of the factory' whose depositary is the proletariat, which in turn is only one part of the factory; and the difficulty relating to the 'disparity of attitudes and stands on the part of the workers', which the Marxist sociologist would resolve by giving preference to 'certain types of

conduct', 'based on a more general schema relating to capitalist society as a whole'. The second difficulty exists, to be sure, but it is by no means a malediction specific to Marxist sociology; it exists for all scientific thought, for all thought as such, as well as for the most ordinary, everyday discourse. Whether I speak about sociology, economics, meteorology or the behaviour of my butcher, I am constantly forced to distinguish what appears to me to be significant from the rest, to give preference to certain aspects and to slide over others. I do this in accordance with certain criteria, rules and conceptions which can always be argued about and which are periodically revised – but I could cease to do so only if I were to cease to think. The fact that preference is given to *these particular* types of behaviour can be concretely criticized, but not the fact of according preference as such. It is distressing to note once again here that the alleged advances over Marxism are in most cases clear regressions based not on new knowledge but on the forgetfulness of what had previously been learned – poorly learned, it would seem.

20 For the justification of what is stated here, we must refer the reader to Mothé, 'L'Usine et la gestion ouvrière', quoted above, as well as to S. Chatel's article, 'Hiérarchie et gestion collective', *Socialisme ou Barbarie*, nos. 37 and 38 (July and October 1964).

21 See 'Le Mouvement révolutionaire sous le capitalisme moderne', *Socialisme ou Barbarie*, no. 31, pp. 69–81. [Now in *Capitalisme moderne et révolution*.]

22 Up to a certain point, a considerable increase in 'aid' to underdeveloped countries could also help to alleviate this problem.

23 What is actually at issue in all this is the fact that we are living the *beginning of the end of the economic* as such. Herbert Marcuse, in *Eros and Civilization*, (London: RKP, 1956) and Paul Goodman in *Growing Up Absurd* (New York: Random House, 1960) were the first, to my knowledge, to examine the implications of this potential upheaval – to which we shall return later.

24 For the possibility of an organization and management of the economy in this sense, see 'Sur le contenu du socialisme I et II', *Socialisme ou Barbarie*, no. 17 (July 1977), pp. 33–49 (Now in *Le Contenu du Socialisme* and forthcoming English edition, University of Minnesota Press). The extent to which these problems are at the heart of the current economic situation is evident in the fact that the idea of the 'automatization' of a great part of the management of the global economy, formulated in *Socialisme ou Barbarie* in 1955-7, inspires since 1960 one of the 'reforming' tendencies of Russian economists, concerning the 'automatization' of planification (Kantorovich, Novozhilov, etc.). However, the realization of this solution is scarcely compatible with the continuing power of the bureaucracy.

25 The demand for a comprehensible economy *precedes* logically and even politically that of an economy in the service of human beings; no one can say in the service of whom the economy is functioning, if this functioning is incomprehensible.

26* This question is discussed at length in part two, chapter 6.

27 See, for example, Allen Wheelis, *The Quest for Identity* (London: Victor Gollancz, 1959) in particular pp. 97–138. This is also the sense of David Riesman's analyses in *The Lonely Crowd* (New Haven: Yale University Press, 1950).

28* As 'Marxists' should have done – and actually did – in this case.

29 The passage in which this sentence occurs, at the end of the third (31st in the consecutive numbering adopted by Freud) of the 'lectures' of the *New Introductory Lectures on Psychoanalysis*, reads as follows: '[The] intention [of the therapeutic efforts of psychoanalysis] is, indeed, to strengthen the ego, to make it more independent of the super-ego, to widen its field of perception and enlarge its organisation, so that it can appropriate fresh portions of the id. Where id was, there ego shall be. It is a work of culture – not unlike the draining of the Zuider Zee.' (*S.E.*, 22, p. 80). Jacques Lacan renders the *Wo Es War, soll Ich werden* by 'Là où fut ça, il me faut advenir' (Where that was, I must come to be) ('L'Instance de la lettre dans l'inconscient' in *Écrits*, (Paris: Le Seuil, 1966) p. 524) and he adds, concerning 'the end which Freud's discovery proposes to man': 'This is one [an end] of reintegration and harmony, I could even say of reconciliation [Versöhnung]. (*Écrits, A Selection* (London: Tavistock Publications, 1977) p. 171).

30 In *The Book of the It* by G. Groddeck, translated by V. M. E. Collins, (London: Vision Press, 1950; New York: Vintage Books, 1961).

31 It would be fairer to say: concerning the clarification and the exploration of the profound dimension of the psyche, which neither Heraclitus nor Plato was unaware of, as even the most superficial reading of the *Symposium* reveals for all to see.

32 '... the nucleus of our being, but it is not so much that Freud commands us to seek it as so many others before him have with the empty adage "know thyself" – as to reconsider the ways that lead to it, and which he shows us.' Jacques Lacan, *Écrits, A Selection*, pp. 173–4.

33 See Jacques Lacan, 'Remarques sur le rapport de D. Lagache', in *Psychoanalyse*, no. 6 (1961), p. 116. 'A pole of attributes – this is the subject before its birth (and perhaps one day it will suffocate under their mass). Attributes, that is to say, signifiers tied more or less closely together in a discourse ...' (*Écrits*, Paris: Seuil, 1966, p. 652).

34 This is obviously the essential difference in relation to other forms of the imaginary (such as, for example, art or the 'rational' use of the imaginary in mathematics) which do not become autonomous as such. We shall return to this at length later. [The term 'imaginary' here and in the two pages that follow is still used in an ambiguous sense, bearing its common usage.]

35 [This is also indicated by Freud's abandonment of the hypothesis of 'infantile seduction' as well as, more especially, by the gradual – although never definitive – questioning throughout the account of the analysis of *The Wolf Man* of the 'reality' of the primitive scene.] This is not a matter of 'reality' or of the 'demands of life in society' as such, but of what becomes of these demands in the discourse of the Other (which, moreover, is by no means a neutral vehicle) and in the imaginary elaboration of the latter by the subject. This obviously does not deny the capital importance, for the *content* of the discourse of the Other and for the specific tenor which its imaginary elaboration will take on, of the concrete character of the society considered, nor the importance of the excessive and irrational nature of the social formulation of these 'requirements' with respect to the frequency and the seriousness of pathogenic situations: on this matter, Freud was extremely clear (cf. in particular, *Civilization and its Discontents*). But at this level we encounter once again the fact that these 'requirements' of society cannot be reduced to the demands of 'reality', to those of 'life in society' in general, or even, finally, to those of a 'society divided into classes' but instead go beyond what these demands would rationally imply. Here we find the point of connection between the individual imaginary and the social imaginary – a topic to which we shall return later.

36 'An ethic announces itself ... through the advent not of fear but of desire.' Jacques Lacan, *Écrits* (Seuil), p. 684.

37 This is not a description of the empirical–psychological conditions of the functioning of the subject but an articulation of the logical (transcendental) structure of subjectivity: there is no thinking subject except as the disposition of contents, every particular content can be bracketed but not some content as such. The same thing is true concerning the problem of the genesis of the subject, considered in its logical aspect: at any given instant the subject is a producer produced and 'at the origin' the subject constitutes itself as that which is simultaneously given all at once as Self and as Other. [The subject in question here is the one that is established with the break up of the psychical monad. See below, chapter 6.]

38* This ultimately leads to denying that the traditional distinction between 'activity' and 'passivity' possesses any originary signification. I shall return to this in the second part of this book.

39 As that doing which is aimed at the other or at others as autonomous beings. See above, pp. 71–9.

40 Political praxis has a second foundation, which shall be distinguished later: the possibility of institutions that favour autonomy.

41 The author of this statement [J.-P. Sartre] was no doubt certain that he carried no trace at all of another within himself (otherwise, he might just as well have said that Hell was himself). He has, moreover, recently confirmed this interpretation by stating

that he had no super-ego. How could we object to this, as we have always thought that he spoke of matters on this earth as if he were a being arriving here from another planet.

42 By this expression we are intending the unity of the twofold multiplicity of dimensions, in 'simultaneity' (synchrony) and in 'succession' (diachrony) which are traditionally denoted by the terms 'society' and 'history'. We shall at times speak of the social or of the historical, without specifying them further, depending on the aspect we wish to underscore. [We shall return to this matter at length in the second part of this book.]

43 In a society of alienation, even for those rare individuals for whom autonomy has a meaning, it can only be truncated, for it runs up, in material conditions and in other individuals, against continually renewed obstacles whenever it is to be embodied in an activity, unfold and exist in the social dimension; autonomy can be manifested in the actual life of these individuals only in uneven openings, occurring by chance or through a certain skill.

44 It is hardly necessary to recall that the idea of autonomy and that of responsibility of each individual for his life can easily become mystifications if they are severed from the social context and posited as self-sufficient responses.

45 This delegation poses multiple and complex problems which it is impossible to discuss here. There is, obviously, at once homology and an essential difference between the 'family' relation and class relations, or power relations in society. Freud's basic contribution (*Totem and Taboo* or *Group Psychology and the Analysis of the Ego*, that of W. Reich (*The Function of Orgasm*), and the numerous contributions of American anthropologists (in particular, Kardiner and M. Mead) are far from exhausting the question, inasmuch as they relegate the properly institutional dimension to a secondary level.

46 If factory workers wanted to question the existing order, they would run up against the police and, if the movement were to spread, the army. Through historical experience we know that neither the police nor the army are impermeable in the face of widespread movements; can they hold fast against the essential part of the population? Rosa Luxemburg said: 'If the entire population *knew*, the capitalist regime would not last 24 hours.' Never mind the 'intellectual' resonance of the statement: let us ascribe to *knowing* its full depth and let us connect it to *willing*. Is it not true beyond the shadow of a doubt? Yes and no. The yes is obvious. The no follows from that other fact, which is equally obvious, that the social regime, precisely, *prevents* the population from knowing and from willing. Unless one is to postulate a miraculous coincidence of positive spontaneities from one end of the country to the other, every seed, every embryo of this knowing and this willing which can be manifested in a given place in society is constantly hampered, combatted and, finally, crushed by the existing institutions. It is for this reason that the purely 'psychological' view of alienation, the one which seeks the conditions for alienation solely in the structure of individuals, in their 'masochism', etc. and which would finally say: if people are exploited, it is because they want to be, is itself unilateral, abstract and, ultimately, false. People are this *and* something else, but in their individual life the combat is grotesquely uneven, for the other factor (the tendency towards autonomy) has to confront the entire weight of instituted society. If it is essential to recall that heteronomy must in each case also find its conditions in each exploited individual, it has to find them to the same extent in social structures, which make the individuals' 'chances' (in Max Weber's sense) of knowing and willing practically inexistent. Knowing and willing are not purely a matter of knowing and willing, we are not dealing with subjects which would be pure will to autonomy and entirely responsible, for if this were the case there would be no problem in any domain whatsoever. It is not simply that the social structure is 'designed for' instilling passivity, respect for authority, etc. even before an individual's birth. It is that institutions are there, in the long struggle of each person's life, to place blocks and obstacles in the way at every instant, to direct the waters in a certain sense, and finally to rage against whatever might be manifested as autonomy. This is why the person who says he

wants autonomy while refusing the revolution in institutions knows neither what he is saying nor what he wants. The individual imaginary, as we shall see later, finds a correspondence in a social imaginary embodied in institutions, but this embodiment exists as such and it is also as such that it must be attacked.

47 See 'Le Mouvement révolutionaire sous le capitalisme moderne', in *Socialisme ou Barbarie*, no. 32, in particular p. 94ff. (Now *Capitalisme moderne et révolution*, p. 120ff., and forthcoming University of Minnesota Press).

48 It is, moreover, very hard to evaluate the actual role they played in the case of workers or even of militants. It is certain that both have always been much more preoccupied with the problems posed by their condition and their struggle than with the need to define a 'final' objective; but it is equally certain that something like the image of a promised land, or of a radical redemption, has always been present to them, carrying the ambiguous signification of an eschatological Millennium, a Kingdom of God without God *and* of the desire for a society in which man would no longer be the main enemy of man.

49* These are the features of the social dimension which are at the root of the impossibility of reflecting on it for itself – without reducing it to what it is not – in inherited thinking. We shall return to this at length in the second part of this book.

3 THE INSTITUTION AND THE IMAGINARY; A FIRST APPROACH

1 Thus, according to Bronislaw Malinowski, at issue here is 'the explanation of anthropological facts at all levels of development by their function, by the part which they play within the integral system of culture, by the manner in which they are related to each other within the system, and by the manner in which this system is related to the physical surrounding ... The functional view of culture insists therefore upon the principle that in every type of civilisation, every custom, material object, idea and belief fulfils some initial function, has some task to accomplish, represents an indispensable part within a working whole.' (*Encyclopaedia Britannica*, 13th edn., 1926, suppl. vol. 1, pp. 132–3). See also A. R. Radcliffe-Brown, *Structure and Function in Primitive Society* (London: Cohen and West, 1952).

2 This is, finally, also the Marxist view, in which institutions always represent the adequate means by which social life is organized in accordance with the requirements of the 'infrastructure'. This view is tempered by certain considerations:

a Social dynamics rests on the fact that institutions do not adapt themselves automatically and spontaneously to the evolution of technology; instead, institutions display passivity, inertia and recurrent 'delay' with respect to the infrastructure (which each time has to be shattered by a revolution);

b Marx clearly saw the autonomization of institutions as the essence of alienation – but he finally had a 'functional' view of alienation itself;

c the requirements of the logic specific to the institution, which can sever themselves from functionality, were not neglected; but the relation to the requirements of the social system in each case, and in particular to 'the requirements of the domination of the exploiting class' remains unclear, or else is jumbled together (as in Marx's analysis of the capitalist economy) with the system's *contradictory* functionality.

We shall return to these different points later. They do not prevent the critique of functionalism formulated in the following pages, although it is situated on another level, from holding for Marxism as well.

3* 'Internal' historical collapses of particular societies – Rome, Byzantium, etc. – provide counterexamples to the functionalist view. In another context, see the cases of the Sherentes and the Bororos described by Claude Lévi-Strauss, *Anthropologie structurale*, pp. 137–9, 141 (on the non-functional character of clans). *Structural Anthropology* (New York: Basic Books, 1963) pp. 158–60.

4 Thus Malinowsky says, 'Functional always signifies the satisfaction of a need.' 'The Functional Theory', in *A Scientific Theory of Culture* (University of North Carolina Press: Chapel Hill, NC, 1944) p. 159.

5 'Signifier' and 'signified' are taken here and in what follows *latissimo sensu*.

6 'In a modern State, the law must not only correspond to the general economic situation and be its expression, it must also be a systematic expression of it so that it does not inflict a denial upon itself due to its internal contradictions. And, to succeed in this, it reflects less and less faithfully the economic realities.' Engels, in a letter to Conrad Schmidt, 27 October 1890. Reprinted in Marx and Engels, *Selected Works in One Volume*, New York: International Publishers, 1968, p. 697.

7 In *Exodus*, the Law is formulated in four chapters (20–3) but the ritual and the instructions concerning the construction of the Temple take up eleven chapters (25–30 and 36–40). Injunctions concerning the ritual, moreover, return repeatedly; cf. *Leviticus*, 1–7; *Numbers*, 4, 7–8, 10, 19, 28–9, etc. The construction of the Temple is also described with a wealth of details on several occasions in the historical books.

8 This is a consequence of the basic law that all symbolism is *diacritical* or acts 'by means of difference': a sign can emerge as a sign only against the background of something that is not a sign or that is a sign of something else. However, this does not permit us concretely to determine where the dividing line should pass in every instance.

9 This excessive, redundant functionality is, in fact, a dysfunctionality, and the Byzantine emperors will, a number of times, have to reduce Justinian's cumbersome codification by summarizing it.

10 The word *ritual* must be used here because the religious cast of the transactions is incontestable at the outset.

11 '*Ex nudo pacto inter cives Romanos actio non nascitur*.' On the acrobatics praetors went through to make this rule considerably more flexible, without ever daring, for all that, to do away with it completely, one may consult any history of Roman law, for example, R. von Mayr, *Römische Rechtsgeschichte* (Leipzig: Göschenverlag, 1913) vol. II, 2, II, pp. 81–2: vol. IV, p. 129, etc.

12 'There is an effectiveness of the signifier that escapes psycho-genetic explanation, for this signifying, symbolical order is not introduced by the subject but encountered by it.' Jacques Lacan, *Séminaire* 1956–7, reviewed by J. B. Pontalis, *Bulletin de psychologie*, vol. X, no. 7, April 1957, p. 428.

13 *Quasi*-rational: rational to a large extent, but as in the social (and not the scientific) use of symbolism, 'displacement' and 'condensation' as Freud said (metaphor and metonymy, as Lacan says) are constantly present, the logic of social symbolism cannot be identified purely and simply with a 'pure logic', or even with the logic of lucid discourse.

14 It evidently takes a simple mind, like Einstein's, to write: 'It is a veritable wonder that we can carry out this business without getting into the greatest difficulties [covering a flat marble surface by a network of straight rods forming equal squares, as in Cartesian co-ordinates] ... [In doing this] I am now no longer able to adjust the quadrilateral so that its diagonals may be equal. If they are equal of their own accord, then this is an especial favour of the marble slab and of the little rods, about which I can only be thankfully surprised.' *Relativity* (London: Methuen, 1960) p. 84. The various deterministic tendencies in the 'social sciences' have long ago outgrown this childlike surprise.

15 Conservative French economist, chief economic advisor to de Gaulle [Ed.].

16 It is in itself a vast problem to decide up to what point (and why) people behave 'rationally' in each case, considering the real and the institutional situation. Cf. Max Weber, *Economy and Society I* (New York: Bedminster, 1968) pp. 6–7. However, even the distinction Weber makes between the actual course of an action and its ideal-typical course in the hypothesis of perfectly rational behaviour, has to be specified: there is, on the one hand, the distance between the actual course of an action and the 'positive rationality' (in the sense in which we speak of 'positive law') of the society considered at a given moment, that is to say the degree of understanding

this society has reached concerning the logic of its own functioning; and there is, on the other hand, the distance between this 'positive rationality' and a rationality as such concerning *this very* institutional system. The Keynesian technique of using the budget to regulate the economic balance was just as valid in 1860 as in 1960. But there is not much sense in imputing 'irrational' behaviour to capitalist leaders before 1930, who, when faced with a depression, acted counter to what the situation called for; they acted, as a general rule, in accordance with what was the 'positive rationality' of their society. The evolution of this 'positive rationality' raises a complex problem that we are unable to enter into here; let us recall simply that it is impossible to reduce it to mere 'scientific progress', to the extent that class interests and situations, along with 'gratuitous' prejudices and illusions that belong to the imaginary, play an essential role in it. The proof of this is that today, 30 years after the formulation and diffusion of Keynesian ideas, substantial numbers of the dominant groups – and at times even a majority of them – stubbornly defend outmoded conceptions (such as strictly balanced budgets or the return to the gold standard) whose application would sooner or later plunge the system into crisis. [What would one have to say after 1974–1986!] [Author's addition to the English translation.]

17 They do not express, as Marx thought, insurmountable 'internal contradictions' (cf. in no. 31 of *Socialisme ou Barbarie*, 'Le mouvement révolutionnaire sous le capitalisme moderne', pp. 70–81 (now *Capitalisme moderne et révolution*) for the critique of this conception), but the fact that, for a long time, the capitalist class was superseded by the logic of its own economic institutions. See the preceding note.

18 An obvious example is that of the penalties set by penal laws. If one can, up to a certain point, interpret the scale of gravity of the infractions and crimes established by each society, it is obvious that the scale of corresponding penalties, whether it be precise or imprecise, includes an unrationalizable arbitrary element – at least once we have gone beyond the *lex talionis* (an eye for an eye). The fact that the law establishes this or that penalty for armed robbery or pimping is neither logical nor absurd; it is arbitrary. See also below the discussion on the Mosaic Law.

19 Consider, for example, the opposition between the excessive wealth of symbolism concerning 'daily life' in most traditional Asiatic cultures and its relative poverty in European cultures; or again, consider the variability of the borderline separating law and mores in various historical cultures.

20 In the same way, one sometimes has the impression that certain contemporary psycho-sociologists forget that the problem of bureaucracy far surpasses the simple differentiation of roles in the primary group even if the bureaucracy finds in it an indispensable counterpart.

21 'Les rapports de production en Russie', in *La Société bureaucratique*, 1, pp. 205–82.

22 V. Rudolf Stammler, *Wirtschaft und Recht nach der materialistischen Geschichtsauffassung*, 5th edn (Berlin: de Gruyter, 1924), in particular pp. 108–51 and 177–211. See also Max Weber's severe critique in the *Gesammelte Aufsätze zur Wissenschaftslehre*.

23* See the second part of this book, in particular chapters 5 and 7; also 'Le dicible et l'indicible' in *L'Arc*, no. 46 (1971), pp. 67–69. ('The Sayable and the Unsayable', *Crossroads in the Labyrinth*, pp. 119–44).

24 Cf. what we said above regarding Roman law.

25 One might attempt to distinguish in the accepted terminology between what we term the ultimate or radical imaginary, that is the capacity to make arise as an image something which does not exist and has never existed, and the *products* of this imaginary, which could be designated as the *imagined*. The grammatical form of this term, however, might lead to confusion, and I prefer to speak instead of the actual imaginary.

26 'Man is this night, this empty nothingness which contains everything in its simplicity; a wealth of representations, images, infinite in number, none of which emerges precisely in his mind, or which are not always present. What exists here is night, the interiority of nature: *pure Self*. In fantastic representations, night is all around; here, there emerges a bloody head, there another white figure; and they disappear just as suddenly. It is this night that one perceives when one looks a man in the eye: a night

which becomes *terrible*; what is then facing us is the night of the world. *The power of drawing images out of this night or of letting them slip away into it, (this is) the fact of positing oneself, internal consciousness, action, division.*' Hegel, *Jenaer Realphilosophie* (1805–6) (Berlin: Akad. Verlag, 1969).

27 It would, obviously, have corresponded much more closely to the 'logic' of capitalism to adopt a calendar with 'decades' affording 36 or 37 days of rest per year instead of keeping weeks and 52 Sundays.

28 As an easy and brief example, and certainly the most commonplace one, consider the goddess 'of the Earth', the Earth-Goddess, Demeter. The most probable etymology (others have been suggested as well; cf. H. G. Liddell and Robert Scott, *Greek-English lexicon* (Oxford: Clarendon Press, 1940) is Ge-Meter, Gaia-Meter, Earth-Mother. Gaia is the name at once of the Earth and of the first goddess, who, with Uranus, lies at the origin of the line of gods. The Earth is seen from the start as an originary goddess, nothing indicates that it was ever viewed as an 'object'. This term (*Gaia*) which denotes the Earth connotes at the same time the 'properties' or rather the Earth's essential modes of being: fertility and source of nourishment. This is what is connotated by the signifier *mother* as well. The connection or rather the identification of the two signifieds: Earth-Mother is obvious. This first, imaginary moment is indissociable from the other: the fact that the Earth-Mother is a divinity, and anthropomorphic – for good reason, since she is a Mother! The imaginary component of the individual symbol is of the same substance, so to speak, as the global imaginary of this culture – what *we* term the anthropomorphic divinization of the forces of nature.

29 '... The highest laws, born in the heavenly ether, Olympus alone is their father, they were never begotten by the mortal nature of men nor will they ever fade into forgetfulness; for in them lies a great god, who never grows old.' *Oedipus Rex*, 865–71.

30 '... a definite social relation between men ... assumes, in their eyes, the fantastic form of a relation between things. In order, therefore, to find an analogy, we must have recourse to the mist-enveloped regions of the religious world. In that world the productions of the human brain appear as independent beings endowed with life, and entering into relation both with one another and the human race. So it is in the world of commodities with the products of men's hands. This I call the Fetishism which attaches itself to the products of labour, so soon as they are produced as commodities ...' And again: '... value ... converts every product into a social hieroglyphic.' *Capital*, translated by Samuel Moore and Edward Aveling (New York: International Publishers, 1967) vol. 1, pp. 72, 74. [We shall return later to the implications of the 'fetishism of commodities'.]

31 This is certainly the point of view of the later works: 'The religious reflex of the real world can, in any case, only then finally vanish, when the practical relations of everyday life offer to man none but perfectly intelligible and reasonable relations with regard to his fellowmen and to Nature. The life process of society, which is based on the process of material production, does not strip off its mystical veil until it is treated as production by freely associated men, and is consciously regulated by them in accordance with a settled plan. This, however, demands for society a certain material ground-work or set of conditions of existence which in their turn are the spontaneous product of a long and painful process of development.' (*Capital*, 1, pp. 79–80.) This is also found in the text, published posthumously, 'Introduction to a Critique of Political Economy' (written at the same time as the *Contribution to the Critique of Political Economy*, completed in 1859): 'Every mythology tames, dominates and shapes the forces of nature in the imagination and through the imagination and disappears as soon as one manages actually to dominate them.' If this were so mythology would never disappear, not even the day when humanity would be able to play dance master with the billions of visible galaxies within a radius of thirteen billion light-years. [The irreversibility of time and a few other trifles would still remain to be 'tamed and dominated'.] Nor could one understand how the mythology concerning nature disappeared long ago from the Western world; if Jupiter was

ridiculed by the lightning rod and Hermes by a Savings and Loans, why did we not invent a cancer-god, an atheroma-god, or a minus-omega god? Marx has more substantial things to say about this in the *Fourth Thesis on Feuerbach*: '[The fact] that the secular basis [of the regular world] detaches itself from itself and establishes itself as an independent realm in the clouds can only be explained by the cleavages and self-contradictions within this secular basis. The latter must, therefore, in itself be both understood in its contradiction and revolutionized in practice. Thus, for instance, after the earthly family is discovered to be the secret of the holy family, the former must then itself be destroyed in theory and in practice.' The imaginary would then be the fantasized solution of real *contradictions*. This is true for a certain type of imaginary, but merely a derivative type. It is not sufficient for understanding the central imaginary of a society for reasons which will be given later on in the text, and which can be summed up in this way: the very constitution of these real contradictions is inseparable from this central imaginary.

32 See 'Le mouvement révolutionnaire sous le capitalisme moderne' in *Socialisme ou Barbarie*, no. 33, p. 75ff. (Now *Capitalisme moderne*, p. 159ff. and University of Minnesota Press, forthcoming.)

33* It is obvious that needs in the social–historical sense (which is not that of biological necessities) are a product of the radical imagination.

The 'imaginary' which compensates for the non-satisfaction of these needs is, therefore, only a second-order and derived imaginary. This is also how the matter is seen by certain tendencies in psychoanalysis today, for which the imaginary 'sutures' an originary gap or cleavage in the subject. But this gap exists only *through* the subject's radical imaginary. We shall return to this at length in the second part of this book.

34 To be sure, someone could always say that these historical creations are simply the progressive discovery of the possibilities contained within a 'preconstituted', ideal and absolute system. However, as this absolute system of all possible forms, by definition, can never be displayed, and as it is not present in history, the objection is gratuitous and amounts, finally, to a dispute over words. After the fact, one could say about anything that has been realized that it was also ideally possible. But this is an empty tautology, which teaches no one anything.

35 The traumatic event is real as an event and imaginary as a traumatism.

36 Marx's phrase about religion [Ed.].

37 '... to say that a society functions is a truism; but to say that everything in a society functions is an absurdity.' Claude Lévi-Strauss, *Structural Anthropology*, (New York: Basic Books, 1963) p. 13.

38 Even this involves certain problems: we have already recalled the existence of dysfunctional institutions, in particular in modern societies, as well as the absence of institutions necessary for certain functions.

39 As Lévi-Strauss seems increasingly tempted to do. See in particular *Le Totemisme aujourd'hui* (Paris: 1962) and the discussion with Paul Ricoeur in *Esprit* (November 1963), in particular p. 636: 'You say that *The Savage Mind* chooses syntax against semantics; for me, there is nothing to choose ... meaning is always the result of the combination of elements which are not in themselves meaningful ... meaning is always reducible ... behind every meaning there is non-sense and the contrary is not true ... signification is always phenomenal.' Also, *The Raw and the Cooked* (London: Cape, 1970) p.12: 'I therefore claim to show, not how men think in myths, but how myths operate in men's minds without their being aware of the fact. And ... it would perhaps be better to go still further and, disregarding the thinking subject completely, proceed as if the thinking process were taking place in the myths, in their reflection upon themselves and their interrelation. For what I am concerned to clarify is not so much what there is *in* myths ... as the system of axioms and postulates defining the best possible code, capable of conferring a common significance on unconscious formulations ...'. As for the significance: 'And if it is now asked to what final meaning these mutually significative meanings are referring – since in the last resort they must refer to something – the only reply to emerge from this study is that myths signify

the mind that evolves them by making use of the world of which it is itself a part'. *The Raw and the Cooked*, p. 341. Since for Levi-Strauss, as we know, the mind means the brain, the latter belonging clearly to the order of things, except for the fact that it possesses the strange property of being able to symbolize other things; one reaches the conclusion that the activity of the mind consists in symbolizing itself in so far as it is a thing endowed with symbolizing power. What concerns us here, however, are not the philosophical aporias to which this position leads but the essential aspects of the social–historical it allows to escape attention.

40 Lévi-Strauss's phrase [Ed.].

41 Lévi-Strauss, *Le Totemisme aujourd'hui*, p. 128.

42 Linguistics, the science which operates so to speak on the ground floor of symbolism, once again tries to pose to itself this question. Cf. Roman Jakobson, *Essais de linguistique générale* (Paris: Editions de Minuit, 1963). Chapter VII ('The phonological aspect and the grammatical aspect of language and their interrelations'). One can even less avoid posing this question in other areas of historical life, to which F. de - Saussure would never have thought of extending the principle of the 'arbitrary character of the sign'.

43 See Lévi-Strauss, *Structural Anthropology*, pp. 206–31.

44 Lévi-Strauss, *The Raw and the Cooked*, passim.

45 As Lévi-Strauss does in *Esprit*.

46 Lévi-Strauss, *The Raw and the Cooked*, p. 194.

47 Lévi-Strauss in *Esprit*, pp. 637, 641.

48 It could, of course, be maintained that a lucid use of symbolism is possible on the individual level (for language, for instance) and not on the collective level (in relation to institutions). But this would have to be demonstrated, and this demonstration could obviously not be based on the *general nature* of symbolism as such. We are not saying that there is no difference between the two levels, nor that this difference would simply be a matter of degree (the greater complexity of the social, etc.). We are simply saying that it stems from factors other than symbolism, namely from the much more profound (and difficult to extricate) character of social imaginary significations and their 'materialization'. See below.

49* The critique of 'structuralism' sketched out here replied to no 'internal necessity' for the author but simply to the need to combat a mystification which, ten years ago, few people were able to escape. It could easily be extended and amplified, but this is not a pressing task inasmuch as the smoke of structuralism is dissipating.

50 We have presented our case elsewhere concerning the relativity of the concept of reification; cf. 'Le Mouvement révolutionnaire sous le capitalisme moderne', in particular, *Socialisme ou Barbarie*, no. 33, pp. 64–5 (now, *Capitalisme moderne*, pp. 152–4); also 'Recommencer la révolution', in *L'Expérience du mouvement ouvrier*, 2, (Paris: Editions 10/18, 1974) pp. 317–18. It is the *struggle* of slaves or of workers which questions reification and relativizes it as a category and as a reality.

51 There is an 'essence' of the Centaur: two definite sets of possibilities and of impossi-bilities. This 'essence' is 'representable': there is nothing imprecise about the 'generic' physical appearance of the Centaur.

52 Value and non-value, licit and illicit are constitutive of history and in this sense, as abstract structuring oppositions, they are presupposed by all history. But *that which* in each case is value and non-value, licit and illicit, is historical and has to be interpreted, as far as posisble, in terms of its content.

53 The fundamental role of the imagination, in the most radical sense, had been clearly seen in classical German philosophy, by Kant but also in particular by Fichte, for whom *produktive Einbildungskraft* is a '*Faktum* of the human mind' which, in the final analysis, is not founded and is not capable of being founded, and which makes possible all the syntheses of subjectivity. This is at least the position of the first *Wissenschaftslehre*, where the productive imagination is that upon which 'is founded the possibility of our consciousness, of our life, of our being for us, that is to say of our being as I.' See, in particular, R. Kroner, *Von Kant bis Hegel*, 2 Aufl. (Tübingen, 1961) vol. I, p. 448ff., 477–80, 484–6. This essential intuition was later obscured (even

in Fichte's own subsequent works), especially by a return to the problem of general validity (*Allgemeingültigkeit*) of knowledge, which appears to be almost impossible to conceive of in terms of imagination. [This question is considered at length in the second part of this book.]

54 I believe that this is the perspective from which most of the material examined by Claude Lévi-Strauss in *The Savage Mind* should be considered, for otherwise the structural homologies between nature and society, for instance, in totemism ('true' or 'so-called') remain incomprehensible.

55 This is actually a tautology, for one cannot see how society could 'represent' itself without *situating itself* in the world; and it is evident that all religions insert humanity in one way or another in a system to which the gods and the world also belong. It is also known, at least since Xenophones (H. Diels and W. Kranz, *Fragmente der Vorsocratiker* (Berlin: Weidmann, 1952, 6th ed.)) that men create gods in their own image, by which we are to understand in the image of their actual relations, which bear the imprint of the imaginary, and in the image of the image that they have of these relations (the latter being for the most part unconscious). The work of G. Dumézil has shown over the past 25 years, on the example of Indo-European religions, the precise homology of the articulation between the social universe and the universe of the divinities. It is in contemporary society where, for the first time, while this connection persists in many different forms, it comes to be questioned because the image of the world and the image of society are detached from one another, but especially because each of them tends to become dislocated in itself. This is one of the aspects of the crisis of the [instituted] imaginary in the modern world, a matter to which we shall return later.

56 'These creatures, degraded by misfortune, were repulsive.' Jules Verne, *Les Enfants du Capitaine Grant* (Paris: Hachette, 1929) p. 362ff. Verne must, as was his custom, have borrowed the elements of his story from a traveller or explorer of the period. [See now Colin Turnbull, *The Mountain People*, (New York: Simon and Schuster, 1972).]

57 As Sartre thinks, *Critique of Dialectical Reason*, translated by Alan Sheridan-Smith. (London: NLB, 1976), p. 122ff. Sartre goes so far as to write: 'Thus, in so far as body is function, function need, and need praxis, one can say that *human labour* ... is *entirely* dialectical' (p. 90). It is amusing to see Sartre criticize at length the 'dialectic of nature' in order to end up, by means of the successive identifications, body = function = need = praxis = labour = dialectic, himself 'naturalizing' the dialectic. What must be said is that we are cruelly lacking a theory of praxis for hymenoptera, which perhaps the sequel to the *Critique of Dialectical Reason* will provide.

58 From the point of view of generality, not of chronology. In the writings of Marx and Engels both principles of explanation exist together and intersect. At any rate, in *The Origin of the Family*, etc. (1884) – a fascinating work which provides more to think about than most modern ethnological works – Engels clearly underscores the *increase in productivity* permitted by 'the first great social divisions of labour' (animal husbandry, agriculture) and which are supposed 'necessarily' to have led to slavery. This 'necessarily' is the whole question. As for the rest, throughout the chapter on 'Barbarism and civilization', where the question of the appearance of classes should have been treated, Engels continually speaks of the evolution of technique and of the corresponding division of labour, but nowhere does he tie this evolution of technique *as such* to the birth of classes. But then how could he, since his subject-matter leads him to consider simultaneously the first stages of animal husbandry, agriculture and crafts, activities based on *different* techniques and leading to (or compatible with) the *same* division of society into masters and slaves (or with the absence of such a division)? The appearance of animal husbandry, agriculture and crafts can in themselves lead to a division into professions not into classes.

59* As soon as a society produces a 'surplus', it swallows up an essential part of it in absurd activities such as funerals, ceremonies, wall paintings, the construction of pyramids and so forth.

60* On the opposition between Marx's historical descriptions and his construction of the 'concept' of class, see 'La Question de l'histoire du mouvement ouvrier', in *l'Expéri-ence du mouvement ouvrier*, 1, pp. 45–6.

61 Engels came close to touching on this idea: 'We saw above how at a fairly early stage in the development of production human labour-power obtains the capacity of producing a considerably greater product than is required for the maintenance of the producers, and how this stage of development was in the main the same as that in which divisions of labour and exchange between individuals arise. *It was not long then before the great 'truth' was discovered that man also can be a commodity; that human energy can be exchanged and put to use by making a man into a slave.* Scarcely had men begun to practise exchange when already they were exchanged themselves.' *The Origin of the Family* (London: Lawrence and Wishart, 1943;) pp. 200–1 (author's italics). This great 'truth', essentially the same as the 'deception' denounced by Rousseau in the *Discourse on the Origin of Inequality*, is itself neither truth nor deception, and can neither be 'discovered' nor 'invented'; it had to be *imagined and created.* – Having said this, it will be remarked that Engels presents slavery, in this text and elsewhere, as an extension of the exchange of objects between men, whereas its essential moment is the transformation of men into 'objects' – and this is precisely what is not reducible to 'economic' considerations.

62 It has recently been estimated that the cost of changing the models of private automobiles in the United States each year amounts to 5 billion dollars per year *at the minimum* for the period 1956–60, more than 1 per cent of the country's national product [and far superior to the annual national product of Turkey, a country of 30 million inhabitants], without taking into account the increase in petrol consumption (in relation to the savings that could have been realized through technological progress). The economists who presented this analysis to the 47th annual meeting of the American Economic Association (December 1961) do not deny that these changes may also have contributed improvements or that they may have been 'desired' by consumers. 'Nevertheless, the costs estimated seemed so staggeringly high that it seems worthwhile presenting the bill and asking whether it was worth it in retrospect.' F. M. Fischer, Z. Griliches and C. Kaysen, *American Economic Review*, May 1962, p. 259.

63 Reification, as it is analysed by Lukács (*History and Class Consciousness*) is obviously an imaginary signification. But it does not appear so in Lukács because the *res* has a mystical philosophical value, to the extent, precisely, that it is a 'rational' category capable of entering into an 'historical dialectic'.

64 From this point of view there is indeed a sort of 'functionality' of the actual imaginary inasmuch as it is a 'condition for the existence' of society. But it is a condition for the existence of society as *human society*, and this existence as such replies to no function; it is an end for nothing and has no end.

65 This is what appears to me to be the essential contribution, despite his expressed intentions, of Claude Lévi-Strauss, in particular in *The Savage Mind*, much more than the kinship between 'archaic' thinking and bricolage, or the identification between the 'savage mind' and rationality as such. As to the vast problem on the most radical philosophical level concerning the relation between the imaginary and the rational, the question whether the rational is simply a moment of the imaginary or whether it expresses man's encounter with a transcendent order, this we can only leave open here, doubting, moreover, that we shall ever be able to do otherwise. [This problem is discussed at length in the second part of the present work.]

66 This is not affected by the fact that every society necessarily distinguishes between what *for it* is real–rational and what *for it* is imaginary.

67 As linguists would say, these languages do not have simply a cognitive function; and only cognitive contents [I would now say identitary contents] are wholly translatable. Cf. Jakobson, *Essais de linguistique générale*, pp. 78–86.] The total dialectic of history, implying the possibility of an exhaustive translation, in principle, of all cultures into the language of the 'higher' culture implies this reduction of history to the cognitive. From this point of view, the parallel with poetry is absolutely rigorous; the text of history is an indissociable mixture of cognitive and poetic elements. The extreme

structuralist tendency holds more or less: I cannot translate *Hamlet* into French for you, or can do so only poorly, but what is much more interesting than the text of *Hamlet* is the grammar of the language in which it is written and the fact that this grammar is a special case of a universal grammar. One can reply: no thanks, poetry interests us to the extent that it contains something more than grammar. One can also ask: And why then is English grammar not directly this universal grammar? Why are there *many* grammars? To be sure, the poetic elements themselves, although they cannot be translated rigorously, are not inaccessible. But this access is a re-creation: '... poetry, by definition, is untranslatable. Creative transposition alone is possible' (Jakobson, *Essais de linguistique générale*, p. 86). Even beyond cognitive content, there is reading and approximate comprehension across various historical phases. This reading, however, must accept the fact that it is always someone's reading.

4 THE SOCIAL–HISTORICAL

1 Thus, for example, all that Marx has to say which is true, profound, important and new about society and history, he says *despite* this 'elsewhere' which governs his entire thought: the fact that history *must* (*muß, soll* and *wird*) lead to a classless society. It results from this that what is essential in his discovery cannot fit within his own system. See 'La Question de l'histoire du mouvement ouvrier', in *L'Expérience ouvrier*, 1, pp. 11–120.

2 The difficulty or the impossibility of satisfying this requirement has been recognized, we know, at least as early as Plato's *Sophist*. Aristotle's effort in the *Metaphysics* was aimed essentially at surmounting the multiple meanings of: being, what he called *pollachos legomenon*. Intending this meaning as *one* will then govern all of later philosophy, and this will almost always lead to translating the differences in the meanings of: being by gradations in the quality of being or in the 'ontological intensity' accorded to corresponding types of entities.

3 We know that, as early as the *Republic*, Plato examines the alteration in the order of the city as an historical process, and that, at the other end, Marx's effort concerns the determination of the relation between the organization and the functioning of social systems and their dynamics, or their history. It will be evident later that what I mean by the unity and indivisibility of the social–historical is situated on another level. The examples of Husserl and Heidegger still show to what extent the separation is ingrained and deeply rooted in inherited thought. For both of them, although in different ways, an (impoverished) question of history appears as a philosophical question – but never a philosophical question of society.

4 If a justification for these formulations is sought, one may refer to what was stated above concerning the historical emergence of capitalist society and its unity, or the establishment of an asymmetrical division of society into classes (p. 45–54).

5 Hegel, *Wissenschaft der Logik* ed. by Georg Lasson, (Leipzig: Felix Meiner, 1923), vol. II, pp. 426–9.

6 *Philebus*, 17 b–18 d.

7 Claude Lévi-Strauss, *Race et Histoire*, collection Méditations, (Gonthier, 1967).

8 '... it is a law of nature that the same cause, provided it remain in the same condition always produces the same effect,' Aristotle, *On Generation and Corruption*, II, 336 a 27–8. The same, under the same conditions, produces the same: the set formed by the cause, the conditions and the effect contains these as its parts. Cf. *Metaphysics*, E. 1026 a 16–17: 'Now all causes must be eternal ...'

9 The meaning of this term will be discussed at length in chapter 5.

10 See, in addition to the first part of this book, 'La Question de l'histoire du mouvement ouvrier'.

11 This is what Claude Lévi-Strauss now does explicitly: '... structural interpretation ... alone knows how to account at once for itself and for the others.' *L'Homme nu* (Paris: 1971) p. 561.

12 Chapter 5 is devoted to clarifying these two terms. *Legein* is the identitary dimension of social representing/saying: *legein* (from which comes *logos*, logic) signifies distingui-shing-choosing-positing-assembling-counting-saying. In language, *legein* is represented by the component *code*; the signifying component of language will here be termed *langue*. *Teukhein* is the identitary (or functional, or instrumental) dimension of social doing: *teukhein* (from which comes *technē*, technique) signifies assembling-adjusting-fabricating-constructing.

14 See 'La Question de l'histoire du mouvement ouvrier', pp. 32–7.

15 Machines, locomotives, railways, etc. are 'instruments of the human brain, created by the hand of man, materialized organs of knowledge', Marx wrote in the *Grundrisse*: *Foundations of the Critique of Political Economy*, translated by Martin Nicolaus (Harmondsdworth: Penguin, 1973).

16 We shall return to this at length. See below chapter 6.

17 Cf. D. Park, *Contemporary Physics* (New York: Harcourt Brace, 1964) pp. 131–49.

18 The fact that this permanence is no longer viewed within the framework of the fixed and unchanging Aristotelian *phusis* but as limited and relativized through evolution, changes nothing at bottom. The living being is nothing if it is not a stable *eidos*, and this stability is essentially determined as the capacity for self-preservation and self-reproduction, in the repetition of the same.

19 Thus the bourgeoisie establishes a new *mode of being* of production and a new type of relation between production and the rest of social life, which is *its* creation – and which Marx retrospectively projects over all of history. See 'La Question de l'histoire du mouvement ouvrier', pp. 45–66.

20 See below, chapter 7, pp. 341ff.

21 Set-theory, like all mathematics, formally presupposes a logic, the so-called formal or symbolic logic, and is based on it; but formal or symbolic logic presupposes that the objects it speaks about to begin with, the propositions it treats as unanalysable and indifferent with respect to their content, are themselves a set, an ensemble, on which a particular relation, implication is defined. The situation is basically the same when, in an alleged second stage, quantifiers are introduced. There is, thus, a logico-mathematical circle, evident also in the fact that one cannot do formal logic without a numbering system – and which is eliminated only in words when it is asserted that the numbers involved here are 'other' than the numbers of arithmetic. Logic and mathematics are indissociable, posited together, two aspects of the same – of the identitary–ensemblist.

22 This has been a torture for commentators, forced to speak of 'essential accidents'; in fact, there are, for Aristotle, essential accompaniments and accidental accompani-ments.

23 It is obviously not by chance that a genuine particularizing of time in relation to space begins to appear in physics only when the schema of complete determination has to be abandoned, namely in thermodynamics, where the vector of time is identified with increasing probability and an irreversibility of time is introduced and interpreted as extreme improbability (whereas mechanical phenomena as such are reversible). We shall return later to the question of the irreversibility of time from the social–historical point of view. It is enought to note here that the probabilist definition of physical time is also, in the final analysis, an identitary–ensemblist definition (such is the logico-ontological foundation of any theory of probability) and that thermodynamic 'time' is a 'time' of equalizing and of un-differentiating (growth of entropy).

24 The recent development of work in ethno-history tends to show that the denial of the historicality of so-called 'archaic' societies was erroneous and ideologically determined. Cf. also Claude Lefort, 'Sociétés "sans histoire" et historicité', in *C. Int. Soc.*, vol. 12 (1952).

25 The following is a summary of a study of the *Timaeus* which I hope to publish soon.

26 Plato, *Philebus*, 32 b.

27 Ibid., 37 d.

28 Plato, *Timaeus*, 27 d–48 e.

29 Ibid., 48 a–52 e.

30 Ibid., 50 b.

31 Aristotle, *Physics*, IV, 10–14, in particular 219 b 16–25, 220 a 9–21, 222 a 13; see also *De anima*, III, 6, 430 b 6–14. Kant, *Critique of Pure Reason*, § 6 b. See also Jacques Derrida's rigorous text, 'Ousia and grammē', in *Margins of Philosophy* (Brighton: Harvester, 1982) pp. 29–68.

32 Plato, *Timaeus*, 52 b.

3 Speaking of mathematical reasoning, Galileo says: 'Now these steps which our intellect makes with time, moving stage by stage, the divine intellect, after the manner of light, crosses them in an instant, which is the same thing as saying that it is always present to all of them.' *Dialogue on the two greatest systems of the world*, (Milan: Opere, R. Ricciardi, 1953) vol. III, p. 183; quoted by Alexandre Koyré, *Études galiléennes*, 1986, p. 286.

34 N. Bourbaki, *Elements of Mathematics, Set Theory* (Paris: Hermann, 1966) vol. 1. Introduction E.I.8. We know that this is a chimaera, pursued for some time by some great mathematicians, but abandoned for 40 years, and which has now reappeared as the broken-down horse mounted by successive waves – ethnological, linguistic, psychoanalytic, semiotic – of Parisian fashion.

35 The origin (*archē*) is 'the first point from which a thing either is or comes to be or is known,' Aristotle, *Metaphysics*, △, 1.

36 As we know, Aristotle defines time as 'the number of motion in respect of "before" and "after"' (*Physics*, IV, 219 b 1–2; cf. 220 a 3–4) and motion as 'the fulfilment of what exists potentially, in so far as it exists potentially' (201 a 10–11) or, more precisely, 'of the movable *qua* movable' (202 a 7). This signifies that the movable (or that which changes, etc.) acquires, through the action of a being in act the *eidos* to which it was *pre-destined*. Cf. *Physics*, III, 202 a 7–12: '... the full-formed man begets man from what is potentially man.'

37 'Now it happens that these two Rules (the rules 'according to which we must think that God causes nature to act') manifestly follow from the sole fact that God is unmovable, and always acting in the same way, he always produces the same effect' (Descartes, *Le Monde ou Traité de la Lumière* in *Oeuvres de Descartes*, ed. Charles Adam and Paul Tannery (Paris: J. Vrin, 1964), vol. XI, p. 43). Also: 'From the fact too that God is never subject to change and that he always acts in the same way, we may arrive at knowledge of certain rules, which I call the laws of nature ...' (*Principes de Philosophie*, v. IX, 2, p. 84). It is easy to see that Aristotelian physics (the impossibility of any change of place in the absence of a cause) and Galilean–Cartesian–Newtonian physics (the impossibility of any change of velocity in the absence of a cause: inertia) are but two concrete realizations of identity and determinacy, following two different interpretations of that which is characteristic of the determinations peculiar to material things: their 'natural place' or their 'state of motion'. The second interpretation becomes possible only by positing in a strictly identitary fashion that space is perfectly homogeneous, without any privileged and 'natural' 'place', pure self-difference of the identical. The principle of relativity follows from this 'immediately'.

38 *Symposium*, 205 b–c; *Sophist*, 219 b; 265 b–266 d.

39 Except for Kant in the *Critique of Judgement*, where, nevertheless, what is finally recognized as the creativity of the imagination (in the work of art) has no ontological weight. It is certainly not by chance that in *Kant and the Problem of Metaphysics*, a work devoted for the most part to the role of the imagination in Kant, Heidegger takes absolutely no account of the third *Critique*.

40 Plato, *Timaeus*, 29 b.

41 Ibid.

42 Ibid., 31 b.

43 Ibid., 265 e.

44 Actually, the complexity and the ambiguity of Aristotle's formulations on this subject are impressive; I attempted to provide some indications on this subject elsewhere ('Technique', *Encyclopaedia Universalis*, vol. 15, 1973, p. 803ff.) See also *Metaphysics*, λ, III, 1069 b–1070 a; (*Crossroads in the Labyrinth*, pp. 229ff.).

45 See *Kant and the Problem of Metaphysics, passim.* The same thesis is nuanced but not abandoned for all that in *Vom Wesen des Grundes.*

46 In this respect, Aristotle's much criticized categories in his treatise of the same name, categories which are indeed oriented in accordance with the necessities of *legein* in general and of Greek *legein* in particular, correspond to something less uncertain than, for example, the Kantian categories, 'deduced' from the pure necessities of the transcendental unity of apperception but, in truth, not 'deduced' at all, expressing merely a particular grammatical–logical–metaphysical concreteness and, of course, just as *dated.* Let it be noted in passing that what truly functions as categories in Aristotle is presented by him not in the treatise on the *Categories* but in book △ of the *Metaphysics.*

47 *Physics* IV, 219 b 12–15; 220 a 21–2. The *peras,* the limit, term, determination *implied* by the present essentially excludes time; *it only happens* to be found 'in time'.

48 In this sense, Heidegger's interpretation of being as 'presence' in traditional ontology is well founded, but derivative. Presence, at once as congruence or coincidence *and* as eternity, atemporality, is required by determinacy. And it is because being means being determined – even if that which is is elsewhere, far away, in the past, yet to come, hence non-present – that the fact of being, that is to say determinacy, must be transformed into different forms of 'presence', including virtual presence. I shall show elsewhere (in *L'Élément imaginaire*) that this requirement governs what continues to be (for example in Aristotle's *De anima*) the implicit presupposition of 'true vision': vision is 'true' to the extent that it is 'close'; there is a canonical–optimal–absolute distance for 'seeing truly' – and this distance, ultimately, can only be 'zero distance'. The truth of vision *is* congruence, 'spatial' coincidence.

49 In fact, such a harmony is always tacitly postulated by idealist philosophers; for materialist philosophers, it is 'explained', the explanation being available on demand from the absolute scientific Spectator, who, unfortunately, is constantly changing addresses.

50 To be sure, the actual time of capitalism is not 'pure' either; for a long time it is superimposed upon and coexists with, without being able to break it, the actual temporality of earlier social formations and levels which survive beneath capitalism or alongside it.

51 *Thucydides* I, 70.

52 Ibid., II, 2.

53 *Ecclesiastes* 3, 1–8.

54 Ibid., 3, 10; 3, 14.

55 Such is the strange condition of language, that there is not a single word which does not contain within it the seed of its own destruction, something like a machine to overturn its own meaning.' Jean Paulhan, *Le don des langues,* Oeuvres complètes (Cercle du livre précieux), v. III, p. 390. Quoted by Serge Viderman, *La Construction de l'espace analytique,* 1970, p. 94. Viderman provides an excellent clarification of the irreducibility of the significations of the analytic field to any sort of logical schemata.

56 The terms code and *langue* are discussed at length below (see chapter 5).

5 THE SOCIAL–HISTORICAL INSTITUTION: *LEGEIN* AND *TEUKHEIN*

1 Philosophies which attempted to posit an absolute starting point or an unconditioned origin, a foundation which founds itself, have always contained, from *this* point of view, logical fallacies – in the case of Descartes – or else were never actually able to get out of this 'origin' and of that which it tautologically implies – as happens, more or less, to Husserl.

2 In what follows, I am referring to the so-called 'naive' theory of ensembles (set theory) for reasons which shall become apparent in the text, and which I have

developed, from another point of view, in 'Modern Science and Philosophical Interrogation' (*Crossroads in the Labyrinth*, pp. 208–20).

3 *Beiträge zur Begründung der transfiniten Mengenlehre*, 1, *Math. Annalen*, 46 (1895), p. 481.

4 Needless to say the term 'union' does not have the meaning here which is given to it in the development *of* set theory; just as the terms 'separation' and 'discrete' used here and later on do not have the meaning ascribed to them in topology.

5 Even the minimum condition mentioned does not absolutely go without saying, except in a neo-Darwinian sense: a society which absolutely inhibited heterosexual desire would quickly become unobservable. Concerning the possibility for a society to go to the very limit of self-extinction, cf. Colin Turnbull, *The Mountain People*, (London: Cape, 1973).

6 Let us recall that automaton signifies something quite different from a 'robot' or a mere 'machine': automaton means that which moves of *itself*.

7 Why this is so is another question. The apparatus, like all apparatuses of the living being, seems to be able to exist only with a considerable excess capacity or redundance. We know in part the importance of this redundancy, in its various forms, for the survival of the individual and of the species – and for evolution; but this is obviously not an 'explanation' for it. In any event, it is likely that the classifying of the information received by the living being into the categories relevant/non-relevant is neither 'fixed' nor 'definitive', and this itself is indicative of one of the limits of the description of the living being as an identitary automaton.

8 The term 'recognize' is here a violent abuse of language; it covers the stereochemical mechanism whereby, in a cell, a particular molecule is 'recognized' as belonging to a given class of molecules as well as a dog or a horse 'recognizes' its master. The distinction is of no importance for the present discussion.

9 Lévi-Strauss [Ed.].

10 The term 'symbolic' as it is used in France by certain currents in psychoanalysis actually corresponds to a component of certain social imaginary significations, to their instituted normativity. Although these significations are, in each case, instituted with a specific content, what is implied (and what we are led to believe) is that behind them stands a non-positive normativity (which does not follow from the particular institution of society), thereby producing the illusion of a normativity which would at once be 'materially defined' and stand as trans- or meta-cultural. In this way, for example, one speaks of the 'symbolic father' – which means nothing more than the instituted father.

11 The term 'code' is not used here in the sense commonly understood in linguistics since Saussure (and which simply repeats the notion of system). It is used in the sense it has in the expressions of deciphering a code, of cryptographic code; or in Shannon's formula, 'meaning is what remains invariant when one passes from one code to another' – a formula which is, obviously, a definition of *code* and not of *meaning*. A code is not a good code, and is not even a code at all, unless its terms are in bi-univocal correspondence with those of another code. In the case of language as code, the bi-univocal correspondence is that between the signifiers (words or sentences) and the elements *designated* by these (signifieds as they form an ensemblist–identitary system).

12 Bourbaki, *Eléments de mathématique* (Paris: Hermann, 1968). E.I.9–E.I.10.

13 We get around this in appearance only when we posit as an axiom that 'there exists an infinite set' (for example, Bourbaki, *Eléments de mathématique*, E.III.45), whether one defines as 'infinite' a set which is not finite (such that its cardinal number a $\neq$ a + 1), or whether one defines as infinite a set which is equivalent to one of its own parts. In both instances one is granting the (unrealizable) possibility of an indefinite iteration of the same operation.

14 See, for example, Bourbaki, *Eléments de mathématique*, E.I., pp. 16–38.

15 If Newton and Leibniz had had the misfortune to know the criteria for formalized mathematics, they would never have dared to publish their discoveries in differential calculus. Analysis was, logically, a seamy place for a century and a half, until the

situation was cleaned up by Cauchy and Weierstrass. Cf. Abraham Robinson, *Non-standard Analysis* (Amsterdam: North Holland Pub. Co. 1966) pp. 260–82. Likewise, it is known that several of the demonstrations provided by Galois for basic and true propositions were actually false.

16 Cf. for instance *Metaphysics*, Γ, 4.

17 In a flash of genius, an eminent linguist one day wrote: 'mare = horse + female.' If, as is common usage, the sign + in this expression indicates the operation of an additive group, then it results that, for L. Hjelmslev, a female is a mare from which horseness has been subtracted.

18 Allow me to stress 'socially'; I am not saying that signification is the totality of associations which a word may provoke in a given individual.

19 H. Diels, *Fragmente der Vorsokratiker* (Berlin: Weidmann, 1952, 6th ed.) Fr.9, 26, 125.

20 *De anima*, III, 8, 432 a 9–10.

21 Speaking of mutual implication here would, obviously, be more than an abuse of language in relation to the estabished usages in logic and in mathematics. To say of two propositions that they mutually imply one another is to say that they are identical or the same. Separation and reunion, however, are not possible without one another, nor without the other operative schemata discussed below, they *require one another*, each arising due to the very fact that the other appears. It would be meaningless, though, to say that they are the 'same'. We shall speak of reciprocal inherence or of circular implication, for lack of any more appropriate terms.

22 Separation/union can also be expressed as exclusion/inclusion, or as discreteness/continuity; in this we implicitly posit inside and outside, borderline and proximity.

23 This could not be otherwise unless syntagmata containing an *arbitrary* number of words were allowed – which is absurd. For a language which includes a million words, and which would allow as the maximum length syntagmata of 100 words, the number of possible syntagmata is *at most* $1\ 000\ 000^{100} = 10^{100}$. Although it is considerable – the 'number of particles in the universe' is only, it seems, 10^{80} – this number would nevertheless be posited as on the order of zero in any mathematical question where it would be compared to the poorest infinity, the power of the denumerable (the 'number' of natural whole numbers 1, 2, 3 ...). And all these syntagmata are 'given together' with the code, its basic signs and syntagmatic rules. So there is no sense in speaking of 'the creativity of speaking subjects', if one places this in the combinatories of a finite set.

24 Let us note, without being able to elaborate here, that even in this case ensemblist–identitary logic is far from accounting for all the aspects of the language function as *legein*. This possible non-value is still situated in a sphere of general value, and it is never pure nothingness, simple non-value but always continues to be a social datum. A poorly pronounced word, a poorly constructed or incoherent sentence are still 'signs', not natural occurrences. The transgression of rules can result in a defect which diminishes the use-value without cancelling it out – bad pronunciation, an incorrect yet 'comprehensible' sentence – or in the 'perversion' or abolition of the *canonical* use-value: nonsense, absurdity, materially false ....

25 We know that this question tortured Greek philosophy, from beginning to end. To this day it has lost neither its meaning nor its sharpness.

26 This is still the case where 'different languages' (according to caste or sex/generation) are instituted within a society: there is an equivalence between the individuals belonging to the linguistic sub-groups formed in this way, and even a general equivalence since these groups must all be in possession of their respective languages.

27 This is what I should like to call Aristotle's postulate: 'Spoken words are the symbols of mental experience and written words are the symbols of spoken words. Just as all men have not the same writing, so all men have not the same speech sounds, but the mental experiences (*pathemata*), which these directly (*protos*) symbolize, are the same for all ...' (*De Interpretatione*, I). I shall return later to the connection between imagination and language, which is posed implicitly, though certainly, by Aristotle, and later taken up by Plotinus.

28 This obviously concerns what in mathematics is called an arrangement, a combination in which the order of the terms is not indifferent.

29 Thus, there can be no mathematics without a relation of well-ordering, presupposed in the arrangement of signs and propositions, and this is also true for a metamathematics or any sort of metalanguage. What is presented in the construction of formalized mathematics as a special case of the relation of order in general, the relation of well-ordering, is, from another point of view, what is presupposed in every relation of order and even simply in every relation, which can be generated only by using the well-ordering.

30 Kant, *The Critique of Pure Reason*, translated by Max Müller (New York: Anchor, 1966) p. 388 (italicized in the original).

31 Kant saw this in part: the 'persistence' of the object through the phases of its constitution is a function he ascribes – correctly in his egological frame of reference – to the imagination. However, even in this frame of reference, it is impossible to insert this 'object' in experience – without which it is nothing – without the representation (*Vertretung*) of other objects by means of *terms*, products of *legein*. I shall return to this question in *L'Élément imaginaire*.

32 See the article on 'Technique' quoted in note 44 of chapter 4.

33 Even *legein* does not realize fully this bipartition, it *tends towards* it. The logic of *legein* as code is oriented towards this division – which, in actuality, is unrealizable. This is already enough to destroy the structuralist postulates, which *require* that whatever is not mandatory be forbidden. In French *vèche* does not exist, without being forbidden. Calling it a 'phonological word' changes nothing here.

34 *De anima*, III, 9–12, in particular 434 a 5–15.

35 The expression is de Gaulle's [Ed.].

36 *Prometheus*, v. 506.

37 A. Leroi-Gourhan, *L'Homme et la Matière* (Paris: 1971) p. 318.

38 Teleology has recently been rediscovered in biology – and baptized teleonomy. What would become of the metaphysics of positive scientists without the linguistic resources of Greek?

39 Lewis Mumford, *The Myth of the Machine* (New York: Harcourt, Brace and World, 1966) chapter 9.

6 THE SOCIAL–HISTORICAL INSTITUTION: INDIVIDUALS AND THINGS

1 See 'Modern Science and Philosophical Interrogation', in *Crossroads in the Labyrinth*.

2 The term 'representation' – employed by Freud almost as many times as the number of pages in his writings – lends itself to debate to the extent that it leads one to understand that 'that which' is posited in and through representation represents something else (*Vertretung* in German). The German word *Vorstellung* (from *vorstellen*, 'put', 'pose', 'place before') would be less liable to mislead; this did not prevent Heidegger from denouncing it as a manifestation of the modern tendency 'to forget Being', in various texts which, whether they have actually been read or not, continue to produce devastating effects among cultivated Parisian ladies who have taken to hold representation in abhorrence. I was tempted by the terms position/presentation or, even more so, by *phantasma*. But it is best to limit as far as possible any changes of vocabulary; the reader who knows how to read will quickly understand in what sense the term is used here.

3 I have attempted to show that this separation is impossible in 'Epilegomena to a theory of the soul which has been presented as a science', in *Crossroads in the Labyrinth*, pp. 3–45.

4 Mélanie Klein, *Narrative of a Child Analysis* (New York: Basic Books, 1961), p. 70.

5 See below, chapter 7, p. 346–54.

6 Cf. 'Epilegomena to a theory of the soul'.

7 *Die Traumdeutung, Gesammelte Werke* II, p. 116 note 1 and pp. 529–30. The translations of the second passage, both in the Standard Edition (V, p. 525) and in the
French edition (ed. of 1967, p. 446) contain a blatant error.

8 'Formulations on the Two Principles of Mental Functioning' (1911), *G.W.* VIII,
p. 234; *S.E.* XII, p. 219. The derivation of 'thought' on the basis of representation
is clearly formulated, ibid., *G.W.*, VIII, p. 23; *S.E.* XII, p. 221.

9 'A contribution to the psychogenesis of manic-depressive states', in *Contributions to
Psycho-analysis*, 1950, p. 282.

10 Jean Laplanche and J.-B. Pontalis, 'Fantasme originaire, fantasmes des origines,
origine du fantasme', *Les Temps Modernes*, no. 215, April 1964, p. 1834.

11 Susan Isaacs, 'Nature et fonction du phantasme', *La Psychanalyse*, no. 5, 1959,
p. 125ff.

12 In their article quoted above.

13 *Draft L.* Analogous formulations occur in *Draft M* (*S.E.* 1, 248–53).

14 'I call such phantasies – of the observation of sexual intercourse between the parents,
of seduction, of castration, and others – 'primal phantasies'; and I shall discuss in
detail elsewhere their origin and their relation to individual experience.' 'A Case of
Paranoia Running Counter to the Psychoanalytic Theory of the Disease' (1915),
G.W., X, p. 242; *S.E.*, XIV, p. 269.

15 Ibid., pp. 1861, 1868. 'Syntax' is evidently here an effect of structural–linguistical
seduction. This is not a matter of a 'syntax' that can be isolated but of the global
arrangement of the scene, where the organization and *that which* is organized are not
separable.

16 In the sentence quoted in note 14, Freud speaks of *observing* the 'primal scene'.

17 This is already the case in writings as early as *Draft N* (*S.E.* 1, 254–257); cf. also
G.W., X, p. 294, *S.E.*, 14, p. 196 or *G.W.*, XII, 156, *S.E.*, 17, p. 120.

18 Laplanche and Pontalis, 'Fantasme', p. 1865.

19 *G.W.*, V, p. 123, *S.E.*, 7, p. 222.

20 *G.W.*, XVII, p. 115. The italicized word appears in the German text.

21 Laplanche and Pontalis, 'Fantasme', p. 1867.

22 See for example 'Das Interesse an der Psychoanalyse', *G.W.*, VIII, p. 416; *S.E.*, 13,
p. 186: '... the neuroses themselves have turned out to be attempts to find *individual*
solutions for the problems of compensating for unsatisfied wishes, while institutions
seek to provide *social* solutions for these same problems' (italicized in the text).
The expression *Wunschkompensatorische Phantasien*, desire or wish compensating
phantasies, returns often in Freud's writings.

23 'A starving man dreams of bread,' says a Greek proverb.

24 Plato in the *Symposium* (200 c–e) stated more correctly that one can desire something
one does not lack in the sense that one wishes to continue possessing it.

25 This term has been translated here, as often as possible, by *leaning on* [Ed.].

26 Cf. the letter to Fliess dated 21 September 1897 and 'Formulations on the Two
Principles of Mental Functioning', *G.W.*, VIII, p. 230ff.; *S.E.*, XII, p. 218ff.

27 'Formulations on the Two Principles of Mental Functioning', *G.W.*, VIII, p. 233;
S.E., XII, p. 221 (translation modified).

28 Cf. Freud, *G.W.*, II–III, pp. 571–4, *S.E.*, 5, pp. 556–9. [There is no being] capable
of appetite without possessing imagination' Aristotle stated (*De anima*, 433b 29).

29 'Formulations on the Two Principles of Mental Functioning', *G.W.*, p. 232, note;
S.E., pp. 219–220, note. This note should be quoted *in extenso*, for here Freud affirms
(against the 'objection of reality') that the infant, including maternal care, constitutes
a psychical system wholly under the domination of the 'pleasure principle'; and where
he also states that a fine example 'of a psychical system shut off from the stimuli of
the external world' and which even satisfies its needs for nourishment 'autistically (to
use Bleuler's term)' is provided by the bird in its egg; and that the 'devices' by means
of which the system, living in accordance with the pleasure principle, can shelter
itself from the excitations of reality 'are merely the correlative of "repression", which
treats internal unpleasurable stimuli as if they were external – that is to say, pushes
them into the external world.' In contrast to what may have been said about it, the

theme of an 'originary narcissistic investment' of the self is present in Freud up to the end – as can be confirmed in the *Outline of Psycho-analysis*, which was never finished (for instance, *G.W.*, XVII, p. 115; *S.E.*, XXIII, p. 141ff.).

30 Laplanche and Pontalis, 'Fantasme', p. 1868.

31 Note dated 12 July 1938 (London), *G.W.*, XVII, p. 151; *S.E.*, 23, p. 141ff.

32 See the quote from Freud, note 29 above.

33 Hegel's phrase [Ed.].

34 Plato, *Philebus*, 16 c–d: 'All things ... that are ever said to be consist of a one and a many, and have in their nature a conjunction (*symphyton*) of limit (*peras*) and unlimitedness (*apeirian*).'

35 In *La Violence de l'interprétation – Du pictogramme à l'énoncé* by Piera Castoriadis-Aulagnier (Paris: PUF, 1975) one finds a similar conception, from the perspective proper to the author, which by no means diverges from the one adopted here.

36 Freud, *S.E.*, 23, p. 141ff.; *G.W.*, XVII, p. 115: 'The breast is certainly not at the start distinguished from the infant's own body and when it is separated from the body and has to be shifted to the 'outside', because it is so often missing for the infant, it carries with it as '*object*' part of the originary narcissistic libidinal investment' (italicized in the original). *An Outline of Psycho-analysis* is, as we know, Freud's last text, interrupted by his death.

37 Cf. also Serge Vidermann, *La Construction de l'espace analytique*.

38 The perspective and the specific preoccupations which govern the discussion of the history of the psyche attempted here prevent me from examining several important questions in the scope they require, and first and foremost among these, the question of sexuality. The profoundly imaginary character of human sexuality (beyond any 'phantasizing' in the ordinary sense of the term) that is to say, human sexuality as an imaginary creation (at once psychical and social–historical) would require an entire book all by itself. I must confine myself to noting that the absolute and actual erotogenicity of the entire surface of the body during the monadic phase, just as the virtual erogenicity of this surface throughout the life of the individual, go far beyond the resources of the notion of anaclisis and translate the autistic investment of the somato-psychical monad. The 'first' pleasure of the monad, undifferentiated somato-psychical pleasure, shows that the erotization of the totality of 'one's own body' *is already present even before 'one's own body' exists* as 'separate'. The 'second' pleasure, that of the triadic phase, corresponds to the 'specific' erotization of particular corporeal zones, relating to the corresponding 'partial objects'for which the mediation of the imaginary other (as a general rule, the mother) is essential. Finally, after 'reality' has been established, the stabilizing and increasing specificity (in 'normal' cases) of the various kinds of 'corporeal pleasure' goes along with the appearance of the enigma of 'non-material' pleasure (Freud has the courage to call it *intellektuelle Lust* in *Formulations on the Two Principles of Mental Functioning*, *G.W.*, p. 236; *S.E.*, p. 224) connected in particular to sublimated activities in which we find once again pure representation as the source of pleasure.

39 In this way, for example, overnight for millions of communists in France and throughout the world, Tito was transformed from the glorious leader of a popular democracy into an outlaw spy and agent of imperialism – for so decreed the Master of signification, the late Joseph Stalin.

40 For anyone who knows how to read, it is blindingly obvious (without word-play) that the problem that Freud posed in the theme of the 'Oedipus complex' and the 'murder of the father' was the problem of the socialization of the psyche. As early as 1964 (see above, p. 144–6) I wrote, and I was probably not the first, that the solutions he gives to it remain mythological because he thought he could deduce the institution from the functioning of the psyche. But this changes nothing about the fact that this socialization includes an uneliminable psychogenetic or idiogenetic dimension, and that this can only be conceived of on the basis of Freud's work and his fundamental discoveries. Discoveries which are not cancelled out by Freud's socio-cultural horizon or, and this amounts to the same thing, by his scientism and his positivism (cf. 'Epilegomena to a theory of the soul'). Proof of this can be found in the fact that

they are endlessly pillaged and parasitized by the impostors who chuckle today over 'papa-mama' (perhaps children of the future will have free access to desire if only they learn to babble 'dede-gaga'). To have brought to light this signification of the 'Oedipus complex' over and beyond Freud himself has been one of the important contributions of Jacques Lacan. For anyone who knows how to see, this cannot be masked by the pernicious mirages in which he wanders, and leads others astray as well, for a number of years now.

41 See above, p. 95–101.
42 As is well known, the polemic on this subject begins with Malinowski at the start of the 1920s and is already fully developed in W. Reich.
43 'Words mean what I want them to mean,' as Humpty-Dumpty used to say.
44 *G.W.*, XIV, p. 457 (*Civilization and its Discontents, S.E.*, 21, p. 97). On sublimation, Freud says the most astonishing and the most contradictory things. In this way, for instance, in the *Ego and the Id, G.W.*, XIII, p. 258; *S.E.*, 19, p. 30: the internalization of the abandoned object is held to be 'a kind of sublimation'. The difference between sublimation and idealization ('Introduction to Narcissism', *G.W.*, X, p. 161ff.; *S.E.*, 14, p. 69ff.) will not be considered here.
45 As are most of those appearing in *Group Psychology and the Analysis of the Ego*, Freud purely and simply identifies there the social element with 'the influence of a large number of people'.
46 *G.W.*, IX, p. 92. (*Totem and Taboo, S.E.*, XIII, p. 74). Cf. also *G.W.*, XIV, pp. 439–440; *S.E.*, 21, p. 81.
47 'Triebe und Triebschicksäle,' *G.W.*, X, p. 223; 'Instincts and Their Vicissitudes', *S.E.*, 14, p. 131.
48 'On Narcissism: An Introduction', *G.W.*, X, p. 161; *S.E.*, 14, p. 69ff. On the other hand, in the 32nd of the 'New Introductory Lectures . . .,' Freud distinguishes between sublimation and inhibition with respect to their aim and affirms that neither of these is caused by repression.
49 Proof of this fact lies in the numerous societies in which homosexuality has been an explicit institution.
50 'A satisfaction of this kind (that tied to artistic creation or to science) . . . has a special quality which we shall certainly one day be able to characterize in metapsychological terms,' Freud wrote in 1930 (*Civilization and its Discontents, S.E.*, 21, p. 79; *G.W.*, XIV, p. 438).
51 Even Socrates says to Crito (*Crito*, 53 e) that, if he were to escape to go 'roistering in Thessaly', he may hear many humiliating comments about himself. True, this is not all he says to Crito. But throughout the entire discourse which Socrates addresses to himself, speaking in the name of the laws of Athens, finally, there is no way totally to separate 'one must not contradict oneself' from 'I cannot give others the image of myself as someone who contradicts himself.'
52 '*Triebe und Triebschicksäle*', *G.W.*, X, in particular pp. 215–19; *S.E.*, 14, in particular, pp. 122–5.
53 Balzac's character [Ed.].
54 It is this social–historical institution of things and of a world which in fact constitutes Husserl's *Lebenswelt*; and this *Lebenswelt*, barely disguised, stands behind what Heidegger has to say about beings, Dasein and Being.
55 'To die – to sleep; – To sleep! perchance to dream: – ay, there's the rub; For in that sleep of death what dreams may come . . .' (*Hamlet*, III, 1).
56 The relation of referral may be considered as an *optional* pseudo-equivalence. If *a* can refer to *b* and *b* can refer to *c*, then *a* can refer to *c*. The relation is therefore 'optionally transitive'. In the same way, if *a* can refer to *b*, *b* can refer to *a*. The relation is 'optionally symmetrical'. If the mast makes me think of the boat, the boat can make me think of the mast. And if the boat makes me think of the *Chancellor*, the mast can make me think of the *Chancellor*. [A Jules Verne novel, named after the ship the *Chancellor*. – Ed.] If to this we add the apparently inoffensive hypothesis that the relation of referral is reflexive (that *a* refers to *a*), we then have a relation of optional pseudo-equivalence; and the representations related in this way can be

said to be optionally pseudo-equivalent *modulo* this relation. This must not be confused with genuine mathematical equivalence, which is expressed as follows: for any x, y, z belonging to a set, xRy necessarily entails yRx (symmetry); xRy *and* yRz necessarily entail xRz (transitiveness); and it is always true that xRx (reflexivity).

57 *Topics*, I, 4, 101 b; *Posterior Analytics*, II, 3, 90 b.

58 *De anima*, 430 b 27–31.

59 And necessarily leads to Aristotle's God – Thought, to Hegel's Spirit or to an ultimate being-a-being of the same nature. Althusser and other *Normaliens* who were 'working over concepts' and 'producing concepts' under the cover of 'Marxism' seem to have never noticed this. The deep-seated deterioration of the quality of university-level teaching in France can be seen to have begun long before May 1968.

60 The concept is identity, or unity, of being and of essence: *Wissenschaft der Logik* (ed. Georg Lasson), (Leipzig, Felix Meiner, 1923) II, pp. 213, 235.

61 The Platonic soul *theorei*, gazes at, the *eidē*, aspects/figures. When Heidegger translates Parmenides' *noein* (which usually means: thinking) by *vernehmen*, perceiving (which in German gives *Vernunft*, reason), which is actually one of its most ancient meanings, he puts his finger, whether he knows it or not, (and aside from the fact whether or not one can stop at this in the case of Parmenides) on the instituted social–historical origin of the interpretation of thinking. *Was heißt Denken?* (Tübingen, Niemeyer Verlag, 1954) p. 124. It is not difficult to see, moreover, that the relation to being is always thought by Heidegger implicitly in accordance with the schema of perception. The same thing is true, but here it is explicit, about Merleau-Ponty in *The Visible and the Invisible*, in particular in his notes.

7   SOCIAL IMAGINARY SIGNIFICATIONS

1 See 'Modern Science and Philosophical Interrogation', in *Crossroads in the Labyrinth*, pp. 217–20.

2 In addition to the quote from the *Philebus* given in note 34, p. 402, this can also be seen in *Philolaos* (Diels Fr. 1 and 2) who says practically literally the same thing.

3 *De anima*, I, 3, 407 b 24–5.

4 Kant, *Critique of Judgement*, translated by J. C. Meredith (Oxford: OUP, 1952), p. 23.

5 See 'Modern Science and Philosophical Interrogation'.

6 In such a perspective, language being *only* a system of differences, no term is ever given unless the totality of the others is given at the same time.

7 Author's addition to English translation.

8 *Euthydemus*, 283 c–d.

9 *Sophist*, 259 a–d.

10 *Nicomachean Ethics*, VI, 12, 1143 a 35ff.

11 *Metaphysics* Γ, 6, in particular 1011a 15–24.

12 For example, W. V. O. Quine, *Mathematical Logic*, revised edn (New York: Harper and Row, 1962) p. 50ff.

13 *Metaphysics* Γ, 2, 1004 b 22–25. Asking for a demonstration of everything including principles (*archai*) is, he says further on, characteristic of *apaideusia*, of the lack of *paideia* (1006 a 4–11), that is to say, of that which makes a human human, and a human living in the city.

14 See for example *Economy and Society*, pp. 3–13.

15 Lévi-Strauss's phrase [Ed.].

Index